Families in the Urban Environment

Understanding Resilience

Bassim Hamadeh, CEO and Publisher

Mieka Portier, Acquisitions Editor

Sean Adams, Project Editor

Natalie Piccotti, Senior Marketing Manager

Kassie Graves, Vice President of Editorial

Jamie Giganti, Director of Academic Publishing

ISBN:978-1-5165-2515-7 (pbk) / 978-1-5165-2516-4 (br)

First Edition

———

Families in the Urban Environment

Understanding Resilience

EDITED BY Jason Plummer

California State University—Los Angeles

Contents

Introduction 1

■ **Part I** Theories of Resilience..15

READING 1 A Family Resilience Framework: Innovative Practice
Applications.. 17
Froma Walsh

READING 2 Family Social Capital and Health—A Systematic Review
and Redirection 35
Elena Carrillo Alvarez, Ichiro Kawachi, and Jordi Riera Romani

READING 3 Resilience to Discrimination Stress Across Ethnic Identity
Stages of Development 67
*Andrea J. Romero, Lisa M. Edwards, Stephanie A. Fryberg, and
Michele Orduña*

■ **Part II** Family in the United States....................................85

READING 4 The American Family 87
John Iceland

READING 5 Immigration and Growing Diversity.....................107
John Iceland

READING 6 It's Not Fair: The Pecking Order in Immigrant
Families.. 133
Joanna Dreby

■ **Part III** Marriage and Partnership 161

READING 7 Pair Bonding: Dating, Marriage, and Long-Term
Relationships 163

Frederick Brown and Cynthia LaJambe

READING 8 Negotiating Marriages... 207

Gene H. Starbuck and Karen Saucier Lundy

READING 9 Same-Sex Couple Relationship Strengths:
A Review and Synthesis of the Empirical
Literature (2000–2016) 247

Sharon S. Rostosky and Ellen D. B. Riggle

READING 10 The Experience of Resilience for Adult Female
Survivors of Intimate Partner Violence:
A Phenomenological Inquiry................................. 275

Sara E. Crann and Paula C. Barata

■ **Part IV** Family and Work Life...297

READING 11 Family Budgets: Staying in the Black, Slipping into
the Red.. 299

*Sarah Halpern-Meekin, Kathryn Edin, Laura Tach, and
Jennifer Sykes*

READING 12 Constructing a Feminist Reorganization of the
Heterosexual Breadwinner/Caregiver Model: College
Students' Plans for their Own Future Families................... 329

*Megan Fulcher, Lisa M. Dinella, and
Erica S. Weisgram*

READING 13 Parenting Stress, Dinnertime Rituals, and Child
Well-being in Working-Class Families 353

*Yesel Yoon, Katie Newkirk, and Maureen
Perry-Jenkins*

■ **Part V**   Urban Factors..373

READING 14   The Challenge of College Readiness 375
William G. Tierney

READING 15   Educating Homeless and Highly Mobile Students:
Implications of Research on Risk and Resilience 393
Ann S. Masten, Aria E. Fiat, Madelyn H. Labella, and
Ryan A. Strack

READING 16   Family Resources as Protective Factors for Low-Income
Youth Exposed to Community Violence 413
Cecily R. Hardaway, Emma Sterrett-Hong,
Cynthia A. Larkby, and Marie D. Cornelius

Introduction

The Urban environment and Positive development: A Review of Developmental Tasks and Psychosocial Development

> He thus learns to persuade himself that it is better to do nothing, or as the psychologist would say, "to inhibit his motor impulses." When the same boy, as an adult workman, finds himself confronted with an unusual or untoward condition in his work, he will fall back into this habit of inhibition, of making no effort toward independent action (Addams, 1909, 1972).

Although Jane Addams and Urie Bronfenbrenner were not contemporaries, they both understood how one's social context mattered. For Addams, she understood that "in rural America the quest for adventure led to harmless pranks, but in the city the same impulse resulted in arrest and jail" (Addams, 1909, 1972, p. xxvi). For Bronfenbrenner, as a theorist, any discussion of human development without an investigation of the physical/social environment is a study out of context (Rosa & Tudge, 2013). Bioecological systems theory posit that human development is affected by the interactions between a person and the environments; specifically, process, person, context, and time act simultaneously to affect developmental outcomes (Rosa & Tudge, 2013). Further, the environment in which a person interacts can include both risk and protective factors (Table 1). Risk factors are measurable characteristics or hazards that increase the likelihood of an adverse outcome; in contrast, protective factors are internal and external forces that help to resist or reduce risk (Allen-Meares & Fraser, 2004). In the third phase of Bronfenbrenner's systems model, he viewed proximal processes as influencing developmental outcomes by either promoting competence or diminishing the possibility of dysfunctional outcomes (Rosa & Tudge, 2013). Thus, it is through proximal process that one's context influences human development. For example, in terms of parenting (the proximal process), parents (the context) have to convert their human capital into social capital for their children (the person). Consequently, in our assessment of urban families, we have to assess how the urban environment can either facilitate or hinder completion of family tasks. Lastly, I posit that understanding how families use the resources of the urban environment to raise children requires using a positive youth development framework.

The Positive Youth Development (PYD) framework has two tenants: 1) internal (factors associated with family and individual systems) and external (factors associated with neighborhood and societal systems) assets facilitate development, and 2) individuals and communities vary in the quality of the developmental assets to which they have access (Benson, P., 2008; Benson, Scales, Hamilton, & Sesma, Jr., 2007; Sherrod, 2008). PYD practitioners and scholars have used the framework to explain the plasticity of human development and the importance of the interaction between an individual and his or her social environment (Silbereisen & Lerner, 2008). To that end, PYD focuses on analyzing the individual context that promote thriving (Lewin-Bizan, Bowers, & Lerner, 2010). In terms of outcomes, youths with a positive developmental process are those who possess competence and confidence, are caring, and connected to and able to make positive contributions to their community; however, the quality of physical and social environments in which youth and families live vary.

Social problems are not restricted by geography. Phillips (2017) notes that whether we are discussing suburban, rural, or urban areas, social problems exist everywhere and may interfere with children's completion of developmental tasks. But owing to the population density in urban areas, we are obliged to focus on the urban environment. Specifically, Phillips notes that problems such as homelessness, gang activity, and violent crime may be exacerbated by the urban environment. Consequently, the word *urban* in this book is meant to suggest an urbanized area/community that, according to Delgado (2002), exists within a city that includes its residents and institutions. And the term *family* is meant to designate a group of two or more individuals who provide ongoing instrumental and emotional support to one another (Canary & Canary, 2013). This definition encompasses family in all its various forms. As Alvarez, Kawachi, and Romani (2017) note, a group of college students sharing a dorm room would not constitute family. In terms of the definition provided here, such a living arrangement does not create equivalent ties (i.e., there is no societal expectation that roommates would provide for the emotional or instrumental well-being for one another). Alvarez and colleagues' (2017) review of the literature provides definitions of the terms *instrumental* and *emotional support*, concluding that instrumental support is "the exchange of help and assistance with tangible resources" and emotional support is characterized by "care, affection, and perceptions of empathy and guidance." This support is necessary for converting a family's human capital into social capital for their children. Moreover, such tangible support in times of need is a factor necessary for promoting resilience.

In our common language, it is easy to confuse the terms *cope* and *resilience*. Both relate to how one handles adversity; however, for this text, I am defining adversity as an event that threatens the successful completion of a developmental or familial task. Havighurst (1974) defines a developmental task as one that occurs during a particular stage of life and whose successful achievement leads to social approval, the likely accomplishment of future tasks, and personal happiness. According to this definition, a development task has biological, psychological, and cultural roots. These definitions enable researchers to apply the bioecological systems approach to the study of urban families, or how micro-, mezzo-, and macrosystem influences affect a great variety of factors (i.e., personal health, family process, neighborhood characteristics, public policy) and how they facilitate or hinder the successful completion of developmental tasks. Such an approach views the family unit (and its individual members) as engaged in a bidirectional interactive system.

The American Psychological Association (APA) describes *resilience* as the ability to adapt in the face of adversity, trauma, tragedy, threats, or significant sources of stress. Further, the APA posits that *self-efficacy*, positive self-image, and internal locus of control along with age-appropriate verbal and cognitive skills, emotional regulation/social-emotional competence, and tangible support in times of need are factors that promote resilience. The organizing theme of this book frames resilience as successfully completing familial and individual tasks in the face of adversity. Youth and families engage in a process of securing and using what PYD scholars would call ecological and internal assets to avoid or minimize risk.

"Part 1" of this text provides the reader with an overview of resilience. First, resilience is not an individual trait. It is a process, which Walsh deftly reviews in her approach to working with families. Walsh's discussion of family resilience centers the conversation of working with vulnerable families on assessing their strengths. This strengths-based approach is consistent with positive psychology. Alvarez, Kawachi, and Riera Romani, in this text, describe social capital as deriving from one's social network. There are two key points from their investigation that is important for assessing the stressors and strengths within families in an urban context: 1) parents have to make their human capital available to their children. To do this, parents have to be available to their children and there has to be positive interactions between them and their children; and 2) The concepts of collective efficacy, informal control, and social cohesion are factors of social capital that are associated with health and psychological well-being. This underscores how neighborhoods matter in promoting resiliency. Within their social networks, who are the caring adults that children can access? Who can parents turn to as resources?

Romero, Edwards, Fryberg, and Orduna use ethnic identity development and resilience theory to assess how identity development stages may affect one's response to discrimination stress. Shelby (2015) notes that self-esteem consists of self-worth, secure convictions that one's purposes are worthwhile, and self-efficacy, confidence in one's ability to realize his or her purposes. In terms of Romero, Edwards, Fryberg, and Orduna's research on the stress that results from discrimination, youth development and social service professionals should be concerned since, as Shelby notes, discrimination can erode one's self-esteem. This is important since a positive self-concept and self-efficacy are factors that promote resiliency.

"Part 2" focuses on family and immigration. John Iceland contributes two readings in this section: one on the changes in family composition within the United States, and a second on immigration. Joanna Dreby provides a second reading on immigration that provides insight on how immigration policy directly affects the lived experience of families. Iceland's reading on family skillfully provides an overview of family composition in the United States and how it had changed. In doing so, he highlights how structural forces have influenced how one makes decisions about family formation. Although "Part 2" does not focus on resiliency, it does highlight how policy decisions shape the resources available to families in order to complete developmental and psychosocial tasks. Essentially, "Part 2" should be viewed as an exploration of proximal processes and chronosystems.

"Part 3" addresses relationship formation. As Alvarez and colleagues noted in "Part 1," the family unit, however one defines it, is the primary source of affection and protection for children. The majority of the readings in this section focus on characteristics of healthy relationships. The last reading, however, focuses on intimate partner violence and factors for successfully exiting an abusive relationship. "Part 4" and "Part 5" are topical investigations into common stressors found within the urban environment and how families and individuals navigate them. Since no text can cover all stressors, the remainder of this chapter describes the tasks of families and individuals along with the optimal outcomes of task completion. The goal of this review is to provide the reader with an overview of the psychosocial tasks associated with human development.

TABLE 1 Social ecology of risk (adapted from Allen-Meares and Fraser, 2004)

Domain	Variable
Family process	Support for autonomy
	Effectiveness of discipline
	Parental investment
	Family climate
Parental characteristics	Educational attainment
	Parental efficacy
	Resourcefulness
	Mental health
Family structure	Marital status
	Household size
	Economic status
Community connectedness	Institutional involvement
	Informal networks
	Social resources
Neighborhood characteristics	Neighborhood socioeconomic status
	Crime rates/neighborhood problems
	School climate
Peers	Prosocial
	Antisocial

Tasks of Families[1]

Patterson identifies the primary tasks of families as follows: providing a sense of belonging (membership and family formation), providing economic support, instilling social values, and protecting its members (Canary & Canary, 2013). In terms of parenting, Cherlin (2017) describes the role of parents as supplying love and developing a sense of trust in other human beings, providing children with skills needed to become more autonomous and the opportunities to practice/use those skills, and providing guidance, discipline, and support. Thus, the chief task of parenting is to prepare children to become competent members of society. Table 2 provides an overview of parenting styles and corresponding behavioral and moral reasoning outcomes.

Specific tasks

1. Identify who does and does not belong to the system by selectively admitting people into the system, developing and maintaining relationships with extended kin, preventing intrusion on family resources by nonfamily members, and differentiating between advice-giving and decision-making powers of extended family members.
2. Develop deep commitment to the welfare of the family unit as a whole and to its individual members. This commitment is demonstrated by a willingness to postpone, delay, and/or sacrifice one's own gratification for the development of another family member, and balancing one's own rights as a person against those of other members and against one's responsibilities.
3. Maintain open communication for expression of needs, values, frustrations, disappointments, excitements, ideas, interests, etc. Demonstrate respect for the expression of feelings and needs of family members. Provide and protect individualized time for each subunit and also time for family sharing/family conferencing time.
4. Appreciate and support the uniqueness of each member through assistance with the identification of and support for each member's interests, needs, talents, relationships, and goals. Provide for protection and respect of each person's ideas, property, privacy, values, territory, and time.
5. Establish common values, philosophies, and goals while simultaneously protecting the right and responsibility of family members to develop their own rules, values, talents, interests, etc. This task may be accomplished by providing opportunities for family work, relaxation, and play (i.e., social interactions that foster moral reasoning). In terms of caregiver-child interactions, primary caregivers/parents should provide joint decision-making opportunities to resolve conflicts and frustrations associated with daily life, problems, careers, education, spiritual development, etc. Discussions

---

[1]   Unless cited otherwise, developmental and family tasks were adapted from Rita Ledesma (personal communication, April 10, 2014), who has curated multiple scholarly sources on child and family development.

TABLE 2 Parenting styles and effects on children. Sources: Canary, H. E., & Canary, D. J. (2013). Family conflict. Cambridge, MA: Polity Press; Havighurst, R. J. (1974). Developmental tasks and education (3rd ed.). New York: David McKay Co.; and Zastrow, C., & Kirst-Ashman, K. (2001). Understanding human behavior and the social environment (5th ed.). Belmont, CA: Wadsworth/Thomson Learning.

Parenting/Conflict Style	Characteristics	Effects on Moral Development
Authoritarian **Consensus/Competitive**	Restrictive punitive style; sets firm limits and encourages effort; discussion, if permitted, serves advance parent's belief system. The nature of resolving conflict is win-lose.	Average social skill; cognitive competencies; fearful, unhappy vulnerable to stress; possess self-control, altruism, self-esteem. Moral reasoning at a conventional reasoning level.
Authoritative **Pluralistic/Win-Win**	Warm, nurturing, accepting; encourages independence, compromise, and reason; responsive to the needs of child.	High social, cognitive competences; cope well with stress; curious, self-controlled, cooperative with adults, energetic, friendly, self-reliant. Social orientation, compliance, self-esteem, conscience, altruism, and moral reasoning (post-conventional reasoning)
Permissive Indulgent **Protective**	Very involved in child's life; few demands placed on child, but parents expect obedience when demands are placed.	Low self-control, difficulty focusing own behavior; expect to get his or her own way; poor social, cognitive competence. Endorsement of pre-conventional reasoning—moral judgments based on the tangible punitive consequences or rewarding consequences of an act for the actor rather than on the relationship of that act to society's rules and customs.
Permissive Indifferent **Laissez-faire**	Very uninvolved in child; few demands placed on child; lax control; since there are limited interactions, there are limited opportunities to test moral reasoning and prosocial behavior.	

of community, social, national, and world issues and problems to further the ethical and moral development of members should occur as well.

6. Establish rules regulating conduct and relationships consistent with family values and goals. These rules should outline approaches to conflict negotiation. Family members should role model and train children how to establish and maintain relationships

with persons outside the family. Discipline within the family unit should focus on instilling the philosophy and approaches for enforcement of rules.

7. Divide responsibilities for maintenance of family as an effective functioning unit—i.e., the family should focus on what are the tasks (chores) necessary for each member to perform to contribute to the group's well-being. As children (younger members of the family) mature, offer increasingly complex challenges. Balance division of family resources according to individual need.

Tasks of Infancy

Psychosocial

The psychosocial crisis for this period of human development (birth to 1 year) is basic trust versus mistrust, in which the optimal outcome, hope, is defined as optimism tempered by realism. Specifically, infants must learn to trust others to care for their basic needs, which results in an openness to new experiences tempered by a wariness of danger. If caregivers are rejecting or inconsistent in their care, the infant may view the world as a dangerous place (Zastrow & Kirst-Ashman, 2001).

Developmental

Davies (2004) summarizes the overall tasks of infancy as developing attachments and dyadic strategies for maintaining them, gradually gaining control over motor skills, and developing the ability to regulate arousal and affect.

Specific tasks of infancy

1. Establish a meaningful emotional/social relationship: recognize primary caregivers, develop trust in caregivers, develop attachment behaviors.
2. Learn how to learn: orient to objects and stimuli, activate curiosity, develop exploration skills, attend to details, predict and practice obtaining responses from environment, integrate sensory input.
3. Develop social communication skills: begin vocalizing, recognize the social signals of others, participate in vocal and social turn-taking activities.
4. Develop voluntary control of neuromuscular systems: eye-hand coordination, object manipulation, balance responses, mobility.
5. Establish rhythms for activities of daily life: eating, sleeping, and elimination.
6. Recognize oneself as a person, physically separate from attachment objects: engage in physical exploration and comparison, experiment with separation and reunion, begin to understand and trust one's own sensations, begin to meet one's own needs (e.g., positioning, self-comforting, obtaining objects, feeding).

Developmental Tasks of the Toddler/Preschooler

Psychosocial

The psychosocial crisis for toddlers (ages 1 through 3) is autonomy versus shame and doubt. Children must learn to be "autonomous"—to feed and dress themselves, to look after their own hygiene, and so on—resulting in a sense that the child can act intentionally (Zastrow & Kirst-Ashman, 2001). Thus, for Erikson, the optimal outcome is "will," defined as agency, making free choices, and acting independently. Failure to achieve this independence may force the child to doubt his or her own abilities and to feel ashamed.

The psychosocial crisis for preschool-aged (3 to 6 years) children is initiative versus guilt, in which children develop the capacity to have a purpose, characterized as interdependence/leadership. Children of this age will engage in attempts to act grown up and try to accept responsibilities that are beyond their capacity to handle. They sometimes undertake goals or activities that conflict with those of parents and other family members, and these conflicts may make them feel guilty. Successful resolution of this crisis requires balance: the child must retain a sense of initiative and yet learn not to infringe on the rights, privileges, or goals of others. The result is that the child learns how to cooperate with others on a shared task (Zastrow & Kirst-Ashman, 2001).

Developmental

Davies (2004) describes the overall tasks of preschool development as development of play as a vehicle for exploring reality, and transitioning from an egocentric world view and magical thinking to one that is more logical and reality-based.

Specific developmental tasks of toddlers and preschoolers

1. Recognize self as a person, psychologically separate from attachment objects, learn to tolerate separation, recognize and express will, develop skills to entertain self, learn to manage separation anxiety.
2. Learn how to harness and focus energies: identify goals, invest in activities, increase attention span, begin to persist, resist distractions, listen actively.
3. Learn expected social behaviors: imitate and practice roles, responsibilities, and relationships observed in the family and environment; share attention, begin to delay gratification, begin to demonstrate respect for others, learn cooperation and basic social skills, develop and express empathy.
4. Develop communication skills, including receptive comprehension and expressive communication; use language to express ideas, feelings, and thoughts; by age 3 be able to carry on a conversation.
5. Develop self-control, be aware of one's own affective state, learn culturally acceptable ways of communicating feelings, cooperate with adults and be able to follow simple rules, develop self-protective behaviors and safety precautions.

6. Learn to appreciate consequences, recognize simple cause-effect relationships, make simple decisions about daily life, project decisions into the near future.
7. Develop coordination, including gross and fine motor skills: become aware of physical self and physical space; strive for mobility; acquire the ability to manipulate objects and tools; refine motor skills (dexterity, running, jumping, climbing, throwing, hopping, skipping, bouncing a ball, etc.).
8. Learn basic values of family and culture along with socially and culturally acceptable roles and rules for daily life.
9. Engage in self-care: eating, dressing, toileting, simple chores.
10. Seek information and understanding: the child learns to question, experiment, tease, make jokes, persist, seek verification of knowledge and understanding, and practice skills.

Developmental Tasks of the School-Age Child

Psychosocial
The psychosocial crisis for this age group (6 to 12 years) is industry versus inferiority. Successful resolution of this crisis results in competence, defined as self-efficacy. Specifically, children must master important social and academic skills. This is a period when the child compares himself or herself with peers (Zastrow & Kirst-Ashman, 2001). If sufficiently industrious, children will acquire the social and academic skills to feel self-assured, resulting in self-efficacy. Failure to acquire these important attributes leads to feelings of inferiority.

Developmental
The overall developmental tasks for this age group are to develop emotional regulation, real-world skills, and a sense of competence and to establish oneself in the world of peers (Davies, 2004).

Specific developmental tasks

1. Develop sense of belonging through affiliations with others: participate in family activities/responsibilities; socialize with peers; experience similarities and differences; identify and build special relationships; offer contributions to group.
2. Learn how to work: commit self to task; organize schedule; defer relaxation/fun in service of goals; persist, persevere, and evaluate; learn from mistakes; enjoy process.
3. Establish a conscience: recognize the importance of rules; distinguish between right and wrong; develop and demonstrate respect; develop empathy and compassion; practice self-discipline, delay gratification, modify behaviors in light of morality.
4. Master necessary basic skills of culture: literacy, math, social skills, and computer use.
5. Develop competence in selected areas: sports, hobbies, music, reading, etc.
6. Develop appreciation of social and cultural roles relative to gender, expectations.

7. Participate in and identify with cultural traditions: holidays, family, and community.
8. Balance issues of dependence, independence, and interdependence: appreciate self; function independently to the extent possible; manage limitations; seek help; function as part of a group/team; learn from experience; generalize, hypothesize.
9. Continue to develop communication skills (grammar, vocabulary, humor).
10. Continue to elaborate gross and fine motor skills.

Developmental Tasks Associated With Adolescence

Psychosocial

Identity versus role confusion is the psychosocial crisis for individuals between the ages of 13 and 20. Successful resolution of this crisis results in the development of fidelity, marked by the creation of the prosocial self. This is the crossroads between childhood and maturity. The adolescent grapples with the question "Who am I?" and answers by developing a self that respects others and has a healthy self-concept. Adolescents must establish basic social and occupational identities or they will remain confused about the roles they should play as adults (Zastrow & Kirst-Ashman, 2001).

Developmental

The overall developmental task of adolescence is to develop an identity and become a productive adult. In terms of positive youth development, adolescents have to acquire a healthy self-concept and maintain healthy interpersonal relationships, transition from school to work (acquire an occupational identity), and form positive relationships with the larger community (forming a civic identity).

Specific developmental tasks

1. Adolescents begin to appreciate individuality by developing skills and interests, recognizing differences from others, recognizing strengths and limitations, and building upon existing skills.
2. Adolescents develop independent and consistent identity by developing a self-concept and self-esteem, exploring and examining different aspects of the self.
3. Adolescents develop their own values by exploring alternatives, developing decision-making skills, operationalizing values in daily life, and establishing a balance between personal, family, and cultural values.
4. Adolescents begin to develop self-reflective capacities by evaluating personal behaviors and assessing process, developing empathy and compassion, and examining the dynamics of relationships with others.
5. Adolescents begin to function independently (individuation) by assuming greater responsibility for behaviors with regard to work/finances, time management, decision-making capacity (moral and logical reasoning), personal and social behaviors.

6. Adolescents begin to develop a philosophy for life and the skills necessary for adult functioning with regard to relationships, career/work, education, support systems, interactions with others; they begin to establish relationships with others outside of family of origin; they prepare themselves to establish intimate relationships by exploring levels of intimacy via social and familial relationships.
7. Adolescents begin to examine issues associated with a matured physiology and need to assume greater responsibility for self-care.

Developmental Tasks of Young/Emerging Adults

Psychosocial

The psychosocial crisis of young adulthood is intimacy versus isolation. Successful resolution of this crisis results in the capacity to form intimate relationships. Such intimate relationships are more than just sexual but are characterized by relationships in which the person is able to share and give to another person without fear of sacrificing his or her identity (Zastrow & Kirst-Ashman, 2001).

Developmental

According to the APA, emerging adulthood is a distinct period within the life span (Munsey, 2006). Specifically, Arnett describes it as distinct from adolescence and adulthood. In terms of developmental tasks, emerging adults have to learn how to accept responsibility for oneself, make independent decisions, and become financially and residentially independent (Arnett, 2000).

Specific developmental tasks

1. Achieve independence (financial, residential, health maintenance) from family or establish mutually compatible interdependent relationships.
2. Organize personal identity, evaluate self-concept, and internalize identity separate from external or material conditions.
3. Develop capacities to share self via emotional connections with others; articulation of goals, needs, fears, insecurities, and conflicts.
4. Organize philosophical perspective via development of concepts regarding spirituality or meaning of life, identification of life goals, and affiliations with others, deferring to others, and committing to others.
5. Establish satisfying social relationships: develop capacity to be with self, seek affiliations with wide spectrum of people, differentiate between love and friendship and between emotional and erotic intimacy; establish meaningful relationships with a selected few, explore thoughts regarding relationships, marriage, and children; reengage with family of origin.

6. Balance between personal needs and interests with expectations and resources of culture: engage in productive activities, learn to relax, explore career options that reflect self, balance personal rights with community responsibilities, and seek outlets for creativity.

7. Develop capacities for independent decision making: develop evaluative capacities and knowledge of personal limitations, seek assistance and consultation; examine alternatives, examine motivations, develop reflective capacities, modify personal behavior as insight develops, develop short- and long-range planning skills, assume responsibility for decisions.

8. Develop needed expertise and knowledge to fulfill social roles (i.e., parenting, career preparation, education), seek mentors, evaluate and redirect life course as indicated.

References

Addams, J. (1909, 1972). *The spirit of youth and the city streets.* Chicago, IL: University of Illinois Press.

Allen-Meares, P., & Fraser, M. W. (2004). *Intervention with children and adolescents: An interdisciplinary perspective.* New York, NY: Pearson.

Arnett, J. J. (2000, May). Emerging adulthood: A theory of development from the teens through adulthood. *American Psychologist, 55*(5), 469–480.

Benson, P. (2008). Developmental assets: An overview of theory, research, and practice. In R. K. Silbereisen, & R. M. Lerner (Eds.), *Approaches to positive youth development* (pp. 43–67). Thousand Oaks, CA: Sage Publications.

Benson, P. L., Scales, P. C., Hamilton, S. F., & Sesma, Jr., A. (2007). Positive youth development: Theory, research, and applications. In W. Damon, & R. M. Lerner (Eds.), *Handbook of Child Psychology* (6th ed., Vol. 1, pp. 894–941). Hoboken, NJ: John Wiley and Sons.

Canary, H. E., & Canary, D. J. (2013). *Family conflict.* Cambridge, MA: Polity Press.

Cherlin, A. J. (2017). *Public and private families: An introduction* (8th ed.). New York, NY: McGraw-Hill.

Davies, D. (2004). *Child development: A practioner's guide* (2nd ed.). New York, NY: Guilford Press.

Delgado, M. (2000). *New arenas for community social work practice with urban youth: Use of the arts, humanities, and sports.* New York, NY: Columbia University Press.

Havighurst, R. J. (1974). *Developmental tasks and education* (3rd ed.). New York, NY: David McKay.

Hutchinson, E. D. (2010). *Dimensions of human behavior: The changing life course* (4th ed.). Thousand Oaks, CA: Sage Publications.

Lewin-Bizan, S., Bowers, E. P., & Lerner, R. M. (2010). One good thing leads to another: Cascades of positive youth development among American adolescents. *Development and Psychopathology, 22,* 759–770.

Munsey, C. (2006, June). *Emerging adults: The in-between age.* Retrieved from apa.org: http://www.apa.org/monitor/jun06/emerging.aspx

Rosa, E. M., & Tudge, J. (2013, December). Urie Bronfenbrenner's theory of human development: Its evolution from ecology to bioecology. *Journal of Family Theory and Review, 5,* 243–258.

Sawhill, I. V., Winship, S., & Searle Grannis, K. (2012). *Pathways to the middle class: Balancing personal and public responsibilities.* Washington, DC: Center on Children and Families at Brookings.

Shelby, T. (2015). Liberalis, self-respect and troubling cultural patterns in ghettos. In O. Patterson, & E. Fosse (Eds.), *The cultural matrix: Understanding black youth* (pp. 498–532). Cambridge, MA: Havard University Press.

Sherrod, L. (2008). Civic engagement as an expression of positive youth development. In R. K. Silbereisen, & R. M. Lerner (Eds.), *Approaches to positive youth development* (pp. 68–82). Thousand Oaks, CA: Sage Publications.

Silbereisen, R. K., & Lerner, R. M. (2008). Approaches to positive youth development: A view of the issues. In R. K. Silbereisen, & R. M. Lerner (Eds.), *Approaches to positive youth development* (pp. 16–41). Thousands Oaks, CA: Sage Publications.

Zastrow, C., & Kirst-Ashman, K. (2001). *Understanding human behavior and the social environment* (5th ed.). Belmont, CA: Wadsworth/Thomson Learning.

I

Theories of Resilience

A Family Resilience Framework

Innovative Practice Applications

BY FROMA WALSH

Over the past 2 decades, the field of family therapy has refocused attention from family deficits to family strengths (Nichols & Schwartz, 2000). This shift rebalances the longstanding overemphasis on pathology and assumptions of family causality in the field of mental health heavily influenced by the medical model and psychoanalysis. The therapeutic relationship has become more collaborative and empowering of client potential, recognizing that successful interventions depend more on tapping into family resources than on therapist techniques. Assessment and intervention are redirected from how problems were caused to how they can be resolved, identifying and amplifying existing and potential competencies. Therapists and clients work together to find new possibilities in a problem-saturated situation and overcome impasses to change and growth. This positive, future-oriented stance focuses on bringing out the best to enhance functioning and well-being.

A family resilience approach builds on these developments to strengthen family capacities to master adversity (Walsh, 1996, 1998b). A basic premise guiding this approach is that stressful crises and persistent challenges influence the whole family, and in turn, key family processes mediate the recovery and resilience of vulnerable members as well as the family unit. Interventions aim to build family strengths as problems are addressed, thereby reducing risk and vulnerability. As the family becomes more resourceful, its ability to meet future challenges is enhanced. Thus, each intervention is also a preventive measure. Here an overview of a research-informed family resilience framework is presented and discussed to guide intervention and prevention efforts.

The Concept of Family Resilience: Crisis and Challenge

Resilience—the ability to withstand and rebound from adversity—has become an important concept in mental health theory and research over the past 2 decades. It involves a dynamic process encompassing positive adaptation within the context of significant adversity (Luthar, Cicchetti, & Becker, 2000). Researchers have found increasing evidence that the same adversity can result in different outcomes. For example, although many lives are shattered by childhood trauma, others emerge from similar high-risk conditions able to live and love well, evident in the finding that most abused children do not become abusive parents (Kaufman & Ziegler, 1987).

To account for these differences, early studies focused on personal traits associated with resilience, or hardiness, reflecting the dominant cultural ethos of the rugged individual. Resilience was viewed as inborn or acquired on one's own, as in the "invulnerable child" thought to be impervious to stress because of inner fortitude or character armor (Anthony & Cohler, 1987). As research extended beyond situations of parental mental illness or maltreatment to multiple adverse conditions (e.g., socioeconomic disadvantages, urban poverty, community violence, chronic illness, and catastrophic life events), resilience came to be viewed in terms of an interplay of risk and protective processes over time, involving individual, family, and larger sociocultural influences (Garmezy, 1991; Masten, Best, & Garmezy, 1990; Rutter, 1987; Werner, 1993).

Notably, emerging studies of resilient individuals remarked on the crucial influence of significant relationships with caring adults and mentors, such as coaches or teachers, who supported the efforts of at-risk children, believed in their potential, and encouraged them to make the most of their lives (for a review, see Walsh, 1996). However, the prevailing narrow focus on parental pathology blinded many to the resources that could be found and strengthened in family relational networks, even where a parent is seriously impaired. Attention focused on building extrafamilial resources, often dismissing the family as hopelessly dysfunctional.

A family resilience perspective fundamentally alters that deficit-based lens from viewing troubled families as damaged and beyond repair to seeing them as challenged by life's adversities. Rather than rescuing so-called "survivors" from dysfunctional families, this approach engages distressed families with respect and compassion for their struggles, affirms their reparative potential, and seeks to bring out their best. Efforts to foster family resilience aim both to avoid or reduce pathology and dysfunction and to enhance functioning and well-being (Luthar et al., 2000). Such efforts have the potential to benefit all family members as they fortify relational bonds.

A family resilience framework can serve as a valuable conceptual map to guide prevention and intervention efforts to support and strengthen vulnerable families in crisis. Family resilience involves more than managing stressful conditions, shouldering a burden, or surviving an ordeal. This approach recognizes the potential for personal and relational transformation and growth that can be forged out of adversity. By encouraging key processes for resilience, families can emerge stronger and more resourceful through their shared efforts. A crisis can be a wake-up call, heightening attention to what matters. It can become an opportunity for reappraisal of priorities, stimulating new or renewed investment in meaningful relationships and life pursuits. In fact, families report that through weathering a crisis together their relationships were enriched and more loving than they might have been otherwise (Stinnett & DeFrain, 1985). In other words, members may discover untapped resources and abilities they had not recognized.

Ecological and Developmental Perspectives: Family Coping, Adaptation, and Resilience

A family resilience approach to clinical practice is grounded in family systems theory (Walsh, 1996), combining ecological and developmental perspectives to view the family as an open system that functions in relation to its broader sociocultural context and evolves over the multigenerational life cycle (Carter & McGoldrick, 1998; Falicov, 1995). This approach is guided by a bio-psycho-social systems orientation, viewing problems and their solutions in light of multiple recursive influences involving individuals, families, and larger social systems. Using a stress-diathesis model, problems are seen as resulting from an interaction of individual and family vulnerability to the effect of stressful life experiences and social contexts. Symptoms may be primarily biologically based, as in serious illness, or largely influenced by sociocultural variables, such as barriers of discrimination. Family distress may result from unsuccessful attempts to cope with an overwhelming situation. Symptoms may be generated by a crisis event, such as traumatic loss. A pile-up of internal and external stressor events can overwhelm the family and heighten the risk for subsequent problems (Boss, 2001; McCubbin & Patterson, 1983).

A multisystemic assessment may lead to a variety of interventions or a combination of individual, couple, family, and multifamily group modalities depending on the relevance of different system levels to problem resolution. Putting an ecological view into practice, interventions may involve community agencies, or workplace, school, health care, and other larger systems.

A developmental perspective also is crucial. A family resilience approach attends to adaptational processes over time, from ongoing interactions to family life cycle passage and multigenerational influences. Life crises and persistent stresses can derail the functioning of a family system, with ripple effects to all members and their relationships. In turn, family processes in dealing with adversity are crucial for coping and adaptation (McCubbin, McCubbin, McCubbin, & Futrell, 1998; McCubbin, McCubbin, Thompson, & Fromer, 1998); one family may be disabled, whereas another family rallies in response to similar life challenges. How a family confronts and manages a threatening or disruptive experience, buffers stress, effectively reorganizes, and reinvests in life pursuits will influence adaptation for all members and their relationships.

Family functioning is assessed in context of the multigenerational system as it moves forward over time, coping with significant events and transitions, including both predictable, normative stresses (e.g., birth of the first child) and unpredictable, disruptive events (e.g., the untimely death of a young parent). To assess symptoms in temporal context, as well as family and social contexts, a family time line and a genogram (McGoldrick, Gerson, & Shellenberger, 1999) are essential tools, enabling clinicians to schematize relationship information, track system patterns, and guide intervention planning.

Frequently symptoms of dysfunction coincide with stressful transitions or nodal events that pose new challenges and require boundary shifts and role redefinition (Walsh, 1983). Therefore, it is crucial to note the concurrence in timing of symptoms with recent or impending events that have disrupted or threatened the family. For instance, a son's drop in school grades may be precipitated by his father's recent job loss, even though family members may not note the connection. Also, it is important to attend to the wider kin network beyond the immediate household, as well as the context of multiple losses. For example, a young women's serious depression may follow the death of her godmother, who was her mainstay while growing up in a chaotic household. In the case of marital tensions that escalate into violence, the context may be one where the couple has experienced multiple losses: the failing of their small business and subsequent loss of friends and community with relocation. In such cases, too often treatment focuses narrowly on a destructive cycle of interaction without attending to its context. Thus, in assessing the impact of stress events, it is essential to explore how family members handled the situation: their proactive stance, immediate response, and long-term "survival" strategies. Some approaches may be functional in the short term but rigidify and become dysfunctional over time.

The convergence of developmental and multigenerational strains heightens the risk for dysfunction. Distress increases exponentially when current stressors reactivate painful issues from the past (Carter & McGoldrick, 1998). Unresolved conflicts and losses may surface when similar challenges are confronted. Transgenerational patterns are noted (e.g., a daughter becoming sexually active at age 15, the same age her mother had become pregnant with her). Such issues from the past influence future expectations and catastrophic fears. Clinical experience demonstrates that many families function well until they reach a point in the life cycle that had been traumatic a generation earlier. For example, a woman whose father died suddenly at age 50 may have catastrophic fears of losing her husband (as her mother did) when he reaches the same age. Other families may lose their perspective of time when a problem arises, as members become overwhelmed by an immediate crisis or catastrophic fear. They may conflate immediate situations with past events, become fixated on the past, or disengage emotionally from painful memories and contacts.

Clinicians using a resilience-based approach make covert linkages overt through respectful curiosity. They help clients heal and learn from a past that cannot be changed to differentiate the present, and they also help clients seize opportunities to handle current and future situations more effectively. Whereas clinicians typically use genograms to focus on problematic family-of-origin patterns, the approach advocated here also searches for positive examples of dealing with past adversities and encourages clients to seek out models and mentors in their kin network to support their best efforts.

Advantages of a Family Resilience Framework

Assessment of "healthy" family functioning is fraught with dilemmas. Recent postmodern perspectives have heightened awareness that views of family normality, pathology, and health are socially constructed (Walsh, 1999). Clinicians (and researchers) bring their own assumptions into every evaluation and intervention, which are embedded in cultural norms, professional orientations, and personal experience.

Moreover, the concept of the "normal" family has undergone redefinition with the social and economic transformations of recent decades. Although changing gender roles and a multiplicity of family arrangements have broadened the spectrum of families (Coontz, 1997), the persistent myth that one family form is essential for healthy child development (i.e., the idealized 1950s intact nuclear family, headed by a breadwinner father and supported by a homemaker mother) continues to stigmatize other family forms and make them appear abnormal. In fact, family diversity is common throughout history and across cultures (Coontz), and a growing body of research reveals that well-functioning families and healthy children are found in a variety of formal and informal kinship arrangements (Walsh, 1999). What matters most are family processes, involving the quality of caring, committed relationships.

Research on healthy family functioning over the past 2 decades has provided empirical grounding for assessment to identify key processes that can be fostered in intervention with distressed families (Walsh, 1993). However, most empirical measures have been standardized on White, middle-class, intact families who are not under stress. Too often, family distress and differences from the norm are readily assumed by clinicians to be pathological (Walsh, 1993). Furthermore, family typologies tend to be static and acontextual, not attending to a family's emerging challenges over time and in social context.

Clinicians' use of a family resilience framework offers several advantages. By definition, the framework focuses attention on family strengths under stress rather than on pathology. Second, it assumes that no single model fits all families or their situations. Thus, functioning is assessed in context, relative to each family's values, structure, resources, and life challenges. Third, processes for optimal functioning and the well-being of members are seen to vary over time, as challenges unfold and families evolve across the life cycle. Although no single model of family health fits all, a family-resilience-based approach to practice stems from a strong conviction that families have the potential to recover and grow from adversity.

A family resilience framework was developed (Walsh, 1996, 1998b) to guide clinical practice. This framework is informed by research in the social sciences and clinical practice seeking to understand crucial variables contributing to individual resilience and well-functioning families (Walsh 1996, 1998b). Essentially a metaframework, it can be used with a variety of models of intervention. It offers a conceptual map to identify and target key family processes that reduce the risk of dysfunction, buffer stress, and encourage healing and growth from crisis. The framework draws together findings from numerous studies, identifying and synthesizing key processes within three domains of family functioning: family belief systems, organization patterns, and communication processes (Walsh, 1998b). Table 1.1 outlines the key processes. Although it is beyond the scope of this article to describe these processes in detail, a few examples follow.

TABLE 1.1 Key processes in family resilience

Belief Systems

1. Making meaning of adversity
   - Affiliative value: resilience as relationally based
   - Family life cycle orientation: normalize, contextualize adversity and distress
   - Sense of coherence: crisis as meaningful, comprehensible, manageable challenge
   - Appraisal of crisis, distress, and recovery: Facilitative vs. constraining beliefs

2. Positive outlook
   - Hope, optimistic view; confidence in overcoming odds
   - Courage and encouragement; focus on strengths and potential
   - Active initiative and perseverance (can-do spirit)
   - Master the possible; accept what cannot be changed

3. Transcendence and spirituality
   - Larger values, purpose; future goals and dreams
   - Spirituality: faith, communion, rituals
   - Inspiration: envision new possibilities; creativity
   - Transformation: learning and growth from adversity

Organizational Patterns

4. Flexibility
   - Capacity to change: rebound, reorganize, adapt to fit challenges over time
   - Counterbalanced by stability: continuity, dependability through disruption

5. Connectedness
   - Mutual support, collaboration, and commitment
   - Respect individual needs, differences, and boundaries
   - Strong leadership: nurture, protect, guide children and vulnerable family members
     - Varied family forms: cooperative parenting/caregiving teams
     - Couple/co-parental relationship: equal partners
   - Seek reconnection, reconciliation of troubled relationships

6. Social and economic resources
   - Mobilize extended kin and social support; models and mentors
   - Build community networks
   - Build financial security; balance work-family strains

Communication Processes

7. Clarity
   * Clear, consistent messages (word and actions)
   * Clarify ambiguous information: truth seeking and truth speaking

8. Open emotional sharing
   * Share range of feelings (joy and pain; hopes and fears)
   * Mutual empathy; tolerance for differences
   * Responsibility for own feelings, behavior; avoid blaming
   * Pleasurable interactions; humor

9. Collaborative problem solving
   * Creative brainstorming; resourcefulness
   * Shared decision making and conflict resolution: negotiation, fairness, reciprocity
   * Focus on goals; take concrete steps; build on success; learn from failure
   * Proactive stance: Prevent problems; avert crises; prepare for future challenges

Examples: Family belief systems. Family resilience is fostered by shared beliefs that help members make meaning of crisis situations; facilitate a positive, hopeful outlook; and provide transcendent or spiritual values and purpose. Families can be helped to gain a sense of coherence (Antonovsky & Sourani, 1988) by recasting a crisis as a shared challenge that is comprehensible, manageable, and meaningful to tackle. Normalizing and contextualizing members' distress as natural or understandable in their crisis situation can soften their reactions and reduce blame, shame, and guilt. Drawing out and affirming family strengths in the midst of difficulties helps to counter a sense of helplessness, failure, and despair as it reinforces pride, confidence, and a "can-do" spirit. The encouragement of family members bolsters efforts to take initiative and persevere in efforts to overcome barriers. As such, therapists also can help family members focus efforts on mastering the possible and accept that which is beyond their control. Spiritual or religious resources, through faith practices such as mediation or prayer and religious or congregational affiliation, now have empirical support for their healing power. Many find strength and recovery through more soulful connection with nature or through artistic expression. Although spiritual resources have been largely neglected in clinical practice, they can be tapped as wellsprings for resilience (Walsh, 1999).

In family organization, resilience can be fostered through flexible structure, shared leadership, mutual support, and teamwork in facing life challenges. Families in transition are assisted in navigating disruptive changes and structural reorganization, as with the loss of a parent or with postdivorce and stepfamily reconfigurations. Clinicians can help families counterbalance disorienting changes with stability. Especially valuable are strategies that reassure children and other vulnerable family members by coaching behaviors that reflect strong leadership, security, continuity, and dependability.

Communication processes that clarify ambiguous situations, encourage open emotional expression and empathetic response, and foster collaborative problem solving are especially important in facilitating resilience. Therapeutic efforts are future directed, helping families "bounce forward" (Walsh, 1998b). Families become more resourceful when interventions shift from a crisis-reactive mode to a proactive stance, anticipating and preparing for the future. Most important, interventions help families in problem-saturated situations to envision a better future and take concrete steps toward achieving their hopes and dreams (Walsh, 1998b).

Applications of Family Resilience Approaches

Family resilience-oriented intervention in clinical practice builds on the principles and techniques common among strength-based approaches are included. Additionally, a resilience orientation requires that clinicians attend more centrally to the linkage between presenting symptoms and family stressors, focusing on the family coping and adaptational pathways in dealing with and recovery from adversity. Interventions are directed to reduce vulnerability and master family challenges. Even when used with brief problem-solving models (Nichols & Schwartz, 2000), this approach also attends to the suffering clients have endured. In this context, resilience does not mean bouncing back unscathed, but rather it is reflected in clients who effectively work through and learn from adversity and who attempt to integrate the experience into their lives (Higgins, 1994). Clinicians can encourage family members to share their stories of adversity, often eliminating the silence or secrecy around painful or shameful events to build mutual support and empathy. For example, a son, finding it difficult to care for his dying mother because of lingering anger at her alcohol abuse and neglect during his childhood, can be helped to see her in a more compassionate light by learning about her abandonment as a child, coming to appreciate her struggles and courageous efforts alongside her limitations. Clinicians come to see all family members as "heroes on life journeys" who are challenged along the way. Not every family member may be as successful in overcoming adversities, but all are seen to have worth and dignity.

Clinical experience suggests that use of this approach more readily engages resistant families, who often are reluctant to come for mental health services out of beliefs (frequently based on prior experience) that they will be judged as disturbed or deficient and blamed for their children's problems (Walsh, 1995). Instead, family members are viewed as intending to do their best for one another, albeit in misguided ways, and struggling as best they know how with an overwhelming set of challenges. Therapeutic efforts are directed at mastering family challenges through collaborative efforts.

Resilience-based family interventions can be adapted to a variety of formats including periodic family consultations or more intensive family therapy. Psychoeducational multifamily groups emphasize the importance of social support and practical information, offering concrete guidelines for crisis management, problem solving, and stress reduction as families navigate stressful periods and face future challenges. Therapists can identify specific stresses the family confronts and then help members to develop more effective coping strategies, gaining success in small increments and maintaining family morale. Brief, cost-effective psychoeducational modules timed for critical phases of an illness or persistent life challenge encourage families to accept and digest manageable portions of a long-term coping process (Rolland, 1994).

Offering a nonpathologizing approach to stress, coping, and adaptation, the family resilience framework advocated here can be applied with a wide range of problematic situations. Families typically come for help when in crisis, but they often do not connect the presenting problem or one member's symptoms to stressful events and concerns that are relevant. For example, one inner-city mother sought help for her daughter's school problems. During the assessment it was learned that the eldest son in the family had recently been shot and killed in gang crossfire. The family cohesion had been shattered, each member going off separately to deal with the loss: The father isolated himself and drank; a brother sought revenge in the streets; the daughter was upset at school; and the mother, alone in her unbearable grief, focused on her daughter's school problems. Family therapy sessions focused on building mutual support for the family to surmount the tragedy of this unanticipated death together (Walsh, 1996).

All clinical training and services at the Chicago Center for Family Health (CCFH) are grounded in a family resilience orientation to practice. The framework outlined in Table 1.1 guides assessment and intervention planning to foster coping and adaptation in response to normative and nonnormative challenges across the family life cycle, ranging from early parenting to care-giving for the elderly. Valuable application of the family resilience framework is evident in the development of several innovative programs addressing: (a) changing family forms and challenges (e.g., divorce and stepfamily reorganization, gay and lesbian couples and families), (b) job loss and workplace transition, (c) serious mental and physical illnesses, (d) end-of-life challenges and loss, and (e) war-related trauma recovery. A brief overview of these programs follows.

Changing Families in a Changing World: Navigating New Challenges

A resilience framework is especially timely in helping families with unprecedented challenges as they and the world around them change at an accelerated pace (Walsh, 1998b). Family cultures and structures have become increasingly diverse and fluid. Over a lengthening family life cycle, children and their parents are likely to move in and out of varied and complex family configurations, each transition posing new adaptational challenges (Walsh, 1998a). Thus, amid the social and economic upheavals of recent decades, families are dealing with many losses, disruptions, and uncertainties.

As families move into uncharted territory, many are creatively reworking their family life in a variety of households and kinship arrangements (Stacey, 1990). Yet changing patterns can be stressful and can contribute to individual symptoms and relational stress. Myths of the ideal family can compound the sense of deficiency for families in transition, making their adaptations more difficult. Clinicians can assist members to grieve their actual and symbolic losses, such as the loss of the intact family with divorce, and help them find coherence in the midst of complexity and continuities in the midst of upheaval.

Clinicians assess and address couple and family distress, as well as symptoms of individual members, in this larger context of social change. Too often, clients experience these stresses as their own personal deficits or a failed relationship. The numbers of dual-earner two-parent families and of single-parent households is growing, and they face daunting challenges in juggling workplace, household, parenting, and eldercare demands (Hochschild, 1997). Women's efforts for equality and men's desires for more involvement in childrearing are difficult to put into practice, straining relationships and requiring help in renegotiation and rebalancing of traditional gender-role constraints.

Families undergoing divorce may need help, in particular, with myriad challenges over time and initially in the midst of the immediate upheaval of separation, to effective reorganization in single-parent households and coparenting issues. Most face further challenges associated with stepfamily integration. One CCFH program trains family mediation professionals to assist with the resolution of divorce, custody and visitation, and postdecree issues through mediation. Our experience is that many families are anxious and guilty because of the widely held but faulty assumptions that divorce and single-parent households inevitably damage all children. Such generalizations, based on flawed studies (e.g., Wallerstein & Blakeslee, 1989), fail to account for the multiple influences over time that can make a difference in children's adaptation, including the predivorce climate, postdivorce coparenting, and financial security strains (Walsh, Jacob, & Simon, 1995). Research that identifies key factors distinguishing families and children who do well from those who fare poorly over time can inform prevention and intervention efforts for optimal postdivorce adaptation (e.g., Hetherington & Kelly, 2000). For instance, findings that children do better when their parents contain couple conflict, help them prepare for the separation, reassure them that it is not their fault and that they will be cared for, buffer transitional dislocations, and form a cooperative postdivorce parental alliance (e.g., Whiteside, 1998) can be applied to clinical efforts. Therapeutic and mediation approaches can facilitate amicable divorce processes and planning for ongoing care, contact, and support of children (Walsh et al., 1995). Later consultations can address such emerging challenges as custody changes or parental relocation. Specifically, we might encourage a postdivorce father in developing parenting competencies and a more nurturing relationship with his children than he had—or believed he was capable of—when he previously had relied on his wife for parenting in their intact family with traditional gender roles.

Furthermore, gay and lesbian couples and parents are expanding definitions of marriage and family to a broader view of committed relationships, yet these relationships face obstacles of stigma and discrimination that can erode them. Our center is collaborating with two community-based agencies, Howard Brown Health Center and Horizons Community Services, to offer training to mental health professionals to better understand and respond to the pressing issues and needs of lesbian, gay, bisexual, and transgender clients and their families. Application of a family resilience lens can normalize and contextualize their struggles, affirm their desires for loving relationships, and applaud their courage and perseverance in forging new models of human connectedness despite the barriers they face.

Transitional Stresses of Job Loss, Reemployment, and Welfare-to-Work

Another application of a family resilience-based program has been directed to the transitional adjustment of displaced workers when jobs are lost because of factory closings or company downsizing. CCFH resilience-based support groups and counseling services are provided in partnership with a community-based agency, Operation Able, that specializes in transitional services of job retraining and placement of displaced workers. Agency staff sought our resilience approach because it became clear that the ability of workers to rebound from job loss involved many interwoven transitional stresses that interfered with their ability to gain, succeed at, and retain new employment. The simultaneous losses of income and breadwinner status, as well as uncertainty about reemployment success, often fueled anxiety, depression, substance abuse, and couple and family conflict. This pileup of stress over many months, in turn, reduced the ability of family members to support the efforts of the worker. In one case, with the closing and relocation of a large clothing manufacturing plant, more than 1,800 workers lost their jobs. Most were African American or Latino breadwinners for their families, many of whom were single parents with limited education or skills for employment in the changing job market. Psychoeducational support groups and counseling addressed the personal and familial impact of losses and transitional stresses from a resilience perspective. This approach also addressed family strains and rallied family members as a resource to support the best efforts of the displaced worker. Group sessions focused on keys to resilience, such as identifying constraining beliefs (e.g., "No one will ever hire me, because of all my deficiencies—lack of skills, poor English, limited education"), to ultimately identify and affirm strengths (e.g., pride in doing a job well, attention to detail, and personal qualities of dependability and loyalty). The group offers support and encouragement to take initiative and persevere in job search efforts. When a group member fails to get a job or loses a position, s/he is supported to view it as an experience from which to learn and to redouble efforts to overcome obstacles and seize other opportunities. Our experience indicates that the "can-do" spirit is contagious, turning the cycle of hopelessness and despair into hope and determination to succeed.

A similar resilience-based program has been developed to address the adaptational challenges of single mothers in a Welfare-to-Work government program. Most of these mothers must overcome vulnerabilities and multiple barriers to sustained employment, many involving their families and household. Too often these mothers are seen through a deficit lens as unmotivated and underfunctioning and too readily labeled as character disordered. In contrast, a resilience approach views these mothers as underresourced and overwhelmed by multiple and persistent stressors in all aspects of their lives. A family-centered approach accounts for child-care arrangements that must be managed around new employment demands. Counseling assists them in mastering particular challenges associated with raising a child with special needs, caring for a disabled elder, stabilizing a chaotic household, or ending a troubled relationship that heightens risks of substance abuse or violence. Potential kin and social supports, including religious or spiritual resources, are identified and accessed. The resilience-based orientation shifts mothers' outlooks from hopeless despair to affirmation of their strengths and potential. It encourages their active initiative, perseverance, and mastery of the possible in their efforts to make a better life for themselves and their children.

Living Well With Serious Illness

Serious physical or mental illness poses a myriad of challenges for families, requiring considerable resilience for coping and adaptation. A family resilience approach uses concepts and language that humanize the illness experience and accompanying challenges as it encourages optimal functioning and personal and relational well-being.

Although particular features of specific illnesses may differ, there are many commonalities related to psychosocial demands and the timing of an illness in the life of an individual and his or her family. The family-system-illness model developed by CCFH co-director John Rolland (1994), provides a useful framework for resilience-oriented assessment and intervention with families dealing with chronic illness and disability. The model casts the illness in systemic terms according to its expectable pattern of psychosocial challenges over time. The unfolding of a chronic condition is viewed in a developmental context, with the interweaving of illness, individual, and family life cycles. It offers families a psychosocial map to normalize and contextualize their experience. Our experience is that family members find this of particular value because they tend to feel abnormal and deficient in comparison to "normal," "healthy" peers who are not dealing with an illness situation. Assessment and intervention are attuned to family challenges in relation to three dimensions: (a) the expectable demands of varied psychosocial types of illness (i.e., patterning of onset [acute vs. gradual], course [progressive vs. constant vs. relapsing], and outcome [fatal vs. shortened life expectancy or possible sudden death vs. no effect on longevity]); (b) the challenges accompanying varied illness phases (acute, chronic, and terminal) over time; and (c) key family system variables, such as beliefs and multigenerational legacies of past experience coping with illness and other adversity.

This framework can be used to guide periodic family consultations or "psychosocial checkups" to foster optimal coping and adaptation as salient issues and priorities surface and change over time. For instance, in the crisis phase of an illness, family tasks include creating a meaning for the condition that preserves a sense of mastery, grieving the loss of the preillness family identity, undergoing short-term crisis reorganization, and developing flexibility in the face of uncertainty and possible threatened loss (Rolland, 1994). Gradually, families need help in coming to accept the persistence or permanence of the condition, learning to live with illness-related symptoms and treatments, forging an ongoing relationship with health care professionals, and navigating the often-frustrating maze of managed care. In the chronic phase, families must learn to pace themselves and to find respite to avoid burnout, manage relationship skews (as in caregiving), and juggle competing needs and priorities of all family members (Rolland). They may need help in finding ways to preserve or redefine individual and shared goals within the constraints of the illness, as well as ways to sustain intimacy in the face of threatened loss.

Facing Death and Loss

Coming to terms with death and loss is the most painful challenge a family must confront, with ripple effects for all family members and their relationships (Walsh & McGoldrick, 1991). Although there is considerable diversity in individual, family, ethnic, and religious approaches to death and mourning, we can identify common family adaptational challenges that clinicians can help families to master (Walsh & McGoldrick). These include (a) sharing the experience of death, dying, and loss through acknowledgment of the reality, memorial rituals, and open communication of the range of feelings and attempts to make meaning by family members; and (b) reorganization of the family system and reinvestment in other relationships and life pursuits. Clinicians should be alert to a heightened risk of complications in circumstances such as ambiguous, sudden, or untimely loss; violent death or suicide; conflictual relationships at the time of death; and social stigma, as in cases of AIDS (Walsh & McGoldrick). Early intervention is important to prevent marital or family breakdown, precipitous replacement, or long-term dysfunction (Walsh & McGoldrick).

Even when death is anticipated and comes in the later years of life, medical advances pose anguishing dilemmas about the quality of life, suffering, and control over the dying process. We have found family consultations to be especially important to clarify information and options and to assist members in voicing different feelings and resolving conflict on sensitive issues. A resilience-oriented practice approach facilitates, wherever possible, important end-of-life conversations and collaborative decision making. It encourages family members to make the most of limited or uncertain time together. By focusing on mastering the possible and accepting that an impending death is beyond control, family members are encouraged to take active part in enhancing the quality of life to the greatest extent possible, with palliative care to minimize pain and suffering.

A conjoint family life review (Walsh, 1998a) can be valuable as family members reflect together on significant milestones, hopes and dreams, the challenges faced, and their successes and disappointments, thereby gaining a larger perspective incorporating different vantage points (Walsh, 1998a). Therapeutic consultations can assist estranged family members in efforts to heal old wounds or seek reconciliation and forgiveness of past grievances. Even when physical healing is no longer possible, psychosocial and spiritual healing can be deeply meaningful for all. When family members are encouraged to be fully present for one another, they commonly report that this most painful of times also has been the most precious in their relationship (Walsh, 1998b). Although clinicians observe that the death of a child poses a heightened risk for parental divorce (Walsh & McGoldrick, 1991), many couples report that their relationships grew stronger by pulling together to deal with their painful loss. In the aftermath of loss, survivors are helped by finding ways to transform the living presence of a loved one into cherished memories, stories, and deeds that carry on the spirit of the deceased and of their relationship.

Recovery From War-Related Trauma and Loss

In 1998, CCFH was called on to develop resilience-based multifamily groups for Bosnian refugees in Chicago (home to 20,000 Bosnian refugees) and the following year for ethnic Albanians arriving from Kosovo. As a result of the Serbian genocidal campaign of "ethnic cleansing," families in both regions experienced the devastating bombing and destruction of homes and communities; they suffered and witnessed widespread atrocities, including brutal torture, rape, murder, and the disappearance of loved ones. Our family resilience approach was sought because traditional mental health services were viewed in the refugee community as unhelpful and pathologizing, particularly in their deficit-based psychiatric diagnostic categories and narrow focus on treating "traumatized individuals." Often social services offered assistance to immigrants in adaptation to the United States but tended to be less attuned to refugees' experiences of trauma and losses and their deep need for connection to their community and cultural roots.

In contrast, our family resilience approach was experienced as respectful, healing, and empowering. This program, called CAFES for Bosnian and TAFES for Kosovar families (Coffee/Tea And Family Education, Support) used a 9-week multifamily group format. CAFES and TAFES Projects were funded by a National Institute of Mental Health research program to understand and address the mental health consequences of genocide and torture with Stevan Weine, MD, as the principal investigator and codirector of the Project on Genocide, Psychiatry, and Witnessing at the University of Illinois. The program worked well (Rolland & Weine, 1999) because it tapped into the strong family-centered values in their culture. It offered a compassionate setting to encourage families to share their stories of suffering and struggle while drawing out and affirming family resources (e.g., their courage, endurance, and faith; their strong kinship networks and deep concern for loved ones; and their determination to rise above their tragedies to forge a new life). Kosovar refugees faced the additional challenge of uncertainty about whether to remain in the United States or to return to Kosovo, a hazardous and unstable war zone. To foster a spirit of collaboration and develop resources within their community, Bosnian and Kosovar paraprofessional facilitators were trained to co-lead groups.

The positive response to these projects led to the development of the Kosovar Family Professional Educational Collaborative, an ongoing partnership between mental health professionals in Kosovo, through the University of Pristina, and teams of American family therapists, through the auspices of the American Family Therapy Academy, CCFH, and the University of Illinois. The project is co-led by Stevan Weine, John Rolland (MD, co-director, CCFH and clinical professor, Department of Psychiatry, University of Chicago), and Ferid Agani (MD, associate director of clinical services, University of Pristina and Mental Health Assistant to the World Health Organization). The overall aim of this project is to provide resilience-based, family-focused education and training in Kosovo. The primary purpose of the education and training is to enhance the capabilities of mental health professionals and paraprofessionals in addressing overwhelming service needs in their war-torn region by strengthening family capacities for coping and recovery in the wake of trauma and loss. In describing the value of this approach, Rolland and Weine (2000) noted,

> The family, with its strengths, is central to Kosovar life, but health and mental health services are generally not oriented to families. Although "family" is a professed part of the value system of international organizations, most programs do not define, conceptualize, or operationalize a family approach to mental health services in any substantial or meaningful ways. Recognizing that the psychosocial needs of refugees, other trauma survivors, and vulnerable persons in societies in transition far exceed the individual and psychopathological focus that conventional trauma mental health approaches provide, this project aims to begin a collaborative program of family focused education and training that is resilience-based and emphasizes family strengths, (p. 35)

Over an initial 12-month period (April 2000 to April 2001), five teams of American family therapists conducted weeklong training sessions in Pristina. Bringing varied approaches to family therapy (e.g., structural and narrative models), they all emphasized a resilience-based perspective to address family challenges, encouraging Kosovar professionals to adapt the framework and develop their own practice models to best fit their culture and service needs. Readings found to be valuable were sustained through e-mail and collaborative writing. One piece written by a member of the writing group told of a family in which the mother had listened to the gunshots as her husband, two sons, and two grandsons were murdered in the yard of their farmhouse. She and her surviving family members talked with team members in their home about what kept them strong.

> *Surviving son:* We are all believers. One of the strengths in our family is from God. ... Having something to believe has helped very much.
>
> *Interviewer:* What do you do to keep faith strong?
>
> *Son:* I see my mother as the "spring of strength" ... to see someone who has lost five family members—it gives us strength just to see her. We must think about the future and what we can accomplish. This is what keeps us strong. What will happen to him [pointing to his 5-year-old nephew] if I am not here? If he sees me strong, he will be strong. If I am weak, he will become weaker than me.
>
> *Interviewer:* What do you hope your nephew will learn about the family as he grows up?
>
> *Son:* The moment when he will be independent and helping others in the family—for him, it will be like seeing his father and grandfather and uncles alive again. (Becker, Sargent, & Rolland, 2000, p. 29)

In this family, the positive influence of belief systems was striking; particularly strong was the power of religious faith and the inspiration of strong models and mentors. Other families saw their resilience as strengthened by their cohesiveness and adaptive role flexibility:

> Everyone belongs to the family and to the family's homeland, alive or dead, here or abroad. Everyone matters and everyone is counted and counted upon. ... When cooking or planting everyone moves together fluidly, in a complementary pattern, each person picking up

what the previous person left off. ... A hidden treasure in the family is their adaptability to who fills in each of the absented roles. Although the grief about loss is immeasurable, the ability to fill in the roles ... [is] remarkable. (Becker et al., 2000, p. 29)

Unlike many other international trauma-training projects in which foreign experts descend on a war zone to dispense knowledge and then leave, this program has emphasized ongoing collaboration with respect for Kosovar professionals' knowledge about their own culture, values, and service needs. U.S. colleagues gained firsthand knowledge of the impact of the war through orientation sessions arranged by the Kosovar professionals and visits with families in villages and towns throughout the war-torn region. As a product of this collaboration, the Kosovar and American colleagues plan to develop a manual for resilience-based, family-centered training and intervention that can be adapted to other settings worldwide.

Conclusion

Family research and clinical practice must be rebalanced from focus on how families fail to how families can succeed if the field is to move beyond the rhetoric of promoting family strengths to facilitate key processes in intervention and prevention efforts. Both quantitative and qualitative research contributions are useful in informing such approaches and in systematically evaluating their effectiveness. As Werner, a leading pioneer in resilience research, has recently affirmed, resilience research offers a promising knowledge base for practice; the findings of resilience research have many potential applications; and the building of bridges between clinicians, researchers, and policy makers is of utmost importance (Werner & Johnson, 1999).

The family resilience framework presented here can be valuable in guiding clinical practice with families in crisis and those facing persistent adversity. This integrative strength-promoting orientation involves a crucial shift in emphasis from family damage to family challenge. This approach is founded in the conviction that individual and family adaptation, recovery, and growth can be achieved through collaborative efforts. Interventions are targeted to foster family strengths as presenting problems are resolved. As a broad metaframework, a family resilience approach can be integrated with a variety of practice models and modalities and usefully applied with a wide range of populations and problem situations with respect for family and cultural diversity.

In addition to the projects described here, CCFH faculty are involved in innovative resilience-based approaches to family-school partnerships for the success and well-being of at-risk youth, as well as community-based efforts to reduce the risk of adolescent violence. We hope that such programs can serve as models to inspire efforts elsewhere. Programs need to be developed proactively to meet emerging global challenges, including increasing caregiving and end-of-life dilemmas for families with the aging of societies. In every case, we must help families avert breakdown and seize opportunities for recovery and growth out of crisis. With the tremendous social and economic upheavals of recent decades and widespread concern about the survival of the family, useful conceptual models such as a family resilience framework are needed to guide efforts to strengthen couple and family relationships.

In sum, resilience-oriented services foster family empowerment as they bring forth shared hope, develop new and renewed competencies, and build mutual support and collaborative efforts among family members. From this perspective, it is not enough to solve a presenting problem (By strengthening family resilience, we build family resources to meet new challenges more effectively. In this way, every intervention is also a preventive measure.)

References

Anthony, E. J., & Cohler, B. J. (1987). *The invulnerable child.* New York: Guilford Press.

Antonovsky, A., & Sourani, T. (1988). Family sense of coherence and family adaptation. *Journal of Marriage and the Family, 50,* 79–92.

Becker, C., Sargent, J., & Rolland, J. S. (2000, Fall). Kosovar Family Professional Education Collaborative. *AFTA Newsletter, 80,* 26–30.

Boss, P. (2001). *Family stress management: A contextual approach.* Thousand Oaks, CA: Sage.

Carter, B., & McGoldrick, M. (1998). The expanded family life cycle: Individual, family, and social perspectives (3rd ed.). Needham Hill, MA: Allyn & Bacon. Coontz, S. (1997). *The way we really are: Coming to terms with America's changing families.* New York: Basic Books.

Falicov, C. (1995). Training to think culturally: A multidimensional comparative framework. *Family Process, 34,* 373–388.

Garmezy, N. (1991). Resiliency and vulnerability to adverse developmental outcomes associated with poverty. *American Behavioral Scientist, 34,* 416–430.

Hetherington, E. M., & Kelly, J. (2000). *For better or for worse: Divorce reconsidered.* New York: Norton.

Higgins, G. O. (1994). *Resilient adults: Overcoming a cruel past.* San Francisco: Jossey-Bass.

Hochschild, A. R. (1997). *The time bind: When work becomes home and home becomes work.* New York: Metropolitan Books.

Kaufman, J., & Ziegler, E. (1987). Do abused children become abusive parents? *American Journal of Orthopsychiatry, 57,* 186–192.

Luthar, S. S., Cicchetti, D., & Becker, B. (2000). The construct of resilience: A critical evaluation and guidelines for future work. *Child Development, 71,* 543–562.

Masten, A. S., Best, K. M., & Garmezy, N. (1990). Resilience and development: Contributions from the study of children who overcame adversity. *Developmental psychopathology, 2,* 425–444.

McCubbin, H., McCubbin, M., McCubbin, A., & Futrell, J. (Eds.). (1998). *Resiliency in ethnic minority families: Vol. 2. African-American families.* Thousand Oaks, CA: Sage.

McCubbin, H., McCubbin, M., Thompson, E., & Fromer, J. (Eds.). (1998). *Resiliency in ethnic minority families: Vol. 1. Native and immigrant families.* Thousand Oaks, CA: Sage.

McCubbin, H., & Patterson, J. M. (1983). The family stress process: The Double Helix ABCX model of adjustment and adaptation. In H. McCubbin, M. Sussman, & J. M. Patterson (Eds.), *Social stress and the family: Advances in family stress theory and research* (pp. 7–38). New York: Haworth.

McGoldrick, M., Gerson, R., & Shellenberger, S. (1999). *Genograms: Assessment and intervention* (2nd ed.). New York: Norton.

Nichols, M., & Schwartz, R. (2000). *Family therapy: Concepts and methods* (5th ed). Needham Heights: Allyn & Bacon.

Rolland, J. S. (1994). *Families, illness, and disability: An integrative treatment model.* New York: Basic Books.

Rolland, J. S., & Weine, S. (2000, Spring). Kosovar Family Professional Educational Collaborative. *AFTA Newsletter, 79,* 34–35.

Rutter, M. (1987). Psychosocial resilience and protective mechanisms. *American Journal of Orthopsychiatry, 57,* 316–331.

Stacey, J. (1990). *Brave new families: Stories of domestic upheaval in late 20th century America.* New York: Basic Books.

Stinnett, N., & DeFrain, J. (1985). *Secrets of strong families.* Boston: Little, Brown.

Wallerstein, J., & Blakeslee, S. (1989). *Second chances: Men, women, and children a decade after divorce.* New York: Ticknor & Fields.

Walsh, F. (1983). The timing of symptoms and critical events in the family life cycle. In H. Liddle (Ed.), Clinical implications of the family life cycle (pp. 120–133). Rockville, MD: Aspen Systems.

Walsh, F. (1993). Conceptualizations of normal family processes. In F. Walsh (Ed.), *Normal family processes* (pp. 3–69). New York: Guilford Press.

Walsh, F. (1995). From family dangers to family challenge. In R. Mikesell, D. D. Lusterman, & S. McDaniel (Eds.), *Integrating family therapy: Handbook of family psychology and systems theory* (pp. 587–606). Washington, DC: American Psychological Association.

Walsh, F. (1996). The concept of family resilience: Crisis and challenge. *Family Process, 35,* 261–281.

Walsh, F. (1998a). Families in later life: Challenge and opportunities. In B. Carter & M. McGoldrick (Eds.), *The expanded life cycle* (pp. 307–326). Needham Heights, MA: Allyn & Bacon.

Walsh, F. (1998b). *Strengthening family resilience.* New York: Guilford Press.

Walsh, F. (Ed.). (1999). *Spiritual resources in family therapy.* New York: Guilford Press.

Walsh, F., Jacob, L., & Simon, V. (1995). Facilitating healthy divorce processes: Therapy and mediation approaches. In N. Jacobson & A. Gurman (Eds.), *Clinical handbook of couple therapy* (pp. 340–365). New York: Guilford Press.

Walsh, F., & McGoldrick, M. (Eds.). (1991). *Living beyond loss: Death in the family.* New York: Norton.

Werner, E. E. (1993). Risk, resilience, and recovery: Perspectives from the Kauai longitudinal study. *Development and psychopathology, 5,* 503–515.

Werner, E. E., & Johnson, J. L. (1999). Can we apply resilience? In M. D. Glantz & J. L. Johnson (Eds.) *Resilience and development: Positive life adaptations* (pp. 259–268). New York: Academic Press/Plenum Press.

Whiteside, M. (1998). The parental alliance following divorce: An overview. *Journal of Marital and Family Therapy, 24,* 3–24.

Family Social Capital and Health—
A Systematic Review and Redirection

BY ELENA CARRILLO ALVAREZ, ICHIRO KAWACHI,
AND JORDI RIERA ROMANI

Introduction

Several definitions of social capital have been advanced, most of them including concepts of trust, shared norms, reciprocity and resources accessed by individuals as a result of their membership in social networks. As a concept, social capital includes both, the resources accessible through direct, individual connections—more related to social support, information channels and social credentials; as well as the ones that are available to all the members of a given network thanks to the relationships within the network itself—such as norms, trust and reciprocity (Kawachi and Berkman 2014).

Two main approaches exist with regard to its measurement, which are generally referred to as the social cohesion[1] and the network-based views[2] (Islam *et al.* 2006, Villalonga-Olives and Kawachi 2015). When social capital is approached through the social cohesion perspective, it focuses on the extent of closeness and solidarity within groups, and as such, the most used measures tap into indicators such as sense of belonging, trust, and norms of reciprocity. Carrasco and Bilial (2016) have argued that researchers often subsume the concept of social cohesion into social capital, and that that the conflation of social capital with social cohesion results in an individualising tendency that is antithetical to cohesion. We argue however, that social capital and social cohesion are not the same concepts. Nor is social cohesion being subsumed into social capital. To the contrary, social cohesion is a broader concept than social capital, and is defined by two overarching features of society, namely, the absence of latent conflict—whether in the form of economic inequality, or tension/conflict between groups defined by race, ethnicity, religion, immigrant status; as well as the presence of strong social bonds and solidarity—of which social capital is one aspect (Kawachi and Berkman 2000). Thus, one can have social capital without social cohesion (as Carrasco and Bilal 2016 argue), but one cannot have social cohesion without social capital.

In contrast to the cohesion school, the network-based approach to social capital is focused on measuring the resources that are accessed by individuals through their social network. This approach focuses on examining the network positions of individuals, and the resources embedded in those network ties, which are classified according to different types, including instrumental support, emotional support, appraisal support, and informational support (House 1981). Although an ongoing debate exists between these two schools and whether both can co-exist under the social capital umbrella, the prevailing tendency is to consider the two of them as complementary streams of social capital research (Kawachi and Berkman 2014).

The level (or scale) at which social capital can be conceptualised and measured potentially ranges from the macro-level (regional or country level), to the meso-level (neighbourhoods, as well as organisations such as workplaces and schools), down to the individual level. Social capital has been linked to a variety of health outcomes, including all-cause mortality (Kawachi *et al.* 1997—social capital measured at state level), self-rated health (Kawachi *et al.* 1999—social capital measured at state level; Rose 2000—social capital measured at individual level), mental health (Harpham *et al.* 2004—social capital measured at community level; Rose 2000—social capital measured at individual level), cardiovascular disease risk (Sundquist *et al.* 2006—social capital measured at community level), cancer (Lynch *et al.* 2001—social capital measured at country level) and obesity (Holtgrave and Crosby 2006—social capital measured at state level), among others.

In health research, most of the empirical research on social capital has focused on the neighbourhood as the unit of interest, that is, the potential health benefits (as well as downsides) accruing to the residents of communities as a result of their being connected to their neighbours. However, one glaring gap in the empirical literature on social capital and health has been the level of the family, which is remarkable since individuals are primarily nested in families, and family social capital has been posited by many authors as a cornerstone of social capital (Bourdieu 1986, Coleman 1988, Fukuyama 1999, Newton 2001, Putnam 1995). Family social capital is referred to here as the social capital that can be drawn from the family environment.

This lack of research on family social capital does not entail that the family context has not been investigated in the health field: the relevance of family has been actually widely acknowledged and there are notorious contributions on the effect of family functioning and family cohesion on health, especially from behavioural and developmental sciences, but these have not been much explored through the lenses of social capital.

One might ask whether referring to 'family social capital' is pouring old wine into new bottles. What the social capital discourse can add to the study of the family as a determinant of health has to do with achieving a more comprehensive understanding of the influence of intra-familial processes and structure—such as relationship dynamics, the resources embedded within them, and the connections with the environment outside the family.

Because this is still an under-explored field, this article has the potential to draw attention to research on the family field and to offer new areas on where to act to improve individuals and community's health.

Concept of family social capital

Coleman was one of the earliest scholars to bring social capital discourse into the family environment. To him, the main function of family social capital is to make the parent's human capital available to children, and it depends 'both on the physical presence of adults in the family and on the attention given by the adults to the child' (Coleman 1988: S111). Bourdieu (1986) also draws from a similar concept, when he describes social capital as another form of capital (along with material capital and cultural capital), that enables families to successfully manage the material and symbolic resources that they possess for the benefit of its members (Furstenberg and Kaplan 2004). For both of Coleman and Bourdieu, family social capital is seen as the means through which parental human capital can be accessed by the child, and in the case of Coleman two dimensions are distinguished, one referring to the structure and another to the function: high family social capital entails not only the physical presence of adults in the household (e.g. two parent households, i.e., the structural dimension), but also the presence of supportive interactions between parents and their children (which does not always exist even if the parents are physically present, namely, the functional dimension).[3]

In his work 'Social capital in the creation of human capital' (1988), Coleman explores how family social capital is relevant to the educational achievement of children. Despite the description of the different forms of social capital made in the first part of this paper, however, a distinction between them is not made in the empirical work. Family social capital is, then, estimated through the use of four indicators: (i) the ratio of parents to children; (ii) the frequency of talking to parents about personal experiences; (iii) the frequency of discussions with parents about personal matters and (iv) the mother's expectations about the child's education. His results showed that the ratio of parents to children and maternal educational expectations were associated with a decreased risk of dropping out of school, while the frequency of talking to parents about personal experiences was not related.

Several critiques have been made to Coleman's operationalisation and measurement of family social capital, which can be summarised in three main aspects. The first aspect refers to the omission of the multifaceted nature of social connections, which may be relevant to health outcomes. In the last fifteen years, the Australian Institute of Family Studies has made a considerable effort to provide further foundation to family and community social capital, resulting in two comprehensive publications in which Winter (2000) and Stone (2001) discuss, respectively, the concept and measurement of these two kinds of social capital. In both texts, a point is made that Coleman's measures are biased, since they only gather information related to the structural component of social capital, failing to take into account the quality of those relationships, and consequently not capturing elements of 'trust' and 'norms' within family relationships. The inclusion of an item reading 'the frequency of discussions with the parents about personal matters' could be interpreted as an attempt to measure the quality of family relationships but Winter's argument, which we agree on, is that using this item as the only indicator to assess quality fails to reflect the true nature of such interactions and eludes the dimensions of these social connections that may be most relevant to the studied outcome.

The second point is related to the attribution to children of a passive role in the construction of social capital. In examining the existing accounts of the creation of family social capital, Morrow (1999) has argued that the concept is scarcely developed as it relates to the role of children and that a youth's perspective on family social capital is missing in the scientific literature; that is, they are most often viewed as mere receptors of social capital without contributing to its creation. This is most clear in Coleman's work when he emphasises the negative effects of an increasing number of children in the family, while he recognises the relevance of other adult family members in the household on the available social capital. In this sense, we join Morrow (1999:751) in advocating for 'a more 'active' conceptualisation of children drawing on the sociology of childhood' that would allow an exploration of 'how children themselves actively generate, draw on, or negotiate their own social capital or indeed make links for their parents or even provide active support for parents'.

Third, the non-consideration of socio-demographic features as potential co-variables. Authors such as White (2008) or Morgan (2011) have shown how the significance of social capital is influenced by personal characteristics such as gender, age or ethnicity, as well as by parental (or other family members') beliefs and behaviours, as they are likely to set the norms and values of the group.

Notwithstanding these debates and critiques, Coleman's original work has undeniable merit in drawing attention to the concept of social capital in the family context, although this area of study has been rather overlooked in health sciences. Our aim in this review is to examine the family as the 'missing level' in studies on social capital and health by conducting a systematic review on the use and measurement of this notion in the health literature, with the final intention of articulating a direction for future research on the field.

Methods

A systematic search in PubMed, Web of Science and Sociological Abstracts databases was conducted in September 2015, using different search strategies built with the assistance of a medical librarian. The Boolean operators were built specifically for each of the databases and included different terms for the concept of 'family', plus the term 'social capital'. No time limits were applied. Inclusion criteria with regard to the conceptualisation of family were not set, as one of the interests of this review was to explore how had the notion of family been approached. The decision of limiting the sample to studies mentioning explicitly 'social capital' was made with the intention of specifically investigating the use of the social capital theory to study the influence of family dynamics on health. Additionally, only quantitative studies were included so that it was possible to extricate in a comparable way the items used to measure it. The conceptualisation and operationalisation of family in this context is a critical issue, as we shall see later. Because of the exploratory character of this review, at least in its first part, a decision was made to include all the papers indicating that family social capital was measured, independently of how 'family' had been operationalised. In this way, we sought to have a broad overview upon which to build our subsequent redirection.

The search provided 718 references, which resulted in 317 documents after removing duplicates. Four inclusion criteria were used to distinguish the relevant literature: (i) papers based on quantitative empirical research; (ii) measuring social capital within the family; (iii) having a documented health outcome—which include both mental and physical health, health behaviours and health care access and (iv) with full text accessible.

The 317 references yielded after the duplicate removal were first title and abstract screened by one coder, who judged whether each paper met the inclusion criteria. For each of the references, a 'yes', 'no' or 'can't tell'. The movement of references with one or more 'can't tell' to the full text screening phase was discussed with the other authors of this paper. The process was repeated in the full-text stage, with the 47 references that conformed to the inclusion criteria.

A total of 30 papers conformed the final sample and were tabulated to facilitate the analyses. Table 2.1 shows the full list of references together with their descriptive data.

Results

Family social capital in the health literature

From the review of the papers in our sample, it can be learnt that family social capital in the health literature has been mostly operationalised by adapting the concept of social capital to fit the boundaries of family. The depth of the analyses varies, from some authors using simple indicators such as the frequency of parents playing games with their children (Berntsson et al. 2007), to others even attempting to differentiate between the structural and cognitive dimensions of social capital or bonding, bridging and linking relationships within the family (Gonsalves 2007, Widmer et al. 2013). In short, we can say that the approach described begs two questions: (i) how is 'social capital' conceptualised? and (ii) what is the definition of 'family'?

Reflecting the broader 'state of the art' social capital research, in which multiple definitions of social capital are used, a variety of definitions of social capital have been also applied to the family context, drawing on those elaborated by Bourdieu (1986), Coleman (1990), Putnam (1993) or Lin (2001), among others. All of them have in common, in that try to capture the extent and nature of family-based network ties, but as well as within the broader literature on social capital and health, two distinct streams have emerged, namely, the social cohesion and the network conceptions of social capital (Kawachi and Berkman 2014, Kawachi et al. 2010).

TABLE 2.1 Characteristics and measures used in the 20 papers reviewed

	Paper	Country	Sample	Health-related outcomes	SC conceptualisation	Family conceptualisation	Constructs	Items
1	Litwin and Stoeckel (2014)	16 European countries	28,697 persons aged older than 65.	Well-being	Collection of social contacts that give access to social, emotional and practical support	Couple, children, relatives.	Network extent	Name generator in response to the question 'Looking back over the last 12 months, who are the people with whom you most often discussed important things?'
							Network composition	Type of relationship: (i) spouse or partner; (ii) children; (iii) other family; (iv) friends and (v) others.
							Proximity	Proportion of members living within 5 km of the respondent's residence.
							Frequency of contact	Daily, several times a week, about once a week, about every two weeks, about once a month, less than once a month
							Emotional closeness	Proportion of cited persons with whom the respondent felt very or extremely close.
2	Dufur et al. (2013)	United States	10,585 students	Adolescent alcohol and marijuana use	Following Coleman (1990), resources that inhere in the relationships among actors and that facilitate a range of social outcomes.	Parents and children	Interconnection	–How often students discuss (a) school programs, (b) school activities, (c) school classes. –How often parents check home-work.
							Trust	–How much do you trust your children?
							Parental interaction with school	–Parental attendance at parent-teacher meetings –Parental attendance at school events
3	Widmer et al. (2013)	Switzerland	48 individuals (24 young adults with mild intellectual disability and psychiatric disorders and 24 young	Psychological adjustment	Relational resources embedded in social networks that are mobilised in purposive actions.	List of persons considered as significant family members by the respondents at the time of the interview.	Family ties	Using the Family Network Method, participants are asked to provide a list of persons that they consider as significant family members at the time of the interview.
							Emotional support	'From time to time most people discuss important personal matters with other people. During routine or minor troubles, who would give emotional support to X?' (all individuals included by the respondent in his or her list of family members were considered one by one)

#	Study	Country	Sample	Outcome	Definition		Dimension	Items
			adults with mild intellectual disability but without psychiatric disorders)					
4	Eriksson et al. (2012)	Sweden	3,926 11–15 years old children	Subjective health complaints Subjective well-being	Social capital refers to people's participation in social networks and associations, and the norms of trust and reciprocity that arise from these interactions.	Parents and children		–How easy do you find it to talk to your father? –How easy do you find it to talk to your mother?
5	Han (2012)	Korea	3,449 adolescents	Health-risk behaviours	Following Coleman (1988), the embodiment of relations between parent and youth.	Parents and youth	Parent-youth communication	–Parents and I candidly talk about everything –I frequently speak outside experiences and my thought to parents
							Parental knowledge of youth's activities	–When I go out, parents usually know who I am with. –When I go out, parents usually know what I am doing.
6	Li and Delva (2012)	United States	998 Asian Amerian Men	Smoking behaviour	Features of social life – networks, norms, and trust – that enable participants to act together more effectively to pursue shared objectives. Following Putnam it refers to social connections and the attendant norms and trust.	Referred in the text as a 'Family' and 'relatives', not further defined.	Family connections	–How often do you talk on the phone or get together with relatives? –How much can you rely on relatives for help with a serious problem? –How much can you open up to family and talk about your worries?
							Family cohesion	10 items evaluating sense of family: –Family members respect for one another –Value sharing among family members –Trust among family members –Loyalty to family

(Continued)

TABLE 2.1 *Continued*

	Paper	Country	Sample	Health-related outcomes	SC conceptualisation	Family conceptualisation	Constructs	Items
							Family conflict (as a lack of SC)	–Pride of family – ... 5 more 5 items concerning attitude towards one's family: –Personal goals that conflicted those of the family –Arguing over different customs –Feeling lonely and isolated because of lack family unit – ... 2 more
7	Rothon et al. (2012)	England	13–14y.-old adolescents from 13,539 households.	Psychological distress	Coleman's conceptualisation is used, with some modifications based on critiques which have emphasised the need for some agency to be attributed to young people rather than using parental social capital as a proxy.	Parents	Quality of parent-child relationship/ Adults interest in the adolescent	–How well get on with (step-) mother/father –How often fall out with (step-) mother/father –How often talk to (step-) mother/father about things that matter to young person –How true it is to say (step-) mother/father likes young person to make own decision –How many times have you eaten evening meal with family in last 7 days?
							Parental surveillance	–How often parents know (children) where going out in evening –Whether parents ever set curfew on school nights.
8	Morgan et al. (2012)	England, Spain	3,591 15 y-old adolescents	Life satisfaction	The social capital framework used here was adapted from Morrow's original qualitative work exploring the concepts relevance to young people.	Parents	Family sense of belonging	–How often family do things together: watch TV or video; play indoor games; eat meals; go for a walk; going places together; visiting friends or relatives; play sports; sitting and talking
							Autonomy and Control	–How often mother/father let me do the things I like doing, like me to make my own decisions, try to control everything I do, treat me like a baby.
							Family social support	My mother/father (asked separately): –is loving: –understands my problems and worries: –makes me feel better when I am upset –helps me as much as I need

#	Study	Country	Sample	Outcome	Definition	Family definition	Social capital dimension	Items
9	Lau and Li (2011)	China	1306 sixth-grade primary school children and their parents	Subjective well-being	Resources embedded in social relations and social structure.	Parents and children	Structural social capital	–Discussing important issues between parents and children –Interpersonal interactions with parents and children
							Cognitive social capital	–Children perceived parentchild relationship –Level of trust with family members
10	Li and Delva (2011)	United States	2071 Asian American adults	Smoking behaviour	Individuals' objective social network and their subjective evaluation of family and neighbourhood environment.	Referred in the text as a 'family' and 'relatives', no further defined.	Social ties with relatives	–Frequency of talk on phone with relatives –Reliance on relatives for serious problem –Open up to relatives to discuss worries
							Family cohesion	10 items: –share values –work well as a family – …
							Family conflict	Five items –argue with family, –personal goals conflict with family – …
11	Litwin (2011)	United States	1350 old adults	Depressive symptoms	The array of social contacts that give access to social, emotional and practical support	Referred in the text as a 'family' and 'relatives', no further defined.	Subjective quality of relationships	–How often can you open up to member of your family if you have a problem? –How often can you rely on them if you have a problem? –How often of members of your family make too many demands on you? –How often do they criticise you?
							Structure of social network	–Marital status/cohabitation –Number of children –Number of close relatives

(Continued)

TABLE 2.1 *Continued*

	Paper	Country	Sample	Health-related outcomes	SC conceptualisation	Family conceptualisation	Constructs	Items
12	Moxley et al. (2011)	Philippines	361 adults	Nutrition and health knowledge	Putnam's conceptualisation of social capital, as features of social organisation such as networks, norms and social trust that facilitate coordination and cooperation for mutual benefit.	Parents and children	Reflections of symbolic bonding	–Are children living away from home? –Are you separated?
							Family Solidarity	–Does your family eat dinner together? –Does your family go to religious services together? –Does your family have birthday parties for children? –Does your family have birthday parties for adults? –Does your family go to the movies together? –Does your family go on picnics together?
13	Pettit et al. (2011)	United States	Longitudinal study: 459 children from kindergarten to 24 years old and their families.	Life adjustment outcomes: behavioural adjustment, educational attainment, and arrests and illicit substance use.	Following Furstenberg and Hughes (1995): the complex and variegated social mechanisms that parents garner to advance their children's chances of success.	Parents	Global relationship quality	–From 1 to 10 rate your relationship with your mother/father relationship (asked separately)
							Support from parents	–How much does your mother/father provide for your emotional needs? –How much does your mother/father take care of your practical needs? –How much does your mother/father act as an advisor/mentor?
							Parental involvement	–How often does your mother/father talk with you about ordinary daily events in your live ... and 6 more items
14	Bala-Brusilow (2010)	United States	102,353 children	Childhood obesity	Resources accrued and/or accessed from social relationships/ social bonds at multiple levels including the individual, family, neighbourhood, community or nation.	Household	Family structure	–Family structure in the household (two parent biological/adoptive family; two parent step family; single parent/other)
							Family size	Number of persons under the age of 18 living in the household
							Family eats together	Number of days during the last week that the family ate at least one meal together
							Parent know child's friends	Proportion of child's friends that parent has met

#	Author (year)	Country	Sample	Outcome	Definition	Family members	Construct	Items
15	Farrel (2010)	United States	3150 youth	Suicidal behaviour	Set of resources derived from social relationships that allow individuals to implement and accomplish otherwise elusive tasks.	Parents and youth	Parental warmth	About respondents mother and father: –I usually count on her/him to help me out if I have some kind of problems. –She/he usually keeps pushing me to do my best in whatever I do –We do fun things together –She/he usually helps me if there is something I don't understand –When she/he wants me to do something, she/he usually explains the reasons why –She/he spends time just talking with me.
16	Litwin and Shiovitz-Ezra (2010)	United States	1,462 old adults	Well-being, as measured on three separate constructs: loneliness, anxiety, and happiness.	The array of social contacts that give access to social, emotional, and practical support, according to Gray (2009)	Couple, children, relatives.	Network type	–Marital status –Number of children –Number of close relatives
17	Wu, Xie, Chou, Palmer, Gallaher, Johnson (2010)	China	5,164 11–19 years old adolescents.	Depressive symptoms	Following the seminal work of Coleman, social capital refers to the resources inherent in social relationships that facilitate a social outcome.	Parents and siblings	Quality of parent-child relationship Parental monitoring	–On days when no adults is home after school, how many hours are you at home without an adult there? –How many days a week do you eat dinner with your parents? –Are you allowed to go out with friends that your parents don't know? –How often do your parents check whether you've done your homework?
18	Ferlander and Mäkinen (2009)	Russia	1190 adults	Self-rated health	Resources accessed through personal social contacts.	Referred in the text as a 'Family' and relatives, no further defined.	Informal family social capital	–Marital status: a) Married (or cohabiting) b) non-married (divorced, widowed or single) –Do you tend to visit relatives?

(Continued)

TABLE 2.1 Continued

	Paper	Country	Sample	Health-related outcomes	SC conceptualisation	Family conceptualisation	Constructs	Items
19	Keating and Dosman (2009)	Canada	2407 adults aged 65 years and older	– Care assistance	Relying on Putnam's conceptualisation: the resources or 'stock' developed over time through trust and norms of reciprocity which facilitate coordination and cooperation for mutual benefit.	Referred in the text as a 'Family' and 'relatives', no further defined.	Network structure	–gender composition (proportion of the care network comprised of women) –age composition (proportion of the care network between –45 and 64 and proportion of the care network over 65); –relationship composition (Lone spouse, children at home or spouse and children) –proximity (proportion of the care network residing with the senior recipient and proportion of the care network more than 1/2 day's travel away from the senior recipient); –employment (proportion of the care network employed full or part time); –Network size (number of members of the care network)
20	Morgan and Haglund (2009)	England	6425 young people aged 11, 13 and 15.	– Self-reported health and wellbeing-Health-promoting behaviours-Risk taking behaviours (two)	The social capital framework used here was adapted from Morrow's original qualitative work exploring the concepts relevance to young people.	Parents and children	Family sense of belonging	How often do you do the following activities together with your family? –Going for a walk –Sitting and talking about things –Visiting friends and relatives –Going places
							Parental control	Father/mother asked separately: –How often does your mother or father try to control everything you do?

#	Author	Country	Sample	Health outcome	Social relationships	Family composition	Dimension	Items
21	Bassani (2008)	Japan	6,985 respondents	Self-rated health	Social relationships	Parents, children and grandparents (3 generations)	–	–Number of children parent has –Living in multigenerational homes
22	Berntsson et al. (2007)	Nordic countries	10,291 children in 1984 and 10,317 children in 1996	Psychosomatic complaints	Networks, norms and social trust that facilitate co-operation for mutual benefit and in turn lead to a broader social cohesion	Parents and children	–	–How often do you, spouse/partner and the child play games together?
23	Glendinning and West (2007)	Russia	637 15–21y old youth	Measures of mental health and self-rated general health: feelings of self-worth and depression.	Not described	Parents and children	Feelings of support Control Autonomy	e.g. My parent/s understand my problems and concerns e.g. My parent/s try to control everything I do e.g. My parent/s like me to make my own decisions
24	Gonsalves (2007)	United States	1983 adolescent	Alcohol use, depressive symptoms and global health ratings	Resources established through relationships	Referred in the text as a 'Family' and 'relatives', no further defined.	Bonding/Structural Bonding/Cognitive	–Household roster –How far in school did mother/father go? –What kind of work does mother/father do? –How much do you feel that people in your family understand you? –How much do you feel your family pays attention to you? –How close do you feel to mother/father? –Number of things have talked with mother/father about in the past four weeks. –Number of activities have done with mother/father in the past four weeks.
25	Jokinen-Gordon (2007)	United-States	2003 National Survey of Children's Health	Well-being	[Family social capital] Bond between youth and their parents, encompassing the time, efforts, resources and energy that parents invest in their youth, following Coleman (1988)	Parents and youth	–	–How close parents perceive their relationship with the youth. –Number of times in the past week that all members of the family have eaten a meal together.

(Continued)

TABLE 2.1 *Continued*

	Paper	Country	Sample	Health-related outcomes	SC conceptualisation	Family conceptualisation	Constructs	Items
26	Kirst (2007)	Canada	80 drug users	Drug-use related health behaviours	Coleman's individual-level definition of social capital, incorporating elements of Burt's (2001) and Lin's (2001) conceptualisations.	Not specified	Structure of social networks Resources in social networks	–Name and resource generator type questions regarding; size, density, type, multiplexity and closeness. e.g. How often for you see (name) in person? e.g. How often does (name) do a favor for you? –Name and resource generator type questions regarding social trust, social support (emotional, financial, informational), social learning and social norms/informal control: e.g. do you know anyone who can help you if you overdose on drugs? e.g. how often do you share needles with (name)? e.g. how many times in the last month have you used a needle after someone else had already used it?
27	Helliwell and Putnam (2004)	3 different surveys reporting data of 49 countries, including United States, Canada	Adults	Subjective well-being	Social networks and the associated norms of reciprocity and trust.	Not specified	–	Marital status Relations with the extended family
28	Novak et al. (2015)	Croatia	3427 17–18 years old students	Self-rated health	Resources embedded in a social structure which are accessed and/or mobilised in purposive actions	Not specified	–	Do you feel your family understands and gives attention to you?
29	Runyan et al. (1998)	United States	667 2–5 years old children	Well-being, developmental skills and child behaviour.	Benefits that accrue from social relationships within communities and families.	Parents	–	Presence of two parents residing within the home Presence of no more than two children in the home

30	Furstenberg and Hughes (1995)	United States	252 youth interviewed in a 20-year follow up.	Robust mental health and avoided live birth before age 19, as indicators of young adult success.	The complex and variegated social mechanisms that parents garner to advance their children's chances of success.	Parents	
						Family cohesion	Do you receive/give emotional support from/to your own mother?
							Do you see your siblings weekly?
							Do you see your grandparents weekly?
							Presence of biological of long-term stepfather at home
							Parents help with homework
							How often child does activities with parents
							Parent's expectations for school performance
							Mother's educational aspirations for the child
							Mother's encouragement of child
							Mother attended school meetings
							Number of child's friends mother knows

Research on family social capital and health has relied on both the social cohesion and the network approaches. However, there are notable differences in the use of the two approaches in relation to the subjects' life stage and characteristics: for example, research on the elderly as well as people with disabilities have almost exclusively relied on the study of networks and social support, as opposed to investigations in children and youth, which have tended to adopt the social cohesion approach.

One reason why the network approach has not been developed as much as the social cohesion approach may be the way in which 'family' has been defined in these studies. As previously discussed—taking off from Coleman's work—a good part of the research on family social capital has focused on how certain parent-child relations make resources available to children. Seen in this way, the network structure is something that does not need to be defined, since it is already implicit: at the structural level, the family network is constituted only by the children and their parents, and, somehow, the quality of these ties has been estimated preferentially through general questions about cohesion or sense of belonging between members. We agree with Furstenberg and Kaplan (2004), that a further exploration of the characteristics of these ties and what they can provide to health is missing.

In our sample, the study by Widmer *et al.* (2013) provides one of the few examples in which a thorough assessment of the family network was actually conducted. In their research, they applied the family network method, a specific sort of name generator. As in other name generators, participants are asked to provide a list of persons—in this case, persons whom they consider significant 'family members'– for whom they also answer some questions about emotional support, conflict and influence in their own relationships as well as between the other family members previously identified.

The question of what constitutes a family is not a trivial one. Given the heterogeneity of family roles and structures even in western societies (European Communities 2003, United States Census Bureau 2011), a straightforward adoption of the household and/or conjugal family as a unique form of family is, to say the least, biased.

The nuclear family is only one possible conceptualisation of family. In many cultures— for example, in Asia as well as the Mediterranean—the definition of 'family' extends out to a much broader set of connections. The extended network of relatives in these cultures can provide different kinds of social support that certainly ought to be construed as a part of family social capital. In fact, authors like Donati (2007), Prandini (2007), Rava-nera and Rajulton (2010) or Widmer *et al.* (2008), make the point and provide examples which show that the way in which family was defined in terms of structure had a great influence on the level of social capital. Besides, with the increase of divorce and remarriage and the high predominance of single parent families, it is increasingly difficult to set the boundaries of families (Buehler and Pasley 2000). Following Riera (2011), the family is the primary core of affection and protection, and as such the form that this institution takes is more and more a subjective experience. Furthermore, the problem about using the household as a proxy of the family is not only that it is likely to be incomplete (since many family members may be residing outside the household, for example, working in a foreign country and sending remittances back home), but it may also not capture what the individual feels is his or her family, as we can see in Widmer *et al.*'s (2008) work, in which some individuals identified their care-givers as family members. Whether unrelated individuals ought to be considered as 'family' members is debatable. They are certainly 'household' members, and to the extent that they share the same domicile, they could be considered as sharing the same resources, values, and norms within that environment. However, our own position is that 'family social capital' should be primarily restricted to blood ties or in-law relations. Otherwise the boundary between family and external contexts become once again blurred. For example, a group of university students sharing the same flat does not constitute family social capital; rather, their family social capital is accessed through their connections to family members who are living elsewhere. This raises the issue that virtual connections are likely to change the meaning and boundaries of social capital, but *a priori* it might appear that some geographical stability is needed in order to cultivate strong bonds.

Last, but not least, caution must be exercised in equating single parents with a lack of family social capital. Jennings and Sheldon (1985) argue that due to the high collinearity between family composition and other socioeconomic factors, it is not possible to attribute variations in health only to family structure, an observation that Lareau (2003) expands to the strong association between social class and parenting approaches. It has also been noted how informal networks of care outside the household can compensate and even provide greater care assets than the nuclear family itself (Hansen 2005), which reinforce the need of considering the whole constellation of relationships if we are to elucidate the effect of and the pathways through which family social capital on health.

Actually, few of the 29 studies reviewed discuss the mechanisms through which family social capital can affect health. Yet we can find interesting parallels with the broader discourse regarding social capital at the neighbourhood level. According to Kawachi *et al.* (2010), three mechanisms seem to mediate the relationship between social capital and health at the individual level: social influence/social control; social engagement and the exchange of social support. In our literature review, these also appear to be important with regard to the family context. In their study, Moxley *et al.* (2011) found that the main dietary decision maker within more cohesive families was more likely to make healthy choices, suggesting that strong family bonds can encourage their members to gain knowledge about health and learn how to take care of others. They also observed that families with strong ties are more prone to eat meals together where information and behaviours about healthy eating can be reinforced. Pettit *et al.* (2011), in turn, highlight the effect of closer families of protecting their children from high-risk activities (e.g. substance abuse) by facilitating their involvement in other more positive activities. Perceived closeness between parent and child was a strong predictor of youth well-being scores in the study by Jokinen-Gordon (2007); however it was not possible to elucidate whether this association was due to family social capital *per se*, or if it was the result of parents spending more time with their children.

These pathways seem coincident with the work done on family functioning and health outside the social capital approach. Family cohesion, one of the most studied dimensions of the family environment—especially from the fields of mental health and behavioural sciences, has been shown to have an important impact on different aspects of health through mechanisms such as informal control of health-related behaviours, sense of belonging and secure attachment (see Landale *et al.* 2013, Martin, 2008).

The measurement of family social capital

Table 2.1 illustrates the items and constructs used in the different studies that examined family social capital. Measures to capture family social capital vary to a great extent, depending on authors' definition, their notion of family, and the life stage of the respondent. In addition, similar items are used differently across studies, to the extent that the same particular item was used to measure different constructs depending on the author. For instance, the frequency of talking with family members about personal things is categorised as 'family connections' by Li and Delva (2012), as 'quality of parent-child relationship and adult interest' by Rothon *et al.* (2012), as 'parental involvement' by Pettit *et al.* (2011) and as 'family sense of belonging' by Morgan and Haglund (2009).

Also, as noted by Kawachi *et al.* (2014) a certain degree of overlap exists between the constructs used by the social cohesion and network approaches, and we may further add that this also happens with regard to the subscales. With the intention to systematise the measures employed to assess family social capital, we present in Table 2.2 the different items used in the papers reviewed, grouped according to different constructs and subscales widely applied in the study of social capital and health at other scales as proposed by Lochner *et al.* (1999) and Kawachi and Berkman (2014).

TABLE 2.2 Measures of family social capital grouped according to different constructs and subscales widely applied in the study of social capital and health.

Construct	Subscale	Items	Adapted from
Family cohesion	Collective efficacy	−Perception of working well as a family	Li and Delva (2011)
	Informal control	−Number of hours children are at home without any adult after school. −Frequency parents know (children) where going out in evening, −Allowance to go out with friends that your parents don't know −Parents know who the children are with when they go out. −Parents know what children are doing when they go out. −Parents setting curfew on school nights. −Number of child's friends mother knows −Frequency parents check whether you've done your homework	Bala-Brusilow (2010) Dufur et al. (2013) Furstenberg and Hughes, 1995) Hay (2012) Rothon et al. (2012) Wu et al. (2010)
	Social interaction	Frequency of doing the following activities along with family members: −watching TV or video −playing indoor games −doing fun things together −eating meals/eat dinner −going for a walk −going to the movies, to a concert, on a picnic . . . −working on a project −shopping −visiting friends or relatives −playing sports −sitting and talking (about things, about dates, about school problems . . .) −going to religious services −having birthday parties for children −having birthday parties for adults −Talking on the phone (with family or with specific family members) −Visiting relatives (or specific family members)	Bala-Brusilow (2010) Berntsson et al. (2007) Dufur, Parcel and McKune (2013) Farrel (2010) Ferlander and Mäkinen (2009) Furstenberg and Hughes (1995) Gonsalves (2007) Han (2012) Jokinen-Gordon (2007) Lau and Li (2011) Li and Delva 2012) Morgan and Haglund (2009) Morgan et al. (2012) Rothon et al. (2012) Wu et al. (2010)

(Continued)

TABLE 2.2 *Continued*

	Sense of belonging	−Family members respect for one another −Family members get on well −Value sharing among family members −Trust among family members −Loyalty to family −Pride of family −Closeness (to family or to specific family members) −Perception of family paying attention to oneself −Satisfaction of family relationships	Dufur *et al.* (2013) Gonsalves (2007) Jokinen-Gordon (2007) Lau and Li (2011) Li and Delva (2011) Li and Delva (2012) Petit *et al.* (2011) Rothon *et al.* (2012)
Family support	Emotional support	−Facility to talk to family or to specific family members −Facility to open up and talk about worries (to family or to specific family members) −Reliability on relatives for help with serious problems −Receiving counselling (from family or specific family members) −Perception of empathy (from family or specific family members) −Receiving/giving love and warmth (from family or from specific family members)	Eriksson *et al.* (2012) Farrel (2010) Furstenberg and Hughes (1995) Glendinning and West (2007) Gonzalves (2007) Li and Delva (2011) Li and Delva (2012) Litwin (2011) Morgan *et al.* (2012) Pettit *et al.* (2011) Rothon, Goodwin and Stansfeld (2012) Widmer *et al.* (2013) Novak (2015)

Construct	Subscale	Items	Adapted from
	Instru-mental support	−Parents helping with homework −Mother/father (asked separately): helps me as much as I need; −She/he usually helps me if there is something I don't understand	Farrel (2010) Kirst (2007) Morgan *et al.* (2012) Wu *et al.* (2010
	Family conflict	−Frequency in which family make too many demands −Frequency of critiques between family members −Frequency of arguing −Personal goals conflicting those of the family −Feelings of loneliness and isolation because of lack of family unit	Li and Delva (2010) Li and Delva (2012) Litwin and Sciovitz-Ezra (2011) Litwin (2011) Widmer, Kempf, Sapin and Galli-Carminati (2013)

Family network	Network structure	−Extension: number of members of the network −Density: Number of connections within the network −Centrality: Proportion of connections within the network for which the respondent is an intermediary.	Bala-Brusilow (2010) Bassani (2008) Ferlander and Mäkinen (2009) Furstenberg and Hughes (1995) Gonsalves (2007) Helliwell and Putnam (2004) Keating and Dosman (2009) Litwin (2011) Litwin and Shiovitz-Ezra (2011) Litwin and Stoeckel (2014) Runyan *et al.* (1998) Widmer *et al.* (2013)
	Quality of family ties	−gender composition −age composition −Relationship composition (lone spouse, children at home, spouse and children, close relatives, step-parents) −Proximity: proportion of cited persons living within a specific distance range. −Frequency of contact −Emotional closeness: proportion of cited persons with whom the respondent feel very or extremely close −Employment	Bala-Brusilow (2010) Bassani (2008) Ferlander and Mäkinen (2009) Furstenberg and Hughes (1995). Helliwell and Putnam (2004) Keating and Dosman (2009) Kirst (2007) Litwin (2011) Litwin and Sciovitz-Ezra (2011) Litwin and Stoeckel (2014) Runyan *et al.* (1998) Widmer *et al.* (2013)

Measures used in the family cohesion approach include items grouped into four subscales: collective efficacy, informal control, social interaction and sense of belonging.

Collective efficacy has been defined by Zaccaro *et al.* (1995) as 'a sense of collective competence shared among individuals when allocating, coordinating and integrating their resources in a successful concerted response to specific situational demands'. Only one article in our sample assessed collective efficacy as an indicator of family social capital. In their investigation about the association between social capital and smoking behaviour, Li and Delva (2011) asked their participants about their perception of working well as a family, as a part of a family cohesion scale. They measured social capital through different measures of individual social connectedness and subjective assessment of family and neighbourhood environment (i.e. family and neighbourhood cohesion, family conflict). Results of multivariate logistic regression analyses showed increased odds of smoking only for family conflicts or higher levels of connectedness with family members.

Indicators of informal control have been only used in studies conducted in adolescents with regard to mental health outcomes. Wu *et al.* (2010) and Rothon *et al.* (2012) conceptualised informal control as 'parental surveillance or monitoring' using measures such as the frequency that parents know teenagers are going out in the evening, whether teenagers were allowed to go out with friends parents do not know, and the frequency parents checked teenagers' homework. In both cases, an association was found between high levels of parental surveillance and lower odds of poor mental health and depressive symptoms. In the study by Furstenberg and Hughes (1995), the specific relationship between their measure of informal control and mental health is not described, but their results suggest that family social capital is indeed associated with more robust mental health in adulthood.

The dimension most widely measured among the papers drawing upon the social cohesion approach is social interaction and they basically capture activities that families (or specific family members) do together. Some of them ask whether certain activities are done in the family (yes/no answer) and others refer to the frequency. Activities here are very diverse and include, among others, sitting and talking, watching TV, going for a walk, going to a concert, going on a picnic, going to the movies, playing sports, working on a project, having birthday parties or eating meals together (Bala-Brusilow 2010, Berntsson *et al.* 2007, Dufur *et al.* 2013, Farrell 2010, Ferlander and Maekinen 2009, Furstenberg and Hughes 1995, Gonsalves 2007, Han 2012, Jokinen-Gordon 2007, Lau and Li 2011, Li and Delva 2012, Morgan and Haglund 2009, Morgan *et al.* 2012, Moxley *et al.* 2011, Rothon *et al.* 2012, Wu *et al.* 2010) . Morgan and Haglund (2009) did not find a significant association between family social interaction and life satisfaction in teenagers, but other studies showed a positive effect between doing joint activities with family and health-related outcomes such as overall self-reported health (Ferlander and Maekinen 2009, Morgan *et al.* 2012), the likelihood of obesity in children (Bala-Brusilow 2010) or the consumption of fruits and vegetables (Morgan *et al.* 2012). Particularly, having at least a meal together was related with better mental health (Rothon *et al.* 2012), and lower odds of depression (Wu *et al.* 2010).

The last subscale capturing family cohesion is sense of belonging. Sense of belonging is a psychological construct that can be defined as 'the experience of personal involvement in a system or environment so that individuals feel themselves to be an integral part of that system or environment' (Hagerty *et al.* 1992). In the papers we reviewed it has been operationalised through family members' respect for one another, value sharing, trust, loyalty, pride, satisfaction and closeness. In teenagers, when measured by parental relationships satisfaction and parental perceived closeness to the child, it was significantly associated with improved mental health (Rothon *et al.* 2012) and wellbeing scores (Jokinen-Gordon 2007). However, research by Li and Delva (2011, 2012) did not show any association between sense of belonging (measured using a combination of different items, namely value sharing, respect, pride and closeness, among others) and smoking habits among Asian Americans.

Turning to the measures used within the network approach, two constructs capture social capital: social networks and social support. Social networks represent the structure and nature of social relationships, while social support denotes the resources embedded in those networks and accessed by members. According to Lindgren (1990: 469) social support 'allows one to believe that he or she is cared for and loved, esteemed and valued, and belongs to a network of mutual obligation'. She is here referring to emotional social support, but other subtypes of social support are normally identified, including emotional but also instrumental, appraisal and informational support (House 1981). In our categorisation we have also incorporated negative social support, since it was used in several papers. By contrast, none of the studies referred to informational support as a relevant part of family social capital.

Emotional family support was the subscale more widely used to assess social support. Questions about the ease of talking to and relying on family members when facing serious problems or worries, perceptions of empathy and receiving counselling were asked to all ages ranges and in general results showed differences in correlations with health outcomes. Eriksson *et al.* (2012), found in their study on Swedish children that the ease of talking to parents explained about 6 per cent of the variance in subjective health complaints as well as 10 per cent of the variance in subjective wellbeing, with higher levels of emotional support associated with lower levels of subjective health complaints as well as higher levels of subjective wellbeing. By contrast, Litwin's (2011) paper on the association between social network relationships and depressive symptoms among older Americans reported no relation between the perceived family network quality variables and the presence of a high level of depressive symptoms. Introducing a gender perspective, results of a study on smoking behaviours among Asian Americans by Li and Delva (2011) showed that higher levels of family connectedness (as measured by the frequency of talking on the phone or getting together, the reliance on relatives when having a serious problem, and the possibility of opening up to family members to talk about worries) were associated with increased odds of being a current smoker and that this correlation was stronger for women than for men. Even if the cross-sectional nature of this study makes necessary to take these results cautiously, they are aligned with other literature on the double-edged nature of social capital (Portes and Landolt 2002, Moore *et al.* 2009). It is distinctly possible that being closely connected to other family members may result in a downside to health if others also happen to be engaged in unhealthy behaviours. In other words, social reinforcement is a powerful influence on health behaviours; if your parents are smokers, children who feel close to them may express their solidarity by smoking with them.

Alternatively, Li and Delva (2012) hypothesise that the higher likelihood of smoking found in Asian American women with higher levels of family connectedness may be the result of greater levels of stress rather than a negative effect of emotional family support, since women are more prone than men to share their distress with family members and friends.

Instrumental support refers to the exchange of help, aid or assistance with tangible resources such as labour in kind or cash (Berkman and Glass 2000, House 1981). Two of the papers reviewed assessed instrumental support, both among teenagers. Wu *et al.* (2010) asked whether parents helped children with homework, while the question by Morgan *at al.* (2012) was much more open-ended: 'Mother/father (asked separately) help me as much as I need'. In both studies, instrumental support was related with positive health effects, namely fewer depressive symptoms and better life satisfaction. Wu *et al.* (2010) noted that family social capital had not only a direct effect on depressive symptoms, but it also functioned as an important mediator between contextual factors and this mental health outcome, providing significant clues on how parents can modulate the effect of family economic conditions, parent's educational attainment and the resources available at the neighbourhood.

Family conflict was assessed in five of the papers in our sample, conceptualised primarily as family members making excessive demands or having conflicting goals. Again, studies by Li and Delva (2011, 2012) showed higher odds of smoking in Asian Americans to be associated with family conflict. Studies by Litwin (2011), Litwin and Stoeckel (2014) Litwin and Shiovitz-Ezra (2010) and Widmer *et al.* (2013) explore how different network configurations relate to psychological outcomes in older and intellectually disabled individuals. They compare the composition of these networks in terms of family members, acquaintances, friends and even professionals, confirming that more diverse networks in terms of their members (i.e. more bridging social capital) provide greater health benefits.

Studies of family networks fall roughly into two groups. One group of studies, following the work by Coleman (1988), considers marital status, the number of adults, and number of children in the household (Ferlander *et al.* 2009, Furstenberg and Hughes 1995, Helliwell and Putnam 2004, Runyan *et al.* 1998). Another group of studies by Keating and Dosman (2009), Litwin (2011, 2014), Litwin and Shiovitz-Ezra (2010), Litwin and Stoeckel (2014), Moxley *et al.* (2011), and Widmer *et al.* (2013) draw upon network analyses and delve deeper into the study of family ties, also considering dimensions such as density (the number of connections within the network) and centrality (the proportion of connections within the network for which respondent is an intermediary). Concerning the set of papers studying family networks in adults, both the density and diversity of family ties appear to have a positive effect on health. In children, the main measure used has been the ratio of children/adults as an indicator of the availability of parental resources allocated within the family. However, no strong relationships were found between this measure and health outcomes in terms of overall wellbeing or mental health, contrary to the seminal results by Coleman (1988) in the realm of educational achievement.

There are a few items that, in our opinion, do not properly belong to the construct of social capital. For example, the mother's educational aspirations for the child does not seem to be a direct measure of family social capital. While for some, they might be understood as an asset which children can benefit from (Furstenberg and Hughes 1995, Rothon *et al.* 2012), we are close to Morrow's (1999) theoretical model of the relationships between social capital and child welfare outcomes in which social capital (within and outside the family) is assessed by the extent of networks, support received from those networks, perceived trust and reciprocity, shared norms and balance of bonding versus bridging social capital. Parental values and norms, as well as parental decisions to invest in a child would be here intermediate variables that can be conditioned by social capital, but would not be social capital *per se*.

Discussion

The present review is, to our knowledge, the first attempt to systematise the study, conceptualisation and measurement of family social capital in the health sciences. With the growing interest on the effects of social capital on health and the recognition that the social capital embedded in different contexts is associated differently with health outcomes, we suspect that more scholarship on how family social capital affects health is long overdue.

Of course, there is a large body of research on family functioning and health from disciplines such as psychology and social work, but the approaches notably tap into different elements of family life. These divergences become evident when one explores two of the most widely used questionnaires to assess family functioning in psychology: the Family Adaptability and Cohesion Evaluation Scale (FACES; Olson *et al*. 1979) and the Family Environment Scale (Moos and Moos 1994). Family cohesion is a central element in both approaches, but they clearly differ in their attention to dimensions such as adaptability, communication and parental styles—highlights from the psychological point of view—or social networks and social support from the social capital perspective. As discussed above, the focus on family can provide a more integrative approach to understanding how this institution and its links with other community resources and organisations can influence health.

The first step in this endeavour should be to clearly delimit what is 'family'; which is not an easy task, as previously argued. For us, family should be confined to blood and in-law relationships, always taking into account cultural variations in the degree of separation that people consider for inclusion within the bounds of family. For instance, in Spanish culture it is quite common for the definition of 'family' to extend to one's grand-parent's cousins, while this might not be valid in other cultures. In this sense, the definition of family itself would be a great differentiator of the social capital that can be accessed.

It has been almost two decades since Coleman first introduced the notion of family social capital; yet in the field of public health, most of the attention has been devoted to neighbourhood social capital (and more recently, workplace social capital). Some limitations of Coleman's initial conceptualisation have been noted and overcome. Yet, other questions remain to be figured out. Authors like Harpham *et al*. (2002), Morrow (1999) and White (2008) have argued persuasively for considering children as active agents within the social capital discourse. Also the family social capital of adults and the elderly is increasingly being studied. Nonetheless, there is still a lack of recognition of social capital provided by siblings. This is a tendency with roots in Coleman's work, in which a greater number of children was interpreted as diluting parental attention, thus diminishing the resources available to them. In contrast to this view, siblings can play an important role in family social capital from childhood to adulthood by increasing the network size and substituting for resources that parents may not be able to offer in different stages of life, from help in doing homework, to cash loans or emotional support. Above all, a life-course approach needs to be adopted in the study of (family) social capital, as factors influencing health behaviours (not only social influence but also the existence of social norms and shared values and social modelling) are expected to operate distinctly at different stages of life (Coleman 1988, Laub and Sampson 1993, Rackett and Davison 1995).

The mechanisms through which family social capital promotes (or hinders) health behaviours and outcomes is something that needs to be further investigated too. A good starting place is to consider the mechanisms that have been put forward for social capital in other contexts, such as neighbourhoods. From childhood, families provide instrumental and affective-cognitive support that will influence children's health and well-being beyond adolescence (Norton *et al.* 2003, Schor and Menaghan 1995). In adulthood, more cohesive communities—and the same could be expected from family—help their members to cope with stressful situations, can be a significant source of information influencing health and can shape health-related behaviours through informal control and peer influence. Mixed results on the effect of peer influence have been identified for different health behaviours. Christakis and Fowler found that obesity has a contagious effect through social networks—increasing the odds of being overweight when people to which one is connected is obese (Christakis and Fowler 2007), while the effect is the opposite with regard to smoking cessation: when an individual stops smoking there is an increase in the probability that his close contacts will stop smoking too (Christakis and Fowler, 2008).

In this way, those interested in studying family social capital and its relation to health should aim at using measures to estimate not only the global level social capital in this context, but also the different constructs, social cohesion and social networks, and their respective sub-scales, as they are likely to be differently related to health outcomes. The development and validation of instruments to such aim is essential in this process.

There is also an urgent need to understand the downside of family social capital. Portes and Landolt (2002) put light into the so called 'dark sides' of neighbourhood social capital, which included in excessive demands by the members of cohesive groups, restrictions on individual freedom, exclusion of out-group members, and the downlevelling of members' aspirations. In our reviewed papers only Litwin (2011) tried to capture some of these down-sides, but it seems likely that family social capital—like other forms of social capital—can have both health-promoting and health-damaging aspects.

In summary, our findings are consistent with the notion that family social capital is multidimensional and that its components most likely have distinct effects on health. In agreement, we identify four main directions for future research on family social capital and health: (i) the investigation of whether family structure may condition social capital; (ii) research including the different constructs and subscales of social capital, that may allow to further understand how each of these are associated with different health outcomes; (iii) the adoption of a life-course approach that considers the contribution that all the members in the network make in the creation of social capital, as well as the possible different relationship of each social capital indicator and health at different ages and (iv) the consideration of the dark side of social capital.

Ultimately, a social capital approach may shed light on how the family is a critical context that lies between the individual and more upstream contexts, including neighbourhoods and the state, and can provide clues to develop upstream politics for healthier environments. As noted by Litwin and Stoeckel (2014) since notable differences exist in the family dynamics among countries, family social capital could also be an added element to take into account when explaining cross-country health differences.

Address for correspondence: Elena Carillo Alvarez, Universitat Ramon Llull—FCS Blanquerna, Padilla, 326–332 Barcelona 08025, Spain. E-mail: elenaca@blanquerna.url.edu

Notes

1 Scholars using the social cohesion approach include Robert Putnam, Francis Fukuyama and Ichiro Kawachi.
2 Scholars advocating for the social network perspective comprise Pierre Bourdieu, Richard Carpiano, Nan Lin and Spencer More.
3 Besides these two main dimensions, Coleman also talked about additional manifestations of social capital, namely: (i) obligations, expectations and trustworthiness of structure; (ii) information channels; (iii) norms and effective sanctions; (iv) closure of social networks and (v) appropriable social organization, which could also be thought of as subconstructs of social capital or potential mechanisms through which social capital influences health.

References

Bala-Brusilow, C. (2010) A study of the associations between childhood obesity and three forms of social cpital. Wayne State University. Available at http://search.proquest.com.ezp-prod1.hul.harvard.edu/doc-view/818805039?accountid=11311 (Last accessed 16 July 2015).

Berkman, L. and Glass, T. (2000) Social intergration, social networks, social support and health. In Berkman, L. and Kawachi, I. (eds) *Social Epidemiology*. New York: Oxford University Press.

Berntsson, L.T., Köohler, L., Vuille, J.C. and Kholer, L. (2007) Health, economy and social capital in Nordic children and their families. A comparison between 1984 and 1996. *Child: Care, Health & Development*, 32, 4, 441–51.

Bourdieu, P. (1986) The forms of capital. In: Richardson, J. (ed.) *Handbook of Theory and Research for the Sociology of Education*. Westport: Greenwood Press.

Buehler, C. and Pasley, K. (2000) Family boundary ambiguity, marital status, and child adjustment, *The Journal of Early Adolescence*, 20, 3, 281–309.

Carrasco, M. and Bilal, U. (2016) A sign of the times: To have or to be? Social capital or social cohesion? *Social Science & Medicine*, 159, 127–31.

Coleman, J.S. (1988) Social capital in the creation of human capital. *American Journal of Sociology*, 94, Suppl. 1, 95–120.

Coleman, J.S. (1990) Foundations of social theory. Boston, MA: Harvard University Press.

Collins, W.A. and Laursen, B. (2004) Changing relationships, changing youth: Interpersonal contexts of adolescent development, *Journal of Early Adolescence*, 24, 1, 55–62.

Christakis, N.A. and Fowler, J.H. (2007) The spread of obesity in a large social network over 32 Years, *The New England Journal of Medicine* 357, 4, 370–9.

Christakis, N.A. and Fowler, J.H. (2008) The collective dynamics of smoking in a large social network, *New England Journal of Medicine*, 358, 21, 2249–58.

Donati, P. and Prandini, R. (2007) Family and social capital: European contributions, *International Review of Sociology/Revue Internationale de Sociologie* 17, 2, 205–8.

Dufur, M.J., Parcel, T.L. and McKune, B.A. (2008) Capital and context: Using social capital at home and at school to predict child social adjustment, *J Health Soc Behav*, 49, 2, 146–61.

Eriksson, U., Hochwalder, J., Carlsund, A., Sellstrom, E., *et al.* (2012) Health outcomes among Swedish children: The role of social capital in the family, school and neighbourhood, *Acta Paediatr*, 101, 5, 513–7.

European Communities (2003) *The Social Situation in the European Union 2003*. Luxembourg: European Communities.

Farrell, C.T. (2010) The impact of social support and social context on incidence of suicidal behavior in low-income African American adolescents: A longitudinal study. University of Alabama. Available at http:// search.proquest.com.ezp-prod1.hul.harvard.edu/docview/1018362861?accountid=11311 (Last accessed 10 August 2015).

Ferlander, S., Maekinen, I.H. and Ma, I.H. (2009) Social capital, gender and self-rated health: Evidence from the Moscow Health Survey 2004, *Social Science & Medicine*, 69, 1323–32.

Fukuyama, F. (1999) Social capital and civil society. In: *IMF Conference on Second Generation Reforms*. Available at: https://www.imf.org/external/pubs/ft/wp/2000/wp0074.pdf. (Last accessed 15 July 2015). Furstenberg, F.F. and Hughes, M.E. (1995) Social capital and successful development among at-risk youth, *Journal of Marriage and Family*, 57, 3, 580–92.

Furstenberg, F.F. and Kaplan, S. (2004) Social capital and the family. In Richards, M., Scott, J. and Treas, J. (eds) *Blackwell Companion to the Sociology of Families*. Oxford: Blackwell Publishing Ltd.

Glendinning, A. and West, P. (2007) Young people's mental health in context: Comparing life in the city and small communities in Siberia, *Social Science & Medicine*, 65, 6 1180–91.

Gonsalves, L. (2007) Do relationships matter? The role of social/relational capital during emerging adulthood. Brandeis University. Available at http://search.proquest.com.ezp-prod1.hul.harvard.edu/ docview/ 61793501?accountid=11311 (Last accessed 13 July 2015).

Grzywacz, J.G. and Marks, N.F. (1999) Family solidarity and health behaviors: Evidence from the National Survey of Midlife Development in the United States, *J Fam Issues*, 20, 2, 243–68.

Hagerty, B.M., Lynch-Sauer, J., Patusky, K.L., Bouwsema, M., *et al.* (1992) Sense of belonging: a vital mental health concept, *Archives of Psychiatric Nursing*, 6, 3, 172–7.

Han, Y. (2012) Mental health and health-Risk behaviors in adolescence: An examination of social relationships. University of Michigan. Available at http://search.proquest.com.ezp-prod1.hul.harvard. edu/ docview/1520333678?accountid=11311 (Last accessed 13 July 2015).

Hansen, K.V. (2005) *Not-so-nuclear Families: Class, Gender, and Networks of Care*. New Brunswick: Rutgers University Press.

Harpham, T., Grant, E. and Rodriguez, C. (2004) Mental health and social capital in Cali, Colombia, *Social Science & Medicine*, 58, 2267–77.

Harpham, T., Grant, E. and Thomas, E. (2002) Measuring social capital within health surveys: key issues, *Health Policy and Planning*, 17, 1, 106–11.

Helliwell, J.F. and Putnam, R.D. (2004) The social context of well-being, *The Science of Well-being*, 359, 1449, 1435–46.

Holtgrave, D.R. and Crosby, R. (2006) Is social capital a protective factor against obesity and diabetes? Findings from an exploratory study, *Annals of Epidemiology*, 16, 5, 406–8.

House, J.S. (1981) *Work Stress and Social Support*. Reading, MA: Addison-Wesley Longman, Reading, MA.

Islam, M.K., Merlo, J., Kawachi, I., Lindstrom, M., *et al.* (2006) Social capital and health: Does egalitarianism matter? A literature review, *International Journal for Equity in Health*, 5, 3, 1–28.

Jennings, A.J. and Sheldon, M.G. (1985) Review of the health of children in one-parent families, *The Journal of the Royal College of General Practitioners*, 35, 279, 478–83.

Jokinen-Gordon, H. (2007) State of being: An analysis of risk and capital among Arkansas youth. University of Arkansas. Available at http://search.proquest.com.ezp-prod1.hul.harvard.edu/docview/60363912?accountid=11311 (Last accessed 15 July 2015).

Kawachi, I. and Berkman, L. (2014) Social cohesion, social capital and health. In Berkman, L., Kawachi, I. and Glymour, M. (eds) *Social Epidemiology*, 2nd edn. New York: Oxford University Press.

Kawachi, I., Kennedy, B. and Glass, R. (1999) Social capital and self-rated health: A contextual analysis, *American Journal of Public Health*, 89, 8, 1187–93.

Kawachi, I., Kennedy, B.P., Lochner, K. and Prothrow-Stith, D. (1997) Social capital, income equality, and mortality, *American Journal of Public Health*, 87, 9, 1491–8.

Kawachi, I., Subramanian, S.V. and Kim, D. (2010) Social capital and health: A decade of progress and beyond. In Kawachi, I., Subramanian, S.V. and Kim, D. (eds) *Social Capital and Health*. New York: Springer.

Keating, N. and Dosman, D. (2009) Social capital and the care networks of frail seniors. *Can Rev Sociol*, 46, 4, 301–18.

Kirst, M.J. (2007) *The influence of social capital on drug use-related health behaviours: A study of marginalized drug users*. University of Toronto, Canada.

Landale, N.S., McHale, S.M. and Booth, A. (eds) (2013) *Families and Child Health*. New York: Springer.

Lareau, A. (2003) Unequal childhoods: Class, race, and family life. University of California Press. Available at http://books.google.com/books/about/Unequal_Childhoods.html?id=3rmmj3lKATAC&pgis=1 (Last accessed 21 November 2014).

Lau, M. and Li, W.X. (2011) The extent of family and school social capital promoting positive subjective well-being among primary school children in Shenzhen, China, *Children and Youth Services Review*, 33, 2, 1573–82.

Laub, J.H. and Sampson, R. (1993) Turning points in the life course: Why change matters to the study of crime, *Criminology*, 31, 3, 301–26.

Levin, K.A. and Currie, C. (2010) Family structure, mother-child communication, father-child communication, and adolescent life satisfaction: A cross-sectional multilevel analysis, *Health Education*, 110, 3, 152–68.

Li, S. and Delva, J. (2011) Does gender moderate associations between social capital and smoking? An Asian American study, *Journal of Health Behavior and Public Health*, 1, 1, 41–9.

Li, S. and Delva, J. (2012) Social capital and smoking among Asian American men: An exploratory study, *Am J Public Health*, 102, Suppl, 212–21.

Lin, N. (2001) Building a network theory of social capital. In Lin, N., Cook, K. and Burt, R. (eds) *Social Capital*. New Brunswick: Theory and Research. Transaction Publishers. 3–39.

Lindgren, C.L. (1990) Burnout and social support in family caregivers *Western, Journal of Nursing Research* 12, 5, 69–82.

Litwin, H. (2011) The association between social network relationships and depressive symptoms among older Americans: What matters most? *International Psychogeriatrics*, 51, 2, 379–88.

Litwin, H. and Shiovitzezra, S. (2010) Social network type and subjective well-being in a national sample of older Americans, *The Gerontologist*, 51, 3, 379–88.

Litwin, H. and Stoeckel, K.J. (2014) Confidant network types and well-being among older Europeans, *The Gerontologist*, 54, 5, 762–72.

Lochner, K., Kawachi, I. and Kennedy, B.P. (1999) Social capital: A guide to its measurement, *Health and Place*, 5, 4, n259–270.

Luecken, L.J., Roubinov, D.S. and Tanaka, R. (2013) Childhood family environment, social competence, and health across the lifespan, *Journal of Social and Personal Relationships*, 30, 2, 171–8.

Lynch, J., Smith, G.D., Hillemeier, M., Shaw, M., *et al.* (2001) Income inequality, the psychosocial environment, and health: Comparisons of wealthy nations. *Lancet* 358, 9277, 194–200.

Martin, M.A. (2008) The intergenerational correlation in weight: How genetic resemblance reveals the social role of families, *American Journal of Sociology*, 114, Suppl. 1, 67–105.

Moore, S., Daniel, M., Gauvin, L. and Dub e, L. (2009) Not all social capital is good capital, *Health & Place*, 15, 4, 1071–7.

Moos, R. and Moos, B. (1994) *Family Environment Scale Manual: Development, Applications, Research*, 3rd edn. Palo Alto: Consulting Psychologist Press.

Morgan, A. (2011) *Social capital as a health asset for young people's health and wellbeing: definitions, measurement and theory*. Karolinska Instituet, Stockholm, Sweden.

Morgan, A. and Haglund, B.J.A. (2009) Social capital does matter for adolescent health: Evidence from the English HBSC study, *Health Promot Int*, 24, 4, 363–72.

Morgan, A.R., Rivera, F., Moreno, C. and Haglund, B.J.A. (2012) Does social capital travel? Influences on the life satisfaction of young people living in England and Spain. *BMC Public Health*, 12, 138–50.

Morrow, V. (1999) Conceptualising social capital in relation to the well-being of children and young people: A critical review, *Sociological Review*, 47, 4, 744–65.

Moxley, R.L., Jicha, K.A. and Thompson, G.H. (2011) Testing the importance of family solidarity, community structure, information access, and social capital in predicting nutrition health knowledge and food choices in the Philippines, *Ecology of Food and Nutrition*, 50, 3, 215–39.

Newton, K. (2001) Trust, social capital, civil society, and democracy, *International Political Science Review*, 22, 2, 201–14.

Norton, D.E., Froelicher, E.S., Waters, C.M. and Carrieri-Kohlman, V. (2003) Parental influence on models of primary prevention of cardiovascular disease in children, *European Journal of Cardiovascular Nursing*, 2, 2, 311–22.

Novak, D., Suzuki, E. and Kawachi, I. (2015) Are family, neighbourhood and school social capital associated with higher self-rated health among Croatian high school students? A population-based study. *BMJ Open*, 5, 6. doi:10.1136/bmjopen-2014-007184.

Olson, D.H., Sprenkle, D.H. and Russell, C.S. (1979) Circumplex model of marital and family system: I. Cohesion and adaptability dimensions, family types, and clinical applications, *Fam Process*, 18, 1, 3–28.

Pettit, G.S., Erath, S.A., Lansford, J.E., Dodge, K.A., *et al.* (2011) Dimensions of social capital and life adjustment in the transition to early adulthood, *International Journal of Behavioral Development*, 35, 6, 482–9.

Portes, A. and Landolt, P. (1996) The downside of social capital. *The American Prospect*, 26, 1, 18–23. Prandini, R. (2007) Family's social capital: Definition, measurement and subsidies, *Sociologia e Politiche Sociali*, 10, 1, 41–74.

Putnam, R.D. (1993) The prosperous community: Social capital and public life, *The American Prospect*, 3, 10, 35–42.

Putnam, R.D. (1995) Bowling alone : America's declining social capital, *Journal of Democracy*, 1, 1, 65–78.

Rackett, K.C. and Davison, C. (1995) Lifecourse and lifestyle: The social and cultural location of health behaviours, *Social Science and Medicine*, 40, 629–38.

Ravanera, Z.R. and Rajulton, F. (2010) Measuring social capital and its differentials by family structures, *Social Indicators Research*, 95, 1, 63–89.

Riera, J. (2011) Les famílies i les seves relacions amb l'escola i la societat davant del repte educatiu, avui. *Educaci o Social. Revista d'intervenci o S ocioeducativa*, 48, 1, 11–24.

Rose, R. (2000) How much does social capital add to individual health? A survey study of Russians, *Social Science & Medicine* 51, 1421–35.

Rothon, C., Goodwin, L. and Stansfeld, S. (2012) Family social support, community 'social capital' and adolescents' mental health and educational outcomes: A longitudinal study in England, *Social Psychiatry and Psychiatric Epidemiology*, 47, 5, 697–709.

Roustit, C., Campoy, E., Renahy, E., King, G., *et al.* (2011) Family social environment in childhood and self-rated health in young adulthood. *BMC Public Health*, 11, 2–9.

Runyan, D.K., Hunter, W.M., Socolar, R.R., Amaya-Jackson, L., *et al.* (1998) Children who prosper in unfavorable environments: The relationship to social capital, *Pediatrics*, 101, 1, 12–8.

Schor, E.L. and Menaghan, E.G. (1995) Family pathways to child health. In Amick, B.C., Levine, S., Tarlov, A.R. and Walsh, D.C. (eds) *Society and Health*. New York: Oxford University Press.

Stone, W. (2001) Measuring social capital : Towards a theoretically informed measurement framework for researching social capital in family and community life, *Australian Institute of Family Studies*: Melbourne.

Sundquist, J., Johansson, S.E., Yang, M. and Sundquist, K. (2006) Low linking social capital as a predictor of coronary heart disease in Sweden: A cohort study of 2.8 million people, *Soc Sci Med*, 62, 4, 954–63.

United States Census Bureau (2011) America's families and living arrangements: 2011. Available at https://www.census.gov/hhes/families/data/cps2011.html (Last accessed 17 August 2015).

Villalonga Olives, E. and Kawachi, I. (2015) The measurement of social capital, *Gaceta Sanitaria*, 29, 1, 62–4.

White, A.M. (2008) Reframing family social capital from a developmental perspective. Arizona State University. Available at http://search.proquest.com.ezp-prod1.hul.harvard.edu/docview/61785436? accountid=11311 (Last accessed 15 July 2015).

Widmer, E.D., Kempf-Constantin, N., Robert-Tissot, C., Lanzi, F., *et al.* (2008) How central and connected am I in my family? Family-based social capital of individuals with intellectual disability, *Res Dev Disabil*, 29, 2, 176–87.

Widmer, E.D., Kempf, N., Sapin, M. and Galli-Carminati, G. (2013) Family beyond parents? An exploration of family configurations and psychological adjustment in young adults with intellectual disabilities, *Res Dev Disabil*, 34, 2, 207–17.

Winter, I. (2000) *Towards a Theorised Understanding of Family Life and Social Capital*. Melbourne: Australian Institute of Family Studies.

Zaccaro, S.J., Blair, V., Peterson, C. and Zazanis, M. (1995) Collective efficacy. In Maddux, E. *Self-efficacy Adaptation and Adjustment Theory Research and Application*; Springer, New York, 305–28.

Zaccaro, S.J., Blair, V., Peterson, C. and Zazanis, M. (1995) Collective efficacy. In *Selfefficacy Adaptation and Adjustment Theory Research and Application*. pp. 305–28.

Resilience to Discrimination Stress Across Ethnic Identity Stages of Development

BY ANDREA J. ROMERO, LISA M. EDWARDS, STEPHANIE A. FRYBERG, MICHELE ORDUÑA

Prejudice and discrimination are significant factors to consider in the normative development of ethnic minority youth (Eccles, Wong, & Peck, 2006; García Coll et al., 1996). As early as 10 years of age, children perceive discrimination and prejudice against their ethnic group (Spears Brown & Bigler, 2005). By adolescence, discrimination and prejudice are not only common, but also stressful (Eccles et al., 2006; García Coll et al., 1996; Jackson et al., 1996; Spears Brown & Bigler, 2005). Furthermore, stress due to prejudice and discrimination is associated with lower self-esteem, more depressive symptoms, and more risky behaviors during adolescence (Adams, Fryberg, Garcia, & Delgado-Torres, 2006; Eccles et al., 2006; Edwards & Romero, 2008; García Coll et al., 1996; Romero, Carvajal, Valle, & Orduña, 2007; Romero, Martínez, & Carvajal, 2007; Romero & Roberts, 2003a, 2003b; Spears Brown & Bigler, 2005; Szalacha et al., 2003). There is evidence that ethnic identity may buffer the negative influence of discrimination; however, some studies suggest ethnic identity may increase vulnerability to discrimination (García Coll et al., 1996; Greene, Way, & Pahl, 2006; Major & O'Brien, 2005; Romero & Roberts, 2003b; Sellers, Copeland-Linder, Martin, & Lewis, 2006; Sellers & Shelton, 2003). The existing research on adolescents has not always taken a *developmental perspective* to understand how ethnic identity stages may vary in their influence on mental well-being and discrimination stress during this age period (Phinney, 1991). In the current study, we use both ethnic identity development theory and resilience theory to study how ethnic identity development stages may protect or increase vulnerability to discrimination stress among ethnic minority adolescents.

Andrea J. Romero, et al., "Resilience to Discrimination Stress Across Ethnic Identity Stages of Development," Journal of Applied Social Psychology, vol. 44, no. 1, pp. 1-11. Copyright © 2014 by John Wiley & Sons, Inc. Reprinted with permission.

Ethnic identity development

Ethnic identity is typically defined by social psychologists as a social identity that represents the sense of belonging to one's ethnic group (Phinney, 1991). Social identity theory argues that self-esteem is derived from positive social identities and positive social comparisons; the majority of empirical research has found that ethnic identity is associated with higher self-esteem, particularly among ethnic minorities (Phinney, 1991; Tajfel & Turner, 1986; Umaña-Taylor, Yazedjian, & Bámaca-Gómez, 2004). Based on psychoanalytic theory and identity formation theory, scholars have argued that racial and ethnic identity is developmental in that it changes over time and can progress through multiple stages of development (Erikson, 1968; Marcia, 1980; Phinney, 1990). Thus, we argue that depending on the stage of ethnic identity development adolescents will be more or less resilient to discrimination stress. The four stages of *ethnic* identity development are categorized based on two key factors of exploration and commitment: (1) diffuse; (2) foreclosed; (3) moratorium; and (4) achieved (Phinney, 1990; Umaña-Taylor et al., 2004). *Diffusion* is the first stage when youth have not explored their history and have not committed to their ethnic group. *Foreclosure* is when individuals have committed to their ethnic identity without actively exploring their cultural history, traditions, or language. During the third stage, *moratorium*, individuals spend time learning more about the culture, history, traditions, and language of their ethnic group. Youth have not fully committed at this stage, but it is seen as a required stage before reaching achieved identity. Youth who have not explored or committed to their ethnic identity may be more vulnerable to negative effects of discrimination on their negative affect (depressive symptoms) or overall sense of self-worth (self-esteem).

The final stage of ethnic identity development, *achieved*, is when youth have already explored and committed to their sense of ethnic belonging. It is likely that they have resolved any internal conflicts about their ethnicity and their identity is likely to be more permanent. An achieved identity may be more likely to have protective effects on youth mental well-being because it is based on a developmental process of internal acceptance of one's own personal identity and information about ethnic history and traditions. Youth who explore and commit to their identity tend to have higher self-esteem and are more likely to be resilient to conflicts (Erikson, 1968; Marcia, 1980; Phinney & Alipuria, 1990). We argue that the achieved stage is more likely than other stages to protect mental well-being from discrimination stress.

Distinct from the four developmental stages is the construct of *ethnic affirmation*, which is the affective component of ethnic identity.Previously,an emphasis had been placed on the positive component of this variable in terms of pride and happiness (Lee & Yoo, 2004; Roberts et al., 1999). Recent work has identified the negative component of ethnic affirmation as the negative emotional sense of belonging to one's ethnic group, which may include shame and desire to not belong to one's ethnic group (Marsiglia, Kullis, Hecht, & Sills, 2004; Umaña-Taylor et al., 2004). Ethnic affirmation is not theoretically linked with any one particular developmental stage, rather it can occur at any stage of development.

However, ethnic affirmation has been found to be associated with higher stages of ethnic identity development (Lee & Yoo, 2004; Umaña-Taylor et al., 2004).

Resilience theory

Previous research has found that ethnic identity and ethnic affirmation positively buffer the negative effects of discrimination on psychological well-being among minority adolescents (Branscombe, Schmitt, & Harvey, 1999; Greene et al., 2006; Major & O'Brien, 2005; Oyserman, Kemmelmeier, & Fryberg, 2003; Romero & Roberts, 2003b; Sellers & Shelton, 2003). Yet, a few other studies suggest that certain dimensions of ethnic identity may actually increase vulnerability to discrimination resulting in significantly worse mental health status (Greene et al., 2006; Oyserman et al., 2003). We argue that ethnic identity development and ethnic affirmation may help adolescents respond positively to adverse situations of discrimination, that is, be resilient. However, given that the effectiveness of resilience factors may differ based on the intensity of the stressor, we use resilience theory to understand and hypothesize when ethnic identity may enhance well-being, or when it may increase vulnerability in the face of discrimination (Luthar, Cicchetti, & Becker, 2000; Masten, 2001). For example, resilience is comprised of many different factors, and may include protective factors,

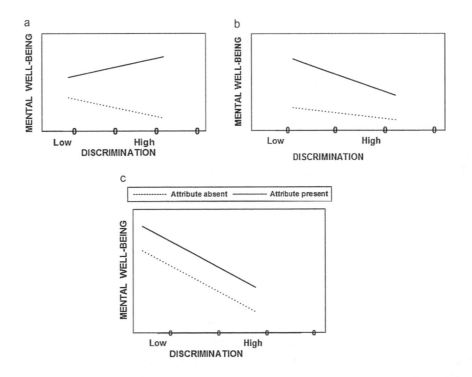

FIGURE 3.1 Graph (a) represents the predicted *protective-enhancing* moderating effect of ethnic affirmation. Graph (b) represents the predicted *protective reactive* effect of ethnic identity stages. Graph (c) represents the direct protective effect of ethnic identity.

vulnerability factors, or moderating factors (Luthar et al., 2000) (see Figure 3.1). *Protective factors* that have a *direct effect* will protect individuals and stabilize well-being at all levels of stress. *Moderating factors* confer more specific advantages under high-risk or low-risk conditions, and these advantages can be described as either enhancing, stabilizing, or reactive (Luthar et al., 2000). *Protective-enhancing factors* will moderate the effect of stress on mental well-being, such that at resilience may increase higher levels of stress when youth have a more achieved ethnic identity. *Protective stabilizing factors* may stabilize well-being at all levels of stress, but when the factor is not present individuals may be vulnerable particularly at high level of stress. *Protective reactive factors* will moderate stress in a manner that may be protective at low levels of stress, but will actually increase vulnerability at higher levels of stress. Extant literature of ethnic identity provides some insight into the possible resilience effects of ethnic identity development and affirmation. Research has found that resilience effects can be very different for positive mental health compared to mental illness. Previous research has demonstrated that ethnic identity and discrimination are associated with depressive symptoms and self-esteem; however, we will explore each hypothesis separately for these two mental well-being outcomes.

While relatively little research has included all four stages of ethnic identity development in relation to discrimination and self-esteem among adolescents, one study examining stages found a moderating effect of ethnic identity achievement on self-esteem. Achieved stage was associated with lower self-esteem under high levels of peer discrimination, with a protective-reactive effect that increased vulnerability at high intensity of stress (Greene et al., 2006).Yet, the majority of previous research suggests that individuals who have a less developed ethnic identity are the most vulnerable to the negative effects of high levels of discrimination (Sellers, Caldwell, Schmeelk-Cone, & Zimmerman, 2003; Sellers & Shelton, 2003; Sellers et al., 2006; Wong, Eccles, & Sameroff, 2003). Thus, we argue that it is more likely that a diffuse stage of ethnic identity development will be associated with protective-reactive effects that increase vulnerability at high levels of stress; however, we will also investigate the protective moderating effects of achieved ethnic identity on self-esteem.

Ethnic affirmation appears to provide a protective effect on depressive symptoms at all levels of discrimination stress (Greene et al., 2006; Sellers et al., 2006). However, in one study, ethnic affirmation increased vulnerability with a protective-reactive effect on depressive symptoms among Korean American students (Lee, 2005). Studies linking ethnic affirmation and self-esteem appear to suggest that positive affirmation is associated with higher self-esteem. Yet, other studies have consistently demonstrated a protective-enhancing effect. Romero and Roberts (2003b) report that Mexican American youth with high ethnic affirmation under high levels of discrimination stress have higher self-esteem (protective-enhancing effect). Greene et al. (2006) also found in a longitudinal study of adolescents of African American and Puerto Rican descent that ethnic affirmation had a protective-enhancing effect on self-esteem at high levels of discrimination (Greene et al., 2006). Additionally, three different studies exploring academic outcomes reported that a positive view of one's ethnic group buffered the negative effect of discrimination among African American and

American Indian adolescents with a protective-enhancing effect on education (Eccles et al., 2006; Oyserman et al., 2003; Wong et al., 2003). Thus, it appears that the resilience effect of ethnic affirmation may even be enhanced at high levels of discrimination stress. Overall, we anticipate that at high levels of discrimination stress, positive ethnic affirmation is likely to have a protective-enhancing effect on youth well-being.

In sum, ethnic identity developmental stages and ethnic affirmation may be a form of resilience for ethnic minority adolescent well-being; however, moderating effects may differ depending on the level of intensity of discrimination stress. We utilize ethnic identity developmental stage theory and resilience theory to investigate the following hypotheses in the current study with a sample of minority adolescents of Mexican and Native American descent.

> *Hypothesis 1.* Ethnic affirmation will have protective-enhancing effects on self-esteem and depressive symptoms. At high levels of discrimination stress, youth with high ethnic affirmation will also report high levels of self-esteem/low levels of depressive symptoms.

> *Hypothesis 2.* Diffuse ethnic identity will have a protective reactive resilience effect on self-esteem and depressive symptoms. Diffuse youth at high levels of discrimination stress will report significantly lower self-esteem and higher depressive symptoms. Achieved stage will have a protective-enhancing effect on self-esteem and depressive symptoms. Achieved youth at high levels of discrimination will report higher self-esteem and lower depressive symptoms.

Method

Participants

A total of 125 adolescents (13–18 years old, $M = 15.53$, $SD = 1.40$) completed surveys at local urban youth afterschool centers. Youth reported that they were Mexican descent (74%), Native American descent (9%), or a mix of these backgrounds (17%). Age (between 13 and 18 years old) and parental consent were the only participation criteria. All parents signed active consent forms to allow their children to participate in the study and all youth participants signed assent forms prior to completing the survey. The Human Subjects Protection Program approved the study.

Measures

Demographics
Subjects completed a demographic questionnaire that included items about age, gender, and ethnicity. Generation levels are based on Cuéllar, Arnold, and Maldonado's (1995) definitions of generations as 1st = respondent was born in a country other than United States; 2nd = respondent was born in United States with at least one parent is born in a country other than United States; 3rd = respondent and both parents were born in United States and

all grandparents were born in a country other than United States; 4th = respondent, both parents born in United States with at least one grandparent born in a country other than United States; 5th = respondent, both parents, and all grandparents born in United States.

Language preference
Preference for Spanish or English was measured by an 8-item version of the bi-dimensional acculturation scale (Marin & Gamba, 1996). Youth were asked "How often do you speak English?"; "How often do you speak Spanish?"; and "How often do you speak English/Spanish (language) with friends/home?" Response items regarding language preferences ranged from 1 (*never*) to 4 (*always*). Four items from this scale measure English preference (α = .76) and four items from the scale measure Spanish preference (α = .90). The responses were averaged across the three items per language. English and Spanish preferences were then dichotomized into "high" or "low" separately based on the median score. Three levels of language preference were created based on the following categories: (1) Spanish preference (low English); (2) bilingual preference (high English and high Spanish); and (3) English preference (high English and low Spanish).

Discrimination stress
The discrimination subscale from the Bicultural Stressors Scale (Romero & Roberts, 2003a) was utilized to assess the frequency and perceived stressfulness of various discrimination experiences. Nine discrimination items were included in this scale (e.g., "Sometimes I feel it is harder to succeed because of my ethnic background," "I am not accepted because of my ethnicity,"and"I do not like it when others put down people of my ethnic background"). The possible range of responses to each stressor are *does not apply* (coded as 0), *not stressful at all* (1), *a little bit stressful* (2), *quite a bit stressful* (3), and *very stressful* (4). These items provide information on whether youth experienced the stressors (does not apply or is present) and the level of stressfulness. A total score representing how many stressors youth had experienced was determined by taking a sum score after items were dichotomized, providing a range from 0 to 9. A mean score was also computed with the continuous responses such that a higher score represents more stress on a scale of 0–4. The internal consistency of the continuous discrimination scale for the current sample was α = .81.

Ethnic affirmation
Ethnic affirmation assesses the degree to which participants felt positive and negative about their ethnic group. Three items were taken from Lee and Yoo's (2004) affirmation subscale on positive affect and an additional five negative affect items were taken from Marsiglia et al. (2004) to address all of the dimensions of ethnic affirmation. The *affirmation* scale consisted of eight items (e.g.,"I am happy that I belong to my ethnic group,""I have a lot of pride in my ethnic background,""Sometimes I wish I looked like someone from a different ethnic group," and "Sometimes I am embarrassed by the way that people from my ethnic group act"). The eight items had a high internal consistency of α = .88 with the current sample.

Ethnic identity stage

Ethnic identity stages were assessed with 11 items from the Multigroup Ethnic Identity Measure (Phinney, 1992). Response items ranged from 1 (*strongly disagree*) to 4 (*strongly agree*). The exploration and commitment subscale items were averaged with high score indicating more agreement. The *exploration* subscale was comprised of five items with an internal consistency of $\alpha = .86$. The *commitment* subscale consisted of six items with an internal consistency of $\alpha = .81$. Ethnic identity stages were based on those outlined by Marcia (1980) and Phinney (1991) (diffuse, foreclosed, explored, and achieved) and constructed based on exploration and commitment subscales of the Multigroup Ethnic Identity Measures (Seaton, Scottham, & Sellers, 2006; Umaña-Taylor et al., 2004; Yip, Seaton, & Sellers, 2006). The ethnic identity stage consisted of the following categories based on media splits of the subscales: 1 = diffusion (low exploration/low commitment), 2 = foreclosed (low exploration/high commitment), 3 = moratorium (high exploration/low commitment), 4 = achieved (high exploration/high commitment).

Depressive symptoms

An 8-item shortened version of the Center for Epidemiological Studies-Depression Scale was used to assess depressive symptoms (Radloff, 1977). The measure includes assessments of the frequency of experiencing four major symptom domains of depression within the past week: negative affect, absence of positive affect (reversed scored), somatic complaints, and interpersonal problems (Crockett, Randall, Shen, Russell, & Driscoll, 2005; Rushton, Forcier, & Schectman, 2002). There is good evidence for the measure's relevance for ethnic minority adolescents (Carvajal, Evans, Nash, & Getz, 2002; Crockett et al., 2005; Roberts, Lewinsohn, & Seeley, 1991). Items referred to the past 7 days and responses were coded as 0 (*never*), 1 (*less than 1 day*), 2 (*1–2 days*), 3 (*2–4 days*), or 4 (*5–7 days*). A mean value was taken with the items to create a continuous scale of depressive symptoms that ranged from 1 to 5. The internal consistency of the scale was .76 with the current sample.

Self-esteem

The Rosenberg (1965) scale was used to measure self-esteem. The 7-item scale (1 = *never*, 5 = *almost always true*) was reliable in previous studies with adolescents (Rosenberg, 1965, 1979), particularly with Mexican Americans. Cronbach's alpha ranged from .73 to .87 (Cervantes, Padilla, & Salgado de Snyder, 1990,1991; Joiner & Kashubeck, 1996).A sample item is "I feel that I have a number of good qualities." For this sample, the scale was sufficiently reliable, $\alpha = .62$. An average self-esteem score was computed.

Procedure

Bilingual and bicultural trained project staff administered the surveys afterschool at local youth centers. Surveys were available in both English and Spanish. Participants had the option to answer the survey in either language (80% completed the survey in English,20% completed the survey in Spanish). The questionnaire was first developed in English and then translated into Spanish by a professional translator. The translations were then back-translated from Spanish to English by local native Spanish speakers (Brislin, 1976; Brislin, Lonner, & Thorndike, 1973). The survey took approximately one and a half hours to complete.

Results

Descriptives and demographic differences Sample demographics are reported in Table 3.1 and descriptives for variables of interest in Table 3.2. Ethnic identity stage was distributed as follows: diffuse ($n = 36$, 30%), foreclosed ($n = 20$, 16%), moratorium ($n = 21$, 17%), and achieved ($n = 45$, 37%). Based on one-way analysis of variance (ANOVA) results, ethnic identity stages differed significantly by self-esteem, $F(3, 117) = 10.48$, $p < .001$; age, $F(3, 118) = 8.00$, $p < .001$; and ethnic affirmation, $F(3, 118) = 21.78$, $p < .001$. Post hoc Bonferroni tests indicated the significant differences as follows: achieved youth ($M = 4.18$, $SD = .54$) reported significantly higher self-esteem compared to diffuse ($M = 3.46$, $SD = .66$; $p < .001$) or explored youth ($M = 3.53$, $SD = .65$; $p < .01$). Achieved youth were also significantly older than other stages (achieved, $M = 16.29$, $SD = 1.34$; diffuse, $M = 15.08$, $SD = 1.13$, $p < .001$; foreclosed, $M = 15.15$, $SD = 1.39$, $p < .01$; and explored, $M = 15.10$, $SD = 1.34$, $p < .01$). Ethnic affirmation differed significantly by ethnic identity stage: Achieved youth ($M = 3.99$, $SD = .10$) had significantly higher affirmation than diffuse ($M = 3.28$, $SD = .63$, $p < .001$) or explored youth ($M = 3.28$, $SD = .70$, $p < .001$). Foreclosed youth ($M = 3.87$, $SD = .23$) were significantly higher on affirmation than diffuse ($p < .001$) or explored youth ($p < .01$). Based on one-way ANOVA analysis, there were no ethnic identity stage differences for discrimination stress or depressive symptoms. No gender differences were found for ethnic identity stage based on t-test analysis. No generation differences were found for ethnic identity stages based on chi-square analysis.

TABLE 3.1 Sample characteristics

	n	%
Gender		
Male	61	49
Female	64	51
Generation		
Immigrant	29	23
Child of at least one immigrant parent	45	36
Both parents born in United States	44	35
Language preference		
English	42	34
Bilingual	39	31
Spanish	44	35

TABLE 3.2 Means, standard deviations and ranges of variables

	M (SD)	Range
Depressive symptoms	2.12 (.74)	1.0–4.5
Self-esteem	3.80 (.70)	2.3–5.0
Discrimination stress	1.16 (.77)	0–3.6
Ethnic affirmation	3.42 (.54)	1.0–4.0
Exploration subscale	2.73 (.71)	1.0–4.0
Commitment subscale	3.29 (.59)	1.0–4.0

Note. The exploration and commitment subscales are from the ethnic identity measure and were combined to create the ethnic identity stages used in further analyses.

TABLE 3.3 Pearson product moment correlation table for continuous variables of interest

	1	2	3	4	5	6
1. Explore	1.00					
2. Commit	.38***	1.00				
3. Affirmation	.27**	.77***	1.00			
4. Discrimination stress	.04	.10	.10	1.00		
5. Self-esteem	.33***	.50***	.37***	−.10	1.00	
6. Depressive symptoms	−.17	−.13	−.13	.25**	−.34***	1.00

Note. *$p < .05$. **$p < .01$. ***$p < .001$.

Based on one-way ANOVA analysis, discrimination stress significantly differed by language preference, $F(2, 122) = 7.73, p < .001$. English speakers reported significantly less stress ($M = .40, SD = .30$) compared to bilingual ($M = .64, SD = .25, p < .01$) or Spanish-speaking youth ($M = .56, SD = .30, p < .05$). One-way ANOVA tests for language preference differences were not significant for depressive symptoms, self-esteem, ethnic identity stages, or affirmation. See Table 3.3 for Pearson product moment correlations for variables of interest. Depressive symptoms were significantly positively associated with discrimination stress, $r(124) = .25, p < .01$, and negatively significantly associated with self-esteem, $r(123) = −.34, p < .001$.

Hypotheses

Multiple linear hierarchical regression models were conducted to test the two hypotheses (see Table 3.4). In order to test interactions, the key variables were transformed into z scores so that the coefficients could be properly interpreted. Hypothesis 1a, that ethnic affirmation will have a protective-enhancing effect on self-esteem in response to discrimination stress, included the following steps: age at step 1, discrimination stress at step 2, affirmation at step 3, and the interaction between affirmation and discrimination stress at step 4. The final model for self-esteem accounted for 57% of the variance, where age, affirmation, and the interaction were significant. Hypothesis 1a was supported, ethnic affirmation had a significant protective-enhancing effect ($p < .05$) on the relation between discrimination stress and self-esteem (see Figure 3.2). Youth with higher rates of affirmation with high scores on discrimination stress reported high levels of self-esteem; youth with low rates of affirmation and high discrimination stress reported significantly lower levels of self-esteem.

Hypothesis 1b. The regression to test if ethnic affirmation would have a protective-enhancing effect on depressive symptoms in response to discrimination stress included the following steps: age at step 1, discrimination stress at step 2, affirmation at step 3, and the interaction between affirmation and discrimination stress at step 4. The final model for depressive symptoms accounted for 33% of the variance, where discrimination stress and affirmation had direct effects, but no significant interaction. Hypothesis 1b was not supported for a protective-enhancing effect, but higher ethnic affirmation was directly associated with fewer depressive symptoms.

Hypothesis 2a. To test the hypothesis that a diffuse identity would have a protective-reactive effect on self-esteem, and achieved identity protective-enhancing effects, multiple linear hierarchical regression steps were: age at step 1, discrimination stress at step 2, ethnic identity stages (dummy coded) at step 3, and interaction between achieved stage and discrimination stress and interaction between diffuse stage and discrimination stress at step 4. The overall model for self-esteem was significant and accounted for 48% of the variance, with age, discrimination stress, and achieved interaction significant (see Table 3.4). Hypothesis 2a was partially supported in that achieved identity stage was protective stabilizing for self-esteem ($p < .05$) (see Figure 3.3). Achieved youth were more likely to maintain a stable level of self-esteem even under high discrimination stress compared to other ethnic identity stages where youth's self-esteem was significantly more vulnerable to the negative effect of high discrimination stress. Diffuse youth were not necessarily significantly more vulnerable compared to other stages.

Hypothesis 2b. To test the hypothesis that a diffuse identity would have a protective-reactive effect, and achieved identity a protective-enhancing effect, on depressive symptoms, multiple linear hierarchical regression steps were: age at step 1, discrimination stress at step 2, ethnic identity stages (dummy coded) at step 3, and interaction between achieved stage and discrimination stress and a second interaction between diffuse stage and discrimination stress at step 4. The overall model for depressive symptoms was significant and accounted for 31% of the variance, with discrimination stress being the only significant variable (see Table 3.4). More discrimination stress was significantly associated with more depressive symptoms. Hypothesis 2b was not supported because ethnic identity stage was not significant and interactions were not significant.

TABLE 3.4 Multiple linear hierarchical regressions

Regression step	R	Adjusted R^2	Δ Adjusted R^2	ΔF	B	SE	Std. β	t
Hypothesis 1a: Ethnic affirmation will have a protective-enhancing effect on the relation between discrimination stress and self-esteem. Self-esteem, $F(4, 112) = 13.34$, $p < .001$								
1. Age	.36	.12	.12	16.99	.09	.66	.19	2.23*
2. Discrimination stress	.38	.13	.01	−7.36	−.03	.06	−.04	−.48
3. Affirmation	.51	.24	.11	3.82	.27	.06	.39	4.62***
4. Interaction	.57	.30	.06	−.11	.12	.05	.20	2.40*
Hypothesis 1b: Ethnic affirmation will have a protective-enhancing effect on the relation between discrimination stress and depressive symptoms. Depressive symptoms, $F(4, 112) = 4.39$, $p < .01$								
1. Age	.04	−.01	−.01	.22	.08	.05	.10	1.05
2. Discrimination stress	.26	.05	.06	3.76	.14	.07	.23	2.60*
3. Affirmation	.33	.08	.03	.53	−.18	.07	−.22	−2.29*
Hypothesis 2a: Diffuse stage will have a protective reactive effect on self-esteem. Achieved stage will have a protective-enhancing effect on self-esteem. Self-esteem, $F(7, 116) = 6.50$, $p < .001$								
1. Age	.34	.11	.11	15.23	.10	.05	.21	2.29*
2. Discrimination stress	.36	.12	.01	−6.38	−.22	.08	−.32	−2.81**
3. Diffuse	.48	.20	.08	−1.97	−.19	.16	−.12	−1.16
Foreclosed					.13	.19	.07	−.69
Achieved					.43	.17	.30	2.60*
4. Diffuse interaction	.52	.23	.03	−.78	.23	.17	.13	1.41
Achieved interaction					.31	.17	.27	2.56*
Hypothesis 2b: Diffuse stage will have a protective reactive effect on depressive symptoms. Achieved stage will have a protective-enhancing effect on depressive symptoms. Depressive symptoms, $F(7, 113) = 2.32$, $p < .05$								
1. Age	.06	−.01	.01	.38	.06	.05	.11	1.07
2. Discrimination stress	.25	.04	.05	3.38	.31	.09	.42	3.34**
3. Diffuse	.31	.06	.02	−1.31	.26	.19	.16	1.35
Foreclosed					.13	.22	.07	.60
Achieved					−.12	.19	−.08	−.63

Note. *$p < .05$. **$p < .01$. ***$p < .001$.

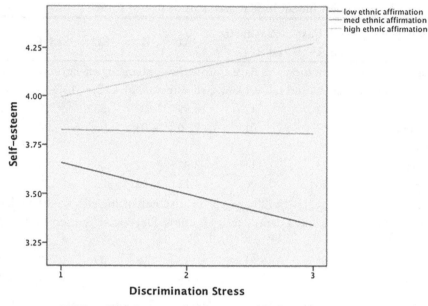

LOWZ = −1SD below mean, MEDZ=at mean, HIGHZ=+1SD above mean

FIGURE 3.2 Hypothesis 1: ethnic affirmation will moderate the relation between discrimination stress and self-esteem.

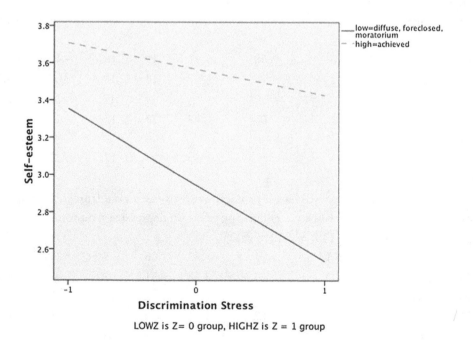

LOWZ is Z= 0 group, HIGHZ is Z = 1 group

FIGURE 3.3 Ethnic identity stage will moderate the relation between discrimination stress and self-esteem.

Discussion

Our study examined the resilience effects of ethnic identity stages and ethnic affirmation on self-esteem and depressive symptoms among minority adolescents. Our results demonstrate that discrimination stress continues to be common and stressful for ethnic minority adolescents and is significantly associated with more depressive symptoms and lower self-esteem. Our findings indicate that ethnic affirmation had a protective effect on depressive symptoms and a protective-enhancing effect on self-esteem. Achieved ethnic identity stage had a protective-stabilizing effect on self-esteem, such that youth self-esteem remained stable at high levels of discrimination stress for achieved ethnic identity stage compared to all other stages (diffuse, foreclosed, moratorium) that were more vulnerable at high levels of discrimination stress. Depressive symptoms were not associated with ethnic identity stages.

Ethnic affirmation, or feeling positive toward one's ethnic group, was generally protective with respect to self-esteem and depressive symptoms. Moreover, there was a protective-enhancing effect for self-esteem, where youth with more positive affirmation reported higher self-esteem at higher levels of discrimination stress compared to youth with low ethnic affirmation whose self-esteem was significantly lower at high levels of discrimination stress (Luthar et al., 2000). In other words, ethnic affirmation further enhanced the global sense of self-worth when youth were faced with high levels of discrimination stress. The protective effect of ethnic affirmation is consistent with previous self-esteem research with Mexican American youth (Romero & Roberts, 2003b), African American and Puerto Rican adolescents (Greene et al., 2006), and with academic outcomes in African American adolescents (Eccles et al., 2006; Wong et al., 2003). These results are also consistent with previous research with African American youth (Greene et al., 2006) that a positive sense of one's ethnic group is associated with fewer depressive symptoms. However, they are inconsistent with Lee's (2005) findings with Korean American young adults; Lee notes that the normative depressive rates for Korean American college students are unique and that types of prejudice will vary between ethnic groups. The current study adds to our understanding of ethnic identity development among Mexican and Native American descent youth; however, the small sample size limits generalizability and future studies with larger samples are needed to explore these effects among these populations. Our findings suggest that a positive identity may contribute to positive adolescent development, and that a less positive or even negative view of one's ethnic group may be detrimental, especially at high levels of stress.

In the current study, results indicate that achieved stage of ethnic identity development provided a protective stabilizing effect on self-esteem for minority youth. Youth who had reached an achieved stage were able to maintain high self-esteem even at high levels of discrimination stress compared to all other ethnic identity stages (diffuse, foreclosed, moratorium) whose self-esteem significantly dropped at high levels of discrimination stress. Youth at the achieved stage, who had spent time exploring their identity and felt resolved and committed to their ethnic group, were more likely to be older, more likely to report higher self-esteem, and more ethnic affirmation in general. These findings are consistent with Erikson (1968) and Marcia's (1980) theories of identity development that self-esteem is high after exploring and committing to one's ethnic identity. Furthermore, these findings are also consistent with Tajfel and Turner's (1986) theory of social identity, which states that a stronger sense of positive belonging to one's social group is likely to lead to a more positive sense of global self-worth or self-esteem. While we did not find that diffuse youth were any more vulnerable than other stages, it is worth noting that even when youth had either explored (moratorium) or committed (foreclosed) they were still significantly more vulnerable compared to youth who had both explored and committed (achieved). We suggest that it is the developmental aspect of youth having actively sought out information about their ancestry and having resolved any internal conflicts that leads to an overall better sense of self and stability even when faced with discrimination stress.

While the majority of previous studies have found that achieved identity and higher identity (more exploration and more commitment) are associated with positive outcomes, a couple of previous studies reported that achieved ethnic identity increased vulnerability (Greene et al., 2006; Oyserman et al., 2003); in the current study, we find that achieved ethnic identity was significantly protective stabilizing compared to all other ethnic identity stages. Our findings may differ from these results in part because of their focus on peer discrimination (Greene et al., 2006), whereas our measure included multiple contexts of peer, school context, and community context (Romero & Roberts, 2003b). The adolescent period is particularly marked by a desire for peer approval, which may heighten the effect of prejudice and negative comments from peers on self-esteem. Additionally, our discrimination measure included immigration concerns and linguistic concerns identified by Mexican American, Asian, and Native American youth (Fryberg & Townsend, 2008; González, 1997; Romero & Roberts, 2003a; Rosenbloom & Way, 2004), whereas previous research focused on racial discrimination effects on African American youth (e.g., Jackson et al., 1996). We find that youth who speak English report less discrimination stress, which may suggest that language differences play a role in experience of discrimination; future studies may also investigate how resilience factors may vary by type of discrimination.

Social identity theory and identity development theories were not originally developed to predict negative mental health; thus, it is not surprising that ethnic identity stages were not significantly associated with depressive symptoms. Resilience models have found that protective factors may function differently for negative mental health outcomes compared to positive well-being (Luthar et al., 2000). Given the cross-sectional nature of the study and the limited sample, we cannot generalize our findings or assume the direction of causality. It may be that more depressed youth are more likely to have negative affect in general, which may also create a more negative view of their ethnic group. Future research with longitudinal samples and larger sample sizes will advance our understanding of the interplay between mental well-being and identity development and affirmation over time for individuals.

We conclude that ethnic affirmation and achieved ethnic identity stage are sources of resilience that help ethnic minority youth respond positively to adverse situations created by discrimination stress. Ethnic affirmation has protective effects on depressive symptoms and protective-enhancing effects on self-esteem. Achieved ethnic identity stage, indicated by having both explored and committed to one's ethnicity, is associated with a protective-stabilizing effect on self-esteem compared to other ethnic identity stages that demonstrate vulnerability to high levels of discrimination stress. Ethnic identity developmental stages represent developmental shifts in understanding and exploring one's ethnic background and appear to also provide an important source of resiliency for ethnic minority adolescents in the face of stress due to discrimination and prejudice. The developmental aspect of ethnic identity is critical to understanding the resilience of ethnic minority adolescents and their healthy development.

References

Adams, G., Fryberg, S. A., Garcia, D. M., & Delgado-Torres, E. U. (2006). The psychology of engagement with indigenous identities: A cultural perspective. *Cultural Diversity and Ethnic Minority Psychology, 12*, 493–508.

Branscombe, N. R., Schmitt, M. T., & Harvey, R. D. (1999). Perceiving pervasive discrimination among African Americans: Implications for group identification and well-being. *Journal of Personality and Social Psychology, 77*, 135–149.

Brislin, R. W. (1976). *Translation: Applications and research*. New York: Gardner Press Inc.

Brislin, R. W., Lonner, W. J., & Thorndike, R. M. (1973). *Cross-cultural research methods: Comparative studies in behavioral science*. New York: Wiley and Sons.

Carvajal, S. C., Evans, R. I., Nash, S. G., & Getz, J. G. (2002). Global positive expectancies of the self and adolescents' substance use avoidance: Testing a social influence mediational model. *Journal of Personality, 70*, 421–442.

Cervantes, R. C., Padilla, A. M., & Salgado de Snyder, N. (1990). Reliability and validity of the Hispanic Stress Inventory. *Hispanic Journal of Behavioral Sciences, 12*, 76–82.

Cervantes, R. C., Padilla, A. M., & Salgado de Snyder, N. (1991). The Hispanic Stress Inventory: A culturally relevant approach to psychosocial assessment. *Psychological Assessment, 3*, 438–447.

Crockett, L. J., Randall, B. A., Shen, Y., Russell, S. T., & Driscoll, A. K. (2005). Measurement equivalence of the center for epidemiological studies depression scale for Latino and Anglo adolescents: A national scale. *Journal of Consulting and Clinical Psychology, 73*, 47–58.

Cuéllar, I., Arnold, B., & Maldonado, R. (1995). Acculturation Rating Scale for Mexican Americans-II: A revision of the Original ARSMA Scale. *Hispanic Journal of Behavioral Sciences, 17*, 275–304.

Eccles, J. S., Wong, C. A., & Peck, S. C. (2006). Ethnicity as a social context for the development of African-American adolescents. *Journal of School Psychology, 44*, 407–426.

Edwards, L. M., & Romero, A. J. (2008). Coping with discrimination among Mexican descent adolescents. *Hispanic Journal of Behavioral Sciences, 30*, 24–39.

Erikson, E. (1968). *Identity: Youth and crisis*. New York: Norton.

Fryberg, S. A., & Townsend, S. M. (2008). The psychology of invisibility. In G. Adams, M. Biernat, N. R. Branscombe, C. S. Crandall & L. S. Wrightsman (Eds.), *Commemorating Brown: The social psychology of racism and discrimination* (pp. 173–193). Washington, DC: American Psychological Association.

García Coll, C., Lamberty, G., Jenkins, R., McAdoo, H. P., Crnic, K., Wasik, B. H., et al. (1996). An integrative model for the study of developmental competencies in minority children. *Child Development, 67*, 1891–1914.

González, G. M. (1997). The emergence of Chicanos in the twenty-first century: Implications for counseling, research, and policy. *Journal of Multicultural Counseling and Development, 25*, 94–106.

Greene, M. L., Way, N., & Pahl, K. (2006). Trajectories of perceived adult and peer discrimination among Black, Latino, and Asian American adolescents: Patterns and psychological correlates. *Developmental Psychology, 42*, 218–238.

Jackson, J. S., Brown, T. N., Williams, D. R., Torres, M., Sellers, S. L., & Brown, K. (1996). Racism and the physical and mental health stage of African Americans: A thirteen year national panel study. *Ethnicity and Disease, 6*, 132–147.

Joiner, G. W., & Kashubeck, S. (1996). Acculturation, body image, self-esteem and eating disorder symptomatology in adolescent Mexican-American women. *Psychology of Women Quarterly, 20*, 419–435.

Lee, R. M. (2005). Resilience against discrimination: Ethnic identity and other-group orientation as protective factors for Korean Americans. *Journal of Counseling Psychology, 52*, 36–44.

Lee, R. M., & Yoo, H. C. (2004). Structure and measurement of ethnic identity for Asian American college students. *Journal of Counseling Psychology, 51*, 263–269.

Luthar, S. S., Cicchetti, D., & Becker, B. (2000). The construct of resilience: A critical evaluation and guidelines for future work. *Child Development, 71*, 543–562.

Major, B., & O'Brien, L. T. (2005). The social psychology of stigma. *Annual Review of Psychology, 56*, 393–421.

Marcia, J. E. (1980). Identity in adolescence. In J. Adelson (Ed.), *Handbook of adolescent psychology* (pp. 159–187). New York: John Wiley.

Marin, G., & Gamba, R. J. (1996). A new measurement of acculturation for His-panics: The Bidimensional Acculturation Scale for Hispanics (BAS). *Hispanic Journal of Behavioral Sciences, 18*, 297–316.

Marsiglia, F. F., Kullis, S., Hecht, M. L., & Sills, S. (2004). Ethnicity and ethnic identity as predictors of drug norms and drug use among preadolescents in the US southwest. *Substance Use & Misuse, 39*, 1061–1094.

Masten, A. S. (2001). Ordinary magic: Resilience processes in development. *The American Psychologist, 56*, 227–238.

Oyserman, D., Kemmelmeier, M., & Fryberg, S. (2003). Racial-ethnic self-schemas. *Social Psychology Quarterly, 66*, 333–347.

Phinney, J. S. (1990). Ethnic identity in adolescents and adults: Review of research. *Psychological Bulletin, 108*, 499–514.

Phinney, J. S. (1991). Ethnic identity self-esteem: A review and integration. *His-panic Journal of Behavioral Sciences, 13*, 193–208.

Phinney, J. S. (1992). The multigroup ethnic identity measure: A new scale for use with diverse groups. *Journal of Adolescent Research, 7*, 156–176.

Phinney, J. S., & Alipuria, L. L. (1990). Ethnic identity in college students from four ethnic groups. *Journal of Adolescence, 13*, 171–183.

Radloff, L. S. (1977). The CES-D Scale: A self-report depression scale for research in the general population. *Applied Psychological Measurement, 1*, 385–401.

Roberts, R. E., Lewinsohn, P. M., & Seeley, J. R. (1991). Screening for adolescent depression: A comparison of depression scales. *Journal of the American Academy of Child and Adolescent Psychiatry, 30,* 58–66.

Roberts, R. E., Phinney, J. S., Masse, L. C., Chen, Y. R., Roberts, C. R., & Romero, A. J. (1999). The structure and validity of ethnic identity among diverse groups of adolescents. *The Journal of Early Adolescence, 19,* 300–322.

Romero, A. J., Carvajal, S. C., Valle, F., & Orduña, M. (2007). Adolescent bicultural stress and its impact on mental well-being among Latinos, Asian Americans, and European Americans. *Journal of Community Psychology, 35,* 519–534.

Romero, A. J., Martínez, D., & Carvajal, S. C. (2007). Bicultural stress and adolescent risk behaviors in a community sample of Latinos and non-Latino European Americans. *Ethnicity and Health, 12,* 443–463.

Romero, A. J., & Roberts, R. E. (2003a). The impact of multiple dimensions of ethnic identity on discrimination and adolescent's self-esteem. *Journal of Applied Social Psychology, 33,* 2288–2305.

Romero, A. J., & Roberts, R. E. (2003b). Stress within a bicultural context for adolescents of Mexican descent. *Cultural Diversity and Ethnic Minority Psychology, 9,* 171–184.

Rosenberg, M. (1965). *Society and the adolescent self-image.* Princeton, NJ: Prince-ton University Press.

Rosenberg, M. (1979). *Conceiving the self.* New York: Basic Books.

Rosenbloom, S., & Way, N. (2004). Experiences of discrimination among African American, Asian American, and Latino adolescents in an urban high school. *Youth & Society, 35,* 420–451.

Rushton, J. L., Forcier, M., & Schectman, R. M. (2002). Epidemiology of depressive symptoms in the National Longitudinal Study of Adolescent Health. *Journal of the American Academy of Child and Adolescent Psychiatry, 41,* 199–205.

Seaton, E., Scottham, K., & Sellers, R. M. (2006). The status model of racial identity development in African American adolescents: Evidence of structure, trajectories, and well-being. *Child Development, 77,* 1416–1426.

Sellers, R. M., Caldwell, C. H., Schmeelk-Cone, K. H., & Zimmerman, M. A. (2003). Racial identity, racial discrimination, perceived stress, and psychological distress among African American young adults. *Journal of Health and Social Behavior, 44,* 302–317.

Sellers, R. M., Copeland-Linder, N., Martin, P. P., & Lewis, R. L. (2006). Racial identity matters: The relationship between racial discrimination and psychological functioning in African American adolescents. *Journal of Research on Adolescence, 16,* 187–216.

Sellers, R. M., & Shelton, J. N. (2003). The role of racial identity in perceived racial discrimination. *Journal of Personality and Social Psychology, 84,* 1079–1092.

Spears Brown, C., & Bigler, R. S. (2005). Children's perceptions of discrimination: A developmental model. *Child Development, 76,* 533–553.

Szalacha, L. A., Erkut, S., Garcia Coll, C., Alarcon, O., Fields, J. P., & Ceder, I. (2003). Discrimination and Puerto Rican children's and adolescents' mental health. *Cultural Diversity and Ethnic Minority Psychology, 9,* 141–155.

Tajfel, H., & Turner, J. C. (1986). The social identity theory of intergroup behavior. In S. Worchel & W. G. Austin (Eds.), *Psychology of intergroup relations* (pp. 7–24). Chicago, IL: Nelson-Hall.

Umaña-Taylor, A. J., Yazedjian, A., & Bámaca-Gómez, M. (2004). Developing the ethnic identity scale using Eriksonian and social identity perspectives. *Identity: An International Journal of Theory and Research, 4*, 9–38.

Wong, C. A., Eccles, J. S., & Sameroff, A. (2003). The influence of ethnic discrimination and ethnic identification on African American adolescents' school and socioemotional adjustment. *Journal of Personality, 71*, 1197–1232.

Yip, T., Seaton, E. K., & Sellers, R. M. (2006). African American racial identity across the lifespan: A cluster analysis of identity status, identity content, and depression among adolescents, college students, and adults. *Child Development, 77*, 1504–1517.

II

Family in the United States

The American Family

BY JOHN ICELAND

Changes in the American family over the last half century have been astonishing. The idealized view of the American family consisting of a married mom and dad with two children has nearly gone by the wayside, and we have instead seen a large increase in the number of single-parent families and people living alone or with housemates. Jason DeParle, a journalist who has written extensively about household living arrangements and poverty, described one woman's path to single parenthood: Jessica Schairer, a mother of three, grew up in a traditional small town outside Ann Arbor, Michigan.

> Her father drove a beer truck, her mother served as church trustee and her grandparents lived next door. She knew no one rich, no one poor and no one raising children outside of marriage. "It was just the way it was," she said.
>
> William Penn University, eight hours away in Iowa, offered a taste of independence and a spot on the basketball team. Her first thought when she got pregnant was "My mother's going to kill me." Abortion crossed her mind, but her boyfriend, an African-American student from Arkansas, said they should start a family. They agreed that marriage should wait until they could afford a big reception and a long gown. . . .
>
> Ms. Schairer has trouble explaining, even to herself, why she stayed so long with a man who she said earned little, berated her often and did no parenting. They lived with family (his and hers) and worked off and on while she hoped things would change. "I wanted him to love me," she said. She was 25 when the breakup made it official: she was raising three children on her own.[1]

Jessica represents one of the growing number of women in the United States who are raising children either on their own or in untraditional household arrangements. But just how much have American marriage and childbearing patterns actually changed? What factors explain these changes? What are some of the consequences of these changes? This chapter addresses these questions and examines the broad diversity in life course transitions that Americans experience today, including cohabitation, marriage, and childbearing.

The Traditional Family

Traditional notions of the family have evolved over time. What we now consider the 1950s traditional family of the male breadwinner working outside the home and the stay-at-home mother taking care of the kids in fact differed from traditional families of the colonial era and much of the nineteenth century. In pre-urban, preindustrial times, a husband and wife often worked together on a farm. As Richard Gill and his coauthors describe the colonial-era family: "Although the husband was considered the head of the family and although there was a sexual division of labor in terms of kinds of work, the sharp division between provider-husband and homemaker-wife did not exist."[2] Family members all contributed to economically productive tasks in and around the home. This included children, who, after the age of six or seven, were expected to do their fair share. That men and women both worked in and around the home is not to say that this was a period of gender equality; families were still strongly patriarchal, and women lacked many rights.[3]

Industrialization and urbanization were key catalysts in spurring changes in the economic functioning of families. Industrialization led to the growth in employment in places more physically removed from the home. Among families with children, the husband was more likely to be employed in a wage-paying job. Since he was more removed from the home, the wife took on the tasks involved in what is often called home production: caring for the children and maintaining the home. Single women often worked outside the home in occupations including domestic service, teaching, and as secretaries, but once they married the strong expectation was that the woman would leave the labor force—if the family could afford it—and take care of the home and children.[4]

Changes In Household Living Arrangements in Recent Decades

There have been several trends in family living arrangements in recent decades. These include a rising age at marriage, a decline in fertility, an increase in divorce, cohabitation, same-sex unions, and nonmarital childbearing. These patterns are collectively termed the *second demographic transition* (the first demographic transition consisted of the decline in fertility and mortality[...]). One result of these trends is that only 49 percent of all households contained a married couple in 2012, down from 78 percent in

1950.[5] The underlying causes of all of these trends have been much discussed and debated, as have their consequences. These issues are the focus of the rest of this chapter.

Age at First Marriage and Fertility

Figure 4.1 shows trends in age at first marriage, by gender, from 1890 to 2011. The first half of the twentieth century saw small declines in the median age at marriage for both men and women. In 1950, the median age was just 23 for men and 20 for women. The decline has been attributed to the growth of well-paid wage labor employment for men that accompanied industrialization. This provided men with a sufficient income to support a family, even at a relatively young age.[6] Not by chance, the years with the youngest ages at first marriage (1950 and 1960) coincided with the baby boom. Early marriage is typically associated with greater fertility, because childbearing in these circumstances tends to begin at younger ages. Since 1960 the median age at first marriage has been rising. By 2010, the median age had risen to nearly 29 for men and 27 for women. In addition to marrying later, since about 1990 an increasing proportion of men and women have not married at all by the age of 45.[7]

FIGURE 4.1 Median age at first marriage, by gender, 1890–2011. Source: U.S. Census Bureau 2011g.

Chapter 1 described the long-term decline in U.S. fertility rates from a time when American women were having, on average, 7.0 children in 1800 to just under 2.0 children today. A growing proportion of women today are also having no children. Whereas among women born in the 1930s, about 10 percent had no children by the time they reached their early forties, among those born in the 1960s this proportion was up to 19 percent.[8] Similarly, while 35 percent of women in the earlier cohort had four or more children, the same could be said for only about 10 percent of the more recent cohort of women. Overall, fertility levels have been fairly stable at near-replacement levels (where women have on average about 2.0 children) since about 1980, though with a small dip since the late 2000s.

Divorce

Divorce rates were historically low in the United States, with well under one in ten marriages ending in divorce in 1870. This percentage crept up over the twentieth century and then rose rapidly in the 1960s and 1970s before declining modestly since. Whereas about one in four marriages that began in the 1950s ended in divorce, close to half of those that occurred in the 1970s are predicted to end in divorce. Somewhere between 40 and 50 percent of more recent marriages are expected to end in divorce, given current patterns.[9] The probability that a marriage will end in divorce varies considerably by education and ethnicity. Divorce rates have continued to increase for women with no high school diploma but have actually declined for college-educated women since the late 1970s. Among marriages that began in the early 1990s, 46 percent of those involving women with no high school diploma ended in divorce ten years later compared with only 16 percent of marriages among women with a college degree (see Figure 4.2).[10] Divorce rates are also higher among blacks than whites.[11] Much of the difference in divorce rates by educational attainment can be attributed to the early age of marriage among less educated men and women (people who marry young are more likely to divorce), plus the diverging economic prospects of Americans of different educational levels.[12] The latter issue is discussed at greater length below.

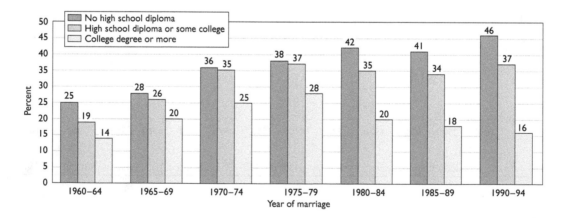

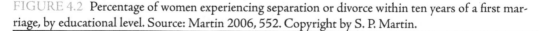

FIGURE 4.2 Percentage of women experiencing separation or divorce within ten years of a first marriage, by educational level. Source: Martin 2006, 552. Copyright by S. P. Martin.

Cohabitation

Cohabitation before marriage is now normative. Of all first marriages between 1965 and 1974, only 11 percent were preceded by cohabitation. During 2005–9, this was up to two-thirds of all first marriages (see Figure 4.3). Cohabitation has risen for all racial and ethnic groups. As of 2009–10, 62 percent of white women ages 19 to 44 have cohabited, compared with 60 percent of black women and 59 percent of Hispanic women. However, there are important differences by educational attainment. About 74 percent of women with less than a high school education have cohabited, compared with 50 percent of women with four years of college or more, who are more likely than other women to proceed directly to marriage rather than to cohabit first.[13]

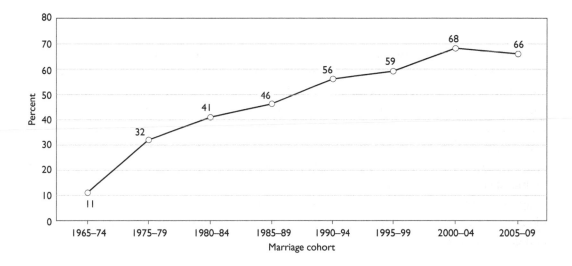

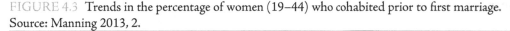

FIGURE 4.3 Trends in the percentage of women (19–44) who cohabited prior to first marriage. Source: Manning 2013, 2.

Cohabiting relationships tend to be less stable than marriages. According to 2002 data, about 50 percent of children born to cohabiting parents experience a breakup of the household by the age of 9, compared with about 20 percent of children born to married parents.[14]

Qualitative research has indicated that many young adults "slide" into cohabitation rather than carefully plan for it. Sociologists Wendy Manning and Pamela Smock report the following conversation with a respondent when he was asked how he started living with his partner: "It began with, first, I had an apartment and she lived with her parents. And it began with her just spending more and more time, staying overnight, um, basically just out of the, you-know, just gradually becoming a fixture and uh, there was never any discussion of the matter. When my roommate moved out and I didn't have a roommate, it just sort—well, it had become permanent even before that, probably, but just wasn't said."[15] Similarly, another respondent describes how he finally realized that he was in a cohabiting relationship: "She stayed at my house more and more from spending the night once to not going home to her parents' house for a week at a time and then you know further, um, so there was no official starting date. I did take note when the frilly fufu soaps showed up in my bathroom that she'd probably moved in at that point."[16]

In an era in which life course transitions are not as clear-cut as in the past, cohabitation has become a lower-risk option than marriage for many people to see if living together works for them or not. Likewise, the commitment to partners tends to be more provisional in cohabiting relationships than in marriage. However, with the increase in cohabitation, the distinction between cohabitation and marriage could erode in the future, much as it has in a few European countries where cohabitation is close to becoming an outright substitute for formal marriage.[17]

Same-Sex Unions

Same-sex unions have also become a lot more common in recent years. Estimates of the size of this population are complicated by challenges in gathering accurate data, but a careful Census Bureau analysis suggests that in 2010 there were an estimated 650,000 same-sex couple households in the United States, up from 360,000 in 2000 (an 80 percent increase). Of the 650,000 couples in 2010, a few over 130,000 consisted of married spouses, while the rest were unmarried partners living together.[18] Just over half of same-sex couples consisted of women living together.[19] Among same-sex couple households, about 1 in 6 (16 percent) included children, with female couples more likely to have children (22 percent) than male couples (10 percent).[20] The number of same-sex unions, including those with children, will likely continue to increase with the growth in public acceptance of same-sex relationships and gay marriage.

Nonmarital Childbearing

Having children outside marriage is no longer uncommon. Whereas in 1940 only 2 percent of births were to unmarried women, by 2009 this figure had risen to 41 percent (see Figure 4.4). Moreover, more than half of births to young women (those under 30 years old) occur outside marriage. These percentages have been growing for all racial and ethnic groups. The proportion of all white births to unmarried women increased sharply over the past two decades, from 20 percent in 1990 to 36 percent in 2009. Among black women, increases occurred earlier; from 1970 to 1990 the proportion of black births to unmarried women jumped from 38 to 67 percent, before gradually continuing to drift upward to 72 percent in 2009. In 2009, over half of Hispanic births (53 percent) were to unmarried women. Only among Asians is the corresponding figure much lower—17 percent in 2009.[21]

However, complicating the picture of trends in nonmarital childbearing is that much of the rise in recent years has occurred among cohabiting couples. In fact, more than half of nonmarital births occur within cohabiting relationships, compared with 29 percent in the early 1990s.[22] Thus, the actual percentage of families headed by single women living alone (without a coresident partner) has not changed much since about 1995. As of 2010, 26 percent of all families, 21 percent of white families, 29 percent of Hispanic families, and 55 percent of African American families were headed by a single woman living with no other parent present in the household.[23] As mentioned earlier, however, the unions of cohabiting couples are more than twice as likely as marriages to dissolve, even though in many ways they resemble married families.[24]

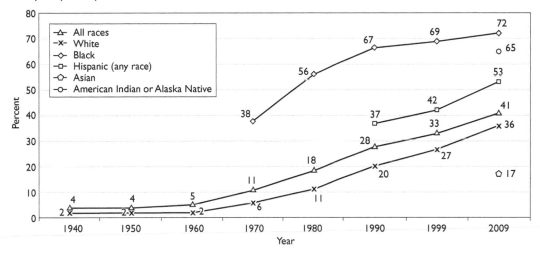

FIGURE 4.4 Percentage of births to unmarried women, by race and Hispanic origin, 1940–2009. Sources: Ventura and Bachrach 2000; Martin et al. 2011.

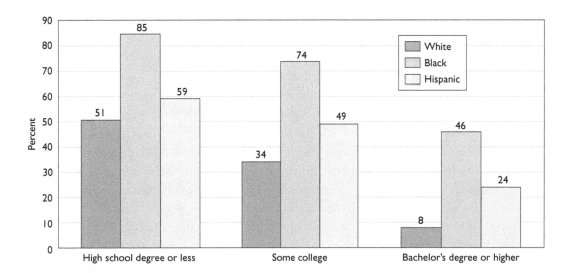

FIGURE 4.5 Percentage of births to unmarried women (ages 20–29 years), by race/ethnicity and level of education, 2009. Source: Child Trends 2012.

Notably, differentials in nonmarital births by educational status are about as prominent as those by race and ethnicity and have become more pronounced over time. Over half (51 percent) of all births to white women without a high school degree occur outside marriage; in contrast, the figure for white women with a bachelor's degree or more is only 8 percent (see Figure 4.5). The percentage of births among African American women with a bachelor's or more that occur outside marriage is fairly high (46 percent) but nevertheless much lower than among African American women with a high school diploma or less (85 percent).[25] The percentage for Hispanics is in between those of whites and African Americans.

International Comparisons

The dramatic changes in family living arrangements over the past few decades have not been confined to the United States alone. Many wealthy countries around the world have experienced a second demographic transition, including delays in marriage and childbearing and increases in cohabitation, divorce, nonmarital childbearing, and women's employment.[26]

Total fertility rates, for example, are below replacement level (which is 2.1 births per woman) in almost all OECD countries, their average being 1.7. (The Organisation for Economic Co-operation and Development consists of a group of mainly wealthy countries.) Women are having children later in life, and more are having no children at all. Fewer people are getting married, divorce rates are up, and more children are born outside marriage than in the past. Cohabitation is often seen as an acceptable alternative to marriage in much of the developed world. Table 4.1 illustrates these patterns by showing the distribution of children living in different kinds of families in OECD countries. Topping the list of countries with the highest percentage of families with two married parents is Greece (92 percent of children live with two married parents); at the bottom is Sweden, where about half (51 percent) live with two married parents. The United States, at 68 percent, is a little lower than the average across the 27 OECD countries (73 percent).[27]

Notably, the table also shows while only half of children in Sweden live in married-couple households, just 18 percent actually live in a household with only one parent. (The OECD average is 15 percent.) Most of the rest live in cohabiting households (31 percent); indeed, Sweden has the highest percentage of children living with cohabitors. The United States has the highest percentage of children living in households with only one parent (26 percent) and a fairly modest percentage living in cohabiting couple households. It should be noted that the table somewhat understates the percentage of U.S. children living in cohabiting households.[28] Recent analyses with better data indicate that about 6 percent of U.S. children live with cohabiting parents rather than the 3 percent indicated in the table.[29] Even with the correction, however, the United States still has a lower percentage of children living with cohabiting parents and a higher percentage living with a single parent than OECD averages.

While these changes in family formation patterns initially began in western Europe, Canada, Australia, and the United States, such changes have begun to spread to central and eastern Europe and several developed countries in Asia, including Japan, South Korea, Taiwan, Hong Kong, and Singapore. All five of these Asian countries, for example, have very low total fertility rates, in the 1 to 1.3 range. The age at first marriage has increased in most East Asian countries, as has the percentage of never-married women. The percentage of men and women who have cohabited has also increased in countries such as Taiwan and Japan. For example, in just the six-year period between 1998 and 2004, the percentage of women aged 20 to 49 reporting a cohabitation experience increased from 11 to 20 percent in Taiwan. Japanese women born during 1975–79 were more than twice as likely to have reported that they had ever cohabited (21 percent) than women born during 1954–59 (10 percent), according to a survey taken in 2004.[30]

TABLE 4.1 Distribution of children, by household type, in selected OECD countries, 2007

ARRANGED BY RANKING OF TRADITIONAL HOUSEHOLDS

	Percentage of children living with			
	2 married parents	2 cohabiting parents	1 parent	0 parents
Greece	92	1	5	1
Slovak Republic	85	4	11	1
Italy	84	5	10	1
Spain	84	8	7	1
Luxembourg	83	7	10	0
Poland	79	9	11	1
Germany	78	6	15	1
Czech Republic	76	8	15	1
Austria	76	7	14	2
Netherlands	76	13	11	0
Portugal	76	10	12	3
Hungary	74	10	15	1
OECD 27 average	73	11	15	1
Slovenia	69	20	10	1
Finland	69	16	14	1
Ireland	68	6	24	2
United States	68	3	26	4
Belgium	68	14	16	3
Canada	67	11	22	0
Denmark	66	15	18	2

France	65	21	14	1
United Kingdom	65	13	22	1
Estonia	53	24	22	2
Sweden	51	31	18	1

Source: OECD 2011a, TABLE 1.1.

Why Have Family Living Arrangements Changed?

Here I focus on the forces that have shaped family living arrangements in the United States, though many of these conditions also exist in other developed countries that have experienced the second demographic transition. Two general arguments have been offered to explain the growth in untraditional families over the past several decades: cultural versus economic perspectives. Below I review both of these explanations, but it should be noted that economic and cultural shifts have occurred hand in hand, and it is thus difficult to draw a definitive distinction between the effects of each.

Culture refers to shared values, expectations, and modes of behavior. Culture is learned in childhood and transmitted through families and communities, and it includes habits of thought and action. Marriage culture in the United States traditionally had two bases: (1) marriage is a given—everyone is expected to marry, and it is the proper thing to do; and (2) marriage is forever. Clearly marital norms have shifted, and today less stigma is attached to being unmarried or divorced than in the past.[31]

Conservative commentators in particular point with alarm to cultural changes that have promoted family dissolution. Some emphasize that misguided government policies aimed at helping the poor have provided work disincentives and encouraged dependency on benefits. According to this view, these policies have also lowered the incentive for marriage and led to all sorts of other wayward behaviors, such as single parenthood and illegitimacy, criminal activity, and drug and alcohol abuse. These patterns are most evident in poor, inner-city African American neighborhoods.[32]

Charles Murray, in his book *Coming Apart: The State of White America, 1960–2010*, focuses on recent family formation patterns among whites. He argues that cultural norms in America have sharply diverged since the early 1960s. Specifically, today we have a group consisting of affluent, highly educated whites who overwhelmingly decide to get married before having children and who live in residential enclaves surrounded by like-minded people. They value marriage, hard work, honesty, and religiosity, and this allows them to enjoy secure and affluent lives. Their choices are also a function of their higher cognitive abilities, which allow them to plan ahead and envision the consequences of their actions.

The second group is the less-educated lower class, which has experienced an erosion of family and community life and for which having children outside marriage has become the norm. Murray attributes the declining fortunes of the lower class to the corresponding decline in the traditional values just named. This population finds itself at or near the bottom of the economic ladder because, according to Murray, its members, on average, have less cognitive ability—and are thus less well equipped to resist the lure of the sexual revolution and doctrines of self-actualization. They live in different neighborhoods from those of the elite and therefore lack appropriate role models. They thus succumb to higher rates of family dissolution, nonmarital births, work avoidance, and criminality. Murray sharply criticizes liberal elites because they do not do enough to publicly defend and affirm the traditional values to which they personally subscribe, and this has both served to exacerbate growing class divisions in society and will lead inexorably to America's decline unless this unhealthy dynamic is reversed.

Murray's thesis has drawn two criticisms. One, focusing on *cultural* values, is that while there has obviously been some shift in normative practices, the institution of marriage is still held in high esteem and most people strive to attain it. In other words, a wholesale cultural turn against marriage has not occurred, even among those with less education. Sociologist Andrew Cherlin holds that in contemporary American society we can describe marriage culture as consisting of the following four elements: (1) marriage is the best way to live one's family life; (2) a marriage should be a permanent, loving relationship; (3) a marriage should be a sexually exclusive partnership; and (4) divorce should be a last resort. Cherlin draws upon survey data (e.g., 76 percent of Americans agreed with the statement that "marriage is a lifetime relationship that should never be ended except under extreme circumstance") and detailed interviews to form conclusions about the continued importance of marriage in society. For example, one low-income unmarried respondent said, "If I get married, I wanna be with this person for the rest of my life. I don't wanna just get married and then our relationship goes wrong, and then I have to go and get a *divorce!*"[33]

A second criticism of Murray's analysis is that it does not focus enough on the role of *economic* factors in driving the growth in nonmarital births. The economist Gary Becker (writing before Murray) has argued that marriage is in large part an economic arrangement, and that its chief benefit arises from the interdependence of men and women. In colonial times, as previously stated, husbands and wives often worked together on family farms. During the heyday of industrialization men were the primary breadwinners in the labor market, and women were in charge of home production. As women's labor market prospects increased over time, the economic incentive to get married declined.[34] As is reflected in the increase in divorce rates in the post–World War II period, women today are also less likely than in the past to be trapped in bad marriages.[35]

Moreover, not only are women's economic prospects increasing, but also those of less-educated men have declined in the United States. Deindustrialization, globalization, and the decline in unionization have led to lower employment levels and wages for men with less than a college degree, many of whom were previously employed in relatively well-paying blue-collar occupations. This in turn has led to a decline in the number of "marriageable" men and further reduced women's incentive to marry.[36] The recent divergence in trends in divorce by education described earlier likely results from people with lower incomes and high economic insecurity experiencing more stress, which increases their likelihood of divorce.[37]

In elucidating the view that economic factors have driven changes in family formation patterns—and as a direct response to Murray—columnist Nicholas Kristof writes:

> Eighty percent of the people in my high school cohort dropped out or didn't pursue college because it used to be possible to earn a solid living at the steel mill, the glove factory or sawmill. That's what their parents had done. But the glove factory closed, working-class jobs collapsed and unskilled la -borers found themselves competing with immigrants. ... So let's get real. A crisis is developing in the white working class, a byproduct of growing income inequality in America. The pathologies are achingly real. But the solution isn't finger-wagging, or averting our eyes—but [economic] opportunity.[38]

A fair reckoning of these two arguments—one economic and the other cultural—is that both help explain recent trends. Sociologists Pamela Smock and Fiona Rose Greenland argue that unmarried couples with children articulate at least three perceived obstacles to marriage: concerns about financial stability, relationship quality, and fear of divorce, with financial concerns often the most paramount.[39] Men and women value marriage and aspire to it but believe, because of fears of divorce, that marriage should occur after financial stability is achieved. Low-income women, because of their expectations of low earnings, have less to lose by having children early and outside marriage, and they also place a very high value on children as adding meaning to their lives.[40] Good mothering is seen not as something that requires tremendous resources but as something that involves being there for the children (an approach to parenting that differs from that of the middle class).[41]

Finally, Smock and Greenland also note that cohabitation offers a marriage-like relationship with many of the same advantages of marriage, such as companionship, shared expenses, sexual access, childbearing, and childrearing. With cohabitation available as an increasingly normative option, the incentive to get married has declined. This helps explain rapid increases in cohabitation in recent years.

A news story on rising nonmarital births in the United States offers the following anecdote, which is consistent with the view that both economic conditions and culture shape family formation patterns:

> Over the past generation, Lorain [a city in Ohio] lost most of two steel mills, a shipyard and a Ford factory, diminishing the supply of jobs that let blue-collar workers raise middle-class families. More women went to work, making marriage less of a financial necessity for them. Living together became routine, and single motherhood lost the stigma that once sent couples rushing to the altar. Women here often describe marriage as a sign of having arrived rather than a way to get there.
>
> Meanwhile, children happen. Amber Strader, 27, was in an on-and-off relationship with a clerk at Sears a few years ago when she found herself pregnant. A former nursing student who now tends bar, Ms. Strader said her boyfriend was so dependent that she had to buy his cigarettes. Marrying him never entered her mind. "It was like living with another kid," she said.

When a second child, with a new boyfriend, followed three years later—her birth control failed, she said—her boyfriend, a part-time house painter, was reluctant to wed. Ms. Strader likes the idea of marriage; she keeps her parents' wedding photo on her kitchen wall and says her boyfriend is a good father. But for now marriage is beyond her reach. "I'd like to do it, but I just don't see it happening right now," she said. "Most of my friends say it's just a piece of paper, and it doesn't work out anyway."[42]

In short, many studies indicate that there has been a cultural shift in American's views of marriage and especially of nonmarital childbearing. While single parenthood is generally not something people aim for—most would like to be in committed, fulfilling unions—it is nevertheless generally socially accepted when it occurs. There is greater emphasis today on individualism and self-actualization than on community and conformity. Nevertheless, the decline in marriage and increase in nonmarital childbearing are also rooted in economic changes that have served to decrease the employment and earnings of men with less than a college degree at the same time that those of women have increased. The traditional economic foundations of marriage have eroded.

Ron Lesthaeghe, who has written at length about the "second demographic transition" in Western and a growing number of non-Western countries, argues that structural factors, including economic conditions, and cultural changes are interconnected and have likewise effected changes in families across a broad array of wealthy nations. Increases in female education have led to greater economic opportunities for women. Similarly, he argues, "the rise of individual autonomy and freedom of choice has legitimized the adoption of non-traditional living arrangements in a very short time. … Furthermore, one should also realize that mass media are producing a 'world culture' in which individual autonomy and self-actualization have a very prominent, if not dominant place, and that these provide both motivations and justifications for the onset of the [second demographic transition]."[43]

Thus, not just the American family is changing; so are families in a large number of nations, particularly wealthy countries, where individuals now feel less constrained by traditional cultural practices. People's choices about their living arrangements, however, have important implications for the well-being of not only the individuals themselves but also their families and communities.

Consequences of Changes In Family Living Arrangements

Changes in household living arrangements in the United States (and other countries) have been met with hand-wringing by many public commentators. The "breakdown" of the American family has been implicated as a cause of rising child poverty, increasing household inequality, and lower educational outcomes among children born in single-parent families. Many bemoan cultural shifts in nonmarital childbearing, feeling that these are indicative of moral decay and foreshadow the country's fall from its lofty position as the global economic superpower. Before I analyze some of these arguments and review evidence that supports the notion that single-parent families are indeed more economically vulnerable than other families, it is first worth noting some of the positive aspects of changes in household living arrangements.

Perhaps most important, to the extent that people enjoy having a broader array of socially acceptable choices available to them, the crumbling of the more restrictive norms of past generations is a good thing. These norms were particularly restrictive of the choices available to women, who were for the most part expected to focus on getting married, bearing children, and taking care of the home. The barriers for entering high-level professional positions (scientists, lawyers, corporate managers) were very high, and the related stereotypes of women's intelligence and emotional stability were degrading. As Cherlin notes, "The increase in personal choice has brought important benefits. It has broadened the opportunity for wives to realize their full potential in paid employment as well as in the home. It has made marriage more egalitarian, with husbands and wives sharing more responsibility for home and wage earning. … Gone are the days when husbands could beat their wives with little fear of prosecution, demand sex at any time, or decide to sell their wives' property. Most people view all of these changes positively."[44]

Cherlin also notes that men's options have broadened as the stigma attached to men caring for their children full time has declined. For example, a *New York Times* story on the growing numbers of stay-at-home dads recounts the following:

> There was little discussion of male ego when David Worford, a former Web editor in Fort Collins, Colo., and his wife, Cherie, an obstetrician and gynecologist, agreed that he would stay home with their young sons a few years ago. "Most of my income was going directly to child care," he said. "Throw on that I was handling most of the domestic workload anyway because of the hours Cherie was working. It just made sense to make the move both economically and for family life. It was great to have a constant at home."[45]

In the same story, another stay-at-home dad related the following observation about rapidly changing social norms: " 'Just a few years ago, I was usually the lone dad on the playground during the day,' Mr. Somerfeld, 39, said on a recent sunny Wednesday morning, while hanging out with eight other dads at the Heckscher Playground in Central Park. 'The moms and nannies gawked at me like I was an exhibit at the zoo. Now, I'm the new normal.' "[46]

In addition to changes in the household division of labor among couples, exiting highly unsatisfying marriages or not entering one at all is also generally more acceptable for both men and women. Young people have the option, and are indeed often encouraged, to explore their wants and needs before settling down. Cohabitation allows one to try on different relationships in a less threatening and permanent way than usually implied by marriage. More people are living alone than at any time in the recent past in the United States and a number of other countries. The proportion of households with a single person has increased from 9 percent in 1950 to 27 percent in 2010. In Scandinavia, between 40 and 45 percent of households contain a single person.[47] Of these changes, conservative-leaning commentator David Brooks notes, "At some point over the past generation, people around the world entered what you might call the age of possibility. They became intolerant of any arrangement that might close off their personal options. The transformation has been liberating, and it's leading to some pretty astounding changes. For example, for centuries, most human societies forcefully guided people into two-parent families. Today that sort of family is increasingly seen as just one option among many."[48]

However, greater choice does not always bring greater happiness or fulfillment. More choice can mean greater uncertainty and anxiety. Brooks, after introducing the notion of the age of possibility, goes on to argue against its potentially positive aspects: "My view is that the age of possibility is based on a misconception. People are not better off when they are given maximum personal freedom to do what they want. They're better off when they are enshrouded in commitments that transcend personal choice—commitments to family, God, craft and country."[49]

Analysts have also noted that the movement in and out of relationships among adults can be particularly disruptive for their children. Children who experience a series of changes in their parents' partnerships are more likely to act out, be delinquent, or become pregnant at a young age.[50] Divorce has the potential to produce considerable turmoil in people's lives. However, it should be noted that divorce can benefit some individuals (particularly if they are exiting an abusive relationship) or can lead to only temporary declines in well-being. How people respond often depends on the presence of various protective factors, such as having the educational and financial resources and the active skills to cope, as well as support from family and friends.[51] Overall, however, evidence indicates that children growing up in a stable two-parent family are less likely to experience a wide range of cognitive, emotional, and social problems both as children and later on as adults than other children. This finding can be explained by the tendency for children in these stable two-parent families to have a higher standard of living, receive more effective parenting, be emotionally closer to both parents, and experience fewer stressful events.[52]

Changes wrought by the second demographic transition have been linked with broader patterns of poverty and inequality. Some changes, such as the delay in childbearing and the increase in maternal employment, have likely served to increase the economic security among women and children. Other trends, however, including divorce and nonmarital childbearing, have served to depress women's well-being. Sociologist Sara McLanahan has argued that these developments have led to diverging trajectories for women. And because women with the most opportunities and resources to begin with tend to follow the more beneficial trajectory and women with the fewest opportunities and resources follow the more harmful one, these trends as a whole have reinforced and exacerbated economic inequality in the United States. She notes:

> Children who were born to mothers from the most-advantaged backgrounds are making substantial gains in resources. Relative to their counterparts 40 years ago, their mothers are more mature and more likely to be working at well-paying jobs. These children were born into stable unions and are spending more time with their fathers. In contrast, children born to mothers from the most disadvantaged backgrounds are making smaller gains and, in some instances, even losing parental resources. Their mothers are working

at low-paying jobs. Their parents' relationships are unstable, and for many, support from their biological fathers is minimal.[53]

Similarly, McLanahan also finds diverging trajectories for women in other wealthy countries. Specifically, she finds that single motherhood (where there is no marriage or cohabitation) is most common among mothers with the least education in countries like Sweden, Norway, Germany, and Italy. In all countries she studied, fathers in the top educational category were also spending more time with their children than the least educated fathers.[54]

Many researchers have drawn a specific link between single parenthood and poverty in particular. W. E. B. DuBois's 1899 study of the African American community in Philadelphia documented high levels of family disorganization and instability in black families, and he linked this to the legacy of slavery, in which families were sometimes split up and its members sold at will. DuBois's groundbreaking study was followed over the years by a number of others that described the contribution of family instability to black poverty.[55] For example, Daniel Patrick Moynihan's 1965 report *The Negro Family: The Case for National Action* set off an explosive debate on the issue. Critics of the report charged that it put too much blame on ghetto culture for family instability rather than on structural conditions, such as deeply entrenched racism, discrimination, and the lack of economic opportunities for blacks in the wake of deindustrialization in many cities in the Northeast and Midwest. More recently, the link between single parenthood and disadvantage among white families has been highlighted by Charles Murray, who, as discussed above, also emphasized the role of culture in producing these changes.[56]

The culture-structure argument aside, these commentators all rightly note that single-parent families are considerably more likely to be poor than other families. In 2011 the poverty rate among married-couple families with children in the United States was 8.8 percent, compared with 40.9 percent among female-headed families with children.[57] Poverty is high among female-headed families for several reasons. Single parents often face the challenge of supporting a family on one income, as well as running a household alone and finding and paying for child care while they work. Lower average levels of education among women who head such families also significantly contribute to their lower earnings. Furthermore, women tend to earn less than men, and mothers tend to accumulate less work experience than others in the workplace. Finally, single mothers often receive only marginal child support from their children's absent fathers, because fathers sometimes don't make enough money to provide much child support.[58]

Cross-national comparisons likewise suggest that single-parent families are more vulnerable to poverty than others, though their poverty rates varied greatly across countries in the mid-2000s. If a relative poverty line equaling 50 percent of the national median income is used, the poverty rate for children in single-mother families across twenty countries in Europe and Latin America as well as Australia, Canada, and the United States ranged from a low of 8.2 percent in Denmark to a high of 50.5 percent in the United States. The United States is known for having high levels of poverty more generally in comparison to other wealthy countries because of its weaker safety net.[59] In nearly all countries poverty rates in single-mother families were considerably higher than among two-parent families. Poverty rates in single-parent families in Anglophone countries (Australia, Canada, Ireland, the United Kingdom, and the United States) averaged 41 percent, compared with 10 percent in two-parent families. Even in low-poverty Nordic countries (Denmark, Finland, Norway, and Sweden), poverty rates among single-mother families averaged 11 percent, compared with 3 percent among two-parent families.[60] These countries with low poverty rates rely significantly on generous government programs such as universal child allowances, food assistance, and guaranteed child support for single parents to keep their poverty rates low.[61]

Conclusion

The first demographic transition[...]—declining mortality and fertility—has been followed by momentous changes in family living arrangements of the second demographic transition. These changes include delays in marriage and childbearing, increases in cohabitation, divorce, and nonmarital childbearing in many wealthy countries. These trends have been driven by both cultural and economic changes. Culturally, the emphasis on individualism and self-actualization has been ever growing, making people less likely to want to conform to traditional familial roles. Economically, greater gender equality in the labor market, mainly fueled by the increasing labor force participation of women, has made women less dependent on men, thus reducing the economic incentive to marry. Meanwhile, the economic fortunes of less-educated men in the United States have fallen in recent decades, in large part as a result of deindustrialization and globalization. This has reduced the number of "marriageable" men and further dampened the incentive for women to marry. While people generally still value the institution of marriage and aspire to it, many low-income Americans feel it is out of reach, because marriage should happen only after a certain level of financial stability has been achieved.

These trends have consequences for the well-being of individuals and their communities. On the one hand, the greater diversity in family living arrangements and the growing emphasis on individualism mean that people have a greater range of socially acceptable choices available to them than in the past. Women in particular are no longer confined to the very circumscribed gender roles that once anchored them to the home. Likewise, men who choose to spend more time in the home raising their children do not face the level of scorn that they might have in the past. On the other hand, this degree of choice has a dark side, especially when it involves the disruption of families and instability for young children and adolescents. Children living with single parents fare worse by a number of measures (e.g., educational attainment, delinquency) than children living in stable two-parent households. Growing economic inequality today contributes to, and is in turn exacerbated by, changing family living arrangements, such as less-educated men and women being less likely to marry and stay married than highly educated men and women, which serves to reinforce their disadvantaged socioeconomic position. Single parents are also considerably more likely to be poor, given that they often have to rely on only one income and often struggle to obtain affordable child care for their children. Poverty rates among single parents are particularly high in the United States, where government benefits tend to be less generous than in many other wealthy countries.

Americans therefore generally view these changes in family living arrangements with some ambivalence. Many conservative commentators are alarmed by these trends and seek to reinforce traditional values. For the most part, however, people cherish this liberty and their own pursuit of self-actualization. This move toward greater individualism is increasingly characteristic of most modern, wealthy countries, and so the growing diversity of family living arrangements is unlikely to reverse any time soon.

Notes

1 DeParle 2012c.
2 Gill, Glazer, and Thernstrom 1992, 147.
3 Gill, Glazer, and Thernstrom 1992, 148.
4 Gill, Glazer, and Thernstrom 1992, 149–50.
5 U.S. Census Bureau 2012l.
6 Fitch and Ruggles 2000, 63–65.
7 Elliott et al. 2012.
8 Jacobsen, Mather, and Dupuis 2012, 9.
9 Cherlin 1981, 2010; Stevenson and Wolfers 2011, 96–108.
10 Martin 2006.
11 Isen and Stevenson 2010.
12 England and Bearak 2012.
13 Manning 2013, 2–3.
14 Kennedy and Bumpass 2008.
15 Manning and Smock 2005, 998.
16 Manning and Smock 2005, 995.
17 OECD 2011a.
18 O'Connell and Feliz 2011, 31.
19 Krivickas 2010.
20 Burgoyne 2012.
21 Ventura and Bachrach 2000; Martin et al. 2011; see also Wildsmith, Steward-Streng, and Manlove 2011; DeParle and Tavernise 2012.
22 Smock and Greenland 2010.
23 U.S. Census Bureau 2011e.
24 Kennedy and Bumpass 2008.
25 Child Trends 2012.
26 Lesthaeghe 1995.

27 OECD 2011a, table 1.1.

28 OECD 2011a, table 1.1.

29 Kennedy and Fitch 2012, 1494.

30 Findings reported in Lesthaeghe 2010. Other sources for the figures include Raymo, Iwasawa, and Bumpass 2008; and Jones 2005.

31 Much of the discussion below also appears in Iceland 2013, ch. 6.

32 See Murray 1984; Rector 1993.

33 Cherlin 2009, 25–26.

34 Becker 1981.

35 Ruggles 1997.

36 For one example of this argument, see Krugman 2012.

37 England and Bearak 2012.

38 Kristof 2012.

39 Smock and Greenland 2010; see also Gibson-Davis, Edin, and McLanahan 2005.

40 See Edin and Kefalas 2005.

41 See Lareau 2003.

42 DeParle and Tavernise 2012.

43 Lesthaeghe 2010, 33–34.

44 Cherlin 2009, 189.

45 A. Williams 2012.

46 A. Williams 2012.

47 Kotkin 2012, 6; Klineberg 2012; the 2010 figure for the United States is from U.S. Census Bureau 2012e, table 61.

48 Brooks 2012a.

49 Brooks 2012a.

50 Cherlin 2009, 190.

51 Amato 2000, 1282.

52 Amato 2005, 75.

53 McLanahan 2004, 608.

54 McLanahan 2004, 616.

55 Frazier 1932, 1939; Myrdal 1996; Moynihan 1965; Bianchi 1990; Hogan and Lichter 1995, 93–139; Lichter 1997.

56 Murray 2012.

57 U.S. Census Bureau 2012h.

58 Bianchi 1999; O'Hare 1996; CONSAD Research Corp. 2009.

59 Gornick and Jantti 2012, 564.

60 Gornick and Jantti 2012, 564.

61 See Rainwater and Smeeding 2003.

Immigration and Growing Diversity

BY JOHN ICELAND

The United States is often said to be a land of immigrants—and with good reason. Immigration from a wide variety of other countries has continuously changed the character of this country. The initial wave of colonial settlement from England and around it—along with the large number of involuntary immigrants from Africa sold into slavery— eventually gave way to immigration from the rest of northern and western Europe in the early to mid-1800s. The stream of immigration then shifted to eastern and southern Europe by the end of the nineteenth century. Immigration slowed to a trickle after the passage of restrictive laws in the 1920s, aided and abetted by two world wars and a deep depression, before once again accelerating in the last decades of the twentieth century. During this last wave, immigrants came from an even broader array of countries spanning the globe— millions from Asia, Latin America, and Africa.

For a land of immigrants, however, the subject of immigration has long been a source of considerable political contention in the United States. Debates have generally centered around two issues: (1) the extent to which immigrants are assimilating and (2) the overall social and economic impact of immigration on the nation. New groups of immigrants from differing origins have long been viewed with suspicion by a substantial portion of the native-born population. Many have worried that immigrants weaken the character of the country or that they are too different from the native born to assimilate or, worse yet, indifferent to assimilating altogether. Others have fretted that immigrants are a drain on the economy, or that they bring crime and social disorganization to our nation's cities and communities, or that they take jobs away from native-born Americans. These debates on immigration have echoed across generations.

For example, many nativists reacted with alarm to the increasing immigration of Catholics from Germany and Ireland in the early eighteenth century. Catholics, who were associated with the pope and other monarchies of Europe, were viewed by some as an internal threat who might undermine the republic. As historian Roger Daniels recounts:

> When relatively large numbers of Irish and German Catholic immigrants, many of them desperately poor, began to arrive in the late 1820s and early 1830s, what had been a largely rhetorical anti-Catholicism became a major social and political force in American life. Not surprisingly, it was in eastern cities, particularly Boston, where anti-Catholicism turned violent, and much of the violence was directed against convents and churches. Beginning with the burning down of the Ursuline Convent just outside Boston by a mob on August 11, 1834, well into the 1850s violence against Catholic institutions was so prevalent that insurance companies all but refused to insure them.[1]

By the end of the century, when immigrants from southern and eastern Europe were pouring in, the targets of the nativists changed, though many of the underlying concerns were the same. As Daniels again relates:

> But lurking behind and sometimes overshadowing these [religious and economic] objections to continued immigration was a growing and pervasive racism, a racism directed not against non-white races, but against presumed inferior peoples of European origin. ... According to one of its founders [of an immigration restriction league], the question for Americans to decide was whether they wanted their country "to be peopled by British, German and Scandinavian stock, historically free, energetic, progressive, or by Slav, Latin and Asiatic races (this latter referred to Jews rather than Chinese or Japanese), historically down-trodden, atavistic and stagnant."[2]

As immigration from non-European countries picked up steam after changes in immigration policy enacted in 1965, many commentators again raised the alarm of immigration's effect on the character of the nation. Writing in 1995, immigration policy critic Peter Brimelow argued that the 1965 law resulted in immigration that is "dramatically larger, less skilled, and more divergent from the American majority than anything that was anticipated or desired ... is probably not beneficial to the economy ... is attended by a wide and increasing range of negative consequences, from the physical environment to the political ... [and] is bringing about an ethnic and racial transformation in America without precedent in the history of the world—an astonishing social experiment launched with no particular reason to expect success." Indeed, he asks, "Is America still that interlacing of ethnicity and culture we call a nation—and can the American nation-state, the political expression of that nation, survive?" Given that his book is titled *Alien Nation: Common Sense about America's Immigration Disaster*, one may not be surprised to find out that Brimelow offers a pessimistic answer to this question.[3]

The rest of this chapter addresses issues raised in these immigration debates by tackling the following basic questions: To what extent is immigration changing the racial and ethnic composition of the country? Are immigrants being successfully integrated into society? What is the economic and social impact of immigration? How does America's experience with immigration compare with those of other countries? A review of the research on these issues can give us a better sense of the types of policies the United States should consider pursuing, keeping in mind that policy is usually driven by a diverse set of constituents with sometimes competing goals.

Immigration Policy and Current Immigration Patterns

From the founding of the country until about 1875 the United States had an open-door immigration policy. The Naturalization Act of 1790 allowed immigrants to acquire citizenship after several years of residence in the United States, and there were no legal restrictions on the number of immigrants or on places of origin. From time to time throughout the nineteenth century there was serious opposition to immigration—or at least to immigrants from certain origins—but these efforts did not have a significant impact on national policy. As noted above, the feeling was sometimes quite vehement, resulting in periodic violence against certain groups, such as Roman Catholics from Ireland.[4]

By the end of the nineteenth century there was considerable debate about the number of immigrants from southern and eastern Europe. In addition, on the West Coast many opposed immigration from China and Japan, as these immigrants were seen as undercutting the economic prospects of the native born.[5] In all cases, racism undoubtedly played a role, for these groups were often considered inferior to the native stock, and the extent to which they could assimilate into American society was also questioned. After the passage of mainly minor laws that barred the entry of convicts and prostitutes in 1875, Congress passed the Immigration Act of 1882, which prohibited immigration from China.[6] Japanese immigration was later limited in 1907 with the "Gentleman's Agreement," in which Japan was pressured to agree not to issue passports to Japanese citizens interested in immigrating to the United States, and the United States agreed to accept the presence of Japanese immigrants already in the country.

The Immigration Act of 1921 was the first law to put a ceiling on the overall number of immigrants allowed entry into the United States, followed by the even tougher Immigration Act of 1924. The 1924 law limited the number of immigrants from any country to 2 percent of the number of people from that country who were already living in the United States in 1890. By using 1890 as the base year for the quotas, the law had the effect of reducing the number of immigrants from southern and eastern Europe, who came in large numbers to the United States especially after that time. Levels of immigration plummeted after these legislative acts and remained low also in part because of the Great Depression in the 1930s and World War II in the early 1940s.[7]

Immigration policy generally became less restrictive in a number of small ways during and after World War II. Perhaps in part a reaction to the racist excesses of Nazism, overt racism in the United States increasingly fell out of favor. In general, many Americans felt that more effort should be made to harmonize policies with basic American ideals of liberty and equality of opportunity.[8] President Franklin Delano Roosevelt, for example, passed an executive order in 1941 that forbade racial discrimination by defense contractors. The

Chinese exclusion laws were repealed in 1943, and the Luce-Celler Act of 1946 prohibited discrimination against Indian Americans and Filipinos, who were accorded the right to naturalization. The Immigration and Nationality Act of 1952 revised the quotas, basing them on the 1920 census (rather than the 1890 census).

In the meantime, immigration from Mexico began increasing in the 1940s and 1950s, largely as a result of the Bracero Program, which aimed to bring contract laborers temporarily to the United States to fill labor shortages, especially in agriculture. Workers were paid low wages, often endured difficult working conditions, and were expected to return to Mexico after their contract expired. The Bracero Program was extended several times before formally ending in the mid-1960s.[9]

At about this time another momentous piece of immigration legislation was passed—the 1965 amendments to the Immigration and Nationality Act (also known as the Hart-Celler Act). This act did away with the discriminatory national quota system and instead set more uniform annual quotas across countries. While supporters of the bill sought to make immigration policy less discriminatory, they did not think it would drastically affect immigration patterns. Senator Edward Kennedy, chair of the Senate Immigration Subcommittee that was managing the bill, asserted, "First, our cities will not be flooded with a million immigrants annually. Under the proposed bill, the present level of immigration remains substantially the same. … Secondly, the ethnic mix of this country will not be upset."[10] The bill set an overall cap of 170,000 visas per year, later raised to 290,000. A number of people were, and continue to be, exempt from quotas, including spouses, children, and parents of U.S. citizens, as well as refugees and other smaller categories of immigrants. In 2009, for example, about 47 percent of the 1.1 million people who gained legal permanent residential status in the United States were immediate relatives of U.S. citizens who were exempt from the numerical quotas.[11]

Senator Kennedy's assurances notwithstanding, the most significant effect of the Hart-Celler Act was that it spurred immigration from countries that had little recent history of sending immigrants to the United States, especially Asia and later Africa. (Immigration from Latin America had been in increasing in the years before the passage of the law, so it is not clear whether the law was responsible for spurring any further migration from that region.)[12] Figure 5.1 shows the number and changing origins of the immigrant population from 1900 to 2009. While the number of immigrants arriving annually was higher between 1900 and 1909 than in the middle decades of the twentieth century, by the 1990s the number of immigrants arriving surpassed all previous levels. The United States received a historical high of over 1 million legal immigrants annually in the 2000s, with many more undocumented immigrants as well. (About 11 million undocumented immigrants lived in the United States in 2011.)[13] However, because of the smaller population base at that time, the proportion of the population that was foreign born in 1910 (15 percent) was still higher than the proportion foreign born a hundred years later in 2010 (13 percent).[14]

Whereas 92 percent of all legal immigrants were from Europe in the 1900–1909 period, this dropped to just 19 percent in the 1970s and 13 percent in the first decade of the 2000s. Meanwhile, the proportion of immigrants from Latin America grew from only 2 percent in 1900–1909 to 23 percent in the 1950s to a peak of 51 percent in the 1990s, before dropping back to 41 percent in the 2000s. The proportion of immigrants from Asia grew rapidly in the 1960s through the 1990s; by the 2000s Asians constituted about a third of legal immigrants. Since 2009, the number of immigrants from Asia has surpassed the number from Latin America.[15] Immigration from Africa was negligible over most of the period,

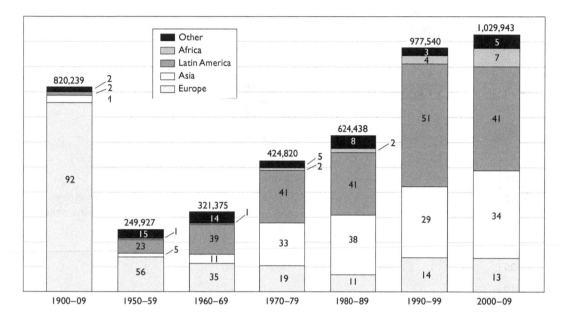

FIGURE 5.1 Annual number of legal U.S. immigrants, by decade, and their percentage distributions, by region of origin, 1900–2009. Note: The Y axis demarcates numbers of immigrants in increments of a hundred thousand. The shadings and numbers *within* the graph's bars indicate percentages of immigrants from the different regions of origin. The Latin America category includes Mexico, Central America, the Caribbean, and South America. The Other category consists mainly of immigrants from Canada in the 1950–59 and 1960–69 periods, though it also includes immigrants from Oceania and a small proportion of immigrants whose origin was not known in the 1980–89 and 2000–2009 periods. Source: U.S. Department of Homeland Security 2012.

though it has increased in the last couple of decades, such that African immigrants made up 7 percent of all immigrants in the 2000s.[16]

Changing immigration patterns and differential fertility rates (higher fertility rates among minority groups than among whites) have had a major effect on the racial and ethnic composition of the U.S. population. Figure 5.2 shows that 63 percent of the population was non-Hispanic white in 2011, down from 83 percent in 1970. The percentage of the population that is African American held steady, constituting 12 percent of the total population in 2011. Meanwhile, the percentage of the population that is Hispanic has increased rapidly, from 5 percent in 1970 to 17 percent in 2011. The Asian population has likewise increased significantly, from 1 to 5 percent over the period. The U.S. Census Bureau projects that by 2060, just 43 percent of the population will be non-Hispanic white, 13 percent will be African American, 8 percent will be Asian, and 31 percent will be Hispanic.[17] These projections, however, should be viewed with caution, as they incorporate assumptions about immigration trends, fertility rates, and future patterns of racial and ethnic identification. For example, recent research has shown that Latino fertility rates may not be as high as commonly thought, and that how people view their identity over time and across generations often changes.[18] Nevertheless, it is safe to say that racial and ethnic diversity in the United States will continue to increase in the coming decades.

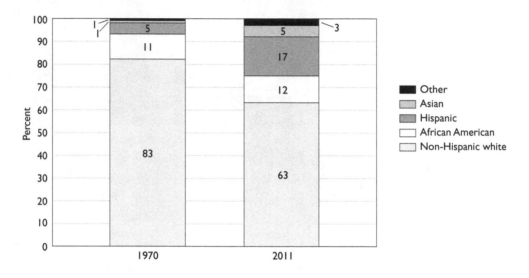

FIGURE 5.2 Racial/ethnic composition of the United States, 1970 and 2011. Sources: 1970 data from Martin and Midgely 2010, 3; 2011 data from Motel and Patten 2013, table 1.

Immigrant Assimilation

What does assimilation mean in the United States today? Researchers and commentators have struggled with the concept, as have immigrants themselves. A newspaper article from the 1990s relates the following story:

> Night is falling on South Omaha, and Maria Jacinto is patting tortillas for the evening meal in the kitchen of the small house she shares with her husband and five children. Like many others in her neighborhood, where most of the residents are Mexican immigrants, the Jacinto household mixes the old country with the new.
>
> As Jacinto, who speaks only Spanish, stresses a need to maintain the family's Mexican heritage, her eldest son, a bilingual 11-year-old who wears a San Francisco 49ers jacket and has a paper route, comes in and joins his brothers and sisters in the living room to watch "The Simpsons."

Jacinto became a U.S. citizen last April, but she does not feel like an American. In fact, she seems resistant to the idea of assimilating into U.S. society. "I think I'm still a Mexican," she says. "When my skin turns white and my hair turns blonde, then I'll be an American."[19]

The article goes on to argue that the changing demographics of the country challenge the notion that immigrants will be able to assimilate, because many newcomers are visible minorities, and, unlike in the past, many immigrants themselves resist assimilation, not wanting their children to assimilate into a culture that they view as being different from and in many ways inferior to their own.

While debates on these issues are far from settled, the evidence tends to indicate—contrary to the implications of the article above—that immigrants in the newest wave are successfully integrating into American society, though the pace and extent of integration vary significantly across groups. In the next section I delve into these issues by defining assimilation, reviewing the empirical evidence on the issue, and describing why the pessimism expressed in the article above is for the most part unwarranted.

What Is Assimilation?

Assimilation refers to the reduction of ethnic group distinctions over time. In the past the term has sometimes been used to mean Anglo conformity; that is, assimilation occurs when an immigrant group adopts the mores and practices of old-stock native-born white Americans. More recent assimilation theorists emphasize that assimilation need not be a one-way street on which minority members become more like the majority group members. Rather, assimilation involves a general convergence of social, economic, and cultural patterns that typically also involve the upward mobility of immigrants and their children.[20]

Assimilation is often not a conscious decision in which an immigrant decides to shed his or her cultural practices and heritage in the pursuit of another culture's. Rather, as Richard Alba and Victor Nee note, assimilation is a lengthy process that typically spans generations: "To the extent that assimilation occurs, it proceeds incrementally as an intergenerational process, stemming both from individuals' purposive action and from the unintended consequences of their workaday decisions. In the case of immigrants and their descendants who may not intentionally seek to assimilate, the cumulative effect of pragmatic decisions aimed at successful adaptation can give rise to changes in behavior that nevertheless lead to eventual assimilation."[21]

Commentators who believe that immigrants of old were eager to assimilate—unlike contemporary immigrants—are not well acquainted with the historical record. Historian Roger Daniels describes how German immigrants in the nineteenth century came mostly for economic reasons, remained very proud of their homeland, and sought to retain their cultural practices:

Indispensable for most cultural institutions that were intended to endure beyond the immigrant generation was some way of ensuring that the second and subsequent generations learn and use the ancestral language—what scholars now call language maintenance. ...

> Beginning with parochial schools, largely but not exclusively Lutheran and Catholic, Germans eventually turned to the public schools and political action in [an] attempt to make German instruction in all subjects available when enough parents wanted it. In such public schools, English might be taught as a special subject as if it were a foreign language, which, of course, it was and is to many young children of immigrants raised in essentially monolingual homes. And in many parochial schools, English was not taught at all.[22]

Daniels notes that German culture remained very strong and proudly expressed until World War I, when the conflict pitting Germany against England, France, and eventually the United States led to strong anti-German feeling in many quarters. Still, even today many communities in the Midwest have strong German roots and cultural heritage.

Ties to the United States were also, at least initially, weak among many immigrants from a number of other sending countries. For example, of the 4.1 million Italians recorded as entering the United States between 1880 and 1920, anywhere from about 30 percent to nearly half returned to Italy.[23] Over the years, many immigrants have been attracted primarily by economic opportunities rather than by the notion of becoming American. Italians, like many other immigrant groups, were also concentrated in particular neighborhoods of particular cities (such as Little Italy in New York City), and they were concentrated in specific occupations as well, such as in low-and semiskilled trades like construction and pushcart vending. Many native-born Americans stereotyped Italians as criminals, pointing to tight-knit criminal organizations such as the Mafia.[24] Here we see that contemporary concerns with crime in immigrant communities (e.g., Hispanic gangs today) and the stereotyping of immigrant groups are nothing new.

Still, just because immigrants of previous waves of immigration from Europe assimilated does not mean that more recent immigrants from Latin America, Asia, and Africa will have the same experience. Commentators have pointed to a number of differences in the conditions under which these different waves have arrived in the United States.[25] Perhaps the most prominent of the arguments is that immigrants today are racially more distinct than those in the past. The counterview is that despite our perception of previous waves of immigrants from Europe as essentially "white," historical accounts indicate that many among those immigrant groups, including the Irish, Jews, and Italians, were perceived to be racially distinct from the majority of native-born Americans. As Daniels writes: "However curious it may seem today, by the late nineteenth century many of the 'best and brightest' minds in America had become convinced that of all the many 'races' (we would say 'ethnic groups') of Europe one alone—variously called Anglo-Saxon, Aryan, Teutonic, or Nordic—had superior innate characteristics. Often using a crude misapplication of Darwinian evolution, which substituted these various 'races' for Darwinian species, historians, political scientists, economists, and, later, eugenicists discovered that democratic political institutions had developed and could thrive only among Anglo-Saxon peoples."[26] The idea that immigrants from different European countries constituted different races diminished only over time as various groups achieved socioeconomic mobility.[27]

Nevertheless, a number of people remain skeptical about the successful integration of many of today's immigrant groups into American society. A competing theoretical perspective—*ethnic disadvantage*—holds that even if new immigrants learn the language and customs of their new country, they may still not be able to achieve significant socioeconomic mobility or acceptance by the white mainstream. Discrimination, for example, may put many educational opportunities or jobs out of reach for newcomers.

One viewpoint somewhere between the two (assimilation and ethnic disadvantage) is *segmented assimilation*. This perspective focuses on divergent patterns of incorporation among contemporary immigrants.[28] It asserts that the host society offers uneven possibilities to different immigrant groups, some of whom might achieve upward mobility and be successfully assimilated into the mainstream, others who will be marginalized and will adopt harmful cultural practices of disadvantaged native-born groups and experience downward mobility, and yet others who will retain strong ethnic ties and still achieve high levels of socioeconomic success. According to this perspective, racial discrimination and the range of economic opportunities available in a particular place at a particular time may shape assimilation trajectories of immigrants and their children. A number of studies have tested these perspectives.

Evidence on Assimilation

While one could study many different dimensions of assimilation (social, political, economic, etc.), I will focus on three dimensions of broad interest that are indicative of immigrants' general position in U.S. society: education, earnings, and residential segregation patterns. Taking generational change into account is critical in these comparisons, as assimilation is thought to occur mainly over time and across generations. Beginning with education, Figure 5.3 shows years of education for different ethnic groups by generation and age averaged over the 1995 to 2007 period. (Multiple years of Current Population Survey data were needed to have large enough samples of relatively small groups, such as second-generation Puerto Ricans, to calculate reliable averages.) It should be noted that individuals born in Puerto Rico, although U.S. citizens at birth, are considered to be "foreign-born" in the analysis on the basis of their shared experiences as newcomers to the mainland United States, whereas their children and subsequent generations are "native-born." On the left-hand side of the figure, we see that third- and higher-generation whites age 50 and over have, on average, 13.1 years of education. This number is higher than the figure among similarly aged immigrants of all origins except South Asians, indicating a general educational advantage among the native-white population.

However, we see that the second generation has experienced considerable increases in mean education levels compared with the first generation, and that most groups have closed the gap or surpassed the educational attainment of third- and higher-generation whites of the same age. For example, while the third-generation or more whites of ages 25 to 39 averaged 13.9 years of education, this figure was 14.3 among children of white

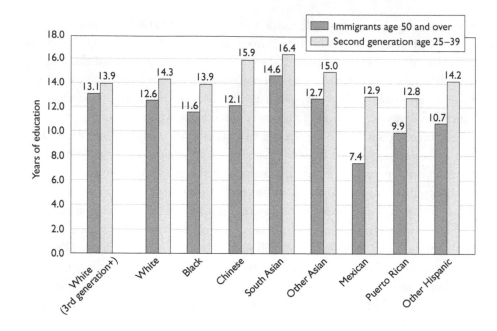

FIGURE 5.3 Years of education, by generation, age, and ethnic origin, among U.S. native born and immigrants, 1995–2007. Note: The first set of bars refers to native-born populace; all others refer to immigrants or their offspring. Following the same key that pertains to the other categories, the first bar in the set for 3rd generation+ whites refers to whites 50 and over, and the second bar refers to 3rd-generation whites ages 25–39. Source: Reitz, Zhang, and Hawkins 2011, table 1, using Current Population Survey data.

immigrants, 13.9 among second-generation blacks, 15.9 among second-generation Chinese, and a high of 16.4 among second-generation South Asians. The two second-generation groups that had lower levels of educational attainment than third-generation or more whites were Mexicans (12.9 years) and Puerto Ricans (12.8 years). However, even though these groups did not reach parity with whites, they far surpassed their respective first generations (7.4 years among Mexican immigrants age 50 and over and 9.9 years among similar Puerto Ricans). The second generation of many groups often does better than third-generation whites, because their parents—especially those with high education themselves—are often a "select" group: many immigrated to the United States because they sought economic mobility, and they push their children to excel in school.[29] These general findings about the upward mobility across immigrant generations are in line with the conclusions of other studies that have analyzed this issue with other approaches and nationally representative data. In other words, while many immigrant groups are initially quite disadvantaged compared with the native mainstream, their upward trajectory suggests that some measure of integration is occurring.[30]

These findings do not mean that there is no cause for any concern. First, the immigrants themselves and their children vary considerably in their educational attainment. The United States attracts both very highly educated professionals (e.g., computer programmers and engineers in Silicon Valley) and low-skill laborers who toil away on farms or construction sites across the country. Even among Hispanics we see considerable variation, with Mexicans having the lowest initial levels of education, while education among "Other Hispanics" is considerably higher.

Second, while generational progress among the Mexican-origin population is impressive, Mexican American educational attainment at this time still lags behind other groups. The lack of documentation among many Mexican-origin immigrants tends to impede integration, because such individuals and their children do not have the same means to access the full range of jobs and educational opportunities that others can in the United States.[31] Researchers Michael White and Jennifer Glick find that adolescents from lower socioeconomic backgrounds tend to lag behind their more advantaged peers regardless of racial and ethnic background, and this can serve to slow continued educational progress across generations. White and Glick further note that while the effect of race may be declining in American society, the effect of race and ethnic origin on educational attainment has not disappeared altogether, even after accounting for many other family background factors.[32]

Turning to the second dimension of assimilation, income, figure 5.4 shows differences in household income by age and generation for the same ethnic groups shown in figure 5.3. The

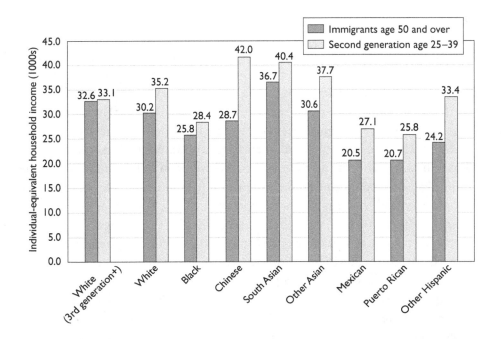

FIGURE 5.4 Household income (adjusted for household size), by generation, age, and ethnic origin, 1995–2007 (in 1,000s of dollars). Note: The first bar in the set for 3rd-generation+ whites refers to whites age 50 and over, and the second bar refers to 3rd-generation of whites ages 25–39. Income is in constant 2001 dollars. Household income is divided by the square root of the number of persons in the household. Source: Reitz, Zhang, and Hawkins 2011, table 3, using Current Population Survey data.

household income measure is adjusted for household size to produce an "individual-equivalent" measure. Some groups have larger households on average, so this measure provides more of a per capita household income estimate that also takes into account economies of scale enjoyed by larger households.[33] Figure 5.4 shows that second-generation households have higher incomes, on average, than first-generation ones among all ethnic groups. In addition, whereas all first-generation immigrant groups except South Asians had lower incomes than third-generation+ whites, the second generation of many groups (whites, Chinese, South Asians, other Asians, and other Hispanics) had higher average incomes than third-generation+ whites in the same age range. Second-generation blacks, Mexicans, and Puerto Ricans all continued to have lower incomes than whites, even if the gap (as compared with the first-generation white gap) was narrower. More sophisticated analyses that take into account differences in education, marital status, and geographic location across groups tend to find small to negligible differences between whites and Asians but lower incomes among African Americans and Hispanics.[34] Other research confirms lower earnings for African Americans, though more mixed findings for Hispanics once many background factors are taken into account.[35] It is not clear why the gap between whites and African Americans, and perhaps Hispanics, exists, though labor market discrimination might play a role. Some studies have found higher levels of disadvantage particularly among blacks and darker-skinned Hispanics, suggesting the existence of a black-nonblack divide in American society abetted by discrimination.[36] American color lines are discussed in more detailed in the following chapter.

With respect to the final dimension of assimilation to be discussed, immigrant residential patterns, I previously conducted research on this issue by examining how levels of residential segregation vary by racial/ethnic group and nativity. The conventional wisdom has long been that new immigrants prefer to settle in ethnic enclaves so that they can live near people who share their common history and culture. Living among friends and family can bring comfort to those in a very unfamiliar environment. Immigrants' social networks also draw them to live in particular neighborhoods. According to the assimilation perspective, however, immigrants would be more likely to move out of these enclaves the longer they are in the host country, and certainly we would expect to see later generations living in a broader array of neighborhoods with groups other than immigrants themselves.

I used the most common indicator of residential segregation, the dissimilarity index, to measure the distribution of different groups across neighborhoods in metropolitan areas across the United States. The index ranges from 0 to 100, where 0 indicates complete integration (ethnic groups are evenly distributed across all neighborhoods) and 100 indicates extreme segregation (ethnic groups live wholly homogeneous neighbor-hoods with co-ethnics). The general rule of thumb is that scores above 60 are considered high in absolute terms, a score between 30 and 60 indicates moderate segregation, and scores under 30 are quite low.

Figure 5.5 shows average levels of segregation of Hispanics, Asians, and blacks from native-born non-Hispanic whites (hereafter termed "whites") across metropolitan areas in the United States, as calculated with 2000 census data. We see that in general, blacks are highly segregated from whites (an overall dissimilarity score of 67), followed by Hispanics

(52) and Asians (43). Of particular relevance to testing the assimilation perspective, native-born Hispanics, Asians, and blacks are less segregated from whites than their immigrant counterparts.[37] In additional analyses, I found that, consistent with the assimilation perspective, some of these differences by nativity are explained by the average characteristics of the foreign born that are generally associated with higher levels of segregation, such as their lower levels of income and English-language fluency, meaning that gains in those attributes generally translate into greater residential integration. I also found that immigrants who have been in the United States for longer periods of time were generally less segregated from whites than new arrivals.[38]

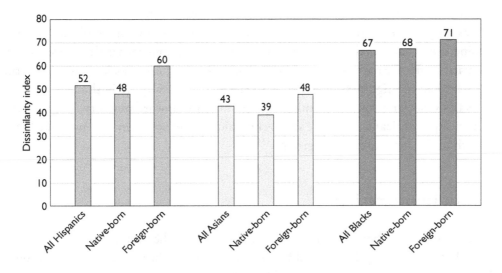

FIGURE 5.5 Segregation of racial/ethnic groups from native-born non-Hispanic whites, by nativity, according to the dissimilarity index, 2000. Source: Iceland and Scopilliti 2008, table 1.

Nevertheless, we do see that patterns vary across racial and ethnic groups, with very high levels of segregation between blacks and whites regardless of nativity. On the one hand, this could provide some support for the segmented assimilation perspective. Clearly, blacks tend to live in very different neighborhoods from those of whites, especially in metropolitan areas in the Northeast and Midwest such as Detroit, Milwaukee, Chicago, and New York.[39] On the other hand, as will be shown in chapter 7, [...] black-white segregation has been declining significantly over the years (this also shows up in 2010 census data), such that the residential (and social) distance between blacks and whites will likely continue to narrow in the coming years.

Despite these findings on the generational improvement in education and income and the decline in residential segregation, some commentators remain skeptical about whether all immigrant groups are assimilating. They rightly point out, for example, that Hispanic immigrants have been met with considerable hostility in many communities and question whether Hispanics will eventually be accepted into American society.[40] Many people also view strict anti-illegal immigration laws passed in states such as Arizona (2010) and Alabama (2011) as condoning racial profiling against Hispanics. Others base their skepticism about assimilation on research; one large study of a sample of Mexican-origin individuals in San Antonio and Los Angeles found that while there was considerable linguistic assimilation among Mexican Americans (i.e., most native-born Mexican Americans were fluent in English), educational and earnings mobility was only modest between the first and second generation, with little additional progress thereafter.[41]

Studies using nationally representative data, however, tend to show slow but steady generational progress among Mexicans. In a careful comparison of assimilation patterns of Mexicans in recent years with Italians and other southern and eastern European groups a century ago, Joel Perlmann concludes that Mexican socioeconomic mobility is slowly progressing such that it may take them "four or five generations rather than three or four to reach parity with the native-white mainstream."[42] That is, the low socioeconomic starting point of Mexican immigrants, combined with the fact that many are in the United States without valid visas (and thus have limited opportunity for upward mobility), suggests that while Mexican Americans will make socioeconomic progress over time, it may take longer for them than for other immigrant groups.[43]

Impact of Immigration

In addition to concerns about assimilation, some question whether immigrants have a positive impact on U.S. society. While one could potentially examine the impact of immigration on just about any aspect of American life, here I focus on the effects of immigration on three areas of broad interest and concern: the economy, social solidarity and social capital, and crime.

Economic Impacts

One economic issue frequently raised is whether immigrants drive down the wages of native-born workers. The answer comes down to whether immigrants are *complements* to American workers or *substitutes* for them. If they are complements, they are not directly competing for existing jobs. Instead, they work in jobs that employers have trouble filling with existing native-born workers (such as in agriculture in some parts of the country), they work in jobs that only marginally compete with native-born businesses (e.g., bodegas that serve ethnic communities), or they even generate job growth because they are entrepreneurs or consumers of goods and services produced by native-born workers. In these cases, immigrants are complementing the existing native workforce and not taking away their jobs. However, if immigrants are substitutes, they are essentially replacing native-born workers or competing enough with them to drive down their wages.

Economists have debated this issue at length over the years, as different methodological approaches have at times yielded different findings. A number of years ago a National

Academy of Sciences panel of accomplished social scientists investigated this issue and concluded that the effect of immigration on the earnings of the native-born workforce is on the whole quite small. Immigration does not reduce the earnings of most native-born workers. Those most susceptible to the negative effects of immigration are low-skill workers, including less-educated African Americans, but even here the effects are small. The evidence suggested that immigrants tend to compete most with immigrants from earlier waves of immigration, for whom the recent immigrants are at times substitutes in the labor market.[44] The findings of the panel have been supported by a more recent review of the research on this topic as well.[45]

The fiscal impact of immigration depends on whether immigrants pay more in taxes than they consume in public services. Calculating the overall impact is quite complicated, as taxes are paid at the federal, state, and local levels via a variety of mechanisms (e.g., income taxes, payroll taxes, sales taxes, etc.), and public services are likewise offered by different levels of government. Moreover, the effects of immigration are both short term and long term, with the latter depending on not only the tax and consumption patterns of current immigrants but also those of the children of immigrants. Both the National Academy of Science panel mentioned above and more recent work have concluded that once all of these elements are balanced, the fiscal effects of immigration are generally small, and they depend on the characteristics of immigrants. Less-educated immigrants tend to consume more public services and contribute less in taxes, as do immigrants over the age of fifty. The federal government tends to benefit from immigration in the form of payroll taxes paid, because even many illegal immigrants with counterfeit Social Security cards have such taxes withheld from their paychecks. Meanwhile, local governments are more likely to bear the brunt of the costs of immigration (at least in the short run), such as in the form of staffing public schools with sufficient support services for immigrant children and health care for a growing local population.[46]

Immigration has a number of other economic benefits to the United States. Immigrants tend to lower the cost of many goods and services as a result of low wages. Higher-income consumers may benefit the most from this because they consume more "immigrant-intensive" products and services, including child care, restaurant food, and landscaping.[47] Among other economic benefits, immigrant entrepreneurs contribute to economic growth, immigration can boost struggling industries and cities, immigrants strengthen America's commercial ties with the rest of the world, immigrants contribute to the United States' engineering and scientific prowess, and immigration counteracts the aging of the native-born population.[48]

Regarding the first of these additional benefits—the contribution of immigrant entrepreneurs—immigrants to the United States have long been economic innovators. Among them, readily recognizable today are Andrew Carnegie (in the steel industry), Alexander Graham Bell (communications), and John Nordstrom (retailing).[49] Even today immigrants are more likely than native-born Americans to start companies. Immigrants, for example, make up 18 percent of all small business owners in the United States, though they are 13 percent of the U.S. population and 16 percent of the labor force.[50] Their impact on the rise of technology businesses and corporations in Silicon Valley in recent years has been immense. One study estimated that immigrants were on the founding teams of just over half of all technology companies in Silicon Valley, including companies such as Google, Sun Microsystems, and SpaceX.[51] In debates about immigration policy, one point many observers agree upon is that high-skill immigrants should be able to get visas to come to the United States more easily than current policy rules allow. As Alex Salkever and Vivek Wadhwa argued in a column on immigrant entrepreneurs:

> Allowing skilled immigrant entrepreneurs to more easily enter America, where they can create good jobs and pay taxes, is the closest thing to an economic free lunch that we are likely to get. In the words of New York Mayor Michael Bloomberg, we are committing "economic suicide" by making it hard for skilled immigrants to stay in the U.S. and contribute to our economy. ... [Foreign-born inventors are most prevalent] in cutting-edge fields such as semiconductor device manufacturing, where 87 percent of patents named an immigrant inventor; information technology, where 84 percent of patents named an immigrant inventor. ... Unfortunately, difficulties in obtaining visas are forcing many founders and innovators to either delay their start-up dreams or to relocate to more hospitable countries.[52]

Illustrating this very point, an article in the *Washington Post* recounted the following visa woes of two aspiring entrepreneurs who were postdoctoral mechanical engineers at MIT and, by extension, the impact this problem might have on our economy if it persists:

> Anurag Bajpayee and Prakash Narayan Govindan, both from India, have started a company to sell the[ir water decontamination] system to oil businesses that are desperate for a cheaper, cleaner way to dispose of the billions of gallons of contaminated water produced by fracking.
>
> Oil companies have flown them to Texas and North Dakota. They say they are about to close on millions of dollars in financing, and they expect to hire 100 employees in the next couple of years. *Scientific American* magazine called water-decontamination technology developed by Bajpayee one of the top 10 "world-changing ideas" of 2012.
>
> But their student visas expire soon, both before summer, and because of the restrictive U.S. visa system, they may have to move their company to India or another country. "We love it here," said Bajpayee, a cheerful 27-year-old in an argyle sweater and jeans. "But there are so many hoops you have to jump through. And you risk getting deported while you are creating jobs."[53]

Immigration has also boosted struggling industries, such as the fruit and vegetable industry in California and the garment industry in New York, and has revitalized many inner cities, such as Miami, Los Angeles, New York, and Philadelphia.[54] In Philadelphia, for example, the immigrant population grew by 113,000 just between 2000 and 2006, by which time immigrants constituted 9 percent of the total population. Audrey Singer and her coauthors conclude that immigrants are revitalizing the city by bringing "fresh energy, entrepreneurship, and vibrancy to many parts of the region. They are breathing life into declining commercial areas, reopening storefronts, creating local jobs, and diversifying products and services available to residents. Immigrants are repopulating neighborhoods on the wane and reviving and sustaining housing markets. Across the region, they are helping to make greater Philadelphia a more global, cosmopolitan center, with stronger connections to economies and cultures abroad."[55] On the other hand, Singer also notes that immigration produces challenges for local institutions, such as in the overcrowding of public schools and the need for more services targeted at non-English-speaking individuals. On the whole, however, immigration has been an economic boon for the city. Recognizing the economic potential of immigration, many other places, such as Dayton, Ohio, Michigan, and Iowa, have tried to lure more immigrants.[56] For all of these reasons, the National Academy of Sciences panel concluded that immigration delivers a significant net economic gain for U.S. residents.[57]

Social Cohesion and Social Capital

The arrival of a large number of immigrants naturally changes the dynamics of communities. Many long-standing community members may view the newcomers with distrust and perhaps fear that immigrants are going to change the character of a familiar place. Sometimes animosity can arise in a struggle for power, as established residents may wish to keep their control over resources while new groups fight for recognition and for what they view as their fair share. For example, discussing racial and ethnic tensions in Los Angeles in the 1990s, researcher James Johnson and his colleagues argued, "Tensions, conflicts, and community instability associated with heightened immigration—especially of nonwhite immigrant groups—threaten to balkanize America. … We believe that the undercurrent of racial and ethnic intolerance that undergirds the nation's changing demographic realities strongly challenges, and may very well threaten, our ability to establish viable, stable, racially and ethnically diverse communities and institutions."[58]

Johnson and his colleagues provide the example of neighborhood change in the city of Compton, a suburb of Los Angeles. It was initially an all-white community that experienced racial tension and white-to-black population succession in the 1960s. In the following decades, Hispanic migration to the area caused new schisms. On the one hand, black residents resented having to share social services and social institutions with the newcomers. On the other hand, newly arriving Hispanics complained about the lack of access to municipal jobs and leadership positions in the local government and about staffing positions in the school system and the content of the school curriculum.[59]

In 2006, in what was viewed by many as a law targeting Hispanics as a whole, Hazleton, Pennsylvania, passed a law that penalized employers for hiring illegal immigrants and landlords for renting to them. The law was declared unconstitutional in 2010 by a federal appeals courts, but the next year the U.S. Supreme Court upheld a similar law in Arizona and ordered a court of appeals to review Pennsylvania's law. Hazleton is a largely white, conservative community that had experienced a slow demographic decline since the 1940s in large part because of the decline of local industries (coal mining and the garment industry). In the 2000s it became a new destination for immigrants, who have in many ways revitalized the city. Hispanics made up 37 percent of the population in 2010, up from only 5 percent just ten years earlier. But this immigration has also been a source of tension, as it has changed the character of the city.

As a news story looking at relations in Hazleton reported, "Hispanic residents said they felt their entire population was stigmatized by the crackdown on illegal immigrants. Felix Perez, a Walmart employee with two daughters, 2 and 9, recalled a time he hesitated at the wheel of his car, unsure which way to turn, and the non-Hispanic driver behind him got out with a gun in his hand. 'He saw my face, he knew I was Spanish,' Mr. Perez said. 'They believe we are all the same because we look the same.' "[60]

According to the same story, some longtime residents are not entirely happy with the changes in their community. "The people in this town, we're becoming a minority," said Chris DeRienzo, 30, a wedding photographer who opposes a pathway to citizenship for illegal immigrants. "It hurts. I grew up here. It's not what it used to be."

One recent study by the well-known political scientist Robert Putnam examined the effect of diversity on social solidarity and social capital. He found that social cohesion was indeed lower in more diverse communities, at least in the short run. As he puts it, "In ethnically diverse neighbor-hoods residents of all races tend to 'hunker down.' Trust (even of one's own race) is lower, altruism and community cooperation rarer, friends fewer."[61] For example, survey respondents in relatively homogeneous areas, such as Bismarck, North Dakota, and Lewiston, Maine, were more likely to report that they trust their neighbors "a lot" than those in diverse places like San Francisco, Los Angeles, and Houston. Putnam also cites Richard Alba and Victor Nee, who note, "When social distance is small, there is a feeling of common identity, closeness, and shared experiences. But when social distance is great, people perceive and treat the other as belonging to a different category."[62]

While Putnam's main analysis focuses on this point, he does provide a word of optimism at the end of his published lecture, saying that these low levels of trust might be fleeting. "In the long run, however, successful immigrant societies have overcome such fragmentation by creating new, cross-cutting forms of social solidarity and more encompassing identities. Illustrations of becoming comfortable with diversity are drawn from the US military, religious institutions, and earlier waves of immigration."[63] It should be said that Putnam's analysis should not be taken as the last word on these issues. The results of his study have been criticized on both conceptual and methodological grounds, though empirical studies have tended to support (though not uniformly) his general conclusion about the negative association between diversity and social solidarity.[64] Thus, immigration can lead to a decline in social cohesion, at least in the short run, though a negative long-term impact is far from inevitable.

Regarding a related issue, the effect of immigration on the incidence of crime, conventional wisdom has long held that immigration is associated with social disorganization, ethnic gangs, and many types of criminal activity. However, an emerging consensus among scholars is that immigration to the United States in recent decades has generally not increased crime and in fact has often served to reduce it.[65] For example, sociologist

Robert Sampson, one of the leading scholars in this area, found that, controlling for individual and family background characteristics, first-generation Mexican immigrants in Chicago were considerably less likely to commit crimes than later generations. He also found that living in a neighborhood of concentrated immigration was directly associated with lower violence, once a number of other neighborhood attributes were accounted for. More generally, he notes that immigration was increasing in the 1990s just when national homicide rates were plunging. He concludes that the beneficial (or at least unharmful) association between immigration and crime may be due to immigration's role in helping to revitalize many declining inner-city neighborhoods and to the positive influence that many immigrants may have on local cultures, given that immigrants themselves are not prone to crime or violence and for the most part do not come from particularly violent cultures.[66]

International Comparisons

International migration has been increasing around the globe in recent decades. Most of the discussion below focuses on comparisons between the United States and other peer (mainly wealthy) countries of Europe and the OECD, but it should be noted that many countries in a wide variety of regions have very high net migration rates, ranging from the United Arab Emirates on the Arabian Peninsula to Singapore in Southeast Asia to Botswana in sub-Saharan Africa.[67]

Many European countries that had been senders of migrants (and colonizers) in the nineteenth century became destinations for immigrants in the post–World War II period. Germany, for example, experienced labor shortages in the 1950s as it continued to rebuild and grow after World War II. It first looked to southern Europe, then Turkey, and then North Africa for temporary laborers. Other European countries with guest-worker policies included, among others, Austria, Switzerland, and Sweden. Some countries, particularly Great Britain, France, the Netherlands, and Belgium, also received immigrants from their former colonies. When a sharp recession hit Europe in the early 1970s, countries with guest-worker programs terminated them. However, a significant proportion of supposedly temporary immigrants did not wish to be repatriated to their countries of origin and stayed in their adopted countries. Many European countries have struggled with their growing diversity, and public opinion remains divided on appropriate levels of immigration. Nevertheless, immigration to many European countries both from their neighbors and from non-European countries continues.[68]

The United States continues to attract more immigrants than any other OECD country. For example, the United States had nearly 40 million foreign-born persons in 2010, followed next by Germany, with nearly 11 million.[69] However, because the United States has a much larger total population than any of these other countries, the percentage of its population that is foreign born is lower than in many others, as shown in Figure 5.6. Countries with the highest percentage of foreign-born residents in 2010 were Australia (26.9 percent), Israel

(24.5 percent), and Switzerland (26.5 percent). Canada (19.0 percent) also had a higher proportion of foreign-born residents than the United States (12.9 percent). A number of OECD countries had a relatively low percentage of foreign-born residents, such as Mexico (0.9 percent), Chile (2.2 percent), and Hungary (4.5 percent). Overall, however, immigration is both bolstering the populations of many countries that would otherwise be facing the prospect of future demographic decline because of low fertility and also transforming the character of these countries.

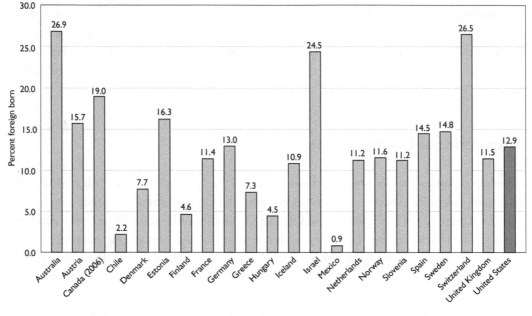

FIGURE 5.6 Percentage of the population foreign born in selected OECD countries, 2010. *Source:* OECD 2013d.

A few of the OECD countries, such as Canada and Australia, have long histories of immigration, whereas for others it is a much more recent phenomenon. The extent to which immigrants are assimilating and otherwise affecting OECD countries varies, for the countries themselves vary considerably in terms of the timing of immigration, the composition of the immigrants, their policies toward immigrants, and the economic and social conditions at the time of reception.

In terms of differences in immigration policy, Germany, for example, initially denied citizenship to all immigrants who could not trace their familial roots back to Germany. Over time this became untenable, as many guest workers originally from Turkey and North Africa, and then their children, were clearly in Germany to stay. Thus, laws regarding citizenship were eventually reformed in 1999 to make it easier for immigrants to gain German citizenship.[70] The United Kingdom had more multicultural policies from the 1970s onward, recognizing the rights of different groups and their claims on public resources. In recent years there has been some backlash against multiculturalism—many feeling that it is divisive—and a greater emphasis on promoting integration and community cohesion.[71]

France, in contrast, has long had an assimilationist approach to immigration, expecting that immigrants should adopt French customs and culture. This approach informed the 2004 passage of what is sometimes referred to as "the veil law," which forbade any visible sign of religious affiliation in schools, and a 2010 law that banned the wearing of veils that cover the face in public places. Despite policies strongly promoting assimilation, many immigrants and their children in France, especially if they are "visible" minorities (those perceived as different because of skin color, language, accent, self-presentation, or surname), report that others perceive them as not being French, though they do experience at least some measure of integration over time and across generations.[72]

Concerns about immigrant integration in many European countries, such as the United Kingdom, France, the Netherlands, and Sweden, frequently focus on the assimilability of Muslim immigrants in particular. There is a broad fear of Islamic radicalism and a skepticism about whether the values of religious immigrants are compatible with the culture of secular humanism that predominates in many European countries.[73] Muslim immigrants in turn often feel that they are viewed with suspicion and discriminated against by the native-born mainstream.[74]

Studies that have systematically investigated immigrant incorporation into Europe and other OECD countries for the most part find that the second generation often does better than the first, as in the United States, though significant variation occurs across immigrant groups. One study of education, unemployment, and occupational attainment outcomes among the second generation in ten countries in Europe (Austria, Belgium, Great Britain, Denmark, France, Germany, the Netherlands, Norway, Sweden, and Switzerland) finds that upward mobility occurs among the second generation but that second-generation minorities from non-European countries still tend to experience some disadvantage, such as those of Turkish ancestry in Belgium, Germany, and the Netherlands; those of Moroccan or other North African ancestry in Belgium, France, and the Netherlands; individuals of Caribbean or Pakistani ancestry in Britain; and those of Surinam ancestry in the Netherlands.[75]

Another cross-national comparison of immigrant integration into the United States, Canada, and Australia finds common patterns of high achievement among the Chinese and South Asian second generation in these countries. Children of black immigrants tend to fare less well in all contexts, though the second generation still does better than the first. Across these host countries, some specific differences appear in relation to the starting points of the immigrants and the extent of generational change, but on the whole the similarities among these countries seem to outweigh the differences.[76] In short, in many different contexts, children from low-status immigrant families lag behind the children from native families, but immigrant incorporation is the dominant trend.[77]

A Final Note on Immigration Policy

Immigration reform has been discussed from time to time in recent years in the United States, mostly focusing on reducing the number of illegal immigrants currently in the country and attracting immigrants that would boost our economy. In some quarters, support for an expanded guest-worker program in the United States is considerable, especially among large businesses that would like to recruit low-wage workers for agricultural work or other labor-intensive work. While there may be good short-term economic reasons to have a guest-worker program, the entry of a large number of temporary, low-skill workers with relatively few rights or prospects for legal incorporation through citizenship may result in the growth of a socially, economically, and politically marginalized constituency. As indicated above, the record of guest-worker programs in western European countries suggests that such immigrants are not usually content to simply go home after they are no longer needed. In fact, approximately 25 to 40 percent of undocumented immigrants in the United States are visa overstayers rather than people who crossed the border illegally.[78] For similar reasons, providing the means for current undocumented immigrants to eventually attain citizenship will likely help them and their children more easily integrate into American society.

On the other hand, policies that favor admitting more immigrants on the basis of education and skills could serve to boost our economy, as such immigrants often engage in highly productive work. They are also more likely to have a positive fiscal impact on national, state, and local budgets through the higher taxes that they pay as compared with lower-skill immigrants. As noted above, the children of high-skill immigrants are also more likely to do well in school and in the labor market and are thus less likely to be marginalized and isolated. Of course, it should be said that immigration policy should not be shaped only on the basis of economic cost-benefit analyses. Immigration policy has long had an important humanitarian component that should help inform policy decisions as well. For example, many countries, including the United States and those of Europe, have policies that allow refugees from dangerous, war-torn countries to immigrate, believing that it would be inhumane to allow them to face extreme hardship or death if they remained. Over the years, such groups have included Jewish refugees during World War II, Vietnamese refugees from the Vietnam War, and Somali refugees in the 2000s seeking to escape the anarchy and clan warfare occurring in many parts of the country.

Conclusion

Immigration has contributed to increasing racial and ethnic diversity in communities across the United States. While the United States is a land of immigrants, fears about the impact of immigration and whether new immigrants are capable of assimilating have been frequently expressed over the years and continually crop up in policy debates on the issue. Research on the recent, post-1965 wave of immigration tends to show that immigrants are by and large being integrated into American society. The second generation tends to have higher levels of education and earnings than their immigrant parents, and that generation also achieves greater parity with whites. The native-born second generation also tends to be less residentially segregated than the first generation. Nevertheless, there is significant variation across immigrant groups, with Asians having the highest levels of attainment. Asian immigrants tend to have relatively high levels of education, and this confers advantages to their children in school and in the labor market. Hispanic immigrants come with relatively low levels of education, and while their children tend to do better than their parents, on average they do not achieve parity with whites. The children of black immigrants likewise achieve some measure of mobility but remain disadvantaged relative to the mainstream; racial discrimination may impact their life chances.

Many studies have also examined the economic and fiscal impacts of immigration. They have generally found that immigrants do not have much of an impact on the employment or wages of most of the native born, though there might be a small negative effect on the wages of low-skilled native-born workers. This effect is generally small because immigrants are often complements of rather than substitutes for American workers; also immigrants often create jobs and are consumers too, which can spur economic growth. Indeed, immigrants are more likely to be entrepreneurs than native-born workers, and high-skill immigrants have been crucial in spurring innovative economic activity in science and technology, such as in Silicon Valley.

The fiscal impact of immigration is small in the aggregate. Immigrants consume government services (such as public education), but they also pay taxes. Highly educated immigrants tend to pay more than they consume in public services. The federal government budget may benefit from immigration, because a large majority of immigrants (including many illegal immigrants with fake Social Security cards) pay federal payroll taxes, though some local governments are harder hit because of small tax collections from immigrants and the cost of locally financed services (such as schools).

More diverse areas sometimes experience intergroup conflict and have less social cohesion and social capital than more ethnically homogeneous areas, at least in the short run, but communities that can successfully incorporate immigrants often forge larger, more inclusive identities over the long run. In the United States at least, immigration in recent decades has not been associated with more crime; immigrants themselves often contribute economically to poor communities and are not particularly prone to criminal activity or violence.

International migration is increasing worldwide. Many European countries that used to send migrants elsewhere in the nineteenth century have, in the post–World War II period, received many immigrants from abroad. These countries struggle with many of the same issues that immigration raises in the United States, such as the considerable concern about whether immigrants and their children—particularly those who are "visible minorities"—will integrate into society. While different host countries and different immigrant groups experience considerable variation, there are signs that integration is occurring in many European countries as well. These trends have not silenced debates on immigration in the United States or abroad, as many are still concerned about how immigration will continue to change the character of their country and how immigrants of the future will fare.

Notes

1 Daniels 2002, 266.

2   Daniels 2002, 275–76.

3   Brimelow 1995, 9 and 232.

4   Daniels 2002, 267–69.

5   Martin and Midgley 2006, 12. See also Daniels 2002, 271.

6   Martin and Midgley 2006, 12.

7   Daniels 2002, 287.

8   Daniels 2002, 329.

9   Daniels 2002, 310–11.

10 Brimelow 1995, 76–77.

11 Martin and Midgley 2010, 2.

12 Daniels 2002, 311.

13 Passel and Cohn 2012.

14 Daniels 2002, tables 6.4 and 16.2; Migration Policy Institute 2012b.

15 Pew Research Center 2013.

16 U.S. Department of Homeland Security 2012.

17 U.S. Census Bureau 2012i.

18 Parrado 2011; Parrado and Flippen 2012; Duncan and Trejo 2011b.

19 Branigin 1998.

20 Alba and Nee 2003, 11.

21 Alba and Nee 2003, 38.

22 Daniels 2002, 159.

23 Daniels 2002, 189.

24 Daniels 2002, 195–98.

25 See Alba and Nee 2003 for a detailed discussion of these issues.

26 Daniels 2002, 276.

27 Alba and Nee 2003, 131–32.

28 Portes and Zhou 1993; Zhou 1999, 196–211.

29 Reitz, Zhang, and Hawkins 2011, 1064.

30 Park and Myers 2010; White and Glick 2009; Bean and Stevens 2003. For a careful and fascinating study of immigrant assimilation in New York, see Kasinitz et al. 2008; and Kasinitz, Mollenkopf, and Waters 2004.

31 Bean et al. 2013; Brown 2007.

32 White and Glick 2009, 111.

33 Specifically, individual-equivalent household income is calculated by dividing household income by the square root of the number of persons in the household. For more details, see Reitz, Zhang, and Hawkins 2011, 1054.

34 Reitz, Zhang, and Hawkins 2011, table 5.

35 White and Glick 2009, 148.

36 J. Lee and Bean 2007, 2012; Golash-Boza and Darity 2008; Frank, Akresh, and Lu 2010.

37 Note that the bar for All Blacks is below that of both Native-born and Foreign-born blacks. While the average segregation for the group as a whole is typically between the segregation experienced by the two component groups, it does not have to be. Each of the component groups could live in

different segregated neighborhoods, but if combined into one group, they may be spread across a broader array of neighborhoods.

38   Iceland and Scopilliti 2008.
39   Iceland, Sharp, and Timberlake 2013.
40   Lippard and Gallagher 2011, 1–23.
41   Telles and Ortiz 2008.
42   Perlmann 2005, 117.
43   See also Brown 2007.
44   Smith and Edmonston 1997, 6.
45   Holzer 2011.
46   Smith and Edmonston 1997; Holzer 2011.
47   Holzer 2011, 10.
48   Smith and Edmonston 1997.
49   Immigrant Learning Center 2013.
50   Fiscal Policy Institute 2012.
51   Salkever and Wadhwa 2012.
52   Salkever and Wadhwa 2012.
53   Sullivan 2012.
54   Smith and Edmonston 1997.
55   Singer et al. 2008, 29.
56   Jackson 2011.
57   Smith and Edmonston 1997, 4.
58   Johnson, Farrell, and Guinn 1997, 1055–56.
59   Johnson, Farrell, and Guinn 1997, 1074–75.
60   Gabriel 2013.
61   Putnam 2007, 137.
62   Alba and Nee 2003, 32.
63   Putnam 2007, 137.
64   Portes and Vickstrom 2011.
65   M. T. Lee and Martinez 2009; Sampson 2008; Martinez, Stowell, and Lee 2010; Stowell et al. 2009; Wadsworth 2010.
66   Sampson 2008, 28–33.
67   Central Intelligence Agency 2013.
68   Hansen 2003.
69   OECD 2013d.
70   Hansen 2003.
71   Modood 2003; BBC News 2011.
72   Simon 2012, 1.
73   See Caldwell 2006; Modood 2003.
74   Modood 2003; Simon 2012.
75   Heath, Rothon, and Kilpi 2008, 218.
76   Reitz, Zhang, and Hawkins 2011, 1063–64.

77 Alba, Sloan, and Sperling 2011.
78 Passel 2005.

It's Not Fair

The Pecking Order in Immigrant Families

BY JOANNA DREBY

> In each American family there exists a pecking order between siblings—a status hierarchy, if you will. This hierarchy emerges over the course of childhood and both reflects and determines the siblings' positions in the overall status ordering in society. It is not just the will of the parents or the "natural" abilities of the children themselves that determines who is on top in the family pecking order; the pecking order is conditioned by the swirling winds of society, which envelop the family.
>
> Dalton Conley, *The Pecking Order*

I'm exhausted by the time we make it to the park. I've persuaded Temo and Dylan to come along by buying them vanilla ice cream cones, ordering them to lick the cones quickly so the drips don't end up on the gray fabric seats of the car. Once I park in the now abandoned school lot, I relax. It is six o'clock. The heavy late afternoon air makes the ice cream drips come more quickly as we climb out. But now the seats won't be ruined by the melting. And all the rushing has been for nothing. I do not see the coach or any nine-and ten-year-olds running around in the long, uncut grass in front of the four steel-posted goals, all missing nets, staggered in different parts of the city park, none belonging to a proper soccer field. Not sure where the practice will be held, I can see that the team captain Camilo—a star who stands out both on and off the field—is not here. I am not late.

When Camilo's father Carlos invited my nine-year-old son Temo along to practice with his son's soccer team, I was elated. It was the perfect setup. Even if only for a month, while taking Temo to the practices and games I could spend more time with the family. But when

Joanna Dreby, "It's Not Fair: The Pecking Order in Immigrant Families," Everyday Illegal: When Policies Undermine Immigrant Families, pp. 99-131, 232-235. Copyright © 2015 by University of California Press. Reprinted with permission.

Temo heard the invitation in Spanish, which he clearly understood with his basic Spanish skills, he groaned, "I am *not* going!" as soon as Carlos and Camilo were out of earshot.

"Yes, you are." I replied, "It is important to me." The standoff continued until a few days later we set up a contract, written out in black Crayola marker.

"It's not fair," Temo had argued. "Why is it always me? Why doesn't Dylan have to do stuff like this?" I'm impressed by the allusion to inequalities between him and his brother, inequalities I came to learn also plagued Camilo and his siblings.

Still, Temo signed his name, in cursive, with a faded green marker and handed the contract over to me. I signed too. And so we have come to soccer so I can observe Camilo doing the activity he loves most, and excels at, procuring much of his parents' resources and time.

Camilo reminds me of the Energizer bunny, his schedule like those of middle-class children whose multiple activities academics posit as having both positive and negative consequences.[1] "He does dance practice on Mondays, three soccer practices a week, and then the games on the weekend," Camilo's father, Carlos—who ferries him to all these various activities—told me.

"He doesn't get tired?" I once asked his mother, Milagros.

"*Como quisiera.* How I wish he would, but no. *El sigue,* he always wants more."

By most accounts, Camilo is a success story. At age nine, Camilo plays for two of the city teams. With the U10 group, his peers, he plays center—a striker. For the older team, the U12s, he plays goalie. But Camilo excels in more than just soccer. He dances with the Mexican folkloric troop at his elementary school. He is among the most popular third graders in his class—well liked by both students and teachers. When I asked to hang out in his classroom for a few days, the teacher didn't object but simply asked, "Why him? He is one of our best students." "Every trimester he gets diplomas and medals," said his father Carlos. His mother Milagros added, "He has tons of medals, he even has one on his key chain."

An archetype of the mixed-status family, Camilo's household epitomizes a pattern in the contemporary United States, and the ensuing complexities that legal status creates. Camilo, the youngest in the family, is a US-born citizen. His two older siblings and his parents are unauthorized migrants. Although families often are loath to outwardly discuss such vast inequalities between siblings and children in the same peer groups, inequality is a hallmark of the current immigration system, which intensifies existing pecking orders among children.

Camilo enjoys a number of advantages, aiding his success as an elementary school–age child in his neighborhood. These advantages are, however, tempered by his status as the child of unauthorized immigrants because in many ways the odds stack up against Camilo. Camilo is the youngest of three, born and raised in a city where one in four survives below the poverty line.[2] The state's median household income is $69,711; in this city it is just $44,543.[3] Camilo's parents' combined income is less. Camilo's father earns a little over the minimum for a manufacturer of realistic-looking white plastic dining plates and pseudo-steel utensils. Although his mother Milagros taught elementary school back in Mexico, like twenty-two of the eighty-one mothers I interviewed, her occupational prestige declined after migration:[4] she now works as a factory temp. "She makes paper for me," Camilo boasts, showing me his math notebook. "I like it because it has pockets on it. That's what I like mostly about it, 'cause it has pockets on it and when I finish something I just put it in here."

The family rents a three-bedroom apartment for $1,100, which they afford with the economic contribution of Camilo's seventeen-year-old brother, Silvio. Silvio was born in Mexico and came to the United States when he was twelve, just a little older than Camilo is now. He works two shifts at a mechanic shop and is rarely at home. I am not even really sure what he looks like, having glimpsed him striding in or out of the apartment only once or twice.

Camilo shares his bedroom with his fourteen-year-old sister, Rebecca, who, also born in Mexico, attends a vocational-technical school and aspires to be a beautician. She is slim; her complexion is a clear milky brown, *café con leche*. With thin lips widening into a gentle smile and carefully lined hazel cat-eyes, Rebecca is a cover girl image for *Seventeen* magazine. I think she might succeed in her goals, if she graduates. At the vocational school she attends, only three out of four incoming students finish with a degree.[5] Still this is higher than at the public high school where her brother Silvio studied. There the graduation rate is only 68 percent and only 19 percent of those graduates expect to attend a four-year college.[6] This is particularly dismal in a state that boasted a graduation rate of 87.2 percent in 2009–10.[7]

Camilo's prospects seem better. He too attends a struggling public school in the district. But he has time. So far, he stands out, having exceeded all expectations.

Legal-Status Distinctions

Immigrants and native born alike share a lasting commitment to the American dream;[8] popular mythology dictates that high-achieving children like Camilo will succeed later in life despite modest upbringings. Yet social inequalities are stubborn. Research shows that racial gaps in education and wealth still endure and income inequalities continue to rise.[9] Camilo is Hispanic and of Mexican origin, comes from a low-income family, lives in a relatively poor community, and attends a low-achieving school. Because inequalities pass down from generation to generation no matter how hard Camilo works, or how well he does in school, if he overcomes the barriers of his background, he will be an anomaly, the result of what Robert C. Smith would describe as an exceptional combination of intrafamilial dynamics and extrafamilial support.[10] Because racial and class disadvantages cling to families, more often than not these disadvantages come to affect children's chances over the long run.[11] Intergenerational social mobility in the United States declined dramatically at the end of the twentieth century.[12]

Theoretically, legal-status distinctions should work differently than race and class: obtaining legal status should be an administrative process similar to applying for a library card. The differences between those who have a library card and those who do not certainly shape one's daily routines, access to books, DVD collections, computers, and—in the case of some libraries—day passes to regional museums. Access to a library card alters one's resources. However, because obtaining a library card is an option for nearly all those who meet the rather simple criteria for proving residence at a particular address, we hardly think of this as the source of deep social status distinctions. Of course, the requirements for a library card prove more difficult for some, such as the homeless population who may not have a permanent address, than for others. Typically, however, most can eventually meet the criteria. Those who do not can access many library resources on site.

Legal status in a restrictive immigration policy environment, in contrast, becomes much more than an administrative hurdle. Because so many individuals have been excluded from the criteria necessary to legally live in the United States, illegality has begun to accrue a social significance similar to that of racial or class background. When no line exists for those who want to legalize, social mobility later in life becomes ever more difficult for unauthorized youth, like Rebecca and Silvio, and even for US citizen children like Camilo living in mixed-status families. Under an inflexible immigration system, legal uncertainty becomes the source of family-based social status inequality, with specific costs for children.

Illegality has numerous consequences for children's development.[13] For one, unauthorized children face educational barriers. Under *Plyer v. Doe* all children, regardless of legal status, are entitled to public school education.[14] However, when states have implemented local laws that target the unauthorized—like Alabama, which ordered schools to ask for citizenship status (a measure that was ultimately overturned)—children in immigrant families grow nervous at the threat of deportation, resulting in significant drops in school attendance.[15] More strikingly, unauthorized youth's education is constrained once they enter high school and begin to make plans for after graduation, since often they are ineligible for student loans, instate tuition benefits, and other programs that will finance their college education.[16]

Children I met described educational barriers as significantly affecting their daily lives at even earlier ages. One seventh grader, for example, described the limitations his legal status created for his educational goals, already a prime concern: "Actually, I am a bit sad about this. Because of the two years I got left back [due to his transition to the US school system], when I am eighteen I will only be in the eleventh grade. I think then they are going to send me to the adult school. I want to finish high school like any other kid. I also want, when I am of age, to drive. But I cannot. I cannot get a license. There are things I want to study, in the university. I would love to go to the university here."

I asked him if he thought about going back to Mexico instead to study.

"Yes, but I cannot tell you an answer about that yet. If I go to Mexico, I can study there. But the career in Mexico will only be valid in Mexico. I want to be a chef, and maybe I can do it there, but it is going to cost a little more than here. And if I study here it will be valid in other countries, they would recognize the degree. It would be better. I would speak Spanish and English. For this reason I would love to stay here and study. But because I don't have papers, I don't know."

"Does this stress you out?" I asked him.

"A lot of stress, a lot of sadness."

"During a normal day, how much do you think about it?"

"Every day. Every single day."

Educational barriers may create low levels of stress about future prospects that children may experience on a daily basis. Over time, knowledge of these limitations may affect children's motivation to succeed in school.

Unauthorized children also may lack access to adequate health care: since they are often uninsured, their parents may forgo preventative care appointments and resort to emergency room care for routine illnesses.[17] Of the 212 children living in the eighty-one families I interviewed, legal status was the primary indicator of insurance coverage. While nearly two-thirds of US citizen children were insured, *none* of the forty-eight unauthorized children in the families I met had health insurance coverage. Although unauthorized children lack insurance, they may have greater health needs, with new studies suggesting that unauthorized youth suffer from greater anxiety and depression because of their status.[18]

Unauthorized children may also experience food insecurity.[19] Among children in families I interviewed, one in ten of the US-born children received food stamps and a little over half received WIC. None of the legal migrant children or the unauthorized children had received benefits under either program. This is not to say that they didn't have similar economic needs, since many of those I interviewed lived in the same households as US-born children. And the unauthorized children in the families I interviewed did rely heavily on school-based food programs; eight out of ten unauthorized children ate lunch through a free program at school, while only just over half of the US-born children did. And while nearly one in three unauthorized children ate breakfast at school, only 15 percent of US-born children did.

Illegality, however, does not affect only unauthorized immigrant children. The citizen children of unauthorized immigrants may face stunted prospects of social mobility. Hiro Yoshikawa, for example, finds that parents without legal status may have fewer resources for their US-born children than parents with legal status. Illegality limits parents' access to social services, curtails their informal social support, and magnifies the economic stressors associated with parenting.[20] These in turn shape children's learning, socioemotional well-being, and physical health. Economic factors stand out; national estimates suggest that one-third of the children of the unauthorized live in poverty, as compared to 18 percent of children with US citizen parents.[21]

Unauthorized parents face a myriad of economic constraints related to their employment prospects and lack of benefits. These factors undoubtedly shape the types of environments US-born citizen children grow up in. Consider home ownership, often used by sociologists as one measure of social inequality.[22] Among the families I interviewed, forty-three of the forty-five unauthorized children lived in rented apartments or homes, whereas one in four US-born children lived in homes their parents owned. Significantly, these patterns were stronger for children living in mixed-status households. The majority of US-born children with unauthorized parents lived in rented dwellings (eighty-seven of ninety-eight), while the majority of US-born children who shared a legal status with their parents lived in homes their parents owned (eighteen of twenty-nine). Strikingly, among those I interviewed there was a similar pattern in health insurance coverage. Eight out of ten US-born children with legal-status parents had health insurance, while only six in ten US-born children with unauthorized parents were insured.

Legal status is not simply a matter of having papers, or *papeles*, as the families I interviewed often referred to legal status. Rather, it creates a social hierarchy—what Dalton Conley describes as a pecking order[23]—among children. Family members experience disadvantages due to the threat of deportation and the dependencies caused by illegality. Yet legal-status differences also shape the long-term prospects of children growing up in the United States, causing insidious inequalities even between siblings, like Camilo and his older siblings Silvio and Rebecca and the twenty-three other families like them whom I interviewed. Research on sibling inequalities typically focuses on factors such as birth order, gender, personality, parental preferences for resource distribution, and changes in family resources over time.[24] For siblings who vary in legal status, all of these factors may matter, but they are overshadowed by much more obvious inequalities.

Camilo, a US-born citizen with a gregarious personality, is the youngest male child in the family. Yet personality and birth order are not the only factors at play because legal status marks Camilo's experiences when compared to those of his older siblings and other unauthorized children. And it does so in more complex ways than simply the presence or absence of a Social Security number. Camilo's citizenship status shapes, at the very least, the rhythms of his daily life, including language usage and participation in housework, his relationship to the migratory process, his resources and subsequent schooling pathways, and his emerging identity as a Mexican American growing up in the United States. These experiences differentiate the lives of unauthorized and citizen children.

Language In Children's Daily Lives

I first met sometimes shy nine-year-old Camilo at an impromptu Sunday afternoon gathering. He was tagging along with his father, Carlos, who sipped a Coca-Cola while chatting with friends who downed Corona after Corona. Camilo stared listlessly for over an hour at the Nintendo DS he had brought with him. He barely acknowledged anyone else in the room, leaning into his game, hiding behind shaggy bangs. His dark brown locks hung in the style of Messi,[25] who plays for Barcelona and is Camilo's inspiration. "I mean, I always wanted to play soccer, but it was Messi that really inspired me. When I saw him play, the way he moves, that's what I want to be," he once told me. But Camilo plays soccer with the light-footed energy—and poacher's mentality—of Chicharrito, a star on Camilo's favorite team, the Mexican Nationals.

Camilo enters a room with a vibe of detached aloofness that contributes to his allure, until you get to know him and find out that he is a nonstop talker. I imagine him unaware of the effect he has on others, although his mother tells me that he knows that girls find him attractive. Camilo denies having a girlfriend, but he lists off the girls at his school who have crushes on him. "At church the girls are always coming up to me and asking me, 'Where's your son, where's Camilo?' " recounts his mother Milagros, laughing.

I think that Camilo intimidates Temo, which is why he does not want to go to soccer practice with Camilo. At the field, after he finishes his ice cream, Temo rolls his eyes again, looking at me as if to say, "I told you so." What he does say is, "So ... where *is* this practice?"

"I'm not sure," I answer on an exhale. "Why don't we take a little walk?" We make a big circle around the park, starting at the side near the elementary school, a sprawling one-story building. It is another ten or fifteen minutes before the boys start to arrive, one by one, congregating by a goal that they help the coach move into position. Camilo and Carlos arrive now too. I walk over with them to meet the coach, who is around my height, somewhat stocky, sporting gleaming white Nike trainers and a pair of navy Adidas pants with two white lines stitched down the sides. Camilo takes Temo with him out to the field and joins in the center of the action, stealing the ball away from one of the others and taking it down to score.

I sit with Carlos, who pushes mirrored sunglasses up onto black hair, spiked short, hard with gel. He smiles broadly, introducing me to others, at ease, making small talk. But Carlos doesn't stay, saying he promised to give a friend a ride, confirming that I have his number before leaving. He asks me to drop Camilo off if he isn't back in time. For the next hour I fend off the mosquitoes as I sit in uncut grass. I watch.

The scrimmage is chaotic, a free-for-all. The coach splits the boys up but does not assign positions. The boys order themselves, some drawn into the pack following the ball, while others—like Temo—play back, in positions, anticipating the movement on the field. The coach, in the middle of the boys, belts out encouragement as he runs along with the play. "*Ataque, ataque*" (Attack, attack), he yells, "*Adelante, así es*" (Go forward, that's it). Off the field, the boys all speak English to each other. On the field, they use Spanish. Physical space and generation pattern children's language usage on and off the field.[26] So does legal status.

In general, children of all legal statuses primarily spoke Spanish with their parents. Approximately three out of four children reported speaking all or mostly Spanish with their mothers, and over half spoke Spanish with their fathers. With other children, they spoke English: approximately three out of four spoke all or mostly English with their peers, and half spoke only English with their siblings. At one nine-year-old's birthday party, for example, the adults sat in a circle on chairs in the main room while the children played in the back bedroom. When one child ventured into the main room to ask for a piece of cake and another to complain to his father about a sibling, the children spoke Spanish. Walking back into the bedroom to collect my boys to leave, I found the children jumping on the beds, rattling off to each other in English, some more fluently than others, some with strong accents, while playing a wild game of basketball and with SpongeBob blaring, in English, on a small nineteen-inch box TV on the dresser. An eleven-year-old summarized the common practice: "I speak Spanish with my mother and my father. But with the other kids, in English."

Camilo is fluent in both Spanish and English. He is not in bilingual classes, so he mostly speaks English at school, although I have watched him switch comfortably into Spanish occasionally in the lunchroom and at recess, as he is doing now on the soccer field. At home, Camilo sometimes speaks English with his dad; his mother has taught him to read and write in Spanish. They prefer that he be bilingual, and Camilo says he likes Spanish and English equally. Indeed, *regardless of legal status*, children in interviews reported similar levels of English proficiency, with approximately six out of ten US-born and unauthorized children reporting that they were either near-fluent or fluent in English. They also reported nearly identical language preferences, with a little over half preferring English and more than a quarter preferring both.

Language usage, as opposed to English proficiency or preference, was different for US-born and unauthorized children. Nearly half of the unauthorized said they spoke all Spanish at home, while only one in ten of the US-born children did. And while very few unauthorized children spoke mostly English at home, almost a third of the US-born children did. Language use across settings also varied by legal status, with unauthorized children much more often reporting that they spoke all or mostly Spanish with their siblings or friends than did US-born children. US-born children reported speaking all English at school more frequently than did unauthorized children. Because children reported similar levels of English proficiency, it is possible that Spanish proficiency explains these differences: while eight out of ten unauthorized children reported being near-fluent or fluent in Spanish, only four out of ten US-born children did.

Researchers often use language as a primary measure of assimilation.[27] However, the greater use of Spanish by unauthorized children does not indicate greater isolation. Both US-born and unauthorized children reported a similar prevalence of cross-racial friendships with whites, Asians, other Latinos, and Middle Easterners. In fact, unauthorized children reported friendships with blacks twice as frequently as US-born children did. And unauthorized children much more often reported that friends came over to their houses to play and that they did sleepovers, a consistent pattern across age categories.[28] Clearly, legal status does not inhibit children from forming friendships with other children in their communities. Unauthorized children do not experience greater isolation from their peers because of their greater use of Spanish and their Spanish-language proficiency. If anything, unauthorized children are more adept at speaking Spanish and thus more frequently use Spanish with their parents and siblings.

Home-Based Activities

Legal status also patterns children's activities within the home [...]. Individual families have different approaches to child rearing and expectations of their children.[29] While class background shapes parenting significantly, research suggests that class does not affect children's contributions to housework in the United States, nor does family structure and maternal employment.[30] Rather, within-family factors, including child's age and gender, consistently matter, with older children and girls helping out more than boys and younger children.[31]

Scholarship does suggest that children's housework contributions may vary by race and immigrant status. Children in Hispanic families have been found to help out more in the home than others; scholars hypothesize that a cultural propensity toward "familism" may explain these greater contributions.[32] Similarly, case studies show that children in immigrant families work hard to help their parents as they adapt to life in a new country.[33] Among the children in Mexican immigrant households I interviewed, however, I found variations in patterns of housework contributions by children's legal status. This suggests that housework may be more about children's relative position within their family than a cultural propensity toward familial cooperation among Hispanics or among immigrants as a group.

Among children aged six through seventeen in the families I interviewed, children who were unauthorized helped out in the home with domestic tasks, including cleaning, cooking, and laundry, more frequently than US-born children. They also more often helped with child care for siblings (Table 6.1).

TABLE 6.1 Percentage of children who *never* helped with domestic tasks

| | Unauthorized Children (n = 45) | US-Born Children | |
		No Mixed-Status Siblings (N = 106)	Mixed-Status Siblings (N = 38)
Chores			
Laundry	52	83	90
Shopping	61	86	92
Cooking	61	89	97
Cleaning	9	55	79
Child care	52	85	95

On average the unauthorized children I interviewed were older than the US-born children yet I found these patterns to be consistent across many different age groups, even though the numbers of children in each specific age group were small. Perhaps even more tellingly, US-born children in households with siblings of mixed legal statuses reported never helping out with laundry, shopping, cooking, cleaning, and child care more frequently than US-born children who didn't live with mixed-status siblings. In other words, US-born children who have unauthorized siblings may contribute the least to family housework.

This is the case in Camilo's family. When I ask about chores, Camilo offers, "Clean my bed, other stuff. Or sometimes help my brother or sister clean the bathroom … Like sometimes, sometimes I need to like, if I get punished or something I need to clean my room every single day for like a month or two." But Camilo's sister, Rebecca, frequently does stuff in the house. According to her mother, Milagros, "Even here, in the house, she helps me with household. She on her own says, 'Mommy, what are you doing? Can I help you?' If I am cooking, she helps." Of course, there gender differences are perhaps at play, as girls tend to do more housework than boys. In Camilo's family, however, father Carlos models male involvement in housework, cooking and cleaning on days when he is not working.[34]

One might also attribute Camilo's fewer contributions to housework to his being the youngest, the baby of the family; age significantly shapes children's contribution to chores.[35] The conflation of birth order and legal status—as unauthorized youth are often older siblings—helps explain why US-born children contribute less to household chores. Yet the experiences of another family suggest that legal status may yield certain disadvantages for children, effectively increasing their responsibilities in the home.

Anita's family, previously described, was a legal anomaly because both parents and the eldest daughter María had naturalized while the younger four siblings remained unauthorized. In this family, María did not contribute as much to work in the home as her younger sisters. This was because María had won a scholarship to a college preparatory high school. Her parents encouraged her involvement in the school's extracurricular activities, and every day after school she spent two to three hours on her homework and didn't have time to do anything else. Instead, Carmen, the second oldest, supervised her younger siblings while her parents were at work; she directed the others in completing daily chores, including vacuuming the living room and cleaning the kitchen after school. This pattern continued even over the summer when María was out of school. One summer she was invited by a friend to attend a weeklong sleepaway camp, and the following summer she worked at a part-time job as a restaurant hostess.

Why would parents view unauthorized children as resources in the home much more than US-born children? US citizen children may, as this case suggests, have greater opportunities outside the home, whether employment based or at school, that parents hope to support. Anita and her husband wanted María to take full advantage of her scholarship, and other opportunities that unfolded, and thus did not require her to help out as much at home. Similarly, Camilo is an extremely talented soccer player. So Carlos and Milagros support his athletic development by taking him to practices and games nearly all week long. Camilo surely returns home tired from these events, with little time to do anything more than complete his homework. In short, parents may find themselves unknowingly investing more in their US citizen children's activities outside the home because their US citizen children have opportunities that their unauthorized children cannot access. Unauthorized children, at home and available, pick up the slack.

Unauthorized children may help with housework for other reasons aside from fewer opportunities outside the home. They may have a very different type of relationship with their parents than US-born children. Unauthorized children, after all, migrated just as their parents did; they understand the difficulties of adjustment to life in the United States more poignantly as they share this history with their parents. Drawing on this shared history, children may view their relationships with parents as more cooperative. Rebecca may have brought with her from Mexico different expectations about her place in the home and thus may voluntarily offer to help her mother Milagros with housework because, to her, it seems natural to do so. One unauthorized eleven-year old told me, for example, when I asked her what chores she did at home, "Sometimes I help my mother. I ask her, 'How can I help you?' and she says, 'You can pick up the clothes.'" Unauthorized children may feel they should help with chores.

Although Rebecca shares the migration history of her parents, she did not migrate with them. In fact, more than eight in ten unauthorized children in the families I interviewed experienced a period of physical separation from one or both of their parents, while only one in five US-born children did. In Camilo's family, I come to learn on the soccer field, experiences of separation have had long-term repercussions that have continued to affect Camilo's siblings long after reunification. The aftermath of family separations may also help explain the different trajectories of unauthorized and US-born children growing up in the United States.

The Aftermath of Family Separation

It is not at this first practice, but at the next one a few days later, at the same park, swatting at some of the same mosquitoes, that I learn more about the ways Camilo's experiences diverge so significantly from those of his brother and sister. I sit with Carlos making the type of small talk parents often do at such events, about how busy the kids keep us. "But don't you want another?" Carlos asks, teasing, "a little girl this time?"

I laugh too; this isn't the first time I've been asked this question. "Nah," I break into my standard response, "I like kids and all, a lot, but two is about all I can manage on my own." I do not add as I sometimes do, with women, that I would need a good man first.

Perhaps it is implied, because Carlos now asks about how involved Temo and Dylan's dad, Raúl, is in their lives. Carlos has met Raúl before. I feel uncomfortably pressed. "He didn't used to visit at all," I answer truthfully. "But now he sees them a lot more," I add, monitoring my voice, trying to keep superficial.

And now the unexpected: Carlos begins to tell me how hard it was when his two older children came up from Mexico. They are not Carlos's biological children, he explains. This I suspected, not because Carlos mentioned it before, but because Rebecca called him her stepfather, repeatedly, in our interview.

Carlos met Milagros when Silvio was just three and Rebecca under a year old. He had been working on an engineering construction project in the small town on the coast of Guerrero where Milagros worked as a schoolteacher. They moved in together until, in 2000, he came—alone—to the United States. Within a year he saved enough money so that Milagros could join him. For four years, Rebecca and Silvio lived with an aunt and uncle and their cousins in Mexico.

In the United States, Carlos and Milagros had Camilo, and then, when Camilo was three, they sent for the older children. "At first they didn't want to come," Milagros had told me, "but then they decided to because the older one began to complain that I wasn't there." They also wanted to meet their little brother, Camilo. "When they were in Mexico, he was really little, and he couldn't talk well. But still, they talked to each other on the phone. They wanted to have some contact with their little brother. And when they came, Camilo waited for them anxiously."

They imagined the reunion would be easier than it was. "We didn't recognize each other." This is Rebecca talking about her arrival. "I remember just standing there and looking at them because I remembered that when my mom left them she was all skinny and then she got a little fat here. It took about a month to get used to living with them again."

While we sit in the itchy long grass in the park, Carlos tells me how difficult it was for the boys to adjust to each other. Camilo admired Silvio and wanted to be like his older brother. But Silvio felt jealous of Camilo for being the baby in the family. "For two or three months he [Silvio] cried almost every night, uncontrollably." Silvio resented that his mother had left him back in Mexico and had gone on to have another child. "We didn't know what to do," Carlos says. "He even had suicidal thoughts. He said he was going to get a knife and cut himself and hurt himself and his siblings."

The emotion in Carlos's voice disarms me. I gulp, thinking about what I don't want to talk about, about the choices I have made and the consequences these choices have had for my children, and Raúl's. The idea of fundamental inequality between siblings plagues me; Temo's claims that "it's not fair" always hold double meaning. I wonder if Carlos also worries about the intrinsic inequality between his two boys: one born in Mexico, the other here, one a biological son he has always lived with, the other a stepchild from whom he lived apart for five years.

Raúl's Children

Much as Carlos's children have diverging opportunities given their different pathways to the United States, over time the differences between Raúl and my children have seemed to only become more noticeable. Unlike in Carlos's family, Raúl's two children from his previous marriage remain in Mexico. When I first met Raúl, I accepted them as my own, or rather, thought I did. But since then I have been awkward in my ex-stepmother role and have not done much to parent them. When Raúl's oldest son Facebook-friended me at age eighteen, the unexpected emotional turmoil brought me to tears. We reconnected online and then visited in Mexico for the first time in eight years. I felt the family connection so strongly, snapping photos of Temo and him leaning forward over their knees in the same fashion next to each other on the sofa, laughing when they each separately asked me quietly, "Do I really look like my brother?"

Raúl and I had planned to bring the boys to live with us in the United States when we married. At the time they lived with their maternal grandmother; in Mexico we visited, buying them new sets of clothes and school supplies. Raúl decided to wait to apply for them until he became a US citizen, allowing time for custody issues to get sorted out. Also, this way no wait times would be attached to their application.[36] When Raúl's citizenship jammed, so did their opportunity to reunite. Adamantly opposed to their unauthorized migration, like most parents Raúl wants his children to have a different—better—life than he had when he migrated north unauthorized as a teenager. Raúl's oldest finished high school after moving in with Raúl's parents but now works a low-wage retail job. The other, living with his maternal grandmother still, also works. Neither has yet attended college. Their prospects growing up in Mexico look so different from those of their siblings in the United States.

You see, Raúl, now remarried, has three more children—aside from Dylan and Temo— growing up in a community similar to that of Camilo and his siblings. Living with both of their parents seems an advantage, one that Raúl's children in Mexico never had. They have traveled to visit family in Mexico, as Raúl has covered the 2,600-mile route by van quite a few times, yet Raúl's children in Mexico cannot migrate legally or even obtain a tourist visa to visit their father. They cannot see with their own eyes life in *el norte*. In contrast, like Temo and Dylan, Raúl's youngest children are US citizens.

Even so, experiences diverge given that they live with Raúl, a former unauthorized migrant, and Temo and Dylan live with me, a US-born citizen. My boys, sons of an academic, squirm as they listen to me read these sections of my book out loud to them. They constantly have to field my questions on what happened in school on a particular day, how they feel about—well—almost everything, and which kids "love each other" and have started dating—I'm curious since I teach a class on the sociology of childhood every year. My stable salary provides opportunities; we travel frequently, often in conjunction with conference or research trips. When Raúl's children travel to Mexico, it is to the house Raúl built for his parents with remittances; they never stay in hotels as we do.

Our children's daily activities also differ. My boys have played hockey, even though it stretches our budget, and travel team soccer. Raúl's son has played rec soccer, but only in the spring, and occasionally he and his sisters participate in folkloric dance events, the cost free. They attend a struggling urban school, similar to the ones children I interviewed attended. In contrast, my boys first attended excellent public schools in a middle-income, white college town in Ohio, and then attended even better schools in the economically and internationally diverse middle-to high-income town where we lived in New Jersey for six months. At lower-performing, diverse urban schools in upstate New York, they benefit from my flexible schedule; I am home most days right after school. And, after Temo spent sixth grade struggling to keep a low profile and avoid fights at the expense of his schoolwork, we have decided to move to a private school for seventh and eighth grade. In New Jersey, Raúl's children share a bedroom in a two room apartment located across the street from a bar on a dangerous city block, while Temo and Dylan each have their own bedrooms in the house I own in one of the nicer neighborhoods in Albany.

My boys enjoy visits to their father, practically glowing in the love they feel from participating in Raúl's family. When the weather is nice, they play soccer outside together enthusiastically, go to the park, and ride bikes up and down the sidewalk. Raúl's children eagerly and affectionately hug Penny, our little Boston terrier, when I drop the boys off, asking in accented English for her to stay with them and their own little poodle, Chiquis—at least they did before Chiquis jumped out of Raúl's Chevy Astro and ran off. They help my boys when they struggle to understand Raúl's quick speech in a Veracruz accent.

Rarely do Temo and Dylan comment on the differences between us and their stepsiblings, differences I know they must notice. After all, they so often comment on the things their friends have that we don't: the backyard trampoline, the home movie theater, the seasonal ice rinks that enthusiastic fathers construct of treated wood and fill by the garden hose in their large backyards when the temperature drops below freezing. Perhaps they downplay their understandings of the class differences between Raúl and me for my benefit, or perhaps for their own. It is surely easier for them to enjoy their connections with their siblings by not thinking too much about it. That one father has three sets of children facing such unequal pathways feels a little uncomfortable. So many factors at play, some that we control and others that we do not. But one, illegality, has come to frame our children's experiences in ways we never anticipated when Raúl and I first met.

Family Migration Patterns

Temo's and Dylan's daily lives, so different from those of their siblings, suggest that children's position in the family pecking order may arise from a combination of the timing of migration and parents' formation of conjugal relationships. In fact, that siblings with different legal statuses sometimes had different biological fathers—as Silvio and Rebecca do—was not uncommon among the families with mixed-status siblings I met.

The factors surrounding women's migration north help explain why children may have different fathers. Migrant mothers from Mexico are often unmarried single mothers or divorced women who seek migration north as a means out of economic difficulties.[37] This was the case for one mother, Elvira. "I married good, with the father of my daughter," she explained, "in the church and everything." But the marriage fell apart while Elvira was seven months pregnant. Her husband came home one evening to their room drunk, and when she refused his advances, uncomfortable in her pregnant body, he dragged her by her hair and pushed her. In the morning, he left. So Elvira moved back in with her own parents, as a single mother; they supported her through the birth of her daughter and after. Two years later Elvira met her current partner, who unconditionally accepted her daughter as his own. "She has always known him as her father." But then he migrated to New Jersey, and the couple separated. Elvira grew desperate at her economic situation and decided to migrate as well to make ends meet. She lived alone in New Jersey for a time but reconciled with her ex when they met at a party. Now they had two US-born children, whom they were raising along with Elvira's first daughter.

Women spoke highly of their new partners who accepted their children from a previous marriage, much as Carlos readily accepted Silvio and Rebecca. Their praise hinted at the pride felt for partners acting differently from the perceived typical *machista* male who does not accept children from previous relationships.[38] I learned from a third party that Ana had a fifteen-year-old daughter in addition to the three children under age six that I met. In our formal interview—in which I spoke with both Ana and her current partner—the existence of this older daughter never came up in the conversation, even when I explicitly asked each about their children. Perched on the edge of the sofa, Ana occasionally glanced over at her husband, I now think for cues about how much to tell. Later with me informally, Ana spoke openly about her daughter. Ana had split with her daughter's father in Mexico. She had migrated to the United States, leaving her daughter with her mother. Her ex-husband also had come to work in New Jersey, but Ana did not have contact with him until she sent for her daughter and when, after arriving, her daughter had problems living with Ana and her new husband. So the daughter moved in with her father, visiting with Ana every other weekend. Although Ana was not ashamed of her daughter, that she did not mention her daughter in our interview illustrates the worst-case scenario. When new partners do not welcome children from previous relationships, inequalities between unauthorized and US-born siblings potentially become even more pronounced.

Transnational separations had specific consequences for children and were fairly common among the families I interviewed. Nineteen of the eighty-one mothers I interviewed had been separated from their children at some point during the migratory process. Seventeen of these migrant mothers had been separated from their own parents as children because of US migration. Nearly half of the fathers—thirty-eight—had been separated from children during the families' migratory process.

Carlos's confessions about Silvio's difficulties after family reunification surprised me, though the story of family separation was familiar. I interviewed so many parents who had left their children in Mexico, and so many children in Mexico whose parents lived in the United States.[39] Parents described feeling guilty at having left their children but believed the sacrifice was worth it. Yessenia, a mother to one child in Mexico and two in New Jersey with her, said, "I feel bad about my son in Mexico. Sometimes sadness overcomes me, and I feel like crying. I have my two children here, but it isn't the same." Yessenia did not communicate this sadness to her son over the phone. Instead, she rationalized the separation of mother and son as something that had been good for the family and important to their survival. She explained,

> I tell him, "Do you remember when I was there and you wanted something; I couldn't buy it for you? My mom gave me something, but it wasn't enough. I had to work to buy you things." … He [son] has never told these things to me [over the phone]. But at school he writes poems. My aunt said she found them. My mom said she found the papers from May 10th [Mother's Day], from the Day of the Child, [and he writes] that he feels sad, and alone. That sometimes he wants to tell his mom that he feels alone, that he loves her very much. But when I talk to him, he doesn't tell me this.

Yessenia's son colluded in the narrative of familial sacrifice, although he, like his mother, seemed upset by her prolonged absence.

For both parents and children, years living apart weigh heavily. Family reunification promises to soften parent-child tensions. For parents, family reunification validates the period of separation as ultimately worthwhile; they view the period of time living apart, and the distance it created, as surmountable with time together.[40] But resentment often clings to children during periods of separation and beyond, no matter how well they get along with their parents and caregivers in Mexico, and no matter how clearly they understand the circumstances surrounding their parents' migration.[41]

Even adults, who had lived apart from a parent years earlier as children described ongoing feelings of detachment in these relationships. One woman at age thirty-two, for example, described her relationship with her mother as close and with her father as distant. "It was very sad," she told me describing the time he had been away. "Because I didn't have my father and because the kids younger than me were always crying." For five years her father had nearly no communication with his family in Mexico. "I remember that day. … We were outside playing in the yard just like the kids now are outside playing. And we saw this man coming towards us, and he had on some ugly clothes and his hair down to the middle of his back, and he was walking all crooked. We thought he was a robber and we ran inside to hide."

The man, of course, turned out to be their father. She said her youngest brother had slapped him and hit him when her mother tried to hug him. "He wasn't like a normal father. We always saw him as really distant." Another woman tracked down her own mother who had left her as a child to raise her younger siblings. When she found out that her mother been living on the streets of Chicago she worried about her mental health and brought her to live with her husband and son. The reunion was not as she expected. "It was like she was never used to living with us and we argued all the time about … that she didn't like anything. … and that—all the time she felt like I hated her." Ongoing guilt and apprehension of resentment by the mother led to many fights and strained their relationship until her mother decided to move out.

For parents the time away may be stressful, but it amounts to a small fraction of their adult lives. For children, like for Silvio and Rebecca, periods apart from their parents represent, at times, more than half of their short lifetimes. And, although many lived with relatives whom they loved dearly, children told me again and again that living with their relatives was not the same as living with parents. "I missed my mother [Milagros] a lot. I didn't feel like I could talk to my aunt the same way that I talk to my mother," Rebecca explained. Similarly, a nineteen-year-old I interviewed in New Jersey said of the two years she had lived without her parents, between the ages of eleven and thirteen, "It was really hard at the beginning." This was because, as other children also told me, "I didn't have the same kind of *confianza* [trust] with my grandmother as I did with my mother." Later in the interview she specified, "To a parent you can say, [with childish voice] 'No, I don't want to eat this.' And with your grandmother it's 'No, you have to eat this.' "

Imagine, then, what it was like for Silvio, who had not lived with his parents since the time he started school in Mexico, to move, at the age of twelve, to the United States, entering a classroom where he didn't speak the language and a household where he didn't know his parents or their routines. No wonder Silvio wanted to be Camilo. Camilo, born in the United States, had lived with both his parents, always, the baby of the house. Camilo had it made.

On Subsequent Resources and Future Prospects

Silvio and Rebecca came up from Mexico during the summer. Worried about their transition, Milagros snuck Silvio and not Rebecca—because he was older—into adult ESL classes before school started. "At school he adapted well," she told me. "At home, he became a bit rebellious … because 'we had abandoned him.' " Milagros and Carlos worried about him. "At school he was an exemplary child. I even went to his school to talk to his teacher because at home it was a total disaster. But they didn't believe me because he was so well behaved." Milagros explained, "Sometimes he didn't do well. When he was mad at me he would say, 'I am going to get all Fs.' And he did. Then he would say, 'Don't worry, Mommy. I am going to get good grades.' And he would bring home As and Bs and honor roll certificates. He is very smart." Milagros and Carlos eventually got him into therapy. But it is unclear whether it was the therapy or early fatherhood that turned things around.

> It was when he started in the tenth grade. He just wanted to go out with his friends. At first I let him go out. … Then he just wanted to do what he wanted to do, without asking,

at any time he felt like it. He skipped school so he could go hang out. Then he started going out with this girl. When she finished middle school, it came out that she had gotten pregnant. We went to talk to her parents and everything. They said if she wanted to come live with us. So she decided to come here. Living here, she started high school. We sent them both. But neither wanted to keep studying. They wouldn't go. So I said, no. "If you don't want to study and you want to work instead, well, work."

Carlos and Milagros continue to help with child care, when needed, but now expect Silvio to contribute to the household on his own.

The transition for Rebecca was less problematic. "I don't know why," says Milagros. "Maybe because she is younger. Her sentiments are very different. She is very different." Mother and daughter are especially close; Rebecca spends more time at home than her siblings. She doesn't participate in any extracurricular activities, like Camilo. Instead, Rebecca often helps with Camilo; since both her parents are already at work when the children wake up in the mornings, she is the one to make sure that Camilo gets off to school. Since reunification she seems to be "making up for lost time."[42] So far, adolescence has been easier for Rebecca than for Silvio, whether because of her age at migration, gender, or personality—which both Milagros and Carlos describe as being much less emotional.

Camilo is different. His hectic schedule dictates the routines of the family.[43] On school days he walks himself to school, where he has breakfast; when school lets out, he often stays at the free after-school program and does his homework there. But if he doesn't feel like staying he walks himself home and does his homework. The rest of the evening, he spends time with his dad, Carlos. On Mondays, "I go to dance. If not, I tell my dad to take me to, um, my cousins' house." Other days, he has soccer practice. The weekends are taken up by soccer as well. "When I don't have school I go to my soccer games." Milagros and Rebecca take Camilo to his soccer games on the weekends because Carlos works. Carlos ferries Camilo to and from all the after-school activities during the week.

Of course, Carlos and Milagros love all three of their children. But, as most parents do, they invest their energies into each in different ways. Because unauthorized and US-born children's experiences within the family migration history are different, their needs differ. As the oldest, Silvio spent formative years away from his parents who sought economic stability via international migration. Reunification, however, did not erase the resentment Silvio felt about the separation. Ongoing resentments carried over into his schooling and affected his emotional well-being more broadly and, seemingly, his motivation to excel in school specifically. Not only did Silvio's unauthorized status affect his prospects in the United States, but so did the decisions he made as a result of the process by which he arrived to live with his parents in the United States after what was, for him, a prolonged period of separation. Silvio at a young age opted out of any academic track by dropping out of high school. After an early entry into fatherhood, Silvio joined his parents as a full-time worker and contributor to the joint household with his parents and partner and daughter. According to Milagros, "Now that he is working he says, 'If I had the opportunity to get my papers, it would be easier to find a better job.' In one place he was working, they wanted to keep him, but they asked for his papers."

Silvio has not ultimately been able to translate his parents' sacrifice via migration into tangible benefits in terms of educational achievement and, in fact, has a lower educational level than both of his parents. He is a proud father of a lovely boy and supports his partner and son with full-time employment. Nonetheless, he has experienced what sociologists describe as downward mobility as a result of the family's migration.[44]

For Rebecca, the middle female child, the transition to the United States proceeded more smoothly than it did for Silvio. Surely aware of her brother's adjustment difficulties, Rebecca has demanded less of her parents' time and energy and helped out more in the home. Although she too lacks legal status and was separated from her parents for as long as Silvio, Rebecca is not a wave maker. She plans to finish high school but is not thinking about college. For this reason she chose to go to the vocational-technical high school; she wants to leave high school with a career, since she knows she will not be able to attend college in the United States because of her lack of papers. Rebecca explains, "It isn't fair that there are kids who don't have opportunities because of the papers." She is disappointed that the DREAM Act, which would allow students, like her, who do well in US schools, has not yet been passed. It is likely that she will benefit from the Deferred Action for Childhood Arrivals, as long as she stays in school and graduates.[45] "When I graduate I want to try to start my own business, have my own beauty salon. I don't know if I can, but I want to here. If I can't, I may have to go back to Mexico to do it." Though Silvio has already opted out of formal school after family reunification and therefore will not be eligible for deferred action, it remains to be seen how Rebecca's legal status and her educational experiences will pan out in terms of her employment prospects over the next five or six years.

Camilo, the youngest, was born into a different family than Silvio and Rebecca because his parents, although still unauthorized low-wage workers, stabilized the family's economic situation during his lifetime.[46] Camilo wants to be a soccer player or a singer when he grows up, goals that—typical of young children—may not be all that realistic. Yet his parents have invested money and time into Camilo's love for the sport. In fact, in the fall after I met him, Camilo was selected on scholarship to play for a Premier League, one that typically costs $2,000 per season. Of course, he probably will not play professionally, but the opportunity may make him eligible for a sports scholarship, if not to college perhaps to a private high school, if he continues to excel. Camilo continues to do well in school. His parents are considering moving to a different school district by the time he reaches middle school so that he doesn't experience the same problems as his older brother did in school. As is the case with Rebecca, Camilo's long-term prospects remain to be seen. But he has direct access to his parents' resources—now supplemented by his older brother's income—and may ultimately be able to benefit from their migratory sacrifice.

Children's Identity and Status Differences

Unauthorized and US-born children's citizenship status also has consequences for the ways they come to terms with growing up as members of Mexican immigrant families. Camilo, as a third grader, tells me that he is Mexican American, " 'Cause I'm, my family is Mexican. That makes me half Mexican, and I was born here so that makes me American too. So I'm half Mexican and half American." I asked all the children I interviewed to pick the best ethnic or racial descriptor. They identified with a diverse set of labels, including *black, white, Hispanic, Latino, Spanish, Spanish American,* and more. Most often, children of all legal statuses chose *Mexican* or *Mexican American*. However, more unauthorized children than US-born children chose the label of *Mexican*. A fourteen-year-old girl explained, "Because I was born in Mexico and I guess you could say I am more Mexican. Even though I was technically raised here in America, I'd still consider myself Mexican." More US-born children, like Camilo, than unauthorized children chose the label of *Mexican American*.

Children matter-of-factly described the differences between themselves and their family members and defined their identities as being tied to their nativity, which they described in very concrete terms. Nearly all were able to correctly tell me where they had been born and also where their parents and siblings had been born. And place of birth, in their minds, extended to their understandings of ethnic identity even at young ages.[47] Carlitos, an eight-year-old, said that he was Spanish American but that his mother, father, and older sister were "Mexicans" and that his brother was, like him, "American, Spanish." When I asked why, he explained, " 'Cause we were born here, and me and my brother were born here, and my sister was born in Mexico." And when I asked an unauthorized nine-year-old, "How come you say your parents and your brother are Latino but your little brother's American?" He explained, " 'Cause my brother, my little brother is from Ohio and he looks like, more lighter. And we look like more darker." For children, race and/or ethnicity was tied to their varying citizenship statuses.

Scholars suggest that factors such as peer relationships, school context, perceived discrimination, parental support, and language proficiency shape the identity formation of ethnic minority youth.[48] Age also may be especially important, with sociologists finding that children develop a sense of symbolic ethnicity as they grow older and that pan-ethnic identification becomes particularly strong for college-aged students.[49] Children's accounts suggest that legal status also may shape children's identity formation, and the way they understand belonging, and that this process may occur at earlier ages than for those not confronted with such differences.[50]

Despite identifying their different citizenship statuses, siblings resisted assigning any social significance to these differences. When I asked Carlitos point blank if he thought his older sister was different from him because she was born in Mexico and he wasn't, he answered, "No, 'cause we're related to each other." Similarly, eleven-year-old Lupe explained that she and her siblings went to different doctors, "well, because they have those little cards, they go to a specific doctor."

"You don't have one?" I asked.

"No, because they were born here."

When I suggested that maybe it wasn't fair, Lupe responded quickly, "That doesn't matter to me."

Siblings were reluctant to call any attention to the meanings of these status differences: that their place of birth—something that children clearly understood—brought advantages. As Lupe's observation suggested, she knew of these differences, although she claimed they did not matter. Just as parents like to talk about treating their children equally, children resist the idea that structural inequalities give them different opportunities, possibly because children are so often determined to ensure that relations in families be as fair as they can be.[51]

Yet it isn't fair, and children know it. Health care access, for one, strikingly differentiates children of varying legal statuses. Patricia, fifteen, explained when I asked where she went if she got sick, "There's a clinic. We have to apply for … I don't know. It's something. I think it's like a discount. Because otherwise it's expensive. We haven't had the time to go."

"Do you ever worry about getting sick?" I asked.

Patricia nodded yes.

In Camilo's family, he is the only one to have health insurance through the state Medicaid program. His sister Rebecca cautiously admits, "It is a little unfair because my brother gets health insurance and I don't." Camilo too knows of the difference. He explains, "My sister and brother were born in Mexico. My whole family actually. I'm the only one that was born here." I ask Carlos and Milagros, "So does he know there is a difference between him and his siblings because of the papers?"

"He is beginning to notice," Milagros answers.

"What does he say?"

"He asks why we cannot go [to Mexico]. We say we don't have papers. 'Why does this happen?' We'll tell him the truth." This is Carlos.

"[He asks,] Why don't you get the papers?" adds Milagros. "Why haven't you gone to do it? Is it expensive?"

"How do you explain?" I ask.

"He has to understand," Milagros says. "He is born here; he is a citizen of this country. His brother and sister, no, because they were born in Mexico. It is very difficult for them to get their papers. They can work and study, but they don't have the same rights as he has."

As children grow up in the United States, they learn that legal status affords differential access to services, health and otherwise. An unauthorized fifteen-year-old explained, "I don't know. It seems like a lot of doors close on you."

"What kind of doors?" I asked her.

"You can't go to a good college. I can't have a good health insurance. You can't drive when you're old enough."

"Have you felt those doors close on you?"

"Yes. For summer programs, sometimes you need a Social Security card." Similarly, a teenage sister, unauthorized, with an eight-year-old US citizen brother explained, "It's hard. You feel different from others. Others have more opportunities. You feel different."

Aside from access to services, children know that illegality curtails educational opportunities. A fourteen-year-old Mexican-born sister to two US-born younger brothers, for example, explained,

> It's kind of, um, how would I say it, like it's kind of unfair for us because, for example, I want to become a doctor. ... But I probably can't do college here because first of all, it's so expensive and you need to like have papers, I guess. My, well, my mentality has been, well, I'm not going to do college here, I'm going to do it in Mexico. But to the kids that want to do it here, that's not fair for them. Especially if they're like really good in school, I feel like it's not fair because they have worked for so long to be like at the point where they're done with high school but they want to go to college but they can't. I feel that's unfair.

Clearly her brothers will not have to return to Mexico if they decide to study medicine. Similarly, Anita's daughter Carmen—described earlier as the unauthorized, second-oldest daughter in a family where the oldest daughter was a US citizen—avoided directly talking about how legal status affected her own life. She denied feeling jealous of her naturalized older sister. But during my visits with the family for approximately six months, I often asked about school. Carmen alluded to the scholarship her sister had received as an opportunity she would not be able to take advantage of despite her better grades.

Understanding Mexico

Children also know that legal status limits travel opportunities. Of all the children in the families I interviewed, nearly one in three US-born children had been back to visit Mexico, while only three of forty-seven unauthorized children had (nine of fourteen legalized children had been back to visit). Children, and parents, most openly discussed differences between siblings related to travel. One teen born in Mexico felt she was the same as her US-born siblings except that "I just feel different at the fact that they actually get to go to Mexico and see my family because I haven't seen them in so long. But other than that, no." In Anita's family, the eldest daughter, María, had been back to Mexico periodically with her parents, usually once or twice a year. Anita told me that after she and María had returned to Mexico recently for two weeks for an aunt's graduation, "The others complain[ed], how come you don't take us?"

Camilo has yet to visit Mexico, "He wants to go," Milagros explains, "but he doesn't want to go alone. He wants to go with his brother and sister. But . . ." The conversation about travel has spurred Milagros and Carlos to explain to Camilo about the legal differences between him and his siblings.

Mexico, for US-born children, may be a vacation spot, a place to visit family. For unauthorized children, Mexico represents the place they are from, a place they feel intimately connected to. Although the unauthorized children I spoke with did not travel back to Mexico, they described more frequent contact with families in Mexico, with one in four saying they chatted with family members in Mexico or sent e-mail, compared to just one in ten US-born children. Unauthorized children in the families I interviewed also participated in two types of extracurricular activities more frequently than did US-born children: youth church groups (nearly half of unauthorized youth and just 23 of 144 US-born children) and dance classes (ten of forty-six unauthorized children and just 9 of 144 US-born children). With only one or two exceptions, the dance classes these children participated in, both in Ohio and in New Jersey, were with Mexican folkloric dance troupes. Unauthorized children engaged much more frequently in activities related to their Catholic and Mexican heritage. These activities signaled a difference in identity formation between the children who had been born in the United States, like Camilo, and those who had not. However Mexico, for unauthorized children, was also a place they could not visit, which was perhaps why the ability to travel arose most significantly in children's minds when they discussed the differences between themselves and their US-born siblings and friends.

Unauthorized children also talked openly about potential permanent returns to Mexico—the result of a deportation or enforcement act. Regardless of their own legal status, children spoke about their fears of deportation. Yet children distinguished between what would happen to themselves and to their siblings, aware that illegality potentially could determine where they would live in the future, shaping their life course. Recall the comments of Moisés and his cousin Andrés from chapter 2. When I asked if it was scary to have immigrants in his family, Moisés, an unauthorized migrant said it was "because, what happens if some cops come to our house and they want to see our papers? We don't have it. And my little brother and my four cousins have it. And we have to go. That's what's scary about it." Andrés, his US citizen cousin, explained, "No, well, yes. if everyone leaves, it's only going to be me and my sister, my little cousin that you were just talking to and my little sister and my little cousin." Similarly, another eleven-year-old US citizen told me it was scary, " 'cause if they get caught, her, if my mom or dad get caught, my sister and me and Luís would have to get a passport to get back. 'Cause we have passports and they don't."

Legal status differentiates siblings and they know it. Unauthorized children grow up longing to connect with Mexico, which they do through participation in folkloric dance classes and church youth groups, as well as via Internet communication with family members back home. They consider themselves Mexican as they sense their political exclusion from the United States. Yet they cannot travel to Mexico. They grow up aware that they are different from US citizen children; they don't have health insurance and cannot participate in the same types of programs as US citizen children. They must forge different educational goals that take into consideration their limitations. Siblings perhaps do not like to think that status makes their identity any different from that of their brothers and sisters, with whom they share so much. But it does.

It's Not Fair

Dalton Conley writes about the inequality between siblings that we like to ignore, as it is somewhat embarrassing to think that we—as parents—give greater advantages to one of our children when we usually feel that we love all equally. Ultimately, though, the pecking order within the family is not about the love that we give our children. Rather, "The pecking order is conditioned by the swirling winds of society, which envelop the family."[52]

Silvio, Rebecca, and Camilo face extremely different prospects. Inequality due to illegality has already marked the young lives of these siblings and others like them. US-born and unauthorized children have different daily routines. Although they both speak English, unauthorized children use Spanish more than US-born children, as they report speaking better Spanish. They also participate in household tasks to differing degrees; unauthorized children help parents the most with housework. Perhaps this is due to US-born children's greater opportunities outside the home and parents' efforts to invest in these opportunities. Or perhaps it is unauthorized children's different experiences during migration that lead them to take on more active roles in the household. Unauthorized children, who so often have been separated from their parents during migration, may feel more invested in what Rob Smith calls "the immigrant bargain":[53] they may help at home because they feel much more a part of the project of familial sacrifice during migration than do US-born children.

Family separation shapes children's trajectories in other ways as well. Because separation can be so difficult, with ongoing feelings of guilt and resentment, there may be a powerful and harmful emotional impact on children even after reunification.[54] Children like Silvio may be smart but may fall behind in school as they come to terms with the complex feelings around family separation and reunification.[55] Many feel strong ties to Mexico, their birthplace, but they cannot travel to visit their former homes. Still, they may seek connection, sending e-mails and chatting with family and friends, dancing with folkloric dance troupes, attending church youth group meetings.

Over time, without opportunities in the United States and unable to physically connect in Mexico, they may begin to feel lost. Schools foster the belief in equal opportunity for both unauthorized students and those with legal status.[56] Yet their opportunities are not equal. Ultimately excluded, some, like many undocumented youth activists, may develop an oppositional consciousness.[57] Others, like Silvio, will join their parents as low-wage workers struggling to make ends meet in the US economy. This seems the most likely outcome, as recent research suggests that unauthorized Mexican and Central American youth are less likely to enroll in college and more likely to drop out of high school than those with legal status.[58]

US-born children, like Camilo, have been born into different types of families than their unauthorized siblings, families that are settled, even if still experiencing precarious employment and lacking economic resources. Camilo considers his ties to be both to the United States and to Mexico. But Mexico, for him, is home to his favorite soccer team, and a place he may visit in the future, not his home. Instead, as time goes on he may seek future opportunities in the United States, opportunities that will further differentiate him from his siblings as long as immigration policy continues to block family sponsorship for those who entered the United States by walking across the border, without inspection.

To some extent Camilo experiences advantages from being the youngest. Yet the advantage of his legal status is likely to become more pronounced, not less, over time. Despite

Carlos and Milagros's best intentions, Silvio is now an unauthorized low-wage worker, like themselves. Rebecca, although still in school, will follow a similar path unless some sort of immigration decision makes deferred action permanent and grants her the right to stay in the United States legally. But Camilo, and other US-born children like him, have a different trajectory. Of the three he is the only one with the chance of experiencing some level of social mobility due to his parents' migration. While explained to some extent by birth order, at a time when immigration policy is stagnant, Camilo's future prospects are shaped most strongly by one overwhelming factor: legal status. Like race, class, and gender, illegality is likely to shape children's mobility, and their place in US society's pecking order, over time.

Numerous factors influence the unequal prospects of these siblings, as they unequally affect those of my children and the other children of Raúl, the two living in Mexico and his US-born children growing up in New Jersey. That our children, and others, have diverging pathways does not mean that one pathway is necessarily better than another. But opportunities certainly differ. And while economic stability, education, birth order, and even personality affect these pathways, so too—it seems quite clear—does illegality. Whether immigration restrictions result in not migrating to avoid becoming illegal, as in the case of Raúl's children in Mexico, being "illegal" in the United States, or having illegal—or even previously illegal—parents, it shapes children's experiences differently even as they live in the same families. And, as Temo reminded me when we first sought Camilo out on the soccer field, this hardly seems fair.

Notes

The chapter epigraph is from Conley (2004: 8).

1   Lareau (2003); Levey (2013).

2   Information on the neighborhood where Camilo lived with his family is available via American Factfinder. However, because I am keeping the location confidential I do not cite the specific website here.

3   See the previous note.

4   This is true among both legal and undocumented migrants. See Akresh (2008); Chriswick and Hurst (1998); Segura (1989); Sullivan (1984).

5   Information on the schools in this city and statewide is available on the New Jersey Department of Education website. Because I am keeping the site confidential, I do not cite the specific website here.

6   See the previous note.

7   See note 5.

8   Extensive scholarship outlines the extent to which the concept of the American dream shapes US society. For an interesting treatment of this shared dream, see J. Hochschild (1996).

9   Abowd and Killingsworth (1985); Danziger and Gottschalk (1993); Farley and Allen (1987); Keister and Moller (2000); Kirschenman and Neckerman (1991); Oliver and Shapiro (2006); Reimers (1985); Waters and Eschbach (1995).

10 Smith (2008). For general information on the intergenerational transmission of social inequality, see Bowles and Gintis (2001, 2002). For intergenerational inequality among immigrant groups, see Portes and Zhou (1993); Zhou (1997b).

11 Alexander, Entwisle, and Olson (2014); Huston (1991); Lareau (2002).

12 See, for example, Beller and Hout (2006).

13 Meir, Slone, and Lavi (2012); Ortega et al. (2009); Suárez-Orozco et al. (2011); Yoshikawa (2011); Yoshikawa and Kalil (2011).

14 Maria López (2005).

15 For more on the controversy in Alabama, see Fox News Latino (2012). For general attendance issues faced by immigrant students, see Driscoll (1999); Suárez-Orozco and Suárez-Orozco (2001); Zhou (1997b).

16 Abrego (2006); Eckstein (2009); Gonzales (2011); Ruge and Iza (2004); Seo (2011); Vandenhole et al. (2011).

17 Nandi et al. (2008); Yoshikawa (2011); Yoshikawa and Kalil (2011).

18 Gonzales, Suárez-Orozco, and Dedios-Sanguineti (2013); Potochnick and Perreira (2010).

19 See Chilton et al. (2009); Hadley et al. (2008); Van Hook and Balistreri (2006).

20 Yoshikawa (2011). See also Yoshikawa and Kalil (2011).

21 Passel and Cohn (2009).

22 Flippen (2001); Keister and Moller (2000); Krivo and Kaufman (2004); Rosenbaum and Friedman (2007).

23 Conley (2004).

24 Dahan and Gaviria (2003); Rosenzweig (1986); Yamauchi (2006).

25 Of course, Messi has sported various hairstyles over the years.

26 For more on code switching, see Portes and Schauffler (1994); Reyes (2004); Vu, Bailey, and Howes (2010).

27 See Waters and Jiménez (2005).

28 The pattern did not hold among fourteen- and fifteen-year-olds, as all of the US-born children had had friends over but only four of the six unauthorized children had.

29 Lareau (2003).

30 Bianchi and Robinson (1997); Cogle and Tasker (1982); Hofferth and Sandberg (2001).

31 Cogle and Tasker (1982); Gager, Sanchez, and DeMaris (2009).

32 Hofferth and Sandberg (2001).

33 Katz (2014); Orellana (2001); Song (1999).

34 Some research suggests that the experience of immigration makes men more open to helping out with domestic tasks. See DeBiaggi (2002); Hondagneu-Sotelo (1994); Pribilsky (2004).

35 Cogle and Tasker (1982).

36 Legal permanent residents can petition for their minor children, but they are put on a waiting list. Citizens who petition for minor children avoid the waiting list, although it still can take one to two years for an application to process.

37 Cerrutti and Massey (2001); Dreby (2010); Kanaiapuni (2000).

38 Note that the great majority of the men I met accepted their nonbiologically children seamlessly, at least in public.

39 Dreby (2006, 2010).

40 See Dreby (2010) on the ways children and parents experience time differently while living apart. Also see Bernhard, Landolt, and Goldring (2005) on mothers' experiences of reunification with their children.

41 Research suggests hardship during periods of separation for children. See Aguilera-Guzmán et al. (2004); Dreby (2007); Parreñas (2005). Some research suggests long-term impacts of separation after reunification. See Artico (2003); Gindling and Poggio (2009); Suárez-Orozco, Todovora, and Louie (2002). For some children in other cultural contexts, separations may not be nearly so devastating. See Olwig (1999).

42 Suárez-Orozco, Todorova, and Louie (2002).

43 Lareau (2003).

44 Gans (1992); Smith (2006); Portes and Zhou (1993); Waldinger and Feliciano (2004); Waters et al. (2010); Zhou (1997b).

45 To be eligible for deferred action, youth must be between the ages of fifteen and thirty-one and be in school or have graduated from high school. See US Citizenship and Immigration Services, "Consideration of Deferred Action for Childhood Arrivals," www.uscis.gov/portal/site/uscis/menuitem. eb1d4c2a3e5b9ac892 43c6a7543f6d1a/?vgnextoid=f2ef2f19470f7310VgnVCM100000082ca60aR-CRD &vgnextchannel=f2ef2f19470f7310VgnVCM100000082ca60aRCRD#guidelines (accessed August 29, 2014). For more on how deferred action has affected children, see Gonzales and Ter-riquez (2013).

46 Conley (2004).

47 Research by Bernal et al. (1990) suggests that ethnic identity formation corresponds to developmental stage, with Mexican American children developing an understanding of ethnic identity before they reach the age of seven or eight.

48 Bernal et al. (1990); Brown and Chu (2012); Phinney et al. (2001); Portes and Schauffler (1994); Umaña-Taylor and Fine (2004).

49 On children's development of a sense of ethnicity, see Gans (1979). On teenagers' development of a pan-ethnic identity, see D. López and Espiritu (1990). On Mexican American adolescents' ethnic identity formation, see Umaña-Taylor and Fine (2004).

50 Most literature on identity formation focuses on the adolescent years. For example, Phinney (1989) suggests three stages in children's identity development and states that for minorities ethnic identity develops most strongly in adolescence. Some sociologists have suggested that children develop understandings of race and ethnicity at earlier ages. See, for example, Van Ausdale and Feagin (1996).

51 For a fascinating study of children's preoccupation with fairness during divorce, see Wade and Smart (2003). Children's preoccupation with fairness has also been extensively studied in psychological and economic literatures. For example, see Almas et al. (2010); Evans et al. (1994).

52 Conley (2004).

53 Smith (2006).

54 Artico (2003). For more on transnational family reunions, see Ramirez, Skrbis, and Emmison (2007). For more on the emotions involved in the maintenance of transnational families, see Baldassar (2007, 2008); Svasek (2008).

55 Gindling and Poggio (2009).

56 Gleeson and Gonzales (2012).
57 On the marginality of undocumented youth, see Silver (2012). On activism among undocumented youth, see Gonzales, Heredia, and Negrón-Gonzales (2013); Negrón-Gonzales (2013).
58 Greenman and Hall (2013).

III

Marriage and Partnership

Pair Bonding

Dating, Marriage, and Long-Term Relationships

BY FREDERICK BROWN AND CYNTHIA LAJAMBE

Part 1: Pair Bonding and Love

"Love is patient, love is kind. It does not envy, it does not boast, it is not proud. It does not dishonor others, it is not self-seeking, it is not easily angered, it keeps no record of wrongs. Love does not delight in evil but rejoices with the truth. It always protects, always trusts, always hopes, always perseveres. Love never fails." (1 Cor. 13:4, Bible, New International Version, 2011)

Preview

Although this description of the highest form of love was written nearly 2,000 years ago, it is still just as meaningful today. The focus of this chapter is on the pairing of humans for a deep, long-term relationship based upon love for each other. Falling in love with another person is one of the most irrational experiences that can change our life entirely. But what greater wish fulfillment of life could a person want than to reach a mutual level of supportive, caring, and protective intimacy with another person? As the quotation above indicates, love is not just some abstract romantic sentiment. Rather, the true extent of love has definite measurable attitudes and behaviors, like acceptance, compassion, and caring for another. Some theorists argue that our need for love and belonging is simply a way that we can give love to others, who also have the same need for love. [...] we need to be in intimate social contact with others to grow to our full potential as humans.

Pair Bonding

The term **pair bonding** refers to a type of strong association various organisms can have for each other, including humans. *Pair bonding* is a term used by sociobiologists and evolutionary psychologists to describe self-selected associations, often for reproduction. Among nonhumans, the powerful survival force for reproductive mating is produced by unlearned hormonal and physiological cycles. Many animal breeding cycles are fixed by the seasonal light from the sun or the light-dark phase of the moon (Brown, 1988). These are different from the psychosocially learned human attractions [...]. As for love, although this binding force is usually thought of exclusively as a human emotion, that may not be completely true. However, science cannot yet state whether nonhumans feel love the way humans do. It is well documented that some nonhumans bond for life, and even after their mate dies, will not mate again.

Love and Liking

Since one of the three pillars of positive psychology is the institution of a strong family, our focus will be on the sociopsychological relationship of marriage. This is because historically, marriage is the most intimate long-term relationship most people will have, and it provides many benefits that enhance the quality and length of life for the partners. No relationship is perfect, however, and within marriage, difficult challenges can occur that the couple must handle if the relationship is to last. We'll look at the major disruptions happening in pair bonding that lead to separation and divorce, as well as the effects of re-pairing into another relationship. Finally, the option of remaining single will be discussed. But first—as an old love song of the 20th century mused, "What Is This Thing Called Love?" (Porter, 1929)— we'll discuss three current theories of love.

Diamond's Romantic and Passionate Love Distinctions
First, *loving* and *liking* are two different concepts. Where **love** is an intense positive feeling, **liking** is a milder feeling, a feeling of being pleased with a relationship. In our discussion of love, we must recognize that there are many different views of love. On one side are psychosocial theories of intimacy and commitment. In contrast are strong biological theories, where those in love are not in control of their emotions, but are driven by internal forces toward each other. In most cases, many of these factors are probably working together, and are very likely to change as people get older.

   a. Romantic love. In this first classification, two kinds of love are distinguished by Dr. Lisa Diamond (2004), **romantic** and **passionate**. *Romantic* love involves positive strong emotions focused on the person who is loved and a strong desire to be with them, not necessarily for sex. According to Gonzaga and coworkers (2006), "... *we define romantic love as a motivational state associated with feeling of attachment and the inclination to seek to commit to one partner ...*" (p. 163). According to Meyers (2002), men tend to fall more readily in love than women, perhaps because they are more romantic, and women are more realistic [...]. However, women seem to be surer of being in love and can express it with more certainty than men. Also, men, more than women, tend to see the one they love as almost perfect.

b. Passionate love. Passionate love is the intense biologically driven sexual arousal caused by the physical presence of the other. According to Gonzaga and coworkers, "*... passionate love ... involves powerful feelings of attraction, desire, passion, and infatuation ...*" (p. 163). Dr. Diamond asserts that this passionate love is fairly fixed in men with what their sexual orientation is, whether it be heterosexual or homosexual. However, she considers that women have a greater passionate love flexibility; their sexual orientation can range widely, depending upon many biological factors at various times.

Over time, the fires of sexually passionate love decrease naturally to less intensity. Like it or not, as with any *eustress*, the human body eventually adapts to intense stimuli. Nothing has gone wrong. Many of us will discover, or rediscover, in our partners the *companionate* love, the "liking" of the other person that was the early reason for our long-term relationship. People now can feel affectionate toward, and liking for, each other as good friends as well as lovers (Hatfield, 1988). A study done over 40 years ago by Cimbalo, Faling, and Mousaw (1976) of the two types of love between long-term couples indicates that many begin with passionate love. These researchers rated passionate love in couples who had been married for up to three years. On a scale of 100, these couples averaged over 98 points. However, those married more than 10 years reported somewhat lower passionate love scores at 84. Of most interest was the fact of no changes between the two different sets of couples in their *liking* scores. Research about 20 years ago tended to confirm these findings about passionate love: After about two years of marriage, expressions of affection decreased to about one-half (Huston & Chorost, 1994). On a more global level, the rate of divorce peaks at about four years (Fisher, 1994).

Lee's Six-Type Model of Love
What has now become a standard classification scheme is Lee's six-type model of love (1988; Gonzaga & coworkers, 2006), which can be distinguished by measured behavior (Fehr & Russell, 1991; Hendrick & Hendrick, 1992). These are listed in Table 7.1:

TABLE 7.1 **Lee's Six Types of Love.**

Sensual—Eros
Game playing—Ludus
Friendship—Storge
Practical—Pragma
Possessive—Mania
Selfless—Agapé

1. Sensual love (*Eros*)—emphasis is on the perceived beauty of the partner; exciting mutual sexual fulfillment through right "chemistry," including "love at first sight"; pain when separated; hurt by a lover's criticism; almost fantasy-like in intensity.

2. Game playing (*Ludus*)—the main feature is enjoying each other by having fun together; recreational activities; teasing and joke playing with very little seriousness or commitment; quick hookups; high probability of breaking up; infidelity; or possible sexual addiction.

3. Friendship (*Storge*)—the main feature is family ties and close friend companionate love, with support, caring, and bonding together in defense of each other.

4. Practical love (*Pragma*)—rational and goal oriented to fulfill set purposes, like arranged marriages in collectivistic societies with interdependency of needs.

5. Possessive (*Mania*)—an obsession or codependency feeling, with overwhelming need for the beloved; can't live without them, who somehow rescues them from their lesser state; considered abnormal love.

6. Selfless love (*Agapé* = **ah-GAH-peh**)—the main emphasis is generosity, giving to the other without wanting anything in return; feeling extremely fortunate to have this person, with caring, forgiving, and patience for the beloved. The love described in the opening quotation would be considered companionate, if not *selfless* love, rather than romantic or erotic love.

Sternberg's Triangular Model

The third classification of love is Sternberg's well-accepted triangular model or theory of **consummate** love (1986, 1998), the most fulfilling and completely satisfying love. The three separate sides show sexually *passionate love*, *intimacy*, and *commitment* (Figure 7.1). Most pair-bonded relationships have various combinations of these three. They form eight distinct love relationship types, from non-love to consummate love, as depicted in Table 7.2. If any component is missing, what remains would not be considered as a *consummate love* relationship. *Intimacy* alone is the basic substance of a friendship. *Passion* alone would be the irrational erotic "crush," or infatuation. *Commitment* alone could be Lee's "practical" love that could fulfill the obligation of some promises or vows. Passion and intimacy without commitment are the conditions for the fantasy of a "no-strings" Lee-type "game-playing" love. In contrast, intimacy and commitment without passion compose companionate love, similar to Lee's "friendship" love. Love with passion and commitment, but no intimacy, has no real substance to it. It is *fatuous*, or foolish, love.

As we consider these three theories, love can come in many forms, something for everyone. Some early research

FIGURE 7.1 Robert Sternberg's triangular theory of consummate love.

Robert Sternberg, "Triangular Theory of Consummate Love," Adapted from "A Triangular Theory of Love," Psychological Review, vol. 93, no. 2, pp. 119–135. Copyright © 1996 by American Psychological Association.

suggested that men were more likely to show the game-playing type of love, while women were more likely to start with friendships or practical relationships (Hendrick & Hendrick, 1995). However, research by Howard (1988) suggested that the reason for the apparent conservativism of females has been from lack of equal status, and that bad outcomes can be more negative for them. Importantly, how long a couple has known each other is a major factor in determining whether companionate love goes along with the early "being in love." In permanently bonded relationships, the passionate love does not disappear from the companionship!

TABLE 7.2 Sternberg's triangular theory of love form eight distinct love relationship types, from non-love to consummate love.

Decision and Type of Love	Intimacy	Passion	Commitment
None-Love	LOW	LOW	LOW
Liking	HIGH	LOW	LOW
Infatuate Love (CRUSH)	LOW	HIGH	LOW
Empty Love (DUTY)	LOW	LOW	HIGH
Romantic (EMOTIONAL)	HIGH	HIGH	LOW
Fatuous Love (FOOLISH)	LOW	HIGH	HIGH
Companionate Love	HIGH	LOW	HIGH
Consummate Love	HIGH	HIGH	HIGH

Robert Sternberg, "Taxonomy of Kinds of Love," Adapted from "A Triangular Theory of Love," Psychological Review, vol. 93, no. 3, pp. 119–136. Copyright © 1987 by American Psychological Association.

To summarize this section briefly, *consummate love* promotes growth, both in each partner and in their relationship. Each person keeps their sense of self, as well as develops a reliance on their mate to fulfill the emotional needs that drew them into the relationship in the first place. If love is genuine, most people have a basic desire to promote the growth, wellbeing, and interests of the person whom they love (Branden, 1980).

Choosing a Mate

Initial Pool of Potential Mates

For most of us, our relationship usually starts with those people we 1) are in *more frequent contact* with, either physically or electronically; 2) find *attractive*; 3) can *communicate effectively* with; and 4) find similar to our self in some ways and add to our self (complementarity) in other ways. After all, long-term pair-bonded relationships are just a type of serious interpersonal relationship. Also, there now may be the start of some irrational, probably even biological, component called *love*. For many people now, romantic love is the final essential ingredient in their long-term pair-bonded relationship. However, as Dr. Sternberg's *triangular theory of love* pointed out, it takes much more than empty (fatuous) love to ensure such a satisfactory relationship.

Given today's telecommunication possibilities, countless people exist whom we could contact for their availability for a possible relationship. Realistically, that number is quite small in which the conditions of interpersonal attraction can begin to work [...]. However, an increasingly popular way to seek a mate is *online dating*. It often includes an initial screening process. In that way, potential partners can be prescreened based on preferred attributes, possibly increasing the likelihood of a good fit. In a large representative study of US adults married between 2005 and 2012 (N=19,131), over one-third met their mate online (Cacioppo et al., 2013). Those who met offline met most frequently at work (21.7 percent) or through a friend (19.1 percent), then at school (11.0 percent) or a social gathering (10.0 percent), and least, at a bar or club (8.7 percent). In contrast to "back in the day," only 6.8 percent met their spouse through family connections, childhood friendships (7.6 percent), or through the church (4.1 percent)(see adjacent Perspective).

Other findings from the study were that divorce was higher for offline (7. 7 percent) than for online (6.0 percent) couples. Also, marital happiness was lower for those who met offline (5.5 percent) than online (5.6 percent). But because a large sample was studied, the practical difference is very small, even though it is statistically significantly different (Nuzzo, 2014). So, it's not yet known which type of dating leads to better marriage outcomes. Finkel and colleagues (2012) evaluated a number of popular online dating sites to see if their claims of being better were true for finding a mate online than offline. Their results showed that access to potential partners online was greater. However, their claims that their secret mathematical matching programs they used were scientifically superior were not supported. The researchers concluded that online dating likely will improve as the programs improve. Until then, time and money are important to consider before using online dating services to find a mate.

Preferred Mate Characteristics

What features do we want our mate to have if we are to be pair bonded with them with any permanency and stability? What features are not only desirable, but nearly essential? A massive worldwide study by Buss and 50 coworkers (1990) surveyed 37 different cultures around the world, looking at desirable features in a mate. They sampled more than 10,000 people over six years between 1984 and 1989, rating 18 desirable characteristics in a possible mate (see adjacent *Perspective*. *Mutual love attraction* was ranked the most desirable characteristic cross-culturally, although not unanimously by far. However, following closely were *dependable character*, *emotional stability and maturity*, and *pleasing disposition*. Ranked furthest down in importance were *prior sexual experience*, *similar religious background*, and last, *similar political background*. Incidentally, at one time, these three topics, sex, religion, and politics, were so controversial in the United States they were not to be discussed in public.

This major study ranked how desirable were other features females and males would want in a mate. Males wanted *physically attractive* mates who could *cook* and were *careful with finances*. In contrast, women valued a mate with high positive social traits of *consideration*, *kindness*, *honesty*, *dependability*, *understanding*, and *well liked by others*. For family survival characteristics, they preferred a man who *cares for children*, has a *steady income*, is *ambitious*, and is *career oriented*. Why these preferences? More recent conclusions by Buss (1994) offer a very reasonable, but far more controversial, explanation. From his team's exhaustive studies that crossed many social and psychological differences, their conclusions are that these preferences are a part of our inborn biological preferences from evolution to ensure survivability of the offspring. Incidentally, for themselves personally, these women preferred a tall man!

What people report finding most attractive and desirable in a mate to some extent depends upon the questions asked in the research study. In an earlier study with single college students, Buss and Barnes (1986) asked them to rank 13 spousal characteristics on the basis of their desirability in a mate, from the first most desirable to least desirable (see Table. 7.3). The first three ranked items were 1) *kind and understanding*; 2) *exciting personality*; and 3) *intelligent*. Interestingly, men ranked physical attractiveness significantly more important at fourth place than women did, who ranked it lower at sixth place. In contrast, women valued more than men did long-run survival attributes, ranking as eight a male being a *college graduate* and as nine having a *good earning capacity*. In similar surveys, with several hundred nearly all unmarried college students across several semesters between 2010 and 2015, your first author confirmed the ranking of both the top three and bottom two spousal characteristics! In addition, a recent survey by McClintock (2014) suggests that *cultural similarity* and *education* are more important in mate selection than trading up for attractiveness. In a very recent study, the top desirable mate characteristics for both females and males were *mutual attraction or love*, *dependable character*, and *emotional stability and maturity*, while men ranked *good looks* at eighth and women ranked it twelfth (Boxer, Noonan, & Whelan, 2015). Furthermore, when Pearce and colleagues (2010) examined whether US and Russian students considered positive psychology attributes—the six virtues and their related strengths—as important characteristics of a person for mate selection, they reported that students from both cultures listed *love*, *dependability*, *happiness*, *kindness*, and *humor* as particularly important qualities when considering a potential mate. Taking these findings together, it can be concluded that most people rate positive internal personal characteristics to be more important for mate selection than external or sociocultural considerations.

TABLE 7.3 Averages ranked for 13 desirable spouse characteristics by 100 male and female US college students. Only "physically attractive," "college graduate," and good earning capacity" were significantly different.

Spouse Characteristic	Desirability Ranking	
	Male	Female
Kind and understanding	1	1
Exciting personality	2	2
Intelligent	3	3
Physically attractive	4	6
Healthy	5	5
Easygoing	6	4
Creative	8	7
Wants children	7	10
College graduate	9	8
Good earning capacity	11	9
Good heredity	10	11
Good housekeeper	12	12
Religious	13	13

Source: D.M. Buss and M. Barnes (1986), "Desirability Ranking," Adapted from "Preferences in Human Mate Selection," Journal of Personality and Social Psychology, vol. 50, no. 3, pp. 559–570.

Actual Mate Selection

Despite our preferred mate characteristics, this does not mean that our eventual mate will possess these characteristics. In fact, what we say we want in a mate and who we eventually choose as a mate may be quite different. Research indicates that during the mate selection process, initial pairing is often a consequence of a spontaneous romantic emotional response. The mate characteristics, or *ideal partner preferences*, come at a later relational stage (Eastwick et al., 2014). In addition, since most Americans say that they would not marry someone they didn't love, emotions appear to override the need to find a partner who possesses a majority of preferred mate characteristics. Then, too, ideal partner preferences prior to meeting a romantic partner may not be what a person uses to evaluate the partner, once face-to-face interactions have occurred. Even when an eventual mate does not possess the preferred mate characteristics, this does not necessarily lead to subsequent marital problems. Instead of differences in ideal versus actual characteristics, marital dissatisfaction resulted from other factors such as low levels of agreeableness, emotional stability, and intellect-openness (Botwin, Buss, & Shackelford, 1997).

    a. Short-term mate selection. Short-term mating includes dating and hookups, including casual sexual encounters. For brief encounters, women are more concerned about male physical attractiveness than other attributes potentially important to mate selection (Schmitt, 2014). This desire to find an attractive male peaks around the time of ovulation, when women are likely to feel more attractive and may dress and behave in a more receptive manner. Women tend to increase their selectivity for short-term mate selection based on physical attractiveness associated with "good genes," while men tend to be less selective in order to increase sexual access.

    b. Long-term mate selection. According to the biological hypothesis by Buss et al. (1990), for long-term mate selection, females usually preferred older established males to ensure offspring survival. Their observations were that "*… in 36 of the 37 cultures, women placed significantly greater value on financial prospects than did men*" (p. 249). Males preferred physically attractive and younger women for a personal kind of survival by being more fertile and able to bear offspring with their genes. In all 37 cultures worldwide, men place a high value on the physical appearance of women. Despite what appears as a totally objective and calculating *social balance model* explanation, Buss et al. observe the following: "*Men do not look at women simply as sex objects, nor do women look at men simply as success objects. One of our most robust observations was that both sexes place tremendous importance on mutual love and kindness when seeking a long-term mate*" (p. 249). To summarize this section, it appears that we don't just look for someone who has our ideal partner preferences and then choose a match. The process is complicated, and no mathematical or theoretical models can predict with high probability that two people are "made for each other" or will end up together.

Marriage and Alternatives to Marriage

In the next section, the institution of marriage will be examined, since it is still the most prevalent long-term intimate relationship known around the world. We must realize that humans can make other committed, informally agreed-upon marriage-type associations. These can be made for set lengths of time based upon various reasons, including love, and for various purposes including reproduction. According to husband-and-wife research team psychologist Dr. David Barash and psychiatrist Dr. Judith Lipton (Barash & Lipton, 2001), at least six types of pair bonding exist, of which humans are known to engage in, and are listed in the adjacent *Perspective*. Even the term *pair bonding* does not cover all of the possible associations for humans, since history records persons with multiple wives (polygamy) and/ or lower-status mistresses, or husbands (polyandry), or same-sexed partners. Briefly discussed near the end of the chapter will be the *polyamory* relationship favored by some.

PERSPECTIVE

Six Types of Pair Bonding
Short-term—for deliberate reproduction or for recreation
Long-term—part of another's life for various reasons
Lifelong—exclusive life partnership
Socially—for economic or territorial reasons
Secret—usually for recreational sex
"Swinging"—couples exchanging partners for recreational sex

Traditional Marriages
For generations in the United States, a **traditional** marriage was only considered acceptable between a female and a male. It referred to the social roles of husband and wife, based solely upon reproduction potential. The male was usually older and was expected to be the family provider. Often with less education, women married usually before age 20 and had most of their children before age 30, becoming "stay-at-home-moms." They were to be dependent upon their husbands and stay home taking care of all aspects of the house and children. Any possessions of hers were assumed his; she was to fulfill his sexual expectations, and any major decisions were finally his. By the 1970s, preference for traditional marriages had dropped to about 43 percent (Lamanna & Riedmann, 1985).

Although current first marriages occur later in age than in previous decades, they are earlier in people's total lifespan, since people are now living much longer. A hundred years ago, people were marrying when about half of their lifespan, less than age 50, was over. Now most are marrying when only about one-third of their lifespan (at about age 80) is over, and the wait until marriage is increasing. First marriages can average over 50 years, which a century ago was the average lifespan!

As of June 26, 2013, the United States Supreme Court struck down the one-man and one-woman definition of marriage as unconstitutional for imposing "... *a disadvantage, a separate status, and so a stigma upon all who enter into same-sex marriages ...*" (Deakins, 2013). Not only did the gender designation change for who could marry, but also other changes had already taken place. Over the last two generations, more women became high school and college graduates, until women outnumbered men as college graduates. Also, according to the 2010 US government census data, women's marrying age averaged just over 26 and men's over 28 and will continue to increase as women become more educated. Current news sources list average age increasing to 27 for females and 29 for males (see the *Perspective* on the age change).

Today, some couples raised in traditional homes are just fine with continuing that structure in their marriage. For those females who choose to stay at home, the term *housewife* is more acceptable now rather than *stay-at-home-mom*, a term that many women apparently detest (Bloom, 2014). *Housewife* implies more creative activities in the home, neighborhood, and the school district. It is being chosen by more women, with a rise from a low of 23 percent in 1999 to a current 29 percent in 2012 (Cohn, Livingston, & Wang, 2014). However, as a growth model for women, the traditional marriage has certain limitations (Scanzoni, 1972). The major issues are equality in decision making, in family responsibilities, and in the marital relationship.

Modern Marriages

What brought about the change from traditional to "modern marriage" was a series of events, an "awakening" of issues of inequality for women that brought about major changes throughout the 20th century. These included women winning the right to vote (1920); women taking the place of men in heavy industry factories during World War II (1940s); the "feminist movement" and "sexual revolution" (1960s); the founding of NOW (National Organization of Women) (1966); Presidential Executive Order 11246 prohibiting employment discrimination (1967); the proposed Equal Rights Amendment (1968); and the Abortion Counseling Service of Women's Liberation began operating in Chicago in 1969. Most of today's young women have little comprehension of how major these events were. Many modern, but socially conservative, Eastern as well as Western societies now recognize that marital gender roles are a matter of personal choice and custom. They are not caused by innate biological differences between men and women. However, apparently women who work outside of the home still do at least one-third more of the home chores and child caretaking than men do. This is known as the double burden, or *double load*, of women (Wedderburn, 1990).

Marriages Now

Apparently, just like gender variability, marriages come in a wide variety that spans both types. A search online results in a listing of various types of families described by anthropologists and sociologists that appear to have developed more recently as societies have become more accepting of them. We start with the historical *extended family* unit that is composed of all genetic and married relatives across at least three generations. Now is the very common unit, the *nuclear family*, composed of two parents and their offspring. Historically, there also has been the *stepfamily*, now known as *blended family*. It is a combined family by partners with children from a former relationship. The most recent family structure, developed among the lesbian, gay, bisexual, transsexual, and queer community, is referred to as the *family by choice* (Ahern & Bailey, 1996). It describes a family of adopted children, live-in partners, relatives of household members, and close friends. This one is now included in the legal system after same-gender partners were allowed to marry. Also, families by choice include partners and their children choosing to live together without a legal marriage contract.

PERSPECTIVE

Types of families now
Nuclear
Extended
Blended
Family by choice

Reasons for Marrying

A search of current popular media can find dozens of reasons to marry, with the most common general reason as bringing *stability* to a relationship, including less anxiety or worry about abandonment. With a legal marriage contract, most couples psychologically begin thinking of themselves as a unit, with a willingness to pool resources to strengthen the unit for greater financial security, providing for the security of the other, and for support of any children. What follows is a detailed description of four standard reasons commonly given for marrying: 1) consummate love, including companionship; 2) psychological support, including escape from loneliness; 3) increased sexual fulfillment, including reproduction and child rearing; and 4) the possibility of increased economic and legal security (see list in *Perspective*).

Before we further explore the reasons for marrying, we might want to consider some of the implications for the changes in marriage rates. In the 20th century, the "golden age" of marrying was in the 1950s, with only about 6 percent of women remaining single. Currently, despite the economic prosperity in the United States, the rate of marrying has decreased to the level of that during the Great Depression of the 1930s (Mather & Lavery, 2014), which was the lowest between 1920 and 1960. The reason given in a 2010 national survey for this decrease is that traditional marriage is being seen by about 40 percent of Americans as becoming "obsolete" (Pew Research Center, 2010). The trends away from long-term pair-bonded marriages are significant because stable marriage is associated with many benefits for families and individuals, including higher income, better health, and longer life expectancy. One reason for these benefits may be that people with higher potential earnings and better health are "selected" into marriage, resulting in better outcomes for married couples. However, most researchers agree that marriage also has an independent, positive effect on well-being. The decline in marriage may affect conditions for the younger generation because of the growing number of children born to unmarried parents. In 2008, nonmarital births accounted for 41 percent of all births in the United States. Although roughly half of these nonmarital births are to cohabiting couples, these unions tend to be less stable and have fewer economic resources compared with married couples. Therefore, declining marriage rates put more children at risk of growing up poor, which can have lasting consequences for their health and future economic prospects.

Consummate Love

Although we have just learned that love can be analyzed into many different types, *consummate love* is the most complete and satisfying love. When asked in 2010 to rank the following reasons for marrying, married and unmarried people placed "being in love" at about 89 percent in importance for marrying (Pew Research Center, 2015). In contrast, until about 150 years ago at the last half of the 19th century in western European countries and the United States, love was considered very secondary to other reasons for marrying (Coontz, 2005). In contrast, Brazilians indicated that, by far, they would divorce if love was not present in the relationship. Following far behind Brazil were Mexico, Hong Kong, and Japan. The United States was in the middle (Levine, 1993). Research at about that same time by Dr. John Gottman (1994) showed that Americans tend to emphasize "love" in the form of *consummate love* as the most important factor for marriage. It seems that only as societies have become more liberal and young people freer of old, more limited traditions, choice by love has become the main reason for marrying. Yet, Buss's (2000) research of historic literature indicates that love as a big factor in pair bonding extends back almost as far as written history, if not further back. Historically, how long love has been the primary reason for marrying is anybody's guess.

Companionship

Married people want their mate to be their good, if not their best, friend, someone whom they can count on regardless. In that way, they will know they will never be alone. Since deep companionship usually includes intimacy, this involves sharing not only thoughts, but momentary emotions, deepest feelings, and a growing history of shared memories. Assuming that two people know each other quite well, their companionship would include similarities and complementarities that started the relationship. In a sense, the companionship relationship can assume a position of two people standing together, regardless of the rest of the world. Companionship was rated at 72 percent as a reason for marrying (Pew Research Center, 2015).

Sexuality

Prior to the present generation in the United States and in many other western European cultures, a widespread middle-and upper-class expectation was that women especially would remain uninitiated into sexual activity until their marriage. Apparently, that was an ideal more than an actuality. In the 1700s in colonial America, about one-third of females were pregnant before marriage, and in England, roughly half were pregnant (Gardner, 2007). The idea of not being sexually experienced before marriage motivated American satirist H. L. Mencken's cynical comment (in paraphrased form), that the height of morality rested on the fact that two people come to the marriage bed totally ignorant of each other! Yet, sexual innocence until marriage still serves three practical purposes:

1. to prevent sexually transmitted diseases like syphilis, gonorrhea, human papilloma virus, genital herpes, and the lethal effects of AIDS;

2. to promote cultural and ethnic "purity" by knowing who a child's father is; and
3. more importantly, to decrease accidental pregnancies and decrease stress on children raised by poverty-stricken single-parent mothers.

Regardless of how it is viewed currently, surveys indicate more frequent sexual activity and more sexual variety engaged in by married partners than by singles (National Survey of Sexual Health and Behavior, 2010). Current research shows that more than 60 percent of females and males are sexually active by age 19 [...]. Marriage for sex seems to be no longer a main reason for marrying.

Child-Rearing

Until the last century, marriage in Western societies has been the main socially approved relationship for "bearing and caring" for children, assuming that these two behaviors are beneficial "moral" acts for society. A woman with children outside of marriage was branded by society as being "immoral," regardless of whether she wanted sex or had been made pregnant by rape. Worse still, the innocent child was punished legally for inheritance purposes for having no father or was classified as unacceptable by various religious institutions. One can be reminded of this social ostracism by reading the two great American classics, Nathaniel Hawthorne's *The Scarlet Letter* (1850) and Thomas Hardy's *Tess of the d'Urbervilles* (1892).

Good parenting for effectively raising children involves enormous amounts of time (upward of 25 years per child), educational and financial resources, and both physical and emotional energy. For example, a child born in 2012 will cost about $243,340 per child, excluding birth costs and college education costs (US Dept. Agr., 2014). The highest costs will be in the urban Northeast and the lowest costs in the urban South and rural regions of the United States. A stable pair-bonded marriage provides a means to share all aspects of raising their children, as well as provide some occasional relief for each parent.

Today, the childbearing situation has changed dramatically. One of every three children (15 million) is being raised without a father, and nearly half of them live below the poverty line (US Census Bureau, 2013). A substantial number of pregnancies occur among unmarried, uneducated teenagers with few marketable job skills, making it difficult for them to provide for themselves and their babies. Reasons vary for these pregnancies. Some are just accidental, out of ignorance or carelessness. For others, it is a means of developing financial "independence" by relying upon social services instead of family for support. Still for others, it provides a misguided means of psychological fulfillment of being needed or of having someone to love. In contrast, a small number of financially secure women are actually choosing to raise children without any involvement by a father. These children are well cared for. Nonetheless, the majority of children in most societies today are still the product of traditional two-person cultural marriages. The Pew Research Center (2010) survey found the marriage rate at about 60 percent for having children.

Economic and Legal Security

In earlier generations, extending back into the dim beginnings of human history, large inter-married families became strong economic units to enhance the survival of the individual, the family, and the tribe. The males banded together for hunting, for warring to increase resources for better survival, and then for protecting their families and their resources. Meanwhile, the females stayed in the home territory with the children. In more industrialized times, males worked outside of the home to bring in money for family survival. Married females went to work because the family needed the money, and their jobs were usually supportive to men's occupations, typically in service or helping positions. The exception was the professional or career-oriented woman. Today, more women are now highly educated and are able to lead independent lives, making marrying for economic security a less important reason. However, a two-income family can result in reaching economic goals perhaps sooner, such as being able to buy a house, providing more for children's education and self-development, and saving for a comfortable retirement. Yet, increased financial stability as a main reason now for marrying was ranked recently at a low of 30 percent (Pew Research Center, 2015).

Legal security is another important benefit of marriage. Beyond financial considerations, there are instances when the legal right to advocate for a spouse is crucial, due to illness or incapacitation. In the event of a serious illness requiring assistance from family members, a life partner who is not a spouse may be denied access to a hospitalized loved one, as the formal medical system may not recognize them legally as a family member.

The Challenges of Marriage

[...] the Holmes-Rahe Stress Response Recovery Scale places marriage right at the middle with a score of 50. For most people, it is a major step in their life because their view of themselves often changes forever. It is not an accident that one of the common marriage traditions is for the bridegroom to carry the bride through the doorway of their new home. It is not the doorway itself, but its threshold that is important. The concept of the threshold separates one space (outside) from another (inside) and symbolizes the change from the former life state of being single to the new one of being married.

With marriage, psychological changes often occur, unlike interpersonal relationships with friends, colleagues, coworkers, and so on. Partners in long-term committed relationships more often now see themselves as a unit, referring to themselves as "we," "us," and "ours," rather than "you" and "me" and "yours" and "mine." A major focus in the life of each partner now is on the other partner in this pair-bonded relationship. Often, statements of commitment are made to the other, either in private or public, about caring for each other across the ups and downs of their lives together. Given the current improvements in health and medicine, the total time with a mate can be as long as 60 to 80 years, essentially more than the length of two full generations and nearly twice the length of a person's lifetime 200 years ago. Many changes can be expected to happen across this length of time. But, what has to be worked out quite quickly is the routine of day-to-day living. Then what can result is a reasonable degree of satisfaction from living together.

After the Commitment

If the premarriage time together was long enough, each partner may become aware of the "real" other person, aside from the pleasant side they may have tried to show. Personal behaviors that we may not be aware of may turn out to be an unintentional irritant to the other. What each has come to expect from other relationships before their marriage, such as with parents or friends, may not work any longer. As one young married woman stated, *"If he wants his socks washed, he is going to have to crawl under the bed and get them. His mother may have done it for him, but not me!"* In turn, after living the life of a bachelor, he may complain, *"Where does all the toilet paper go—it seems to be gone so soon,"* and all she says is, *"What did you expect? I'm a woman!"*

Neither of these examples is a major event, yet there will be countless similar events that need to be resolved if they are going to stay together. If the basic *companionate* relationship holds, then the many minor events will be solved. Then they each can spend their energy working on the more important major challenges that are bound to take place over the life of their relationship. These major changes often involve adequate financial stability and management, dealing with family obligations, maintaining work and professional schedules, children, changes in physical well-being, maintaining good mental health conditions, and changing sexual needs and desires with age.

Good Communication

[...] when discussing the structure of good relationships, how to communicate clearly was shown to be the most important. Most marriage counselors agree that a major key to a successful marriage is open communication. Hopefully, partners are intimate enough that they can share nearly everything with each other, especially if one has questions that affect their union. It would be very rare for two people to agree about everything. Humans are just not made that way. When differences occur and the scene gets uncomfortable, the sooner they are brought out in the open, the sooner they possibly can be resolved. It is known that the communication skills learned in Chapter 7 can be used to resolve most reasonable issues. These include four effective interpersonal communication skills:

1. clear, unambiguous messages;
2. active listening by paraphrasing back what the speaker just said;
3. maintaining respect and caring for the speaker; and
4. accurately interpreting what the spouse was trying to say (Boyd, 1976).

More recently, investigations have focused on positive psychology principles as they relate to healthy relationships. Studies show that when partners share positive daily experiences (when good things happen) with each other, they have greater positive emotions, as well as happiness, life satisfaction (Lambert et al., 2010), and well-being (Gable et al., 2004). The researchers found that these effects are strongest when the partner who listens then responds in an active and constructive way, rather than in a passive or negative way. Also, one study found that a romantic relationship can be enhanced further by sharing an exciting activity together for as little as 90 minutes a week (Coulter & Malouff, 2013). The effect of romantic excitement after four weeks of engaging together in exciting activities had a positive effect on a relationship even four months after the activities ended. According to Ramsey and Gentzler (2015), not only do positive emotions (*affect*) and positive close relationships enhance well-being, but positive emotions are important contributors to building positive close relationships between parents and children, friends, and romantic partners. Those authors suggest that when couples experience conflict and enter therapy to deal with negative affect, at the same time there should be a focus on increasing positive processes and positive affect in the relationship.

Finally, relationships require some adjustment based on the age of those involved. Isaacowitz, Vaillant, and Seligman (2003) found that life satisfaction varied by age group: for young adults, hope for the future was most important, while loving relationships mattered most for middle-aged adults. Older adults derived life satisfaction from hope and loving relationships, as well as citizenship. Strong relationships can address the individual needs of each age group and enhance life satisfaction.

Causes of Disagreement

During the premarriage phase while attempting to impress our potential partner, there may seem to be no real causes for lasting disagreement with them. In the highly irrational time of passionate love, disagreements may be easily overlooked and quickly forgiven. Unrealistically, we may assume that any problems can be dealt with quite easily when together more permanently. This *tender-minded* view will have to be replaced with a more *tough-minded* approach if the relationship is to survive. Here is where open communication involving respect for each other's views will be tested.

a. Areas for potential conflict. Go to the Web and search on the topic "marital problems." Although researchers, marital counselors, and psychologists may disagree on the exact ranking of the most common subjects that are potentials for conflict, the 10 issues listed in Table 7.4 in alphabetical order have not changed much over the last generation (Knox, 1979; Meyers, 2013).

TABLE 7.4 Areas of potential conflict.

Children
Expectations
Families (including in-laws)
Friends—including opposite gender
Household responsibilities
Irritating habits
Money and credit card spending
Religion
Sex and infidelity
Time apart (including recreation)

Nobody comes into a committed relationship with another without some life experiences that they are very familiar with. Since very few people have prior training to deal with each of these issues, most people rely on their background experiences. This is what is known as coming into the relationship with "personal baggage." Assuming that most people have had significant experiences living in a parent's home until they graduated from high school, what has been learned and expected may be quite different from what a mate has experienced and now comes to expect. Let's assume that the precommitment time a couple had was long enough to get to know some of the important things about the other in open and honest discussions. Some, but not all, of the differences between them probably will have been worked on to an agreeable solution. Not until people begin living together on a daily basis will the full extent of meaningful differences start to have their impact, for good or for bad. And as mates grow older, their needs and desires will change the types of differences that will happen.

b. Different needs. How do you know your partner cares for you? What would you want from them to show you that they really care? Each person has the need to feel wanted by their partner. This is especially true after the heat of sensual love has cooled and the deep friendship of companionate love is being further developed. Just how that need is filled may be very different between partners. In a highly popular marriage manual, marriage counselor Dr. Gary Chapman suggests that each person needs at least one of five types of psychological needs listed in Table 7.5 to be filled by their partner, to feel loved by them (2010). Other sources may list more or less than five classes of needs. For our purposes, a brief consideration of his observations may sensitize us to become aware of what our partners, or we, may feel is missing in our relationship. This may have been filled with our families growing up, but may not be present in our new relationship. An important aspect is that people may not even know they have this need and cannot communicate to their mate what they need and are missing now. Surprisingly simple in what these "love languages" are, they are not difficult to provide to a mate who is loved and cared for.

TABLE 7.5   Dr. Gary Chapman's five love languages.

1. Words of affirmation
2. Quality time
3. Receiving gifts
4. Acts of service
5. Physical touch

1) Words of affirmation. This is a strong positive statement that something is good. Many people like to hear at least occasionally, if not more often, someone say to us, "*You did a great job—well done,*" or "*Thanks, it was the best ever.*" Dr. Chapman states that how appreciation is stated can take many forms, or "dialects." The best way may be similar to the way one was used to being told they were appreciated when they were young. Perhaps it is written in a note of thanks or a hand-written poem, telling the person that what they do is more than "just okay."

2) **Quality time.** Spend enough time alone with one's mate without distractions from phone, TV, others, or multitasking. The purpose is to listen and hear what they have to say, what is concerning them, what is important to them, what they want to share with you. If this person is committed to you, then part of their love is to spend time with you. "*You never seem to have any time to listen to me,*" or "*Why do we always have to have family or friends with us when we go out?*" If other things seem more important than spending time with your mate, then the message they get is that they are less valued by you.

An additional aspect in spending quality time with one's mate is in the currently widely discussed concept referred to as *venting*. It is the detailed talking about an event or situation, like a recent everyday *hassle* that has some emotional aspect to it. It is not as intense like talking about a serious personal trauma or memory that can occur in psychotherapy (Kennedy-Moore & Watson, 1999). Sometimes, people just want to be heard, also to hear for themselves what they are saying. By talking about their topic, they may gain insights into what is on their mind or at least reduce some tension that may relate to it. As for its long-term effectiveness, clinical researchers differ in their estimates of the usefulness of *venting*, especially if it does not lead to any insights regarding causes or solutions. Nevertheless, there is a gender difference in that females seem to have a greater need to *vent* than do males. Instead, what males try to do is "fix" what to them seems to be broken. It may go like this—He: "*It seems to me that if you do this or that, it ought to take care of your problem, right?*" She: "*I'm not asking you to fix it; just listen, okay?*" If a person says, "*I need to vent/just talk, can you listen?*" and you do really listen, they are receiving a valuable love gift from you.

3) **Receiving gifts.** To give a gift takes some thought, some time, and some effort. In most societies across the ages, gifts are exchanged as an indication that the person who receives the gift is considered important to the gift giver. If the person who wants gifts as an indication of their importance to another, knows how to give gifts, then they also know that thought, time, and effort involved in giving the gift all were a part of any gift they receive. Here is where the phrase "*it's the thought that counts*" makes the receiver feel valuable to the giver. Dr. Chapman emphasizes that there is no one specific type gift or how often. Instead, one needs to develop a sensitivity to one's partner's likes and appropriateness of time to give a gift, and give them often enough as an indication of continuing love.

4) **Acts of service.** This one is probably used more in traditional marriages in which the social roles are fairly structured and separate. In a female/male relationship, where she takes care of the in-house maintenance and he takes care of the repairs and outside maintenance, to switch off occasionally may seem like a gift. Not only may it ease the burden of the caretaker when they might be overwhelmed by other chores, it also says to their partner "*I care, and I just don't take you for granted.*" Sometimes humor has to go along with the switch-off because things may not be done exactly the way the usual caretaker takes care of things! Yet, here is where partners can give each other an A for effort, rather than a C for lack of perfection!

5) **Physical touch.** In the classic book, *Touching: The human significance of the skin* (1971), psychologist and anthropologist Dr. Ashley Montagu describes how our skin is the largest sensory organ of our body, and from birth onward we will not survive without physical contact from others. How, when, where, and by whom we are touched communicates much

information. A kiss, a caress, a hug, a shove, a slap, and beating, each says something about who did it. [...] females are more sensitive and welcoming to hand holding and hugging than males. Sitting quietly together within occasional touching distance sends the message of wanting to be with one's partner. Not all people want to be or need to be constantly touched. If a partner goes out of their way to avoid touching the other, this usually indicates an emotional distancing. If one's partner enjoys physical touching, then this can be a gift to give to them. Although some males may claim that sexual activity is enough physical touch from their partner to indicate care, not all males think this is so, especially as they get older.

Dr. Chapman cautions that part of the effectiveness of providing the needed "something" for the other is not to assume that their need is the same as yours. If you and your partner have the same need to be filled the same way, then fine. However, with an understanding of these five classes of needs, an open discussion with your partner may determine whether what they are doing is enough, or that a different, more effective offering is needed. Using this method of satisfactory assessment of what you are doing is similar to Dr. Richard Lazarus's three-stage *transactional model of stress assessment* [...] when coping with stressors. In this case, stage one, *primary assessment*, is to find out which of the needs must be filled; stage two, *secondary appraisal*, is to select and try out ways to fill that need; and stage three, *evaluate the outcome*, to determine if your approach is successful or not. If it is not quite right, then go back to stage two as many times as necessary to get it finally right. After all, a long-term positive relationship is a process to be worked on every day.

c. Resolving differences. One of the major potential conflict topics listed above is unrealistic expectations of what long-term pair bonding will involve. A system will have to develop for *accommodation* of differences between partners. Assuming that neither partner is always getting their own way, which is not partnership, then the development of a give-to-get procedure will have to be constructed to resolve differences that are absolutely guaranteed to arise. This will be crucial for major topics if the relationship is to survive. Some minor issues may have to be accepted or overlooked if they can be lived with without being a constant source of irritation.

To resolve differences, partners need to develop their open and honest communication with each other. The same skills discussed in Chapter 7 for being a good listener fit here, and may need to be reviewed. These included 1) *effective listening without interrupting;* 2) when feedback is asked for, *don't give advice;* 3) *forgive* if regrets are expressed; 4) *stay on the topic;* 5) do not generalize, but *be specific about what actions need to change;* and 6) *do not expect immediate solutions.*

d. Compatibility and incompatibility.
1) Compatibility. If our filtering has been successful, we are now pair bonded with a person whom we consider **compatible** with our interests and needs. That is, we have a relationship that works quite well, has few serious problems, and tends to generate calmness and peacefulness with good "vibes." On the other hand, if events are not going smoothly and attempts to resolve issues are not working, anxiety may occur, perhaps depression. The problem may be one or several of the areas of potential conflict that were described above.

Negative emotions may develop for one or both partners in the relationship, that may end with a lack of enough compatibility to resolve the issues, reaching a level of **incompatibility**.

2) **Sexual incompatibility.** One of the areas of conflict that most often uses the term *incompatibility* is for sexual *incompatibility*. It has grown into the status of being serious enough that it can be the legal reason for divorcing. Unfortunately, the term *sexual incompatibility* is used very loosely, referring only to differences between partners in such areas as frequency of sexual activity, types of activity, levels of sexual satisfaction, and so on. To think that each couple will have the same sexual needs over the lifetime of their partnership is like thinking that the same couple will have the same food, clothing, hobby, or work interests. Each person's uniqueness makes that nearly, if not actually, impossible! Once the early passionate phase of being "in love" slows down a little and the companionate phase begins to settle in, personal priorities may also begin to change for the relationship. This is not saying sexual activity is no longer important, since it is a main reason people marry. If one of the main expectations for a person to marry is to have unlimited sexual activity and that is not fulfilled, that can lead to disillusionment and result in exiting the relationship.

Men and women differ in their needs and reasons for sex (Peplau, 2003). One major gender difference is that a woman's sexual arousal varies biologically with the hormonal rhythms of her menstrual cycle, something that men do not have. Also, with age, sexual activity tends to decrease. Among males, sexual need peaks in late adolescence and early adulthood and slowly declines after that into old age. Females peak later, usually in their late 30s or early 40s, and then decline. Perhaps the reason is that as she nears menopause, this is a last potential time to have children. Other reasons for changes in sexual frequency include illnesses, each partner's work demands, increasing needs of children beyond the home in school and other extracurricular activities, and perhaps increasing care of elderly relatives. As the sexual needs of partners change, this is no different from any other type of physical changes with age. These are not sexual incompatibility issues, just natural changes in partners' needs to be *accommodated*.

Then, too, changes in sexual activity may not be at all related to the bedroom activity. As one old-timer said, *"If things are going well in bed, most likely things are going well out of bed, and vice versa."* When a relationship is going well and a couple considers themselves to be sexually compatible, the sexual relationship is usually going well, and sexual differences in needs or difficulties between mates are able to be resolved with caring and love.

3) **Infidelity a symptom—not the cause.** Another major gender difference is this: For men, sexual dissatisfaction is a large factor for seeking compatible sexual satisfaction outside of the relationship. If the feeling is from perceived indifference or no positive emotions of sexual desire from their partner, this often is taken as a judgment against their maleness. In contrast, for women, how she is treated by her partner with intimacy, commitment, and communication is more important than the physical sexual satisfaction. Without these psychological necessities, a woman will find it difficult to keep interest and involvement with her partner. This may lead her to search for fulfillment outside of the relationship. In each of these cases, the love needs are not being met by their partner. However, it does not mean that sexual activity outside the partnership is always involved. For either partner,

these lacks can lead to decreases in the former exclusive intimate communication they had, resulting in *infidelity*, or unfaithfulness. The unfaithfulness is a "symptom" of an unresolved problem, not the problem itself. If, through working out the unresolved issues by the couple or with outside help with a professional counselor, the relationship can be healed, then the symptoms of infidelity usually disappear. A carefully constructed survey two decades ago on sexual activity among committed couples indicates that for them, the percentages of marital infidelity are relatively low: Eighty percent of woman and 65 to 80 percent of men claimed *no other sexual partner* than their spouse while they were married (Michael, Gagnon, Laumann, & Kolata, 1994). More recently, Blow and Hartnett (2005) conducted an extensive review of infidelity studies and concluded that less than 25 percent of heterosexual married couples engaged in infidelity, more often for men than for women.

Romantic Jealousy and Possessiveness

Romantic jealousy can be described as an emotion involving negatively threatening or fearful thoughts of loss and abandonment by someone of high value to a person. According to Buss et al. (2000), "*Jealousy is activated by perceived or real threats to romantic relationships ... Despite the extensive suffering it creates, it served our ancestors well in the competitive currency of reproduction ... deterring a mate from straying, backing off interested rivals, and perhaps even communicating commitment to a partner*" (p. 18). Let's expand the meaning of this quotation.

> **jealousy**—a negative emotional reaction to possible loss of one's significant partner

The 1990 worldwide study by Buss and his 49 coauthors, discussed earlier in the chapter, strongly suggests that jealousy is not just a learned emotion and attitude, but also has an inborn genetic component to it. But it has not yet been clearly separated just how much of the gender difference in jealousy is genetic (Dijkstra, 1998) and how much has been socioculturally conditioned (Pines, 1998). *Jealousy* needs to be clearly understood as different from *envy*. Envy is a strong resentment or a bad feeling a person has toward someone who already has what the envious person wants. It could be power, attractiveness, wealth, position, or an attractive partner. In contrast, jealousy is aroused by whatever draws a partner's attentions and energies away from their mate. Reasons can include attraction to another person, a hobby more pleasant than spending it with a partner, the enjoyment and involvement of a person's work, or even the children of partners. The threat is to a person's self-confidence and how much they are valued by their partner.

Clear gender differences appear in the reasons for sexual jealousy (De Weerth & Kalma, 1993), [...]. Cross-culturally, for males, a partner's infidelity calls out the greatest jealousy, because they focus more on the sexual act and see sexual infidelity as a threat to their own attractiveness. Females are more threatened by a potential emotional relationship with a rival that could damage the relationship with their partner (Buss et al., 1990; Buunk et al., 1996; Pines, 1998). Evolutionarily, a man's jealousy increases the limitation he attempts to put on his mate. By doing that, he is trying to make sure that the children born to her are his. For a woman, jealousy increases the limitation she attempts to put on her mate so that he will provide for their offspring and not someone else's.

According to Buss (2000), apparently, a little jealousy occasionally is a good thing. It says to the partner that they are valued and and do not want to be lost. But it also says that some sort of boundary has been reached that has produced a feeling of threat. Here, open communication between partners can be used to come to an acceptable resolution for both. In contrast, *intense* jealousy can become destructive, coming from strong feelings of a serious threat of losing one's partner. If emotions are extreme, the jealous partner may try to use power to limit them. Continued attempts at control by males result in millions of females each year being battered (Wilson & Daly, 1996), [...]. In the United States, it is no longer an acceptable type of behavior, regardless of culture or religion, because it is now considered a domestic crime. The *Perspective* box offers some ways of attempting to deal with jealousy suggested by clinical psychologist Dr. Peter Salovey (1991).

PERSPECTIVE

Characteristics of Jealousy
1. Often from low self-esteem or insecurities (perhaps fearing abandonment, isolation from a partner).
2. Often occurs when one feels they are putting more into the relationship than their partner.
3. Often occurs when serious doubts arise about partner's commitment to the relationship.
4. Males less likely to express jealousy, but are more likely to express anger toward rival.
5. Females more likely to become depressed, work harder to be more attractive to partner.

Coping with Jealousy

Develop self-reliance—Learn to control expressions of sadness, embarrassment and anger, become more committed to partner.

Engage in positive self-comparisons and self-bolstering—Focus on own good qualities and do something nice for yourself.

Engage in selective ignoring—Perhaps come to the point of deciding that the desired person or objects is just NOT that important.

Part 2: Alternatives to Marriage

Although one-man, one-woman marriage is the most frequent type of pair bonding worldwide, it is not the only way people develop consummate love relationships. Historically, other conjugal arrangements have been tried, including *open marriages*, communal marriages, *bigamy* (marrying a person while still legally married to another) and *polygamy* (being married to more than one person at the same time), and *cohabitation* (living together). The United States has now legalized marriage between two same-sex partners, but not these others. While brief descriptions will be given for most of these arrangements, the first two to be discussed in some detail will be, *cohabitation*, and a recent (or revived) plural arrangement of *polyamory*.

Cohabitation

Cohabitation, living together without a legal marriage contract, has become the fastest growing alternative to traditional marriage in the United States. The majority of couples marrying today cohabit first (Bumpass & Lu, 2000). Data from the US Census Bureau indicate that around 8 million households have two unmarried adults of the opposite sex (see Figure 7.2).

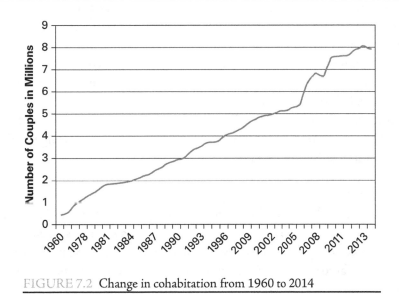

FIGURE 7.2 Change in cohabitation from 1960 to 2014

Reasons for Cohabiting
Reasons for living together are several. *Cohabitation* is seen as a reasonable response to the rise in the divorce rate. Given the disappearing of the old "double standard" where it was accepted for men to have premarital sex, but not women, two results have occurred. First, women now are more willing to "trial run" to determine whether the relationship will last. The second factor is increased sexual opportunities for women. Other reasons include fear

of a legal commitment, more time together, and if the relationship ended, less complications than a legal divorce. Also, a college degree and effective contraceptive methods have decreased the number of first-year cohabitation pregnancies, as compared to women with a high school degree or less. One study found that more commitment and satisfaction occurred in the relationship, with less ambivalence and conflict when the reason for cohabitation was *spending time together* (Tang et al., 2014). However, when the reason for cohabitation was primarily for *"testing the relationship"* or for *convenience*, then the relationship was poorer quality, with lower commitment and higher ambivalence and conflict.

Many men and women also have very mixed feelings about marriage. Reasons given for not choosing marriage can be seen in the following comments:

+ It produces some *loss of personal freedom* and individuality.
+ It *brings new responsibilities*, both to the individual and to the couple.
+ It *requires constant adjustment and adaptation* if it is to succeed.
+ If divorcing, it *leads to complications of separating.*

Cohabiting couples may believe that ending their relationship would be easier and less troublesome than dissolving a legal marriage. However, considering the "six stations of divorce" (discussed in the next section), the breakup is probably as difficult emotionally and socially, if not financially and legally. Furthermore, the successful prosecution of "palimony" suits in the last few years suggests that even the legal distinctions between living together and marriage are disappearing as well. Yet, despite concerns about rising divorce rates and loss of individual freedom, perhaps surprisingly, among cohabiting couples there seems to be no strong aversion to official marriage. Earlier research on this topic found that about 85 percent of cohabiting men and 98 percent of the women expect someday to marry (Risman, Hill, Rubin, & Peplau, 1981). In fact, for those who live together for the first time, the probability of becoming married is 30 percent after one year, then rising to 84 percent after 10 years (Bramlett & Mosher, 2002).

Age and Cohabiting

Although cohabitation is often viewed by a couple as preparation for marriage, previously it was discouraged, due to research suggesting that there was a strong association between cohabitation and subsequent divorce. However, earlier studies of cohabitation may not have considered important factors that made divorce more likely. A recent important scientific reevaluation was made by Dr. Arielle Kuperberg (2014). She reanalyzed 1995 through 2010 data collected from the National Survey of Family Growth, examining several factors that might have led to earlier marriage failures that followed cohabitation. She found the earlier misperception that divorcing was considered as easy as leaving cohabitation, that less religiosity is associated with cohabitation and religious commitments mean little, and that in a marriage, like cohabitation, there is no need to stay and "tough out" a difficult period. However, her most striking finding was that of age of cohabitation. Just as early marriages are associated with increased divorces, earlier age of cohabitation (younger than mid-20s) was associated with higher divorce risk after marriage. When her study adjusted for age and other risk factors for divorce, those who first cohabited and those who directly married were at similar risk of divorce. Her conclusion was that the age of committing to a relationship, married or not, is the strongest predictor of its success. Keep in mind that an older age often goes along with having more education and having a higher-level job with better income.

Other Factors
Another concern about cohabitation before marriage is the quality of the subsequent marriage. A large survey study asked women who cohabitated and then married within the years 1992 and 2006 about the quality of their marriage (Tach & Halpern-Meekin, 2009). Women without children who then married had marital quality similar to those who had directly married. However, for women who had children while cohabiting, their marriage quality was lower. Also, for women cohabitating multiple times, only about one-third of cohabitating relationships resulted in marriage, and divorce was twice as likely when compared with those who only cohabited once with a future husband (Lichter & Qian, 2008).

In general, cohabitating and married couples are equally as affectionate toward, concerned about, and supportive of their partners. They assume roles associated with marriage, such as shared housework and handling finances. The shift from cohabitating to marriage appears to be more symbolic than functional, where marriage is a state that a couple builds up to from moving in together, beginning a career, developing financial stability, and in some cases, even having children prior to the final achievement of marriage (Cherlin, 2004).

Like other aspects of intimate interpersonal relationships, the decision to live together can have both positive and negative effects. On the positive side, people can get to know their partners well and can share in their lives. On the other hand, cohabiting individuals may use their relationship as a *game-playing* love, according to one of Lee's six types of love. Then it is used to avoid long-term emotional commitment to their partners. In essence, the relationship is being used to satisfy their own needs while manipulating the feelings and emotions of the partner.

Alternatives within Marriage

Still keeping the lifetime contract marriage, some researchers have suggested modifications to it. Two of these modifications arose from the 1970s period of the new *no-fault* divorce laws, the high divorce rate of that period, and the liberalizing of sexual behavior. They were *open marriage* and *serial marriage*. Neither has gained any legal status, but both have stimulated thinking about the changes that can take place within married partners over time.

Open Marriage
In 1972, the husband-and-wife anthropologists Nena and George O'Neill wrote the controversial book **Open marriage,** intended to be a manual on marital behavior in a modern age where the husband no longer was the head of the house, with greater overall equality

between spouses. It included discussing how both partners could have friendships with the opposite gender. As for extramarital sexual behavior, they stated they did not recommend it, but also stated that it should not be avoided. That thought, unfortunately, was taken as permission for modern marriages to include non-exclusive sexual behavior. What they had intended was a healthy response to occasional extramarital activity in a non-threatened, non-jealous, noncompetitive way. However, in a later book, Nena O'Neill admitted that if one has deep feelings for one's mate, it is difficult to lose exclusive sexual intimacy and not feel jealous. The concept of an *open marriage* with extramarital sex did not really last. However, the other aspects of a more open and equal marriage have developed into the features of the current modern marriage.

Serial Marriage

The marriages of people now in their early 20s can expect to last upward of 60 to 70 years. When the world was young and people lived only about half the current lifetime, most rules of marriage were first set down. Since then, most couples find that shared goals that have been reached may outlast their usefulness. For example, perfect qualities of shared parenthood are no longer needed when children are grown. Other things must take their place. As an example, octogenarian anthropologist Margaret Mead had reflected on her life as having "three successful marriages!" Marriage to the same person may not always be perfect across a person's changing life experiences. A marriage may come to a natural ending as a phase ends in a person's life journey. Thus, divorce does not have to be seen as failure in marriage, but rather as the necessary conclusion for a finished chapter in a couple's long life. In many ways, the higher divorce rate with a longer life span with a high rate of remarriages suggests that longevity of life is promoting **serial marriages.** Many couples with good early marriages may find the need for a different type of marriage that will sustain them with the same positive benefits as their first successful one.

Polyamory

"Polyamory is … the practice, state or ability of having more than one sexual loving relationship at the same time, with the full knowledge and consent of all partners involved" (Ravenhearts, 2006). This is somewhat similar to open marriage and developed in the Boston area in the 1970s within a loose subculture of other *polys* who are available as support. Polyamory differs from **polygamy**, bigamy, "swinging" (temporary trading of sexual partners), and cohabitation. Communication is the key to maintaining the arrangements, in that all members seem willingly open with each other to make the relationships work. Part of the agreement is that all must be free of sexually transmitted diseases, with secret or illicit affairs extremely rare or not necessary outside of the arrangement. Recent investigation considers *polyamory* not to be a pathological alternative lifestyle because of its openness among participants (Weitzmann, 1999).

polyamory—an open sexual-loving relationship with more than one partner

Singlehood

As of 2014, just over half of the people age 16 or older (about 153 million) in the United States are in **singlehood** (USBLS, 2014). That is, they have never married, are single, or divorced. Many are waiting to get married until after they have completed college degrees or have become established in a career. An increasing number see *singlehood* as a legitimate lifestyle. When asked, they list having few restrictions, ability to set own schedule, able to travel, and freedom in meeting people. Much of this is because of a relatively recent strong national economy, allowing more single people to support themselves alone. Among single people are those who have lost their life partner through death. By age 70, the female-to-male ratio is nearly three to one. For men above age 75, two-thirds (67 percent) are married, while less than one-third (29 percent) of women are (US Census Bureau, 2003). Of those singles who have yet to marry, most will.

> **singlehood**—life lived without a romantic or pair-bonded relationship

Part 3: Divorce and Un-Pairing

Concept of Divorce and Un-Pairing

Definition, Rates, and Types

a. Definition. **Divorce** is the legal ending (called *dissolution*) of a formal relationship between two married people who will no longer have any responsibilities toward each other. Historically, *divorces* are probably as old as written human history, because ancient texts of many cultures outline the procedures for declaring the legal or religious breaking of the contract between a female and a male. Currently, in non-marriage relationships, the legal issues of separating and reestablishing other future relationships can become very complicated, especially concerning financial issues. For our purposes, our discussion of divorce will be confined to those related to legal contractual marriages.

b. Rates. Much distortion has occurred in interpreting divorce rates in the United States because the data are incomplete (Kennedy & Ruggles, 2014). So, we will try to make some sense of what information is available. In the 1970s, yearly divorce rates, regardless of how long people were married, were being compared with marriage rates for each year. For example, in 1981, about 2.4 million people were married, and 1.2 people divorced. That looked like about half (50 percent) divorced, because they were being compared to only one year's marriage rate, regardless of total number married. In reality, of all married people (about 23.4 million), only 5.2 percent divorced that year, although that year was the highest percentage of all years so far recorded. To determine some general probability of divorce over a person's lifetime, a different statistic is needed, and that is only a crude approximation because

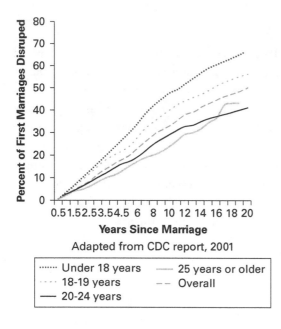

FIGURE 7.3 Percentages of first marriages disrupted by wife's age at marriage.

Copyright in the Public Domain.

those data have not been collected for a long enough time. The following graph gives percent of divorce based upon age of marriage.

Figure 7.3 is an adapted figure from Bramlett and Mosher (2001), which shows percent of people at a given age whose first marriages were disrupted by either separation or divorce within 20 years. By 20 years, the marriage disruption rate overall is 50 percent, but is 67 percent for women who married under 18 years, 55 percent for those 19 and 20, and 41 percent for women who married at age 20 or later. More recent CDC data from 2006–2010 (Copen et al., 2012), showed a somewhat less-than-overall 50 percent trend in disruption of a first marriage. But those numbers are not equally distributed. The percentages differed dramatically, based upon amount of education: In Copen's data, divorce rates were 57 percent for those with less than a high school diploma; 49 percent for those with a high school diploma; 46 percent for those with some college or an associate's degree; but only 24 percent for those with at least a bachelor's degree. The bottom line is, with increased education and a later marrying age, the probability of remaining married is reaching a nearly 80 percent success rate!

c. Two types of legal divorces. First, there are two classes of divorces: *fault* and *no-fault*. Let's deal with the historic *fault* divorce first.

1. **Fault divorce.** These refer to married situations in which clear damage has been done to the relationship. Each state in the United States sets up its own laws for marriage and divorce. For much of the time in the United States, the divorce laws had been very strict, and damage had to be proved. Reasons included abandonment for a fixed length of time, adultery, cruelty (causing emotional or physical pain), inability to have sexual intercourse, and prison confinement. With the rise of *no-fault* divorce, some states now grant only no-fault divorces.

2. **No-fault divorce.** It was between 1975 and 1980 that most states went to "no-fault" divorce laws, and the US divorce rate suddenly increased (NCHS, 1970–1980). That meant that some partners no longer had to agree to make up untrue stories about partner cruelty or adultery to go to court to get a divorce. The greatest number of reasons for divorce are labeled as "irreconcilable differences" or an "irreparable breakdown of

the marriage." This usually means that the couple thinks they can no longer get along, experiencing more negatives than positives now, and expecting more of the same in the future. All states now grant *no-fault* divorces, although some may require that the couple remain separated for a minimum length of time, like a year or so.

d. Two types of divorce settlements. Whether a divorce is fault or no-fault can determine how the finances are distributed between the divorcing partners. If no-fault, then it depends upon whether the state has "common property" or "equitable distribution" laws. If it is a common property state, of which there are only 10, then both assets and debts are divided equally. In the other 40 equitable distribution states, if the couple cannot agree upon a satisfactory arrangement for their assets, then this can be decided upon in court legally, taking into account many factors, like amount each has earned, care of children, and so forth. In that case, one person may receive from one-third to two-thirds of the assets.

Personal Reasons for Divorcing
Log onto the internet and search the topic "marital conflicts," and you will find many sources, including lawyers, marriage counselors, psychologists, psychiatrists, and social workers who list a variety of reasons for divorce. Table 7.6 lists 10 common reasons that divorcing people give, with brief explanations that cover most of the potential sources of conflicts between partners. Next will be a brief discussion of some of the major factors that researchers have uncovered as contributing to divorce.

TABLE 7.6 Ten common reasons for divorcing.

Marrying for the wrong reasons
Loss of personal identity
Getting lost in social roles
Lack of shared visions
Companionship disappears
Unmet expectations
Conflict managing finances
Losing touch with each other
Different priorities and interests
Inability to resolve conflicts

Even with serious unresolved conflict, some couples remain married. This is the type of situation the great American transcendental poet and author Henry David Thoreau (1817–1862), meant when he said some people continue to lead *"lives of quiet desperation"* (*Walden*, 1854). They do so, often either because cultural or religious commitments (see above, Sternberg's "triangular theory" of commitment love) make them afraid to divorce, or because of financial limitations of only one income, or for *the good of the children.* Others do not see themselves better off divorced. Still others do nothing out of habit or lethargy, which is not wanting to be bothered by the divorce process hassle, and just leave their family. Some research indicates that many of the marriages that ended in divorce may not have been as bad as the events that followed (Wilcox, 2009).

Factors Involved
According to demographers, those specialists who describe human characteristics, divorce factors include age, education, race, and religion. Also included are sociopsychological factors of the two people involved, such as their personalities and what motivates them, how they interact with each other, and their marriage expectations. From these considerations, two models were developed to predict the possibility of divorce early in marriage. One was based upon **disillusionment** and the other upon the usual everyday activity, called **enduring dynamics**. But first, let us consider some of the characteristics of the persons who are most likely to divorce, as outlined in Table 7.7.

TABLE 7.7 Who most likely divorces.

Younger, rather than older people—very high for teens
Shorter Dating Length—greater number of divorces
Less or incomplete education—nongraduates of high school or college, training programs or frequent job changes
Lower Occupational Status—more among lower-paid than higher-paid jobs.
Nonreligious highest—religious practitioners lower rate, most conservative lowest rates (Sabini, 1995)
Non-Hispanic Black American women—divorcing more, followed by whites, then Hispanics, with Asians least (Kreider & Ellis, 2011).

On the other hand, with increased democratization of the US population, that is, "people are just people!" especially among the younger generations, factors that are playing lesser sources of potential conflict are the following: 1) differences in age; 2) cultural, (including "race"); and 3) religion. These are definite "in-your-face" facts that confront potential partners as they proceed through the filtering process of mate selection. With adequate open communication, these clear differences are apparently satisfactorily resolved and become non-issues.

Two Early Predictor Models
The basic assumption of these two theories, the *disillusionment* model (Huston, Niehuis, & Smith, 2001) and the *enduring-dynamics* model (Huston, 1994), is that the *causes of divorce* occur very early in marriage, if not before.

   a. Disillusionment model. Not having realistic ideas about what challenges to expect in marriage and how to work at resolving them tends to doom the marriage to early "exiting" (giving up and leaving). This disillusionment sets in early, into an otherwise highly affectionate and deeply-in-love newlywed period. According to Huston et al. (2001), *"It almost seems that early exiters may have entered marriage with the hope that their relationship would improve—that they would become more affectionate and less negative with time—and when these hoped-for improvements were not realized, their fragile bond deteriorated further"* (p. 118).

b. Enduring-dynamics model. This model states that what you see before marriage and during the first two years after marriage turns out to be a quite accurate indicator of the enduring quality of the marriage, whether happy or unhappy. The enduring-dynamics model is similar to what people often refer to as, "what you see is what you get"!

Stations of Divorce

Divorce is not simply stuffing a backpack, packing a suitcase, and walking out on a relationship, making a clean break, and starting over again from zero. More than a generation ago, an analysis was undertaken by anthropologist Dr. Paul Bohannan (1972) on the very complex process of modern divorces. From his observations have come the still widely accepted "six stations," separate components of the divorce process. These components include the emotional, legal, economic, coparenting, community, and psychic aspects. Of these, only the first and last are in any given order. The former family unit changes forever, often with its effects felt most by any children who may be involved, both young and adult. The first-station emotional aspects of divorce have been compared by some analysts with the five-stage theory of grief, as described by psychiatrist Dr. Elizabeth Kübler-Ross (1969). She observed that some people who faced very serious life-threatening illnesses or were confronted with the fact they would soon die would experience some, if not all, of the following emotional states, not necessarily in this exact order:

1. *denial*—not willing to believe it was happening; especially true for divorcing persons who did not see any divorce coming.
2. *anger/resentment*—feelings of unfairness that it should be happening to them, especially when they think they had no part in causing it.
3. *bargaining*—attempting to change things so that the negative events would not happen.
4. *despair*—realizing that the unwanted or unacceptable divorce events were going to happen, no matter what they tried to do.
5. *acceptance*—finally accepting the unavoidable fact that the divorce will happen, and then trying to make the best of a negative ending.

On the other hand, just like people with a healthy perspective on life who are facing death, not all divorcing people go through the first four states, especially when the negative state of their relationship is considered. In those cases, both partners may agree that, although painful, divorcing is probably the best process. These six stations are shown in Table 7.8 with brief descriptions of each.

TABLE 7.8 Six stations of divorce.

3. **Emotional Divorce:** withdrawal of feelings, loss of intimacy—often hurtful words and feelings, without partner support.

4. **Economic Divorce:** separation of all monies (checking, charge, and loan) accounts, settlement and division of all assets and debts.

5. **Legal Divorce:** separation of joint financial rights and obligations, like business contracts, property rights, and inheritance—now easier with no-fault laws.

6. **Coparental Divorce:** establishment of caretaker responsibilities for financial support of children, visitation rights, and schedules.

7. **Community Divorce:** separation or loss of couple-made social relationships, with former friends perhaps taking sides.

8. **Psychic Divorce:** final recognition of self completely separate from former physical, mental, emotional, social, and financial obligations to each other.

Effects of Divorce

Effects on Unpaired Partners

A person who is no longer with a partner may face considerable adjustments, especially if they depended upon another to fulfill major roles. Reacting both with and to anger, bitterness, and disappointment takes effort and is draining. Reaching a level of acceptance with less emotional upheaval will take time; for some people, several years. Research indicates that there is a growing realization that divorce is an extreme action that will not solve all of the conflict problems that arise in marriage. In fact, when people remarry, they may bring with them some of the "old baggage," the same problems, that caused conflicts in any earlier marriages. Many use this time to understand better the reasons why the divorce took place, often with the aid of outside professional help. It may be that the recent decline in the divorce rate over the last few years can be attributed to the fact that the current generation is more willing to accept and use the greater availability of professional resources.

Effects on Children

The issues surrounding divorce effects on children are extremely complex and cannot be adequately discussed in a few paragraphs (Kushner, 2009), since over 7,000 research articles have already been written on this subject. Only a few general comments will be made here to indicate that divorce usually produces greater difficult adjustments for children than their parents. That is because parents are the ones making the active decisions, assuming that divorcing is better than staying together. Children then become a passive partner in whatever are the final decisions, with the effects of divorce being done to them. Some observers claim that effects of a divorce itself on children apparently are no different than serious other family stressors. These include physical and psychiatric illness, death of a parent, or failure of parental attachment to a child (Hartnup, 1996). Yet, divorce can be far more complex than these other situations of family disruption in that, except for the death of a parent, biological parents still are alive, but separated. Often, factors such as personality of the child, resiliency, and culture play significant roles that must be accounted for in adjustment following divorce (Kushner, 2009).

What happens to the adjustment of children following divorce depends upon two major sets of factors: the conditions that led up to the divorce and what happens afterward. The extent of negative factors prior to the divorce depends upon on these factors. They are 1) age of the children; 2) how effective parents were in shielding their children from the partner conflicts; 3) dealing with fears of children about being rejected; or 4) of being the cause of the disruption. After the divorce, the many factors include 1) the stability and arrangements made by the parents for the welfare of their children; 2) whether children remain in a single-parent home; 3) whether the non-caretaker parent has coparenting rights; 4) whether divorced parents remain single or remarry; or 5) whether children go to another relative's home to live. Apparently, the general negative impact upon older children has decreased dramatically from the days of *no-fault* divorces, since divorce is now more common (Emery, 1999).

In general, children may benefit in the short run from living with a single parent who loves them and with whom they have a close relationship. However, according to Dr. W. Bradford Wilcox (2012), director of the National Marriage Project, the data seem quite clear that children raised by a single, divorced mom have a higher probability of difficulties into the teen years and beyond. He refers to the following findings from different sources. Twenty-five percent of children from divorced families did have serious social, emotional, or psychological problems, as compared with 10 percent from intact families (Hetherington & Kelly, 2003). By age 30, more than twice the number of young men growing up without fathers, either from divorce or that the mother never had a mate, have been in jail (Harper & McLanahan, 2004). A study in the United States and New Zealand indicated that girls whose fathers left their home before the age of six were about 30 percent more likely to be pregnant and unwed, as compared with about five percent from a home with a father while they grew up (Ellis & colleagues, 2003). Why the difficulties? Dr. Wilcox believes that it is for the simple reason that single mothers do not have as much time to be involved with and supervise their children as two parents in a home.

Current conclusions, based upon a variety of evidence, are that effects of divorce upon children are not a single result: Divorce can have harmful effects on the intellectual, academic, emotional, and social lives of children. However, negative effects do not necessarily occur for children whose parents were in constant conflict. For them, divorce becomes a relief from such stressfulness (Booth & Amato, 2001), at least in the short run. To summarize, the total context of the family must be taken into account before making a general conclusion about effects of divorce upon children. As of now, there is not a "one-size-fits-all" conclusion that can be made.

Recoupling and Blended Families

Those who divorce hope to remarry better than before, of now "fixing what was broke," or of "getting it right this time." In colonial times nearly 500 years ago in what is now the United States, until within the 20th century, the death of a partner was the reason for remarriage. Today, with recent first partnerships averaging about seven years, recoupling following breakup and divorce has increased. Currently, according to current data from the Pew Research Center (Livingston, 2014), on average about 64 percent of divorced males and 52 percent of divorced females have remarried. Also, age differences indicate that older people are more willing to remarry than those in the 20-to-30-something range. White women are most likely to remarry and black women least likely (Kreider, 2006; Elliott & three coauthors, 2013). Statistics by the US Census Bureau are lacking for those who do not marry but live together, indicating an underestimation of the actual number of combined families.

Reasons for Remarriage

Current data indicate that fewer divorced parents are remarrying than 20 years ago when societal pressures and individual needs steered divorced persons toward remarriage. Nevertheless, a divorced mother may be encouraged to remarry because she is told the children need two parents in the home. Divorced persons often feel awkward in the company of married friends. Divorced men and women may find themselves incapable of handling all the responsibilities of maintaining a household for themselves and their children. Factors such as these, along with the need for affection, adult companionship, and sexual intimacy lead many divorced persons to seek new marital partners.

In considering remarriage, new factors often must be considered. A woman may have children from a previous marriage. She probably will be concerned about how her children will accept their prospective father-by-marriage and how he will relate to them. A man considering remarriage may have financial responsibility for children of a former marriage. If he pays alimony and child support, he may not be in a position to assume the financial responsibilities of an additional family-by-marriage. The individual may also be strongly motivated to overcome the emotional hurt and self-devaluation from the prior divorce. The possibility that one may be marrying "on the rebound" from any or all of these reasons is a factor to be considered carefully.

JUST A THOUGHT

Given the large number of people who are divorced, remarried, or are children of alternative families, what impact does this have on your ideas of having a permanent relationship with someone?

How Successful are Remarriages?

Although most divorced people remarry within five years, and more of them males, the probability of a divorce is greater for a second marriage and is even greater for a third marriage (Kreider, 2006). However, some reports have disputed claims of high failure rates for subsequent marriages. As mentioned earlier, the methods used to collect marriage and divorce data make it difficult to determine reliable statistics.

Blended Families

Many American families are in what are now called **blended families,** also called *stepfamilies.* These terms refer to the combining of families by partners who come into their new relationship with children from a former relationship. In many remarriages, one or both partners have children from a previous marriage. Although no official statistics are available for the actual number of blended families in the United States, a Pew Research Center report (2010) found that 42 percent of families in the United States have at least one step-relative. The partners in these marriages face not only the usual adjustive challenges of parenthood, but also some additional challenges that are unique to blended families. For example, children in blended families have to cope with the disruption of their previous family, as well as the readjustment to the new family. They also may have to adjust to new and different ways of doing things in their own homes. In addition, they may be feeling abandoned and unloved by the absent parent. The children's relationships with their absent parent and their grandparents should be encouraged and supported by both partners in the remarriage. Yet, a child may also feel guilty if they begin to like or love their new parent. As the victims of one unsuccessful marriage, they are also likely to be cautious about investing themselves emotionally in the new marriage.

Parents-by-marriage of blended families also face substantial adjustive problems. It is not easy to love someone else's children, especially if they are withdrawn and seem to resent the presence of a new parent figure. If they try to help their blended children cope with their feelings, it may seem that they are intruding. But if they don't help them, it may seem as if they do not care. Moreover, the way a new parent wants to do something may differ from the accustomed ways of their blended children. New parents have to walk the fine line between insisting that things be done their way or adapting to the old ways of doing things. Spouses also will be coping with the stresses of adjustment to a blended family and will need extra support during the transition period. Estimates are that at least two years is needed for the partners in a remarriage to adjust to each other (Knox, 1985). Then, too, there will be another two or three years before everyone will feel completely comfortable with the new family arrangements.

In the final analysis, as far as developing relationships are concerned, for each person there is a wide variety of available possibilities, from temporary situational events to life-committing pair bonding. Each has its challenges and rewards. One thing is certain—most people will have a committed relationship at some point in their lives. Understanding some of the dynamics of relationships covered in this chapter may help us to make choices that increase the possibility that our relationship not only survives, but also flourishes!

Chapter Summary

+ Three love models were described. First was Diamond's *romantic* versus *passionate*; Lee's six types of love, including *passionate, game playing, friendship, logical, possessive,* and *selfless*; Sternberg's triangular theory of love requires *passion, intimacy,* and commitment for consummate love; absence of one or more of these factors results in seven other types of love.

+ Over 95 percent of US citizens marry sometime in their life.

+ Reasons for marrying include love, companionship, raising children, and economics.

+ Choosing a mate is a process that involves *proximity, availability, complementarity,* and *compatibility.*

+ Marriage requires many individual adjustments to be successful. Problems involve post-honeymoon disillusionment, communication problems, conflict, sexual incompatibility, infidelity, jealousy, problems of power and control, children, and changes in marital sex roles.

+ Cohabitation followed by marriage is more successful if the female is educated and at least in her mid-20s.

+ Polyamory is an open sexual-love relationship of more than two people in which there is little infidelity and low incidences of sexually transmitted disease.

+ *Cohabitation, polyamory, open* and *serial marriages,* and *singlehood* recognize the realities of impermanence, long lives, and change. These alternatives may yield benefits in terms of freedom and choice, but they do not present perfect alternatives.

+ Divorce is a fact of life within 20 years of marriage for at least 40 percent of current marriages.

+ Most likely to divorce are teens, young male adults, short courtships, those with less education and occupational status, the nonreligious, black Americans, those from unhappy or divorced parents.

+ Nonfactors in divorce are differences in age, culture, religion, race, and prior sexual experiences.

+ Reasons given for divorce include physical and mental cruelty, neglect, infidelity, sexual incompatibility, financial problems, and drinking/drugs.

+ Two early-predictor models of divorce include the *disillusionment* and *enduring-dynamics* (what you see is what you get) models.

+ Remarriages occur usually for the same reasons as for originally marrying, with some additional obstacles including children and paying alimony and child support.

+ About 20 percent of US families are *blended families* with children from former marriages.

+ Difficulties may arise between children and new parental figures so severe that the marriages do not last. At least two to five years in the new families are needed for comfortable adjustment.

+ Some people choose singlehood to maintain their independence and live life as they choose.

References

Ahern, S., & Bailey, K. G. (1996). *Family by choice: Creating family in a world of strangers*. Minneapolis, MN: Fairview Press.

Aughinbaugh, A., Robles, O., & Sun, H. (2013). Marriage and divorce: patterns by gender, race, and educational attainment. *U.S. Bureau of Labor Statistics, Monthly Labor Review*, October 2013.

Barash, D., & Lipton, J. (2001). *The myth of monogamy: Fidelity and infidelity in animals and people*. New York: Henry Holt and Company.

Bible (2011). First Corinthians 13:4–8. *New international version*. Colorado Springs, CO: Biblica, Inc.

Bloom, E. (2014). Reclaiming "homemaker." Slate. Published by the Slate Group, a Graham Holdings Company. Retrieved April 26, 2015. http://www.slate.com/articles/double_x/dou-blex/2014/04/_stay_at_home_mom_needs_to_go_let_s_bring_back_homemaker.html

Blow, A. J., & Hartnett, K. (2005). Infidelity in committed relationships II: A substantive review. *Journal of Marital & Family Therapy*, 31, 217–233.

Bohannan, P. (1972). The six stations of divorce. In J. Bardwick (Ed.), *Readings on the psychology of women*. New York: Harper & Row.

Booth, A., & Amato, P. R. (2001). Parental predivorce relations and offspring postdivorce well-being. *Journal of Marriage and Family*, 63, (1), 197–212.

Botwin, M. D., Buss, D. M., & Shackelford, T. K. (1997). Personality and mate preferences: Five factors in mate selection and marital satisfaction. *Journal of Personality*, 65, 107–136.

Bramlett, M. D., & Mosher, W. D. (2002). Cohabitation, marriage, divorce, and remarriage in the United States. National Center for Health Statistics. *Vital Health Statistics*, 23(22).

Bramlett, M. D., & Mosher, W. D. (2001). First marriage dissolution, divorce, and remarriage: United States. *Advance data from vital and health statistics; no. 323*. Hyattsville, MD: National Center for Health Statistics. 2001. DHHS Publication No. (PHS) 2001-1250, 01-0384 (5/01).

Branden, N. (1980). *The psychology of romantic love*. Los Angeles: J. P. Tarcher.

Brown. F. M. (1988). Common 30-day multiple in gestation time of terrestrial placentals. *Chronobiology International*, 5 (3), 195–210.

Bumpass, L. & Lu, H. (2000). Trends in cohabitation and implications for children's family contexts in the United States. *Population Studies*, 54, 29–41.

Buss, D. M. (2000). *The dangerous passion: Why jealousy is as necessary as love and sex*. New York: Free Press.

Buss, D. M. (2000). The evolution of happiness. *American Psychologist*, 55 (1), 15–23.

Buss, D. M. (1994). The strategies of human mating. *American Scientist*, 82 (3), 238–249.

Buss, D. M., & Barnes, M. (1986). Preferences in human mate selection. *Journal of Personality and Social Psychology*, 50 (3), 559–570.

Buss, D. M., et al. (1990). International preferences in selecting mates: A study of 37 cultures. *Journal of Cross-Cultural Psychology*, 21 (1), 5–47.

Buunk, B. P., Angleitner, A., Oubaid, V., & Buss, D. M. (1996). Sex differences in jealousy in evolutionary and cultural perspective: Test from the Netherlands, Germany, and the United States. *Psychological Science*, 7, 359–363.

Cacioppo, J. T., Cacioppo, S., Gonzaga, G. C., Ogburn, E. L., & Van der Weele, T. J. (2013). Marital satisfaction and break-ups differ across on-line and off-line meeting venues. *Proc Natl Acad Sci USA, 110(25),* 10135–10140.

Chapman, G. (2010). *The five love languages: The secret to love that lasts.* Chicago: Northfield.

Cherlin, A. J. (2004). The deinstitutionalization of American marriage. *Journal of Marriage and Family, 66,* 848–861.

Cimbalo, R. S., Faling, V., & Mousaw, P. (1976). The course of love: A cross-sectional design. *Psychological Reports, 38,* 1292–1294.

Cohn, D., Livingston, G., & Wang, W. (2014). After decades of decline: A rise in stay-at-home-mothers. Pew Research Center. Retrieved April 26, 2015. http://www.pewsocialtrends.org/2014/04/08/after-decades-of-decline-a-rise-in-stay-at-home-mothers/

Coontz, S. (2005). *Marriage, a history: From obedience to intimacy or how love conquered marriage.* New York: Viking.

Copen, C. E., Daniels, K., Vespa, J., & Mosher, W. D. (2012). First marriages in the United States: Data from the 2006–2010 National Survey of Family Growth. *Natl Health Stat Report, 49,* 1–21.

Coulter, K., & Malouff, J. M. (2013). Effects of an intervention designed to enhance romantic relationship excitement: A randomized-control trial. *Couple and Family Psychology: Research and Practice, 2,* 34–44.

Deakins, O. (2013). U.S. Supreme Court rules federal law defining "marriage" is unconstitutional. *Lexology.* http://www.lexology.com/library/detail.aspx?g=33053540-8971-4b6f-9ce9-8bf6ed91bfe1

De Weerth, C., & Kalma, A. P. (1993). Female aggression as a response to sexual jealousy: A sex role reversal? *Aggressive Behavior, 19,* 265–279.

Diamond, L. M. (2004). Emerging perspectives on distinctions between romantic love and sexual desire. *Current Direction in Psychological Science, 13* (3), 116–119.

Dijkstra, P. (1998). Jealousy as a function of rival characteristics: An evolutionary perspective. *Personality and Social Psychology Bulletin, 24* (11), 1158–1166.

Eastwick, P. W., Luchies, L. B., Finkel, E. J., & Hunt, L. L. (2014). The predictive validity of ideal partner preferences: A review and meta-analysis. *Psychological Bulletin, 140,* 623–665.

Elliott, D. B., Krivickas, K., Krivickas, M. W., & Kreider, R. M. (2013). Historical marriage trends from 1890–2010: A focus on race differences. Social, Economic, and Housing Statistics Division Working Paper Number 2012-12. Washington, DC: United States Census Bureau.

Ellis, B. J., Bates, J. E., Dodge, K. A., Fergusson, D. M., et al. (2003). Does father absence place daughters at special risk for early sexual activity and teenage pregnancy? *Child Development, 74* (3), 801–821.

Emery, R. E. (1999). *Marriage, divorce, and children's adjustment.* Newbury Park, CA: Sage.

Fehr, B., & Russell, J. A. (1991). The concept of love viewed from a prototype perspective. *Journal of Personality and Social Psychology, 60,* 425–438.

Finkel, E. J., Eastwick, P. W., Karney, B. R., Reis, H. T., & Sprecher, S. (2012). Online dating: A critical analysis from the perspective of psychological science. *Psychological Science in the Public Interest 13(1),* 3–66.

Fisher, H. (1994). The nature of romantic love. *Journal of NIH Research,* pp. 59–64.

Gable, S. L., Reis, H. T., Impett, E. A., & Asher, E. R. (2004). What do you do when things go right? The intrapersonal and interpersonal benefits of sharing positive events. *Journal of Personality and Social Psychology, 87*, 228–245.

Gardner, A. G. (2007). Courtship, sex, and the single colonist. *Colonial Williamsburg Journal.* Williamsburg, VA: Colonial Williamsburg Foundation. Retrieved on May 12, 2015. http://www. history.org/foundation/journal/index.cfm

Gonzaga, G. C., Turner, R. A., Keltner, D., Campos, B., & Altemus, M. (2006). Romantic love and sexual desire in close relationships. *Emotion, 6*(2)163–179.

Gottman, J. (1994). *Why marriages succeed or fail.* New York: Simon & Schuster.

Harper, C. C., & McLanahan, S. S. (2004). Father absence and youth incarceration. *Journal of Research on Adolescence, 14*, 369–397.

Hartnup, T. (1996). Divorce and marital strife and their effects on children. *Archives of Disease in Childhood, 75*, 1–8.

Hatfield, E. (1988). Passionate and companionate love. In R. J. Sternberg & M. L. Barnes (Eds.), *The psychology of love.* New Haven, CT: Yale University Press.

Hendrick, S. S., & Hendrick, C. (1995). Gender differences and similarities in sex and love. *Personal Relationships, 2*, 55–65.

Hendrick, S. S., & Hendrick, C. (1992). *Romantic love.* Newbury Park, CA: Sage.

Hetherington, E. M., & Kelly, J. (2003). *For better or for worse: Divorce reconsidered.* New York: W. W. Norton.

Howard, J. A. (1988). Gender differences in sexual attitudes: Conservativism or powerlessness? *Gender & Society, 2* (1), 103–114.

Huston, T. L. (1994). Courtship antecedents of marital satisfaction and love. In R. Erber & R. Gilmour (Eds.), *Theoretical frameworks for personal relationships* (pp. 43–65). Hillsdale, NJ: Erlbaum.

Huston, T. L., & Chorost, A. F. (1994). Behavioral buffers on the effect of negativity on marital satisfaction: A longitudinal study. *Personal Relationships, 1*, 223–239.

Huston, T. L., Niehuis, S., & Smith, S. E. (2001). The early marital roots of conjugal distress and divorce. *Current Directions in Psychological Science, 10* (4), 116–119.

Isaacowitz, D. M., Vaillant, G. E., & Seligman, M. E. P. (2003). Strengths and satisfaction across the adult lifespan. *International Journal of Aging and Human Development, 57*(2), 181–201.

Kennedy, S., & Ruggles, S. (2014). Breaking up is hard to count: The rise of divorce in the United States, 1980–2010. *Demography, 51* (2), 587–598.

Kennedy-Moore, E., & Watson, J. D. (1999). How and when does emotional expression help? *Review of General Psychology, 5*(3), 187–212.

Knox, D. (1979). *Exploring marriage and the family.* Glenview, IL: Scott, Foresman.

Kreider, R. M. (2006). Remarriage in the United States. US Census Bureau. Poster presented at the annual meeting of the American Sociological Association, Montreal, August 10–14, 2006.

Kreider, R. M., & Ellis, R. (2011). Number, timing, and duration of marriages and divorces: 2009. Current Population Reports, P70-125, US Census Bureau, Washington, DC.

Kübler-Ross, E. (1969). *On death & dying.* New York: Simon & Schuster.

Kuperberg, A. (2014). Age at coresidence, premarital cohabitation, and marriage dissolution: 1985–2009. *Journal of Marriage and Family, 76*, 352–369.

Kushner, M. A. (2009). A review of the empirical literature about child development and adjustment postseparation. *Journal of Divorce & Remarriage, 50* (7), 496–516.

Lamanna, M. A., & Riedmann, A. (1985). *Marriages and families: making choices and facing change.* Wadsworth: Belmont, CA.

Lambert, N. M., Clark, M. S., Durtschi, J., Fincham, F. D., & Graham, S. M. (2010). Benefits of expressing gratitude: Expressing gratitude to a partner changes one's view of the relationship. *Psychological Science, 21,* 574–580.

Lee, J. A. (1988). Love styles. In R. J. Sternberg & M. L. Barnes (Eds.), *The psychology of love.* New Haven, CT: Yale University Press.

Levine, R. V. (1993). Is love a luxury? *American Demographics,* pp. 27–29.

Lichter, D. T., & Qian, Z. (2008). Serial cohabitation and the marital life course. *Journal of Marriage and Family, 70,* 861–878.

Livingston, G. (2014). Four-in-ten couples are saying "I do," again. Pew Research Center. Pew Charitable Trust. Retrieved on May 13, 2015. http://www.pewsocialtrends.org/2014/11/14/four-in-ten-couples-are-saying-i-do-again/

Mather, M., & Lavery, D. (2014). In U.S., proportion married at lowest recorded levels. Population Reference Bureau. Washington, DC: PRB. http://www.prb.org/About.aspx

McClintock, E. A. (2014). Desirability, matching, and the illusion of exchange in partner selection. Retrieved on 12/24/2015 from http://paa2011.princeton.edu/papers/111953.

Meyers, C. (2013). Top 10 causes of marital discord. About.com: Divorce support. http://divorcesup-port.about.com/od/isdivorcethesolution/qt/marital_discord.htm

Meyers, D. G. (2002). *Social psychology.* New York: McGraw-Hill.

Michael, R. T., Gagnon, J. H., Laumann, E. O., & Kolata, G. (1994). *Sex in America: A definitive survey.* Boston: Little, Brown.

Montagu, A. (1971). *Touching: The Human Significance of the Skin.* New York: Columbia University Press.

National Survey of Sexual Health and Behavior. (2010). Findings from the National Survey of Sexual Health and Behavior, Center for Sexual Health Promotion, Indiana University. *Journal of Sexual Medicine, 7,* Supplement 5. http://www.nationalsexstudy.indiana.edu/Nuzzo, R. (2014). Statistical errors. *Nature, 506(13),* 150–152.

O'Neill, N. (1977). *The marriage premise.* Lanham, MD: M. Evans and Co.

O'Neill, N., & O'Neill, G. (1972). *Open marriage: A new lifestyle for couples.* New York: M. Evans and Co.

Pearce, A. R., Chuikova, T., Ramsey, A., & Galyautdinova, S. (2010). A positive psychology perspective on mate preference in the United States and Russia. *Journal of Cross-Cultural Psychology, 41(5–6),* 742–757.

Peplau, L. A. (2003). Human sexuality: How do men and women differ? *Current Directions in Psychological Science, 12* (2), 37–40.

Pew Research Center (2010). The decline of marriage and rise of new families. Washington, DC: Pew Charitable Trust. Retrieved May 5, 2015. http://www.pewsocialtrends.org/2010/11/18/the-decline-of-marriage-and-rise-of-new-families/

Pines, A. M. (1998). Gender differences in romantic jealousy. *Journal of Social Psychology, 138* (1), 54–71.

Porter, C. (1929). "What is this thing called love?" Song from musical "Wake Up and Dream."

Ramsey, M. A., & Gentzler, A. L. (2015). An upward spiral: Bidirectional associations between positive affect and positive aspects of close relationships across the life span. *Developmental Review, 36,* 58–104.

Ravenhearts (2006). Frequently asked questions re: polyamory. www.Mithrilstar.org/Polyqmory%20 FAQ-Ravenhearts.htm

Risman, B. J., Hill, C. T., Rubin, Z., & Peplau, L. A. (1981). Living together in college: Implications for courtship. *Journal of Marriage and the Family, 43,* 77–83.

Sabini, J. (1995). *Social psychology.* New York: W. W. Norton.

Salovey, P. (1991). *The psychology of jealousy and envy.* New York: Guilford Press.

Scanzoni, J. H. (1972). *Sexual bargaining: Power politics in the American marriage.* Englewood Cliffs, NJ: Prentice-Hall.

Schmitt, D. P. (2014). Evaluating evidence of mate preference adaptations: How do we really know what *Homo sapiens sapiens* really want? In V. A. Weekes-Shackelford & T. K. Shackelford (Eds.), *Evolutionary perspectives on human sexual psychology and behavior* (pp. 3–39). New York: Springer.

Sternberg, R. (1998). *Cupid's arrow: The course of love through time.* New York: Cambridge University Press.

Sternberg, R. (1986). A psychological theory of love. *Psychological Review, 93,* 119–135.

Tach, L., & Halpern-Meekin, S. (2009). How does premarital cohabitation affect trajectories of marital quality? *Journal of Marriage and Family, 71,* 298–317.

Tang, C. Y., Curran, M., & Arroyo, A. (2014). Cohabitors' reasons for living together, satisfaction with sacrifices, and relationship quality. *Marriage & Family Review, 50*(7), 598–620.

US Census Bureau (2013). Table FG10. Family Groups. *US Census Bureau Statistics.* Washington, DC: US Government Printing House.

US Census Bureau (2001/2003). *US Census Bureau Statistics.* Washington, DC: US Government Printing House.

US Dept. Agr. (2014). Parents projected to spend $245,340 to raise a child born in 2013, according to USDA report. Release No. 0179.14. Washington, DC: United States Department of Agriculture.

Wedderburn, A. (1990). Women and nightwork. *Bulletin of European Shiftwork Topics, 2,* 15–21.

Weitzmann, G. D. (1999). What psychology professionals should know about polyamory. Presented at the 8th Annual Diversity Conference, March 12, Albany, New York.

Wilcox, W. B. (2012). The kids are not really alright. *Slate.* Published by the Slate Group. Retrieved on May 9, 2015. http://www.slate.com/articles/news_and_politics/slate_fare/2006/08/about_ us.html

Wilcox, W. B (2009). The evolution of divorce. *National Affairs.* Fall 2009, issue 1. Retrieved from http:// nationalaffairs.com/publications/detail/the-evolution-of-divorce on October 6, 2015.

Wilson, M. I., & Daly, M. (1996). Male sexual proprietariness and violence against wives. *Current Directions in Psychological Science, 5,* 2–7.

Negotiating Marriages

BY GENE H. STARBUCK AND KAREN SAUCIER LUNDY

Prelude

Jarrad and Kallia were married 10 years ago. So were Lou and Marina. Although the couples lived in the same city, they did not know each other.

Both couples had children and were reasonably well off financially. Each couple was admired by their friends for having solid marriages. Their children did well in school; the couples were active in their respective religious groups, and they both had supportive family networks.

As nearly as anyone else could tell, they were perfect couples. Things were not going as well, however, in the privacy of their homes. The two couples grew increasingly quarrelsome with each other. The couples still did not know each other, but their situations were similar.

Kallia and Jarrad finally decided that they had better get some help or their marriage would be in trouble. They finally found a marriage counselor who would see them on Sunday, which was about the only time they had free. They could drop their kids off at Sunday school and see the therapist.

After their first tense session with the counselor, Kallia went outside and looked at the congregation leaving the church across the street. The families looked so close and so happy; the couples all seemed like they had no problems in the world. Kallia wished her marriage could be like those of the couples across the street. She admired them.

By coincidence, Lou and Marina were in the congregation across the street. Marina glanced at the counselor's office and saw a woman and man leaving. The couple looked troubled but sincere and determined. Marina wished she and Lou had the nerve to see a counselor about their troubled marriage, like that couple did. She admired them.

Which couple is more likely to improve their marriage?

Even if you love someone, getting used to living with him or her is a major life adjustment. Issues of decision making and power must be worked out, and a variety of role relationships must be developed.

Marital quality can be defined and measured in a variety of ways. While all couples would like to have happy, satisfying, and stable marriages, several factors decrease the chances that they will do so.

Throughout a marriage, there are a number of developmental challenges that must be faced. Couples continually develop and renegotiate their scripts as they live out their marriages.

> **Thinking Ahead** How much independence do you think husbands and wives should have from each other? Which partner, if either, should have the final say in such matters as how to raise children, purchasing new furniture, or where to live? If you think they should have equal say, how will the matter get resolved when they disagree? Says who? How can you measure whether a marriage is good or bad?

The fact that we can find an institution in all societies that we can call marriage does not necessarily mean that the institution has the same meaning for all the participants. Meanings change as societies change.

From the range of roles available in a particular societal script, couples construct their own mutual marital scripts, making each family somewhat different from others (Edgar & Glezer, 1994). This chapter will focus primarily on the husband-wife dyad. [...]

Changing Meanings of Marriage

A wedding creates a marriage between a bride and a groom. These two partners are now legitimately called husband and wife. While both the newlyweds and the community understand that their roles are to change, exactly what those new roles will be varies by time and place.

A wedding finalizes a type of contract, not only between the bride and groom but also among members of their extended families and the entire community. All agree to change their role expectations in accord with the socially acceptable meanings associated with marriage. In late agrarian European societies, for example, young persons who were not married were not supposed to engage in sexual intercourse. After the wedding ceremony, however, it was virtually required that they do so because of strong pronatalist expectations.

Changes in modes of production have brought different ways of enforcing the marriage contract. In hunting-gathering societies, the contractual expectations were informal and were generally enforced by the extended families of the husband and wife. Agrarian societies added the strong influence of religious institutions, some extrafamilial political control, and community sanctions. While such forces continue to operate in industrial and postindustrial societies, the marital contract has become increasingly formalized and enforced by courts and other facets of the political institution.

In many aspects of their married lives, couples are considerably freer from social control now than was the case earlier in American history. Informal controls have weakened, and political laws do not regulate details of everyday married life. As a consequence, the dynamics of marriage have changed. These changes can be illustrated by use of the gender-role continuum that was introduced in chapter 1 (see Figure 8.1).

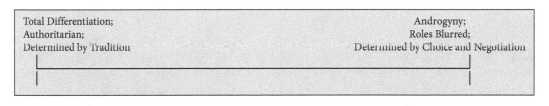

Total Differentiation;	Androgyny;
Authoritarian;	Roles Blurred;
Determined by Tradition	Determined by Choice and Negotiation

FIGURE 8.1 Gender role continuum

Source: Adapted from Adams, Bert N. 1995. *The Family: A Sociological Interpretation*. Fort Worth: Harcourt Brace. Page 108.

As the left extreme of the gender-role continuum indicates, the wedding ceremony in traditional societies carried with it a relatively complete set of instructions about the role relationship between the husband and wife. Couples reached agreement about their roles on the basis of **spontaneous consensus** rather than by discussion and negotiation (Fox, 1974; Scanzoni, 1979). In such a traditional marriage, the parties never discussed the division of labor that might assign home care tasks such as cooking to the woman, and provider tasks like earning a living to the man. Yet this might be what the marriage contract calls for. It was simply assumed that the husband and wife would behave in accord with the expected division of labor.

> **Spontaneous consensus:** Agreement arrived at without consideration by the parties involved, based on commonly held assumptions that are often derived from tradition.

As laws replaced community pressure, the normative marital expectations were sometimes formalized as part of the legal system. The doctrine of *coverture* [...] which assigned responsibility of property ownership to the husband and deprived married women of the right to own many kinds of property, was once part of the Western marital legal contract.

In the United States and other postindustrial societies, the gender-biased expectations of marriage have largely been removed from the legal system. Informal expectations, partly perpetuated by religious beliefs, still have influence, but fewer and fewer role decisions are based on spontaneous consensus. Instead, as there is movement toward the right-hand side of the gender-role continuum, wives and husbands increasingly negotiate their decisions. The gender-role distinctions are increasingly blurred and unclear.

Conjugal Power

Family power has long been of interest to social scientists. We will look at some early sociological perspectives on the topic, then move to more current definitions, measurements, and theories about power.

Family Power and Early Sociology

The changes brought about by industrialization, including those involving conjugal power, were a major topic for 19th-century social theorists. In 1855, the French sociologist Frederic Le Play wrote about what he saw as a rapid decline of the traditional, male-dominated peasant family. He called on the French government to adopt policies that would shore up the patriarchal stem family form.

In 1884, Friedrich Engels argued that the first historical class conflict resulted from the power gained by men over women in the monogamous family. In his view, only the communist revolution would finally enable women to have equal power with men.

Max Weber defined **power** as "the probability that one actor within a social relationship will be in a position to carry out his own will despite resistance" (1925/1964:152). The "probability" part of the definition implies that a powerful person need not always exercise power and might not always be successful at getting his or her own way. If the probability is high, however, power is high.

There has been debate about whether overcoming resistance is an essential component of power. If a wife wants her husband to go to a church service with her, and he does so rather than watching a football game, she got her way. If he actually wanted to go to church and was just waiting to be asked, there was no resistance. By Weber's definition, no power was exerted. On the other hand, the husband might have "wanted to" only because the wife talked him into it. In this case, it could be argued that she had power even though there was no overt resistance.

Alternately, he might have worked out a deal that he would go with her to church if she would watch a later game with him. Now do both have the power, or one more than another, or is it a situation in which both win?

Weber distinguished between **illegitimate power,** which is exercised without permission of the governed or any institutional approval, and *legitimate power* or **authority**. Illegitimate power typically involves force, coercion, or threat, while legitimate power operates in ways that are considered socially acceptable.

Weber was primarily addressing the issue of political power at the macrosocial level, but his distinctions have relevance to the issue of **conjugal power.** If the husband uses force or threat of force to get his favorite dinner, for example, this would be a form of illegitimate power. Other concepts related to power are useful at both the macro and micro levels. Someone with **influence** does not have authority to make the actual decision but can help sway the outcome. At the conjugal level, even if the husband and wife both agree that the husband should make the final decision about what kind of car to buy, the wife can strongly influence the choice.

In spite of considerable theoretical speculation about conjugal power, there were few attempts precisely to define and measure it until the work of Robert O. Blood Jr. and Donald M. Wolfe in the late 1950s. Although their research method has been criticized, they made a major contribution to the study of family power (see Finding Out 8.1).

Power: The probability that one actor within a social relationship will be in a position to carry out his or her own will [despite resistance] (Weber). **Illegitimate power:** Power exercised without the consent of the governed, or in socially unapproved ways, usually by coercion. **Authority:** Power exercised in socially approved ways; legitimate power. **Conjugal power:** The ability of spouses to affect each other's behavior. **Influence:** The ability to shape the thinking and behavior of a decision maker.

Resource Theory

Social exchange theory […], originally developed by George C. Homans (1961) and Peter Blau (1964) to explain social interaction in general, has been applied to issues of marital power and decision making. A key assumption of the perspective is that humans seek to maximize their own rewards and seek relationships that help them do that. Consideration of resources is an important component of the mate-selection process […].

As individuals interact, they develop a sense of trust and abide by a "norm of reciprocity," which prescribes that favors be repaid (Gouldner, 1960). Some sense of equity is established whereby each party to the agreement believes he or she is receiving a fair deal.

Ability to influence others is dependent, in part, on the resources available to reward compliance. The resources might be money, ownership of goods, knowledge, providing services, or even love. If the resources are unequal between the partners, power differences might develop that favor the partner with the most resources. An early application of this perspective was the development of Waller's (1951) "principle of least interest." Among the dating couples he observed, the person most committed to the relationship had the least power. The least-committed person used the other's love as a resource in the social exchange between the two.

Rather than consider emotions, Blood and Wolfe looked at income and social status as resources that could be used to gain power in a marriage. This "resource theory of marital power" has since been widely tested. While Blood and Wolfe found that power was associated with resources such as occupation, educational level, income, and age, other studies have found more complicated, and even contradictory, results (Brinkerhoff & Lupri, 1992;

FINDING OUT 8.1 *BLOOD AND WOLFE'S STUDIES OF CONJUGAL POWER*

All contemporary studies of conjugal power acknowledge their debt to the pioneering work of Blood and Wolfe, published in 1960 as *Husbands and Wives: The Dynamics of Married Living*. Their study brought representative survey research to the study of the family and developed the resource theory that remains a cornerstone of thinking about marital power (Szinovacz, 2000).

Blood and Wolfe believed that, by the late 1950s, American marriages had moved so far in the direction of egalitarianism that traditional patriarchal norms no longer determined the distribution of conjugal power. To test their views, they developed a measure of power that they used to collect data from a sample of 731 urban wives and 178 farm wives in greater Detroit. They asked each wife who made the final decision in each of eight areas of married life.

On each item, respondents were given five choices, each of which was assigned a point value: husband always (5 points); husband more than wife (4 points); husband and wife exactly the same (3 points); wife more than husband (2 points); and wife always (1 point). Each couple, then, had a score ranging from 8 (1 point on each question) to 40 (5 points on each question). This was their "relative authority score." For the entire sample, the relative authority score averaged 26.08, or 3.26 per question. A score of 24, or 3.00 per question, would have been exactly egalitarian. Less than one-half of 1% of husbands made the final decision in all eight areas (a score of 40), and about the same portion of wives made the final decision in all areas (a score of 8).

The following questions, along with their aggregate relative authority scores, were given in order from most to least husband authority (Blood & Wolf, 1960:21).

Who usually makes the final decision about:

What job the husband should take (4.86);

What car to buy (4.18);

Whether or not to buy some life insurance (3.50);

Where to go on a vacation (3.12);

What house or apartment to take (2.94);

Whether or not the wife should go to work or quit work (2.69);

What doctor to have when someone is sick (2.53);

How much money your family can afford to spend per week on food (2.26).

In addition to the relative authority score, Blood and Wolfe also calculated a "shared authority score" for each couple. This score was determined by the number of times the option "husband and wife exactly the same" was chosen. This score could range from 0, with no egalitarian choices, to 8, where egalitarian decision making was used in all areas.

Using a combination of the "relative authority score" and the "shared authority score," each couple could be assigned to one of four categories of conjugal power (Gelles, 1995):

1. *Wife Dominant.* The wife had greater decision making authority if the relative authority score was less than 19.
2. *Husband Dominant.* The husband had greater decision-making authority if the relative authority score was over 28.
3. *Syncratic.* This style was relatively egalitarian and had considerable shared decision making. The relative authority score was between 20 and 28 while the shared authority score was 4 or more.
4. *Autonomic.* This style was also relatively egalitarian but differed from the syncratic style in that husband and wife each had areas in which they had more authority, but the couple had few decisions that were made together. The relative authority score was between 20 and 28, while the shared authority score was 3 or less.

As Blood and Wolfe predicted, most couples (71%) had one of the relatively egalitarian styles. There were, however, more couples in the "husband dominant" category (25%) than in the "wife dominant" classification (3%). To conclude "men have more marital power than women" did not mean that all, or even most, husbands had more power than their wives; 75% did not. Instead, the conclusion means that, when there was a power difference between husbands and wives, it was much more likely to be in favor of the husband.

Since they rejected the idea that patriarchal norms determined power, Blood and Wolfe explained the discrepancy between husband-and wife-dominant marriages by using the "resource theory" of power. They found that husbands who had the most resources, such as money, education, and status, tended to have the most decision-making authority. Similarly, wives who were in the paid labor force were likely to have more power than those who were not. Controlling resources provided a power base.

Although it is still referred to in the literature on family power, Blood and Wolfe's study has been severely criticized from several perspectives. The survey approach itself has been questioned as a way of studying marital power. A second set of criticisms relates to the specific survey approach used by Blood and Wolfe. In their study, and in most follow-up studies, only wives were asked about decision making in their marriages. Other studies have found that, when both husbands and wives are asked, they provide significantly different reports (Safilios-Rothschild, 1969; Cromwell & Cromwell, 1978).

Another concern with the method used by Blood and Wolfe is the number and type of questions used to indicate decision-making processes. They used only eight specific issues, which might not be indicative of the full range of variables in the actual interactions of married couples. The specific issues about which respondents are asked can make a difference in the outcome.

Finally, Blood and Wolfe have been criticized on the grounds that their measure directly concerns decision making, not power, and the two things might not be the same. Some definitions of power require an element of overcoming resistance. On the other hand, Blood and Wolfe generally referred in their study to "authority," as a kind of power in which the wife might not like the outcome, but does not reject the right of the husband to make that decision. In their interviews, most respondents in the Blood and Wolfe study reported that, even when one party makes the "final decision," the other party usually agrees. In other words, agreement has somehow already been arrived at before the "final decision" is made.

Lamousé, 1969; Michel, 1967; Safilios-Rothschild, 1970). Rodman (1972) suggested that the resource model might work in an egalitarian family system, but not in a patriarchal society.

Rank (1982) found that women with high levels of income, education, and occupational prestige had more power in their marriages than women with low levels of such resources. This seems to confirm resource theory. For men, however, increases in resources were actually associated with less marital power. The explanation was that, in the United States, egalitarian norms are more commonly accepted among men in higher class positions.

Brinkerhoff and Lupri (1992) found a clear link between socioeconomic status and the type of egalitarian decision making. As education, occupation, and income of couples increased, a higher percentage of couples were characterized by autonomic rather than syncratic decision making. Rather than making decisions together, married individuals at high socioeconomic status levels were more likely to have independent but equal decision-making authority.

The Brinkerhof and Lupri (1992) results confirmed other studies finding that having more resources at her disposal does increase the wife's autonomous decision-making authority but add that husband's autonomy is increased as well. The joint decision making, as exemplified by the notion of "pooling" resources, is reduced.

Because they studied homosexual couples as well as heterosexual ones, Blumstein and Schwartz (1983) provided an interesting perspective on gender differences, resources, and power. Higher income was a better predictor of power holding in gay male couples than other types; the partner with the highest income had the most power. Among lesbian couples, perhaps because of a conscious effort to establish an egalitarian relationship, income imbalance did not affect the balance of power.

Married heterosexuals fell between the extremes. Husbands were rated more powerful in 33% of cases in which their incomes exceeded their wife's incomes by $8,000 or more. Husbands were more powerful in 18% of cases in which the income was about equal. When the wife's income exceeded her husband's by $8,000 or more, husbands were still rated more powerful in 15% of cases (Blumstein & Schwartz, 1983:54).

Gender-Based Conceptions of Power

The resource theory of power has been criticized from several perspectives. Feminists agree that control of resources influences power. They take exception, however, to Blood and Wolfe's assumptions that social structural variables are no longer relevant and that resources are individual matters (Gillespie, 1971; Glenn, 1987). Feminist scholars point out that men have greater access to high-paying jobs and high status positions in society. In addition, they argue that patriarchal norms still provide more authority to men in general and to husbands in particular. These structural variables give men, by virtue of being born male, resources and power in marriage. Some of this power is invisible. When husbands and wives know each other's answer to particular questions, wives are more likely to conform to their husbands' opinions than vice-versa. Even when it appears that agreement was negotiated, the husbands may have an advantage (Zipp, Prohaska, & Bemiller, 2004). The result is gender inequity.

Other researchers have pointed out that, in the context of social exchange and resource theory, equity and equality are different concepts and must be distinguished from each other (Cate et al., 1982). An exchange might be considered equitable, or fair, in spite of the fact that exactly equal amounts of each type of reward are not provided to each participant. One partner might get more access to leisure time, for example, while the other gets more access to spending money.

Wives spend considerably more time doing housework than do husbands, even when wives are employed. Feminists see this as inequitable because the husband and wife are not doing exactly the same thing. Many couples might see the exchange as equitable, however, because the man is spending more time in paid labor, and the two activities offset each other [...].

Some gender researchers have pointed out that, when role expectations are different, power might be approached in different ways. Lipmen-Blumen (1984) concluded that oppression by men in the public sphere of life resulted in the development of different power strategies by women in the private sphere. Called "micromanipulation," women's strategy is a less direct form of power than that used by men and is based on the woman's superior interpersonal skills. Women might learn to behave as if they are maintaining the husband-dominated definition of marital power, while circumventing, influencing, and subverting that power in interpersonal interaction.

This might help explain why wives report overall satisfaction with their marital role structure in spite of the appearance that men have more power (Biernat & Wortman, 1991; Major, 1993). It might also help explain why men often do not feel like they have the power in relationships (Cancian, 1989; Farrell, 1993).

We discussed Cancian's concept of "feminization of love" in chapter 8. As a counterpart to that concept, Kranichfeld (1987) derived the "masculinization of power." She argued that the resource theory has defined and measured power in a male-biased way by focusing on resources that have traditionally been associated with men. Women have tremendous power over socialization of children and over the kin-keeping role that binds generations of families together. Kranichfeld pointed out that this kind of power has received little attention in the research literature; the result has been the inaccurate image that women are powerless.

From this perspective, it might not be true that employed women, or women with more income, have more power than full-time family workers. Instead, the employed woman's power base and style would be more similar to a man's, and she would appear more powerful by the measures and definitions currently in use. At the same time, the employed wife risks losing her traditionally feminine power base and style.

Little research has been done on the "selection factor" and marital power. The kinds of resources thought to bring power, especially money, status, and age, are precisely the kinds of resources women have traditionally looked for in the process of mate selection [...]. In effect, women choose men who, by standard measures, are likely to develop more power than they themselves will. A complete exchange theory would look at the characteristics women possess that make them desirable and presumably serve as their power base.

Human Capital and Empowerment Theories

The human capital analysis of marriage overlaps both functionalism and resource theory. Gary Becker (1991), the major proponent of this perspective, argued that specialization is more efficient in the family, just as it is in corporations and government. It is a rational choice by couples to maximize their combined rewards by specializing in different activities.

Becker argued that the traditional division of labor maximized rewards from the human capital invested in both household/family labor and wage labor. Wives specialized in family activities partly because biology made them more efficient feeders and tenders of children and because they received less reward from the paid labor force. This left the husband to dedicate himself to maximizing the reward from paid labor. When the couple attempted to develop a parallel role script, both household and paid labor suffered.

Using mathematic models to determine optimum efficiency, Becker concluded that, even in a society that provided truly equal opportunities for men and women, couples would specialize. Although some mixture of roles is efficient, the maximum reward occurs when one partner focuses primarily on wage labor and the other primarily on family work. The primary worker is therefore able to work overtime, to advance in a career more rapidly, and to move to a better job if necessary. The primary family worker can better organize the household, prepare meals more efficiently, and be available to take care of child emergencies. Even in an equal-opportunity society, the primary income earner would still make more money than the primary family worker, and the distribution of decision making would still be affected by the division of labor. It would not necessarily be the case, however, that the roles would always be determined by gender.

In an effort to reformulate the concept of conjugal power, Jack O. Balswick and Judith K. Balswick (1995) proposed an "empowerment model." They pointed out that most theories assume that power is a matter of winners and losers; if one person is to get his or her way, the other person fails to get his or her way. Conjugal power, however, can be viewed as a process in which each partner uses resources to increase the resources of the other partner. Rather than viewing relationships as a series of *quid pro quo* (one thing for another) exchanges, this perspective assumes that relationships can be seen as a condition in which both partners are mutually enhanced.

With the empowerment perspective, home-related tasks can take on a greater value. Cooking nutritious and delicious meals improves life for all family members—and the person doing the cooking can receive the reward of knowing he or she is providing a benefit that does not reduce either partner's power. Likewise with other tasks that families do with and for each other. All are empowered when all are helping.

Another attempt to reformulate questions of power and equity makes a distinction between the "justice perspective" and the "care perspective" (Gilligan, 1982; Noddings, 1984; Thompson, 1991; Giles-Sims, 1994). These theorists associate most traditional analysis with the justice principle, with focus on autonomy, self-interest, rational thoughts, and abstract standards of rights and justice. Such attributes are traditionally associated with men.

The "care perspective," in contrast, sees justice as derived from interactions that meet one's own and one's family's needs through cooperation and empathy in a particular context. The "care perspective" emphasizes elements of mutual script maintenance such as nurturing, understanding, and interdependence. These attributes are more commonly associated with women (Giles-Sims, 1994).

Marital Roles and Scripts

As society moves from rigid, traditional role expectations to egalitarian, negotiated relationships, the individuals involved must make an increasing number of the decisions. Several different role relationships need to be constructed, using communication and negotiation skills that were not as necessary before the postindustrial era. As couples establish these roles, they construct a mutual script that guides various areas of their relationship.

Couple Role Relationships

[...] couples construct a sexual script for themselves. Each person draws on the societal script and his or her own experiences to construct individual scripts. Two such scripts come together in scenes by which couples develop a mutual script that has features unique to that couple.

A Role Typology It is not only in the sexual sphere that this process occurs. Nye (1976), along with Bahr, Chappell, and Leigh (1983), developed a typology of eight family roles that couples must consider in scripting their marriage:

+ *The housekeeper role* includes both management and task aspects of running a household, from meal planning and deciding on cleanliness standards to doing laundry and tidying the house (Mederer, 1993).
+ *The provider role* focuses on supplying the money and material goods necessary to support the family.
+ *The sexual role* involves satisfaction of the sexual wants of the couple.
+ *The kinship role*, also called the kin-keeper role, maintains the place of the couple's nuclear family in a network of extended families.
+ *The recreational role* involves the leisure activities of the couple.
+ *The therapeutic role* deals with emotional and instrumental needs of the couple, providing sympathy, understanding, and advice.
+ *The child-care role* is primarily involved with the physical care of children, including feeding, bathing, and protecting infants and young children.
+ *The child-socialization role* involves the responsibility of instilling the values, attitudes, skills, and behaviors required by the children for success in society at large.

Important additions to Nye's list of role relationships are the *religious role*, which includes the responsibility for formal and informal religious practices, and the *friendship role*, which locates the couple in a network of extrafamilial social relationships. (See Figure 8.2 for a pictorial summary of all ten marital role relationships.)

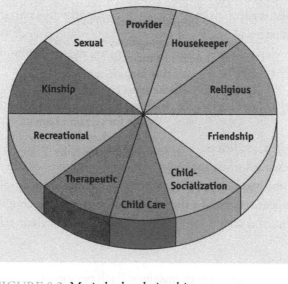

FIGURE 8.2 Marital role relationships

Not all couples are involved in the child-care and child-socialization roles, and some do not make religion part of their role set, but these three roles can be of major importance in other marriages. All couples must deal with the other roles in one way or another. [...]

The Provider and Kinship Roles [...] couples incorporate the provider and housekeeper roles into their relationships. The options ranged from completely complementary ones, in which each person performed a specific role, to completely parallel ones, in which the two were essentially interchangeable.

The provider and housekeeper roles interact in several ways. Money has to be brought into the household, but decisions about how to spend the money also need to be made. Pahl (1989) found five major distributive systems used by couples:

* *The female whole wage system* gives wives sole responsibility for household finances. The husbands hand over all of their wages, except perhaps a personal allowance, to their wives.
* *The male whole wage system* is the reverse of the female whole wage system. If the wife has no independent income, she may or may not receive a personal allowance. Very few couples use this system (Vogler & Pahl, 1994).
* *The housekeeping allowance system* is the second most common system. The husband, who brings in all or nearly all of the money, turns over a fixed amount of money to the wife for specified household expenses. He pays for other items out of his share, which includes his personal spending money. To the extent that the wife has personal spending money, it is the amount she might be able to save from the household expenses account.
* *The independent management system* is relatively rare, but it might be increasing in popularity, especially for couples that include remarried individuals. It is probably the most common system for cohabiting couples. Each partner has an independent income and is responsible for certain expenses. They typically have separate checking and savings accounts but sometimes shift money back and forth between them.
* *The pooling system* is the most common, found in over half of a large sample of British couples (Vogler & Pahl, 1994). The partners pool their resources, usually by a joint checking account, and each has access to the pool. Decision making tends to be egalitarian. Vogler and Pahl further divided their sample into a male-managed pool, a female-managed pool, and a joint pool. The joint pool included about 20% of all couples, while the male-managed and female-managed types included about 15% of couples each.

Vogler and Pahl (1994) found that joint control over pooled resources was associated with the most egalitarian decision making and with the smallest difference between the amount of personal spending money for husbands and wives. The housekeeping allowance system resulted in the greatest discrepancy in personal spending money.

It is not clear exactly how couples decide which financial allocation style to use. When wives have independent incomes, the couple is more likely to use one of the pooled systems or the independent management system. Blumstein and Schwartz (1983) found that wives were slightly less likely to favor pooling. The explanation was that it has long been part of the provider role that the man turn over his earnings to the family. Women are less likely to be socialized to the provider role, so they are more likely to believe that the money they personally earn should fall outside the joint account.

The Recreation Role The issue of independence is also relevant to the recreation role. Orthner (1975) investigated the amount of time couples spent in each of three kinds of recreational activities:

+ *Individual activities,* such as reading books or taking solitary walks do not involve interaction with others and might even discourage togetherness.
+ *Joint activities* require active participation with others. Playing card games and taking weekend trips together are examples.
+ *Parallel activities,* while being done with another person, do not require significant interaction. Watching television or listening to music can be like individual activities done in the company of others.

The distinction is not the activity itself; listening to music or walking can be a joint activity. The important difference is in the amount of interaction. All three types of recreation can provide benefits to individuals and families. Orthner (1975) found particular benefits from joint activities because they encourage communication between partners.

The Therapeutic Role Good communication is a key component of the therapeutic role. Perhaps more than any of the role issues, the importance of the therapeutic role has increased in the postindustrial marriage. Partners in the modern "companionate marriage" (Blood & Wolfe, 1960) are expected to be friends with each other. They are expected to understand each other's problems and provide empathy, reassurance, and affection. Since 1970, hundreds of marital advice books have stressed the importance of marital communication, providing suggestions on how to listen and talk to each other. The theme of such books has been that therapeutic communication is particularly a problem for men who have been socialized into instrumental rather than expressive roles. Although there are inconsistent results, most studies find that women are somewhat better at self-disclosing, picking up nonverbal clues, empathizing, and listening (Basow, 1992). All of these qualities are important to the therapeutic role.

Constructing Postindustrial Marital Scripts

Constructing a marriage today involves an extraordinary number of adjustments and redefinitions of reality, many of which are never consciously addressed by the participants. Individuals receive images of marriage from a variety of sources including their own parents, other relatives, their religion, friends, and the media. These images must be reconciled with the images held by their partners as the two construct their own scripts for marriage.

Even during courtship, couples begin to agree to "secret contracts" about how they would behave during marriage and how they would expect their partner to behave (Stuart & Jacobson, 1985). These tacit agreements are often based on idealized images of each other and of marriage itself. After they marry, the couple cooperate in the construction of a marital reality of their own (Berger & Kellner, 1964). During their first year of marriage, successful couples are likely to tell each other stories about their courtship. These recollections help to construct a couple-based view of the world that increases the stability of the relationship (Orbuch, Veroff, & Holmberg, 1993). A vast variety of matters must be negotiated and made real for the couple (see Highlight 8.1).

Berger and Kellner (1964) use an example from the friendship role to illustrate their point that individuals revise their definitions of reality in favor of a mutually constructed, marital definition of the situation. It usually happens that each married partner gradually interacts less and less with persons who were good friends prior to the marriage. Each person begins to look at former friends through the eyes of his or her spouse. Gradually, the couple will begin to interact with other married dyads rather than with single former "best friends."

Berger and Zellner argue that the negotiation of a shared reality takes place almost automatically, extending not only into the future but into the past as well. In effect, the past is changed because it is seen through the newly created marital lens. Some events become more important, some less so, and the meaning of others is altered. An event that might once have been seen as "a good time" can become "an irresponsible act." Meanings are continually negotiated as a couple cooperates to construct a life together.

Generalized Mutual Scripts

Couples do not take each new day and each event as a totally new phenomenon; they give it meaning in accord with the generalized marital script they have developed over time. [...] the most important element of the sexual script is the "why" of the script. The same might be said for the typology, developed by Cuber and Harroff (1965), of more general marital scripts. They found two basic marriage types, **intrinsic marriages** and **utilitarian marriages,** each of which has subtypes.

Intrinsic marriages exist for the love and intimacy they provide to the partners. This type of marriage, which has both vital and total varieties, is a relatively recent historical ideal.

Vital marriages are, as the term implies, full of life; the word *vital* comes from the Latin *vita*, meaning "life." The recreational script of these couples includes considerable joint activity, but it is the togetherness rather than the activity itself that provides the pleasure. Genuine sharing and excitement in their relationship supplies the central meaning in life for both of them. Similarities rather than differences between the two are emphasized, and when conflict does occur it tends to be settled quickly and without lasting rancor.

Total marriages are like vital marriages except that there are even more areas of sharing. In these rare marriages, all possible activities are joint. If they do not actually work together, they share their work extensively by talking to each other, having lunch together, and traveling together when possible. It is as if the two partners do not have, nor ever had, a truly separate existence. Infidelity would be virtually unthinkable for these couples. Although the matter has not been studied, partners in total marriages probably file more detailed flight plans than other couples but have the plans challenged less often.

Utilitarian marriages exist for economic cooperation, maintaining the extended family line, establishing alliances among *familia*, or other purposes not related to couple intimacy. Until the late industrial period, most marriages were of this type. Cuber and Harroff (1965) found three varieties among contemporary utilitarian couples: conflict habituated, devitalized, and passive-congenial.

Conflict-habituated marriages are a utilitarian type in which the purpose seems to be tension and conflict. A central theme of these marriages is to control and channel the conflict, which rarely exhibits itself in public. It largely consists of verbal arguments, some of which provide running battles for the duration of the marriage. Although it is negative, there is a high energy level in these relationships that might be missed by a partner who got into a more passive, less conflicted, relationship.

Devitalized marriages were once intrinsic but have lost their spirit. Most marriages change over time, but in these there is a clear discrepancy between young marriage expectations and the middle-aged reality. The marriage still serves as a base of operations for each partner, and the couple have their children or other memories. Although the partners sometimes miss the earlier intimacy, they largely accept the changes without developing strong antagonisms.

Passive-congenial marriages are similar to devitalized marriages except that there never was a strong emotional component. Congenial means having similar tastes and habits or being friendly and sociable. Although there is little strong emotion in these relationships, there is also little conflict. This style fits well with dual-career or parallel kinds of marriages.

HIGHLIGHT 8.1 *NEGOTIATING FLIGHT PLANS*

Married couples have a host of major issues with which to deal: handling finances, the division of power and labor in the household, having and raising children, how frequently and in what ways to make love, and what kind of relationships to have with in-laws. In addition to these issues is a dazzling array of decisions about how to go about living together day to day.

Often a set of rules is gradually established about how to handle a particular matter, then there is constant monitoring to see if the rules are followed or if they need to be changed. One such issue could be called the "filing of flight plans."

Before they take off, airplane pilots file a flight plan that indicates their destination, route, and projected time of arrival. If they do not arrive at their destination, rescuers will have some idea about where to begin a search. If they do not arrive roughly when they plan to, they might be asked to account for their tardiness.

Family members file "flight plans" with each other, following a set of rules that they negotiate, often without consciously talking about the rules. One rule prescribes the occasions on which filing a plan is expected. If a husband is simply going outside to pick up the newspaper, he may or may not be expected to file a verbal plan by saying, "I think I'll go get the newspaper." If he is going shopping, he probably will have to let his wife know, especially if she is home when he leaves. If she is not, he might or might not be expected to file a written flight plan in the form of a note on the refrigerator or other predetermined location. Over time, couples develop unspoken norms that are taken for granted but that were initially problematic. The husband might have found out that he was expected to file a flight plan only after he got back from the store one day and was questioned regarding his whereabouts. After that, he filed a flight plan to avoid a disruption in the couple's definition of their marriage as cooperative and happy.

Another issue deals with the length of time covered by particular flight plans. If the wife files a "go to the store" flight plan, and returns in the normative time, her absence will not be questioned. If she returns six hours later, she will probably be expected to provide an account for her long absence by filing an amended flight plan explaining what took her so long. A new set of procedures for filing amended plans via telephone might be instituted. Anytime an account is called for, it is an indication that expectations have not been met (Scott & Lyman, 1968). The result will be negotiation about whether the account will be honored, and perhaps a questioning of the expectation itself.

Another issue is the specificity expected of the flight plan. Some couples expect an almost minute-by-minute, detailed plan: "I'm going to the dentist for a check-up, then I'll drop the cleaning off, then to the mall to look for shoes, then to the post office to buy stamps, then . . ."; for other couples, a loose "I'll be gone all afternoon" will suffice.

Finally, there is the issue of "debriefings," or discussions after the event is over. In some cases, discussion is neither offered nor expected. At other times, the traveling partner is expected to indicate whether the original flight plan was followed exactly or if there were any changes not already noticed.

The husband and wife are not the only family members to file flight plans. Children must also learn the flight plan rules of their family, which change regularly as the child gets older. Flight plans, like other aspects of mutual scripts, are never finally settled, but continue to be changed and negotiated throughout the life of the relationship.

Cuber and Harroff (1965) did not claim that all marriages, even among the upper-class couples they studied, fit clearly into one of their five types. There are borderline cases, and couples can move from one type to another over time. Cuber and Harroff stressed, too, that they did not see any one type as superior to any other or that the participants of any type are more or less happy than other types. None of the couples they used for their typology had ever seriously considered divorce, even the conflict-habituated ones.

> **Intrinsic marriages:** Marriages with the "why" of maintaining the intimacy of the relationship between husband and wife. **Utilitarian marriages:** Marriages with a "why" other than intimate expression; a marriage of convenience for economic or other reasons.

It is possible that, since divorce is much more common now than when they did their study, some of the "bad" marriages would be more likely to end and the "good" ones remain. We would not know that for sure, however, until we developed a valid way of determining what a good marriage is.

Marital Quality

We all know that some marriages seem very good, some seem very bad, and most seem somewhere in between. Family researchers are interested in finding valid ways of measuring the quality of marriages so that variables associated with good marriages can be found. This might help find ways to improve the quality of specific marriages or to help avoid bad marriages.

Measuring Marital Quality

Several concepts are related to measuring good marriages. One approach is to ask whether the partners in the marriage are **happy**. The root of the term relates to a matter of luck, as in mis*hap*, *happ*enstance, and *hap*hazard. This implies that happiness is not something that a person can aim directly for but is an accidental by-product of other phenomena.

To find the variables that are associated with happiness requires a way to measure the elusive concept. Typically, surveys are used to ask someone a question like, "Taken all together, how would you describe your marriage? Would you say your marriage is very happy, pretty happy, or not too happy?" (Davis & Smith, 1972–2002; Glenn & Weaver, 1977). Sometimes the happiness question is asked about one's life in general or one's job. It can also be asked about more specific aspects of marriage such as the household division of labor, the couple's sex life, or their financial situation. Another kind of variation is to word the answer differently, perhaps by having six categories ranging from "Extremely happy" to "Extremely unhappy."

> **Happy:** Characterized by good luck, pleasure, satisfaction, or joy. **Satisfaction:** Fulfillment of a desire, need, or appetite; contentment derived from having needs met. **Adjustment:** The act or means of adapting, corresponding, or conforming. **Stable:** Resistant to change, self-restoring, consistently dependable.

It is easy to think of happiness as something that varies from one person to another. There are, indeed, individual differences; some people just seem happier than others regardless of the position they are in. There are, however, differences based on the role and status of the individual.

Because the concept of happiness seems so elusive, some researchers prefer to ask about marital **satisfaction** instead. As used in surveys, the approach is basically identical except the word *satisfied* is substituted for *happy*. Even though the two words have slightly different meanings, they are often used interchangeably in the research. Both concepts tend to tap into the degree to which a person perceives his or her individual needs to be met in the marriage (Bahr, 1989).

Marital **adjustment** is both an ongoing process and an assessment of a marriage at a particular time. Although several measures preceded it, the best known measure is now the Dyadic Adjustment Scale developed by Graham B. Spanier (1976a), along with his colleagues Robert Lewis, Charles Cole, and Erik E. Filsinger (see Finding Out 8.2).

A final kind of measurement of marital quality is marital **stability** or instability, typically defined as a propensity to divorce. This might include serious contemplation of divorce, talking to friends about the possibility of divorce, or actually taking steps to get a divorce.

The least happy marriages are not necessarily the least stable. Udry (1981) found that a person's perception about marital alternatives was a better predictor of divorce than was marital dissatisfaction. A person in an unhappy marriage might stay with his or her partner if no alternative looks better, and one in a reasonably happy marriage might divorce if an even better alternative is seen. South and Lloyd (1985) tested this possibility using a large, nationwide sample. They found the highest risk of divorce where the husband or wife encountered an abundance of spousal alternatives. Increased labor force participation of women and high geographic mobility both increase marital instability.

Correlates of Quality: Identifying Marital Strengths
Several factors have affected changes in marital quality in the last few decades. Some of these have had a negative influence: increased marital heterogamy, increased premarital cohabitation, and increased job demands and work hours for women. Others may have increased marital satisfaction: increased economic resources, more equality in marital decision making, and more support for the norm of lifelong marriage. One factor in particular has had mixed

effects: increases in the husbands' share of housework have decreased the husbands' marital quality but increased that of their wives (Amato et al., 2003).

Although rates of marital happiness may have declined slightly since the early 1970s, American couples remain quite satisfied with their current marriage. When asked to characterize their marriage as "very happy," "pretty happy," or "not too happy," well over 60% now respond "very happy" (Davis & Smith, 2004). Men (62.9%) are slightly more likely to report "very happy" marriages than are women (60.6%), but only 2.8% of men and 4.6% of women said "not too happy" (Davis & Smith, 2004). These figures vary in ways that help determine correlates of quality.

[...] married men and women have greater happiness with their lives than any category of single people. In fact, marital status is a better predictor of overall life happiness than any other variable included in Table 8.1. Income is second as a predictor when other factors are held constant.

TABLE 8.1 Marital happiness and life happiness of married persons, by selected variables and gender, percent reporting "very happy"

Variable	Marital Happiness		Life Happiness	
	Men	Women	Men	Women
Family Income				
Lower Third	64.3	54.7	35.6	33.0
Middle Third	64.7	63.1	35.8	40.4
Upper Third	67.6	65.0	42.4	45.6
Educational Level				
Not High School Graduate	64.5	56.4	31.7	28.5
High School Graduate	65.4	63.4	30.1	33.2
College Graduate	67.2	65.3	32.6	36.1
Religions Affiliation				
Liberal Protestant	68.4	64.3	41.5	43.2
Conservative Protestant	66.2	61.0	40.1	41.3
Catholic	65.8	61.7	36.2	40.8
Jewish	68.4	67.4	41.3	42.9
None	55.3	57.9	30.7	32.3
Frequency of Attendance at Religious Services				
Never	57.6	58.7	32.7	37.8
Monthly-Yearly	64.0	59.0	35.3	36.6
Weekly	72.5	67.3	46.0	47.9
Age				

Under 30	65.5	67.3	32.9	40.2
30 to 49	63.1	60.4	35.9	40.0
50 and up	69.2	62.7	43.4	44.7
Race				
White	67.0	64.0	39.2	43.0
Black	53.5	46.1	29.1	27.2
Working Status, Self				
Full Time	64.8	61.5	37.7	40.0
Part Time	62.4	60.9	35.9	40.9
Unemployed	57.0	54.1	23.6	26.9
Retired	70.4	64.0	46.1	46.9
In School	64.6	56.6	38.6	40.9
Keeping House	63.9	62.9	31.3	42.3
Working Status, Spouse				
Full Time	63.3	63.7	37.4	42.0
Part Time	65.2	55.1	35.4	37.4
Unemployed	62.3	47.9	23.4	28.7
Retired	72.4	61.1	49.2	44.5
In School	65.2	68.9	34.9	38.8
Keeping House	66.9	54.3	39.2	36.5
Number of Children				
None	69.7	73.7	40.0	44.5
One or Two	64.4	61.6	37.8	41.9
Three or More	66.5	59.5	38.9	40.2
Overall:	65.9	62.5	38.6	41.6

Source: Davis, James Allan, and Tom W. Smith: General Social Survey(s), 72–02. (Machine-readable data file). Principal Investigator, James A. Davis; Director and Co-Principal Investigator, Tom W. Smith; Co-Principal Investigator, Peter V. Marsden, NORC ed. Chicago: National Opinion Research Center, producer, 1998; Storrs, CT: The Roper Center for Public Opinion Research, University of Connecticut, distributor. Microcomputer format and codebook prepared and distributed by MicroCase Corporation, Bellevue, Washington. Analysis by Gene H. Starbuck.

Many researchers have worked to find out what makes people happy in their marriages and their lives as a whole. Table 8.1 summarizes data about married Americans from the General Social Surveys (GSS). One clear finding is that married individuals are considerably happier with their marriages than with their lives in general. It also appears that, while men rate their marriages as slightly happier than do women, married women report

FINDING OUT 8.2 *THE DYADIC ADJUSTMENT SCALE*

Graham B. Spanier and others developed a widely used measurement of the quality of marriage and similar relationships. To develop their scale, they began with a set of 300 questions that could be asked of couples about their marriage. Researchers added some questions of their own and then got rid of duplicate questions and those that did not seem appropriate. This left a questionnaire with 225 items.

This set of questions was asked of a sample of 218 married persons in central Pennsylvania, as well as to every person who had gotten divorced in the same region in the preceding year. Answers were tabulated and scores for the married and divorced group were compared. Any questions that did not receive significantly different answers from the two groups were thrown out. A pool of 32 questions remained; these became the Dyadic Adjustment Scale.

Each question was tabulated as part of one of four separate dimensions of the overall scale:

- *Dyadic satisfaction* is measured by asking how often the couple quarrels, gets on each other's nerves, or confides in their mates, and generally how happy they are in their relationship.
- *Dyadic cohesion* measures the couple's feeling of togetherness. They are asked how often they have a stimulating exchange of ideas, laugh together, or calmly discuss something.
- *Dyadic consensus* asks how frequently the partners agree on such items as handling family finances, recreation, and religious matters.
- *Affectional expression* asks how frequently partners agree on demonstrations of affection and sex relations, and whether these matters have been a problem in the past two weeks.

Based on the answers to each of the 32 questions, an overall score, as well as a score for each of the four dimensions, can be calculated. These scores can then be associated with other questions asked by the researchers about such things as the couple's income, religion, how long they have been married, whether they have children, and a number of other issues. Well over 1,000 separate studies have been reported that used the Dyadic Adjustment scale to learn more about the quality of marriages.

Sources: **Dyadic** Adjustment Scale published in Graham B. Spanier, "Measuring Dyadic Adjustment: New Scales for Assessing the Quality of Marriage and Similar Dyads," *Journal of Marriage and the Family* 38 (1976):15–28.

This summary is based largely on a copy of the scale found in Delbert C. Miller, *Handbook of Research Design and Social Measurement*, 5th ed. Newbury Park, CA: Sage, 1991.

slightly happier lives than do their husbands. When particular couples are considered, however, virtually no difference exists in marital satisfaction between the husbands and wives (Kurdek, 2005).

The data in Table 8.1 reflect the association between other variables and happiness. This information is valuable, but it is not as sophisticated as other studies cited below and should be interpreted with some caution. We must also remember that correlation does not prove causality. We might assume, for example, that having more money "causes" people to be happier. This might be true, but it is also possible that happy people make more money, that is, happiness "causes" the income change. It could also be true that some other variable such as level of education "causes" both more income and more happiness

Socioeconomic Status Lower income and educational levels are generally related to lower rates of marital stability (i.e., more divorce), but the effect of money and social status on marital satisfaction is less clear. Although some studies find no relationship (Bahr et al., 1983; Nye & McLaughlin, 1982), others find a slight positive correlation between social status and marital satisfaction (Lewis & Spanier, 1979; Piotrokowski, Rapoport, & Rapoport, 1987). Unemployment is associated with both lower marital stability and lower marital satisfaction (Larson, 1984).

Conger et al. (1990) concluded that economic hardship could reduce warmth and supportive interaction which, in turn, reduces marital quality. In a longitudinal study, Conger et al. (1999) found that, over time, economic pressure predicts individual distress and marital conflict, which in turn predict marital distress. However, high marital support and effective couple problem solving reduced the negative effect of economic distress.

GSS results also find a correlation between family income and happiness. Higher incomes are associated with higher levels of both marital happiness and overall life happiness. These data also indicate that income appears to make more difference to women than it does to men. This might be a fruitful line of inquiry for future research. Education and income are clearly related variables and have a similar association with happiness. Education makes some difference, more for women than for men.

Race As with Whites, married Blacks have higher levels of happiness than single ones, although not as high as White marrieds (Taylor et al., 1991; Davis & Smith, 1998–2004). This is partly related to lower average levels of economic and educational resources, since Black couples with higher incomes have greater satisfaction with family life than do Black couples with low incomes (Staples, 1988). As a group, however, Blacks report experiencing more negative behaviors from their spouses and are more likely to report that the spouses have affairs, hit or push them, waste money, or do not make them feel loved (Broman, 2005).

Religion Religious beliefs and participation are associated with marital satisfaction. Couples who attend religious services regularly have higher levels of marital satisfaction and stability than those who do not identify with a religion (Heaton & Pratt, 1990). The causality is unclear. Religious beliefs and participation themselves might directly increase happiness in individuals. Since religious services are a form of social interaction, though, it might be the connection with a supportive group of like-minded individuals, more than the religious beliefs themselves, that improve satisfaction. It might also be true that religious participation does not increase happiness, but rather that happy people are more likely to attend gatherings such as religious services.

The GSS findings (Table 8.1) confirm the relationship between frequent involvement in religious activities and higher marital and life happiness. In addition, there appear to be only small denominational differences, except that persons with no religious affiliation have considerably lower happiness levels than those with an affiliation of some kind.

Most studies find that religious homogamy increases marital satisfaction (Heaton & Pratt, 1990). Such studies include persons with no religious preference who might be married to Christians or Jews. When only interdenominational intermarriages among Christians are considered, impact on marital satisfaction is weak or nonexistent (Williams & Lawler, 2003). Lower satisfaction with inter-religious marriages appears more likely among men than women, perhaps because children tend to be raised in the faith of the mother, which could reduce the father's interaction in the family (Shehan et al., 1990).

Class, Age, and Racial Homogamy As with religion, homogamous marriages of other types are generally characterized by higher quality, couple satisfaction, and stability than heterogamous ones (Lewis & Spanier, 1979). The association between social class heterogamy and marital satisfaction is difficult to research because social class is difficult to define and because hypergamy is an accepted part of the mate-selection process (Glenn, Hoppe, & Weiner, 1974). Large social class differences, however, can result in difficulties with in-laws, friends, and leisure interests.

Age seems to be an exception to the general rule about homogamy and marital quality. Large age difference between partners might create difficulties for some couples, but if so, the difference apparently creates offsetting strengths. Analysis of two large sets of data found no significant differences in marital quality as associated with age discrepancies of partners (Vera, Berardo, & Berardo, 1985).

Racial and ethnic heterogamy is more acceptable now, so they might not have as big an effect on marital quality as was once the case. Research in Hawaii found some evidence that mixed marriages were less stable but only under certain conditions and spousal combinations. Marriages in which the bride came from a higher income ethnic group than the groom, for example, were more likely to end in divorce than the reverse case (Ho & Johnson, 1990).

Carter and Glick (1976) looked at census data to determine how many of the marriages of the 1950s were still intact in 1970. Ninety percent of White-White marriages were intact, as were 78% of the Black-Black marriages. By contrast, 63% of Black husband–White wife marriages survived and only 47% of the White-husband Black wife couples were still together. Noting that survival rates of the marriage types are in order from most to least common, Reiss and Lee (1988) suggested that the survival rates reflect the differential in social support that each type receives. In the 1970s, at least, interracial couples faced difficulties of finding appropriate places of residence, lack of close emotional ties toward kin, and negative responses from the public (Golden, 1975). All of these factors can increase marital stress and reduce marital satisfaction.

Part of the difficulty faced by couples from different backgrounds is the possibility of a lack of **role consensus,** or agreement about how the various roles associated with marriage should be played. The greater the degree of role consensus, and the better each spouse meets the role expectations of the other, the better the marital quality (Bahr, Chappell, & Leigh, 1983; Burr, Leigh, Day, & Constantine, 1979). This remains true unless one or both partners base their expectations on socially prescribed perfectionism, in which case marital quality can suffer (Haring, Hewitt, & Flett, 2003). Mutual scripts are easier to construct and maintain if the two partners have similar assumptions about appropriate marital and familial roles. This general finding apparently applies to housekeeping, child socialization, and other marital roles mentioned earlier in this chapter.

> **Role consensus:** Agreement between actors about how a role should be played.

Work/Family Arrangements The entry of large numbers of women into the coprovider role in recent years has led to considerable research on the effect of this trend on family and individual satisfaction. One question was whether wives who were employed outside the home were happier than homemakers. A careful review of six large national studies found no evidence to support the popular assumption that women who worked outside their homes were generally happier and more satisfied with their lives (Wright, 1978). Instead, each option has costs and benefits, and the negative images of homemaking have been emphasized in the research (Eshleman, 1994). Shehan's (1984) study of the mental health of homemakers and wage workers found the majority of both groups to be "well off" psychologically, with no significant differences between the groups in terms of depression, health anxiety, or life satisfaction.

More detailed study, however, revealed that the woman's life goals affected the relationship between homemaking and life satisfaction. Homemakers who wanted careers were less satisfied with their lives than those who never wanted outside careers. Women without career aspirations, however, were happier in general than employed women (Townsend & Gurin, 1981). A review of studies compiled by Spitze (1988) found that the effect of women's employment on marriage and family depended on whether the work was full or part time, whether there were children, the ages of the couple, how long they had been married, their income, and several other factors.

According to the GSS, the most desirable work status, for both men and women, is "retired," while the least desirable is "unemployed." The effect of being in school, or having a spouse in school, is complex. Beyond that, it would appear that both husbands and wives are happiest when the husband works for pay full time and the wife is a housekeeper. Perhaps surprisingly, the few men who are housekeepers appear much happier about their situation than are the women whose husbands do the housekeeping.

The kind of job and amount of time a wife works has an impact on marital stability. In both postindustrial societies like the United States and less developed countries like Thailand, the more hours a wife works outside the home, the higher the rates of marital instability for some types of marriages (Greenstein, 1990; Edwards et al., 1992). Women who work in jobs that are not traditionally held by women have divorce rates almost twice that of women in more traditional positions. Women who make considerably more income than their husbands, and who hold professional jobs requiring advanced levels of education, have less stable marriages (South, 1985; Cooney & Uhlenberg, 1989; Houseknecht, Vaughn, & Macke, 1984).

Role consensus is difficult for couples to achieve in these situations, partially because they are departures from the traditional way of handling the provider role in marriage. Wives in the labor force reported higher marital quality if their husbands were less traditional (Vannoy-Hiller & Philliber, 1989). These attitudes apparently matched the role expectations of the less traditional women.

Quality is affected when gender-role attitudes change during the course of the marriage, according to a longitudinal study by Amato and Booth (1995) of 2,033 married individuals. Wives who developed less traditional attitudes over time believed that their marriage quality went down; they reported less happiness, less interaction, more disagreements, more problems, and higher divorce proneness. When husbands developed less traditional attitudes, however, their marital quality went up slightly. Perhaps increasing non-traditionalism by wives distances them from their husbands, making role consensus more difficult, while increasing nontraditionalism by men brings the couple's views closer together.

The division of labor in family work can also affect marital quality. How much housework is done, and by whom, may not have much impact; but whether the division of labor is considered fair can matter a good deal. If one or both partners believe the house and family work is unfair, the couple has lower overall marital satisfaction and a greater probability of divorce (Voydanoff & Donnelly, 1999; Kluwer, Heesink, & Van de Vliert, 1997). Perceived inequity has a greater impact on wives' dissatisfaction than on husbands' (Frisco & Williams, 2003).

Presence of Children Whether or not the childhood role is enacted makes a difference in marital quality. Women without children, in general, report higher levels of marital satisfaction than mothers (Polenko, Scanzoni, & Teachman, 1982). The GSS results (not shown) confirm that both men and women under 30 who have never had children report much higher levels of marital happiness than those who are parents. For women, this difference remains large throughout the life span. For men over 30, however, there is almost no difference in marital happiness between those who have fathered children and those who have not.

Voluntarily childfree women score especially high on the "marital cohesion" portion of the Dyadic Adjustment Scale. They report more outside interests, more work on projects with their husbands, more frequently having good exchanges of ideas, and more quiet discussions (Houseknecht, 1979).

Couples who do not yet have children, or those whose children have grown up and left home, have higher marital satisfaction than those with children currently in the home (Rollins & Feldman, 1970). Parenting stress negatively affects psychological well-being and perceived marital quality for both husbands and wives. Parenting stress increases as numbers of children increase and as economic problems grow. The household division of labor and whether the wife works or not do not appear to affect parenting stress (Lavee, Sharlin, & Katz, 1996).

On the other hand, the presence of preschool children in the home does have at least a temporary effect on marital stability (Bradbury et al., 2000). Couples with very young children rarely get divorced. They will apparently suffer higher levels of marital unhappiness before they end a marriage than will childfree couples (White & Booth, 1985). Among elderly couples, those who had children reported significantly greater satisfaction with family life, an association particularly strong for women (Singh & Williams, 1981; Greil, Leitke, & Porter, 1988).

Communication, Support, and Sexuality Good communication, both in the therapeutic role and for purposes of negotiating marital roles, is strongly related to marital quality. A review of 20 years of research found that several aspects of communication are associated with high marital satisfaction: higher rates of self-disclosure, expression of love, support and affection, laughter and positive nonverbal communication involving good listening skills and body posture (Boland & Follingstad, 1987). Research specifically on Black couples has reached similar conclusions (Thomas, 1990). When the conflict management style is collaborative rather than competitive, marital happiness is higher (Greef & de Bruyne, 2000).

It is not completely clear whether good communication skills "cause" happy marriages or whether the happy marriages result in good communication. There is some evidence that teaching good communication skills such as self-disclosure to couples can increase the perceived intimacy of their marriages (Waring, Schaefer, & Fry, 1994).

Marital success is associated with the support each partner gives the other in nonmarital matters. This might be particularly true with dual-working couples, who like to see their partner as someone who can support them in their work activities and feelings (Bradbury et al., 2000). When a person turns to a friend, negative feeling about the relationship might actually increase, especially if the friend makes negative comments about the relationship. When individuals believe that their social network is positive about their relationship, however, relationship happiness is higher (Bryant & Conger, 1999; Julien et al., 1994). Wives' marital satisfaction appears to be more affected by their social support than does husbands' (Acitelli & Antonucci, 1994).

The communication that arises from joint leisure activities is important to marital satisfaction (Orthner, 1975). The relationship between shared leisure and good marriages depends, however, on how well each individual enjoys the activity. If one partner dislikes the activity but participates just "for the sake of the couple," marital satisfaction is likely to suffer (Crawford et al., 2002).

Joint decision making and egalitarian communication styles are associated with higher levels of marital satisfaction. Of the nonegalitarian styles, wife-dominant marriages are less happy than husband-dominant ones, especially for women (Olson & DeFrain, 1994).

The sexual role is important to marital quality. Blumstein and Schwartz (1983) concluded that a good sex life is central to marital satisfaction. For people in the same age group, sexual frequency is strongly correlated with marital happiness (Christopher & Sprecher, 2000; Davis & Smith, 1972–98). Again, more frequent sexual activity might not, in itself, cause the happiness. Instead, couples who are getting along well and are otherwise happier probably feel more like having frequent sex than couples the same age who are otherwise miserable.

Satisfaction with sexual communication is probably more strongly associated with overall sexual satisfaction than are frequency of sex, frequency of orgasm, or other aspects of sexuality (Byers & Demmons, 1999; Cupach & Comstock, 1990; Sarrel & Sarrel, 1980). As with other role relationships, it is the perception of communication quality that is important, not objectively measured communication skills, although the two are probably related.

Communication with, and support from, extended kin can affect marital happiness. Living near a close relative improves marital satisfaction if the relative is supportive of the marriage; but if not, the couple is better off without nearby relatives (Perry-Jenkins & Salamon, 2002). The husband's and wife's experience with their own families of orientation affect their own marital adjustments; this is even more true for wives than for husbands (Sabatelli & Bartle-Haring, 2003).

Premarital Prevention Programs It is increasingly recognized that healthy marriages are good for the partners, their children, and society as a whole (Waite & Gallagher, 2000). At the same time, concerns are mounting that marriage is threatened. Consequently, governments, churches, and other entities are increasingly supporting various premarital prevention programs. Fortunately, it turns out that at least some of these programs can be helpful, at least to newlyweds. One review of several programs found that participants in such programs were significantly better off than nonparticipants (Carroll & Doherty, 2003). Clergy and lay leaders may be as successful in conducting the programs as more academically prepared staff (Markmann et al., 2001). The most helpful elements of such programs are often reported to be those that focus on communication skills.

Maintenance Behaviors **Relationship maintenance behaviors** help to continue marriages by preventing their decline, by enhancing them, or by their repair and re-establishment. Canary and Stafford (1992) developed a typology of five common types. *Positivity* involves maintaining positive, cheerful, and uncritical interaction with one's spouse. *Openness* includes communication that directly addresses the nature of the relationship. *Assurances* are behaviors that stress one's interest in continuing the relationship. *Network* means interacting with common friends and relatives. *Sharing tasks* involves doing one's fair share (as each individual defines it) of such responsibilities as household tasks.

> **Relationship maintenance behaviors:** Actions taken by participants to preserve ongoing relationships. **Developmental tasks:** Undertakings or objectives associated with a particular stage in the life of an individual or life cycle of a family.

Canary and Stafford (1994) found that couples who engage in these maintenance behaviors have higher perceptions of such indicators of relationship quality as satisfaction, commitment, and liking each other. Dainton et al. (1994) and Weigel and Ballard-Reisch (1996) have found an association between maintenance behaviors and the love husbands and wives feel for each other.

Haas and Stafford (1998) found that same-sex couples use maintenance behaviors that are similar to that by heterosexual couples. Their use is probably different for men and women. While wives' use is associated with events that occur within the relationship, husbands' use may be more connected to events outside the marriage (Weigel & Ballard-Reisch, 1999). While there is an association between marital quality and use of maintenance behavior, it is not clear which causes what. People in good relationships might be more inclined to engage in the helpful actions. On the other hand, using the behaviors might make the relationships better. Weigel and Ballard-Reich (1999) suggest that the latter is true, and that couples might be able to intentionally improve their relationships by learning and using the five types of maintenance behaviors.

Marriage in the Middle and Later Years

The process of constructing a life together is not something that occurs early in the marriage and is then forgotten. Marital adjustment is a process that lasts throughout the marriage as situations change and are defined and redefined. One way of looking at this process is by use of the developmental perspective.

The Life Cycle of a Marriage

[…] the developmental perspective looks at family relations in terms of definable stages, each of which is associated with particular **developmental tasks.** Successful completion of the task leads to greater life satisfaction and success in later tasks, while failure is associated with unhappiness, failure at later stages, or social disapproval (Havighurst, 1953). For example, if a couple does not successfully adapt to the birth of their first child, the family may well be in jeopardy throughout the remaining stages.

The stages constituting a family life cycle are usually divided by discrete events that typically occur with married couples, but various theorists have used different events to differentiate the stages. For purposes of analysis, the family life cycle has been divided into as many as 24 stages (Rodgers, 1962) and as few as four (Sorokin, Zimmerman, & Galpin, 1931; Rubin, 1976).

Perhaps the most widely used typology was that developed by Duval (1957). Although other terminology is sometimes used, the eight basic stages are:

1. *Couples without children*: from the wedding until the birth of the first child.
2. *Infant*: until the first child is 30 months old.
3. *Preschooler*: oldest child is 30 months to 6 years old.
4. *Elementary School*: oldest child is 6 to 13 years old.
5. *Teenager*: Oldest child is 13 to 20, or leaves home.
6. *Launching*: from the time the first child leaves home until the last child leaves home.
7. *Empty nest*: from the time the last child leaves the home until the husband's retirement.

8. *Retirement*: from the time the husband retires until the death of one or both spouses.

The development model remains a useful framework, but it does have serious shortcomings when applied to postindustrial American families (Mattessich & Hill, 1987). The biggest problem is that the model accurately describes only a minority of marriages. Some couples never have children, so their stage is impossible to determine. Perhaps half of couples divorce before either dies, so they have a "truncated" life cycle. Some have no "launching" stage because they have only one child. Others, including blended families, have children before the wedding, so they have no "childless" stage. Still other couples have no, or little, "empty nest" stage because their adult children continue to live with them. Some middle-aged couples have their elderly parents living with them; and in the increasing number of dual career couples, the wife's retirement is important but not reflected in the typology. Many of these family variations, however, still conform to certain characteristics of the life cycle, so the concept remains a useful tool for family analysis.

Marital Satisfaction and the Life Cycle

The most widely quoted study about marital satisfaction and the life cycle was done by Rollins and Feldman (1970) using an eight-stage developmental typology. Their conclusion is referred to as the "U-shaped" relationship between family stages and life satisfaction. The majority of husbands and wives are very satisfied in the childless and into the infant stage, with the wives being slightly happier than husbands. After that, satisfaction goes down, with the wives' declining slightly faster than the husbands' through the "teenager" stage. After that, satisfaction goes up for both spouses through the retirement stage.

The GSS data in Table 8.1 do not directly test the U-shaped hypothesis, but the age group with the greatest marital happiness is over fifty. The middle age group is slightly least happy, with the youngest group next. This appears to slightly confirm the U-shaped hypothesis, as does the data that "retired" is the happiest job status. This is typical of cross-sectional research, that is, studies done at one time rather than across time. Longitudinal studies, where couples are followed over time to compare their happiness levels, tend to get different results.

Bossard and Boll (1955) found no relationship between marital unhappiness and the marital life cycle. In contrast, Blood and Wolfe (1960) found that marital satisfaction generally declined throughout the course of marriages. White and Booth (1985) followed couples for a three-year period from the childless stage through birth of the first child. The U-shaped hypothesis would predict a decline in happiness during this period, but no such decline was found.

A more comprehensive study followed couples for 40 years. No evidence for a general U-shaped curve was found. Instead, marital satisfaction was relatively stable over time with a slight decrease at about the 20–year period. The researchers concluded that the U-shaped curve is largely an illusion (Vaillant & Vaillant, 1993). Glenn's (1998) longitudinal work found a general decline of happiness early in marriages but no convincing evidence of a general upturn of happiness in older marriages. He concluded that, perhaps, the older people with happier marriages had happier marriages all along than did people who are currently middle-aged. While cross-sectional studies sometimes find that couples married for longer periods of time have fewer conflicts, studies that follow couples over time cast doubt on that conclusion. In fact, during some development periods such as having children in the home, conflict may increase over time. The apparent decrease in conflict for long-term married couples is probably the result of divorce among the couples with more conflict (Hatch & Bulcroft, 2004).

Whether the U-shaped hypothesis or the gradual decline hypothesis is accurate, it has been argued that marriages for love are likely to become less happy after the romance wears off. They would "start off hot and get cold." Arranged marriages, since they are not based on emotional attachment, might be expected to "start off cold and get hot." Robert Blood (1967) tested this hypothesis with a study in Japan. He found no evidence that the arranged marriages got hotter with time; both arranged and love marriages demonstrated a gradual decline in happiness.

A similar study was done in China (Xiaohe & Whyte, 1990). Women who had married for love reported higher levels of satisfaction throughout the life cycle than those in arranged marriages. There was evidence for neither a general decline nor a U-shaped relationship. In both types of marriages, satisfaction was greatest for couples married 20–25 years, with a slight decline in older marriages.

Even studies that do find a general trend regarding marital satisfaction over the life cycle find only small differences, and they find that marital satisfaction for couples at all stages is relatively high (Rollins & Cannon, 1974; Gelles, 1995). Several factors appear to be more important determinants of marital satisfaction than the couple's stage in the marital life cycle.

Postparental Couples
A major change for most couples in middle age is the decreasing amount of time, energy, and money devoted to the childcare and child socialization roles. For this reason, the term **postparental period** is sometimes applied to this stage of married life. Neither the name, nor most of the research, applies to the small number of couples who never had children. Even for parents, however, the name is slightly misleading. They really do not stop being parents even if they have "launched" their last child. There are sometimes "re-entries" of children, and ties are maintained to children who do not move back home. Whether in the home or living independently, their children are now adults and the role relationships change. The major characteristic of these couples is the return to the two-person conjugal family and ultimately to one partner living alone.

Length of time couples spend in postparental families significantly increased during the 20th century. In 1900, the typical couple did not have a postparental period because at least one spouse died before the last child left home. Today, men and women typically marry in their early to mid-20s. The last child is launched in their mid-to late 40s, and a spouse is not likely to die until their early to mid-70s. This leaves the stable couple a postparental period of 20 to 25 years (Eshleman, 1994).

Most persons 65 and older continue to live with their spouses. Because of higher marriage rates and longer life expectancy, Asians (62.1%) are more likely than Hispanics (50%)

and Blacks (38%) to live with their wives or husbands. In addition, elderly Blacks (35%) are more likely to live alone than are Asians (15%) or Hispanics (21%) (see Figure 8.3). Even in the 75-and-older category, 74% of men are still living with their wives or other close family member. By contrast, the percentage of women living with their spouses declines rapidly with age. In the 75-and-older category, only 48% live with their spouse or other close family member (Census Bureau, 2005).

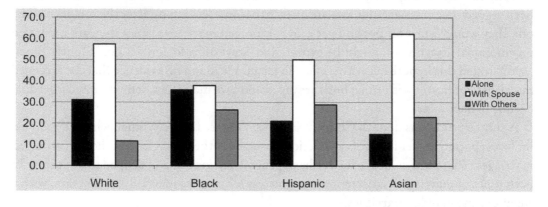

FIGURE 8.3 Living arrangements of persons age 65 and over, by race/ethnicity

Source: U.S. Bureau of the Census. *Statistical Abstract*, *2009*, Table 57. Washington, DC, U.S. Government Printing Office.

The percentage of the population that is in the postretirement years has increased since 1970 and is projected to continue to increase well into the future. Part of this increase is the result of increasing life expectancy. In 2011, however, the first year's crop of baby boomers will hit age 65, bringing an even more rapid increase in the elderly population (see Figure 8.4).

The increase in the numbers of elderly is expected to strain the Social Security system and perhaps other retirement programs. At the macroeconomic level, there will be fewer persons of working age supporting a larger number of post-working-age individuals. This is partially offset, however, by a decrease in the percentage of the population that has not yet reached age 18. The total percentage in the two nonworking-age groups will begin increasing in 2010 and then level off in 2030 at about 48%. Put differently, 52% of the population will be working to support both themselves and the remaining 48%. This compares to 2005, when 40% of the population was in the non-working-age group (see Figure 8.4).

Part of this gap is likely to be made up by the number of persons who continue to work past age 65. That percentage dropped rapidly from 1960 until about 1990, but then began to increase. In 2003, about 20% of men and 13% of women continued to work after age 65. These percentages will probably continue to increase (see Figure 8.5).

An increasingly older population will influence the employment market in the next few decades. Through 2012, four of the five fastest-growing occupations are expected to be

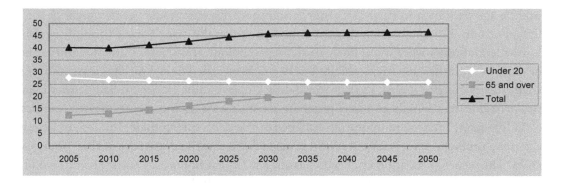

FIGURE 8.4 Percent of U.S. population in young and old non-working age groups, 2005–2050

Source: Calculated from data in U. S. Bureau of the Census. *Statistical Abstract of the United States: 2004–2005.*
Washington, D.C: U.S. Government Printing Office. Table 12.

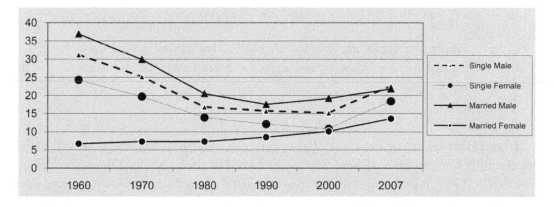

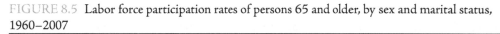

FIGURE 8.5 Labor force participation rates of persons 65 and older, by sex and marital status,
1960–2007

Source: U.S. Bureau of the Census, 1995. *Statistical Abstract of the United States: 1995*, Table 636. Ibid 2009,
Table 576.

medical assistants, physician assistants, social and human service assistants, and home
health aides, all related to the aging population. Network systems and data communications
analysts are the other category in the top five (*Statistical Abstract*, 2004–2005:Table 599).

Post-Launch Transitions

The postparental period can be divided into two developmental stages: the postlaunch stage
and the postretirement period. The popular press, and popular wisdom, report several
problems associated with both stages, for both men and women.

Men in the launch and postlaunch stage are often reported to suffer a "midlife crisis"
involving dissatisfaction with career, family, social position, or self-perception. While men at
all ages have issues of some kind to face, careful research finds little support for a widespread
midlife crisis among Americans. Farrell and Rosenberg (1981) compared 300 men entering

middle age with men in their 20s. They found some discontent and reassessment of their lives, but only 12% of the men displayed the signs generally associated with midlife crisis. Unskilled laborers were more likely to show psychological distress. Skilled workers and other lower middle class men exhibited what might be called denial mechanisms, allowing them successfully to maintain their worldview. Upper middle class men had neither identity problems nor denials and were generally satisfied with their careers and their families.

While many men are temporarily saddened by the departure of their children, it is rarely a serious problem. Exceptions are rural or farm fathers at the departure of their youngest child. The return of an adult child who has already left the home might actually cause more distress than the launch itself (Lewis, Volk, & Duncan, 1989).

It was once thought that the **empty nest syndrome** was widespread among women whose children had left home, especially when their husbands were still in the workforce. Harkins (1978) found that, in the 1960s and 1970s, belief in the empty nest syndrome was so pervasive that medical journals ran ads for antidepressants to combat the alleged problem.

> **Empty nest syndrome:** Role loss after a child has left the home resulting in depression, identity crisis, and lowered well-being. Actually a rare phenomenon.

Attempts to verify the existence of an empty nest syndrome have been mixed. There are certainly some women who are extremely affected by their children's departure. Blood and Wolfe (1960) found evidence of increased marital discord during this stage, and Bart (1971) found some reported depression and feelings of maternal role loss among women who had been overly involved with their children. Other studies found unchanged or increased overall happiness and marital satisfaction at the time of the empty nest (Deutcher, 1969; Rollins & Feldman, 1970).

Norvel Glenn (1975) reviewed results from six national studies. He found that middle-aged women whose children had left home reported greater happiness and well-being than women the same age who still had children in the home. Harkins (1978) found no evidence of effect on physical well-being of the empty nest, and only a small and temporary negative effect on psychological well-being. Apparently belief in the existence of an empty nest syndrome has evaporated; there has been virtually no research on the subject in the past 20 years.

Postretirement Couples
The concept of retirement as an expected part of the life cycle is relatively new. In most hunting-gathering societies, persons who did live to older ages, perhaps forty or so, were revered for their knowledge and participated in production as much as possible until their deaths. In agrarian societies, the elderly who were the owners of land and other means of production maintained their authority and social standing. Persons generally worked until they died or were no longer physically able to do so; they were then supported by

their families as their capacities waned. Government and religious positions were typically lifetime appointments, and women employed in such positions as midwives often continued working well into their 70s (Demos, 1986).

It was not until the 17th century that the English word **retirement** was used to describe withdrawal from a position for purposes of more leisure (American Heritage Dictionary, 1992). Even then, it was something reserved largely for the wealthy.

> **Retirement:** To withdraw from one's paid occupation.

As industrialization proceeded, the elderly began to lose their social standing at the same time that life expectancy was increasing. Rapid social change renders the knowledge base of the elderly less valuable, at least in terms of economic production. Further, elderly workers in factories did not own the means of production and might actually be less productive than younger, more nimble, workers.

In Europe, beginning in England with the Elizabethan Poor Law of 1601, a larger governmental entity began to assume some responsibility for the infirm elderly and others in poverty (Trattner, 1979). This began to remove some of the responsibility of elderly support from children and other family members.

In the United States, it was not until the Great Depression of the 1930s that the federal government assumed major responsibility for older workers. The Social Security Act of 1935 had two goals in this regard: it provided an income that enabled older workers to retire, and it strongly encouraged, even forced, retirement so that more jobs would become available for younger workers. As mandatory retirement became an issue, older workers lobbied to set the age at 70; younger workers wanted the age to be 60. Age 65 became the arbitrary compromise for the mandatory retirement age (Bassis, Gelles, & Levine, 1991). In 1979, federal legislation outlawed mandatory retirement at 65, and now, with a few exceptions, all mandatory retirement policies have been eliminated.

Adjustment to retirement includes, for most persons, a reduction in income. Although this becomes a severe problem for some, poverty rates for the elderly are actually lower than for the country as a whole. In 2002, 12.1% of all Americans were living below poverty level, compared to 10.4% of those 65 and over. While 9.1% of elderly Whites were poor, the poverty rate for elderly Blacks was 26.0% and for elderly Hispanics was 23.8% (*Statistical Abstract*, 2004–2005:Table 696). Because the pensions of many retired persons do not keep up with the rate of inflation, poverty rates increase significantly for older retirees.

For married people, retirement decisions are usually the result of joint decision making (Smith & Moen, 1998; Smith & Moen, 2004). The timing of retirement influences the adjustment of married couples, as Brubaker's (1985) typology of "traditional," "synchronized," and "dissynchronized" retirements suggests. The most common "traditional" or "single" type involves the retirement of the sole breadwinner, usually the husband. The loss of the breadwinner role is a significant adjustment for the husband, and the two partners must renegotiate the housekeeping and other roles. The wife might have difficulty with what she sees as interference with her household sphere of influence.

"Synchronized retirement" occurs when dual breadwinners retire simultaneously (Brubaker, 1985). Both partners suffer the loss of their breadwinner role at the same time, but these couples are probably accustomed to considerable negotiation regarding the housekeeping role.

Two types of dissynchronized retirements are possible. Because men's careers tend to start earlier and be more continuous, and because of age hypergamy, husbands in two-earner couples are more likely to retire first. This results in the "dissynchronized husband initially" couple. Less commonly, perhaps because of ill health or work dissatisfaction, the wife will retire first, resulting in a "dissynchronized wife initially" couple (Brubaker, 1985).

How retirement decisions are made, and who retires first, can affect a couple's satisfaction. Generally, satisfaction is reduced if the retirement transition upsets the authority structure that existed prior to retirement. Retired husbands and wives are more likely to be dissatisfied if their spouses continued to be employed and had more voice in the retirement decision (Szinovacz & Davey, 2005). Couples are most likely to be satisfied when they are both retired and the wife reports that her husband was not primarily influential in her retirement decision (Smith & Moen, 2004).

Because the breadwinner role no longer takes the time it once did and no longer ties the couple to their home, the recreational role expands considerably. It becomes more important whether the couple has developed individual, joint, or parallel leisure activities.

While many circumstances change upon retirement, some do not. For example, the relationship between gender ideology and household tasks is not significantly altered after retirement: men with an egalitarian ideology do not invest more in routine tasks, although women with an egalitarian ideology increase their investment in such activities (Solomon, Acock, & Walker, 2004). Nor does the established structure of marital conflict change much (Davey & Szinovacz, 2004). Interactive mutual scripts developed over long periods of marriage largely continue to operate.

Some of the adjustments associated with retirement are related to changing physical capabilities and the way older persons are perceived in America. Butler (1975) coined the term **ageism** to refer to discrimination against the elderly. He refers to the "myth of senility," which portrays all elderly persons as mentally disabled. When a teenager or young adult forgets where the car keys are, it is attributed to being busy, to being in love, or to other age-acceptable causes. When the same thing happens to a 70 year old, it might be attributed to the age-acceptable cause of senility, even when the person is not senile.

Ageism: Discrimination or prejudice based on age, especially against the elderly. **Bereavement:** The condition of being deprived of a loved one by death. **Grief:** Deep mental and emotional anguish.

In the United States, the elderly are thought to be less competent and intelligent and to have low activity levels and poor health (Levin, 1988). While it is unfair to stereotype all the elderly in this way, health issues are important. Poor health and declining physical abilities do affect many retirees and are a major concern and topic of conversation. Retirement does not cause poor health, however; poor health is more likely to cause retirement (Atchley & Miller, 1983.)

In spite of role transitions and health concerns, Atchley (1992) found no evidence that retirement has a direct overall effect on marital satisfaction. Spanier, Lewis, and Cole (1975) found levels of marital satisfaction equivalent to the earlier stage before the couple had children. We have seen the GSS data indicating that retirement is associated with higher levels of life and marital happiness than any other work status.

Myers and Booth (1996) found several connections between men's retirement and marital quality. Leaving a high-stress job increased marital satisfaction. Gender-role reversals and decreased social support, however, reduced marital quality.

Generally, satisfaction with family life is high for both sexes, and most of the elderly are well integrated into the social and religious life of the community. Contrary to the images that their children and other family members forget the elderly, most have considerable contact. Women are especially likely to have family and religious contacts (Dorfman & Mertens, 1990).

The elderly often adjust by redefining their family situation (Allen et al., 2000). They sometimes add fictive kin to their support system. They also upgrade kin, such as treating a niece "like a daughter." Perhaps because such survival skills were more necessary for Blacks, they are more likely to convert friends into kin than are aging Whites (Johnson & Barer, 1997).

Death, Grief, and Mourning
All marriages that do not end in divorce eventually end in the death of one or both spouses. While this can occur at any age, it is more common among the elderly. **Bereavement** is accompanied by the emotional response of **grief.** Describing this response is perhaps better left to poets, psychiatrists, or clergy, rather than sociologists, but it can include shock, disbelief, overwhelming sorrow, depression, numbness, disbelief, loss of appetite, loss of desire to live, a questioning of the meaning of life or of one's god, a sense of total isolation, inconsolable sadness, anger, guilt, relief, remorse, regret, fear, and a number of other feelings.

Emotional and behavioral reactions are guided by **mourning** customs that vary from one culture to another. The wearing of black armbands for a time is a simple mourning practice. Others are more complex and depend on the culture's meanings of death and the roles expected before and after the loved one's death. The most formal expectations are signified by funeral practices that virtually all societies have but construct differently.

From a functionalist perspective, the funeral is an important ritual with personal, familial, religious, and social functions. A funeral is a rite of passage for the deceased, who is typically believed to be transported to a different form and status. It is also a rite of passage for the survivors because it signifies change in role and status. A wife becomes a **widow**, and a husband becomes a **widower.** These roles redefine the place of the person with respect to other family members and the community at large. In most societies, remarriage is allowed after a specified period has elapsed.

Mourning: The socially constructed expectations regarding reactions to death. **Widow:** A woman whose husband has died. **Widower:** A man whose wife has died (this term reflects the fact that male family terms are typically derived from female terms).

FAMILIES IN THE NEWS *MARRIAGE CLASSES GO TO PRISON*

Oklahoma is one of the nation's leaders in state support of wedded bliss. It's latest program is now offered at Joseph Harp Correction Center.

The Oklahoma Marriage Initiative was started in 1999 by Republican Gov. Frank Keating and has been continued by his Democratic successor, Brad Henry. Nearly 30,000 high school students have received marriage and relationship skills training, in addition to 27,000 participants in workshops held by 1,364 people who have been trained to teach marriage-skills classes. These preachers, county agricultural extension agents, and others have now reached over 1% of the adult population in the state.

Now the program has moved into prisons. Howard H. Hendrick, a human services director explained, "There are 600,000 Americans leaving prison in the next few years, and those guys are all coming to an apartment complex near you."

Not all of the prison's program participants will be leaving. Dunnino Moreland has served 12 years of a life sentence that began when he was 16. He married Tammy two years ago, and worries that she might stop visiting him someday. "I'll be here while there's breath in my body," Tammy responded during a recent class.

Aaron Cosar has served 19 years of his life sentence, and is now an assistant to the chaplain and an instructor in the marriage skills course. He credits the classes for helping him in the marriage he entered long after he started serving his sentence.

The program's curriculum, developed by Colorado researchers Howard Markman and Scott Stanley, focuses on communications skills. It teaches people to slow down and listen to each other before disputes become arguments.

An unanticipated result of the program, say inmates, is that the skills they learn help them improve their relationships with other inmates and guards.

Source: Summarized from Rick Lyman. "Prison Marriage Classes Instill Stability." *New York Times*, April 16, 2005. http://nytimes.com

Considerably more widows than widowers live in the United States. In 2004 there were 11.1 million widows and 2.6 million widowers (Census Bureau, 2005). Average age at widowhood is 66.1 years for women and 68.4 years for men. Widows average another 14.3 years of life, while widowers average 6.6 remaining years (Kart et al., 1988).

In addition to the difficulties associated with grieving, widows often face financial hardship. Average standard of living for women dropped 18% after the death of their husbands, and 10% of women who were above the poverty line before dropped into poverty after their husbands died (Bound et al., 1991). While it is often assumed that widows have more economic problems, some studies have found that widowers are as likely to have economic hardships as widows (Benokraitis, 1993). Children and others are sometimes less likely to offer assistance to widowers because they assume the men have planned and managed their financial affairs better (Smith & Zick, 1986).

Loneliness can be a problem for both but is more severe for men. Widows are more likely to be connected to family, peer, and religious groups than are widowers, who suffer more from depression and other mental illness (Gove, 1972). Widowers have higher suicide rates, and overall death rates, during the year following the death of their spouses than do widows (Smith, Mercy, & Conn, 1988).

The death of a spouse is an extraordinarily difficult life transition. After a period of adjustment, however, most widows and widowers go on to lead highly satisfying lives. Women often make the adjustment by turning inward and becoming more self-confident, assertive, and independent. Men often adjust by becoming more externally oriented and being more appreciative of friends and relationships (Silverman, 1988). Widows who had been most dependent on their spouses experience the greatest gain in self-esteem after their loss. Widowers who had been most dependent on their wives for home maintenance and financial management tasks experience the greatest personal growth following loss (Carr, 2004).

Summary and Conclusion

A wedding announces role changes for the bride and groom. How that happens changes from one time and place to another and has become increasingly vague in the postindustrial era. Today's couples are increasingly free to negotiate their own role relationships rather than arriving at agreement by spontaneous consensus.

Blood and Wolfe conducted pioneering studies of conjugal power. Their resource theory of power remains important. It seems to provide good explanations for differences in power among women but is less explanatory for men. Gender-based theories of conjugal power also have adherents, as do human capital and empowerment theories. Marriage relationships have also become increasingly egalitarian, as determined by different measures of, and theories about, conjugal power.

Newlyweds negotiate several role relationships, working out their own marital scripts using social expectations as a starting point. Utilitarian and intrinsic marriages are determined by the "why" of the marital relationship.

Couples have a number of role relationships to negotiate: sexual, provider, housekeeper, religion, friendship, child socialization, childcare, therapeutic, recreational, and kinship. Couples also develop a generalized script based on the basic "why" of their relationship.

Family scholars have developed a number of indicators of marital quality, including marital happiness and marital stability. Several factors are associated with marital happiness and life satisfaction.

Developmental theories look at the "life cycle" of marriages. Specific points in the life cycle, such as the "empty nest" period and retirement pose challenges for couples. Considerable research has been done on the effect of life-cycle changes on marital quality, with confusing and sometimes contradictory results.

In conclusion, this chapter focused more on the microsociological processes and outcomes involved in marriages. It should be apparent that measuring the "goodness" or "badness" of relationship is difficult, and not all measures get the same results. Some unhappy marriages, for example, are nonetheless quite stable.

Just as a couple negotiates a marriage, their negotiations continue when children must be taken into account. This is the topic of the next chapter.

> **Rethinking in Context** If you could ask a couple five questions to find out how good their marriage is, what would those questions be? Why? Would your questions be different for young than for old couples? Why, why not? Assuming you get married, what you would like to be able to say about your marriage when you look back at it at age 85?

Internet Sites

The American Association of Marriage and Family Therapy http://www.aamft.org/
The Coalition for Marriage, Family and Couples Education http://www.smartmarriages.com/
A British relationship study group http://www.oneplusone.org.uk/
Marriage support http://www.couples-place.com/

Same-Sex Couple Relationship Strengths

A Review and Synthesis of the Empirical Literature (2000–2016)

BY SHARON S. ROSTOSKY AND ELLEN D. B. RIGGLE

Vaughan and Rodriguez (2014) have cogently argued that LGBT research might fruitfully draw upon the "three pillars" of positive psychology (i.e., positive subjective experiences, character strengths and virtues, and positive social institutions) as an organizing framework (Seligman & Csikszentmihalyi, 2000) for examining LGBT strengths. Fincham and Beach (2010) proposed the addition of a fourth pillar of positive relationships in recognition of their centrality to optimal human functioning and flourishing. They challenged the field of relationship science to directly investigate "relationship strengths and how they might be harnessed in the face of stressors and life challenge," and the positive aspects of relationships that extend beyond coping to thriving and flourishing (Fincham & Beach, 2010, p. 7).

The purpose of this article was to identify and summarize empirical research on same-same-sex couple relational strengths. To define and organize the literature for review, we drew on Fincham and Beach's (2010) conceptualization of relationship strengths as internal and external resources that (a) facilitate couples' resilience or their ability to cope effectively with stressors and challenges or (b) contribute to their well-being, thriving, and flourishing. First, we discuss findings related to the internal strengths of couples that promote their well-being and resiliency. Then we discuss external resources that facilitate their relational well-being.

In considering the literature, we note that the social context in which same-sex couples form and maintain their intimate relationships is rapidly changing. In the United States prior to 2000, same-sex couples did not have access to legal state recognition of their relationship (i.e., civil unions or marriage). In our own interviews with same-sex couples in 2000, few imagined that they would one day have access to civil marriage (Rostosky, Riggle, Dudley, & Comer Wright, 2006). That same year, Vermont became the first state to provide civil unions to same-sex couples. This important event marked the beginning of a series of legal changes culminating in the legal recognition of same-sex marriage in all 50 states in 2015.

This changing social landscape has led to significant interest in the study same-sex couple relationships. As predicted by positive psychology's third pillar, social institutions and the evolving social and political landscape since 2000 exerts a profound effect on same-sex couple relationships. We chose 2000 as the starting point for our review of the literature in recognition of the first year that at least some same-sex couples had access to legal state recognition for their relationships. We limited this review to U.S. samples in recognition that same-sex couples create and maintain their relationships in significantly different social, political, and cultural contexts around the world.

To locate the literature for this review, we performed two PsycINFO searches, one of index terms and one of keywords. We limited each search to articles published in English, in peer-reviewed journals, on adult populations (over age 18) in the United States between the years 2000 and 2016. We combined the index term homosexuality (n = 5,016) with an index search of couples or relationship quality or relationship satisfaction or relationship termination (n = 7,285), which yielded 205 records. The keyword search included *any* of the following keywords: same-sex couple, same-sex relationship, same-sex marriage, gay couple, gay relationship, lesbian couple, lesbian relationship. This search produced 532 records. We examined each record and excluded studies that were not empirical, used non-U.S. populations, did not directly focus on same-sex couple relationships, or did not assess a strength of same-sex couple relationships as defined above. As a result, we excluded studies that focused on parenting, advance planning, attitudes toward same-sex couples, negative relationship factors or outcomes such as intimate partner violence, conflict, or minority stress, and risk behaviors related to HIV or substance use. After eliminating records that were clearly not about relationship strengths in same-sex couples and duplicate records from the two searches, we retained 67 abstracts from the index search and 53 abstracts from the keyword search. The authors separately examined each of these abstracts and then met to make a final determination about whether or not each study assessed a strength of same-sex relationships. We agreed on a final dataset of 66 articles for the current review. We then categorized each of these articles according to the strengths that were assessed. In the sections that follow, we summarize the findings on the internal strengths and external resources that support couples' relationships.

In this article, we use the terms "same-sex couples" and "different-sex couples" unless there is a compelling reason to use other terms. A number of studies included in this review appear to assume rather than measure sexual identities. For instance, studies of "lesbian couples" may assume that all female partners in the sample identify as lesbian, or may exclude from analysis those with other identities (e.g., bisexual, queer). In this review, we use *same-sex couple* to refer to research on couples that include two individuals who both identify as male or who both identify as female. One or both of these partners may self-identify as "gay," "lesbian," "bisexual," "queer," or even "straight." Likewise, we use the term *different-sex couples* to refer to research conducted using couples in which one partner identifies as "female" and the other partner identifies as "male" to avoid making assumptions about the individual sexual identities of the partners.

Internal Strengths of Same-Sex Couple Relationships

Of the studies included in this review, 26 focused on at least one of three couple-level relationship processes and 40 focused on at least one of four positive relationship characteristics. Although we discuss each category separately, these processes and characteristics are interrelated rather than discrete. The three positive relationship processes are respecting and appreciating individual differences, generating positive emotions and interactions, and effectively communicating and negotiating. The four positive relationship characteristics are perceived intimacy, commitment, egalitarian ideals, and outness.

Positive Relationship Processes

Respecting and appreciating individual differences

Studies of relationships frequently focus on compatibility, or similarities between couple members (e.g., Becker, 2013; Kilmann & Vendemia, 2013; Kurdek, 1993); however, appreciation and respect for differences emerged as a valued strength in six qualitative studies of same-sex couples. In these studies, couples perceived that cultivating mutual respect, acceptance, and appreciation of within-couple differences in personality, perspectives, preferences, and strengths was important to the quality of their relationship.

Riggle, Rothblum, Rostosky, Clark, and Balsam (2016) interviewed 18 female couples and 13 male couples who were all in legalized relationships (civil unions or marriages) and had been together for an average of 23 years. These couples perceived that their ability to respect and appreciate both their similarities and their differences was an important strength that partially accounted for their relationship quality and longevity. These couples tended to view their different backgrounds, personalities, and skill sets as complementary rather than problematic. Likewise, Dziengel (2012) found that older same-sex couples in long-term relationships saw their differences as valuable assets, rather than deficits, with each partner contributing different strengths to the relationship.

Supporting each partner's individuality is a relational process that enhances effective communication. In two interview studies, female couples reported that respecting and honoring individual differences in perceptions and approaches promoted their "empathic attunement" with each other and their communication competence (Connolly & Sicola, 2005; Littlefield, Lim, Canada, & Jennings, 2000). These couples also viewed their differences as complementary and advantageous to their relationship. In an analysis of conversations, same-sex couples viewed acceptance of their individual differences as an important expression of commitment to their relationship (Rostosky et al., 2006). In another study, couples noted that it was important to their relationship to respect, support, and appreciate each partner's individual spiritual and religious beliefs and activities (Rostosky, Otis, Riggle, Kelly, & Brodnicki, 2008).

Generating positive emotions and interactions

Four studies documented same-sex couples' general use of positivity in their relationships. Kurdek (2008a) found that expressiveness, or the tendency to display positive responses such as understanding, kindness, or tenderness, was associated with higher relationship satisfaction and commitment in 304 same-sex couples. Long-term same-sex couples reported that interacting positively and sharing positive experiences such as fun and laughter was a strength that contributed to the "success" of their relationship (Riggle, Rothblum, et al., 2016). In a study of 53 male couples, the expression of positive emotions in the baseline interview (e.g., warmth, affection, and a sense of "we-ness") predicted relationship satisfaction 4 years later (Boesch, Cerqueira, Safer, & Wright, 2007). Looking specifically at health-related behaviors, same-sex couples, compared with different-sex couples, were found to work more positively and cooperatively to mutually support each other's efforts (Reczek & Umberson, 2012).

Five studies examined couples' positive interactions during conflict. For example, female couples reported higher levels of positive problem solving, or focusing on the problem at hand, compared with the other couple types (Kurdek, 2001). Compared with different-sex parenting couples, same-sex couples without children reported higher levels of symmetrical positive communication, which involved working together to generate solutions to a conflict (Kurdek, 2004).

In an observational study, same-sex couples used more positivity than negativity when discussing a conflict, meaning that their interactions were less domineering, whining, and belligerent, and more humorous, affectionate, joyful, and excited compared with different-sex married couples (Gottman, Levenson, Swanson, et al., 2003). In a follow-up study of only the same-sex couples, expectancy of positive interactions was associated with current relationship satisfaction and also predicted relationship stability 12 years later. For female partners, expressions of affection, and for male partners, validating responses during the interaction task were associated with relationship satisfaction (Gottman, Levenson, Gross, et al., 2003). In another study of couples' interactions, observers rated female couples' interactions as more harmonious than male couples and different sex-couples during a conflict task (Roisman, Clausell, Holland, Fortuna, & Elieff, 2008).

Several studies focused on the stigmatizing social context of same-sex relationships. Gaines and Henderson (2004) found that same-sex couples positively reframed their experiences of stigma and discrimination which kept them motivated to work even harder on their relationship. Likewise, Connolly (2006) interviewed 10 female couples who had been together for at least 10 years and found that these women took a positive perspective, reframing external stresses and challenges as opportunities that kept them unified.

In a study of 40 same-sex couples, dyads recounted how they dealt with stigma and discrimination from their families, coworkers, and communities by positively affirming their relationship and reframing negative experiences as empowering rather than diminishing (Rostosky, Riggle, Gray, & Hatton, 2007). Interracial same-sex couples used positive coping strategies such as making positive meaning out of their experiences of race and sexual identity-related stress and took positive actions to address these stressors (Rostosky, Riggle, Savage, Roberts, & Singletary, 2008). Couples used positive emotions such as humor as a way to alleviate stress (Riggle, Rothblum, et al., 2016; Rostosky, Riggle, Savage, et al., 2008). Same-sex couples who were able to make positive meaning out of their experiences of stigma and discrimination and see these experiences as opportunities to strengthen their bond with their partner (Frost, 2011a) also reported more closeness in their relationship (Frost, 2014).

Effectively communicating and negotiating

Good communication skills are widely considered to be important to satisfying couple relationships (Bradbury & Karney, 2013). However, these skills may take on added importance for same-sex couples who face the challenges of stigmatization. We identified 10 studies that assessed effective communication as part of conflict resolution and decision-making and four studies that focused on effectively negotiating sexual boundaries, religious participation, and outness.

In an interview study of 18 female and 13 male same-sex couples who had been together for an average of 23 years (Riggle, Rothblum, et al., 2016), couples reported that one key to their relationship longevity was communication. These couples reported that they talked frequently about their feelings and communicated with each other to resolve conflicts. A study of 14 same-sex couples' conversations about commitment revealed that couples consider it very important to invest in their relationship by engaging in discussion to solve problems, express their feelings, and negotiate differences (Rostosky et al., 2006).

In a thematic analysis of 220 same-sex partnered individuals' responses to open-ended survey questions, "talking things out" and "working through things together" were valued strengths that benefited the relationship (Degges-White & Marszalek, 2007, p. 112). In a mail survey of 81 male and 223 female couples, higher scores on effective arguing, or the perception that conflicts in the relationship are quickly and constructively resolved, was associated with higher levels of commitment (Kurdek, 2008a).

Other studies have focused on negotiating and resolving conflict through shared decision-making and compromise. Littlefield et al. (2000) interviewed 16 female couples and Connolly and Sicola (2005) interviewed 10 female couples who had been together for 10 years or more. In both studies, couples perceived that being able to negotiate during conflict was one specific communication skill that accounted for the success of their relationship.

Patterson, Ward, and Brown (2013) interviewed eight young women about their current or most recent same-sex relationship. The women in this sample perceived that good communication, specifically the ability to communicate about areas of conflict and come to resolution, was an important component of their relationship. In a daily diary study, constructive communication patterns that included positive discussion, expression, and negotiation, weakened the significant association between negative feelings about a conflict and negative perception of the partners' relationship maintenance behaviors (Ogolsky & Gray, 2016).

Two studies (Dziengel, 2012; Quam, Whitford, Dziengel, & Knochel, 2010) analyzed data collected from a nationally recruited online sample of 156 midlife and older men and women in same-sex relationships of at least 10 years duration. Participants completed a standardized assessment (ENRICH) that included communication and conflict resolution subscales. The sample scored in the high range on the communication and conflict resolution measures, with women scoring significantly higher than men (Quam et al., 2010). The participants also answered 13 open-ended questions about their perceptions of factors contributing to their relationship longevity. Women were more likely than men to report that they and their partners equally shared responsibility for initiating the discussion of areas of conflict (Quam et al., 2010).

In further analyses of the answers to the open-ended questions, couples described the importance of actively negotiating agreements, specifically regarding sexual boundaries and boundaries with unsupportive family members and friends (Dziengel, 2012). In face-to-face interviews, Adam (2006) reported that men in same-sex relationships (N = 70) actively and overtly negotiated detailed sexual agreements about monogamy/nonmonogamy with their partner. Two qualitative analyses of couples' conversations found that couples actively negotiate couple boundaries related to sex and disclosure or "outness" (Rostosky et al., 2006) and activities related to religious/spiritual values (Rostosky, Riggle, Brodnicki, & Olson, 2008).

Positive Relationship Characteristics

Four positive relationship characteristics were assessed across the studies that were reviewed: perceived intimacy, commitment, egalitarian ideals, and outness. The first three characteristics have frequently been studied in comparison to different-sex couples. Disclosure of the same-sex relationship or LGB identity, or outness, is a characteristic unique to same-sex couple relationships.

Perceived emotional intimacy

Emotional intimacy is a relationship strength that involves feelings of deep connection, caring, understanding, and validation of the self that develops from mutually responsive interactions (Gable & Reis, 2006; Reis, 2007). Same-sex couples (Rostosky et al., 2006) and same-sex partnered individuals (Degges-White & Marszalek, 2007) have reported that emotional intimacy is an important strength that they value in their relationship. In an analysis of 14 couples' conversations, emotional intimacy (even more than sexual intimacy) was of primary importance to their committed relationship (Rostosky et al., 2006).

Eleven studies compared same-sex and different-sex couple relationships on some measure of perceived intimacy. Four of these studies found no significant differences between same-sex and different-sex partnered individuals on measures of perceived intimacy (e.g., Cusack, Hughes, & Cook, 2012; Kurdek, 2004), types of intimacy (Frost & Gola, 2015) or intimacy-related goals (Frost, 2011b). Even when mean levels of intimacy and associations with relationship quality do not differ by type of couple, there may still be differences in how intimacy is expressed. For example, same-sex couples reported more frequent use of intimacy-related "bonding" behaviors to maintain their relationship, including spending time together and engaging in discussions about their relationship. Different-sex couples, on the other hand, reported more maintenance behaviors like gift-giving, providing support, and using humor (Haas & Stafford, 2005).

Five of the comparison studies found that same-sex partners reported higher levels of perceived intimacy. In one study, same-sex couples reported being more comfortable with closeness compared with different-sex married couples (Kurdek, 2001). Balsam, Beauchaine, Rothblum, and Solomon (2008) recruited same-sex couples and their different-sex married siblings, creating demographically similar comparison samples (in contrast to Kurdek, who recruited different-sex married couples and same-sex couples separately). In Balsam et al.'s (2008) analyses, same-sex couples reported significantly higher levels of perceived intimacy than different-sex married couples. Consistent with these findings, a sample of men and women ($N = 220$) who responded to open-ended questions in an online survey noted that, compared with their own previous different-sex partnered relationships, they experienced their current same-sex relationship as more emotionally intimate and connected (Degges-White & Marszalek, 2006/2007).

Other studies have documented that same-sex partnered women rate their relationships as significantly more intimate compared with other couple types. For instance, compared with men in same-sex relationships and men and women in different-sex relationships, women in same-sex relationships were more likely to report that psychological intimacy characterized their relationship (Mackey, Diemer, & O'Brien, 2000). In these relationships of more than 15-years duration, "psychologically intimate communication characterized by mutuality of understanding, acceptance, trust and respect based upon an openness and honesty of thoughts and feelings not customarily shared in other social relationships" predicted relationship satisfaction for all couple types (Mackey, Diemer, & O'Brien, 2004, p. 123).

A qualitative interview study (Umberson, Thomeer, & Lodge, 2015) found that same-sex partnered women, compared with different-sex partnered women, described more collaboration in the "emotion work" of maintaining intimacy in their relationship. Same-sex partnered men, compared with different-sex partnered men, also described doing more "emotional work" in terms of being sensitive to their partner's needs for emotional support and autonomy.

Studies have also sought deeper understanding of other intimacy-related constructs in the context of same-sex couple relationships. Trust is an intimacy-related strength that is associated with relationship satisfaction in same-sex couples (Kurdek, 2003). In this study, female partners reported significantly higher trust of their partner than did male partners, although the effect size was small. Trust also emerged as an important part of relationship commitment in four qualitative studies using a range of methodologies (Dziengel, 2012; Gaines & Henderson, 2004; Littlefield et al., 2000; Rostosky et al., 2006).

Measures of intimacy commonly include items about sharing time and activities, an important contributor that also emerged in same-sex couples' narrative descriptions. Five qualitative studies reported that companionship, shared activities, and shared fun were important relationship strengths. Gaines and Henderson (2004) conducted semistructured interviews with 15 male and 15 female couples that included questions about the best qualities of their relationship and how they maintained their relationship over time. These couples reported that spending time together, enjoying common interests, and having fun, were the best characteristics of their relationship. These characteristics aligned with other intimacy-related strengths that couples mentioned including companionship, mutual love and caring, trust and honesty (Gaines & Henderson, 2004).

In conversations about commitment (Rostosky et al., 2006), same-sex couples discussed spending time together in shared activities, which functioned as an important investment in their relationship. These couples linked this investment to a rewarding sense of companionship. Rostosky, Riggle, Brodnicki, et al. (2008) found that shared activities extended to spiritual and religious practices that contributed to a feeling of connection between partners. In an online survey (N = 156) using open-ended questions (Dziengel, 2012) and in interviews with 31 couples (Riggle, Rothblum, et al., 2016), midlife and older adults in long-term same-sex relationships revealed that spending time together having fun was important to their intimate connection.

Couples' shared activities often reflect their shared interests or values. Sometimes couples have similar interests, providing a basis for shared activities that bring them closer together. Couples may also show their value of the relationship by engaging in activities that one partner enjoys and the other partner supports (Riggle, Rothblum, et al., 2016).

Same-sex couples specifically described how shared values and meanings contributed to their perception of intimacy. Female couples who had been together a minimum of 10 years developed intimacy-related qualities of empathy and shared meaning that they said helped them in their communication with each other (Connolly & Sicola, 2005). Shared (positive) meanings have also been associated with feelings of closeness to one's partner (Frost, 2014). Couples may share values related to politics, world view, and money (Dziengel, 2012; Riggle, Rothblum, et al., 2016). Couples make plans together, working toward goals that reflect shared values, such as raising a family or supporting each other's careers (Riggle, Rothblum, et al., 2016).

All of these intimacy-building pursuits contribute to feelings of closeness or "we-ness" (Fergus & Skerrett, 2015). In mixed-method research, intimacy-related qualities such as shared values (Rostosky, Otis, et al., 2008), feelings of closeness (Boesch et al., 2007), and empathy (Gottman, Levenson, Gross, et al., 2003) have been linked to relationship satisfaction. Intimacy-related activities appear to contribute to positive relationship quality over time. In a longitudinal study of male couples, Boesch and colleagues (2007) found that higher levels of secure, intimate attachment to each other was positively associated with higher dyadic-level relationship satisfaction and individual-level commitment 4 years later.

Commitment

Commitment is the intention to persist in a relationship (Rusbult, Agnew, & Arriaga, 2011). We identified seven studies that examined commitment in same-sex relationships. In couple interviews, long-term couples attributed their relationship quality and longevity, in part, to their commitment (Riggle, Rothblum, et al., 2016). A qualitative analysis of same-sex couples' conversations revealed that couples made investments in their relationship that demonstrated their commitment to their relationship. These investments included moving in together, pooling financial resources, publicly disclosing their relationships, making efforts to communicate and work through problems, and making plans for the future (Rostosky et al., 2006).

Kurdek's (2004) longitudinal analyses documented that the predictors of commitment and relationship satisfaction (e.g., perceptions of equality within the relationship, perceptions of social support) were the same for same-sex and different-sex couples. In tests of the investment theory of commitment (Rusbult et al., 2011), commitment has been examined as an outcome of relational investments (Lehmiller, 2010) and as a predictor of relationship satisfaction (Kamen, Burns, & Beach, 2011). In a sample of same-sex partnered and different-sex partnered men, investments of time, effort, and self-disclosure in their current relationship predicted relational commitment in both groups (Lehmiller, 2010). A study of 142 men in same-sex relationships found that commitment was associated with higher relationship satisfaction (Kamen et al., 2011).

In two studies, Johnson's (1999) tripartite model of commitment provided a conceptual framework for examining processes of attraction and constraint that form three types of commitment (personal, moral, and structural). Attractions to the relationship and constraints to leaving the relationship predicted commitment in both same-sex couples and different-sex married couples (Kurdek, 2000). Using a novel concept-mapping approach, Pope and Cashwell (2013) found that same-sex partnered and different-sex partnered individuals had similar perceptions and understanding of moral commitment, or the felt sense of obligation to persevere in a relationship.

Egalitarian ideals

LGBT individuals have noted that one of the positive aspects of their identities is the freedom from rigid gender roles that allows them to create intimate relationships consistent with their values of egalitarianism and equality (Riggle, Rostosky, McCants, & Pascale-Hague, 2011; Riggle, Whitman, Olson, Rostosky, & Strong, 2008; Rostosky, Riggle, Pascale-Hague, & McCants, 2010). Three qualitative studies in the current review documented that same-sex couples and same-sex partnered individuals perceive their commitment to being equal partners as a strength of their relationship (Degges-White & Marszalek, 2007; Patterson et al., 2013; Rostosky et al., 2006). For example, in an analysis of 14 couples' videotaped and transcribed conversations about commitment, couples characterized egalitarianism as a fundamental value and strength that benefited their relationship (Rostosky et al., 2006).

This value of equality may be particularly important to women, who have directly experienced the effects of a male-dominated social hierarchy. Thus, some survey findings suggest that female same-sex couples are more likely than male same-sex couples (Kurdek, 2003) and more likely than different-sex couples (Kurdek, 2001) to report that they contribute equally, treat each other as equals, are equally committed, and have equal power in their relationship.

Compared with different-sex parenting couples, both female and male same-sex couples without children reported higher levels of equality in their relationship (Kurdek, 2004), which was significantly associated with commitment level in all couples. Boesch et al. (2007) found that male couples' perceptions of equality predicted their relationship satisfaction and commitment 4 years later.

Three comparative studies found that equal division of childcare is a strength of same-sex couples relative to different-sex couples. A study of same-sex and different-sex couples who had recently adopted children found that the same-sex couples reported more equal sharing of childcare and housework compared with the different-sex couples (Goldberg, Smith, & Perry-Jenkins, 2012). Likewise, women in same-sex relationships are more likely than women in different-sex marriages to report that they share childcare equally (Solomon, Rothblum, & Balsam, 2004). In a comparison of 33 same-sex female couples and 33 different-sex couples, all of whom were parenting young children, both types of couples reported that they divided household labor equally and that this was ideal; the female couples, however, were more likely to report that they divided childcare evenly and that this division was ideal (Patterson, Sutfin, & Fulcher, 2004).

Compared with findings related to the division of childcare, findings on couples' division of household labor is more mixed. Two studies comparing men and women in same-sex relationships to men and women in different-sex marriages found that those in same-sex relationships reported more equal sharing of household tasks and also more equal sharing of finances and relationship maintenance behaviors (Gotta, Green, Rothblum, Solomon, Balsam, & Schwartz, 2011; Solomon, Rothblum, & Balsam, 2005). However, another study of relationship maintenance behaviors found that committed same-sex and different-sex partnered individuals both reported that their most common shared activity was completing household tasks together, like doing laundry and cleaning (Haas & Stafford, 2005).

Another study of same-sex and different-sex partnered women found that both groups of women reported similar levels of responsibility for cooking, cleaning, and earning income, but same-sex partnered women were more likely to report that this responsibility was always shared equally with their partner (Matthews, Tartaro, & Hughes, 2003). In a comparison of 36 female and 43 male same-sex couples, female couples were more likely than were male couples to share six household tasks equally, and perceived equality in the task sharing was positively associated with relationship satisfaction and stability (Kurdek, 2007).

A study of same-sex partnered fathers who had at least one child under the age of 18 reported that they and their partner actually practiced their ideal of an equal division of household and childcare tasks. Reporting consistency between the ideal and real division of tasks was associated with higher life satisfaction and a stronger parenting alliance 1 year later (Tornello, Sonnenberg, & Patterson, 2015). Some of the results reviewed above suggest that egalitarian ideals may be even more important than actual egalitarian division of household labor. In one of the few ethnographic studies of African American same-sex partnered women, Moore (2011) concluded that the espousal of egalitarian values did not necessarily translate into an equal division of labor. Nevertheless, inequalities in the division of labor were not a source of conflict and were not perceived as a power imbalance. These couples reported that what was most important to their relationship satisfaction was that both partners contributed financially to the household.

Egalitarian values are also evident in couples' communication and decision-making. For instance, female couples who had been together at least 10 years perceived that talking together frequently and learning to deal effectively with conflict were processes that contributed to their sense of equality (Littlefield et al., 2000). In an online sample of male and female couples who had been together at least 10 years ($N = 145$), the majority (87%) reported that they made major decisions together and at least half of the sample indicated that they also shared in deciding on which movie to see, doing dishes, and planning vacations. Female couples, compared with male couples, however, reported significantly more agreement about sharing decision making (Quam et al., 2010).

In a qualitative study of 40 same-sex couples, Jonathan (2009) discovered a central theme of "attuned equality" that featured concern about fairness and equity, equal attention to each partner's needs, mutual decision making, direct communication about problems, and the negotiation of daily chores that took individual interests into considerations. In this study, the couples that were aware of inequities or power imbalances in their relationships ($N = 10$) worked to acknowledge these and somehow rebalanced the relationship by compensating the less powerful partner. Similar interview studies have also found that egalitarianism contributes to positive interactions within same-sex couple relationships. In Connolly and Sicola's (2005) interviews with 10 female couples and Littlefield et al. (2000) interviews with 16 female couples, many couples specifically tied their use of negotiation within their relationship to the value that they placed on being equal partners.

Outness

Unique to same-sex relationships is the extent to which a couple is "out" or discloses their relationship to others. Making decisions about disclosure is part of the minority stress process that affects couple relationships (Rostosky & Riggle, 2016). Being out as a couple may also function as an investment that couple members make in their relationship (Rostosky et al., 2006). Six studies in this review examined outness.

Three qualitative studies found that same-sex partnered women (Patterson et al., 2013) and same-sex couples (LaSala, 2000; Rostosky et al., 2006) perceive that being out as a couple is an important strength in their relationship. In a sample of male couples, LaSala (2000) found that being out to their parents, even when the parents disapproved, was important because it relieved the couples of the stress of trying to conceal their relationship and gave them an opportunity to validate their relationship.

Studies using other methodologies have found positive associations between outness and relationship quality. For instance, Jordan and Deluty (2000) found that same-sex partnered women who were more out about their relationship enjoyed more social support and higher relationship satisfaction. In another survey, same-sex partnered men who were more out reported higher relationship quality (van Eeden-Moorefield, Pasley, Crosbie-Burnett, & King, 2012). In an observational study, same-sex couples who were more out to the world (i.e., straight friends, coworkers, strangers) but not necessarily more out to family (i.e., parents, siblings, extended family) used more positive affect during an interaction task and reported higher relationship satisfaction (Clausell & Roisman, 2009).

External Resources That Support Same-Sex Relationships

The positive psychology framework includes the role of positive social environments and institutions as the third pillar (Seligman & Csikszentmihalyi, 2000). Social support and marriage equality, as well as other forms of relationship recognition, fall into the category of positive social institutions. In this review, the contribution of social support was assessed in 13 studies and the contribution of legal recognition was assessed in 11 studies.

Perceived Social Support

Social support for their relationship has been found to be an important resource that helps same-sex couples create and maintain a satisfying relationship (Kurdek, 2008a; Riggle, Rothblum, et al., 2016). Long-term midlife same-sex couples report that having the support of friends and family members is one of the strengths that contributed to their long and happy relationship (Connolly, 2006; Riggle, Rothblum, et al., 2016). Gaines and Henderson (2004) interviewed male and female same-sex couples and found that women, in particular, perceived that support for their relationships from friends, family, and the gay and lesbian community helped them to cope with social disapproval.

Jordan and Deluty (2000) found that perceived social support from all sources, including family, friends, and coworkers, was associated with relationship satisfaction in same-sex partnered women. In dyadic interviews, a sample of predominately ethnic or racial-minority young adult same-sex couples (mean age 22) perceived that their relationship was strengthened by the social support and resources provided by their parents, friends, and church (Macapagal, Greene, Rivera, & Mustanski, 2015). Same-sex couples have reported that they rely on the support of family members and friends as a specific resource for managing their race-related and sexual identity-related minority stress (Rostosky et al., 2007; Rostosky, Riggle, Savage, et al., 2008).

Social support is an important resource for same-sex couples; however, there is evidence that they have less access to this resource, especially from their families. Although Graham and Barnow (2013) found no differences in same-sex and different-sex couples' perceived social support from family, friends, or partners, other studies have documented differences that disadvantage same-sex couples. For instance, compared with different-sex couples, same-sex couples reported less support for their relationship from their family of origin (Kurdek, 2004). Another study (Solomon et al., 2004) compared same-sex partnered men and women in civil unions or with no legal relationship status to married men and women. Same-sex partnered women reported less social support from family compared with married women. Men (regardless of couple type) did not differ in their perception of social support from their families, however same-sex partnered men perceived more social support from their friends compared with different-sex partnered men (Solomon et al., 2004).

Couples who do not have high levels of family support for their relationship may find ways to accept this lack of support so that it does not interfere with their relationship quality. For instance, LaSala (2000) found that male same-sex couples drew boundaries with their disapproving family members and maintained an emotional independence from them as a way to protect their relationship.

Some evidence in the studies reviewed above also suggests that same-sex couples may compensate for a lack of family support by building stronger social support in their friendship network. Female same-sex couples compared with married different-sex couples (Kurdek, 2001), and male same-sex couples compared with female same-sex couples (Kurdek, 2004), reported more social support for their relationship from friends. Overall satisfaction with social support, rather than overall level of support, predicted commitment and relationship satisfaction in all couples (Kurdek, 2004; Kurdek, 2008a).

Marriage Equality/Legal Relationship Recognition

In general, the literature suggests that a good marriage is associated with greater health, happiness, and life satisfaction (Myers & Diener, 1995; Kiecolt-Glaser, & Newton, 2001). The majority of this research, however, has focused on different-sex couples. Changes in marriage laws since 2000 has allowed researchers to explore the positive impact of marriage equality and other forms of legal relationship recognition, such as civil unions and domestic partnerships, on the well-being of same-sex couples.

Prior to marriage equality in all 50 states in 2015, some studies examined the contribution to couple well-being of other types of legal recognition. For example, Fingerhut and Maisel (2010) found that being in a registered domestic partnership buffered the negative effects of internalized "gay-related stress" on life satisfaction in a sample of same-sex partnered Californians. In a national sample of gay, lesbian, and bisexual individuals, participants who had some kind of legal relationship status (i.e., civil union, domestic partnership, civil marriage) reported more meaning in life, less internalized stigma, fewer depressive symptoms, and less stress than participants who were in committed relationships that did not have legal status (Riggle, Rostosky, & Horne, 2010a, 2010b). Legal recognition for one's relationship has also been associated with relationship stability (Whitton, Kuryluk, & Khaddouma, 2015). In analysis of a nationally representative longitudinal survey, Rosenfeld (2014) found that being in a legally recognized relationship, or even simply considering yourself "married" without any formal status, reduced the odds of relationship dissolution for both same-sex and different-sex couples.

Marriage appears to have psychological benefits for same-sex partners. In an analysis of the 2009 California Health Interview survey, lesbian, gay, or bisexual (LGB) individuals who were in a same-sex marriage (7% of the sample of 1,166 LGB participants) reported less psychological distress than those who were not. Participants who were in different-sex marriages reported the least distress and LGB participants who were not in any legally recognized relationship reported the most distress (Wight, LeBlanc, & Lee Badgett, 2013). In a sample of midlife same-sex couples, those who lived in a state that recognized their civil marriage reported less vigilance, less isolation, less concealment of their LGB identity, and more acceptance of their LGB identity (Riggle, Wickham, et al., 2016). Some same-sex couples perceived that family members became more supportive and accepting of their relationship when they got legally married (Schecter, Tracy, Page, & Luong, 2008).

Same-sex couples perceive that marriage benefits their relationship in a number of ways. Same-sex partnered individuals (*n* 526) in states without marriage equality reported that marriage was important to them because of the financial benefits and legal protections and the social legitimacy that comes with marriage. These respondents also valued civil marriage as an expression of love and commitment (Haas & Whitton, 2015).

These benefits also emerged in qualitative interview studies. Married same-sex couples felt more financially, legally, and emotionally secure, and perceived more social "legitimacy" and "validation" for their relationship after marrying (Lannutti, 2011; Porche & Purvin, 2008; Rostosky, Riggle, Rothblum, & Balsam, 2016; Schecter et al., 2008). They also experienced "an unexpected qualitative deepening of commitment" (Schecter et al., 2008, p. 413). Nevertheless, Lannutti (2011) documented some concerns among older same-sex couples that marriage might increase their vulnerability to discrimination and stigma. These couples felt that civil marriage was unnecessary in their case because they had obtained legal documents that protected their relationship and had participated in commitment ceremonies that pledged their lifelong devotion.

Moving Toward a Positive Psychology of Same-Sex Relationships

For most people, having a satisfying intimate relationship is part of living well, or "living the good life." The quality and stability of one's intimate relationship is positively associated with health (Umberson, Williams, Powers, Liu, & Needham, 2006) and life satisfaction

(Gustavson, Røysamb, Borren, Torvik, & Karevold, 2015). Although research has demonstrated the negative effects of social stigma on same-sex relationships (Doyle & Molix, 2015), in this review we sought to locate research on the strengths of these relationships.

The studies that we located and reviewed revealed internal strengths and external resources that contribute to positive relationship qualities such as satisfaction. These strengths, and probably others that have not garnered empirical attention in the same-sex couple literature such as compassion and awareness, are interrelated and appear to work together to produce the "we-ness" that characterizes resilient couples (Fergus & Skerrett, 2015). Future research on same-sex couples' strengths will benefit from continuing to build on a theoretical and methodological foundation of "we-ness" that is represented by the fourth pillar of positive psychology (Fincham & Beach, 2010).

As Gable and Reis (2006) noted, there is a reciprocal and dynamic interaction that occurs between individual partners and the relationship that they form and maintain. From this vantage point, we discuss the findings of this review with consideration to the four pillars of positive psychology: positive subjective experiences and character strengths and virtues (Pillars 1 and 2) that are assessed at the level of the individual; positive social institutions (Pillar 3); and the strengths of same-sex couples as an interdependent dyad (Pillar 4). The strengths of each pillar interact to support the same-sex couple's well-being as individuals and as a "third entity," an interdependent dyad that is greater than the sum of its individual parts (Fergus & Skerrett, 2015, p. 201).

Individual-Level Strengths of Same-Sex Relationships (Pillars 1 and 2)

The well-being of a couple's relationship and the well-being of the individuals in that relationship are contingent upon each other (Fergus & Skerrett, 2015). Therefore, individual strengths contribute to the well-being of the couple. This review finds strengths consistent with the first (positive subjective experiences) and second (character strengths and virtues) pillars of the positive psychology framework (Seligman & Csikszentmihalyi, 2000). Consistent with the first pillar, positive interaction in general (e.g., Gottman, Levenson, Swanson, et al., 2003) and showing appreciation and respect for individual differences specifically (Rostosky et al., 2006) emerged as internal strengths that are important to same-sex couples' relationship quality. Other positive processes such as positive meaning-making (Frost, 2011a, 2014) and positive reframing (Connolly, 2006; Gaines & Henderson, 2004) appear to be important internal strengths that partners use to cope with minority stress in a social context that stigmatizes their relationship (e.g., Frost, 2014).

The second pillar, character strengths and virtues, has not received much attention in the same-sex couple literature. Two character strengths that did emerge in the current review are same-sex couples' use of humor (Connolly & Sicola, 2005; Rostosky, Riggle, Savage, et al., 2008) and spirituality (Rostosky, Riggle, Brodnicki, & Olson, 2008) to support their relationship. Future research might explore the contribution of other character strengths and virtues such as courage, humility, and forgiveness (Vaughan & Rodriguez, 2014).

Research on other individual-level strengths and their contribution to the well-being of same-sex couple relationships is also needed. For example, research is needed to understand the contribution of positive LGBT identity to healthy same-sex relationships. Only one qualitative interview study mentioned that couples perceived that comfort with their same-sex couple identity was important to the quality of their relationship (Gaines & Henderson, 2004). In a sample of Israeli gay men (not included in this review), Elizur and Mintzer (2003) found that self-acceptance was associated with relationship satisfaction. On the basis of qualitative analyses, Riggle and Rostosky (2012) articulated positive aspects of LGBT identity that include authenticity, compassion/empathy, gender role flexibility, communication, belonging to a community, and engagement in social justice work, activism, and serving as a role model. Future research could assess LGBT identity strengths such as feelings of authenticity and perceptions of social belonging and test their contribution to couple well-being.

Positive Social Institutions (Pillar 3)

The third pillar, positive social institutions, is represented in the current review by research on the external resources of social support and legal recognition. The research suggests that same-sex couples actively negotiate extended family relationships in ways that different sex couples do not (e.g., LaSala, 2000; Rostosky et al., 2007). In contrast to different-sex couples' social support networks, same-sex couples may need to actively create social support through families of choice and may rely more on the support of their friendship networks.

Few studies have examined community-level supports for same-sex couples. One qualitative study in this review found that female couples perceived that support from the larger gay and lesbian community helped them cope with social disapproval (Gaines & Henderson, 2004). Additional research is needed on the contribution of general and LGBT-specific community-level resources and supports to same-sex couples' relationship quality.

A number of studies have examined the contribution to well-being of marriage equality/legal relationship recognition. Specific research is needed on the positive effects on same-sex couples of inclusive policies (e.g., marriage and inclusive nondiscrimination policies), many of which have been enacted relatively recently (Riggle et al., 2010a, 2010b). Future research needs to follow continuing changes in policy and address the contributions of positive institutions and a positive social environment to the health and well-being of same-sex couples and their families.

Couple-Level/Dyadic Strengths (Pillar 4)

In the current review, four relationship characteristics, perceived intimacy, egalitarianism, commitment, and outness, were found to be important to same-sex couple relationships. Three of these internal strengths have received considerable attention in the general relationship science literature that has traditionally focused on different-sex couples, perhaps because they are considered to be highly influenced by gender norms and expectations. Studies that compared these strengths in same-sex and different-sex couples often found no significant differences (e.g., Mackey et al., 2004; Patterson et al., 2004). When studies found significant differences, same-sex relationships, and particularly female relationships, exhibited higher levels of perceived intimacy and empathically attuned communication (e.g., Mackey et al., 2000; Umberson, Thomeer, & Lodge, 2015) and egalitarianism (e.g., Goldberg et al., 2012; Kurdek, 2001, 2003).

Perhaps same-sex couples practice intimacy-related skills more than different sex couples out of necessity, accounting for their self-reported and observed higher levels. Lev (2015) has noted that same-sex couples often forge high levels of intimacy in their relationships using an "us-against-the-world" approach. High levels of emotional intimacy strengthens commitment and provides a consistent and dependable source of support within the relationship that buffers minority stress and promotes thriving (see Feeney & Collins, 2015).

Egalitarianism in same-sex couples has been assessed frequently, and findings suggest it is an important value and strength in many same-sex relationships that is associated with relationship satisfaction (Kurdek, 2007). These studies have built on assumptions about gender roles as enacted in a heteronormative cultural and relational context and may have different meanings and impacts for same-sex couples (Reczek & Umberson, 2012; Umberson et al., 2015). Partners in same-sex relationships may have been similarly socialized in gender role norms and, recognizing the inequalities inherent in these norms, may be more likely to value equality or the negotiation of tasks on the basis of likes/dislikes and skills rather than gender norms.

Future research is needed to explore how same-sex couples enact gender in their relationships and how they use their strengths and skills to creatively form and maintain thriving relationships within a heteronormative society. Future studies may help to clarify distinctions in aspirational values about egalitarianism and their enactment in same-sex couple relationships. Dyadic-level, observational research may complement individual interview studies to achieve this aim (Umberson, Thomeer, Kroeger, Lodge, & Xu, 2015).

Commitment was most often studied through the theoretical lens of the investment model of commitment (Rusbult et al., 2011). Using this framework, few differences in commitment or commitment-related processes have been found when same-sex and different-sex couple relationships are compared (e.g., Kurdek, 2000, 2004). Future research may focus on discovering the meanings of specific types of investments to same-sex couples. Sexual exclusivity, for instance, may not serve the same investment and commitment function in male same-sex couple relationships as it does in female same-sex couple (or different-sex couple) relationships (Gotta et al., 2011).

Comparatively few studies have examined outness as a strength of same-sex couples. Whether outness functions primarily as a commitment-related investment or has other functions in same-sex relationships, it is a relationship characteristic that is unique to same-sex couples. Couples negotiate outness in part to manage stigma and potential exposure to prejudicial acts or discrimination. The role of disclosure and concealment of same-sex couple identity and its contribution to same-sex relationship well-being needs further examination.

Other dyadic-level strengths need to be explored in future research. For example, it may be fruitful to build on the theoretical construct of communal coping (Lyons, Michelson, Sullivan, & Coyne, 1998) that has been used to understand couples' interdependent health behaviors (e.g., Lewis et al., 2006). Communal coping focuses on positive interactions and dyadic level actions that are intended to benefit the relationship rather than the individual. Building on theoretical constructs such as communal coping may inspire further research on the dyadic-level strengths that same-sex couples draw upon to ameliorate minority stress.

Limitations and Recommendations

Methodology

One general limitation of the reviewed studies is the measures used to assess couple well-being. The most frequently assessed outcomes are global relationship quality (e.g., Balsam et al., 2008; Roisman et al., 2008) or relationship satisfaction (e.g., Boesch et al., 2007; Kamen et al., 2011; Kurdek, 2004). Longitudinal studies in this review often focused on relationship stability (Gottman, Levenson, Gross, et al., 2003; Rosenfeld, 2014; Whitton et al., 2015) or change in global relationship quality over time (Kurdek, 2008b). One longitudinal study examined life satisfaction and parenting alliance as outcomes (Tornello et al., 2015). Future research might consider expanding outcome measures to include, for example, aspects of eudaimonic well-being such as purpose and meaning.

Assessing positive outcomes in same-sex couple relationships may require further development of psychometrically validated measures for this population. Most of the typically used measures of global relationship quality and relationship satisfaction, for instance, were originally developed and validated for use with different-sex couples. Given that same-sex couples may have different perceptions of their relationship and what is important to their relationship, additional validation of existing measures and perhaps new measures need to be developed. For example, the unique strengths of same-sex couples, including being out about their relationship and making positive meaning out of minority stress experiences, need valid measures that can be used in survey research. These and other strengths and resources are important to examine at both the dyadic and individual-level of analysis (Umberson, Thomeer, Kroeger, et al., 2015).

The majority of studies in this review can be characterized as correlational survey studies that compared different-sex and same-sex relationships, or exploratory, qualitative studies of same-sex couples that systematically analyze narratives for themes. Studies that directly compared same-sex and different sex couples on relationship strengths have found many more similarities than differences (e.g., Cusack, Hughes, & Cook, 2012; Farr et al., 2010; Gottman, Levenson, Swanson, et al., 2003; Graham & Barnow, 2013; Kurdek, 2000, 2004; Roisman et al., 2008). However, comparative studies do not directly address the stigma that renders same-sex and different-sex relationships fundamentally unequal within the cultural, social, and political context.

Another significant limitation of the research is that the majority of studies are based on predominately White samples. Although persons of color or non-White persons may be involved at similar rates in same-sex relationships, lack of representation in research studies suggests that researchers have not accessed these relationships or communities successfully. For example, Moore's (2011) discussion of Black lesbian identity, including same-sex couple relationships and motherhood, represents a substantive contribution to our understanding of these families and a broadening of our understanding of same-sex couples (see also Moore & Stambolis-Ruhstorfer, 2013). Future research needs to include the perspectives of non-White and non-U.S.-based samples of same-sex couples (for examples of non-U.S. samples, see Badgett, 2009 and van Zyl, 2011). Although accessing these couples may be challenging, exploring the strengths and positive aspects of these relationships will expand our knowledge about same-sex couple relationships and the types of resources and social supports that can help them flourish.

Survey data available for research on the positive qualities and strengths of same-sex couples is not readily available. Social stigma has posed difficulties in recruiting same-sex couples for research studies (Meyer & Wilson, 2009). Population-based studies in the U.S. have rarely included questions to identify same-sex couples or individuals with same-sex partners (see summary and critique in Joyner, Manning, & Bogle, 2016). Only recently have surveys begun to ask directly about sexual identity or even the sex of a respondent's partner, which has often been assumed rather than assessed (see Gates, 2015). Even those surveys, such as Midlife Development in the U.S. (MIDUS), that have included identifying questions often result in very small sample sizes of LGB individuals, suggesting sampling bias (see Riggle, Rostosky, & Danner, 2009). Finally, population-based studies do not commonly include validated measures of relationship strengths (Umberson, Thomeer, Kroeger, et al., 2015), another limitation that needs to be addressed in future research.

Theoretical frameworks

Relevant theory can be used to help contextualize same-sex couples' strengths. For example, *positive marginality* refers to the resiliencies and strengths that may result from the coping efforts of people who carry some form of "outsider" social status (Unger, 1998). Some recent research has used positive marginality as an explanatory framework for understanding the resilience of LGBTQ (i.e., lesbian, gay, bisexual, transgender, queer) individuals (e.g., deVries, 2015; Frost, 2011a), and this concept may be helpful in building a positive psychology of same-sex relationships. Lev (2015) has written about relational resilience as a positive strength of same-sex couples, and this framework may also inspire new research questions and hypotheses to build a positive psychology of same-sex relationships. Concepts such as positive marginality and relational resilience may explain couples' perception that their relationship is strong in part because of the challenges that stigma presents (Rostosky et al., 2007; Riggle, Rothblum, et al., 2016).

Reis (2007) noted that the extensive relationship science literature would benefit from a unifying conceptual framework. Even though the same-sex couple literature is very small in comparison, future research will benefit from conceptual models that integrate and unify the many strengths that emerge in this review. One possibility is to take an integrated view of the four pillars of positive psychology. Integrating the concept of partner responsiveness (Gable & Reis, 2006) might further help to unify the relationship processes and strengths of same-sex couples into a coherent framework. The concept of partner responsiveness to the self assumes the interdependence of partners and the interaction between the development of the self and the close relationship. Thus, the growth and well-being of the individual influences and is influenced by the growth and well-being of the intimate relationship.

Central to this process of growth is the perception that one's partner responds with understanding, appreciation, and support (Gable & Reis, 2006). The internal strengths that emerged from this review can be understood as the means by which partners express and enact their mutual understanding and support. As Gable and Reis (2006) conclude, "perceived partner responsiveness is central both to interpersonal processes involved in intimacy and closeness, and to intrapersonal processes that underlie self-knowledge, self-esteem and personal goal pursuit" (p. 222). Further research could propose and test perceived partner responsiveness as a unifying conceptual framework for the four pillars.

In conclusion, research on same-sex couples' strengths and their contribution to couple well-being can move forward through theoretically driven inquiry, psychometrically sound measurement, and inclusive sampling. Same-sex couples form and maintain their relationships in a social context that still stigmatizes their relationships and subjects them to discrimination and minority stress (Doyle & Molix, 2015; Frost & LeBlanc, 2014; LeBlanc, Frost, & Wight, 2015; Rostosky & Riggle, 2016). Even in this context, same-sex couples create relationships that do not significantly differ from different-sex couples in measures of global relationship quality (Graham & Barlow, 2013; Kurdek, 2008b; Patterson et al., 2004; Roisman et al., 2008). Continuing to move beyond the role of stress to include the role of relational strengths in health and well-being is part of the work that lies ahead.

References

Adam, B. D. (2006). Relationship innovation in male couples. *Sexualities, 9,* 5–26. http://dx.doi.org/10.1177/1363460706060685

Badgett, M. V. L. (2009). *When gay people get married: What happens when societies legalize same-sex marriage.* New York, NY: New York University Press. http://dx.doi.org/10.18574/nyu/9780814791141.001.0001

Balsam, K. F., Beauchaine, T. P., Rothblum, E. D., & Solomon, S. E. (2008). Three-year follow-up of same-sex couples who had civil unions in Vermont, same-sex couples not in civil unions, and heterosexual married couples. *Developmental Psychology, 44,* 102–116. http://dx.doi.org/10.1037/0012-1649.44.1.102

Becker, O. A. (2013). Effects of similarity of life goals, values, and personality on relationship satisfaction and stability: Findings from a two-wave panel study. *Personal Relationships, 20,* 443–461. http://dx .doi.org/10.1111/j.1475-6811.2012.01417.x

Boesch, R. P., Cerqueira, R., Safer, M. A., & Wright, T. L. (2007). Relationship satisfaction and commitment in long-term male couples: Individual and dyadic effects. *Journal of Social and Personal Relationships, 24,* 837–853. http://dx.doi.org/10.1177/0265407507084186

Bradbury, T. N., & Karney, B. R. (2013). *Intimate relationships* (2nd ed.). New York, NY: Norton.

Clausell, E., & Roisman, G. I. (2009). Outness, big five personality traits, and same-sex relationship quality. *Journal of Social and Personal Relationships, 26*(2–3), 211–226. http://dx.doi.org/10.1177/026540 7509106711

Connolly, C. M. (2006). A feminist perspective of resilience in lesbian couples. *Journal of Feminist Family Therapy, 18*(1–2), 137–162. http:// dx.doi.org/10.1300/J086v18n01_06

Connolly, C. M., & Sicola, M. K. (2005). Listening to lesbian couples. *Journal of GLBT Family Studies, 1,* 143–167. http://dx.doi.org/10.1300/ J461v01n02_09

Cusack, C. E., Hughes, J. L., & Cook, R. E. (2012). Components of love and relationship satisfaction: Lesbians and heterosexual women. *Psi Chi Journal of Psychological Research, 17,* 171–179.

Degges-White, S., & Marszalek, J. (2007). An exploration of long-term, same-sex relationships. *Journal of LGBT Issues in Counseling, 1,* 99–119. http://dx.doi.org/10.1300/J462v01n04_07

de Vries, B. (2015). Stigma and LGBT aging: Negative and positive marginality. In N. A. Orel, C. A. Fruhauf, N. A. Orel, & C. A. Fruhauf (Eds.), *The lives of LGBT older adults: Understanding challenges and resilience* (pp. 55–71). Washington, DC: American Psychological Association. http://dx.doi. org/10.1037/14436-003

Doyle, D. M., & Molix, L. (2015). Social stigma and sexual minorities' romantic relationship functioning: A meta-analytic review. *Personality and Social Psychology Bulletin, 41,* 1363–1381. http://dx.doi. org/10 .1177/0146167215594592

Dziengel, L. (2012). Resilience, ambiguous loss, and older same-sex couples: The resilience constellation model. *Journal of Social Service Research, 38,* 74–88. http://dx.doi.org/10.1080/01488376.2011.62 6354

Elizur, Y., & Mintzer, A. (2003). Gay males' intimate relationship quality: The roles of attachment security, gay identity, social support, and income. *Personal Relationships, 10,* 411–435. http://dx.doi. org/10.1111/ 1475-6811.00057

Farr, R. H., Forssell, S. L., & Patterson, C. J. (2010). Gay, lesbian, and heterosexual adoptive parents: Couple and relationship issues. *Journal of GLBT Family Studies, 6,* 199 –213. http://dx.doi. org/10.1080/ 15504281003705436

Feeney, B. C., & Collins, N. L. (2015). Thriving through relationships. *Current Opinion in Psychology, 1,* 22–28. http://dx.doi.org/10.1016/j .copsyc.2014.11.001

Fergus, K., & Skerrett, K. (2015). Resilient couple coping revisited: Building relationship muscle. In K. Skerrett, K. Fergus, K. Skerrett, & K. Fergus (Eds.), *Couple resilience: Emerging perspectives.* (pp. 199–210). New York, NY: Springer Science Business Media.

Fincham, F. D., & Beach, S. R. H. (2010). Of memes and marriage: Toward a positive relationship science. *Journal of Family Theory & Review, 2,* 4–24. http://dx.doi.org/10.1111/j.1756-2589.2010.00033.x

Fingerhut, A. W., & Maisel, N. C. (2010). Relationship formalization and individual and relationship well-being among same-sex couples. *Journal of Social and Personal Relationships, 27,* 956–969. http://dx.doi.org/10 .1177/0265407510376253

Frost, D. M. (2011a). Stigma and intimacy in same-sex relationships: A narrative approach. *Journal of Family Psychology, 25,* 1–10. http://dx .doi.org/10.1037/a0022374

Frost, D. M. (2011b). Similarities and differences in the pursuit of intimacy among sexual minority and heterosexual individuals: A personal projects analysis. *Journal of Social Issues, 67,* 282–301. http://dx.doi.org/10 .1111/j.1540-4560.2011.01698.x

Frost, D. M. (2014). Redemptive framings of minority stress and their association with closeness in same-sex relationships. *Journal of Couple & Relationship Therapy, 13,* 219 –239. http://dx.doi.org/10.1080/15332691.2013.871616

Frost, D. M., & Gola, K. A. (2015). Meanings of intimacy: A comparison of members of heterosexual and same-sex couples. *Analyses of Social Issues and Public Policy (ASAP), 15,* 382–400. http://dx.doi.org/10 .1111/asap.12072

Frost, D. M., & LeBlanc, A. J. (2014). Nonevent stress contributes to mental health disparities based on sexual orientation: Evidence from a personal projects analysis. *American Journal of Orthopsychiatry, 84,* 557–566. http://dx.doi.org/10.1037/ort0000024

Gable, S. L., & Reis, H. T. (2006). Intimacy and the self: An iterative model of the self and close relationships. In P. Noller & J. A. Feeney (Eds.), *Close relationships: Functions, forms and processes* (pp. 212–222). New York, NY: Psychology Press.

Gaines, S. O., Jr., & Henderson, M. C. (2004). On the limits of generalizability: Applying resource exchange theory to gay relationship processes. *Journal of Homosexuality, 48,* 79–102. http://dx.doi.org/10 .1300/J082v48n01_04

Gates, G. J. (2015). *Demographics of married and unmarried same-sex couples: Analyses of the 2013 American Community Survey.* Los Angeles, CA: Williams Institute, UCLA School of Law. Retrieved from http://williamsinstitute.law.ucla.edu/wp-content/uploads/Demographics-Same-Sex-Couples-ACS2013-March-2015.pdf

Goldberg, A. E., Smith, J. Z., & Perry-Jenkins, M. (2012). The division of labor in lesbian, gay, and heterosexual new adoptive parents. *Journal of Marriage and the Family, 74,* 812–828. http://dx.doi.org/10.1111/j .1741-3737.2012.00992.x

Gotta, G., Green, R.-J., Rothblum, E., Solomon, S., Balsam, K., & Schwartz, P. (2011). Heterosexual, lesbian, and gay male relationships: A comparison of couples in 1975 and 2000. *Family Process, 50,* 353–376. http://dx.doi.org/10.1111/j.1545-5300.2011.01365.x

Gottman, J. M., Levenson, R. W., Gross, J., Frederickson, B. L., McCoy, K., Rosenthal, L., ... Yoshimoto, D. (2003). Correlates of gay and lesbian couples' relationship satisfaction and relationship dissolution. *Journal of Homosexuality, 45,* 23–43. http://dx.doi.org/10.1300/ J082v45n01_02

Gottman, J. M., Levenson, R. W., Swanson, C., Swanson, K., Tyson, R., & Yoshimoto, D. (2003). Observing gay, lesbian and heterosexual couples' relationships: Mathematical modeling of conflict interaction. *Journal of Homosexuality, 45,* 65–91. http://dx.doi.org/10.1300/J082v45n01_04

Graham, J. M., & Barnow, Z. B. (2013). Stress and social support in gay, lesbian, and heterosexual couples: Direct effects and buffering models. *Journal of Family Psychology, 27,* 569–578. http://dx.doi.org/10.1037/ a0033420

Gustavson, K., Røysamb, E., Borren, I., Torvik, F. A., & Karevold, E. (2015). Life satisfaction in close relationships: Findings from a longitudinal study. *Journal of Happiness Studies, 17,* 1293–1311.

Haas, A. P., & Stafford, S. L. (2005). Maintenance behaviors in same-sex and marital relationships: A matched sample comparison. *Journal of Family Communication, 5,* 43–60. http://dx.doi.org/10.1207/ s15327698jfc0501_3

Haas, S. M., & Whitton, S. W. (2015). The significance of living together and importance of marriage in same-sex couples. *Journal of Homosexuality, 62,* 1241–1263. http://dx.doi.org/10.1080/00918369.2015 .1037137

Johnson, M. P. (1999). Personal, moral, and structural commitment to relationships: Experiences of choice and constraint. In J. M. Adams & W. H. Jones (Eds.), *Handbook of interpersonal commitment and relationship stability* (pp. 73–90). New York, NY: Kluwer Academic/Plenum Press Publishers. http://dx.doi.org/10.1007/978-1-4615-4773-0_4

Jonathan, N. (2009). Carrying equal weight: Relational responsibility and attunement among same-sex couples. In C. Knudson-Martin, A. R. Mahoney, C. Knudson-Martin, & A. R. Mahoney (Eds.), *Couples, gender, and power: Creating change in intimate relationships* (pp. 79–103). New York, NY: Springer.

Jordan, K. M., & Deluty, R. H. (2000). Social support, coming out, and relationship satisfaction in lesbian couples. *Journal of Lesbian Studies, 4,* 145–164. http://dx.doi.org/10.1300/J155v04n01_09

Joyner, K., Manning, W., & Bogle, R. (2016). *Gender and the stability of same-sex and different sex relationships.* Retrieved from http://www .bgsu.edu/organizations/cfdr

Kamen, C., Burns, M., & Beach, S. R. H. (2011). Minority stress in same-sex male relationships: When does it impact relationship satisfaction? *Journal of Homosexuality, 58,* 1372–1390. http://dx.doi.org/10 .1080/00918369.2011.614904

Kiecolt-Glaser, J. K., & Newton, T. L. (2001). Marriage and health: His and hers. *Psychological Bulletin, 127,* 472–503. http://dx.doi.org/10 .1037/0033-2909.127.4.472

Kilmann, P. R., & Vendemia, J. M. C. (2013). Partner discrepancies in distressed marriages. *The Journal of Social Psychology, 153,* 196–211. http://dx.doi.org/10.1080/00224545.2012.719941

Kurdek, L. A. (1993). Predicting marital dissolution: A 5-year prospective longitudinal study of newlywed couples. *Journal of Personality and Social Psychology, 64,* 221–242. http://dx.doi.org/10.1037/0022-3514 .64.2.221

Kurdek, L. A. (2000). Attractions and constraints as determinants of relationship commitment: Longitudinal evidence from gay, lesbian, and heterosexual couples. *Personal Relationships, 7,* 245–262. http://dx.doi .org/10.1111/j.1475-6811.2000.tb00015.x

Kurdek, L. A. (2001). Differences between heterosexual-nonparent couples and gay, lesbian, and heterosexual-parent couples. *Journal of Family Issues, 22,* 727–754. http://dx.doi.org/10.1177/019251301022006004

Kurdek, L. A. (2003). Differences between gay and lesbian cohabiting couples. *Journal of Social and Personal Relationships, 20,* 411–436. http://dx.doi.org/10.1177/02654075030204001

Kurdek, L. A. (2004). Are gay and lesbian cohabitating couples really different from heterosexual married couples? *Journal of Marriage and the Family, 66,* 880–900. http://dx.doi.org/10.1111/j.0022-2445.2004.00060.x

Kurdek, L. A. (2007). The allocation of household labor by partners in gay and lesbian couples. *Journal of Family Issues, 28,* 132–148. http://dx .doi.org/10.1177/0192513X06292019

Kurdek, L. A. (2008a). A general model of relationship commitment: Evidence from same-sex partners. *Personal Relationships, 15,* 391–405. http://dx.doi.org/10.1111/j.1475-6811.2008.00205.x

Kurdek, L. A. (2008b). Change in relationship quality for partners from lesbian, gay male, and heterosexual couples. *Journal of Family Psychology, 22,* 701–711. http://dx.doi.org/10.1037/0893-3200.22.5.701

Lannutti, P. J. (2011). Security, recognition, and misgivings: Exploring older same-sex couples' experiences of legally recognized same-sex marriage. *Journal of Social and Personal Relationships, 28,* 64–82. http://dx.doi.org/10.1177/0265407510386136

LaSala, M. C. (2000). Gay male couples: The importance of coming out and being out to parents. *Journal of Homosexuality, 39,* 47–71. http:// dx.doi.org/10.1300/J082v39n02_03

LeBlanc, A. J., Frost, D. M., & Wight, R. G. (2015). Minority stress and stress proliferation among same-sex and other marginalized couples. *Journal of Marriage and the Family, 77,* 40–59. http:// dx.doi.org/10 .1111/jomf.12160

Lehmiller, J. J. (2010). Differences in relationship investments between gay and heterosexual men. *Personal Relationships, 17,* 81–96. http://dx .doi.org/10.1111/j.1475-6811.2010.01254.x

Lev, A. I. (2015). Resilience in lesbian and gay couples. In K. Skerrett, K. Fergus, K. Skerrett, & K. Fergus (Eds.), *Couple resilience: Emerging perspectives.* (pp. 45–61). New York, NY: Springer Science + Business Media. http://dx.doi.org/10.1007/978-94-017-9909-6_3

Lewis, M. A., McBride, C. M., Pollak, K. I., Puleo, E., Butterfield, R. M., & Emmons, K. M. (2006). Understanding health behavior change among couples: An interdependence and communal coping approach. *Social Science & Medicine, 62,* 1369 –1380. http://dx.doi.org/10.1016/j .socscimed.2005.08.006

Littlefield, G. D., Lim, M. G., Canada, R. M., & Jennings, G. (2000). Common themes in long-term lesbian relationships. *Family Therapy, 27,* 71–79.

Lyons, R. F., Michelson, K. D., Sullivan, M. J., & Coyne, J. C. (1998). Coping as a communal process. *Journal of Personal and Social Relationships, 15,* 579–605. http://dx.doi.org/10.1177/0265407598155001

Macapagal, K., Greene, G. J., Rivera, Z., & Mustanski, B. (2015). "The best is always yet to come": Relationship stages and processes among young LGBT couples. *Journal of Family Psychology, 29,* 309–320. http://dx.doi.org/10.1037/fam0000094

Mackey, R. A., Diemer, M. A., & O'Brien, B. A. (2000). Psychological intimacy in the lasting relationships of heterosexual and same-gender couples. *Sex Roles, 43,* 201–227. http://dx.doi.org/10.1023/A:1007028930658

Mackey, R. A., Diemer, M. A., & O'Brien, B. A. (2004). Relational factors in understanding satisfaction in the lasting relationships of same sex and heterosexual couples. *Journal of Homosexuality, 47,* 111–136. http://dx .doi.org/10.1300/J082v47n01_07

Matthews, A. K., Tartaro, J., & Hughes, T. L. (2003). A comparative study of lesbian and heterosexual women in committed relationships. *Journal of Lesbian Studies, 7,* 101–114. http://dx.doi.org/10.1300/J155v07 n01_07

Meyer, I. H., & Wilson, P. A. (2009). Sampling lesbian, gay, and bisexual populations. *Journal of Counseling Psychology, 56*, 23–31. http://dx.doi .org/10.1037/a0014587

Moore, M. R. (2011). Two sides of the same coin: Revising analyses of lesbian sexuality and family formation through the study of Black women. *Journal of Lesbian Studies, 15*, 58–68. http://dx.doi. org/10 .1080/10894160.2010.508412

Moore, M. R., & Stambolis-Ruhstorfer, M. (2013). LGBT sexuality and families at the start of the 21st century. *Annual Review of Sociology, 39*, 491–507. http://dx.doi.org/10.1146/annurev-soc-071312-145643

Myers, D. G., & Diener, E. (1995). Who is happy? *Psychological Science, 6*, 10–19. http://dx.doi. org/10.1111/j.1467-9280.1995.tb00298.x

Ogolsky, B. G., & Gray, C. R. (2016). Conflict, negative emotion, and reports of partners' relationship maintenance in same-sex couples. *Journal of Family Psychology, 30*, 171–180. http://dx.doi.org/10.1037/ fam0000148

Patterson, C. J., Sutfin, E. L., & Fulcher, M. (2004). Division of labor among lesbian and heterosexual parenting couples: Correlates of specialized versus shared patterns. *Journal of Adult Development, 11*, 179–189. http://dx.doi.org/10.1023/B:JADE.0000035626.90331.47

Patterson, G. E., Ward, D. B., & Brown, T. B. (2013). Relationship scripts: How young women develop and maintain same-sex romantic relationships. *Journal of GLBT Family Studies, 9*, 179–201. http:// dx.doi.org/ 10.1080/1550428X.2013.765263

Pope, A. L., & Cashwell, C. S. (2013). Moral commitment in intimate committed relationships: A conceptualization from cohabiting same-sex and opposite-sex partners. *The Family Journal, 21*, 5–14. http://dx.doi .org/10.1177/1066480712456671

Porche, M. V., & Purvin, D. M. (2008). 'Never in our lifetime': Legal marriage for same-sex couples in long-term relationships. *Family Relations, 57*, 144–159. http://dx.doi.org/10.1111/j.1741-3729.2008.00490.x

Quam, J. K., Whitford, G. S., Dziengel, L. E., & Knochel, K. A. (2010). Exploring the nature of same-sex relationships. *Journal of Gerontological Social Work, 53*, 702–722. http://dx.doi.org/10.1080/01634372 .2010.518664

Reczek, C., & Umberson, D. (2012). Gender, health behavior, and intimate relationships: Lesbian, gay, and straight contexts. *Social Science & Medicine, 74*, 1783–1790. http://dx.doi.org/10.1016/j. socscimed.2011 .11.011

Reis, H. T. (2007). Steps toward the ripening of relationship science. *Personal Relationships, 14*, 1–23. http://dx.doi.org/10.1111/j.1475-6811 .2006.00139.x

Riggle, E. D. B., & Rostosky, S. S. (2012). *A positive view of LGBTQ: Embracing identity and cultivating well-being.* Lanham, MD: Rowman & Littlefield.

Riggle, E. D. B., Rostosky, S. S., & Danner, F. (2009). LGB identity and eudaimonic well-being in midlife. *Journal of Homosexuality, 56*, 786–798. http://dx.doi.org/10.1080/00918360903054277

Riggle, E. D. B., Rostosky, S. S., & Horne, S. G. (2010a). Does it matter where you live? State non-discrimination laws and the perceptions of LGB residents. *Sexuality Research & Social Policy, 7*, 168–172. http:// dx.doi.org/10.1007/s13178-010-0016-z

Riggle, E. D. B., Rostosky, S. S., & Horne, S. G. (2010b). Psychological distress, well-being, and legal recognition in same-sex couple relationships. *Journal of Family Psychology, 24*, 82–86. http://dx.doi. org/10 .1037/a0017942

Riggle, E. D. B., Rostosky, S. S., McCants, W., & Pascale-Hague, D. (2011). The positive aspects of a transgender identity. *Psychology and Sexuality, 2,* 147–158. http://dx.doi.org/10.1080/19419899.2010.534490

Riggle, E. D. B., Rothblum, E. D., Rostosky, S. S., Clark, J. B., & Balsam, K. F. (2016). "The secret of our success": Long-term same-sex couples' perceptions of their relationship longevity. *Journal of GLBT Family Studies, 12,* 1–16. http://dx.doi.org/10.1080/1550428X.2015.1095668

Riggle, E. D. B., Whitman, J. S., Olson, A., Rostosky, S. S., & Strong, S. (2008). The positive aspects of being a lesbian or gay man. *Professional Psychology, Research and Practice, 39,* 210–217. http://dx.doi.org/10 .1037/0735-7028.39.2.210

Riggle, E. D. B., Wickham, R. E., Rostosky, S. S., Rothblum, E. D., & Balsam, K. F. (2016). Impact of civil marriage recognition for long-term same-sex couples. *Sexuality Research & Social Policy.* Advance online publication. http://dx.doi.org/10.1007/s13178-016-0243-z

Roisman, G. I., Clausell, E., Holland, A., Fortuna, K., & Elieff, C. (2008). Adult romantic relationships as contexts of human development: A multimethod comparison of same-sex couples with opposite-sex dating, engaged, and married dyads. *Developmental Psychology, 44,* 91–101. http://dx.doi.org/10.1037/0012-1649.44.1.91

Rosenfeld, M. J. (2014). Couple longevity in the era of same-sex marriage in the United States. *Journal of Marriage and the Family, 76,* 905–918. http://dx.doi.org/10.1111/jomf.12141

Rostosky, S. S., Otis, M. D., Riggle, E. D. B., Kelly, S., & Brodnicki, C. (2008). An exploratory study of religiosity and same-sex couple relationships. *Journal of GLBT Family Studies, 4,* 17–36. http://dx.doi.org/ 10.1080/15504280802084407

Rostosky, S. S., & Riggle, E. D. B. (2016). Same-sex relationships and minority stress. *Current Opinion in Psychology, 13,* 29–38. http://dx.doi .org/10.1016/j.copsyc.2016.04.011

Rostosky, S. S., Riggle, E. D. B., Brodnicki, C., & Olson, A. (2008). An exploration of lived religion in same-sex couples from Judeo-Christian traditions. *Family Process, 47,* 389–403. http://dx.doi.org/10.1111/j .1545-5300.2008.00260.x

Rostosky, S., Riggle, E. D. B., Dudley, M. G., & Comer Wright, M. L. (2006). Commitment in same-sex relationships: A qualitative analysis of couples' conversations. *Journal of Homosexuality, 51,* 199–223. http:// dx.doi.org/10.1300/J082v51n03_10

Rostosky, S. S., Riggle, E. D. B., Gray, B. E., & Hatton, R. L. (2007). Minority stress experiences in committed same-sex couple relationships. *Professional Psychology, Research and Practice, 38,* 392–400. http:// dx.doi.org/10.1037/0735-7028.38.4.392

Rostosky, S. S., Riggle, E. D. B., Pascale-Hague, D., & McCants, L. (2010). The positive aspects of a bisexual identification. *Psychology and Sexuality, 1,* 131–144. http://dx.doi.org/10.1080/19419899.2010.484595

Rostosky, S. S., Riggle, E. D. B., Rothblum, E. D., & Balsam, K. F. (2016). Same-sex couples' decisions and experiences of marriage in the context of minority stress: Interviews from a population-based longitudinal study. *Journal of Homosexuality, 63,* 1019–1040. http://dx.doi.org/10 .1080/00918369.2016.1191232

Rostosky, S. S., Riggle, E. D. B., Savage, T. A., Roberts, S. D., & Singletary, G. (2008). Interracial same-sex couples' perceptions of stress and coping: An exploratory study. *Journal of GLBT Family Studies, 4,* 277–299. http://dx.doi.org/10.1080/15504280802177458

Rusbult, C. E., Agnew, C., & Arriaga, X. (2011). *The investment model of commitment processes.* Department of Psychological Sciences Faculty Publications. Paper 26. http://docs.lib.purdue.edu/psychpubs/26.

Schecter, E., Tracy, A. J., Page, K. V., & Luong, G. (2008). Shall we marry? Legal marriage as a commitment event in same-sex relationships. *Journal of Homosexuality, 54,* 400–422. http://dx.doi.org/10.1080/ 00918360801991422

Seligman, M. E., & Csikszentmihalyi, M. (2000). Positive psychology. An introduction. *American Psychologist, 55,* 5–14. http://dx.doi.org/10 .1037/0003-066X.55.1.5

Solomon, S. E., Rothblum, E. D., & Balsam, K. F. (2004). Pioneers in partnership: Lesbian and gay male couples in civil unions compared with those not in civil unions and married heterosexual siblings. *Journal of Family Psychology, 18,* 275–286. http://dx.doi.org/10.1037/0893-3200 .18.2.275

Solomon, S. E., Rothblum, E. D., & Balsam, K. F. (2005). Money, housework, sex, and conflict: Same-sex couples in civil unions, those not in civil unions, and heterosexual married siblings. *Sex Roles, 52*(9–10), 561–575. http://dx.doi.org/10.1007/s11199-005-3725-7

Tornello, S. L., Sonnenberg, B. N., & Patterson, C. J. (2015). Division of labor among gay fathers: Associations with parent, couple, and child adjustment. *Psychology of Sexual Orientation and Gender Diversity, 2,* 365–375. http://dx.doi.org/10.1037/sgd0000109

Umberson, D., Thomeer, M. B., Kroeger, R. A., Lodge, A. C., & Xu, M. (2015). Challenges and opportunities for research on same-sex relationships. *Journal of Marriage and the Family, 77,* 96–111. http:// dx.doi .org/10.1111/jomf.12155

Umberson, D., Thomeer, M. B., & Lodge, A. C. (2015). Intimacy and emotion work in lesbian, gay, and heterosexual relationships. *Journal of Marriage and the Family, 77,* 542–556. http://dx.doi.org/10.1111/jomf .12178

Umberson, D., Williams, K., Powers, D. A., Liu, H., & Needham, B. (2006). You make me sick: Marital quality and health over the life course. *Journal of Health and Social Behavior, 47,* 1–16. http://dx.doi .org/10.1177/002214650604700101

Unger, R. K. (1998). Positive marginality: Antecedents and consequences. *Journal of Adult Development, 5,* 163–170. http://dx.doi.org/10.1023/A: 1023019626469

van Eeden-Moorefield, B., Pasley, K., Crosbie-Burnett, M., & King, E. (2012). Explaining couple cohesion in different types of gay families. *Journal of Family Issues, 33,* 182–201. http://dx.doi.org/10.1177/ 0192513X11418180

Van Zyl, M. (2011). Are same-sex marriages un-African? Same-sex relationships and belonging in post-apartheid South Africa. *Journal of Social Issues, 67,* 335–357. http://dx.doi.org/10.1111/j.1540-4560.2011 .01701.x

Vaughan, M. D., & Rodriguez, E. M. (2014). LGBT strengths: Incorporating positive psychology into theory, research, training, and practice. *Psychology of Sexual Orientation and Gender Diversity, 1,* 325–334. http://dx.doi.org/10.1037/sgd0000053

Whitton, S. W., Kuryluk, A. D., & Khaddouma, A. M. (2015). Legal and social ceremonies to formalize same-sex relationships: Associations with commitment, social support, and relationship outcomes. *Couple & Family Psychology, 4,* 161–176. http://dx.doi.org/10.1037/cfp0000045

Wight, R. G., Leblanc, A. J., & Lee Badgett, M. V. (2013). Same-sex legal marriage and psychological well-being: Findings from the California Health Interview Survey. *American Journal of Public Health, 103,* 339–346. http://dx.doi.org/10.2105/AJPH.2012.301113

The Experience of Resilience for Adult Female Survivors of Intimate Partner Violence

A Phenomenological Inquiry

BY SARA E. CRANN AND PAULA C. BARATA

Introduction

Intimate partner violence (IPV) is a complex social problem that affects millions of women worldwide. The World Health Organization (WHO; 2002, 2006a) broadly defines IPV as any behavior within an intimate relationship that causes physical, psychological, or sexual harm including physical aggression, psychological abuse, forced intercourse, and various controlling behaviors (e.g., isolating a person, restricting access to information and assistance). A multi-country study of physical and sexual violence found prevalence estimates of IPV against women ranged from 15-71% among several industrialized and non-industrialized countries (WHO, 2006b). The rates of physical injury as a result of IPV in Canada, where the current data were collected, and the United States are high (23.6% and 26.7%, respectively; Thompson, Saltzman, & Johnson, 2003). In Canada, intimate partners are perpetrators in almost half (45%) of all violent crimes against women reported to police (Sinha, 2013). The pervasiveness and significant consequences of abuse have elicited considerable interest from researchers trying to better understand the causes, interacting factors, and implications of IPV. Previous research on IPV has largely focused on the negative psychological and physical consequences for women. There is, however, a growing body of positive psychological research examining how women cope and move through their experiences of abuse. Psychological resilience has emerged in the literature as an important phenomenon for women who have experienced partner abuse. This is a growing area of research, yet there is relatively little known about the lived experience of resilience for survivors of IPV. Using a phenomenological approach, the purpose of the current study is to examine how psychological resilience is constructed and experienced by adult female survivors of IPV. It is important to note that the term *survivor*, rather than *victim*, is used intentionally throughout this article to describe women who have experienced abuse. Particularly in the context of resilience research, the term *survivor* conveys a sense of strength, resistance, and positivity that is reflected in the experiences of the women who participated in this study.

Resilience and Related Concepts

Broadly, there is disagreement in the literature as to the most appropriate way to define and conceptualize resilience. Previous theoretical and empirical work has conceptualized resilience in different ways (e.g., trait, outcome, process). Although an in-depth discussion of the conceptual complexities of resilience is beyond the scope of this article due to space constraints, critiques and criticisms of the construct have been well-documented (e.g., Luthar, Cicchetti, & Becker, 2000; Roisman, 2005). It has even been suggested that there are no meaningful differences between different conceptualizations of resilience, and any distinction simply reflects the types of questions being asked, duration of stressor, and population under study (Macini & Bonanno, 2006). Not surprisingly, multiple conceptualizations of resilience have subsequently led to the use of various indicators of resilience. Three broad categories of psychosocial indicators of resilience are reflected in the literature: the absence of psychopathology (e.g., lack of a clinical diagnosis or scoring below the clinical cutoff on a measure of psychopathology), the presence of resilience proxy measures (e.g., factors associated with resilience, such as self-efficacy or hardiness), and resilience scale scores (e.g., Connor–Davidson Resilience Scale).

Post-traumatic growth (PTG) is theoretically related to resilience. Tedeschi and Calhoun (2003) argue that PTG is conceptually distinct from resilience because PTG implies a significant and positive change in emotional and cognitive functioning that goes beyond baseline levels. Embedded in their distinction between resilience and PTG is the assumption that resilience is more akin to recovery or homeostaticity. However, the assumption that there is no distinction between recovery and resilience has also been challenged in the literature (Bonanno, 2005). Terms like *growth*, *adaptation*, *coping*, *recovery*, and *thriving* are found throughout the literature on positive functioning after trauma, but are often not clearly defined in individual studies and are defined in various ways across the literature.

Despite disagreement or lack of clarity over theoretical distinctions between resilience and related concepts, it remains an important endeavor to better understand how women cope with and move through their experiences of abuse. The valuable clinical and policy applications of resilience research, especially in the context of IPV, secure its importance and relevance in psychological research. Understanding resilience is important because it can help practitioners build practical strategies, skills, or competencies for women experiencing abuse (Humphreys, 2003). For the current research, and with acknowledgment of the various conceptualizations of resilience and related concepts, resilience was approached as a broad and inclusive construct in a deliberate effort not to constrain participants' understandings and experiences of the phenomenon (Massey, Cameron, Ouellette, & Fine, 1998).

Resilience and IPV Literature

For the purposes of the current research, we draw on previous IPV research that has explicitly examined resilience or made inferences about women's resilience based on the research findings. Previous research examining women's resilience in the context of IPV can be classified broadly as (a) quantitative research testing models of resilience in specific populations (e.g., African American women and women living in shelters), and (b) qualitative examinations of women's resilience following an abusive relationship.

Quantitative research. In quantitative research with adult female survivors of IPV, resilience is often conceptualized as an outcome of protective factors and measured as the absence of psychopathology. Previous research has measured resilience as low levels or the absence of post-traumatic stress disorder (PTSD; Wright, Perez, & Johnson, 2010), depression (Carlson, McNutt, Choi, & Rose, 2002; Wright et al., 2010), anxiety (Carlson et al., 2002), and suicide attempt status (Meadows, Kaslow, Thompson, & Jurkovic, 2005). Some researchers have used multiple resilience indicators. For example, Humphreys (2003) used both a self-report measure of resilience and a measure of general psychological distress to test for a relationship between abuse experience, psychological distress, and resilience in women living in shelters. This body of quantitative research also found support for various protective factors for resilience, including various types of social support (e.g., Carlson et al., 2002), self-esteem (Carlson et al., 2002; Meadows et al., 2005), positive health, religious coping and spirituality, hope, self-efficacy, effectiveness of obtaining resources (Meadows et al., 2005), coping, and empowerment (Wright et al., 2010). Although this body of research has provided invaluable knowledge about the diversity and abundance of protective factors for resilience, inferring resilience from the absence of psychopathology fails to acknowledge the social and cultural context in which the development and expression of resilience is embedded and constrains the complexity of the phenomenon (Almedom & Glandon, 2007). The multidimensional nature of resilience suggests that individuals may fail to meet resilience indicators (e.g., by having a diagnosis of PTSD), yet be functioning well in other domains of adjustment, such as school or work performance (Luthar et al., 2000).

Furthermore, what is considered a resilient outcome or a protective factor for resilience may not be relevant across social and cultural contexts (Masten, 1994; Ungar, 2004). Even within a group, such as survivors of IPV, there can be a range of contexts, supported by the research on stages of abuse (e.g., Doherty, 1997) and the process of leaving an abusive relationship (e.g., Landenburger, 1989). The research on stages has identified the experience of moving through abuse as a fluid process that changes over time (Landenburger, 1989; Merritt-Gray & Wuest, 1995). The conceptualization and measurement of resilience in previous quantitative research does not reflect the fluid and dynamic nature of abuse, omitting the contextualized experiences of survivors from our understanding of resilience. Embedded in existing quantitative approaches to the study of resilience is an assumption that how women develop and experience resilience is largely consistent over time and populations. However, previous research suggests that individual difference (Gallo, Bogart, Vranceanu, & Matthews, 2005) and contextual and environmental factors likely influence an individual's response to stress. While resilience may be a more common response to trauma than previously thought (Bonanno, 2005), it is unlikely that this response is uniform across individuals or context. Some previous quantitative work has already begun to address the importance of paying attention to women's surrounding context when researching IPV (Meadows et al., 2005), but methodologies that acknowledge and reflect context have yet to be fully incorporated into resilience research with adult survivors of IPV.

Qualitative research. There is a need for more qualitative research to further our understanding of resilience (Luthar et al., 2000; Rutter, 2006). This is particularly relevant to IPV because resilience has been so narrowly conceptualized and measured. Qualitative approaches allow researchers to grapple with conceptual and methodological issues inherent in resilience research, including researcher-imposed values about appropriate outcomes, recognition for participant context and subjective experience, and not restricting resilience to an essentialist construct (Massey et al., 1998). According to Ungar (2004), most research on resilience is situated in "positivist modes of inquiry" and locates resilience within an ecological framework that typically uses quantitative methods to make generalizations about causal relationships. Ungar (2004) argues that this approach to resilience research is "unable to accommodate the plurality of meanings individuals negotiate in their self-constructions as resilient" (p. 345) and offers a constructionist interpretation of resilience, which pays greater attention to the relativistic nature of resilience, as an alternative. Social constructionism posits that experiences and their associated meanings are socially produced and historically and culturally specific, rather than direct representations of reality (Burr, 1995). A constructionist approach to the study of resilience generates findings that are meaningful to participants, and protective factors are understood to be "multidimensional, unique to each context, and predict health outcomes as defined by individuals and their social reference group" (Ungar, 2004, p. 344). Ungar et al.'s (2007) multi-country study of resilience in youth found seven "tensions" of resilience. Tensions are specific challenges that the culturally diverse youth were faced with. Youth who were identified as resilient had successfully resolved each tension. The seven tensions are access to material resources, relationships, identity, power and control, cultural adherence, social justice, and cohesion. Although the presentation of these tensions, and the degree of relevance or influence of each tension, was culturally specific, the seven tensions were found across the cultural groups in this study. Ungar's work highlights a common underlying experience of resilience (i.e., the tensions), while demonstrating the influence of the surrounding social and cultural context on the formation and expression of resilience.

Whereas there is a body of qualitative research examining women's experiences of leaving, surviving, and coping with abuse (e.g., Crawford, Liebling-Kalifani, & Hill, 2009; Davis, 2002; Kangagaratnam et al., 2012) that has acknowledged the influence of women's socio-cultural context, there are few qualitative studies that have specifically examined women's experiences of resilience in the context of IPV. One exception is Young (2007), who examined factors and processes related to resilience and PTG in survivors of IPV. Using a grounded theory approach, Young found that resilience following an abusive relationship involved renewed self-perceptions, renewed faith and spiritual beliefs, and a return to baseline levels of functioning. PTG occurred in the form of change in relationships, self-perception, and cognitive appraisals. K. M. Anderson, Renner, and Danis (2012) provided a mixed-method approach to the study of resilience, and in their qualitative analysis reported the importance of religious and informal and formal social support for women's recovery and resilience following abuse. These studies are an important step in increasing qualitative work in this area of research and bringing women's voices into the literature; however, samples were limited to women who had not experienced IPV for at least 1 year. This criterion may limit our understanding of resilience as a phenomenon that only occurs after a certain period of time has passed following trauma. Furthermore, previous qualitative studies have focused largely on the impacts of abuse and the personal and social factors that contribute to recovery and resilience, rather than on the qualities and experience of resilience as a psychological phenomenon. As a result, we still have little understanding of how survivors of IPV understand and experience resilience in their lives.

In both qualitative and quantitative research, researchers often label women's experiences as resilience, and yet we have little knowledge of women's lived experience and personal account of resilience. A deeper understanding of women's lived experience may help to uncover underlying assumptions and presuppositions (Weiss, 2008) about resilience. In light of findings from previous work that suggest resilience is a context-dependent phenomenon, women's own accounts of resilience would meaningfully contribute to our understanding of the phenomenon and enhance the theoretical utility and applicability of resilience research.

Method

Phenomenology is a philosophical approach to the study of phenomena and human experience (Holloway, 1997) and as such, was an appropriate theoretical framework for better understanding the experience of resilience for survivors of IPV. The aim of a phenomenological inquiry is to create a description of the lived experience of a phenomenon without prior assumptions (Holloway, 1997). Entrenched in the method is a "set of existential and phenomenological assumptions by which women are viewed as active meaning makers" (Buchbinder & Eisikovits, 2003, p. 355). The participant's description is taken to directly represent the rich experience of the participant (Holloway, 1997), interwoven with their personal, interpersonal, and social realities (Moustakas, 1994). Phenomenology has been suggested as a method well-suited for providing women with a voice about their experiences (Davis, 2002). The purpose of phenomenological inquiry is not to generalize the findings across all survivors' experiences of resilience and IPV, but to enrich our understanding of the lived experience of resilience within a particular context. Studies using a phenomenological approach use in-depth interviewing with a small number of individuals who have experience or knowledge of the phenomenon (Holloway, 1997).

Procedure

Ethics approval was obtained from the authors' university research ethics board. Sampling was purposive and specifically sought to recruit women who were currently or had previously experienced abuse by an intimate partner. Participants were recruited primarily through the first author's contacts at women's agencies in southern Ontario and advertising through online classifieds (Kijiji). Interested women were asked to contact the first author, at which time they were screened for eligibility and scheduled for an interview. Written informed consent was obtained prior to the interview. Each participant participated in a single, semi-structured interview that lasted 45 min to 1½ hr. Face-to-face interviews were conducted in private meeting rooms located in women's organizations or public libraries. Interviews were audio-recorded and transcribed verbatim. Interview questions asked women to describe how they moved through and coped with their experiences of abuse, to describe a time they did and did not feel resilient after, during, or in spite of abuse, why they consider those experiences to showcase (or not showcase) resilience, and how those experiences have changed over time. Interview questions were designed to elicit women's experiences of resilience both within and following their abusive relationship. The term resilience was not defined for participants so as not to impose any one understanding of the phenomenon and to allow participants the freedom to share their own understanding of resilience. However, it was necessary to explicitly use the term *resilience* in the interview to capture and examine the underlying essence of the experiences that the women, rather than the authors, understood as resilience. Following the interview, women were provided with a list of community resources, given a CDN$30 honorarium, and reimbursed in full for childcare and parking/public transportation.

Participant Characteristics

All 16 women who contacted the researcher expressing interest in the study were eligible to participate because they were 18 years of age or older; could read, write, and speak English; and self-identified as having experienced IPV as an adult (defined as any physical, emotional, psychological, sexual, economic, or other type of abuse by someone you are intimate with). All 16 participants had past abusive relationships, and two of the participants were experiencing abuse from their current partner at the time of the interview. Participant age ranged from 18–55 years. Eight women identified as White/European, two as Caribbean, two as South Asian, one as Latin American, one as First Nations/

Native, and two women identified as bi-racial. All women identified as heterosexual. Other demographic information was diverse, including level of education (*some elementary* to *graduate degree*), household income (*below CDN$19,999* to *CDN$60,000-CDN$79,999*), and religious affiliation (seven different religious affiliations were noted along with five women who had no religious affiliation). Participants reported experiences of physical, verbal, emotional, sexual, economic, spiritual, and legal abuse. The majority of women (*n* = 14) reported experiencing multiple types of abuse. Length of abuse ranged from less than 1-20 years. The majority of women were mothers (*n* = 13) and ages of children ranged from 1-21 years.

Data Analysis

Analysis was guided by Colaizzi's (1978) method, which is grounded in the theoretical and epistemological assumptions of phenomenology. Nevertheless, the authors were aware that the use of a specific method for phenomenological research might be seen as inflexible (Holloway, 1997). To avoid inflexibility, the method described below was used as a guiding and iterative process as opposed to a rigid set of analytical steps.

Each transcript was read carefully to become familiar with the participant's account. Using a detailed line-by-line review of each transcript, aspects that seemed relevant to the phenomenon of resilience were extracted. Each extracted statement was then reviewed to help make sense of it in the participant's own terms. These meanings were then clustered into common patterns and themes. The clusters of themes were compared with the data to confirm and validate the patterns. A detailed description of the participants' feelings and ideas within the themes was created. Finally, the fundamental structure of the phenomenon was described. An additional tenant of the phenomenological philosophy and method is *bracketing*, which is the self-reflective and purposeful acknowledgment of personal biases and assumptions. The first author kept a reflective journal as a way to help acknowledge and clarify personal assumptions and influences on the research process.

Analysis and Discussion

Central to the women's experiences of resilience were cognitive, emotional, and behavioral shifts that occurred throughout the abusive relationship, during the process of leaving, and after the relationship or abuse had ended. The concept of shifts is being used as an organizational device to better understand the underlying structure of the women's resilience. A shift represents a change in the way a woman was thinking, feeling, or behaving with regard to herself, the abuser, the abuse, a relationship, or some other aspect of her life. Shifts occasionally occurred abruptly, but more often developed gradually over time.

Shifts occurred in three distinct, yet highly related theme areas, which have been conceptualized by the authors as *toward resistance*, *in the experience of control*, and *toward positivity*. Women often experienced multiple shifts in one area–for example, a cognitive shift and several subsequent behavioral shifts toward resistance—which individually may seem small and inconsequential, but when aggregated reveal a more robust shift toward resistance. Throughout their narratives women also discussed many internal and external factors and processes that helped them develop or maintain resilience. This is consistent with previous research that has identified various protective or facilitating factors for resilience. Evident in the women's experiences of resilience is the relationship between protective factors and shift experiences; specifically, that protective factors often facilitated shift experiences. For the purposes of the current research, and consistent with some previous work on resilience (e.g., Notter, MacTavish, & Shamah, 2008; Young, 2007), these protective factors and processes have been conceptualized as *pathways* for resilience to better reflect the context-dependent and dynamic nature of the resilience process. The experience of resilience for women in this study encompassed a dynamic relationship between various internal and external pathways that worked to facilitate cognitive, emotional, and behavioral shifts toward resistance, in the experience of control, and toward positivity.

Shifts Toward Resistance

Resistance is being used as a broad term to reflect women's active capacity to oppose, avoid, and push back against the abuse and its negative effects, the abuser and abusive relationships, and the broader social environment that upholds social and cultural norms of violence against women. Shifts toward resistance occurred most often while the abusive relationship was intact and became less frequent once the abuse, fear of abuse, or abusive relationship ended. All the women interviewed spoke about changes they underwent to resist or counter some aspect of their lives related to the abuse. However, as demonstrated in the analysis below, shift experiences varied in how this change was enacted, how abruptly or gradually it occurred, and what types of pathways (i.e., protective factors) facilitated the shift. As such, shifts were highly personal and unique experiences for the women.

Some women experienced shifts toward resistance by deliberately behaving in a certain way with the intention of mitigating, and ultimately resisting, future abuse. This included giving up friends, physically removing herself from certain situations that were likely to become abusive, relocating her home, changing her place of employment, moving into a shelter, contacting the police, and ending the relationship as a way to resist further abuse. These actions demonstrate changes in the women's behaviors because they were often the result of escalating or more frequent abuse. For example, Crystal (pseudonyms are used throughout) talked about a gradual shift in the way she viewed her partner that led her to leave the relationship: "Little by little I realized that's not where I wanted to be anymore [with partner]." She realized she "could not stay another night in the house, not knowing [what] I was going to experience at night." These shifts were often explicitly tied to women's understanding of their resilience. For example, Carmen saw her call to the police as a demonstration of her resilience because it conveyed explicit resistance to the abuse: "For me to actually stand up and like get the police involved too, I think that shows resiliency 'cause it shows I'm not going to put up with it."

For some women, a shift toward resistance manifested through trying to teach their abuser that his behavior was not acceptable. Carmen said she "was trying to educate him on how to treat someone else" and that this man, her second abusive partner, "was younger and he needed a lot of learning." Carmen's behavior was something she had developed as a result of a previously abusive relationship, and she was now trying to teach her new partner that his behavior was not acceptable, demonstrating resistance to the abuse and her abuser. Carmen's example also demonstrates how shift experiences can be developmental and occur across relationships.

Experiencing negative consequences as a result of the abuse, including fear and mental health issues, featured prominently in some women's accounts of abuse and resilience. The women frequently discussed the process of dealing with negative feelings and mental health issues within their accounts of resilience, which detailed shifts toward resisting negative mental health:

> I remember I got up one day and I went to take a shower and I couldn't even stand up, I just felt so sick. And for whatever reason in my head I asked myself "what are you doing here [in mental health facility]? Why are you here? And once I got out of there [facility] I just determined to tell myself that no one on this planet was worth me taking my life. (Wendy)

Experiences of resilience like Wendy's shed light on the ongoing nature of resilience. Wendy was dealing with significant mental health issues, but saw her experience in the mental health facility as part of her resilience. As previously discussed, resilience is often quantitatively measured as the absence of psychopathology, but these accounts support a highly complex process.

Several of the women were first-generation immigrants to Canada and their shifts toward resistance were intertwined with their experiences of immigration and culture. Women spoke about refusing to uphold cultural expectations of women and the normalization of abuse both at home and in Canada:

> The [cultural] community I belong to, if your husband calling you names or hitting you, it's normal. They feel it's normal … that's why I was living in the situation for a long time, but it was very hard to change people's minds. Especially my parents. But now I feel when I left him, I prove he was abusing, I shouldn't have lived with him. (Savita)

In this quote, Savita says that she stayed with her abuser because of the normalization of abuse in her community, but that she eventually shifted away from accepting these norms by leaving her abuser and has continued to resist them by trying to change other people's acceptance of the norms. One of Ungar et al.'s (2007) tensions is adherence or opposition to cultural norms, which functions either as a barrier or pathway to resilience. Within the broader Canadian context in which she was living, Savita's opposition to her community's sociocultural norms and expectations about gender roles, abuse, and marriage was a source of strength and expression of resilience. Savita's experience is also consistent with the *social justice* tension, which reflects resistance to oppression. Her remarks were in response to a question that asked her to describe her experiences of resilience, which highlight the importance of Savita's surrounding sociocultural context on her resilience and emphasize the importance of using research methodologies that capture and reflect this context.

Finally, women experienced shifts toward resistance as a gradual reframing of how they understood their partners and relationships. For example, Monica talked about a slow change in how she viewed her abuser and their relationship:

> It took a lot, it took a lot … it's just one day I started to think clearly. I just realized, you know, this person never cared about me, this person never loved me. Like, who am I fooling? And it took for him to treat me a certain way.

Shifts in the Experience of Control

The term *control* is being used to describe the amount of influence and direction women felt they had over specific aspects or overall outcomes of their lives, relationships, and other experiences. Shifts in the experience of control were understood by women as both positive and negative and occurred throughout different stages of the relationship and the process of leaving. Unlike the other types of shifts, which reflect increases in resistance and positivity, not all changes the women experienced related to control were necessarily feelings of increased control.

Developing a more complex relationship with control was a common experience for women. For some women, this involved becoming more flexible and accepting that some things were not under their control. For example, Wendy said she "got to a point where [she] had to learn that it was okay to fail" and she saw this process as "regaining control in a different way." For other women it involved perceptions of increased control. For example, Jane talked about how she "never used to have control" during her abusive relationships and now if she doesn't have control "it kind of just upsets [her]." She talked about "slowly trying to focus more on things [she can control] instead of other people." Jane acknowledges these difficulties and is continuing to work on them, suggesting that even though gaining control after her abusive relationship has resulted in some negative consequences, she is continuing to actively shift her way of thinking and her subsequent behaviors. This draws attention to the complexities around negotiating control for a woman who has been abused. Resilience is typically considered to be a positive phenomenon, but similar to shifts toward resistance, the women's shifts related to control suggest that resilience is a dynamic process that can include periods of difficulty.

Women's realization that they could not control the attitudes and behaviors of an abusive partner was a prominent cognitive and emotional shift. Although the majority of women spoke about eventually coming to realize they could not change (i.e., control) their abuser, the implications of this shift varied. Initially, this may appear contradictory to women's shifts toward resistance in which they tried to change their partner's abusive attitudes and behaviors. However, women experienced multiple shifts over time and these experiences did not occur in isolation of each other or the context in which they were embedded, highlighting how different elements of resilience can be more or less relevant for women at different times. This provides support for the conceptualization of resilience as a process because shifts that occurred earlier (e.g., shifts in resistance where women tried to change their partner's attitude or behavior) sometimes evolved over time. For some women, there was a point in the process where they underwent a change in how they perceived control in their lives and realized that they were unable to change their abuser's attitudes and behaviors. As demonstrated below in Laura's quote, this shift often facilitated women taking additional steps to end their relationship. This pattern is consistent with that found in previous research on the process of leaving, whereby women undergo a series of complex changes in their cognitive appraisal system (Moss, Pitula, Campbell, & Halstead, 1997).

> But that's the hardest part of getting through it is realizing—and you can ask any woman—realizing that that person is not going to change … once you finally realize this person's not going to change, that's when you're like ok I've got to go. (Laura)

For several women, shifts in the experience of control were about developing perceptions of increased control during and after the abusive relationship. This is one of the most evident examples of Ungar et al.'s *power and control* tension. The power and control tension refers to "the capabilities within, and the resources surrounding, the participants to experience materials and/or discursive power in terms meaningful to their context" (Ungar et al., 2007, p. 298). For example, Monica talked about her gradual realization that she had control because she was the one who could decide whether to visit her incarcerated ex-partner, which ultimately helped her to emotionally "let go" of the relationship and helped her feel like she was "moving on with [her] life." Adrienne talked about the feeling of gaining control as a result of calling the police on her abusive partner, which she says made her feel resilient. Adrienne had also seen her act of calling the police as resistance and a way to fight back, demonstrating a connection between shifts and that a single experience (i.e., calling the police) can serve multiple functions.

The development of personal boundaries, which included learning which attributes and behaviors were "red flags" in partners, was another way women increased control in their lives. Similar to other shifts related to control, the development of boundaries was a highly personal experience because the purpose and outcomes of developing boundaries varied significantly among women. These boundaries were seen as a way for women to develop an increased sense of control over their lives and were often explicitly linked to the experience of resilience. For example, for Susan, "having better boundaries, you know, so that you have healthier relationships in the future" was an important part of her resilience, which she believes keeps survivors from "going back" into a negative mind frame.

Shifts Toward Positivity

The final shift present in women's accounts of their resilience has been conceptualized as *toward positivity*. Positivity is being used as a broad term to reflect women's acknowledgment of progress or positive change in their lives. As demonstrated in the analysis below, shifts toward positivity were often highly connected to other shift experiences. Shifts toward positivity occurred most often after the abuse or the abusive relationship was over and women were starting to rebuild their lives.

Many women spoke about a general shift toward positivity whereby they began to feel good about themselves and have hope for the future. Wendy spoke about the realization that she was "going to be okay again." She knew "it's not the end of the world" even though "it's a very sad, hurtful thing," and she "will live again." These shifts typically occurred over long periods of time and featured most prominently in women who had been away from the abuse or their abuser for a considerable amount of time. A component of feeling good often involved letting go of self-blame:

> I also understand his responsibility in it now, right? And that's because of all the support that I had through getting over it. And I think that's been important to me, to my healing, is being able to understand him and his situation, but also give him the responsibility. (Beth)

Several women identified the refocusing of their energy, time, and thoughts as an important part of their resilience. Some women refocused their energy and care onto themselves and their children, while other women began focusing on the present and enjoying each day. Regaining a sense of their "true selves" was an important way of increasing positivity for some women. This experience is consistent with Ungar et al.'s (2007) *identity* tension, in which the individual regains a sense of themselves and individual identity.

Although shift experiences related to positivity were largely internal experiences, several women spoke of a desire to teach and help others. Sophia acknowledged that now she "can help people too" by doing "volunteer jobs with the women who suffered violence" and for Wendy helping others meant working to change the legal system. She talked about her resilience as "how much can [she] do to try and change this crazy system" and how this desire to make change "has been a burning desire ... that gets [her] up every morning." Ungar et al.'s (2007) *cohesion* tension, which involves a sense of duty to the community's greater good, is evident in these examples of volunteerism and advocacy.

Women also experienced a shift toward positivity by reframing their abusive relationships as learning experiences. They saw these learning experiences as largely positive changes to how they viewed themselves and their surrounding world. Women acknowledged and actively understood their experiences as a learning process and consciously took something positive away from this process. Many women spoke about specific things that they had learned about themselves or the type of relationship and partners they want in the future, whereas other women spoke more generally. Narratives of personal growth and "change for the better," including becoming more compassionate and setting and fulfilling goals, such as going back to school, were common. Learning to identify red flags and develop boundaries were common learning experiences for women. The development of boundaries was also relevant to women's experience of resilience in the context of gaining control over their lives, highlighting again the connection between shifts and the multiple functions of a particular experience.

Pathways for Resilience

Throughout their narratives, women identified various internal and external pathways (i.e., protective factors) that influenced their experience of resilience. A fuller description of the women's pathways for resilience is described elsewhere (Crann, 2012); however, some examples are provided below to demonstrate the relationship between pathways and shift experiences for survivors of IPV. Table 10.1 outlines the specific ways that women experienced shifts and the various pathways that facilitated those shifts.

TABLE 10.1 Shift experiences and examples of pathways participants used to facilitate shifts.

Shift type	Shift experiences	Pathways
Resistance	Changing their behaviors to mitigate abuse	Learning information about abuse
	Contacting the police	Reflection on past experiences
	Ending their relationships	Social support
	Teaching their abuser to not be abusive	Mother as role model
	Resisting cultural norms and cycles of abuse	Connecting with women who had similar experiences
	Resisting abuse sequelae	Protection of their children
	Reframing the relationship	Faith and prayer
		Prioritizing
		Determination
Control	Acknowledgment that the abusive partner would not change	Institutional and personal social support
	Perceptions of increased control	Protection of children
	The development of a new relationship with control	Comparing relationship to other relationships
	The development of personal boundaries	Learning information about boundaries
		Reflecting on previous experience
		Self-esteem
Positivity	Feeling good about themselves	Institutional and personal social support
	Having hope for the future	Getting family and friends' perspectives
	Letting go of self-blame	Connecting with the community
	Refocusing their thoughts and energy	Comparing their situation to other women
	Regaining a sense of self	Self-care
	Helping others	Protection of children
	Personal growth	Determination
	Coming to see their experiences as a learning experience	Emotion and problem-focused coping

Social support, both personal and institutional, was identified as an important external pathway for many women in the current study and has received support as a protective factor for resilience in previous research (e.g., Carlson et al., 2002). Social support is similar to Ungar et al.'s (2007) *relationship* tension, where participants identified the importance of supportive relationships in developing resilience. The pathway of social support facilitated shift experiences across the three theme areas. For example, the support Crystal received from her mother was instrumental in her ability to leave her abusive relationship (i.e., a shift toward resistance): "My mother is a big part of me standing up … why I had to get out of this [relationship]." For Beth, social support helped her let go of responsibility and self-blame (i.e., a shift toward positivity):

> I immediately opened up to family and friends and had all their support throughout it, which was good because they could give me a fresh perspective on what was going on. … So outside perspectives, definitely, had a huge part in my ability to deal with what had happened and to not feel responsible for him or responsible for what happened in the relationship.

Reflecting on previous experiences, abusive or otherwise, was identified by several women as an important internal pathway for resilience. Laura spoke about developing boundaries as a way to gain control over her life (i.e., a shift in control), and that it was through a process of reflecting on previous experiences of abuse that she realized she needed to set boundaries in her life because she saw herself as "too open" and "overwhelmed with other people's needs."

Dynamic and Context-Dependent Process

The women shared the common experience of shifts and mentioned many of the same pathways for resilience, yet demonstrated unique patterns within these shared experiences. This is reflected in how certain factors or processes functioned as pathways that facilitated shifts for some women, but were experienced as the shift for others. For example, Laura says, "there's always been the core of me that's been super strong and I always knew, even through all the crap, that that was still there." Laura's narrative about maintaining her sense of self can be interpreted as a pathway for resilience because her strong sense of self existed prior to her experience of abuse and helped carry her through her negative experiences. However, for other women, regaining a sense of self manifested as a shift because a strong sense of self was not identified as a consistent source of support or help through their experiences, but instead was something that was built up throughout the resilience process. How a particular factor or process manifests and the function it has may therefore depend largely on the specific context of that individual's life.

Women also explicitly spoke about the personalized nature of resilience—about having their own "version of resilience" and how "it's [resilience] different for everybody and for every situation." Rachel elaborated on the personalized nature of resilience:

For some people resilience literally might just mean being able to live, like keep their bodies alive and, say, provide for their children; for others it might look like where they go beyond that and, and start achieving, you know, their dreams or functioning at a higher level or being able to consider self-actualization.

In contrast to Rachel's description of resilience are the discrete (although often disagreed upon) categories of functioning present in the existing literature, such as recovery and PTG. The women's experiences of resilience were much broader and could encompass multiple degrees of functioning, including the struggle with mental health issues that is not typically included in the conceptualization of resilience with survivors of IPV. While theoretical debates about the nuances between various constructs are alive and well in the literature, the lived experiences and lay understandings of resilience for the women in this study do not reflect a concern with such theoretical distinctions.

Both women who saw themselves as resilient and women who were not yet ready to label themselves as resilient spoke about resilience as an ongoing process:

Resilience is something that's ongoing, like it's not like you have all these circumstances and yes you get through them and that's it, they're done. You're always going to have new stuff come up so you're always going to have to deal with how to get through it. (Wendy)

The majority of women spoke about the time-consuming and difficult nature of developing and maintaining resilience. Jane explained that abuse is not something one can "bounce back right after … it does take time" but that she believes she did "bounce back, like not so quick because it did take some time and it like, um, struggle and, and stuff." The overall complexity of the resilience process, as demonstrated by the women's experiences, has significant implications for the way that resilience is measured in survivors of IPV. Considering that resilience is often measured as the absence of psychopathology in this group, the findings of this study highlight the importance of using appropriate indicators of resilience to improve the validity of the research. If researchers fail to incorporate women's understandings and experiences of resilience (e.g., that resilience is not contingent on the absolute absence of psychopathology), the translation of research to clinical and policy applications will be constrained.

The findings of the current research suggest that women who have experienced IPV often have different understandings and experiences of resilience, including multiple ways to describe their own experiences. This is supportive of a social constructionist, rather than essentialist, interpretation of resilience and highlights the influence of social and cultural contextual factors on an individual's experience of resilience (Ungar, 2004, 2008; Ungar et al., 2007). According to Ungar (2004), "a constructionist interpretation explicitly tolerates diversity in the way resilience is nurtured and maintained" (p. 345). The findings also support previous work that has identified resilience as a multidimensional process (Luthar et al., 2000; Ungar, 2008). As evidenced throughout the analysis, many of the experiences of the participants were consistent with Ungar et al.'s (2007) tensions. The *access to resources* tension did not emerge in the current study; however, that may be due to the specific interview questions and focus of the current study on the underlying essence of resilience rather than the factors that contributed to resilience. In line with the culturally specific expressions of the common tensions found by Ungar and colleagues, the findings of the current study show diverse and contextually specific expressions of shifts within the broader shared experience of undergoing the shifts.

Some recent work on resilience has started to conceptualize the experience of resilience as some form of shift or change (e.g., Kidd & Davidson, 2007; Lau & van Niekerk, 2011). A phenomenological study of resilience in survivors of childhood sexual abuse found that positive change over time was a prominent theme in the experience of resilience and that change was ongoing, complex, and non-linear (Baker, 2007). The results of Baker's (2007) study also allude to various internal and external factors as catalysts for positive change, akin to the current studies' framing of pathways as facilitators of shifts. Although this small body of research has begun to frame the experience of resilience as shifts, this conceptualization is still very new and further research is required to better understand resilience as shift experiences across populations and contexts. Resilience research has largely moved toward a process conceptualization (Luthar et al., 2000; Ungar, 2008), and while the finding that resilience is a dynamic process is not a new contribution to the literature, it can inform how resilience is framed and measured in research with survivors of IPV. Framing resilience as a series of shifts can ultimately help evolve the process of conceptualization by shedding light on the underlying mechanisms and reducing the ambiguity in what is meant by researchers when they refer to resilience as a process.

The findings of this study, as well as the work of Young (2007), highlight several parallels between the process of resilience and the process of leaving an abusive relationship. In a review of the process of leaving literature, women reported experiencing a shift in perspective that either occurred suddenly or developed gradually, often facilitated by factors including internal catalysts, such as seeing the influence of the relationship and abuse on their children, and external catalysts, such as support and alternative perspectives from family, friends, and helping professionals (D. K. Anderson & Saunders, 2003). This is highly similar to the current participants' experiences of shifts in several ways, including the experience of cognitive, emotional, and behavioral changes, diversity in these changes occurring either suddenly or over time, various factors and mechanisms that facilitate these changes, and a purposeful effort to make change. The overlap between the process of leaving an abusive relationship and the process of resilience therefore has several implications for the way both processes are understood. Although a relationship appears to exist between these processes, they remain distinct. However, the process of leaving could conceivably be conceptualized as nested within the broader process of resilience, whereby women who undergo the process of leaving an abusive relationship are likely also experiencing resilience, but women do not necessarily need to leave an abusive relationship to experience resilience. The findings of the current study, which provide some support for the process of resilience occurring even while an abusive relationship is still intact, provide initial support for this nested framework. Women's accounts of resilience occurred across various stages of their relationships, suggesting that resilience, at least for these women, is a much broader and encompassing experience than how resilience has traditionally been conceptualized and studied in survivors of IPV.

The conceptualization of resilience as cognitive, emotional, and behavioral shifts has implications for the way in which survivors are positioned in society. Feminist scholars have fought hard to counteract the notion that women are responsible for ending their abuse. The findings of this study suggest that it is shifts within women that encompass the resilience process, creating the possibility that resilience could be viewed as a choice and placing the responsibility on women to pursue such shifts. While acknowledging that there are many interacting and influencing factors and processes that would influence a woman's ability to experience resilience, there seems to be a degree of personal desire to change that is both implicitly and explicitly reflected in the women's experiences, as many women talk about needing to acknowledge and purposefully make change. Acknowledging this balance has already begun and can be seen in feminist literature documenting the shift from viewing battered women through an intra-psychic lens (e.g., learned helplessness) toward consideration for the broader patriarchal social structures and contextual constraints on women's options for seeking help and leaving an abusive relationship (D. K. Anderson & Saunders, 2003; Dobash & Dobash, 1992). Addressed further in the Applications section below, future research on resilience in survivors of IPV should continue to both acknowledge this tension and explore how survivors of IPV understand women's active role in this process.

The women who participated in this study came from diverse cultural, ethnic, religious, and economic backgrounds. Participants were recruited from a large urban center with a high immigrant population, and some considerations are to be made related to the cultural and social context of the research. Considering the high level of cultural diversity within Canada, and particularly within Ontario, the experience of resilience for immigrant women in Canada may be different from those who migrated to countries that place a high value on assimilation or are culturally homogeneous. The underlying common experience of resilience as shifts in resistance, control, and positivity for women in this study, regardless of immigration status, cultural background, and other demographic factors, suggests that there may be broader social, cultural, and institutional factors influencing the development of resilience. For example, there are a number of social services and resources available for immigrant women and for specific cultural communities in the region where participants were recruited. Access to support may have affected women's development of resilience, as well as newcomers' perspectives on social norms related to violence against women in Canada. In this sense, the participants' environment may have provided "access to health-enhancing resources in culturally relevant ways," a key component of resilience (Ungar et al., 2007, p. 288). Immigrant women in the current study often spoke about the normalization of violence against women in their home countries and how they did not recognize their experiences as abuse until they were living in Canada. However, some women spoke of their abuse experiences leading to their decision to migrate as a way to escape or move forward from the abuse, indicating that they acknowledged their experiences as abuse even when living in a context where violence against women was normalized. In addition to indicating that the experience and acknowledgment of abuse are highly influenced by the cultural and social context in which women live, it suggests that overcoming abuse and the resilience process may look very different for a woman who does not perceive her experiences as abuse.

Finally, this study provides a starting point for future resilience research to examine broader contextual influences on survivors' resilience. Whereas the current study focused on personal and relational factors and processes related to resilience, future research should examine the influence of broader social and institutional factors and systems as they relate to resilience. For example, future research should examine and compare the lived experience of resilience in women from various cultural backgrounds living in urban centers with greater access to culturally relevant supports and resources with women living in rural areas, where there are fewer resources available. A health and wellness framework that accounts for influences on health and resilience at micro, meso, and macro levels (e.g., Prilleltensky & Prilleltensky, 2003) may also be useful for conceptualizing future research at a broader contextual level.

Study Limitations

Although a qualitative approach was purposeful in addressing some of the limitations of previous research, the current study has several limitations that require consideration. The sample was self-selected and this may have influenced participants' responses and experiences in that women who participated may have viewed themselves as more resilient or had experiences and understandings of resilience that are markedly different from women who chose not to participate. Several women did acknowledge that while they felt they were on their way, they did not feel comfortable labeling themselves resilient at the time of the interview. It is important to acknowledge that there may be a social desirability effect in identifying as resilient, particularly in this type of interview-based research.

Only one interview was conducted with each woman, so we may not have a good understanding of how resilience changes across time and how women come to name their experiences as resilience. Furthermore, the retrospective nature of this study may have influenced some participants' accounts of their experiences. Although women who were currently experiencing abuse were intentionally recruited for this study, there were only two women in the sample experiencing abuse at the time of the interview. Although interview questions were designed to tap into resilience within the abusive relationship even if women were no longer experiencing abuse, we still have a limited understanding of the shift experiences for women currently being abused and how they come to label their experiences as resilience. Future research should continue to examine resilience in women as they are experiencing IPV and use a longitudinal design to further explore the development and maintenance of resilience over time.

Finally, the use of the word *resilience* in the interview is a potential limitation of this study. Although the authors felt it necessary to orient participants to the specific phenomenon under study to most accurately capture and examine the essence of resilience, it is possible that the explicit use of the term confounded the results by priming participants to socially available understandings of the term rather than their own interpretations.

Applications of Research

Throughout their narratives women often made explicit suggestions about how to better help women experiencing abuse. Several women suggested the police and victim services could provide more detailed explanations of the arrest process and improve their follow-up with women. Women's discussion about the need for change in the justice system supports the conceptualization of resilience involving a shift toward resistance, as women were engaging in resistance against their abuser and the broader legal system by clarifying a need for change in the current system. Furthermore, women's attention to these issues within a discussion on resilience highlights the importance of viewing resilience within the broader social and cultural context, as opposed to through an entirely intra-psychic lens. Women understood resilience as supported through social systems instead of something that resulted entirely from internal processes.

The findings of this study can be applied to clinical practice and programs designed to help women who have been abused. Women may benefit from the conceptualization of resilience as a process that can be fostered and supported in various ways. Clinicians could work with clients to engage a variety of pathways, which may ultimately lead to an increase in shift experiences and an overall experience of more robust resilience. Even beyond a clinical setting, if women are aware of the personalized nature of resilience and encouraged to actively seek different pathways for resilience, it could help to facilitate the resilience process. Furthermore, understanding resilience as a personalized and dynamic process may have implications for how clinicians frame the process of healing and recovery for women who are experiencing abuse. Understanding resilience as an ongoing process may function as a catalyst for resilience in and of itself and may help women better understand their experiences and remain optimistic, even during times of sadness, fear, or other difficulties that arise.

Conclusion

The purpose of this qualitative study was to better understand the experience of resilience for women who have survived intimate partner abuse using a phenomenological approach. Based on a review of the theoretical and empirical work on resilience and IPV, there was a pressing need for women's lived experiences to inform our understanding and subsequent methodological approaches to the study of resilience. Previous research on resilience in survivors of IPV has been constrained by narrow definitions and conceptualizations of the phenomenon. The findings of this study demonstrate how the experience of resilience for adult female survivors of IPV incorporates internal and external pathways as facilitators for cognitive, emotional, and behavioral shifts toward resistance, in the experience of control, and toward positivity that occur during various stages of abuse and the process of leaving.

References

Almedom, A. M., & Glandon, D. (2007). Resilience is not the absence of PTSD any more than health is the absence of disease. *Journal of Loss & Trauma, 12*, 127–143. doi:10.1080/15325020600945962

Anderson, D. K., & Saunders, D. G. (2003). Leaving an abusive partner: An empirical review of predictors, the process of leaving, and psychological well-being. *Trauma, Violence, & Abuse, 4*, 163–191. doi:10.1177/1524838002250769

Anderson, K. M., Renner, L. M., & Danis, F. S. (2012). Recovery: Resilience and growth in the aftermath of domestic violence. *Violence Against Women, 18*, 1279-1299. doi:10.1177/1077801212470543

Baker, S. R. (2007). *Resilience as process among women over 50 who report a history of childhood sexual abuse* (Doctoral dissertation). Retrieved from Library and Archives Canada. (AMICUS No. 37943701)

Bonanno, G. A. (2005). Resilience in the face of trauma. *Current Directions in Psychological Science, 14*, 135–138. doi:10.1111/j.0963-7214.2005.00347.x

Buchbinder, E., & Eisikovits, Z. (2003). Battered women's entrapment in shame: A phenomenological study. *American Journal of Orthopsychiatry, 73*, 355–366.

Burr, V. (1995). *An introduction to social constructionism.* New York: Routledge.

Carlson, B. E., McNutt, L. A., Choi, D. Y., & Rose, I. M. (2002). Intimate partner abuse and mental health: The role of social support and other protective factors. *Violence Against Women, 8*, 720–745. doi:10.1177/10778010222183251

Colaizzi, P. F. (1978). Psychological research as the phenomenologist views it. In R. S. Valle

& M. King (Eds.), *Existential-phenomenological alternatives for psychology* (pp. 48-71). New York, NY: Oxford University Press.

Crann, S. E. (2012). *"Some days I don't know how I got through it, but I did": The experience of resilience in survivors of intimate partner violence* (Master's thesis). Retrieved from Library and Archives Canada. (AMICUS No. 41340607)

Crawford, E., Liebling-Kalifani, H., & Hill, V. (2009). Women's understanding of the effects of domestic abuse: The impact of their identity, sense of self and resilience: A grounded theory approach. *Journal of International Women's Studies, 11*, 63–82.

Davis, R. E. (2002). "The strongest women": Exploration of the inner resources of abused women. *Qualitative Health Research, 9*, 1248–1263. doi:10.1177/1049732302238248 Dobash, R. E., & Dobash, R. P. (1992). *Women, violence, and social change.* New York: Taylor

& Francis.

Doherty, D. C. (1997). *Spousal abuse: An African-American female perspective* (Doctoral dissertation). Retrieved from ProQuest Dissertations and Theses (UMI 9729466).

Gallo, L. C., Bogart, L. M., Vranceanu, A. M., & Matthews, K. M. (2005). Socioeconomic status, resources, psychosocial experiences, and emotional responses: A test of the reserve capacity model. *Journal of Personality and Social Psychology, 88*, 386–399. doi:10.1037/0022-3514.88.2.386

Holloway, I. (1997). *Basic concepts for qualitative research.* London, England: Blackwell. Humphreys, J. (2003). Resilience in sheltered battered women. *Issues in Mental Health Nursing, 24*, 137–152. doi:10.1080/01612840305293

Kangagaratnam, P., Mason, R., Hyman, I., Manuel, L., Berman, H., & Toner, B. (2012). Burden of womanhood: Tamil women's perceptions of coping with intimate partner violence. *Journal of Family Violence, 27,* 647-658. doi:10.1007/s10896-012-9461-1

Kidd, S., & Davidson, L. (2007). "You have to adapt because you have no other choice": The stories of strength and resilience of 208 homeless youth in New York City and Toronto. *Journal of Community Psychology, 35,* 219–238. doi:10.1002/jcop.20144

Landenburger, K. (1989). A process of entrapment in and recovery from an abusive relationship. *Issues in Mental Health Nursing, 10,* 209–227. doi:10.3109/01612848909140846l Lau, U., & van Niekerk, A. (2011). Restorying the self: An exploration of young burn survivors' narratives of resilience. *Qualitative Health Research, 21,* 1165–1181. doi:10.1177/1049732311405686

Luthar, S. S., Cicchetti, D., & Becker, B. (2000). The construct of resilience: A critical evaluation and guidelines for future work. *Child Development, 71,* 543–562. doi:10.1111/1467-9624.00164

Macini, A. D., & Bonnano, G. A. (2006). Resilience to potential trauma: Toward a lifespan approach. In J. W. Reich, A. J. Zautra, & J. S. Hall (Eds.), *Handbook of adult resilience* (pp. 258–280). New York: Guilford Press.

Massey, S., Cameron, A., Ouellette, S., & Fine, M. (1998). Qualitative approaches to the study of thriving: What can be learned? *Journal of Social Issues, 54,* 337–355.

Masten, A. S. (1994). Resilience in individual development: Successful adaptation despite risk and adversity. In M. C. Wang & E. W. Gordon (Eds.), *Educational resilience in inner-city America: Challenges and prospects* (pp. 3–25). Hillsdale, NJ: Lawrence Erlbaum.

Meadows, L. A., Kaslow, N. J., Thompson, M. P., & Jurkovic, G. J. (2005). Protective factors against suicide attempt risk among African American women experiencing intimate partner violence. *American Journal of Community Psychology, 36,* 109–121. doi:10.1007/s10464-005-6236-3

Merritt-Gray, M., & Wuest, J. (1995). Counteracting abuse and breaking free: The process of leaving revealed through women's voices. *Health Care for Women International, 16,* 399–412. doi:10.1080/07399339509516104

Moss, V. A., Pitula, C. R., Campbell, J. C., & Halstead, L. (1997). The experience of terminating an abusive relationship from an Anglo and African American perspective: A qualitative descriptive study. *Issues in Mental Health Nursing, 18,* 433–454.

Moustakas, C. (1994). *Phenomenological research methods.* Thousand Oaks, CA: Sage. Notter, M. L., MacTavish, K. A., & Shamah, D. (2008). Pathways toward resilience among women in rural trailer parks. *Family Relations, 57,* 613–624.

Prilleltensky, I., & Prilleltensky, O. (2003). Towards a critical health psychology practice. *Journal of Health Psychology, 8,* 197–210.

Roisman, G. I. (2005). Conceptual clarifications in the study of resilience. *American Psychologist, 60,* 264-265. doi:10.1037/0003-066X.60.3.264

Rutter, M. (2006). Implications of resilience concepts for scientific understanding. *Annals of the New York Academy of Sciences, 1094,* 1–12.

Sinha, M. (2013). Measuring violence against women: Statistical trends (Catalogue no. 85-002-X). Retrieved from http://www.statcan.gc.ca/pub/85-002-x/2013001/article/11766-eng.pdf

Tedeschi, R. G., & Calhoun, L. G. (2003). Routes to posttraumatic growth through cognitive processing. In D. Paton, J. M. Violanti, & L. M. Smith (Eds.), *Promoting capabilities to manage post-traumatic stress: Perspectives on resilience* (pp. 12–26). Springfield, IL: Charles C. Thomas.

Thompson, M. P., Saltzman, L. E., & Johnson, H. (2003). A comparison of risk factors for intimate partner violence-related injury across two national surveys on violence against women. *Violence Against Women, 9,* 438–457. doi:10.1177/1077801202250955

Ungar, M. (2004). A constructionist discourse on resilience: Multiple contexts, multiple realities among at-risk children and youth. *Youth & Society, 35,* 341–365. doi:10.1177/00441 18X03257030

Ungar, M. (2008). Resilience across cultures. *British Journal of Social Work, 38,* 218–235. Ungar, M., Brown, M., Liebenberg, R. O., Kwong, W. M., Armstrong, M., & Gilgun, J. (2007).

Unique pathways to resilience across cultures. *Adolescence, 42,* 287–310.

Weiss, G. (2008). An interview with Professor Gail Weiss. *International Postgraduate Journal of Philosophy, 1,* 3–8.

World Health Organization. (2002). *Intimate partner violence.* Retrieved from http://www.who.int/violence_injury_prevention/violence/world_report/factsheets/en/ipvfacts.pdf

World Health Organization. (2006a). *Intimate partner violence and alcohol fact sheet.* Retrieved from http://www.who.int/violence_injury_prevention/violence/world_report/factsheets/ft_intimate.pdf

World Health Organization. (2006b). *Summary report: WHO multi-country study on women's health and domestic violence against women: Initial results on prevalence, health outcomes, and women's responses.* Retrieved from http://www.who.int/gender/violence/who_multicountry_study/summary_report/summary_report_English2.pdf

Wright, C. V., Perez, S., & Johnson, D. (2010). The mediating role of empowerment for African

American women experiencing intimate partner violence. *Psychological Trauma: Theory, Research, Practice, and Policy, 2,* 266–272. doi:10.1037/a0017470

Young, M. D. (2007). *Finding meaning in the aftermath of trauma: Resilience and posttraumatic growth in female survivors of intimate partner violence* (Doctoral dissertation). Retrieved from http://scholarworks.umt.edu/cgi/viewcontent.cgi?article=1468&context=etd

IV

Family and Work Life

Family Budgets

Staying in the Black, Slipping into the Red

BY SARAH HALPERN-MEEKIN, KATHRYN EDIN, LAURA TACH,
AND JENNIFER SYKES

What does it really mean to have a social safety net organized around the principle that, if you work you shouldn't be poor? The American poverty line is neither an absolute measure of what it takes to survive—an estimate of what a basic "market basket" of necessities costs—nor a relative measure, like poverty thresholds in Europe that identify households falling below some percentage of the median income; the figure in the European Union is 60 percent. Instead, it is based on 1950s surveys of the cost of a minimally nutritious diet on an "emergency" or short-term basis (which assumed that a family consumed powdered milk and no fresh vegetables), multiplied by three (at that time, the average family spent a third of its income on food). Since the poverty threshold was set in the 1960s based on these calculations, the dollar amount has simply been adjusted for inflation.[1]

Because of the poverty line's odd origins, no one is quite sure what "poor" really means in America, and, perhaps for that reason, hardly anyone likes the official measure. Some on the political right, for example, charge that the threshold is way too high—Robert Rector of the Heritage Foundation argues that it overestimates poverty because few poor Americans truly go without food, most have air conditioners and cable, half have personal computers, and a third even have fancy TVs. "For most people, the word 'poverty' suggests near destitution: an inability to provide nutritious food, clothing, and reasonable shelter for one's family. However, only a small number of the 46.2 million persons classified as 'poor' by the Census Bureau fit that definition," he writes.[2] This is not mere punditry: surveys show that the poor do report possessions that many Americans—especially those of a previous generation—would deem luxuries. Because of this, some economists have called for a new poverty measure based on consumption, not income, arguing that it does the best job of identifying the neediest Americans.[3]

In contrast, those on the political left often complain that the poverty line is much too low—little more than a back-of-the envelope, midcentury calculation based on national patterns of consumption that no longer hold; Americans now spend only about a sixth of their income on food, for example, but more on child care and medical costs than they once did. At this writing, the poverty line for a family of four is just under $24,000 in income, or about $2,000 a month. Critics in this camp ask, is there any place in America where a family of four can actually make ends meet on that amount? Columbia University's National Center for Children in Poverty estimates that, on average, a family would need an income of about *twice* the poverty level to truly get by.[4] Ordinary Americans seem to side with the Columbia University researchers. In 2007, Gallup pollsters asked Americans from across the country: "What is the smallest amount of yearly income a family of four would need to get along in your local community?" The median response was $45,000, with a mean above $50,000.[5]

The EITC was designed to bring a minimum-wage worker and his or her family above the official poverty line. The controversy over the poverty line raises the question of whether this is a worthy goal. Some might argue that, if the working poor have Internet and cable TV, supplementing their incomes with a cash transfer from the government is not an appropriate policy objective. Others might contend that, if the working poor are willing to play by the rules—stay employed—it is unjust, even immoral, not to ensure that they have the wherewithal to provide their children with a minimally decent life, as Americans define it. Indeed, for those meeting this fundamental requirement of the American social contract, just getting by may not be enough; those in this camp might argue that society should ensure that they have the real possibility to reach for more.

Accordingly, this chapter is devoted to examining the finances of working-poor and near-poor households who claim the EITC. At present, one minimum-wage job will provide an income of $14,500 a year, provided the work is full time and full year. The EITC and other tax credits fill the gap between that figure and the poverty threshold. Here we ask which of the two views of the poverty line is correct. Are people below the threshold truly struggling, or are they blowing money on big-screen TVs and cable packages? We'll find that the answer isn't one or the other, but both.

Our logic in addressing this question at the start of the book is simple: if we want to understand the real impact of the EITC, and whether it is worth the cost to taxpayers, getting a detailed look at household budgets is a critical first step. But, as we've indicated, the ultimate question this chapter raises is much larger: What bundle of goods and services is "enough" for those on the front lines of this revolutionary new approach to alleviating poverty, parents who are working but poor? Is it merely about financial need, or should our standard for what is enough be based on American notions of what workers "deserve"? In short, given the fact that these household heads all play by the rules—working, many full time and full year—do they need the EITC, and are they worthy of it?

We devote a later chapter (chapter 3) to comparing the new work-based safety net to the old welfare entitlement system that existed prior to the 1996 reforms, and to the time-limited welfare system that remains. Thus we will not engage in a full discussion of those differences here. Note, however, that the old system, which entitled a family to a certain level of resources based on their need, never came close to pulling families above the poverty line. Today, not one state in our nation offers enough in TANF benefits to raise a family much above even half of the official poverty threshold;[6] in fact, in the majority of states, TANF benefits are limited to less than a third of the poverty line, although TANF beneficiaries usually are also able to claim SNAP (formerly known as food stamps) and Medicaid. Nonetheless, the monthly TANF benefit for a family of three won't even pay the rent:[7] it is less than the cost of a modest two-bedroom apartment in any state, and, in twenty-six states it is not even half of that cost.[8] This shortfall is meaningful given the fact that nationally only a quarter of eligible families get any form of subsidized housing, and families with substantial assets are barred from the welfare rolls.[9]

Clearly, what remains of the traditional need-based safety net is not—and never was—truly about helping families meet all of their needs. Yet few politicians worry in public, and perhaps few even worry in private, that TANF benefits are too low. What standard of living, then, did Bill Clinton envision ensuring when he proposed a massive expansion of the EITC so that working Americans—at least those with kids—would not be poor? Was it bare-bones survival or something more—some notion of a "decent" standard of living that exceeded subsistence? The narratives we present in this chapter raise the question of what kind of reward American workers ought to get from their labor.

We first turn to Ashlee Reed, whose household financial situation is quite typical of that of other households in our study. Ashlee grew up in the South Boston housing projects watching her mother struggle financially while raising three kids on her own. A high school dropout, Ashlee's mom had to take whatever work she could find. Certification as a home health aide translated into long hours taking care of the elderly for little more than minimum wage. Perhaps as a result, she frequently lectured Ashlee and her siblings about the importance of education in the hopes that her children might rise above bottom-of-the-barrel jobs like hers and escape "Southie," the troubled neighborhood in which they lived. Ashlee bought into this message wholeheartedly; she excelled in high school and took out loans so that she could go to college. Four years later, she left with her bachelor of arts degree in hand, becoming the only college graduate in her family.

But life has fallen short of the comfortable living promised by her mother's stay-in-school mantra. Now, seven years after graduation, this twenty-nine-year-old white mother lives with her boyfriend, Adrian—who used to work as a cook in her college cafeteria—and their three young children on a run-down block that's just a stone's throw from the one that she was raised on. She is still saddled with $25,000 in educational debt, which she chips away at bit by bit. Because of the slack job market for teachers, she considered herself lucky when she landed a job at Head Start, earning $532 in gross wages per week, or $357 in take-home pay, during the forty-four-week school year.[10] But the job hasn't left her much better off than her mother.

We first meet this family of five in their small, two-bedroom apartment directly across from a convenience store on a busy street in Dorchester. This mostly black neighborhood borders South Boston, the largely white enclave to the east where Ashlee was raised. Inside the apartment, it is dark; the living room is crowded with outdated but carefully preserved furniture, and a washing machine sits prominently in the kitchen, taking up too much space. Though it's cramped here, order reigns; the only clutter visible is an overflowing pile of bills on the desk in the living room.

Ashlee has a housing choice voucher—a program known colloquially as Section 8, which limits her rent to roughly 30 percent of her income.[11] Without it, she would need to devote nearly all of her take-home pay to rent this modest apartment.[12] During the months that she is employed—all but eight weeks during the summer—her share of the rent is $575 (the government pays the rest). And, in this unit, the rent includes utilities, a lucky break. Years ago, Ashlee applied for a modification to her housing voucher, which would have entitled her to a three-bedroom apartment so that the three kids wouldn't have to all share a room, but she has heard nothing from the Boston Housing Authority about that request. She needs to be close to work—she purchased a car only recently—so Ashlee has ended up in Dorchester, a step down, not up, from Southie. She worries about raising her children here: the block is home to a bar that is open all day, and Ashlee says the street is full of "yelling and broken bottles."

Head Start teachers don't command high wages, but the job does offer some critical perks for this working mother of three. While she must leave her toddler with her boyfriend's mother while she works, she can bring her two older children with her. Though the two kids are not technically eligible for the program (she makes too much money to qualify), Head Start charges her only $300 per month for both children. Elsewhere, she might easily pay three or four times that amount.[13] Another perk is the schedule, which allows her to be home with the kids after school. She firmly believes that "no matter what, my kids have to come first." Despite the nice fit between her family responsibilities and her work schedule, running after a dozen or so preschoolers all day can be tiring, and, for the hard work involved in managing her classroom, she finds the compensation wanting. In an average month, her paychecks show gross earnings of $2,288, although she notes that payroll taxes, deductions for her share of her health care premium, and intentional overwithholding—a decision to "save" made when both she and Adrian were working—bring that amount down considerably.[14]

Employment entails a host of expenses—especially child care and transportation. A busy highway separates Ashlee from her job. Now that she has a car, she drives to work, piloting a dark blue Dodge Caravan older than her children's ages combined—five-year-old Warren, four-year-old Mallory, and three-year-old Johnny. She's proud that this "clunker" is paid off, but it isn't cheap to insure or maintain: in a typical month, she estimates that she pays $401 for transportation, between car insurance, gas, registration, and routine maintenance or the occasional parking ticket. That's nearly a third of her take-home pay.

Ashlee's financial struggles are particularly acute at the moment. Her boyfriend, thirty-three-year-old Adrian, can't pay anything toward the household expenses. After six years of steady work as a cook at her alma mater, he was laid off just before Christmas, along with all of his coworkers, when the college chose a rival food-service provider. By the time of our first in-depth conversation, Adrian's unemployment benefits have run out. And Ashlee is facing another financial hit: it's late June, and she has just been laid off from her job, as she is every summer. She, along with thousands of Head Start teachers across the country, applies for unemployment during the summer months, but unemployment insurance covers only a portion of her lost wages; in any case, the first check takes about four weeks to arrive.[15] While waiting for that check, Ashlee copes by using the only safety net that she has available—credit cards—to pay the bills.

For Ashlee and so many others working lower-wage jobs, there really is no *average* month. Instead, their financial lives are boom and bust. During the "bust," debt accrual is common. Most aspire to save, but the barriers to saving are high; unexpected financial upheavals quickly eat away at one's savings. During the forty-four weeks that Head Start is in session, Ashlee, Adrian, and the kids can count on at least one steady paycheck. But each summer Ashlee's income takes a nosedive. And she has no cheap source of child care available to make a summer job worth her while. Most years, Ashlee manages to limp along until February, tax refund time. In February, when her tax refund arrives, she can catch up on bills that may have been overdue for months, pay off some of her longer-term debt, and, in good years, save for the summer financial crunch.

Falling Behind

We begin by considering Ashlee's financial situation in an "average" month, as if her income and expenses stayed steady throughout the year. In the typical month, Ashlee's expenses exceed her wages from her job. With monthly expenses totaling $2,856—this includes only minimum payments on the credit cards and on her student loans—and average take-home pay of under $1,600, the family is sliding into debt even during the months that she claims her full salary, as long as Adrian is unable to contribute.[16] The weighty load of Ashlee's credit card debt is testimony that she's relied on credit as a safety net in the past.

Ashlee lives as many lower-wage workers do, under a cloud of debt that grows rather than shrinks over time: currently, she owes five credit card companies a total of $4,080.[17] Each month, she tries to make at least the minimum payment on these cards plus a few dollars more, but, with interest rates of more than 20 percent (and one as high as 30 percent), her progress on paying down the balances is slow. Lately, she feels a sense of accomplishment in those months when she manages not to increase the amount she owes. On top of the credit cards, her student loan payment is $360 a month. She tries not to think about how long it will take to pay off the $25,000 that remains. Since Adrian has been unemployed, Ashlee has skipped these payments in order to provide for the family's basic needs.

Boom Time

Last February, Ashlee got a refund check from H&R Block totaling $4,704—more than three times the amount that she brings home in an average month. Ashlee keenly remembers the excitement she felt when she collected that check, walking it straight to the bank. By the time that the refund was in hand, she had spent months planning how she would spend it. She had fallen behind on her student loan during the prior summer and had decided to put that particular debt at the top of the list. Ashlee typically prioritizes her student loan above her credit cards because, "once you go so long without paying, they can default you." Defaulting on a federal student loan triggers garnishment of one's tax refund, a risk she doesn't feel prepared to take: "I didn't want to get there," she says.

After she had gotten up to date on that loan, the remaining $3,204 from the refund allowed Ashlee to pay down some of the principal on her credit cards, which she had also accrued the prior summer, and to catch up on the overdue cable and phone bills. Now, just as she faces another layoff, the savings from her tax refund have nearly run dry. Thus, this year, Ashlee made no progress toward her longer-term goal: "I try to save [a lot of my refund]. My goal usually, even though I don't ever make it, is to have enough money saved up for the summer for when I go onto unemployment, because . . . it takes like four weeks [to get my first unemployment check]. That's four weeks without pay if I don't have anything saved up from when I was working. So I usually have that goal, which is to at least have enough to get me through that [month without any cash coming in]." For Ashlee, having that cushion in savings would decrease her reliance on credit cards and alleviate stress. Given the seasonal ups and downs in Ashlee's financial situation, especially since Adrian lost his job, it is difficult to formulate, much less stick to, a budget.

All of the families we spoke with live on incomes considerably below the American median.[18] All face the pressures of raising kids in a city with high living costs while juggling work and family demands. Where do they work and how much are they earning? How do they choose to allocate their limited resources? When there is money left over after the bills are paid, where is the surplus going? How important is the large infusion of cash from the EITC?

Our goal in this chapter is to trace the flow of money in lower-wage working households. As indicated above, we first present average monthly expense and income figures calculated from detailed financial descriptions of expenditures over the prior year. However, as Ashlee Reed's story shows, averages can be misleading. So we go beyond these figures to describe the ups and downs families experience over the course of the year. Few of our families enjoy predictable incomes and expenditures. Job loss and fluctuations in hours are common, as are unexpected spikes in expenses. Uncertainty is not the exception; it is the rule.

We asked parents to recount their finances in great detail. We tried to account for every dollar that came in, every dollar they spent, and every outstanding IOU. Although it might seem inconceivable to some middle-class readers, many parents were able to provide us with this detailed accounting of their financial lives without much reference to documentation beyond an occasional glance at a credit card statement or utility bill. The strength of the financial recall of the poor puts the spotlight on one potential benefit of living under the constraints of a tight budget.[19] While social scientists have found that being impoverished can be mentally taxing—focusing so much on how to meet immediate needs can create a scarcity of attention for other tasks, like long-term financial planning—the flip side of this coin may be a facility with mental account keeping of the monthly cash flow that would floor many middle-class Americans.[20]

Ordinary Working People

Our families are among the more fortunate of America's lower-income households—they have worked enough during the past year to warrant sizable tax credit refunds from the government. These workers are employed in a variety of jobs that keep the local economy running. But these jobs often require few educational credentials and provide limited monetary rewards.

Some work in restaurants, prepping food in the kitchen or taking orders from sit-down customers. Others serve as receptionists and file clerks. Like Ashlee Reed, some take care of children, while others help the sick and disabled elderly in roles as home health aides, certified nurse's assistants, and medical technicians. In short, these are the ordinary working people who feed the rest of us, ring up our orders and hand over our change, sort our paperwork, watch our kids, care for our older relatives or us when we're sick, and provide many of the other services that are a daily backdrop to our lives.

Table 11.1 shows the range of jobs held by the parents we interviewed. Almost all work in some type of service occupation. About half hold jobs in offices, restaurants, or child care centers. Most of the administrative workers are support staff, such as receptionists or clerical workers. Almost all of those in education work as preschool teachers, as public school teacher's assistants, or in day care centers.

TABLE 11.1 Respondents' and spouses' occupations over the prior twelve months

Occupational Classification	N	Examples of Jobs
Office and administrative support	24	Auto shop receptionist, community college office worker
Education, training, library	23	Head Start staff, teacher's aide
Food preparation, serving	17	Dunkin' Donuts worker, pizza parlor cook
Sales	12	Convenience store clerk, Radio Shack salesperson
Building and grounds cleaning	11	School custodian, housekeeper, office cleaner
Health care support	11	Home health aide, medical assistant, nurse assistant
Transportation and material moving	9	Bus driver, elderly meal deliverer, truck driver
Health care practitioners, technicians	6	Nutritionist, medical coder, emergency medical technician
Construction and extraction	6	Painter, carpenter
Installation, maintenance, and repair	5	Cable TV installer, auto mechanic
Personal care and service	5	Hairdresser, child caregiver

Production	3	Baker, laundromat manager, curtain factory supervisor
Management	3	Assistant building manager, property manager
Business and financial operations	2	Seasonal worker at tax preparation business
Community and social service	2	Unemployment counselor
Total occupations[a]	139	

Note: Occupational classifications derived from Bureau of Labor Statistics occupational categories.

A Occupations total greater than the number of respondents (115) because some individuals hold more than one job, and for some married couples both partners have held employment in the past year.

Among these working-poor households we heard a recurring wish for *better* employment. All desire higher pay and benefits—vacation time, paid sick leave, and a retirement plan. More than that, they want stable hours, job security, some flexibility, full-time hours, and greater respect from employers and their clientele. Mostly, though, they just want steady jobs with a paycheck they can count on—and this was in 2007, before they felt the effects of the Great Recession. One in ten had experienced involuntary unemployment at some point during the prior year. Others, like Ashlee, had boyfriends, their children's fathers, or kin who lost jobs as well. With network support often vital to their financial survival, families felt the pinch of these job losses too.

The service workers we spoke with complained the most about the lack of predictability in their schedules. Rose Alvarez, an immigrant from El Salvador who is raising two teens with limited help from their father, tries hard to put in forty hours a week as a home health aide. Even when she has a full client load, she tries to pick up extra shifts when other aides call in sick. Yet clients come and go, so Rose's hours can change suddenly and dramatically. She explained, "Sometimes I work only five hours a day, so that's no good. But the reason is because when the people get more sick, they get put in a nursing home. Some of them, they go and pass away. . . .

Sometimes I lost ten hours in one week." Rose tries to work as much as she can, but she ultimately has limited control over her schedule. Others have schedules that are more predictable, but the work is seasonal. Some have jobs that depend on favorable weather conditions or a strong economy, such as construction work and house painting. These jobs made financial planning a challenge.

It is an article of faith for most of these families that work will lead to upward mobility. With the arrival of tax season, workers can point to their refunds as evidence that it's worth sticking it out at their jobs. Most insist that their economic situations will improve someday, even if they are not sure how. Some simply believe that, if they stay at a given job long enough, they'll eventually get a raise or an increase in hours. Others predict steady movement up the job ladder—from a nurse's assistant to a medical technician to a registered nurse, for example—imagining they'll somehow manage to acquire the necessary certifications to claim the better-paying occupations they are aspiring to. Some have little hope for mobility in their current occupations but believe that they will manage to find a better job sooner or later. These low-wage employees have not given up on the American Dream.

The Balance Sheet

We interviewed parents who claimed a relatively large earned income tax credit (EITC), which meant they had worked a considerable number of hours in the prior year. Ashlee Reed, whom we met at the beginning of this chapter, had earned approximately $27,500 annually in gross income, placing her above the mean in our sample—the families we studied earned roughly $22,000 on average. But nearly a quarter (24 percent) earned less than $15,000 annually.[21]

Table 11.2 shows income by marital status for parents in the study. Because the EITC has somewhat higher eligibility thresholds for married couples, the single parents we spoke with have lower incomes than the married couples do on average.[22] The typical married couple in our study reports about $29,000 in total income, while the unmarried parents have about $19,000. A few families report somewhat higher incomes than EITC eligibility thresholds should allow. Often these are cohabiters where one partner claims the kids and files as "head of household," just as the IRS forms direct (there is no separate filing status for cohabiters). When Ashlee and Adrian file their taxes, for example, Adrian claims one of their children while Ashlee claims the other two, each filing separately because they are unmarried. Others do not report all of their income to the IRS but were willing to disclose it to us. Income that goes unreported to the IRS is not common, and it isn't usually substantial.

TABLE 11.2 Respondents' annual household earnings, by marital status

Annual Earnings	Single (%)	Married (%)	All (%)
Less than $15,000	32	10	24
$15,001–$20,000	33	8	24
$20,001–$25,000	12	15	13
$25,001–$30,000	7	10	8
$30,001–$35,000	13	28	18
More than $35,000	3	30	12
Number of respondents	75	40	115

Note: Marital status refers to respondents' tax filing status with the IRS. Single respondents used the "head of household" filing status, and married respondents used the "married, filing jointly" filing status. Percentage totals do not equal 100 percent because of rounding.

[…] families' incomes routinely fall short of their expenses. To get by despite this shortfall in earned income, they rely on other sources of support—ex-partners who pay child support, kin and romantic partners who contribute, and government support such as TANF or unemployment insurance. One in six (17 percent) of the households in our study receives child support through the formal system; these payments augment the average household income by an average of $230 for those who receive it. However, those receiving informal child support get even more: $360 on average each month. Some count on assistance from friends and family during lean months—one in five families (20 percent) get financial help from kin or romantic partners, gleaning $194 per month on average. Only a small number of families claimed anything in the past year from cash welfare, TANF, or other programs paying cash benefits, such as Supplemental Security Income (SSI). Many, however, claimed some benefits from SNAP. Taken together, TANF, SSI, and SNAP (when counted as cash) add an average of $271 monthly.[23]

Table 11.3 summarizes the effect of these contributions and government benefits on the typical monthly budget.

As the next chapter will show, tax time is long anticipated and, for many, the only time during the year when income is sure to exceed expenses. Unlike the legions of upper-and middle-class families across America who dread filing their taxes (and who may wait until the April 15 deadline), lower-wage earners as a group tend to file as early as possible, at the end of January or early February when their W-2s come in the mail.

TABLE 11.3 Respondents' average monthly and annual incomes, by marital status

	Single	Married	All
Monthly Income			
Monthly Earned Income (EI)	$1,562	$2,496	$1,887
EI + Child Support (CS)	$1,608	$2,519	$1,925
EI + CS + Gov't Benefits (Gov)[a]	$1,879	$2,861	$2,221
EI + CS + Gov + Kinship Support[b]	$2,013	$3,021	$2,363
Annual Income			
Annual Earned Income (EI ×12)	$18,744	$29,952	$22,644
Tax Refund[c]	$4,545	$4,952	$4,686
Annual EI + Tax Refund	$23,289	$34,904	$27,330
N	75	40	115

Note: *Marital status* refers to respondents' tax filing status with the IRS. Single respondents used the "head of household" filing status, and married respondents used the "married, filing jointly" filing status. Incomes are in 2007 dollars.

[a]Government benefits include TANF, SNAP, SSI, utility assistance, and unemployment insurance. They do not include the value of housing subsidies.

[b]Kinship support includes contributions from adults inside or outside the household (other than romantic partners) and informal child support payments.

[c]Tax refund includes the refundable EITC, the refundable child tax credit, and refunds of paycheck withholding. It includes both federal and state tax refunds.

These working families say tax season feels like "hitting the lottery." It is no wonder. Their refund checks include the earned income tax credit, other federal tax credits, and any taxes overpaid throughout the year (either from their additional withholding or through employers' overestimation of owed taxes), minus any taxes owed. On average, this federal refund check from the US Treasury, taken together with their state refund check, which may contain additional state and local tax credits, boosts the family budget by $4,686 for parents in our study. It is difficult to overstate the importance of tax time in their financial lives. The average refund is equivalent to nearly three months of earnings.[24] Recall that the modern EITC was originally designed to allow a family of three with a minimum-wage, full-time, full-year job to escape poverty, and, for most of the families we spoke to, it does.[25] However, these workers also drew on the extensive in-kind safety net that bolsters needy families' resources: SNAP; the Special Supplemental

Nutrition Program for Women, Infants, and Children (WIC); housing assistance of various sorts; and public health insurance such as MassHealth.

In Massachusetts, SNAP is available to families with children who have incomes under 200 percent of the poverty line.[26] This means that a single parent with two children who has $2,767 or less in monthly income could receive some benefits from the program.[27] In 2006, our study's tax year, a family of three would have been eligible for a maximum $399 per month in food stamps if they had no earnings. Each dollar earned reduces the maximum benefit by 25 cents. Because eligibility for this program continues to be based on need, many of the households in our study qualified for a modest amount from SNAP.[28]

WIC helps pregnant and nursing women and children under five to obtain milk, eggs, baby formula, cereal, and other nutritious foods. The income limit for this program is 185 percent of the poverty line. This program offers in-kind benefits only, but the cash value of the monthly food package can total as much as $100 per month if two members of the household qualify.[29]

Housing subsidies generally come in one of two forms, public housing or housing choice ("Section 8") vouchers. These are not entitlements; they serve only a small fraction of those who are eligible. In many jurisdictions, wait lists for the voucher program are closed or are opened for only a brief period of time when vouchers become available. Qualified applicants are then generally chosen by lottery, though especially needy households, such as those that are homeless, sometimes receive priority. Families pay a portion of their income (generally 30 percent after certain deductions) for rent, and the federal government picks up the rest.[30] Housing choice vouchers can be used to rent market-rate units, providing the landlord is willing to participate in the program, the rent isn't too high, and the unit can pass the housing authority's inspection.[31]

When we launched our study, Massachusetts was the only state in the country with a health insurance requirement (paving the way for the subsequent federal overhaul of the health insurance system). MassHealth, instituted in 2007, is free of charge to children under 300 percent and adults under 133 percent of the poverty line. Other lower-income residents can buy MassHealth insurance at discounted rates.[32] Consequently, many in our study had access to relatively affordable health insurance.

Some families we spoke with reported that someone in their household had drawn income from SSI. This is a federal disability program that offers benefits to disabled adults and their minor children who do not have the work history to qualify for SSDI (Social Security Disability Insurance) or workers' compensation—or to children with disabilities serious enough to qualify them for SSI had they been adults.[33] State offices determine eligibility for disability payments, but the federal government pays for most of the benefits (approximately one-quarter of recipients nationwide—including those in Massachusetts—live in a state that offers an additional supplement). To be eligible, an adult must be deemed so physically or mentally impaired as to be unable to work for at least the next twelve months. Earnings below $300 a month are seen as one form of evidence of the inability to work, and there is also a $2,000 asset limit (for an individual). The federal benefit rate in 2006, the year just prior to our study, was $603 per month for an individual claimant.[34] For children to qualify, they must live in a low-income household and have "marked and severe functional limitations" expected to last for at least a year.[35]

Figure 11.1 shows the number of families in our study who report deriving income from each of these government programs.[36] In this sample of working families, with incomes ranging from well below to significantly above the poverty line, some were eligible for an array of government assistance programs above and beyond the EITC, but others were not, at least at the time of the study. While fifty-one families (44 percent) said they had used cash welfare (AFDC or TANF) at some point in the past, only nine families (8 percent) told us that they had received any cash welfare in the last year. In contrast, forty-five families (39 percent) had received SNAP, and a majority, seventy-three families (64 percent), got some form of housing assistance—a rate that is more than two times the national average among eligible households. In twenty-five families (22 percent), someone received SSI. Thirty-three households (29 percent) drew benefits from the WIC program. Eight families (7 percent) claimed unemployment insurance for a portion of the year. As indicated above, because our

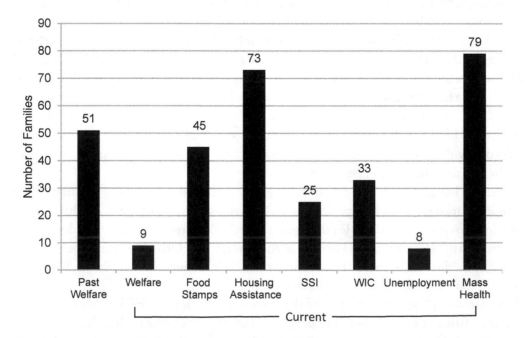

FIGURE 11.1 Number of families in sample using government assistance programs. N = 115 families.

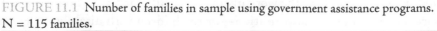

families lived in Massachusetts, in most—seventy-nine—households (69 percent) at least someone was covered by government-subsidized health insurance (usually MassHealth).

These working families are not dependents in the colloquial sense, but they are nonetheless recipients of substantial government assistance, even beyond the EITC. Figure 11.2 shows the number of programs families are currently claiming in addition to the EITC. Only sixteen of our families (14 percent) receive the EITC alone, while fifty-four families (47 percent) draw on three or more government support programs in addition to tax credits. Together, figures 11.2 and 3 show that the government safety net for the working poor extends well beyond the EITC, especially in the city of Boston, where housing costs are unusually high and housing subsidies are in greater supply than elsewhere.

The Expense Side of The Ledger

Despite these various sources of government assistance, expenses exceed income in the typical month for the families in our study (see table 11.4). The average household spends roughly six in ten dollars (59 percent) of their earnings for just three items: housing, food, and transportation. Note that even *after* taking into account housing subsidies and SNAP benefits, families typically spend nearly half (45 percent) of their wages just on housing and food.

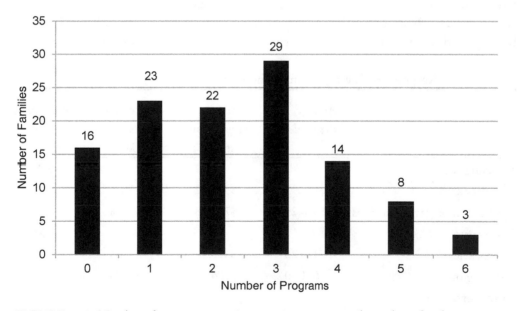

FIGURE 11.2 Number of government assistance programs currently used per family. N = 115 families. Count of government assistance programs excludes the EITC.

Spending among the families in our sample is similar to that of other lower-income families nationwide. Our analysis of the Bureau of Labor Statistics' 2005 Consumer Expenditure

Survey, when restricted to those respondents at or below 300 percent of the poverty line, showed that a household unit of three spent a monthly average of $381 on food at home (versus $398 for our sample), $90 on buying prepared food outside the home ($82 for our sample), $73 on clothing ($123 for our sample), $1,102 on housing expenses ($735 for our sample), $129 on medical costs ($68 in our sample), and $395 on transportation ($355 in our sample).[37] Thus the expenses among our sample of families are broadly representative of the allocations among disadvantaged families across the country.

Housing

As we've already noted, housing costs are higher than average in Boston and contribute heavily to the city's dubious distinction of being "one of the most expensive places to live in the U.S.," as noted in *Forbes*.[38] On average, our families earn $1,887 each month, while an average two-bedroom apartment in Greater Boston costs $1,345 per month, and a three-bedroom unit averages $1,609.[39] So, how do they manage? Very few—27 percent—are paying the full cost of the housing that they occupy. While 64 percent get some form of subsidy, another 11 percent are doubled up, living with family or friends.[40] Housing expenses consume approximately one-quarter of the typical family budget; this is substantial, but it is a fraction of what the figure would be if all paid market rent. The reason so many Boston-area lower-income families have subsidies is that those without one are often priced out of Boston altogether. The Boston Housing Authority, which administers most subsidies, estimates that it provides a subsidy to approximately 10 percent of all city residents.[41]

TABLE 11.4 Respondents' average monthly household expenses

	Average, All Respondents	Average, Respondents with Cost	% Respondents with Cost	Average % of Monthly Budget
Housing costs				26%
Utilities	$139.97	$338.62	73.0%	
Rent or mortgage + utilities	$690.29	$708.78	97.4%	
Food costs				19%
Groceries	$420.26	$420.26	97.4%	
Eating out	$91.40	$104.59	84.3%	
Transportation				14%
Car expenses	$357.00	$743.52	62.6%	
Public transport/cabs	$31.11	$83.58	42.6%	
Medical expenses				3%
Insurance	$57.74	$188.97	28.7%	

Out-of-pocket medical costs	$13.83	$27.43	50.4%	
Other household expenses				19%
Phone (mobile and landline)	$102.18	$123.69	86.1%	
Child care	$89.29	$191.09	43.5%	
Children's school expenses	$43.52	$61.81	60.0%	
Children's clothing	$95.44	$105.67	73.0%	
Adult clothing	$55.51	$73.08	68.7%	
Adult hair care	$26.52	$44.20	54.8%	
Toiletries/cleaning supplies	$46.99	$54.30	39.1%	
Laundry	$28.95	$60.30	10.4%	
Furniture	$10.77	$69.98	13.9%	
Appliances	$6.13	$44.68	12.2%	
Nonessential purchases				13%
Entertainment	$76.06	$177.90	84.3%	
Cable TV	$41.64	$54.86	73.9%	
Internet	$22.09	$36.70	56.5%	
Cigarettes	$28.13	$87.60	30.4%	
Alcohol	$9.29	$34.93	25.2%	
Lottery tickets	$7.94	$30.11	35.7%	
Other	$158.52	$343.24	95.7%	
Debt payments				6%
Credit cards	$73.61	$175.66	38.3%	
Medical bills	$5.73	$37.04	14.8%	
Student loans	$16.05	$93.74	16.5%	
Other debt	$77.21	$267.67	13.0%	
Total monthly expenses	$2,683.19[a]			

Note: N = 115 families. *Debt payments* refers to the amount paid toward debts, not how much is owed. Expense values are in 2007 dollars.

[a]This total does not double count utilities, which appear twice in this column.

In contrast to renters, the home owners among our families pay a premium for their stake in the American Dream. On average, they devote $2,101 per month toward their housing costs—including the mortgage, insurance, and taxes—considerably higher (by more than a thousand dollars) than renters who pay the full market price. Subsidized renters pay the least for their housing expenses, averaging under $400. Adding together housing and utilities, home owners pay about twice what unsubsidized renters pay and five times what those with subsidized housing must lay out each month.

Food

After housing costs, food takes the second-largest bite out of a typical family's budget—$512, or 19 percent on average (see table 11.4). Tamara Bishop—a thirty-three-year-old black single mother who works as an assistant preschool teacher, gets $70 from SNAP each month to help feed her four children—two teenage daughters and two sons still in grade school. But that benefit buys less than a week's worth of groceries, leaving her to cover the rest of the family's food purchases with cash: "You know, my kids, like they like to eat! I cook every day . . . and I don't even buy . . . things that they want, like snacks and stuff. I buy 'food food.' Sometime, like, especially the end of the month, it's like, like last month there was like nothing in the refrigerator; I mean nothing. I had to like borrow the money [from my mom]." Tamara usually spends $250 in cash on groceries each month in addition to SNAP.

Because the working poor and near-poor often live with financial uncertainty, it was not uncommon for us to hear stories of families buying in bulk at discount stores and filling pantries and deep freezers, especially at tax time. These stockpiles help to ensure that food won't run short when money gets tight. Brenda Hutchinson, a thirty-eight-year-old, married, white school lunch aide, explains that, when the tax refund check comes, she takes her two daughters—ages four and eleven—to BJ's Warehouse, a wholesale chain that sells groceries and other items in bulk. This year, they spent over $400 on meat, which she stores in her mother's standalone freezer. They also bought large quantities of pizza bagels and cases of soup. She tells us, "I just keep them like stocked up so you don't have to worry about running out of food, you know?" That families use their EITC money in this way reflects the reality that these parents often have too little income to make it through the month, even with SNAP.

Mariella Ambrosini, a white fifty-seven-year-old whose daughters, ages fifteen, twenty, and twenty-three, all live at home, has severe emphysema and relies on her husband's seasonal earnings as a construction foreman as well as her SSI check to get by. When visiting Mariella in her third-floor walkup in East Boston, we immediately notice that just inside the door is a large metal shelf overflowing with pasta, canned goods, chips, and cereal. She tells us, "My big expense is food, my refrigerator gotta be full all the time. Otherwise I get very depressed." For Mariella and many others, food represents security, and the state of Mariella's pantry serves as an important barometer of how she is faring financially.

Other Necessities

Transportation consumes $388 per month, or 14 percent of the typical family's monthly budget. About two-thirds of our families (63 percent) have cars and spend an average of $744 monthly on automobile-related expenses, including car loans, car insurance, gas, maintenance, excise fees, parking fees, and tickets (see table 11.4). In Boston, public transit is extensive, and more than four in ten families (43 percent) were entirely reliant on it when we spoke with them (including a few with cars that they could not afford to fix or insure). But buses and trains do not always run on time. And low-income neighborhoods in Boston are underserved by subway lines. Thus getting to work or to the store can mean navigating several bus routes, or riding a bus and then the subway.[42] Using public transportation saves money but costs time—time parents can sometimes ill afford while juggling child care or multiple jobs.

Although our families live in Massachusetts and have access to MassHealth, they still report some medical expenses: $72, or 3 percent of total monthly income on average. As noted above, by virtue of their incomes, many qualify for free or subsidized health care coverage under MassHealth. For the 29 percent who pay something toward their health care, the expense is relatively small—$189 on average—probably because so many receive at least a partial subsidy.

In their study of spending practices of low-income single mothers, Edin and Lein found that, when money ran short at the end of the month, the phone bill was one obligation that families let slide—telephone service cost their households only about $30 on average in the mid-1990s, when they conducted their research.[43] What is considered a household "necessity" clearly changes over time; now, a decade and a half later, phone costs have spiraled—averaging $102 among our families. Most (86 percent) have either a cell phone or a landline, and many (71 percent) have both. The cell phone bill is often a high priority because many are locked into one-or two-year contracts with their providers and can be assessed a hefty fee for late payments. Some have pay-as-you-go plans; while this option is relatively expensive for anyone who uses his or her phone very often, they pose no risk of broken contracts and potential late fees.

Child care and educational expenses consume $133 of the typical family's monthly budget. The fifty families with child care expenses (44 percent) pay only $191 each month on average, far below the market rate, because many have managed to secure subsidies. Yet for some, even the assistance they qualify for does not feel like enough. When administrative assistant Corine Samuels, forty-nine, black, and separated from her husband, took in her four-year-old granddaughter, Tamika, she did not anticipate the bite of her share of the child care bill: "They told me when I had custody of my granddaughter that . . . I wouldn't have to pay for child care; this year they told me I gotta pay child care. I have to pay $27.50 a week for her to go to child care. [The caseworker] told me, 'Oh, that ain't nothing!' It's . . . nothing if I had it. When you don't have it, it's something! If you don't have it, [even] $5 is a lot."

Clothing constituted $151 of the typical family's monthly budget. When it comes to shopping for themselves, many parents rely on discount stores such as Target, T.J.Maxx, and Marshalls, but usually only when they absolutely need to shop for something—an outfit for a job interview, a uniform for work, or sneakers when the old pair has holes. Occasionally, though, parents will treat themselves to an inexpensive item of clothing that they don't strictly need. Twenty-six-year-old Rita Ramirez, a Hispanic hairdresser and mother of two children, ages one and nine, whose boyfriend lives out of state, says, given how hard she works, she believes that she's earned the right to a few new $7 T-shirts or a $15 pair of flip-flops.

While adults can put off buying clothes for years, growing children often require new clothes—with chilly Boston winters and humid summers, most children require some new items each spring and fall. Usually, our parents scour the city for sales, supplement with hand-me-downs, and solicit their relatives for clothing as Christmas and birthday gifts.

Another $158 each month goes to hair care, toiletries, and cleaning supplies. This includes trips to the laundromat; families who don't have washing machines at home spend $60 each month on average to wash and dry their clothes. Buying or renting furniture or appliances isn't uncommon; 14 percent of families made a furniture purchase or paid rent on their furniture in the last year, while another 12 percent are making payments on household appliances, such as washers, dryers, refrigerators, or air conditioners.

Nonessential Spending

Though expenses generally exceed incomes, families still devote 13 percent of their budgets to nonessentials (see table 4)—the rare personal indulgence, a drink at happy hour with coworkers, or a treat for the kids, usually no more than a family trip to the arcade. For the most part, this spending is done without apology—after all, they emphasize, for all their struggles, they are *working* families, and being a worker gives one the right to spend on a few special extras every now and then. In keeping with this philosophy, more than eight in ten (84 percent) say they spend something on entertainment, mostly for DVDs, the occasional excursion to a family reunion, or a trip to the movie theater. In addition, half pay for Internet service; these parents typically justify the $37 average monthly cost by explaining that their children need the Internet for homework (although many may also use it for entertainment or to keep in touch with friends and family). Nearly three-quarters of all households have a cable television subscription, a quarter spend something on alcohol in a typical month, nearly a third buy cigarettes, and more than a third play the lottery. Almost all spend on other nonessentials as well: tithing to a church, purchasing pet food, buying gifts, or helping out needy family members or friends.

Debt Payments

Debt plays a pivotal role in the financial lives of these families [...]. For the purpose of creating an average monthly snapshot of their budgets, we asked parents to talk in depth about which debts they pay regularly, which are more hit or miss, and which are ignored altogether. The typical household pays $173 monthly toward outstanding debt, or 6 percent of monthly expenditures (see table 11.4). Note that this does not include rent or regular monthly payments on big-ticket items like furniture, appliances, or cars, which are categorized separately as household expenses. The 38 percent of families who make credit card payments dedicate an average of $176 per month to these bills; just under a third of families are paying on other kinds of debt, usually medical bills or student loans.

Financial Ups And Downs

Averages mask important ebbs and flows in income and expenses. A few families with whom we spoke have a stable pattern of income and expenditure despite their lower earnings. Most, however, live financially precarious lives, without a substantial private safety net (like savings or access to significant financial assistance from kin), and are therefore sensitive to financial *shocks*—sudden shifts in income or expenses.

Many say they have almost come to expect that something will derail them financially at some point during the year. Jerry Morales lives with his wife, Tessa, their three children, ages five, seven, and fourteen, and his mother in a housing project in South Boston. This white thirty-two-year-old works two jobs—full time during the week in the mailroom at a community college and on the weekend as a truck driver for a bakery, a 2:00 A.M. shift delivering doughnuts. Sometimes he gets discouraged by how surprise expenses seem to crop up with such frequency. "My dream basically is to get a house and be settled financially, everything. That's all I ever wanted. No matter how much we try, there's always something that just kicks us in the butt." Jerry's wife, Tessa, recalls the year when they faced a fourfold financial nightmare. First, she lost her waitressing job. Then "My mom passed away. I just had [my youngest daughter]. Jerry got sick [and couldn't work]. So, it was a stressed year."

A car repair, a family member in need, or even something as small as a parking ticket can be the jolt that "kicks us in the butt" when a household is living paycheck to paycheck. Family income may likewise dip abruptly because of lost hours at work or a layoff. Some life events, like illness or pregnancy, increase expenses while decreasing one's ability to earn. In the face of a financial shock, families go without, borrow, skip bills, or turn to their credit cards. A generous tax credit in February can halt the downward spiral or—for those who save some of the refund—prevent a subsequent one.

Struggles With Government Support

By their own definition, these families have fulfilled their part of the American social contract: they work and take care of their children to the best of their ability. [...] they disdain those who are dependent on welfare.[44] Because they view themselves as upstanding citizens and taxpayers who contribute into the system, they believe that they are worthy of a little help from the government—a hand up—when times are tough. This doesn't mean that the help they believe that they deserve is always forthcoming. Despite the plethora of programs one might, in theory, be able to draw on, in their view assistance is often wanting or slow in coming.

Some complain about eligibility and benefits that are based on gross, rather than net, income. Tanya Salazar, a twenty-eight-year-old married black mother of three who range in age from five months to twelve years, works at a clothing factory. She complains, "This apartment['s rent] is based on my income. It's based on my gross, not my net. How can you base my living expenses on money I'm not going to see? Yeah, you know that's why they took my Section 8 away, because gross I was getting like $1,000 [every two weeks]. After taxes I was only getting seven-something. And then, when you just added up my expenses alone, yeah, I had change left over, but once you took the [Section 8] certificate, I'm paying $1,400 [in] rent. It just doesn't add up."

Talisha Watson, a black twenty-five-year-old who lives with her boyfriend, Daven, and her elementary school–aged daughter, Jasmine, recently lost her job as a medical coder. She shares a similar story.

> I have one kid, and they [the welfare department] feel I was making enough money. I didn't feel like I was making enough money. I said, "Okay, you count gross pay. That is a lot. But let's talk about after taxes. . . ." I am paying health insurance . . . and then you have dental. . . . You have your 401k. . . . And God forbid if I work overtime. . . . The taxman get that back. I don't see that money. You know, so it's like . . . I should be able to splurge on something. . . . I work for this, but nooooo!

Talisha decries programs that take, rather than give, as earnings rise, and is even angrier about programs where eligibility abruptly ends once income exceeds a certain level. She echoes what is a key source of frustration for many: doing what's right—trying to better oneself through earnings—earns you a slap if not a shove out the door from "the system." Work ought to be rewarded, not punished, they insist. Ironically, the EITC also declines as earnings rise once families reach the phaseout range in benefits, but the way the total tax refund check is calculated is fairly mysterious to most. Further, the "refund" is adjusted for the ebbs and flows in earnings only once a year. Thus the declines in SNAP or one's housing subsidy are experienced as a "punishment" for working, while any eventual reduction in tax credits is not.

Nonetheless, the most common complaint is that most programs are built around the assumption of a steady income rather than on the ups and downs that are endemic to the financial lives of the working poor. Marissa Lopez is a thirty-one-year-old Hispanic single mother of three, ages five, eleven, and thirteen. She is relatively well educated—she has completed some college course work and is certified as a medical assistant, so her wages are higher than those of most. The catch is that she has not been able to get a full-time job in her field. Instead she's worked for a temp agency for the past seven years, filling in at various hospitals and doctors' offices. It's hard to predict how long any given assignment will last or how many hours she'll get. And there are sometimes weeks, even months, between assignments. "Sometimes I'm able to get forty hours a week. Other times I'm lucky if I get eight hours a week," she explains. SNAP has added to, rather than eased, the ups and downs in income, because the benefits are based on the prior month's earnings. Worse still, each time she is deemed ineligible because of an unusually flush paycheck, she must apply again during the next lean month and then wait for her case to be approved, an often lengthy process. In her words: "My income is not always stable. So one month I could be eligible for food stamps and the next month I'm *not* eligible for food stamps." Marissa must be diligent in updating her caseworker, since failure to report a new job, or any substantial increase in hours or wages, can result in steep sanctions. In some states offenders are barred from future receipt of SNAP benefits.[45]

Bitterness over "unfair treatment" can flow from these experiences. Luanna Fields, a white woman who smiles as she declines to tell us her age, is an education coordinator who is currently working on her master's degree at a local university. She lives with her husband, Colin, the grocery store manager she married a year ago, and her teenage son, Dustin, in a single-family home on a quiet, dead-end street in Malden, a lower-middle-class inner suburb north of Boston. Luanna and Colin have a rent-to-own agreement with their landlord.

The Fields ask us to arrive at eight o'clock on a Saturday morning so that Luanna can keep her promise to take an elderly friend shopping at 10:30 A.M. We move to the kitchen, which is spick-and-span, noting the nautical theme—the lighthouse knickknacks mingling with Colin's collection of wine bottle holders. We sit in the breakfast nook, which looks out over the neighbor's backyard, where Luanna shares strong opinions about the help she gets—and doesn't get—from the government. "I think that people like us that are the middle class [can't get anything from the government]. If you're really rich and you have all this kind of money, then you—I think that they make out somehow better [than us]. And then the lower class, it seems like even though they're all struggling, they get, you know, all those [benefits]. But the middle class, it just seems like we get stomped on. . . . Either you make it or you don't, you know. Trial and error." Until she married her husband, Luanna earned just enough to escape poverty, yet she views herself as part of the middle class—a group that she feels is left out, "stomped on," by the system.

Similarly, thirty-six-year-old Juana Vega, a married Hispanic mother to eleven-year-old Milo, works as a disability specialist at a local preschool and conveys her deep sense of frustration that, because they are doing the right thing (going to work, attempting to support themselves), her family is getting less than those who are less deserving:

> Because we're like a working family, we're like in the middle of everything. Like people who, like my sister-in-law, they're poor by the eyes of the government, they get all this money—welfare—and they get fuel assistance and they get food stamps. And they don't work because it's easy that way. Why go to work and make [money on your own]—she's getting her gas paid. I'm not. I can't get my gas paid because I'm working, you know? And sometimes I feel like, all these people getting all this money without—by lying and doing *nothing*, and the people like me that live check by check. . . . I work so hard, I pay so much in taxes, and maybe it'd be easy if I lie [down] too and just—you know what? I'm gonna live on welfare, I stay home, watch TV all day and I get paid [by welfare], you know? This is a working family; let's give it a relief!

Juana's claims are far from accurate—welfare benefits get a family to only half of the poverty line even in an unusually generous state like Massachusetts, and they are subject to strict time limits and participation requirements (which don't allow one to "stay home, watch TV all day"). And, other than the sales tax imposed on certain purchases, Juana gets back more in her tax refund than she pays in. In fact, the EITC and other tax credits that families like Juana's receive are at least as generous as welfare is to those with no outside income. But this is beside the point. Poor or near-poor workers like Juana often see themselves as the beleaguered "middle class," stuck between those who are eligible for what they imagine are big handouts and those who can truly afford to go without such assistance.

Support From Family And Friends

People often turn to their families and friends for help when times get tough, as is true among those in our study. Since anthropologist Carol Stack's seminal 1974 ethnographic work *All Our Kin*, which showed how crucial kin were in poor families' daily struggles for economic survival, the accepted wisdom is that family and friends play a key role in lower-income people's lives, buffering them from financial hardship.[46] But statistics actually show it is the more advantaged who draw the most resources from their networks. They are more likely than the poor to have friends and family with substantial assistance to offer.[47] This does not mean that the kin support that lower-income families do draw on is unimportant. While it is true that such support seldom compensates for the large gap in resources between the poor and the better off—and almost never offers the leg up that families need to buy cars, make down payments on homes, or save for college or retirement—kin support is often vital for routine survival.

Kin don't usually offer a once-in-a-blue-moon handout when times get particularly tough. Many of our families are involved in ongoing reciprocal and one-way exchanges with family and friends. Being embedded in such a social network, however, comes with the risk that someone else's financial woes can quickly become one's own.[48] Given the financial situations of the households we studied, they are only rarely the most well off in their networks; many are on the receiving end the majority of the time, garnering small loans of a few dollars here and there and, quite frequently, toys, clothes, meals, and special extras for their children. The $20 borrowed here and there to keep the lights on or the extra bag of groceries that appears at the doorstep can't usually make up for a significant shortfall of income, but it can ease stress for households with budgets that come up short. It is important to reiterate, however, that help from family and friends is generally neither asked for nor offered to cover outstanding debts. This ultimately limits the value of kin, who may help to prevent a family from falling further into material hardship but don't—or perhaps can't—aid families when they're trying to dig out from under pressing financial obligations. Debt limits families' abilities to build assets, especially purchasing a home, or to get good credit terms on other big-ticket items like cars, or even to rent an apartment in a more desirable neighbor-hood, because of the impact on credit scores.

Dominique Henderson is a twenty-three-year-old, single, black mother of a preschool-aged daughter and works as a teacher's aide at a local school; she relies on a variety of people who offer her financial help from time to time. When she needed to buy living room furniture, a friend was willing to put the purchases on her credit card with the promise that Dominique would pay her back at tax time. Dominique also wants to save for a home. She's opened a bank account with her brother where she can deposit savings toward this long-term goal;

keeping the account in her brother's name makes withdrawing the money for other purposes more difficult—and this is the point. Her sister lets Dominique use her bus pass that the sister only rarely puts to use (she has a car) to help her save money on transportation; Dominique says she can also borrow that car, or her brother's car, when she needs to. When she missed the deadline for financial aid at community college, Dominique's brother and sister each stepped up with $600 so that she could enroll that semester. When she attempted to reimburse them at tax time, they refused the money. Then her brother bought her a used car and paid the insurance on it for several months. "My brother—anything! He will do it for me." In a sense, Dominique's family and friends are her bank—extending loans and acting as creditors—but they don't charge interest and more readily forgive debts.

Dominique's kin are particularly helpful when it comes to providing for her three-year-old daughter, Tatiana. When Tatiana's swimming lessons went from $30 to $50 per eight-week session, Dominique told her daughter that she would have to quit, but Dominique's brother and sister offered to pay for the lessons. They knew how much their niece loved to swim. Dominique's cousin bought Tatiana a bed, and her brother got a mattress for it; to complete Tatiana's bedroom, Dominique's cousin bought the girl a TV. Her sister also buys clothing for Tatiana using her employee discount at the Gap. Dominique values her family's contributions, noting, "I get lucky."

The benefits that many of our families gain from their networks are not just financial—there are psychological benefits as well. When emergency medical technician LaWanda James, a twenty-three-year-old black single mother with a seven-year-old son, gets stressed from falling behind on bills, she finds solace in the knowledge that she can turn to her sister if she needs to: "My sister has always told me, 'Don't stress! As long as I have, you have.' So I have to say I've been blessed in that, since that I never really want or need for anything. And when it does get to that point, [my sister is] yelling at me like, 'Why didn't you ask me sooner? Here.'" Similarly, when we ask Debra McKinley, an engaged, twenty-eight-year-old white waitress and mother of two little girls, to estimate how much she owes her half sister, from whom she borrows most frequently, she laughs and exclaims, "My life! I couldn't put a dollar amount, you know. And the thing is, she doesn't put a dollar amount to it."

Although Dominique gets a great deal from her network, she also gives quite a lot. If she has money and someone asks for it, she'll always share if she can, even if she knows she's going to need it later on. "Do you know how much money like I have out that I still didn't get back?" she asks rhetorically before estimating that she's loaned out nearly $6,800 that hasn't been repaid. Eight hundred went to a close friend whom she trusts, so she thinks she will eventually get that money back, but she doesn't trust the other friends or her ex-boyfriend—additional recipients of her generosity—to act so responsibly. Her willingness to loan is an essential part of her ability to stay afloat; she loans out money when she can because she knows that if she were to need help, those who were able to would reciprocate. Because family members are generous with loans and gifts, she's more likely to have the income to spare when friends ask her for a loan. In many ways, her generous kin are a boon to her wider network of friends.

Shari Barfield, a married, black, thirty-six-year-old realtor, and mother of three—ages one, five, and twelve—gets cash only here and there from her kin, but she gleans a lot of in-kind support. Her mother watches her youngest child, so she doesn't need to pay for child care. When her daughter was born, her family sent loads of clothes and other baby items. Her sons also benefit from grandparents who "spoil them" with gifts every time they visit. Shari and her husband, in turn, help her brother out financially every now and then when he needs it—they don't expect him to reciprocate. Her husband also gives his ex-wife cash over and above his child support when his children need money for a school field trip or some other unexpected expense. The Barfields' finances, like those of so many, are not independent from those of their family and friends. Rather, they are intertwined, to greater and lesser extents, with money, clothes, toys, and food being passed around from those who can afford to help to those who need a hand.[49] Most of our families are receivers but also givers, sometimes simultaneously.

Not all, however, are so lucky to have family or friends to rely on. Carmen Sanchez, a forty-year-old preschool teacher and mother of four, who emigrated to the United States from Honduras, struggles to get any support from her children's father, from whom she's separated; their children range in age from three to seventeen. Every few weeks he'll give her $20—that is, unless she really pushes him. "I said, 'Look, I cannot be just doing the whole thing by myself. One week I will go [to the grocery store] and the other week you will go.' And he said, 'I don't have the money.' But, then, last week he gave me $100 because I said to him, 'Do you want me to look for another man that can feed my children?' He gave me the $100. I was surprised. I was really surprised. I went and paid my cell phone." In addition to struggles with her ex, Carmen and her mother battle over finances. Her mother lives on the second floor of Carmen's apartment and is supposed to be paying her $700 a month in rent. But it's been almost a year since the woman has paid at all. Recently, her mother promised she'd start paying $50 a week toward the rent; several weeks have passed since this offer was made, but Carmen has yet to see any cash. Rather than serving as a resource, Carmen's mother increases her financial burden.

Carmen's story hints at a darker side of personal ties. They not only smooth consumption in tough times but can be the *cause* of tough times: for example, a grandmother's finances can be thrown into disarray when she must suddenly assume responsibility for her grand-children because her daughter is about to lose custody of her children to the state.[50] Unlike a bank, which is required to disburse money you've deposited, or a government entitlement that must support those meeting its criteria, support from family, friends, and exes can be unreliable and may be subject to their changing emotions and financial circumstances. Furthermore, as we alluded to above, these are often reciprocal relationships. One must be prepared to give as well as to receive. For families like those in our study, who already struggle to make ends meet, giving over even a small portion of their meager resources can be a major hit to an already-strained budget.

Looking at average earnings and spending patterns allows us to get a sense of how much a typical family—such as Ashlee Reed's—earns and spends over the course of a year. But we've also tried to give some sense of the variation that these monthly averages obscure.

Many of our families are living near the financial edge. Because of low earnings and frequent financial surprises, only 11 percent are in good financial shape—they have minimal debts and substantial assets such as personal savings to provide a cushion should a bump in the financial road come along. Though all of the families in our study include at least one worker, earned income does not typically stretch to fully meet monthly expenses. Thus putting away a little each month in anticipation of a rainy day is difficult; families' financial planning more often includes figuring out which bill they can most easily neglect, not what they will do with their surplus funds.

Although most families we spoke to engage in some discretionary spending—a child's birthday present or a weekly lottery ticket—their budgets reveal a good deal of thrift as well. Despite their complaints that the "rules" of various government programs often exclude them or penalize them for working—this is an especially common claim among those with fluctuating work hours, like Marissa Lopez—these families are also the focus of a new, work-based safety net—the EITC—which allows them to claim cash assistance on top of their wages, and not in lieu of earnings, as was the case with the welfare system. And most get at least some in-kind assistance—SNAP, government-subsidized health insurance, a housing subsidy—as well. Many draw considerable aid from their networks, but network support is unevenly distributed and can sometimes be more of a hindrance than a help.

Are families spending and saving beyond what they can afford with their monthly earnings *because* they know the tax refund check is coming? We do see some evidence for this, particularly with heating bills, which parents can put off paying as most jurisdictions prohibit utility companies from discontinuing service because of nonpayment during the winter months. The February refund check happens to be perfectly timed to satisfy these obligations just before the restriction on shutoffs ends in March. Parents also sometimes say they buy Christmas presents on credit in anticipation of the tax refund. However, such behavior is not widespread. This may be because many are unsure of how much they will receive in their tax refund check from year to year—an issue we discuss in the next chapter. Further, financial shocks are so common that families often make spending decisions in response to events beyond their control (a job loss, new brake pads for the car, or a plumber's bill for a clogged pipe). Thus advanced planning of any kind is difficult.

Research on the psychology behind financial decision making has explored whether people make impulsive decisions, rather than well-thought-out plans, because of a lack of willpower, limited cognitive control, or limited attention due to other demands on one's "bandwidth" (how much of our mental capacity is available to us at any given time). Researchers consistently find that those who are operating under strain are less likely to make optimal decisions.[51] Like the dieter who, after avoiding the office candy bowl all day, breaks down at the end of the night and reaches in the freezer for a pint of ice cream, someone operating under tight financial conditions—trying to carefully monitor each dollar coming in and going out—may be more likely to make a rash spending decision that conflicts with her long-term financial goals. The key insight from this research is that a lack of willpower to avoid impulse buys or to align one's behavior to one's long-term financial goals is not characteristic of low-income individuals per se; rather the *condition* of scarcity takes up valuable bandwidth, in turn hampering optimal spending behavior.

Are the families in our study "overspending," even for the basics? Could they secure housing, food, and transportation more cheaply? The question of how much is "enough" is relative, at least in a rich nation like ours. Thus the closest we can come to answering this question is by comparing the expenses among our households to what other lower-income households in the United States spend to meet basic needs. As discussed above, parents in our sample are not engaging in profligate spending relative to their economically constrained peers across the country. While many could potentially trim some of their spending on the basics, not to mention the "extras" they sometimes consume, economic psychology helps us to understand why they fail to do so: making sound economic decisions that are consistent with long-term financial goals requires bandwidth that may be in short supply.

In future chapters, however, we'll argue that the "scarcity" perspective is not sufficient to explain much of the behavior we observe. Rather, spending and saving decisions are guided by the meaning households attach to the EITC. Further, as we will show, what outsiders may deem "frivolous" spending is often deeply meaningful to these parents—and arguably their children—and may have value that can exceed its monetary cost.

Let's revisit the question we opened this chapter with: Do families like the Reeds really need the additional resources the EITC offers? Ashlee Reed takes home about $1,600 in a typical month, but her bills exceed $2,800. Her finances are wildly out of balance right now because Adrian has no job and has run out of unemployment insurance. But, even when he's working, the money doesn't stretch far enough in the summers, when Ashlee goes for two months without a regular paycheck. Currently, shelter, food, transportation, and child care alone exceed her take-home pay.

Still, Ashlee does spend on some "extras," like cable TV and an occasional six-pack of beer. Some might argue that she should be saving that money to guard against circumstances like those in which she now finds herself. Ashlee would probably contend that she is a worker and thus deserves to splurge a little now and then.

At the outset of this chapter, we outlined two views of poverty. On the one hand, many point to the fact that the poverty line falls far short of what most Americans view as the minimum amount necessary to live on. But on the other, the American poor now consume more than ever before. In light of our data, both views of American poverty are correct. Using the lens of consumption, the Ashlee Reeds of the world are consuming more than the generation that came before, even though they hover around the official poverty line. But when we consider expenses relative to income—even for basic necessities like shelter, food, child care, and transportation—many working-poor households are living in the red at least some, and perhaps much, of the time. Since they work, they believe they shouldn't have to live as if they were impoverished. They believe that they earn the freedom from scrimping from time to time. And, as long as they are playing by the rules and working, they also deserve—at least in their own minds—a hand up from the government when income doesn't stretch to meet expenses.

Notes

1. In 2012, the Census Bureau adopted a "supplemental measure" of poverty that adjusted for things like regional variation of living costs, the value of tax credits (which are not counted in the official measure because they are after-tax income), and in-kind benefits.
2. Rector (2012).
3. Meyer and Sullivan (2009, 2007, 2003).
4. National Center for Children in Poverty (2010).
5. Jones (2007).
6. These general patterns held true for AFDC as well, though there was brief period of time—the late 1970s—when benefits were considerably more generous.
7. A unit renting at 40 percent of Area Median Rent.
8. Massachusetts is a best-case scenario—TANF benefits in the state are usually high, so TANF brings a family up to 50 percent of the poverty line (Finch and Schott 2011).
9. Rice and Sard (2009).
10. Ashlee Reed's net earnings are lower than we might expect because she overpays her taxes and opts to contribute 5 percent of her wages to a retirement program through work.
11. Boston Housing Authority (2010). See also Boston Housing Authority (2009). The first document says that, in a Section 8 tenancy, the tenant payment is the amount calculated under the 1937 Act (Section 3(a)(1)) as 30 percent of the family's Monthly Adjusted Income.
12. US Department of Housing and Urban Development (2014).
13. Child Care Aware (2012).
14. The average month has 4.33 weeks. Thus we multiply weekly wages by 4.33.
15. Unemployment benefits in Massachusetts provide approximately 50 percent of a worker's earnings, along with a $25 per child per week benefit. However, there is a one-week period of unemployment before workers become eligible for benefits and another delay of approximately three weeks before benefits get processed (see Massachusetts Executive Office of Labor and Workforce Development 2013).
16. This does not include Ashlee's cohabiting boyfriend's expenses or income. Prior to losing his job, Adrian contributed to the family household expenses, though not on an equal basis. For the most part, Ashlee says that he has his own expenses (his own credit cards, for example) but that he does chip in for household costs when she is short on money. During the time he was employed in the cafeteria, the rent on their Section 8 apartment was higher ($950), but after he lost his job the Housing Authority reassessed their rent and lowered it to $575, on the basis of Ashlee's income alone. Adrian also has the following additional expenses, not listed in Ashlee's budget: $145 for car insurance, $173 in gas, and $50 for his cell phone. While he has been unemployed, Ashlee says that her paycheck has been stretched to cover all of his essential expenses as well.
17. Her boyfriend, Adrian, also has three credit cards with a total balance of $4,835.
18. Nationally, the median household income in the United States in 2007 (the year in which we interviewed families) was $52,673; in Massachusetts, the median household income was $64,815 (Semega 2009).
19. See also Edin and Lein (1997).

20　On the extent to which the stresses of poverty monopolize attention, see, for example, Mullainathan and Shafir (2013).

21　Income figures in this chapter refer to gross income, unless otherwise noted. We sought respondents' gross earnings figures, but in some cases they may have given their net income, resulting in an underestimation of gross income.

22　Because of how the American tax system works, cohabiting parents don't report their partners' income on their tax forms—this allows them to both pool income and enjoy a sizable credit. We count only the tax filing unit's income in our calculations.

23　The assistance received through SNAP would probably be substantially higher among a more disadvantaged group of families. Among families like those in our study, whose earnings are generally in the $20,000 range, SNAP benefits are more minimal than for those in more dire straits.

24　The Census Bureau estimates that the poverty rate would have been 2 percent higher without the EITC, rising from 15.7 percent to 17.7 percent (Yen 2011).

25　See Holt (2006); Meyer (2007, table 4).

26　The federal poverty line for a family of three in 2006 was an annual income of $16,600.

27　Albelda and Shea (2007).

28　Food and Nutrition Service (2013). Note that even the modest benefit levels these families receive from SNAP are quite sizable when summed over the course of the year. However, unlike the EITC check, SNAP benefits are parceled out monthly and can be used only for specific purposes. This means that $1 in SNAP benefits is not equivalent, in parents' minds, to $1 from their tax refund checks.

29　Benefits.gov (2013).

30　US Department of Housing and Urban Development (2013a, 2013b).

31　It is important to note that the EITC doesn't count against public housing rent, which is an added benefit for public housing residents of this form of income.

32　Massachusetts Executive Office of Health and Human Services (2014).

33　Social Security Administration (2014b).

34　Office of Policy, Office of Research, Evaluation, and Statistics (2007).

35　Social Security Administration (2014a, 6).

36　The measure of previous welfare use probably provides an underestimate, as respondents were not extensively interviewed about all of their government program usage throughout their adult lives.

37　Castner and Mabli (2010). The Consumer Expenditure Survey's measure of housing costs is broadly defined to include items such as furniture, while the figure for our study excludes items like furniture.

38　*Forbes* ranks Boston as the eighth most expensive city in which to live in the United States ("America's Most Expensive Cities" 2009).

39　These figures represent 2009 HUD Fair Market Rent for the Boston area (US Department of Housing and Urban Development 2009).

40　The 62 percent figure for those receiving some form of housing subsidy makes our sample stand apart from the common experience nationwide, where only one in four low-income households receives rental assistance (Sullivan 2013). Therefore, although our sample is exceptional in residing in a high-rent area, this disadvantage is balanced out, in a sense, by their greater likelihood of having some sort of housing subsidy.

41 Boston Housing Authority estimates (see Boston Housing Authority 2011).

42 Powers (2013).

43 Edin and Lein (1997).

44 Interestingly, one of the points many families make in claiming this status is that they pay taxes: that is, because they have paid into the system, they have, in a way, paid for their own benefits. This is based on a disconnect in their understanding of the relationship between the taxes they see taken from their paychecks on a weekly basis and the tax refund check they receive on an annual basis. For many, this refund check alone exceeds the taxes they have paid into the system, meaning that their discussions of paying for their own benefits (like SNAP or unemployment insurance, for instance) or their frustration at seeing less deserving people living off the taxes they pay through their hard work are based on a fallacy. However, this points out the psychological importance to people of feeling mainstream. From their perspective they are like other, more economically advantaged workers because they pay taxes; therefore, like these other workers, they are deserving, and their receipt of government support should not be stigmatized.

45 Some states have tried to introduce a degree of flexibility in the SNAP system to help households avoid a seemingly endless process of reporting income fluctuations. Nonetheless, for parents like Marissa who see sizable changes in income—in some months she is eligible and others she is ineligible for SNAP—reporting can still feel onerous.

46 See also, for example, Edin and Lein (1997); Pattillo-McCoy (1999).

47 Jayakody, Chatters, and Taylor (1993); Lee and Aytac (1998); Parish, Hao, and Hogan (1991); Sarkisian and Gerstel (2004); Swartz (2009). See also Harknett (2006).

48 For further discussion, see also Edin and Lein (1997); Stack (1974); Stern-berg Greene, Boyd, and Edin (2010).

49 Such networks of support can help families in tough times but also have the potential to hold families back when times are good, weighed down by the needs of extended family. For example, Heflin and Pattillo (2002) find that having poor family members is associated with lower levels of asset ownership. This implies that programs that aim to help families build assets must think holistically of the entire family system or resource network.

50 Sternberg Greene, Boyd, and Edin (2010).

51 Baumeister, Vohs, and Tice (2007); Mullainathan and Shafir (2013); Shah, Mullainathan, and Shafir (2012); Spears (2011).

Constructing a Feminist Reorganization of the Heterosexual Breadwinner/ Caregiver Model

College Students' Plans for their Own Future Families

BY MEGAN FULCHER, LISA M. DINELLA, AND ERICA S. WEISGRAM

Introduction

Since the industrial revolution, middle-class heterosexual couples in the United States have specialized their labor such that men were primarily responsible for earning money outside the home and women were primarily responsible for the care and nurturing of children: the breadwinner-caregiver model (Bernard 1981). Although widely accepted at the time as the ideal family model, many women were unsatisfied in these prescribed roles as detailed in Friedan's (1963) revolutionary feminist work, *The Feminine Mystique*. Today, most women in the U.S. are involved in careers even while parenting young children (U.S. Department of Labor 2011), and many are primary breadwinners for their families (Wang et al. 2013), resulting in a need for a cultural shift in the organization of both the workplace and the family. Instead, many heterosexual couples in the United States continue to subscribe to the ideal of breadwinner-caregiver family model, although few actually meet the ideal criteria (Cohen 2014). In these families mothers may work to "help" the family financially and fathers may "help" with the children without reconstructing family roles leading to negative consequences for both parents, but women in particular (Gaunt 2005; Hood 1986). This paper draws on a sample of emerging adults in the U.S. to examine students' own plans for using the breadwinner-caregiver model to organize their own future family and work roles.

Megan Fulcher, Lisa M. Dinella, and Erica S. Weisgram, "Constructing a Feminist Reorganization of the Heterosexual Breadwinner/Caregiver Family Model: College Students' Plans for their Own Future Families," Sex Roles, vol. 73, no. 3-4, pp. 174-186. Copyright © 2015 by Springer Science+Business Media. Reprinted with permission.

Squeezing family roles into a model that does not fit may have a particularly negative impact on women (Helms-Erikson et al. 2000). This organization of roles may leave women burdened with work/family conflict and men disconnected from their children. However, the breadwinner-caregiver model is a powerful organizing tool that is difficult for heterosexual couples to reject, and heterosexual couples in the U.S. still use gender as the main criteria for dividing paid and unpaid labor (Mannino and Deutsch 2007; Solomon et al. 2005). Ferree (1990, 2010), in her feminist review of research on the family, argued that gender roles in the family may not be so much *performed* as *required* by the social structures that confine men and women. This paper will examine the impact of such structures in the U.S. on emerging adults' plans for their own family as well as mechanisms for changing family structures that sustain the breadwinner-caregiver model. The family is one such social structure in the United States in which women and men find their behaviors restricted by their gender (Ferree 1990). A feminist family model that does not rely on gender to organize family responsibilities not only benefits parents but reduces the gendered information and modeling available for their children (Mack-Canty and Wright 2004). Therefore, it is important to examine individual differences in young men's and women's plans for dividing paid and unpaid labor in their future families. Because most women in the U.S. plan on working while raising children, it is particularly important to find correlates of men's plans for involvement in childcare. The social-cognitive theory of gender development (Bussey and Bandura 1999) would suggest that young men who remember their own fathers as active in childcare would envision a future in which they divide family labor more equitably. A primary aim of this research is to examine associations between U.S. students' visions of their future families and the remembered division of labor of their parents.

Families do not operate independent of the culture in which they reside. Parents' behaviors are influenced by cultural supports and pressures, often confining parents to conventional behaviors, perhaps even those unaligned with their own aspirations or attitudes (Ferree 1990, 2010; Fox and Murry 2000). Most research cited here, except where noted, relies on samples from the United States. Indeed in the United States, there are many cultural supports in place to sustain the breadwinner-caregiver model (Ferree 1990). U.S. employers, working under the breadwinner-caregiver model, assume that mothers' income is less valuable to the family than men's and that family responsibilities will make mothers less reliable workers. Hence, mothers in the U.S. are paid less than other women (and men), particularly women in lower paying jobs (Budig and Hodges 2014) confining them to helper/supplemental status within their families. Conversely, men who are fathers are paid more than men without children particularly if they are married, heterosexual men (Hodges and Budig 2010). When men are paid more and women less, it is difficult for heterosexual parenting couples to resist cultural pressure to have women more involved in childcare while men work longer and are less available to children.

Thus, U.S. women take more time off work to care for newborn children than do men (Harrington et al. 2011). This early experience may cement the mother as primary caregiver and the expert on childcare. In their position as secondary caregivers (Wall 2007), fathers simply complete childcare tasks as needed and requested by mothers. This management/helper arrangement may continue through parenting pushing fathers out of important caregiving responsibilities. When mothers are cast as managers it is difficult for fathers to construct a caregiving role themselves; this may entrench both mothers' roles as caregivers and fathers' as providers (Meteyer and Perry-Jenkins 2010). If fathers in the U.S. received more cultural and structural support for participation in childcare, there may be less specialization of labor, freeing parents from responsibilities tied to gender.

Impact of the Breadwinner-Caregiver Model

Clinging to the breadwinner-caregiver model may limit women's equality and opportunities in the family and the workforce. It may be difficult for women to make headway in prestigious or gender-nontraditional careers if full participation in a career is influenced by family needs and responsibilities. As noted above, wives' work is often considered supplemental to the family finances and is seen in addition to her normative role as caregiver. In such families women may move in and out of employment as the providing and caregiving needs of their families change in the U.S. and Israel (Gaunt 2005; Hood 1986).

Women's involvement and enjoyment of their work can serve as buffer against depression and marital conflict (Helms-Erikson et al. 2000). However, this buffer only exists for women who see themselves as co-providers for their family. When women framed their work as more supplemental for the family needs, the positive psychological associations with work disappeared (Helms-Erikson et al. 2000). For women and their families to reap the benefits of women's paid labor, it needs to be reframed as an important part of family finances and paired with a more equitable division of childcare. An important component of the breadwinner-caregiver model is that the provider will be cared for and supported by the caregiver. Thus, when women work they often remain supporters and caregivers of their husbands without any support for themselves (Ferree 1990). Working women are left needing a wife (Brady 1972).

However, when women's income is essential for the family, this is often experienced by women as a loss of their freedom to choose nurturing and failure by men to provide for the family and keep the breadwinner-caregiver organization intact (Ferree 1990). For women, especially those who endorse traditional gender roles, being a good parent may mean choosing a job that is flexible enough to still allow for significant childcare responsibilities despite the fact that this job may be lower in salary (Weisgram et al. 2010). Taking time out of work or working part-time often has a negative impact on women's ability to make money and advance within careers in England and the US (Connolly and Gregory 2005; Smithson et al. 2004). It is clear that for women, work and family roles depend on one another and at times are indistinguishable.

There is evidence that young men think less about family roles than do young women, and are less likely to have made decisions about family roles than young women (Friedman and Weissbrod 2005). When men identify their family role as that of the provider or breadwinner, their family role is completely enmeshed with their work role. That is, for men being a good parent means working hard outside of the home in high status, full time occupations (Liu 2002). It may be that both parents are focused on providing for the needs of their family; however, they define these needs differently (Kaufman 2005; Thompson and Walker 1989). Livingston and Judge (2008) found that in contrast to egalitarian men, traditional men felt more guilt when caregiving for their family interfered with their paid work and less guilt when work interfered with family responsibilities. Clearly, traditional men are most comfortable fulfilling the provider needs of their family rather than the nurturing needs. Egalitarian men, however, report more flexible future roles and more planned involvement in the care of young children than traditional men (Kaufman 2005).

Mechanisms of Change

The dual roles of woman and worker often contradict one another, and many women feel they must choose either the "baby or the briefcase" in China and the U.S. (Cheung and Halpern 2010, p. 183). Contrary to media reports (Belkin 2003), research does not indicate that women are dropping out of careers to raise children (Boushey 2007). Instead they are working with employers and family members to negotiate the roles of worker and mother. When women see their family roles outside the breadwinner-caregiver model, they experience caregiving tasks differently. Some women find household tasks (e.g., laundry) to be more meaningful and important than do men (Kroska 2003). This changes as women's paid work hours increase; their feelings about family tasks become more similar to men's feelings, such that they report less meaning in feminine tasks (Kroska 2003). This finding suggests that value placed on household tasks may depend on whether parents perceive their roles as traditional or nontraditional. Under the breadwinner-caregiver model, mothers' paid work may have little meaning, and she may strive to continue to fulfill all of the traditionally feminine tasks as well. It may be that ideas about women's paid labor and financial responsibilities may be changing faster than ideas about men's and women's roles in the family. There is evidence that some men in emerging adulthood see women as economic providers while still not seeing them as equal in other domains (Jaramillo-Sierra and Allen 2013). A feminist reconstruction of family roles would allow men to derive meaning and importance from nurturing tasks as well.

When fathers are given the same access and opportunity to participate fully in the transition to parenthood though paternity leave and extended time off of work, they can move from helper to co-parent. In this co-parenting role, Canadian and U.S. fathers show the same nurturing behaviors as mothers (Rehel 2014). Men who do engage in childcare tasks build efficacy for childcare and are capable caregivers. In a Canadian sample, fathers built competence in childcare tasks as they spend more time with children, particularly if they are exposed to models of such behavior (Magill-Evans et al. 2007). In a Canadian sample, fathers' interactions with toddlers were of the same interactional quality as mothers, particularly when mothers are not present (de Mendonça et al. 2011). When mothers are absent, married fathers are more engaged and engaging with children suggesting that their secondary role when mothers are present is simply culturally constructed (Meteyer, and Perry-Jenkins 2010). In order to reject specialization in family labor, both partners must be open and committed to a feminist approach to marriage (Blaisure and Allen 1995; Mack-Canty and Wright 2004).

Recent research indicates that such successful alternate models do exist; lesbian and gay parents and single parents actively work to construct families with flexible provider and caregiver roles that are not tied to gender (Adamsons and Buehler 2007; Fulcher et al. 2008). Heterosexual couples need to reconfigure their roles in family such that both partners can participate in the financial and emotional care of children and that each type of support will be valued by family members. Single fathers report feeling competent and satisfied with their role as caregiver (Adamsons and Buehler 2007). There is virtually no difference in child outcomes when children (sons and daughters) live with single mothers than when they live with single fathers (Downey et al. 1998). It appears that primary caregiving parents, regardless of their gender, behave in ways that promote child adjustment and well-being. Although the breadwinner-caregiver model defines mothering and fathering by different parenting behaviors, men and women are equally capable of fulfilling all of these parenting roles. When parents are released from these roles they show parenting behaviors that are similar and untied to gender. Mothers and fathers parent differently not because of their gender but because of role constraints placed on them under the breadwinner-caregiver family model (Ferree 1990; Geiger 1996).

An important step in such feminist reconstruction of both work and family roles is to pinpoint attributes of heterosexual families that are associated with emerging adults' adherence to or rejection of the breadwinner-caregiver model—a model that promotes gender inequality. Although work-life balance is an important social and feminist issue examined in a variety of contexts (Arthur and Lee 2008; Carlson et al. 2000; Netemeyer et al. 1996), it is important to look at mechanisms of change to the breadwinner-caregiver model, particularly those that can occur in the individual family. The current study examined how young women and men are planning to divide paid labor and childcare responsibilities as they enter young adulthood, start careers, and begin families. Specifically, this study investigated how nonconventional parental behaviors remembered by young adults may influence the traditionality of their vision of their future work and family life. We are specifically interested in whether young adults' future family roles follow the breadwinner-caregiver model or whether they endorse a reconstructed feminist model in which work and family roles are not tied to gender.

Social Cognitive Theory

The link between parents' conventional division of labor and young adults' ideal division of labor within their future families can be explored via the processes outlined in social cognitive theory. According the social-cognitive theory of gender development (Bussey and Bandura 1999), boys and girls develop ideas about their future family and work roles through modeling, enactive experience, and direct instruction. When modeling adults, boys and girls turn to different models, and these adults respond to the child's own gender typed behaviors. Thus, boys and girls develop efficacy in different domains, which leads to differences in behavior, preferences, activities, and career aspirations (Bussey and Bandura 1999). As children create a vision of their own future family roles, they may use the breadwinner-caregiver model their parents present as a template.

Indeed, when parents divide labor differently, children have different expectations about their future. If girls see mothers more involved with domestic tasks, they tend to plan their future with a bigger emphasis on family rather than career roles. In contrast, when parents divide labor more equitably, children report more flexible attitudes about gender (Fulcher et al. 2008). Young women with employed mothers report expecting to spend less time in family care while sons of employed mothers report expecting to spend more time in family care than did the sons and daughters of non-working mothers (Riggio and Desrochers 2006). It may not only be the amount of paid labor that mothers participate in that is important to children's vision of future families, but also how mothers and their families perceive the mothers' work role (Neblett and Cortina 2006). Daughters of working mothers who viewed themselves as providers reported less traditional gender role attitudes than daughters of working mothers who did not consider breadwinning an important part of their family role (Helms-Erikson et al. 2000).

It is clear that daughters can develop a parenting schema that incorporates the importance of caregiving and providing modeled by their working mothers. Less evidence exists about how parents' division of paid labor impacts sons' work plans. When mothers work, sons may observe fathers who are more involved in childcare, thereby increasing their own efficacy for parenting tasks (Riggio and Desrochers 2006). Fathers' more regular involvement in physical care and not just play has been shown to have several benefits to children's well-being and adjustment (Bronte-Tinkew et al. 2008). However, fathers are more likely to spend time caring for sons than for daughters (Manlove and Vernon-Feagans 2002). Israeli fathers were found to be more in tune with the interactional signals of sons than of daughters (Feldman et al. 2013) and sons seem to benefit more from father involvement (Bronte-Tinkew et al. 2008). Fathers increased involvement in parenting is associated with more psychological health in men (Schindler 2010) and their children. It follows then that fathers' caregiving behaviors may be more influential on sons' than on daughters' visions of their future family lives. Thus social-cognitive theory would suggest that sons who observe their fathers involved in nurturing would build feelings of competence for childcare tasks and would be more likely to envision future family roles that include caring for children. When children have feelings of efficacy in a domain, they are likely to be drawn to activities that include such tasks, practice, and persevere in frustrating circumstances building both real and perceived competence. Thus, when children hold efficacy in a domain they are likely to be working toward a future that includes such tasks (Bandura et al. 2001).

In emerging adulthood, men and women may be planning their future family roles differently. In college, when students work toward future careers and begin serious romantic partnerships, young adults begin to incorporate both family and occupational goals in their visions of their future selves (Fulcher and Coyle 2011). Young women in college report that they intend to be both workers and mothers (Hoffnung 2004) although they may not fully appreciate the difficulty of balancing those roles. Family role responsibilities that are tied to gender are impacting women's career plans much more substantially than men's. Even before marriage and parenthood men and women struggle to evaluate the provider role. When dating young adults negotiate money and paying for dates and activities (Jaramillo-Sierra and Allen 2013). It is important to investigate family characteristics that are associated with emerging adults' lessened adherence to the breadwinner-caregiver model.

The Current Study

The current study was designed to investigate college students' plans for dividing paid and unpaid labor in their future families and how these plans would reflect the breadwinner-caregiver model. Emerging adulthood is a transitional period between late adolescence and early adulthood (Arnett 2000). During this developmental period, emerging adults spend time and energy exploring choices surrounding future work and relationships, and they often make important work and family role decisions that will impact their future lives during this time (Arnett 2000; Kaufman 2005; Lease 2003; Mahaffy and Ward 2002; Stone and McKee 2000). Gender differences in attitudes about social roles and plans may become more distinct during this stage (Fulcher and Coyle 2011).

Of particular interest to this study were the parenting variables that may be associated with a family labor model less tied to gender. This study included a sample of young college men and women drawn from three universities in the Northeast, Southeast, and midwest. There were several hypotheses tested:

1. Male and female college students would plan to divide responsibilities for paid and childcare labor in their future families differently. Women would plan to adhere less to the breadwinner-caregiver model than would men.
2. Reports of parents' traditional division of paid labor would predict students' more traditional plans for the division of paid and childcare labor when they become parents.
3. Reports of parents' traditional division of childcare would predict students' plans for a more traditional division of paid and childcare labor when they become parents.
4. College men who remembered their father as more involved in childcare would feel more competent at childcare tasks.

Method

Participants

The participants in the study were 586 college students (185 males, 401 females). All of the participants were within the age range of 18 to 25 years, with an average age of 19.64

years. Ten participants self-identified as gay, lesbian or bisexual. Participants were recruited from psychology courses at three universities, some students received extra credit for their participation. The sample drew participants from three different universities. One school was a small private rural university in the South, another was a mid-sized private suburban university in the Northeast, and finally, a mid-sized public university in the Midwest. Schools of different types were chosen to increase the demographic characteristics of the families from which the sample was drawn. Indeed differences in families did emerge as a function of school the participants attended. See Table 12.1 for descriptive data by school and gender.

The sample was primarily European American with the mid-sized universities having a less diverse sample (private 90 % White, public 91 % White) than the small private school (78 % White), $\chi^2(582) = 50.57$, $p<.001$. Although, most students were first years or sophomores, every class was represented in each school's sample. Participants from the small private school were more likely to be juniors or seniors, $F(2, 571) = 36.17$, $p<.001$. Most participants reported that their parents were married (76 %), $\chi^2(582) = 12.71$, ns. and this did not differ significantly as a function of school or gender. Mothers of participants at the small private college were less likely to be employed (67 %) than were mothers of participants at the mid-sized universities (83 % private, 89 % public), $\chi^2(582) = 23.55$. $p<.001$. Students reported their mothers had a wide range of occupations including newspaper carriers, teachers and attorneys. Students also reported fathers holding a wide range of occupations including custodians, sales managers, and surgeons. For female participants, fathers at the mid-size public university were more likely to be employed (100 % employed) than fathers of participants at the private university (92 % mid-sized, 89 % small), $\chi^2(365) = 17.83$. $p<.001$, there was no difference for male participants.

To test for differences in parents' work hours, education, and income as a function of school attended and participant gender a MANOVA was performed. No main effect for gender or gender by school interactions emerged. However there was a main effect for school attended on several variables. Mothers of participants at the small private school were reported to be more highly educated than mothers of participants at the mid-sized private or mid-sized public school, $F(2, 429) = 22.62$, $p<.001$. Mothers of participants at the small private university also worked fewer hours each week than did mothers of participants at the mid-sized private and mid-sized public school $F(2, 429) = 12.91$, $p<.001$. Although there was a difference in work hours there was no difference in mothers' income as a function of school participant attended. Fathers of participants at the small private school were also more educated than fathers from the mid-sized private and public university and fathers from the mid-sized private university were more educated than those from the mid-sized public $F(2, 429) = 32.15$, $p<.001$. Fathers of participants at the mid-sized private school worked longer hours than fathers of participants at the small private university and the mid-sized public university $F(2, 429) = 3.67$, $p = .03$. Fathers at the two private schools had higher incomes than did fathers at the public university but were not different than one another, $F(2, 429) = 47.02$, $p<.001$. The school participants were recruited from is controlled for in all hypotheses testing.

TABLE 12.1   Demographic characteristics by gender and subsample

Variable	Males (N = 135)						Females (N = 285)					
	Midsize, Private (N = 47)		Small, Private (N = 35)		Midsize, Public (N = 62)		Midsize, Private (N = 99)		Small, Private (N = 30)		Midsize, Public (N = 156)	
	M	SD	M	SD	M	SD	M	SD	M	SD	M	SD
Mothers' education[b]	3.96	1.85	5.37	1.61	3.82	1.65	3.70	1.62	5.13	1.80	3.54	1.58
Mothers' weekly work hours[b]	37.87	19.01	25.14	25.75	36.74	16.59	34.93	22.60	20.52	22.33	35.89	15.91
Mothers' income	4.64	2.64	4.31	3.73	3.98	1.89	4.38	2.77	4.60	3.46	4.10	2.31
Fathers' education[b]	4.21	1.95	5.71	1.47	3.69	1.78	3.82	1.70	5.40	1.96	3.40	1.65
Fathers' weekly work hours[b]	50.21	13.91	48.06	20.22	45.98	8.40	51.89	14.86	50.23	12.46	47.72	11.19
Fathers' income[b]	8.45	2.09	8.66	3.22	5.97	2.63	8.13	2.55	9.30	2.72	6.01	2.45
Participants' class year[b]	1.96	1.13	2.44	1.14	1.49	.73	1.77	.99	2.30	1.23	1.39	.67
Participant ethnicity[a,b,c]	90		83		97		88		73		86	
% European American												
Parents marital status	68		78		79		78		78		76	
% married												
Mothers employed[b]	86		65		83		81		70		92	
% yes												
Fathers employed[b,c]	96		97		100		92		89		100	
% yes												

Mothers' and fathers' education categories ranges from 1 = some high school to 7 = graduate school, mothers' and fathers' income categories ranged from 1 = $0 – $10,000 to 11 = $100,000+, participants' class year range from 1 = first year to 4 = senior

a indicates a significant main effect for gender

b indicates a significant main effect for school

c indicates a significant interaction effect for gender and school

Measures

Students' Visions of Their Future Work Roles

Students' plans to work when parenting were measured using items from the Plans to Work subscale of the Family Responsibility Scale (Looker and Magee 2000). Participants responded to three items pertaining to work during parenthood (e.g., "Do you think you will work when your children are babies and too little for school?") by endorsing a 5-point Likert response scale that ranged from "definitely" to "definitely not." High scores indicated a plan to work less when parenting young children. Internal consistency as measured by Cronbach's α was .75 for this measure. Students' expectations of the division of paid labor for their family was measured using an item from the Family Tasks subscale of the Who Does What? (Cowan and Cowan 1990). For this item students indicated who would be responsible for "providing financially for the family" by choosing a response ranging from 1 (she will do it all) to 9 (he will do it all). High scores indicate a vision of men being more responsible for providing for the family. Means and standard deviations for this scale can be found in Table 12.2.

Students' Visions of Their Future Parenting Roles

Students' expectations for their future division of childcare tasks were also measured using a subscale of the Who Does What? (Cowan and Cowan 1990). On the childcare task subscale, students indicated who they expected would be responsible for 20 childcare tasks by choosing a response ranging from 1 ("She will do it all") to 9 ("He will do it all"). Example tasks include getting up in the night with child and planning and preparing meals for child. Mean scores were computed, with high scores indicating a vision of dividing childcare where men are more involved, which is thus less traditional. Internal consistency as measured by Cronbach's α was .83 for this subscale. For each of these 20 childcare tasks students also reported their feelings of competence. Responses ranged from 1 (not very competent) to 9 (very competent). Internal consistency measured by Cronbach's α for competence was .93. Means and standard deviations can be found in Table 12.1.

Parents' Division of Paid Labor

Participants answered questions about their parents' occupations, including their parents' job titles and descriptions, work hours, and income levels. A differential score was created for parents' work hours per week (father's hours—mother's hours). A differential score was also computed for parent's income (father's income score—mother's income score). Each of these scores was converted into a z-score and summed. Higher scores indicated more traditional divisions of paid labor (i.e., father works and earns more than mother). Means and standard deviations for this scale can be found in Table 12.1.

TABLE 12.2 Means and standard deviations for variables by gender and subsample

Variable	Males (N = 135)						Females (N = 278)					
	Midsize, Private (N = 46)		Small, Private (N = 28)		Midsize, Public (N = 61)		Midsize, Private (N = 94)		Small, Private (N = 26)		Midsize, Public (N = 158)	
	M	SD	M	SD	M	SD	M	SD	M	SD	M	SD
Future work plans [a,c]	1.66	.67	1.74	.85	1.83	.53	3.05	.88	3.05	.83	2.57	.81
Future financial responsibility [a,b]	5.94	1.33	6.48	1.25	5.72	1.17	5.51	.98	5.43	1.45	5.28	.89
Future childcare responsibility [a,b]	4.62	.52	4.50	.53	4.61	.51	4.14	.51	4.00	.59	4.28	.53
Students' childcare competence [a]	7.25	1.12	7.18	.90	7.32	1.12	7.93	.99	7.81	.92	8.03	.91
Parents' division of childcare [a]	3.74	.81	4.10	.76	3.76	.79	3.52	.90	3.59	.80	3.58	.88
Parents' division of paid labor [a,b]	.14	1.38	.55	2.15	-.44	1.35	.37	1.82	1.18	1.97	-.31	1.32

Students' work plans range from 1 (definitely will work) to 5 (definitely will not work). Students' financial and childcare plans range from 1 (she will do it all) to 9 (he will do it all). Students' childcare competence scores range from 1 (not very competent) to 9 (very competent). Parents' division of childcare ranged from 1 (mother did it all) to 9 (father did it all). Higher values of the parents' division of paid labor indicates fathers' increased responsibilities for paid work

a indicates a significant main effect for gender

b indicates a significant main effect for school

c indicates a significant interaction effect for gender and school

Parents' Division of Childcare Labor

Students reported their perceptions of their parents' division of childcare labor using the Who Does What? Scale (Cowan and Cowan 1990). Students reported what percentage of each of 20 child-care tasks their parents typically performed from 1 ("Mom did it all") to 9 ("Dad did it all"). Example tasks include getting up in the night with a child and planning and preparing meals for a child. Mean scores were computed; high scores indicate a vision of dividing childcare where men are more involved, and thus less traditional. Means and standard deviations for this scale can be found in Table 12.1. Internal consistency was high, $\alpha = .92$.

Results

Preliminary Analyses

Subsample Differences

To test for differences among the variables as a function of the university from which the student was recruited (e.g., small private, mid-sized private, or mid-sized public), a MANOVA was performed. In the overall model, university attended did emerge as a main effect, $\Lambda = .89$, $F(12, 800) = 4.00$, $p<.001$. Specific differences were revealed among students of different schools in their future financial responsibility, $F(2, 411) = 4.14$, $p = .02$, future childcare responsibilities, $F(2, 411) = 3.86$, $p = .02$, and parents' division of paid labor, $F(2, 411) = 113.79$, $p<.001$. Post-hoc analyses revealed that students at the mid-sized public institution reported that they were planning to divide financial responsibility more equitably than did students at the small private or mid-sized private institutions. Post-hoc analyses did not reveal any significant differences between individual schools on future childcare plans finally, students at the small private university reported a more traditional division of their parents' paid labor than did students at the mid-sized private university or the mid-sized public university. Additionally, students at the mid-sized private university reported a more traditional division of paid labor between their parents than students at the mid-sized public university.

There was an interaction between the university attended and participants' genders $F(2, 411) = 7.53$, $p = .001$ for students' plans to work when parents. For women only, participants from the midsized-public school were more likely to plan on working while parenting. Because the university participants attended was associated with several variables, it was controlled for in subsequent analyses. In the following MANCOVAs participants' university was entered as a covariate. In each regression, two dummy coded variables for the university students attended were entered as a first step. In each analysis, the theoretical model improved significantly the demographic model.

Gender Differences

Although gender differences were predicted to emerge as part of the hypotheses, preliminary analyses were conducted to test for gender differences in the traditionality of parents' division of paid and unpaid labor, $\Lambda = .57$, $F(2, 400) = 49.51$, $p<.001$. It was revealed that men remembered their fathers were more involved in childcare than did women, $F(1, 411) = 9.87$, $p = .002$. Also men remembered their mothers to be more involved in paid labor than did women, $F(1, 411) = 4.43$, $p = .04$. Unfortunately the proportion of participants who identified as non-heterosexual (less than 2 %) was too small to test a gender by sexual orientation hypothesis.

Intercorrelations Among Variables
As a preliminary analysis, the intercorrelations among all of the variables were examined separately for men and women (see Table 12.3). Although many of the relations that emerged were part of the hypothesized analyses, many interesting associations between outcome variables also emerged. For example, as men and women envision men more responsible for providing financially for the family, their plans for men to be involved in childcare decreased. Similarly, the predictor variables parents' division of paid labor and parents' division of childcare were also negatively associated with one another.

Hypotheses Testing

Hypothesis 1
Male and female college students would plan to divide responsibilities for paid and childcare labor in their future families differently. Women would plan to adhere less to the breadwinner-caregiver model than would men. A MANCOVA was conducted to test students' plans to work while parenting small children, their plans to divide childcare labor in future families, and their

TABLE 12.3 Summary of intercorrelations of variables

Measure	1	2	3	4	5	6
1. Future work plans	–	.38**	–.26**	–.02	.34**	–.10
2. Future financial responsibility	–.10	–	–.28**	–.03	.09	–.11*
3. Future childcare responsibility	.10	–.36**	–	.03	–.24**	.28**
4. Childcare competence	.08	–.14	.12	–	–.05	–.03
5. Parents' division of paid labor	–.05	.24**	–.23**	–.02	–	–.24**
6. Parents' division of childcare	.03	–.10	.28**	.19*	–.26**	–

Intercorrelations for male participants are represented above the diagonal and intercorrelations for female participants are represented below the diagonal. Students' work plans range from 1 (definitely will work) to 5 (definitely will not work). Students' financial and childcare plans range from 1 (she will do it all) to 9 (he will do it all). Students' childcare competence scores range from 1 (not very competent) to 9 (very competent). Parents' division of childcare ranged from 1 (mother did it all) to 9 (father did it all). Higher values of the parents' division of paid labor indicates fathers' increased responsibilities for paid work

$^*p<.05.$ $^{**}p<.01$

feelings of childcare competence as a function of participants' genders. The overall model was significant, $\Lambda = .56$, $F(2, 554) = 110.74$, $p<.001$. In support of the hypothesis, men were more likely to report planning to work when they had small children than were women, $F(1, 560) = 206.00$, $p<.001$. Men reported planning to divide paid labor more traditionally than did women $F(1, 560) = 31.78$, $p<.001$. Men were also more likely to report a vision of future childcare that was more evenly distributed than did women, whereas women expected a division of labor where they were responsible for more childcare labor, $F(1, 560) = 80.23$, $p<.001$. Finally, men reported feeling less competent at childcare tasks than did women. $F(1, 560) = 79.36$, $p<.001$. Means and standard deviations can be found on Table 12.1.

Hypothesis 2

Reports of parents' traditional division of paid labor would predict students' more traditional plans for the division of paid and childcare labor when they become parents. First, a linear regression was conducted to test the prediction of students' plans to work from parents' division of paid labor, participants' genders, and an interaction term. The model was significant overall, $F(5, 442) = 47.34$, $p<.001$. Parents' division of paid labor ($\beta = .12$, $p = .006$), participants' genders ($\beta = -.52$, $p<.001$), and the interaction ($\beta = -17$, $p<.001$) were all significant predictors of students' work plans. To test the interaction, linear regressions split by gender were run to test the prediction of work plans by parents' division of paid labor. As hypothesized, this model was significant overall for daughters, $F(3,291) = 18.68$, $p<.001$, but, as expected, it was not significant for sons. In particular, a traditional division of parental paid labor behavior positively predicted daughters' plans to work less (or not all) while parenting young children, $\beta = .29$, $p<.001$. The overall model was significant, $F(5, 439) = 17.77$, $p<.001$.

A second linear regression was performed to test the prediction of students' vision of future financial family responsibilities from parents' division of paid labor, participants' genders, and an interaction term. The model was significant overall, $F(5, 441) = 10.51$, $p<.001$. Parents' division of paid labor ($\beta = .14$, $p = .006$), participants' gender ($\beta = .22$, $p<.001$), and the interaction term ($\beta = .10$, $p = .033$) were each significant predictors. To test the interaction, linear regressions split by gender were performed to test the prediction of financial responsibility by parents' division of paid labor. As hypothesized, this model was significant overall for sons, $F(3, 148) = 5.59$, $p = .001$, but not for daughters. Specifically, parents who divided labor less traditionally have sons who are planning to share financial responsibilities more equitably in their future families ($\beta = .18$, $p = .031$).

Finally, a regression analysis tested the prediction of participants' plans for childcare responsibilities from parents' division of paid labor. The overall model was significant, $F(5, 439) = 17.77$, $p<.001$. Participants' genders ($\beta = .35$, $p<.001$), and as expected, parents' division of paid labor ($\beta = -.19$, $p<.001$), predicted students' plans to divide childcare labor. Participants' whose parents divided paid labor more equally planned to have men more involved in childcare.

Hypothesis 3

Reports of parents' traditional division of childcare would predict students' plans for a more traditional division of paid and childcare labor. A first regression predicted students' plans to work as parents from parents' division of childcare, gender, and an interaction term. Although the full model was significant, $F(5, 551) = 45.23$, $p<.001$, the only significant predictor was participants' genders ($\beta = -.68$, $p<.001$). A second regression tested the prediction of participants' plans for dividing financial responsibilities from parents' division of childcare, participants' genders, and an interaction term. The overall model was significant, $F(5, 552) = 8.98$, $p<.001$. Parents' division of childcare labor was the only significant predictor ($\beta = -.11$, $p = .02$), such that parents who divided childcare equally had sons and daughters who planned to divide the financial responsibility for the family more equitably.

Finally, a linear regression was conducted to test the prediction of students' childcare plans from parents' division of childcare, participants' genders, and the interaction. This model was significant overall, $F(5,542) = 30.02$, $p<.001$, as was hypothesized. In particular, the more fathers were involved in childcare, the more participants expected men to be involved in childcare ($\beta = .26$, $p<.001$). Participants' genders also significantly predicted students' childcare plans ($\beta = .29$, $p = .005$). The interaction was not significant.

Hypothesis 4

College men who remember their father as more involved in childcare will feel more competent at childcare tasks. A linear regression was performed to test the prediction of students' competence for childcare tasks from parents' own division of childcare, participants' genders, and an interaction term. The model was significant overall, $F(5, 539) = 16.02$, $p<.001$. Parents' division of paid labor ($\beta = .10$, $p = .04$), participants' gender ($\beta = -.74$, $p<.001$), and the interaction term ($\beta = .43$, $p = .007$) each predicted students' competence for childcare tasks. Linear regressions split by gender were performed to test the prediction childcare competence by parents' division of childcare labor. As hypothesized, men whose fathers participated in more childcare felt more competent in childcare tasks ($\beta = .20$, $p = .01$).

Discussion

Recent research and interventions have targeted young adults' occupational aspirations (Jacobs et al. 2006; Neblett and Cortina 2006). In particular, interventions that encourage women and girls to explore less traditional careers have increased (e.g., Weisgram and Bigler 2006, 2007). Although the cultural messages about gendered roles in the workplace have loosened, little change has occurred in the family domain. Few, if any, interventions have been designed to encourage boys and men to consider less traditional family roles. As more and more women are trained for and committed to careers, they are also expecting and expected to be primarily responsible for child care tasks, including managing a husband in a helper role (Halpern 2005). Even privileged women at selective colleges expect a future of inequality in household work regardless of their plans for paid labor (Fetterolf and Eagly

2011). These women cannot imagine hurdling the breadwinner-caregiver family model that requires gender roles within the family (Ferree 2010).

However women often report feeling less commitment to the breadwinner-caregiver model than do men. Orrange (2002) conducted in-depth interviews of men and women enrolled in law school or masters of business administration graduate programs. Most men in this sample expected to be breadwinners for their families while expecting their wives to be caregivers and responsible for the family. When men envisioned their wives working they perceived their incomes as supplemental and their work as something meaningful to her, not to the family. None of the men expected to be primary caregivers to young children. Conversely, most women expected that their husbands would share in family responsibilities and in paid labor. Other women planned to enter and leave the workforce to respond to the caregiving needs of their families. Finally, there was a smaller group of women who were considering remaining single in order to focus on their careers. No women in this sample intended to be sole caregivers or sole providers for a family or children (Orrange 2002). Our results indicate a similar pattern of mens' and womens' commitment to the breadwinner-caregiver model. Almost all men were planning to work when they were parenting young children (97 % answered that they would definitely or probably work), while women were as likely to report they were planning on staying home with their young children as to say they would work (46 % answered that they would definitely or probably work). This indicates that, as they choose and train for careers, men, unlike women, do not see work and family roles as conflicting. However, it also indicates that almost half of college women are planning on being financial providers for families while very few men envision a caregiving role. Given that women expect to (Fetterolf and Eagly 2011) and are actually likely (Hodges and Budig 2010) to earn less than their male partner they may find themselves thrust into a supplementary provider role rather than one of co-provider. When women's income is seen as supplementary their primary family role is seen as nurturance and childcare, regardless of their work hours.

Given the cultural support for the breadwinner-caregiver model, women have had more opportunity to observe women in childcare than men have to observe men in childcare. Through these observations women build efficacy, or feelings of competence, for the nurturance role (Bussey and Bandura 1999). Thus we find, women in our sample reported feeling more competence for childcare tasks than did men. It is clear that even as college women prepare themselves for careers and work, they also feel prepared to care for small children. At the birth of the first child when child care responsibilities begin, women with feelings of competence are able to launch into primary caregiver role, leaving fathers who may feel less competent in a secondary role before they have any efficacy building hands-on experience with newborns. It may be these early experiences of parenting when roles are strongly gendered that serves to entrench families into the bipolar roles of provider and nurturer (Lee and Waite 2005; Meteyer and Perry-Jenkins 2010), instead of co-provider and co-parent roles that are not tied to gender.

Indeed, men and women in this sample were also envisioning a different division of childcare in their future families. Interestingly, men envision being more involved in childcare than women think that men will be. In fact, on the list of 20 childcare tasks, women and men disagreed on the proportional sharing of 19 tasks, such that men reported more future responsibility than women thought men would have. It is important to note that although men are reporting a vision of future childcare labor that is *more equitable* than do women, both men and women are still envisioning childcare that is *primarily* women's responsibility. Of the 20 tasks, men reported that they would be primarily responsible for only five; women envisioned men being primarily responsible in only one domain (discipline). These expectations match the division of labor arrangements found in heterosexual couples today (Mannino and Deutsch 2007).

When constructing a vision of their future life, children and emerging adults rely on the arrangements of their own parents (Fulcher and Coyle 2011). The gendered family roles defined by the breadwinner-caregiver model are handed down from parents to children. However it is also in parents' behaviors in which we can find tools that children can use to construct a more feminist family model. For example, in our sample parents' nontraditional division of paid labor did predict daughters' plans to work and sons who planned to share more family financial responsibilities. Both sons and daughters of nontraditional parents envision a future family where men are responsible for more childcare. When students reported that their fathers were involved in childcare, they were more likely to plan a division of future childcare where men are more involved. Interestingly, men's and women's memory of an equal division of childcare labor between their own parents predicted their visions of dividing financial responsibilities more equally as well. This represents a break away from the breadwinner-caregiver model, these students are planning for a feminist family not just where women work, but where men and women share parenting and financial responsibilities.

Interestingly, college men who reported their fathers to be more involved in childcare reported more competence in childcare tasks. These sons build efficacy for child care tasks simply by observing their fathers. When men enter parenting with more competence they can avoid treating their wife as expert and create a caregiving role for themselves. If this co-caregiver role is established early neither parent is burdened with *or* precluded from childcare responsibilities. Such competence building may be what men need to abandon the breadwinner-caregiver model. Recent research (Harrington et al. 2011) of almost 1000 middle class U.S. fathers found that these men were interested in a parenting role outside of being a provider. These fathers report that providing love and support and being involved in the child's life are more important aspects of fatherhood than is providing financial security. However, they reported that taking care of childcare tasks were the least important to good fatherhood. Laws and policies that were designed to promote work flexibility may not work and may actually backfire for women (Fernàndez-Kranz and Rodriguez-Planas 2011) and men are less likely to ask for such flexibility (Harrington et al. 2011). It has been suggested that in order to make such policies truly family friendly and non-discriminatory, men should be mandated (or incentivized) to take time off for newborn care. A recent study of Canadian men who were incentivized to take parental leave found that these men who were co-caregivers (and not workers) for a 5 week paid leave were involved in daily domestic labor and spent less time at work throughout their child's childhood (Patnaik 2014).

A feminist family model can only be achieved when structural changes in the work place are tied with changing culture values surrounding family roles. These changes may begin with non-traditional parents. If men and women are able to build efficacy for both providing and nurturing than neither would be relegated to the helper roles that exist under the bread-winner-caregiver model. Men could create nurturing relationships with children without being managed by mothers (Adamsons and Buehler 2007; de Mendonça et al. 2011). This strengthened relationship would benefit men's and children's well-being (Schindler 2010). Women could benefit from work and the provider role (Helms-Erikson, et al. 2000) without perceiving a loss to their children's care (Ferree 1990). There is ample evidence from other family types (gay, lesbian, unmarried) that actual competence for caregiving and nurturing is unrelated to gender (Lamb 2012). It would benefit heterosexual men, women and their children to work to reconstruct family roles without ties to gender. Our sample is largely generalizeable to White college students. It is important for future studies to recruit more diverse samples; it may be that the process of managing work and family roles functions differently in non-White families. Research suggests that, historically, African American mothers are more likely to work and, correspondingly, African American families are more likely to divide labor equitably (Shelton and John 1996). In fact, African American women are less likely to report that working interferes with caregiving and to see maternal work as beneficial to their children (Bridges and Etaugh 1996). It may be that African American couples may already have constructed family roles outside of the breadwinner-caregiver model. However, within samples of African American couples there is variability of egali-tarianism. In African American couples where husbands have more traditional gender roles and participate less in household labor, marital satisfaction is decreased for both spouses (Stanik and Bryant 2012). Future research should include larger samples of African American students to examine the influence of the breadwinner-caregiver model on future plans.

It is also important that changes in White middle class families in the United States has an impact on minority, working class and immigrant families. As middle class mothers become more responsible for providing income, they often delegate some of the child care tasks to paid workers. These workers are often women of color who leave their own children for long spans of time to nurture others (Hochschild 2005). A feminist restructuring of the breadwinner-caregiver model will include men as caregivers and not simply shift nurturing responsibilities from one woman to another.

It is also possible that young adults who are not in college may have different plans for work and family; these men and women may enter the workforce earlier and expect lower paying jobs. Women particularly may feel they do not have an option to choose between working and childcare. A particularly interesting future aim should be to assess how the breadwinner-caregiver model is perceived by children who experienced the recent recession. As providing income became more difficult for parents, it is possible that these students will have observed fathers involved in more care and mothers involved in more work, simply as a function of economics. This may help them build a more flexible family role model or it may be associated with family struggle and drive students to a deeper commitment to the breadwinner-caregiver model.

We asked students to report their memories of their parents' division of paid and unpaid labor. Men were likely to remember fathers' heavier involvement than were women. Although these may be biased memories and fathers are equally involved with sons and daughters, it may also be that students' perceptions (accurate or not) are important in creating schemas about family roles. Future studies should collect division of labor reports from both parents and children. Finally, these findings simply reflect a snapshot of developmental process of career and family formation. A longitudinal study of emerging adults' plans and attitudes would help to define the processes involved in these decisions.

A feminist restructuring of the breadwinner-caregiver model may begin at home and with individual parents but it needs scaffolding and support from surrounding cultural systems. Employers respond to employees' parenthood in gendered ways. In laboratory experiments and audits of real job hiring processes, mothers were less likely to be recommended for hire than childless women. Experiments show that mothers were rated as less committed and competent. Participants offered mothers lower starting salaries and had less expectations of promotions for mothers than for women without children (Correll et al. 2007). Conversely, fathers were offered more money than other men. This sexist practice make it difficult for couples to choose a more feminist family model (Gerson 2009). The undergraduate students studied here will soon be not only parents and workers, but could serve a cultural change makers (Ferree 2010). If these students can conceptualize a feminist family model for themselves, they may also work to hire and promote mothers and fathers differently than the previous generation. In order to shift the cultural family model, fathers' most important task may be to be seen, by their children, their employers, and their peers, doing daily domestic tasks and doing them well.

Compliance with Ethical Standards The research reported on in the manuscript, "Constructing a Feminist Reorganization of the Heterosexual Breadwinner/Caregiver Family Model: College Students' Plans for their Own Future Families" complies with ethical standards for research as directed by the American Psychological Association. The project was approved individually by the Institutional Review Boards of Washington and Lee University, Monmouth University, and the University of Wisconsin, Steven's Point. Participants gave informed consent before participating in data collection.

References

Adamsons, K., & Buehler, C. (2007). Mothering versus fathering versus parenting: Measurement equivalence in parenting measures. *Parenting: Science and Practice, 7*, 271–303. doi:10.1080/15295190701498686.

Arnett, J. J. (2000). Emerging adulthood: A theory of development from the late teens through the twenties. *American Psychologist, 55*, 469–480. doi:10.1037//0003-06X.55.5.469.

Arthur, N., & Lee, C. (2008). Young Australian women's aspirations for work, marriage and family: 'I guess I am just another person who wants it all'. *Journal of Health Psychology, 13*, 589–596. doi:10.1177/1359105308090931.

Bandura, A., Barbaranelli, B., Caprara, G. V., & Pastorelli, C. (2001). Self-efficacy beliefs as shapers of children's aspirations and career trajectories. *Child Development, 72*, 187–206. doi:10.1111/1467-8624.00273.

Bernard, J. (1981). The good-provider role: Its rise and fall. *American Psychologist, 36*, 1–12. doi:10.1037/0003-066X.36.1.1.

Belkin, L. (2003, October 26). The opt-out revolution. *New York Times*. Retrieved from http://www.nytimes.com/2003/10/26/magazine/ 26WOMEN.html.

Blaisure, K. R., & Allen, K. R. (1995). Feminists and the ideology and practice of marital equality. *Journal of Marriage and Family, 57*, 5–19. doi:10.2307/353812.

Boushey, H. (2007, June 9). *Mommies opting out of work: A myth that won't die*. Retrieved from http://www.alternet.org/module/printversion/53464.

Brady, J. (1972). Why I want a wife. In S. Barnet, M. Berman, W. Burto, & M. Stubbs (Eds.), *Literature for composition* (3rd ed.). New York: Harper Collins.

Bridges, J. S., & Etaugh, C. (1996). Black and white college women's maternal employment outcome expectations and their desired timing of maternal employment. *Sex Roles, 35*, 543–562. doi:10.1007/BF01548252.

Bronte-Tinkew, J., Carrano, J., Horowitz, A., & Kinukawa, A. (2008). Involvement among resident fathers and links to infant cognitive outcomes. *Journal of Family Issues, 29*, 1211–1244. doi:10.1177/0192513X08318145.

Budig, M. J., & Hodges, M. J. (2014). Statistical models and empirical evidence for differences in the motherhood penalty across the earnings distribution. *American Sociological Review, 79*, 358–364. doi:10.1177/0003122414523616.

Bussey, K., & Bandura, A. (1999). Social cognitive theory of gender development and differentiation. *Psychological Review, 106*, 676–713. doi:10.1037/0033-295X.106.4.676.

Carlson, D., Kacmar, K., & Williams, L. (2000). Construction and initial validation of a multidimensional measure of work-family conflict. *Journal of Vocational Behavior, 56*, 249–276. doi:10.1006/jvbe.1999.1713.

Cheung, F. M., & Halpern, D. F. (2010). Women at the top: Powerful leaders define success as work and family in a culture of gender. *American Psychologist, 65*, 182–193. doi:10.1037/a0017309.

Cohen, P. (2014). *Family diversity is the new normal. Council on Contemporary Families*. Retrieved from https://contemporaryfamilies.org/wp-content/uploads/2014/09/new-normal-family-diversity.pdf.

Connolly, S., & Gregory, M. (2005). *Part-time work- A trap for women's careers? An analysis of the roles of heterogeneity and state dependence*. University of Oxford Department of Economics Discussion Paper Series, pp. 1471–0498.

Correll, S. J., Benard, S., & Paik, I. (2007). Getting a job: Is there a motherhood penalty? *American Journal of Sociology, 112*, 1297–1338. doi:10.1086/511799.

Cowan, P. A., & Cowan, C. P. (1990). Becoming a family: Research and intervention. In I. E. Sigel & G. H. Brody (Eds.), *Methods of family research: Biographies of research projects, Vol. 1: Normal families* (pp. 1–51). Hillsdale: Lawrence Eribaum Associates.

de Mendonça, J. S., Cossette, L., Strayer, F. F., & Gravel, F. (2011). Mother-child and father-child interactional synchrony in dyadic and triadic interactions. *Sex Roles, 64,* 132–142. doi:10.1007/s11199-010-9875-2.

Downey, D. B., Ainsworth-Darnell, J. W., & Dufur, M. J. (1998). Sex of parent and children's well-being in single-parent households. *Journal of Marriage and the Family, 60,* 878–893. doi:10.2307/ 353631.

Feldman, R., Bamberger, E., & Kanat-Maymon, Y. (2013). Parent-specific reciprocity from infancy to adolescence shapes children's social competence and dialogical skills. *Attachment & Human Development, 15,* 407–423. doi:10.1080/14616734.2013.782650.

Fernàndez-Kranz, D., & Rodriguez-Planas, N. (2011). *Unintended effects of a family-friendly law in a segmented labor market.* Discussion Paper Series (5709), Institute for the Study of Labor, IZA

Ferree, M. M. (2010). Filling the glass: Gender perspectives on families. *Journal of Marriage and Family, 72,* 420–439. doi:10.1111/j.1741-3737.2010.00711.x.

Ferree, M. M. (1990). Beyond separate spheres: Feminism and family research. *Journal of Marriage and Family, 52,* 866–884. doi:10. 2307/353307.

Fetterolf, J. C., & Eagly, A. H. (2011). Do young women expect gender equality in their future lives? An answer from a possible selves experiment. *Sex Roles, 65,* 83–93. doi:10.1007/s11199-011-9981-9.

Fox, G. L., & Murry, V. M. (2000). Gender and families: Feminist perspectives and family research. *Journal of Marriage and Family, 62,* 1160–1172. doi:10.1111/j.1741-3737.2000.01160.x.

Friedan, B. (1963). *The feminine mystique.* New York: W. W. Norton Company.

Friedman, S. R., & Weissbrod, C. S. (2005). Work and family commitment and decision-making status among emerging adults. *Sex Roles, 53,* 317–325. doi:10.1007/s11199-005-6755-2.

Fulcher, M., & Coyle, E. F. (2011). Breadwinner and caregiver: A cross-sectional analysis of children's and emerging adults' visions of their future family roles. *British Journal of Developmental Psychology, 29,* 330–346. doi:10.1111/j.2044-835X.2011.02026.x.

Fulcher, M., Sutfin, E. L., & Patterson, C. J. (2008). Individual differences in gender development: Associations with parental sexual orientation, attitudes, and division of labor. *Sex Roles, 58,* 330–341. doi:10.1007/s11199-007-9348-4.

Gaunt, R. (2005). The role of value priorities in paternal and maternal involvement in child care. *Journal of Marriage and Family, 67,* 643–655. doi:10.1111/j.1741-3737.2005.00159.x.

Geiger, B. (1996). *Fathers as primary caregivers.* Westport: Greenwood Press.

Gerson, K. (2009). Changing lives, resistant institutions: A new generation negotiates gender, work, and family change. *Sociological Forum, 24,* 735–753. doi:10.1111/j.1573-7861.2009.01134.x.

Halpern, D. F. (2005). Psychology at the intersection of work and family: Recommendations for employers, working families, and policymakers. *American Psychologist, 60,* 397–409. doi:10.1037/ 0003-066X.60.5.397.

Harrington, B., Van Deusen, F., & Humberd, B. (2011). *The new dad: Caring, committed, and conflicted.* Boston: Boston College Center for Work & Family.

Helms-Erikson, H., Tanner, J. L., Crouter, A. C., & McHale, S. M. (2000). Do women's provider-role attitudes moderate the links between work and family? *Journal of Family Psychology, 14,* 658–670. doi:10.1037/0893-3200.14.4.658.

Hochschild, A. R. (2005). Love and gold. In L. Ricciutelli, A. Miles, & M. McFadden (Eds.), *Feminist politics, activism and vision: Local and global challenges* (pp. 34–46). London & Toronto: Zed/Innana: Books.

Hodges, M. J., & Budig, M. J. (2010). Who gets the daddy bonus?: Organizational hegemonic masculinity and the impact of fatherhood on earnings. *Gender and Society, 24,* 717–745. doi:10.1177/0891243210386729.

Hoffnung, M. (2004). Wanting it all: Career, marriage, and motherhood during college-educated women's 20s. *Sex Roles, 50,* 711–723. doi:10.1023/B:SERS.0000027572.57049.ff.USA.

Hood, J. C. (1986). The provider role: Its meaning and measurement. *Journal of Marriage and the Family, 48,* 349–359. doi:10.2307/ 352402.

Jacobs, J. E., Chhin, C. S., & Bleeker, M. M. (2006). Enduring links: Parents' expectations and their young children's gender-typed occupational choices. *Educational Research and Evaluation, 12,* 395–407. doi:10.1080/13803610600765851.

Jaramillo-Sierra, A. J., & Allen, K. A. (2013). Who pays after the first date? Young men's discourses of the male-provider role. *Psychology of Men and Masculinity, 14,* 389–399. doi:10.1037/a0030603.

Kaufman, G. (2005). Gender role attitudes and college students' work and family expectations. *Gender Issues, 2,* 58–71. doi:10.1007/ s12147-005-0015-1.

Kroska, A. (2003). Investigating gender differences in the meaning of household chores and child care. *Journal of Marriage and Family, 65,* 456–473. doi:10.1111/j.1741-3737.2003.00456.x.

Lamb, M. E. (2012). Mothers, fathers, families and circumstances: Factors affecting children's adjustment. *Applied Developmental Science, 16,* 98–111. doi:10.1080/10888691.2012.667344.

Lease, S. H. (2003). Testing a model of men's nontraditional occupational choices. *The Career Development Quarterly, 51,* 244–258. doi:10. 1002/j.2161-0045.2003.tb00605.x.

Lee, Y. S., & Waite, L. J. (2005). Husbands' and wives' time spent on housework: A comparison of measures. *Journal of Marriage and Family, 67,* 328–336. doi:10.1111/j.0022-2445.2005.00119.x.

Liu, W. M. (2002). The social class-related experiences of men: Integrating theory and practice. *Professional Psychology: Research and Practice, 33,* 355–360. doi:10.1037/0735-7028.33.4. 355.

Livingston, B. A., & Judge, T. A. (2008). Emotional responses to work-family conflict: An examination of gender role orientation among working men and women. *Journal of Applied Psychology, 93,* 207–216. doi:10.1037/0021-9010.93.1.207.

Looker, E. D., & Magee, P. A. (2000). Gender and work: The occupational expectations of young women and men in the 1990s. *Gender Issues, 18,* 74–88. doi:10.1007/s12147-000-0012-3.

Mack-Canty, C., & Wright, S. (2004). Family values as practiced by feminist parents: Bridging third-wave feminism and family pluralism. *Journal of Family Issues, 25,* 851–880. doi:10.1177/ 0192513X03261337.

Magill-Evans, J., Harrison, M. J., Benzies, K., Gierl, M., & Kimak, C. (2007). Effects of parenting education on first-time fathers' skills in interactions with their infants. *Fathering, 5,* 42–57. doi:10.3149/ fth. 0501.42.

Mahaffy, K. A., & Ward, S. K. (2002). The gendering of adolescents' childbearing and educational plans: Reciprocal effects and the influence of social context. *Sex Roles, 46,* 403–417. doi:10.1023/ A:1020413630553.

Manlove, E., & Vernon-Feagans, L. (2002). Caring for infant daughters and sons in dual-earner households: Maternal reports of father involvement in weekday time and tasks. *Infant and Child Development*, *11*, 305–320. doi:10.1002/icd.260.

Mannino, C. A., & Deutsch, F. M. (2007). Changing the division of household labor: A negotiated process between partners. *Sex Roles*, *56*, 309–324. doi:10.1007/s11199-006-9181-1.

Meteyer, K., & Perry-Jenkins, M. (2010). Father involvement among working-class, dual-earner couples. *Fathering*, *8*, 379–403. doi:10. 3149/fth.0803.379.

Neblett, N. G., & Cortina, K. S. (2006). Adolescents' thoughts about parents' jobs and their importance for adolescents' future orientation. *Journal of Adolescence*, *29*, 795–811. doi:10.1016/j.adolescence.2005.11.006.

Netemeyer, R., Boles, J., & McMurrian, R. (1996). Development and validation of work-family conflict and family-work conflict scales. *Journal of Applied Psychology*, *81*, 400–410. doi:10.1037/0021-9010.81.4.400.

Orrange, R. M. (2002). Aspiring law and business professionals' orientations to work and family life. *Journal of Family Issues*, *23*, 287–317. doi:10.1177/0192513X02023002006.

Patnaik, A. (2014). *Reserving time for daddy: The short and long-run consequences of fathers' quotas (Working paper series)*. doi:10. 2139/ssrn.2475970.

Rehel, E. M. (2014). When dad stays home too: Paternity leave, gender, and parenting. *Gender & Society*, *28*, 110–132. doi:10.1177/0891243213503900.

Riggio, H. R., & Desrochers, S. J. (2006). Maternal employment: Relations with young adults' work and family expectations and self-efficacy. *American Behavioral Scientist*, *49*, 1328–1353. doi:10.1177/0002764206286558.

Schindler, H. S. (2010). The importance of parenting and financial contributions in promoting fathers' psychological health. *Journal of Marriage and Family*, *72*, 318–332. doi:10.1111/j.1741-3737.2010.00702.x.

Shelton, B. A., & John, D. (1996). The division of household labor. *Annual Review of Sociology*, *22*, 299–322. doi:10.1146/annurev.soc.22.1.299.

Smithson, J., Lewis, S., Cooper, C., & Dyer, J. (2004). Flexible working and the gender pay gap in the accountancy profession. *Work, Employment and Society*, *18*, 115–135. doi:10.1177/ 0950017004040765.

Solomon, S. E., Rothblum, E. D., & Balsam, K. F. (2005). Money, housework, sex, and conflict: Same-sex couples in civil unions, those not in civil unions, and heterosexual siblings. *Sex Roles*, *52*, 561–575. doi:10.1007/s11199-005-3725-7.

Stanik, C. E., & Bryant, C. M. (2012). Marital quality of newlywed African American couples: Implications of egalitarian gender role dynamics. *Sex Roles*, *66*, 256–267. doi:10.1007/s11199-012-0117-7.

Stone, L., & McKee, N. P. (2000). Gendered futures: Student visions of career and family on a college campus. *Anthropology and Education Quarterly*, *31*, 67–89. doi:10.1525/aeq.2000.31.1.67.

Thompson, L., & Walker, A. J. (1989). Gender in families: Women and men in marriage, work, and parenthood. *Journal of Marriage and Family*, *51*, 845–871. doi:10.2307/353201.

U.S. Department of Labor, Bureau of Labor Statistics. (2011, March 24). *Employment characteristics of families summary*. Retrieved from http://www.bls.gov/news.release/famee.nr0.htm

Wall, G. (2007). How involved is involved fathering? An exploration of the contemporary culture of fatherhood. *Gender & Society*, *21*, 508–527. doi:10.1177/0891243207304973.

Wang, W., Parker, K., & Taylor, P. (2013). *Breadwinner moms: Mothers are the sole or primary provider in four-in-ten households with children; Public conflicted about the growing trend.* Pew Research Center. Retrieved from http://www.pewsocialtrends.org/2013/05/ 29/breadwinner-moms/.

Weisgram, E. S., Bigler, R. S., & Liben, L. S. (2010). Gender, values, and occupational interests among children, adolescents, and adults. *Child Development, 81*, 778–796. doi:10.1111/j.1467-8624.2010. 01433.x.

Weisgram, E. S., & Bigler, R. S. (2007). Effects of learning about gender discrimination on adolescent girls' attitudes toward and interest in science. *Psychology of Women Quarterly, 31*, 262–269. doi:10. 1111/j.1471-6402.2007.00369.x.

Weisgram, E. S., & Bigler, R. S. (2006). Girls and science careers: The role of altruistic values and attitudes about scientific tasks. *Journal of Applied Developmental Psychology, 27*, 326–348. doi:10.1016/j. appdev.2006.04.0.

Parenting Stress, Dinnertime Rituals, and Child Well-being in Working-Class Families

BY YESEL YOON, KATIE NEWKIRK, AND MAUREEN PERRY-JENKINS

This study examined the extent to which family dinnertime rituals serve a protective role for families experiencing high levels of stress. Using data from a longitudinal study of working-class couples, the role of dinnertime rituals as a moderator of mothers' and fathers' parenting stress and child psychosocial outcomes was investigated. Greater dinnertime rituals reported by fathers moderated the effect of parenting stress on internalizing problems for girls, but not for boys. Fathers' reports of dinnertime rituals were related to fewer behavioral symptoms, internalizing problems and externalizing problems, and greater adaptive skills for girls. No significant interaction effects for mothers' parenting stress or rituals were found, but there were significant main effects of mothers' parenting stress and dinnertime rituals on child outcomes. These findings suggest that dinnertime rituals can potentially moderate the effects of parenting stress on child outcomes and fathers and daughters showed the greatest benefits of these family practices.

F amily rituals and routines are important for enhancing child health and well-being. Fiese et al. (2002) stated that regular rituals and routines contribute to stability and predictability in family life that enhance children's functioning. However, providing consistent, predictable family rituals and routines may be very challenging for the more than 58% of American families with young children in which both parents are employed outside of the home (Bureau of Labor Statistics, 2011). Fiese et al. pointed to the importance of family rituals as potential buffers of parenting distress. A moderation model holds that family rituals may serve as a protective mechanism for families in the presence of stress. If

Yesel Yoon, Katie Newkirk, and Maureen Perry-Jenkins, "Parenting Stress, Dinnertime Rituals, and Child Well-being in Working-Class Families," Family Relations, vol. 64, no. 1, pp. 93-107. Copyright © 2015 by National Council on Family Relations.

family rituals work as a moderator, then interventions focused on enhancing rituals would be a critical method to buffer parenting stress on child outcomes.

In this study, the role of family rituals in the understudied population of working-class families is explored. Rituals may be of even greater importance in dual-earner, working-class families because the work—family challenges facing low-wage workers are often significantly more stressful than for higher income workers. For example, working-class employees are more likely to face stressful work conditions involving mandatory overtime, low autonomy, variable work shifts, time-pressured productivity targets, few sick/personal time benefits, and unpaid family leave than their middle-class counterparts (Perry-Jenkins, 2005). Moreover, these work stressors spill over to affect the well-being and stress of working-class workers, creating unique challenges to family life and parenting (Perry-Jenkins, Smith, Goldberg, & Logan, 2011). For example, more than one third of working-class employees work non-standard shifts or rotating shifts, making it difficult to maintain regular family routines such as family meals and bedtime routines. In addition, mandatory overtime and little job flexibility, characteristics of low-wage work, also affect working parents' ability to maintain consistent family routines. Thus, a significant contribution of this study is its unique focus on working-class parents who face the challenge of managing family life while holding down low-wage and less flexible jobs.

The aim of this investigation is to examine the relationship between parenting stress and children's psychosocial outcomes as children transition to first grade, and to examine whether rituals mitigate the effect of high stress on child functioning.

Parenting Stress and Child Well-Being

Parenting stress has been linked to poorer outcomes in children, as measured by teachers' ratings of behavior problems in the classroom and social competence (Anthony et al., 2005) as well as increased externalizing and internalizing problems (Hart & Kelley, 2006; Rodriguez, 2011). The risk and resilience model supports the notion that risk and protective factors can enhance or undermine children's well-being (Black & Lobo, 2008). Parenting stress is an example of one such risk factor that can have detrimental effects for children's well-being. A family resilience framework extends the notion of resilience to the dynamic interactions of the broader family context and how certain family practices, such as family rituals and routines, can enhance well-being (Walsh, 2003). Based on this framework, this study examines dinnertime rituals as a potential protective factor that may buffer the risk effects of parenting stress.

Nature and Importance of Family Rituals

Fiese (2006) defined *family rituals* as repeated patterns of behavior that facilitate family life, communicate family values, and augment family identity. Fiese developed a self-report measure, the Family Rituals Questionnaire (Fiese & Kline, 1993), to assess family practices across different settings and dimensions to get a holistic measure of family practices that highlights the routinized practice and the symbolic meaning of family rituals. Rituals have a symbolic and affective component, such as dinnertime conversations when family members reflect on their day or discuss sensitive topics (Fiese, Foley, & Spagnola, 2006). In this study, the ascribed symbolic meaning (ritual meaning) and the patterned routine (ritual routine) of family dinnertime rituals are examined.

Mealtime as a Meaningful Family Ritual. Family mealtime rituals encompass the routinized aspects of family rituals, which are the repetition of tasks and roles over time, and the symbolic aspect of rituals, through the interactions that occur between members during the mealtime. Eating together "as a family" may be meaningful to individuals in the family (DeVault, 1994). Family mealtimes increase family connections (Fiese, 2006) and create a sense of family identity and group membership (Eaker & Walters, 2002; Leon & Jacobvitz, 2003). Engaging in family mealtimes has been associated with fewer internalizing symptoms (Fiese, Winter, Wamboldt, Anbar, & Wamboldt, 2010), greater academic success (Spagnola & Fiese, 2007), and fewer adolescent high-risk behaviors (Fulkerson et al., 2006; Sen, 2010). Based on this solid research base, it is hypothesized that family dinnertime rituals are related to better child psychosocial outcomes.

Child Gender and the Effects of Family Rituals. Family mealtimes are a context in which gender roles are enacted and reinforced. Gender socialization research points to the different ways parents interact and socialize with daughters and sons (McHale, Crouter, & Whiteman, 2003). Specifically, the dynamic interactions that take place during mealtimes can be experienced differently for girls and boys depending on how parents socialize their child.

Investigators have found gender differences in the effects of family rituals on children and adolescents although the findings are inconsistent. Levin, Kirby, and Currie (2011) found that frequent family meals were associated with the reduced likelihood of risk behaviors for girls but not boys. In one of the few studies that considered gender and ethnicity, more frequent family rituals were found to protect Latina adolescent girls from cumulative risk factors (Loukas & Prelow, 2004). Additional studies have found family rituals to be related to higher math ability and social competence with peers (Churchill & Stoneman, 2004); lower odds of adolescent risk behavior and depressive symptoms (Eisenberg, Olson, Newmark-Sztainer, Story, & Bearinger, 2004; Levin et al., 2011); and decreased likelihood of initiating drinking in girls, compared to boys (Fisher, Miles, Austin, Camargo, & Colditz, 2007). In contrast, family rituals have been found to be more strongly related to boys' outcomes than girls, including greater social competence (Ferretti, 2011) and better academic and physical health outcomes reported by teachers (Guidubaldi, Cleminshaw, Perry, Nastasi, & Lightel, 1986). Discrepant findings for gender differences in the experience of family rituals make it difficult to conclude whether there are consistent differences in the benefits of family rituals for boys and girls. Overall, there appears to be a pattern of evidence indicating greater benefits of family rituals for girls compared to boys. In this study, a similar pattern is expected to show a stronger benefit of family rituals for girls compared to boys.

Parent Gender and the Effect of Family Rituals. Although women typically spend more time preparing and performing tasks involved in the mealtime (DeVault, 1994), it is unclear whether family mealtimes have differing meanings (i.e., how one feels about the activity) for mothers and fathers. Mothers are typically held to be keepers of family rituals and therefore mothers have most often been recruited as the primary respondent in studies of family rituals, leaving little known about fathers' enactment and meaning associated with family rituals. Empirical studies of family rituals using reports from both parents can illuminate how the experience of family rituals may differ as a function of gender.

Family Rituals as a Moderator of Parenting Stress and Child Well-being

Although research has demonstrated that family rituals are directly related to better child and adolescent outcomes, there are no existing studies that have tested family rituals as a moderator between parenting stress and child outcomes. In one related study, Jacob, Allen, Hill, Mead, and Ferris (2008) found that dinnertime routines buffered the effects of long work hours on work—family conflict. They also found that women were more sensitive than men to the protective effects of dinnertime routines when work—family conflict increased (Jacob et al., 2008). This study aims to address this gap in the literature by testing family rituals as a moderator of the relation between parenting stress and child outcomes.

The Current Study

The proposed study makes a number of significant contributions to the literature. First, it includes reports of family dinnertime rituals from mothers and fathers. The unique and potentially different experience of fathers is measured to provide a more accurate picture of how family rituals are related to parenting stress and child outcomes. Second, this sample was drawn from a larger longitudinal study examining the experiences of working-class, dual-earner families across the transition to parenthood. Few studies have explored family rituals in low-income, dual-earner households who face greater financial stress and have fewer resources than their middle-class counterparts (Perry-Jenkins, 2004). Moreover, this study examines the potentially protective role of family rituals in households pressed for time and resources as parents must juggle the demands of work while caring for young children. The study examines families as their oldest child is entering school when family rituals may become destabilized while parents learn to manage children's schedules. The transition into school has been deemed one of the developmental "sensitive periods" when children may have positive or negative transitional experiences. The presence of stable rituals has been found to protect children against the challenges of this transition (Wildenger, McIntyre, Fiese, & Eckert, 2008). By using teachers' ratings of children's behavior, the study incorporates a unique perspective on the psychosocial and behavioral outcomes related to the presence of family rituals as children transition to the first grade.

The ecological model highlights the importance of the acknowledging how multiple systems, including family and social class, interact to influence children's outcomes. Because the families in this study are working-class families, the experiences of parenting stress and family dinnertime rituals may differ from families of other social classes. Parent—child interactions can be unique given some individual-level factors such as child or parent sex. Additionally, the risk and resilience framework provides a way to understand how family practices such as family dinnertime rituals can play a protective role in the presence of parenting stress. Using a sample of working-class families, this study addresses the following research questions and tests the corresponding hypotheses:

1. Is there a direct relationship between parents' report of dinnertime rituals and teachers' reports of children's psychosocial outcomes? It is hypothesized that greater family dinnertime rituals are related to better psychosocial outcomes in children.
2. Is there a direct relation between parents' report of stress and teachers' reports of children's psychosocial outcomes? It is hypothesized that greater parenting stress is directly related to poorer child psychosocial outcomes.
3. Is the direct relation between parents' report of stress and teachers' reports of children's psychosocial outcomes moderated by parents' report of dinnertime rituals? It is hypothesized that family rituals work as a moderator lessening the negative effects of parenting stress, because theoretically family rituals create a sense of stability and identity for families.
4. Does the relation between parenting stress, family rituals, and child outcomes differ by sex of either parent or child? Based on trends pointing toward greater benefits of family rituals for girls, it is hypothesized that more family rituals are related to better outcomes for girls than boys. Based on what is known about women's greater invested time and effort in family rituals, it is hypothesized the relation between parenting stress and family rituals is stronger for mothers than fathers.

Method

Participants

Participants were part of a larger longitudinal project examining the transition to parenthood among 153 dual-earner working-class couples, with a follow-up family interview when children were in first grade ($n = 121$). For this study, data came from the final time point and was collected from mothers, fathers, and teachers when target children were in first grade. Out of these 121 families, 20 were excluded who were no longer married or cohabiting, 6 families for whom teacher reports were missing, and 2 families who were missing both parents' reports of rituals, leaving 93 families for this study. In comparison to the 60 families not included, the families in this study were more likely to have been married prior to the birth of the target child and had significantly higher household incomes prenatally and when the target child was age 1 year than families lost through attrition. Mothers in this study also worked significantly more hours outside the home when children were age 1 year than mothers who were excluded. No differences were found in fathers' work hours, years married or cohabiting prior to the target child's birth, parents' education level, or in parents' race. Couples were recruited from prenatal classes at hospitals in the New England area during their third trimester of pregnancy. Couples had to meet the following criteria to be included in the study: (a) both members of the couple were employed full-time (35 hours per week or more), (b) both members of the couple planned to resume full-time work within 6 months of the baby's birth, (c) both members of the couple were "working class" as defined by educational attainment of a 2-year associates degree or less, (d) both members of the couple were expecting their first child, and (e) the couple was married or cohabiting for at least one year prior to participation in the study. By the time of the final interview, when target children were entering the first grade, families had an average of 2.1 children, with the majority of target children (87%) having younger siblings and 13% having no siblings. More than one half of the children were female (57%) and children were, on average, age 6.9 years.

Defining and measuring *social class* is a complicated issue; educational level (i.e., no more than an associates' degree), job characteristics (i.e., no supervisory responsibilities, hourly wage), and income were used as screening criteria for the working-class sample in this study. Education was chosen as the primary focus for two reasons. First, education is a precursor of job advancement, and those with low levels of education are likely to remain in low-wage work. Second, income alone is less representative of social class status because many of the fathers hold more than one job. For 16% of women and 28% of men, the highest degree held was a high school diploma or Graduate Equivalency Diploma during the prenatal interview; a majority of the sample (53.8% of women and 55.9% of men) had some type of additional schooling or vocational training after high school (e.g., beautician's school, refrigeration mechanic training). During the prenatal interview, only 28% of women and 15% of men held a 1- or 2-year associate's degree. None of the parents had a college degree when the target child was born; however, 4% of mothers and 5% of fathers had earned a bachelor's degree when the child was entering first grade. Mothers and fathers worked an average of 32 and 44 hours, respectively, at the final interview.

The majority of the sample were dual-earner families, with 83% of families having both partners working at least one job at the final interview. The remaining families relied solely on men's (11%) or women's (6%) earnings. The median self-reported gross individual salaries were $35,725 and $22,100 for men and women, respectively, and the median family income was $59,900 (range $18,304–$134,640). Based on a household of four, 20% of families' household income fell below 200% of the poverty line and would be defined as low-income. Importantly, these estimates represent gross income, thus, after taxes take-home pay is considerably less. Few of these families were in poverty; however, the loss of one partner's income would have moved many families close to or below the poverty line. The most common types of jobs held by men were factory worker, truck driver, and food service worker. Women were employed most often as food service workers, factory workers, and beauticians.

Measures

Parenting Stress. Parenting stress was assessed using the short form of the Parenting Stress Inventory (PSI; Abidin, 1995). This measure assessed mothers' and fathers' levels of stress related to their roles as parents. Mothers and fathers completed the 25-item PSI and the Total Stress Score was used as overall level of parenting stress. Sample items include "I feel trapped by my responsibilities as a parent" and "I find myself giving up more of my life to meet my children's needs than I ever expected." Responses on the scale range from 1 (*strongly agree*) to 5 (*strongly disagree*), with a higher score signifying higher levels of parenting stress. The range of scores for mothers was 36 to 130 and for fathers was 38 to 117. Cronbach's alpha for mothers was .94 and for fathers was .94.

Family rituals were assessed from mothers and fathers using the Dinnertime subscale of the Family Rituals Questionnaire (FRQ; Fiese & Kline, 1993). The FRQ assesses rituals across seven settings and eight dimensions; the dinnertime scale is one of seven settings that are assessed in the overall measure and the subscale used in this study. The FRQ includes eight items that assess eight different dimensions: occurrence, roles, routine, attendance, affect, symbolic significance, continuation, and deliberateness. For more specific definitions of each of the settings and dimensions of the FRQ, see Fiese and Kline (1993).

In this study, the total Dinnertime Ritual subscale represented the sum of the Dinnertime Ritual Meaning and Dinnertime Ritual Routine scores. Ritual Meaning and Ritual Routine were calculated by summing the individual dimension items (e.g., symbolic significance, routine) that correspond to each respective factor. An example of an item that captured ritual meaning is, "In some families people feel strongly about eating dinner together," and an item reflecting the ritual routine is, "In some families, dinnertime is flexible. People can eat whenever they can." Each respondent was asked to indicate how true the statement was for his/her family. Responses on the scale range from 1 to 4, with a higher score endorsing more of the particular dimension of the dinnertime. The range of scores for mothers was 10 to 31 and fathers was 11 to 30. Cronbach's alpha for mothers was .79 and for fathers was .68.

Child Behavioral Outcomes. Children's internalizing problems, externalizing problems, adaptive skills, and behavior symptoms were measured using the Behavioral Assessment System for Children—Teacher Report Scale (BASC-TRS; Reynolds & Kamphaus, 1992) for the age group 6 to 11 years. The BASC-TRS is a 131-item comprehensive rating scale that assesses a broad range of psychopathology in children age 21/2 years and older. Teachers were asked to rate on a 4-point scale (*never, sometimes, often, almost always*) the degree to which each item described the child. The teachers' reports of child outcomes were collected an average of 3 to 4 weeks after the parent interviews and self-report measures were collected.

The BASC-TRS demonstrates good reliability and validity with school-age children, with Cronbach's alphas ranging from .89 to .97 for girls and .90 to .96 for boys (Reynolds &

Kamphaus, 1992). The use of teacher reports was an important strength of the study design as much of the past literature has relied solely on parent reports of child outcomes. T scores (based on general, not gender-specific, norms) for the Externalizing (37 items), Internalizing (26 items), and Adaptive Skills (39 items) composites and the Behavioral Symptoms Index were used. The Externalizing composite includes subscales that measure aggression, hyperactivity, and conduct problems. The Internalizing composite includes subscales that measure depression, anxiety, and somatization. The Adaptive Skills composite includes subscales that measure adaptability, leadership, social skills, and study skills. The Behavioral Symptoms Index is a combination of hyperactivity, aggression, anxiety, depression, attention problems, and atypicality scales from the clinical composites, reflecting overall levels of problem behavior "in much the same way as the overall composite score of an intelligence test measures the underlying dimension of g" (Reynolds & Kamphaus, 1992, p. 52), and overlapping to some extent with the externalizing and internalizing clinical composites. The range of T scores for externalizing scores was 40 to 69, internalizing scores was 39 to 81, adaptive skills was 35 to 73, and behavioral symptoms was 37 to 62.

Child Sex. A dichotomous variable indicating child sex (0 = *boy*, 1 = *girl*) was included as a predictor in order to examine the different effects by child sex.

Control Variables. All control variables were measured at the final interview, when the target child was entering first grade. The number of children in the family was included as a control variable, as it is related to parenting stress (Warfield, 2005) and was correlated with mothers' reports of dinnertime rituals in this sample. A dichotomous variable indicating whether parents worked the same shift as his/her partner, and the total number of hours the parent worked at all of his or her jobs were included as control variables because they were correlated with children's outcomes in this sample, and research has suggested they are related to dinnertime rituals and parenting stress (Jacob et al., 2008; Joshi & Bogen, 2007), with nonstandard work schedules also related to children's behavioral outcomes (Joshi & Bogen, 2007).

Child Care Involvement. Preliminary analyses were run to test whether the relationship between fathers' stress, dinnertime rituals, and child outcomes could be attributed to differences in father involvement in child care. Fathers' and mothers' childcare involvement were measured using the 7-item Daily Childcare Involvement subscale of the Childcare Involvement Scale (Bouchard & Lee, 2000). Parents were each asked to estimate their own and their partner's level of involvement in activities requiring direct interaction with their child, such as putting the child to bed. Participants reported their involvement using a 7-point scale ranging from 1 (*never*) to 7 (*almost always [7 times a week]*) and items are averaged to obtain a mean score. Parents' reports of their own involvement were used. Father's scores on this measure ranged from 1.86 to 6.71 (M = 4.03, SD = 1.04, Mode = 4.0), and mothers' ranged from 3.14 to 7.00 (M = 5.27, SD = .91, Mode = 4.14). Cron-bach's alpha was .79 for fathers and was .66 for mothers.

Results

The means, standard deviations, and intercorrelations among mothers' and fathers' reports of parenting stress and dinnertime rituals, and the four subscales of teachers' reports of child outcomes, are shown in Table 13.1. Casewise deletion was used, resulting in sample sizes ranging from 81 to 91 for analyses. There were no significant differences between mothers' and fathers' reports of parenting stress and family dinnertime rituals. When comparing parents' reports of parenting stress and dinnertime rituals by child sex, ANOVAs revealed a significant difference in dinnertime rituals, with mothers' reporting more family rituals with

TABLE 13.1. Means, standard deviations, and correlations of parent and child study variables

	Mean	SD	N	1	2	3	4	5	6	7	8
Predictors											
1. Mother parenting stress	73.09	19.97	92	—							
2. Father parenting stress	69.83	18.86	90	0.49**	—						
3. Mother dinnertime ritual	21.97	4.86	92	−0.16	−0.15	—					
4. Father dinnertime ritual	21.40	3.86	90	−0.13	−0.10	0.44**	—				
5. Child externalizing problems	46.47	6.80	91	0.20+	0.29**	−0.35**	−0.15	—			
6. Child internalizing problems	48.98	9.20	93	0.09	0.30**	−0.10	−0.09	0.20+	—		
7. Child behavioral symptoms	46.91	7.21	93	0.23*	0.33**	−0.32**	−0.20+	0.79**	0.64**	—	
8. Child adaptive skills	55.64	8.84	85	−0.23*	−0.23*	0.21+	0.25*	−0.42**	−0.36**	−0.65**	—

Note: Parenting stress and dinnertime rituals were all mean centered.

$+p < .10$, $^*p < .05$, $^{**}p < .01$.

girls than boys. There was no significant difference in fathers' reports of family dinnertime rituals depending on child sex. Bivariate correlation analyses (Table 13.1) revealed a positive correlation between spouses' reports of parenting stress ($r = .49$, $p < .01$), and a positive correlation between spouses' reports of family dinnertime rituals ($r = .44$, $p < .01$). Fathers' parenting stress was positively correlated with child externalizing problems, internalizing problems, and behavioral symptoms, and was inversely related to child adaptive skills, whereas mothers' parenting stress was only positively related to child behavioral symptoms, and negatively related to child adaptive skills. Mothers' reports of greater dinnertime rituals were correlated with lower child externalizing problems and behavioral symptoms, whereas fathers' dinnertime ritual reports were correlated with higher child adaptive skills. Child outcomes were highly intercorrelated, with the exception of internalizing and externalizing problems, which were not significantly correlated.

The moderation of the relationship between parenting stress and teacher reports of child outcomes by dinnertime rituals was tested using Baron and Kenny's (1986) approach of hierarchical linear regression analyses, controlling for the number of children in the family, the couples' work shift schedule, and the total number of work hours and including main effects and hypothesized interactions. Interactions with child sex and parenting stress and child sex and rituals were also examined. All of the continuous variables were mean centered prior to being entered into the model so the conditional effects of each variable can be interpreted as the effect of each variable at the mean of other variables. For significant interaction effects, further probing of these interactions was tested using PROCESS, a macro in SPSS (Hayes, 2013), using three conditional values of the moderator: at the mean, one standard deviation below and above the mean value of the moderator.

Dinnertime Rituals and Child Sex as Moderators of Parenting Stress and Child Psychosocial Outcomes

Multiple hierarchical linear regressions were conducted with control variables entered in Step 1, followed by main effects of child sex, parenting stress, and dinnertime rituals entered in Step 2, two-way interaction effects of each predictor in Step 3, and finally the 3-way interaction of child sex, parenting stress, and dinnertime rituals in Step 4. These predictors were regressed on each individual child outcome including externalizing and internalizing problems, behavioral symptoms, and adaptive skills. The results are shown separately by each parent (Table 13.2 for mothers' predictors, Table 13.3 for fathers' predictors).

Mothers' Reports of Parenting Stress and Dinnertime Rituals. It was hypothesized that regular dinnertime rituals would buffer, or reduce, the effects of parenting stress on child psychosocial outcomes. Mothers' greater reports of dinnertime rituals significantly predicted fewer externalizing problems and fewer behavioral symptoms. Mothers' reports of parenting stress were significantly associated with poorer adaptive skills, and greater externalizing

TABLE 13.2. Hierarchical regression models predicting children's outcomes from mothers' reports of parenting stress and family rituals

	Externalizing Problems		Internalizing Problems		Adaptive Skills		Behavior Symptoms Index	
	Model 1	Model 2	Model 1	Model 2	Model 1	Model 2	Model 1	Model 2
Variable	b(SE)	b(SE)	b(SE)	b(SE)	b(SE)	b(SE)	b(SE)	b(SE)
# of children	− 1.56 (1.29)	− 1.06 (1.27)	1.62 (1.76)	2.16 (1.92)	0.50 (1.71)	0.78 (1.77)	− 0.56 (1.38)	− 0.13 (1.38)
Work hours	0.01 (0.05)	− 0.004 (0.05)	− 0.09 (0.07)	− 0.08 (0.07)	− 0.04 (0.07)	− 0.01 (0.07)	− 0.01 (0.06)	− 0.02 (0.05)
Couple shift[a] Child sex[b]	0.40 (1.60)	− 0.20 (1.51) − 3.69* (1.39)	0.72 (2.17)	0.17 (2.27) − 0.15 (2.08)	− 0.12 (2.17)	− 0.36 (2.15) 4.42* (1.99)	0.98 (1.71)	0.41 (1.62) − 3.71**(1.49)
Parenting stress Dinnertime		0.06 + (0.03) − 0.31* (0.15)		0.02 (0.05) − 0.24 (0.23)		− 0.10* (0.05) 0.13 (0.21)		0.07 + (0.04) − 0.32 + (0.16)
ΔR^2	.02	.20	.05	.02	.01	.13	.01	.19
F for ΔR^2	0.66	6.87**	1.52	0.56	0.21	4.00*	0.14	6.51**
R^2	.02	.22**	.05	.07	.01	.14+	.01	.19**

Note: Parenting stress, dinnertime rituals, work hours, and number of children were all mean centered.

a Couple shift: 0 = same shift, 1 = opposite shift. b Child sex: 1 = girl, 0 = boy. + p < .10, * p < .05, ** p < .01.

TABLE 13.3. Hierarchical regression model results predicting children's outcomes from fathers' reports of parenting stress and family rituals

	Externalizing Problems				Internalizing Problems			
Variable	Model 1 b(SE)	Model 2 b(SE)	Model 3 b(SE)	Model 4 b(SE)	Model 1 b(SE)	Model 2 b(SE)	Model 3 b(SE)	Model 4 b(SE)
# of children	−1.64 (1.19)	−1.57 (1.14)	−1.11 (1.17)	−1.11 (1.18)	2.54 (1.61)	2.41 (1.61)	3.18* (1.60)	3.34* (1.53)
Work hours	−0.002 (0.05)	0.03 (0.05)	0.01 (0.05)	0.01 (0.05)	−0.09 (0.07)	−0.06 (0.07)	−0.10 (0.07)	−0.12 + (0.07)
Couple shift	0.44 (1.58)	−0.25 (1.55)	−0.11 (1.60)	−0.09 (1.64)	0.01 (2.15)	−1.37 (2.19)	−0.71 (2.20)	0.59 (2.16)
Child sex (CS)		−3.83** (1.39)	−3.93** (1.39)	−3.93* (1.40)		0.88 (1.95)	0.78 (1.90)	0.45 (1.83)
Stress (PSI)		0.10** (.04)	0.13* (0.06)	0.13* (0.06)		0.17** (0.06)	0.21* (0.08)	0.15 + (0.08)
Dinner (DR)		−0.10 (0.19)	0.25 (0.27)	0.25 (0.28)		−0.29 (0.27)	0.40 (.38)	0.18 (0.37)
PSI x DR			−0.01 (0.01)	−0.01 (0.02)			−0.04* (0.02)	0.001 (0.02)
CS x DR			−0.64 + (.36)	−0.64 + (0.37)			−1.14* (0.50)	−0.89 + (0.49)
CS x PSI			−0.04 (0.08)	−0.03 (0.09)			−0.02 (0.11)	0.09 (0.11)
CS x PSI x DR				−0.001 (0.02)				−0.09** (0.03)
ΔR²	.02	.18	.04	.00	.05	.11	.08	.07
F for ΔR²	0.64	5.82*	1.26	0.003	1.41	3.67*	2.69	7.66*
R²	.02	.20**	.24*	.24*	.05	.16*	.24*	.31*

	Adaptive Skills				Behavioral Symptoms			
Variable	Model 1 b(SE)	Model 2 b(SE)	Model 3 b(SE)	Model 4 b(SE)	Model 1 b(SE)	Model 2 b(SE)	Model 3 b(SE)	Model 4 b(SE)
# of children	0.92 (1.55)	0.15 (1.54)	−0.80 (1.57)	−0.96 (1.57)	−0.52 (1.26)	−0.38 (1.19)	0.22 (1.18)	0.27 (1.18)
Work hours	0.09 (0.07)	0.07 (0.07)	0.08 (0.07)	0.08 (0.07)	−0.05 (0.05)	−0.02 (0.05)	−0.05 (0.05)	−0.06 (0.05)
Couple shift	−0.88 (2.12)	0.46 (2.11)	0.55 (2.15)	−0.12 (2.19)	0.90 (1.69)	−0.39 (1.62)	0.02 (1.63)	0.41 (1.67)
CS[b]		3.91* (1.92)	4.35* (1.89)	4.59* (1.89)		−3.38* (1.45)	−3.46* (1.41)	−3.56* (1.41)
Stress (PSI)		−0.07 (0.06)	−0.12 (0.08)	−0.09 (0.08)		0.13** (0.04)	0.17** (0.06)	0.15* (0.06)
Dinner (DR)		0.51 + (0.26)	−0.08 (0.36)	0.01 (0.37)		−0.27 (0.20)	0.25 (0.28)	0.19 (0.29)
PSI x DR			0.01 (0.02)	−0.004 (0.02)			−0.03* (0.01)	−0.02 (0.02)
CS x DR			1.21* (0.50)	1.14* (0.50)			−0.88* (0.37)	−0.81* (0.38)
CS x PSI			0.10 (0.11)	0.04 (0.12)			−0.03 (0.08)	0.003 (0.09)
CS x PSI x DR				0.05 (0.03)				−0.03 (0.02)
ΔR²	.02	.14	.07	.02	.02	.21	.08	.01
F for ΔR²	0.64	3.96*	2.05	1.91	0.43	7.19**	2.76*	1.16
R²	.02	.16*	.23*	.25*	.02	.22**	.30**	.31**

Note: CS = child sex; PSI = Parenting Stress Index; DR = dinnertime rituals.

PSI, DR, Work hours, and number of children were mean centered.

[a] Couple shift: 0 = same shift, 1 = opposite shift. [b] Child sex: 1 = girl, 0 = boy. +$p < .10$, * $p < .05$, ** $p < .01$.

problems and behavioral symptoms. There was also a main effect of child sex, such that girls had greater adaptive skills and fewer externalizing problems and behavioral symptoms, compared to boys. When testing for moderation, no significant interactions between mothers' reports of dinnertime rituals and parenting stress predicted children's outcomes.

Fathers' Reports of Parenting Stress and Dinnertime Rituals. It was also hypothesized that associations between fathers' reports of stress and child outcomes would be moderated by dinnertime rituals. Fathers' parenting stress was related to greater externalizing problems and behavioral symptoms, and marginally related to greater internalizing problems, for boys. There was no relation between fathers' parenting stress and child adaptive skills.

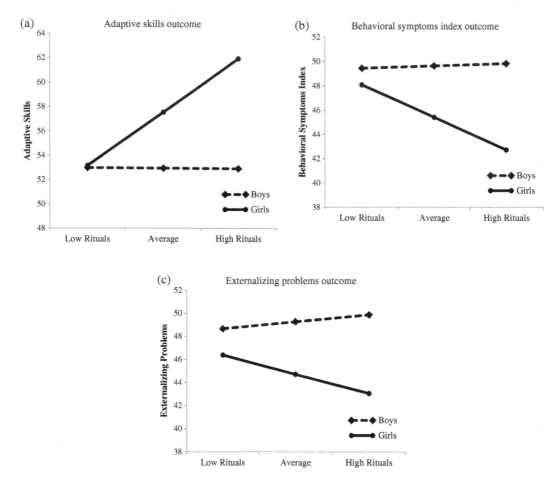

FIGURE 13.1   Two-way interactions of fathers' report of dinnertime rituals and child sex predicting teachers' report of children's adaptive skills, externalizing problems, and behavioral

Second, there were significant interactions between fathers' reports of dinnertime rituals and child sex predicting several outcomes. Fathers' dinnertime rituals were related to greater adaptive skills (Figure 13.1a), fewer behavioral symptoms (Figure 13.1b), and fewer externalizing problems (Figure 13.1c) for girls, but not for boys.

Finally, the hypothesized three-way interaction of parenting stress, dinnertime rituals, and child sex was supported for internalizing symptoms. As shown in Figure 13.2, dinnertime rituals moderated the association between father's parenting stress and internalizing symptoms for girls, but not for boys. A closer look at the three-way interaction revealed that there was a significant positive association between fathers' stress on girls' internalizing symptoms at low levels of fathers' dinnertime rituals. However, the relation between fathers' parenting stress and girls' internalizing symptoms became nonsignificant and changed direction at high levels of dinnertime rituals. In other words, greater dinnertime rituals reported by fathers nullified the effects of high parenting stress on girls' internalizing symptoms.

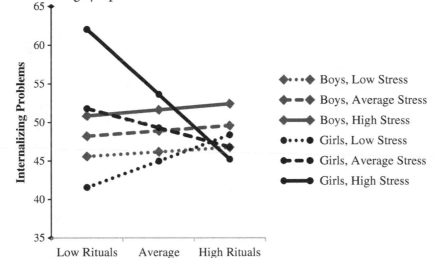

FIGURE 13.2   Three-way interaction of child sex, fathers' report of dinnertime rituals, and parenting stress predicting children's internalizing behaviors.

Exploratory Analyses

One potential explanation for why results only emerged between fathers and daughters with no relationships for sons may be that fathers are generally more involved with sons. Researchers have suggested that fathers' involvement with sons is more expected and scripted (McHale et al., 2003); thus dinnertime may be one of the few, or only, scripted family interactions where daughters and fathers have time together. Based on this line of thinking, it was hypothesized that other, less scripted types of parenting involvement, such as shared leisure together, would be higher for fathers and sons than fathers and daughters. One-way ANOVA comparisons revealed that fathers spent more time in child care involvement with sons than daughters, $F(1, 87) = 5.993$, $p = .016$, confirming the hypothesis that fathers spend more discretionary time with sons than daughters. Mothers' reports of involvement revealed a similar sex effect, with mothers being more involved with daughters than with sons, $F(1, 90) = 5.389$, $p = .023$; however, the mean difference between daughters and sons was smaller for mothers (0.435) than for fathers (-0.531) and mothers were, overall, more involved with children of both sex than were fathers, $t(88) = -7.79$, $p < .001$.

Discussion

The results of this study provide support for direct relationships between family dinnertime rituals and child outcomes, and between parenting stress and child outcomes, as well as some evidence for more complex moderated relationships. Only modest relationships linked mothers' reports of stress or rituals to children's outcomes, and the moderation model was not supported for mothers. Fathers' reports of dinnertime rituals were significantly related to more adaptive skills and lower behavioral symptoms, externalizing problems, and internalizing problems for girls, but not for boys. In addition, fathers' higher reports of dinnertime rituals diminished the effect of high parenting stress on girls' internalizing symptoms. Regardless of whether fathers reported low or high parenting stress, parenting stress was no longer related to girls' internalizing symptoms when fathers reported high dinnertime rituals. The effect of parenting stress and dinnertime rituals was not significant for boys.

Our findings support the existing literature that has more often found effects of family dinnertime rituals for girls compared to boys. Researchers have speculated that girls are more sensitive to nuances in family interactions and factors within the home environment (Churchill & Stoneman, 2004; Eisenberg et al., 2004). In addition, girls may have greater self-regulatory capacities compared to boys' delayed maturation, making it easier for families to establish family rituals with girls (Ferretti, 2011). Another possible explanation for the lack of finding for boys is that household tasks and activities are often sex-typed and boys may benefit from an alternative kind of family ritual other than family dinnertime. Girls tend to spend more time engaged in household tasks and chores than boys, and thus girls may be more engaged in the family dinnertime ritual than boys. The role of context is important when examining gender-specific differences in parent—child interactions (Lindsey & Mize, 2001). Gender-based differences have emerged in the study of parent—child play activities. Fathers' tend to engage in more physical play with boys than with girls and mothers tend to play with their children in a more structured manner with empathic conversations (John, Halliburton, & Humphrey, 2013). This finding poses a possible explanation for how mothers and fathers differ in their behaviors toward their children, and the effect of fathers' engagement with boys may not be accurately reflected in a family ritual such as dinnertime. Another type of family ritual may have gender-specific effects on child outcomes, which can possibly account for the gender differences found in the study. In the future, different kinds of family rituals (e.g., bedtime rituals, family vacations) can be included to investigate whether boys may benefit from a different kind of family activity.

When examining why moderation emerged only for fathers and daughters, it was speculated that family dinnertime rituals represent a major source of scripted time when fathers interact with their daughters. Gender ideology theory posits that parents enact what they view as appropriate roles for men and women, such as paternal beliefs about being more involved and available to sons than daughters (Aldous, Mulligan, & Bjarnason, 1998). Mothers have typically been found to spend more time with their children than fathers (Harris & Morgan, 1991), and fathers typically spend more time with sons than daughters (Manlove & Vernon-Feagans, 2002). Thus, family dinnertime may provide a unique opportunity for fathers to connect with their daughters as one of few family settings in which fathers can regularly be available emotionally and physically for their daughters. In working-class families, fathers may have limited opportunity to interact with their daughters outside of dinnertime, thus making dinnertime rituals particularly important for girls. This explanation of results is consistent with past findings that fathers are more involved in caregiving tasks and more available to sons than daughters (Manlove & Vernon-Feagans, 2002). In our sample, fathers spend more time with boys than girls, and mothers spend more time with girls than boys, supporting the notion that fathers are enacting their gendered views of spending time differently with boys versus girls.

The protective function of family rituals may be attributed to the sense of meaning that it brings to individuals in the family. When trying to explain why moderation only emerged for fathers and daughters, it may also have to do with the amount of meaning these interactions hold, especially for daughters, as this may be one of the few established times fathers get to spend with their daughters. When family dinnertime interactions are characterized by meaningful and genuine interest in children's well-being, children are less likely to experience internalizing symptoms (Fiese et al., 2006). Similarly, fathers' reporting greater family dinnertime rituals, thus more meaningful interactions with their daughters, also reduces the effect of stress on internalizing symptoms. Thus, the dinnertime rituals are serving as an important setting for positive and meaningful emotional exchanges with their fathers.

It is difficult to reduce the amount of stress that parents experience, especially low-income parents who must work long hours to support their families. Findings from this study show that families with stable rituals, like a set dinnertime, may protect some children from the adverse effects of stress. From the risk and resilience framework, family dinnertime rituals are an example of one important protective factor that can promote resilience even in the face of parenting stress within a working class context. The fact that fathers' time and emotional investment in a meaningful regular family activity can help protect daughters from internalizing problems sheds light on the unique dynamic that may be taking place between this dyad. Although there are parenting interventions targeting fathers' involvement in their children's lives, father involvement can matter in unique ways depending on child sex. Creators of parent interventions and father involvement programs should consider what specific activities can be implemented to best cater to the unique gendered dynamic between parent and child. Although this study examined family dinnertime rituals in particular, what may really matter most is time set aside for fathers to be involved in their daughters' lives in a way that is meaningful and consistent. Future research studies should incorporate a wider range of family rituals, and ask specific questions that can expand upon the gendered nature of parent—child dynamics that is taking place during dinnertime rituals. Also, future research should focus more attention on the role of fathers in promoting better outcomes for their children as well as how and why fathers' involvement may differ by child gender as the results of this study found that the relation between fathers' dinnertime rituals and stress were not the same across both girls and boys.

It is interesting that dinnertime rituals did not moderate the relationship between maternal stress and either sons' or daughters' outcomes. Revisiting the traditional gender roles and socialization of children, mothers are typically thought to be the ones assigned to organizing, preparing, and carrying out the dinnertime ritual, so dinnertime rituals may not buffer their parenting stress as it does for fathers. What may be considered as unique time together for fathers and daughters may not be unique for mothers and their children. Furthermore, mothers are more likely to compensate for stress by doing their best to have quality time with their children whenever they can, possibly explaining the lack of interaction for mothers' reports and child outcomes. Fathers may be more likely to allow work stress to detract from the quantity and quality of their time with their children, again making the dinnertime ritual a special opportunity to benefit the family, particularly between the father and his child. It will be important to learn more about how mothers and fathers differ in terms of their experiences with family dinnertime rituals—if mothers feel these family rituals add to their level of stress because of how much they are responsible for carrying out the ritual, or if there is something else that contributes to the lack of buffering effect of dinnertime rituals for mothers' stress on child outcomes. In this study, the focus was on the effect of family dinnertime rituals on child outcomes, however, future research can explore if dinnertime rituals may moderate the relationship between parents' stress and their own psychosocial outcomes. The positive benefits of family dinnertime rituals may extend to multiple family members, and it will be important to empirically examine this relationship.

Limitations of This Study

Our findings should be interpreted with caution given several limitations. The sample size was small and limited to working-class and low-income families, therefore the generalizability of the findings are limited. The small sample size gave modest power to detect significant effects. Future studies should examine families in other cultural contexts, as values about gender roles may change the dynamic between parents and children. Also, though the data are from a larger longitudinal study, the analyses are cross-sectional. However, within the one time point of data collection, teacher reports of child outcomes were collected after the parents' report of parenting stress and dinnertime rituals. Therefore, the presence of the time lag, albeit a small one, and multiple sources of data (mothers, fathers, and teachers) help reduce the possibility that the associations between parenting stress and child behavior problems could be in the opposite direction. Although casual attributions cannot be made, the importance of the effects found should not be discounted as there was some time sequence and multiple sources of data. It will be useful to replicate this study with longitudinal data to investigate change over time in the relationship between parenting stress and child outcomes.

Dinnertime rituals are but one example of family rituals, and there are other settings of family rituals that should be considered in the future such as weekends or bedtime rituals.

Conclusion

Despite the limitations of the study, our findings suggest that for fathers experiencing stress, family rituals serve a protective role for girls' psychosocial outcomes. The families in this study exist within a social context of having multiple jobs and having limited financial resources. Despite these contextual risk factors, it is evident that when fathers reported more family dinnertime rituals, this family practice significantly buffered the negative effects of stress on their daughters' psychosocial outcomes. Importantly, family dinnertime rituals, as a protective and stabilizing mechanism in family life, may be especially important for fathers and daughters, as this could be the only time fathers get to routinely interact with their daughters. The findings of this study add to the limited literature on the protective moderation relationship between parenting stress, family rituals, and child psychosocial outcomes. Future research should expand upon these findings to dig deeper in terms of the unique dyads that exist within family systems, and the role of meaningful and predictable family time together.

Note

1 This research is supported by a grant from the National Institute of Mental Health to Maureen Perry-Jenkins (R01-MH56777).

References

Abidin, R. R. (1995). *Parenting Stress Index: Professional manual* (3rd ed.). Odessa, FL: Psychological Assessment Resources.

Aldous, J., Mulligan, G. M., & Bjarnason, T. (1998). Fathering over time: What makes the difference? *Journal of Marriage and the Family, 60,* 809–820.

Anthony, L. G., Anthony, B. J., Glanville, D. N., Naiman, D. Q., Waanders, C., & Shaffer, S. (2005). The relationship between parenting stress, parenting behaviour and preschoolers' social competence and behaviour problems in the classroom. *Infant and Child Development, 14,* 133–154. doi:10.1002/icd.385

Baron, R. M., & Kenny, D. A. (1986). The moderator-mediator variable distinction in social psychological research: Conceptual, strategic, and statistical considerations. *Journal of Personality and Social Psychology, 51,* 1173–1182. doi:10.1037//0022-3514.51.6.1173

Black, K., & Lobo, M. (2008). A conceptual review of family resilience. *Journal of Family Nursing, 14,* 33–55. doi:10.1177/1074840707312237

Bouchard, G., & Lee, C. M. (2000). The marital context for father involvement with their preschool children: The role of partner support. *Journal of Prevention and Intervention in the Community, 2,* 37–54. doi:10.1300/J005v20n01_04

Bureau of Labor Statistics. (2011). *Employment characteristics of families summary.* Retrieved from http://www.bls.gov/news.release/pdf/famee.pdf

Churchill, S. L., & Stoneman, Z. (2004). Correlates of family routines in Head Start families. *Early Childhood Research & Practice, 6.* Retrieved from http://ecrp.uiuc.edu/v6n1/churchill.html

DeVault, M. L. (1994). *Feeding the family: The social organization of caring as gendered work.* Chicago, IL: University of Chicago Press.

Eaker, D. G., & Walters, L. H. (2002). Adolescent satisfaction in family rituals and psychosocial development: A developmental systems theory perspective. *Journal of Family Psychology, 16,* 406–414. doi:10.1037/0893-3200.16.4.406

Eisenberg, M. E., Olson, R. E., Neumark-Sztainer, D., Story, M., & Bearinger, L. H. (2004). Correlations between family meals and psychosocial well-being among adolescents. *Archives of Pediatric and Adolescent Medicine, 158,* 792–796. doi:10.1001/archpedi.158.8.792

Ferretti, L. K. (2011). *The influence of family routines on the resilience of low-income preschoolers.* Unpublished masters' thesis, Auburn University, Auburn, AL.

Fiese, B. H. (2006). *Family routines and rituals.* New Haven, CT: Yale University Press.

Fiese, B. H., Foley, K. P., & Spagnola, M. (2006). Routine and ritual elements in family mealtimes: Contexts for child well-being and family identity. *New Directions for Child and Adolescent Development, 111,* 67–89. doi:10.1002/cad.155

Fiese, B. H., & Kline, C. A. (1993). Development of the Family Rituals Questionnaire: Initial reliability and validation studies. *Journal of Family Psychology, 6,* 290–299. doi:10.1037//0893-3200.6.3.290

Fiese, B. H., Tomcho, T. J., Douglas, M., Josephs, K., Poltrock, S., & Baker, T. (2002). A review of 50 years of research on naturally occurring family routines and rituals: Cause for celebration? *Journal of Family Psychology, 16,* 381–390. doi:10.1037//0893-3200.16.4.381

Fiese, B. H., Winter, M. A., Wamboldt, F. S., Anbar, R. D., & Wamboldt, M. Z. (2010). Do family mealtime interactions mediate the association between asthma symptoms and separation anxiety? *Journal of Child Psychology and Psychiatry, 51,* 144–151. doi:10.1111/j.1469-7610.2009.02138.x

Fisher, L. B., Miles, I. W., Austin, B., Camargo, C. A., & Colditz, G. A. (2007). Predictors of initiation of alcohol use among US adolescents. *Archives of Pediatrics & Adolescent Medicine, 161,* 959–966. doi:10.1001/archpedi.161.10.959

Fulkerson, J. A., Story, M., Mellin, A., Leffert, N., Neumark-Sztainer, D., & French, S. A. (2006). Family dinner meal frequency and adolescent development: Relationships with developmental assets and high-risk behaviors. *Journal of Adolescent Health, 39,* 337–345. doi:10.1016/ j.jadohealth.2005.12.026

Guidubaldi, J., Cleminshaw, H. K., Perry, J. D., Nastasi, B. K., & Lightel, J. (1986). The role of selected family environment factors in children's post-divorce adjustment. *Family Relations, 35,* 141–151. doi:10.2307/584293

Harris, K. M., & Morgan, S. P. (1991). Fathers, sons, and daughters: Differential paternal involvement in parenting. *Journal of Marriage and Family, 53,* 531–544. doi:10.2307/352730

Hart, M. S., & Kelley, M. L. (2006). Fathers' and mothers' work and family issues as related to internalizing and externalizing behavior of children attending day care. *Journal of Family Issues, 27,* 252–270. doi:10.1177/0192513X0528 0992

Hayes, A. (2013). *Introduction to mediation, moderation, and conditional process analysis: A regression-based approach.* New York, NY: Guilford.

Jacob, J. I., Allen, S., Hill, E. J., Mead, N. L., & Fer-ris, M. (2008). Work interference with dinnertime as a mediator and moderator between work hours and work and family outcomes. *Family and Consumer Sciences Research Journal, 36,* 310–327. doi:10.1177/1077727X08316025

John, A., Halliburton, A., & Humphrey, J. (2013). Child-mother and child-father play interaction patterns with preschoolers. *Early Child Development and Care, 183,* 483–497. doi:10.1080/030044 30.2012.711595

Joshi, P., & Bogen, K. (2007). Nonstandard schedules and young children's behavioral outcomes among working low-income families. *Journal of Marriage and Family, 69,* 139–156. doi:10.1111/j.1741-3737.2006.00350.x

Leon, K., & Jacobvitz, D. B. (2003). Relationships between adult attachment representations and family ritual quality: A prospective, longitudinal study. *Family Process, 42,* 419–432. doi:10.1111/j.1545-5300.2003.00419.x

Levin, K. A., Kirby, J., & Currie, C. (2011). Adolescent risk behaviours and mealtime routines: Does family meal frequency alter the association between family structure and risk behaviour? *Health Education Research, 27,* 24–35. doi: 10.1093/her/cyr084

Lindsey, E. W., & Mize, J. (2001). Contextual differences in parent-child play: Implications for children's gender role development. *Sex Roles, 44,* 155–176.

Loukas, A., & Prelow, H. M. (2004). Externalizing and internalizing problems in low-income Latino early adolescents: Risk, resource, and protective factors. *Journal of Early Adolescence, 24,* 250–273. doi:10.1177/0272431604265675

Manlove, E. E., & Vernon-Feagans, L. (2002). Caring for infant daughters and sons in dual-earner households: Maternal reports of father involvement in weekday time and tasks. *Infant and Child Development, 11,* 305–320.

McHale, S. M., Crouter, A. C., & Whiteman, S. D. (2003). The family contexts of gender development in childhood and adolescence. *Social Development, 12,* 125–148. doi:10.1111/1467-9507.00225

Perry-Jenkins, M. (2004). The time and timing of work: Unique challenges facing low-income families. In A. Crouter & A. Booth (Eds.), *Work-family challenges for low-income parents and their children.* (pp. 107–116). Mahwah, NJ: Lawrence Erlbaum Associates.

Perry-Jenkins, M. (2005). Work in the working class: Challenges facing workers and their families. In S. M. Bianchi, L. M. Casper, K. E. Christensen, & R. B. King (Eds.), *Work, family, health and well-being* (pp. 453–472). Mahwah, NJ: Lawrence Erlbaum Associates.

Perry-Jenkins, M., Smith, J. Z., Goldberg, A. E., & Logan, J. (2011). Working-class jobs and new parents' mental health. *Journal of Marriage and Family, 73,* 1117–1132.

Reynolds, C. R., & Kamphaus, R. W. (1992). *Behavior Assessment System for Children: Manual.* Circle Pines, MN: American Guidance.

Rodriguez, C. M. (2011). Association between independent reports of maternal parenting stress and children's internalizing symptomatology. *Journal of Child and Family Studies, 20,* 631–639. doi:10.1007/s10826-010-9438-8

Sen, B. (2010). The relationship between frequency of family dinner and adolescent problem behaviors after adjusting for other family characteristics. *Journal of Adolescence, 33,* 187–196. doi:10.1016/j.adolescence.2009.03.011

Spagnola, M., & Fiese, B. H. (2007). Family routines and rituals: A context for development in the lives of young children. *Infants and Young Children, 20,* 284–299. doi:10.1097/01.IYC.0000290352.32170.5a

Walsh, F. (2003). Family resilience: A framework for clinical practice. *Family Process, 42,* 1–18. doi:10.1111/j.1545-5300.2003.00001.x

Warfield, M. E. (2005). Family and work predictors of parenting role stress among two-earner families of children with disabilities. *Infant and Child Development, 14,* 155–176. doi:10.1002/icd.

Wildenger, L. K., McIntyre, L. L., Fiese, B. H., & Eckert, T. L. (2008). Children's daily routines during kindergarten transition. *Early Childhood Education Journal, 36,* 69–74. doi:10.1007/s10643-008-0255-2

V

―――

Urban Factors

The Challenge of College Readiness

BY WILLIAM G. TIERNEY

A great deal of discussion has occurred about the need for the United States to increase the number of students who enter a postsecondary institution and graduate with the requisite skills necessary to assume good-paying jobs. The logic of such an assertion is clear and sound. The United States once led the world in the percentage of students who went to and graduated from college and now lags behind other industrialized countries (Lewin 2010). The estimate of the number of jobs in a decade's time that will require skills learned in college far exceeds the estimates of graduates from America's postsecondary institutions. By current estimates, California, for example, in 2025 will have over one million jobs that cannot be filled—especially in the fields of science and technology—because the public post-secondary sector will be unable to meet demand due to capacity constraints and a mismatch between the skills students acquire in college and those skills needed for the workforce (Johnson and Sengupta 2009). To be sure, not everyone needs a four-year college degree, but the assumption has been that simply graduating from high school is no longer good enough (see figure 14.1). Such a point is particularly important for discussions pertaining to education's role in alleviating poverty. By 2020, 39% of workers are projected to need a bachelor's degree to meet economic demand. By 2025, that figure will increase to 41%.

A related problem is that too many students graduate from high school who are not college ready. Roughly 60% of students must take a remedial class in English or math when they enter college, and the percentage is even higher for community college entrants (Bailey, Jeong, and Cho 2009; National Center for Public Policy and Higher Education 2010). The related costs to postsecondary institutions of paying for non-credit-bearing courses and the time involved for students in need of remedial education are considerable. And yet, we know that the lifetime earnings of someone who has a college degree is significantly higher than someone with a high school degree; we also know that during the last recession, unemployment for high school graduates was higher than those with college degrees (Carnevale, Rose, and Cheah 2013; Taylor et al. 2010).

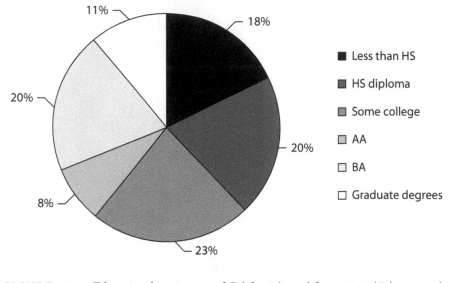

FIGURE 14.1   Educational attainment of California's workforce, 2010 (Johnson and Sengupta 2009)

The response to these issues has been twofold. On the one hand, President Obama, the Gates and Lumina Foundations, and numerous think tanks have issued calls for increasing college enrollment and decreasing the time it takes a student to graduate (Lumina Foundation 2013; White House n.d.). On the other hand, a great deal of discussion has been focused on creating a common core curriculum across the United States that will increase what students learn in high school so that they are better prepared for college. In this light, a common core curriculum might be considered a move toward "college for all," which is why some states have resisted the plans.

Nevertheless, the goals are straightforward and seemingly commonsensical: to increase the number of students attending college and to increase the number of students who graduate from high school college ready. The evidence demonstrates that college graduates earn more than high school graduates, which, in turn, increases tax revenues for states and the federal government (Tierney and Hentschke 2011). Presumably, if the country achieves its goal of having more college graduates, it will be stronger economically, socially, and civically. It will also be better able to face the myriad issues of the twenty-first century.

Such a goal has met with two critiques. First, many have pointed out that such goals are unattainable. The state of American secondary schools will be unable to improve the college readiness of the least ready, argue some, and even if they did, argue others, postsecondary institutions have been unable to increase college capacity by traditional means—building more campuses—and are largely unwilling to consider alternative devices (e.g., online learning) to increase capacity (Tierney and Hentschke 2011; see figure 14.2).

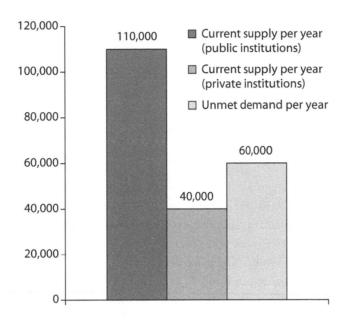

FIGURE 14.2.   Baccalaureates issued per year by California institutions: Current supply vs. demand (Tierney and Hentschke 2011)

Second, some, such as Richard Vedder (2012), have argued that there is no evidence that America needs more college graduates. Others have pointed to a credentialing phenomenon where people with advanced degrees are performing jobs that could be done by people with lesser credentials (Owen and Sawhill 2013). In effect, they are suggesting that rather than needing more college degrees, we need fewer. The assumption is that credentialing individuals drives up educational requirements that are entirely unnecessary to fill certain jobs.

As I elaborate in the following sections, both arguments have a degree of merit. The relationship between high schools and postsecondary institutions has been fraught with miscommunication for over a century. For example, only 10% of high school teachers believe that their students are not well prepared for college-level writing, as opposed to 44% of college faculty members (Sanoff 2006). High school teachers also believe that 63% of their graduating seniors are prepared for college-level coursework, while only 25% were shown to be college ready in ACT testing (Amelga 2012). Similarly, the capacity crisis in higher education has not occurred overnight; neither senior administrators nor faculty have offered long-term plans, however, that do not involve the state simply providing additional funds— something states will not do to a level necessary to meet demand.

The data that the credential proponents call upon are also true. A 2010 investigation of census data reveals that out of 41.7 million employed college graduates, 37% hold jobs that only require a high school degree (Vedder, Denhart, and Robe 2013). From this perspective, the country has workers who cannot find employment because better educated—not better qualified—workers have taken their positions. Moreover, new college-readiness requirements discourage students from taking career and technical education courses, and these requirements depress the ability of those who are trained for a particular job to find employment (Betts, Zau, and Bachofer 2013). From this perspective, it is less a need for more credentials and more a need to align skills with jobs.

Although these arguments are plausible, they also tend to miss the mark. Neither miscommunication nor an inability to increase capacity ought to suggest that the current situation is viable if it is not. If the country will be better off with more college graduates, ways need to be found that enable that to happen, either by policy directives at the state and federal level or through creative action on the part of P–12 schools and postsecondary institutions.

Data that show that some workers have assumed positions for which they are overqualified also does not take into account the fact that other positions are unfilled because of a lack of qualified workers. From this perspective, the problem is not that too many people have a college degree but that they have the wrong kind of degree. Whereas the United States has an urgent need for more individuals who hold degrees in science, technology, engineering, and math (STEM), it has an oversupply of individuals with other sorts of degrees. Those with other degrees may well have assumed positions for which they are overqualified, but they are unqualified for positions that require a bachelor's degree with a particular skill set. Thus, the country needs more college graduates with different degrees.

One question that has not been considered very much, which I turn to here, is a variation of the two critiques: how many high school students should not participate in the postsecondary sector? I wish to consider the consequences for those who do not go on to college. That is, although the data seem undeniable that more people need to participate in higher education, no one has suggested that everyone needs to attend college. The analysis of increasing access to higher education has been fine tuned to the degree that there is a good understanding of how many individuals will benefit from a four-year degree, how many need an associate of arts degree, and how many can get by simply with a postsecondary technical certificate. Such analyses not only help individuals consider what kind of skills they need for employment but also presumably can help the state develop an educational plan.

Such an understanding of the country's postsecondary needs is doubly useful. If one segment of the postsecondary sector only needs certificates, they should qualify for federal and state grants and loans, just like their advanced degree-seeking counter parts. However, such a projection also suggests that not everyone needs a four-year degree, or, for that matter, a two-year degree or postsecondary certificate. According to 2010 data, approximately 72% of the students who attend a postsecondary institution go to a public institution (U.S. Department of Education 2012). Virtually all students who demonstrate a financial need and who attend an accredited institution—public, private nonprofit, or for-profit—receive some form of financial aid (Tierney and Hentschke 2007). Coupled with state subsidies to public institutions, the public investment in higher education is considerable, although many suggest it is not enough.

But virtually no one suggests that public higher education should accommodate everyone who graduates from high school or has a GED. If the country was to support and fund postsecondary education in a manner akin to how public K–12 education is funded, the costs would be enormous. Recall my earlier comment in this chapter about California's situation. California needs to increase its college attainment rate from 31% to 41%, and an additional 20% need to have some form of postsecondary education (Johnson and Sengupta 2009). Such a goal accounts for 60% of high school graduates going on to college, and herein lies the problem I wish to consider in the remainder of this chapter.

A great deal of discussion has involved the need for increasing access to higher education, and it is fair to say that the policy-oriented dialogues have been largely supportive of such goals. The issues have revolved around what policies to take to enable the goals to be achieved. But what happens to those 40% of high school students in the United States who only need to graduate from high school? What becomes of them? Are we suggesting that a certain segment of society shall remain poor, even though additional educational avenues may lift them out of poverty? What are the consequences for them if the country enacts a "college for all" curriculum? And, perhaps most controversially, who decides which students need a college degree versus a high school degree?

Such questions are not only policy dilemmas but also go to the heart of how the country has defined education and democracy. The dilemma of individual achievement and communal responsibility has been an issue since the founding of the country. Accordingly, in what follows, I outline the educational issues surrounding a "college for all" curriculum for those who are least prepared. I consider the philosophical assumptions underpinning what should be learned in high school, even though those assumptions go unrealized. I then turn to a discussion of tracking to demonstrate historically who has gone to college and who has not, as well as who attends community colleges as opposed to four-year institutions. The data will be no surprise in the twenty-first century, but they stand in the way of an argument that says, all things being equal, anyone can go to college. I then contrast the data with how educational systems function in advanced, industrialized European countries to suggest an alternative model. I conclude not with a suggestion that one or another position is correct but that the current road we are on is untenable. As I elaborate later on, we must confront our philosophical inconsistencies before we are able to put forward strategic policies that help improve the country.

To advance this argument, I ground the discussion in delineating what happens to one hundred ninth grade students in California as a whole and in Los Angeles in particular.

The Philosophical Underpinnings of "College for All"

Assume one hundred students enter ninth grade. We know what happens to them now. An overrepresentation of students of color, first-generation, and low-income youth are less likely to graduate from high school and go on to college than Anglo and Asian, middle-and upper-class youth. Of those students who graduate from high school, an overrepresentation of middle-and upper-class, and Anglo and Asian students are more likely to go to a four-year institution than their low-income, first-generation Latino and African American counterparts.

Assume, however, that a degree of latitude exists, and the nefarious influence of tracking based on race and class is moot. What should be the assumption about the educational trajectory of those one hundred ninth grade students? Of related concern is who should determine that educational trajectory? Three primary philosophies undergird how one approaches these issues.

Individuals Have Equal Ability

One philosophic stance is that all children have equal ability if they are provided equal opportunity. From this perspective, if one hundred students enter ninth grade, and they are of unequal ability, it is because children have not been accorded equal opportunities. Those lacking quality educational experiences need to be provided with additional support to enable them to be on par with other children. If society provides adequate support, each child has the potential not only to graduate from high school but also to attend and graduate from a postsecondary institution.

The decision to go to college is made by the individual and his or her parents; that decision need not be made until the twelfth grade, although every opportunity should be afforded to children prior to their senior year so they are ready to apply. Society, as defined by the citizenry and taxpayers, should have a relatively insignificant role in sorting out who attends and who does not. Society has an obligation to pay for a student's education, but the assumption is that, as a public good, education should benefit all citizens equally. As opposed to other public goods, such as clean water or public safety, the assumption about education is that an individual's ability matters. There is no assumption that some people are better consumers of clean drinking water than others, or that how someone drinks water is variable. For other public goods, the quality of the consumer is irrelevant. The goal is to ensure that all individuals have access to the same quality drinking water.

Education, however, inevitably involves the user of the public good in a fundamentally different manner. The state not only needs to ensure that users have access to the public good, but, by ninth grade, if some students are lagging behind others, the state is obligated to provide the requisite resources to bring all students up to an acceptable level that enables them to graduate and, presumably, attend and graduate from a postsecondary institution. With other public goods, such as clean drinking water, the state does not need to train some users how to drink, or assume that some are better drinkers of water than others. Instead, the state simply needs to provide clean water to everyone.

Such an approach combines two public philosophies about the individual and the community. All individuals are alike, and the community's responsibility is to ensure not only equal opportunity but equal outcomes. The practical consequences of this approach are that a "college for all" curriculum should be implemented in all high schools. If all students can attend and succeed in college, the curriculum should be geared toward enabling every student to go to college.

Individuals Have Variable Ability (but Deserve Equal Opportunity)

A second philosophic stance is that those one hundred ninth graders are not all alike. Some are better qualified, as defined by standardized tests, grades, and teachers' judgments, than others. Consequently, some will graduate from high school and go to college, while others will not. However, all students should have the opportunity to attend college, and every effort should be made to enable participation in college. The result has been the creation of programs such as Upward Bound, Talent Search, and Math, Engineering, Science Achievement (MESA). Although many have questioned the effectiveness of such programs (e.g., Haskins and Rouse 2013), the assumption has been that all children need to be provided equal opportunity, which gets defined as the ability to go to college. Nevertheless, by the end of high school, if all students have been provided an equal opportunity, some will go to college and others will not. Moreover, some students will attend selective four-year institutions, whereas others will attend a two-year college; some will graduate with a bachelor's degree, whereas others will attain a postsecondary certificate. In some respects, the Master Plan in California (University of California 2007) was developed with this perspective in mind.

As with the previous stance, the individuals who determine whether a student goes to college are the student and his or her parents. However, where one goes is also shaped by tests that society has sanctioned by way of publicly supported institutions. How one performs on the tests is an indicator to the individual about what society is willing to pay. That is, one cannot simply decide to attend the postsecondary institution of his or her choice. Until twelfth grade, an individual has a great deal of leeway, but, ultimately, standardized tests will most likely be determinative.

Society's role is to enable equal opportunity via a tax structure that supports public education. Differentiation occurs, as judged by a student's ability, such that some will go to a community college and others to an elite four-year institution. The assumption has less to do with everyone having equal ability and more to do with the assurance that everyone has the opportunity to pursue whatever educational avenue they may desire, if they meet the requisite criteria.

This approach has two different stances about the individual and community. Individuals are different, but over time they will be able to sort out what they want to do. The community's responsibility is to ensure equal opportunities that will enable the individual to determine what to do. The result is that a "college for all" curriculum needs to be implemented in every school to ensure equal opportunity. When course offerings, such as Advanced Placement classes, the International Baccalaureate, and the like, are investigated, discrepancies will point out a lack of equal opportunity. What then needs to happen is to assure that students have the exact same educational opportunities. In Los Angeles, for example, what has come to be known as "A–G requirements" is a curricula aimed at students who desire to attend a postsecondary institution. Indeed, if a student successfully completes the A–G coursework, he or she must be admitted to a four-year institution. Until 2012, students had the option of not taking the A–G courses. With the vocal support of the school superintendent, the school board passed a motion in 2012 that stipulated, from 2014 onward, that all students will take the A–G curricula. Such a decision highlights the philosophy outlined here.

Individuals Have Variable Ability (and Should Be Tracked according to Their Ability)

A third philosophic stance is that the one hundred students have different abilities, and these abilities can be assessed by ninth grade. The standard way to determine intellectual difference is through standardized tests, grades, and teachers' evaluations. The result is ability grouping. Students are differentiated according to ability—some will take a college-focused curriculum, and others will take what used to be called vocational education, or a career-oriented curriculum. Thus, some students are expected to apply to four-year postsecondary institutions and receive a baccalaureate degree that prepares them for "white-collar" work, some will go to two-year community colleges for working-class jobs, and still others will only require a high school degree and find employment largely in the service sector.

Although hard work certainly plays a role in how this stance views ability, ultimately the assumption is that some are qualified and others are not. From this perspective, then, a desire to attend college should not play a role in the decision of who actually attends college. The arbiter is the school system, which interprets scores and tests for the state. The state's role is to ensure that the system is fair, equitable, efficient, and effective.

To be sure, the work of Howard Gardner (1993), following in the line of John Dewey (1916), offers a different interpretation. A case can be made that students do not have variable abilities but different abilities. Gardner and others reject standardized tests because they examine one form of intelligence rather than multiple forms. While there is much to be said for this line of work, the ideas have not been implemented. Indeed, high-stakes testing has taken on only increased importance over the last several years, which sorts students into those who are college bound and those who are not.

A long history exists about the misguided attempts to track students according to race, class, gender, and religion rather than ability. A considerable literature also exists about the limited successes of ability grouping (Ansalone 2001; Archbald and Farley-Ripple 2012). A fair amount of research, for example, suggests that high-ability students do just as well in mixed groups, and low-ability students do better in mixed groups rather than in a group of their peers. Others have pointed out the state's long history of privileging the children of the wealthy rather than the poor.

At the same time, the data presented earlier highlight the fact that although we need more people participating in higher education, we surely do not need everyone attending college. Literature also points out that a "college for all" curriculum is more likely to push students who are the least ready out of high school; courses that are oriented for students likely to attend college are also likely to bore students who have no desire to keep studying academic subjects (Rosenbaum, Stephan, and Rosenbaum 2010; Samuelson 2012).

The Consequences of Tracking and Detracking

Tracking

I have described philosophical positions that are absent, if possible, of ideology. That is, I have assumed that we live in a perfect world and put forward positions as if under lying issues such as racism, sexism, and classism do not exist. Absent the history of such issues, a policy analyst may suggest one of these philosophical stances and proceed to implement it. However, one need merely look at college admissions to discover the pernicious outcomes of ability grouping, or what has come to be known as tracking (Ansalone 2001; Oakes 1985, 1987).

The Master Plan for Higher Education in California is a useful case in point (Douglass 2011; Geiser and Atkinson 2013; University of California 2007). Enacted in 1960, the plan has been viewed as a prototype for other states and even foreign countries. Although many suggest that the plan is in need of an overhaul a half a century after its creation, the basic tenet has been widely lauded as a democratic ideal: if an individual wanted to attend a postsecondary institution, then the state would find a place for him or her in the public system. Such an idea is laudable, and moved the ideal of equity forward when the Plan was initiated, yet the implementation of the plan has not been free of the often-implicit, and occasionally explicit, consequences of discrimination.

Even today, for example, African Americans and Latinos are overrepresented in community colleges and underrepresented on the ten campuses of the University of California (UC). Similarly, the poor are overrepresented in two-year institutions and underrepresented at the UC. Within an institution, we also know that poor people of color and women tend to be underrepresented in high-status STEM fields and overrepresented in lower-status fields, such as education and nursing.

To be sure, one possible interpretation of such data is that the postsecondary sector sorts people out in a meritocratic manner. Indeed, a meritocracy is ostensibly what has driven American education for a century. The idea of a meritocracy is, in part, laudable. At the turn of the century, some postsecondary institutions implemented quotas so that they did not have an overrepresentation of Jews in their institutions. Hence, the assumption of a standardized test was that anonymity would sort people according to their ability, rather than by their religious affiliation. Over time, of course, the citizenry came to realize that if attending college was based solely on a standardized test, then some would be privileged and others harmed. As a corrective, programs such as Head Start and public policies such as affirmative action were created. Public policies that tend to help underperforming students have nevertheless come under attack and have largely been curtailed, underfunded, or eliminated.

Those who call for a return to a meritocracy never really face the probable outcome, however. Assumptions that individuals have variable ability and should be tracked accordingly will likely vary by race, income, and gender. That is, the trends that have occurred in a society that has given lip service to the idea that everyone should have equal opportunity are likely to be exacerbated. No one seriously would believe, for example, that equal percentages of poor and upper-class students will be taking Advanced Placement classes, even if they should in theory. Insofar as schools are embedded in a society that provides inherent advantages to some and disadvantages to others, the likely result is that the poor and students of color will be even more overrepresented among non-college-goers, as well as at less elite institutions in the postsecondary sector.

Indeed, even though the most pernicious effects of tracking have ended, many will argue that structural tracking remains (Lucas 1999). From this perspective, the overt placement policies of the 1960s and 1970s that cordoned off educational opportunity for the poor and students of color have largely ended. As Lucas (1999) points out, "Chicago schools used a four-track system composed of honors, regular, essential, and basic programs. All students were assigned to one of the four tracks, and that track assignment determined students' courses" (6). Investigations of this sort of assignment underscored how students in largely middle-and upper-class neighborhoods received one kind of curricula, while students in poorer neighborhoods received another. Although formal segmentation has ended, careful analyses have pointed out how structural inequality enables it to continue; in effect, a hidden curriculum has replaced what was once demonstrably clear. Advanced Placement classes in low-income neighborhoods, for example, may now exist. However, the number of students in those neighborhoods who actually take Advanced Placement tests, much less receive scores high enough to get college credit, is less than half of the number in upper-class neighborhoods.

Others have argued that those who are tracked fall within an "oppositional culture" (Ogbu 2008). According to this position, minority students assume that succeeding in high school conforms to the majority culture and that academic advancement requires Black and Latino students to "act white." Even though this thesis is provocative (and some students may adhere to such an idea), the careful work of Angel Harris (2011) and others has largely debunked the notion of an "oppositional culture." The Black-White achievement gap, he argues, can be more likely attributed to opportunity rather than to any internalized oppression on the part of students of color. In effect, tracking by way of a hidden curriculum in low-achieving schools is what stymies educational opportunity.

Detracking

An alternative view has to do with the consequences of assuming that everyone should take a "college for all" curriculum. Students currently enter ninth grade with varying abilities. In the past, students had varying opportunities to choose college-preparation curricula, but the assumption of "college for all" is that every student—all one hundred students in my hypothetical model—will take such a curriculum. In effect, success in high school gets defined as being prepared for college. Research has shown, however, that a "college for all" curriculum actually may increase the dropout rate in schools (Berliner 2006; Rosenbaum et al. 2010; Rumberger 2011). It is also true, as noted earlier, that all jobs will not require a college certificate or degree (Carnevale, Smith, and Strohl 2010). The result is that an increasing number of scholars have questioned a one-size-fits-all curricular model that expects all students to be prepared to go to college (Symonds, Schwartz, and Ferguson 2011).

Conversely, a fair amount of research questions the utility of a "college for all" curriculum (Roderick, Nagaoka, and Coca 2009). Underperforming students are also at risk of being pushed out of the traditional school system if they do not do well on high-stakes tests (Lin 2006). The San Jose Unified School District, for example, mandated a college preparatory curriculum; the result was that Black and Latino students were disproportionately moved to alternative high schools (Lin 2006). Others point out that at a time when technology and social media have vastly broadened options—consider how citizens receive news and information—that to offer fewer options in education seems wrongheaded.

Many argue that career and technical education increases attendance rates, decreases dropout rates, and improves high school completion rates (Balfanz and Byrnes 2012; Bishop and Mane 2004). As I elaborate in the following paragraphs, international comparisons demonstrate that countries with variable curricular options, including vocational education, have higher completion rates than the United States (Cardoza 2012). From this perspective, then, the curricula of other industrialized countries should be adopted in our schools.

If a potpourri of options exists, the likelihood that students will graduate from high school and assume a variety of careers may increase. One example that Russell Rumberger (2011) has pointed out is Big Picture Learning High Schools. In these schools, Rumberger notes that "learning is tailored to the interests and goals of each student and pursued through a combination of individualized school-based and work-based learning experiences" (272). The point is not merely that students have multiple curricular options but that their graduation is dependent upon what they need to know in their areas of interest. A student who wants to study physics, for example, will not only have a very different curriculum from a student who wishes to be a chef, but what the future physicist needs to master to graduate from college will differ from what someone who wishes to be a chef will need to master. This approach assumes that noncognitive skills (e.g., motivation, grit, time management) are as important as cognitive skills for some students (Heckman, Stixrud, and Urzua 2006). Thus, rather than assume that ability grouping tracks students into a dichotomy of "haves" and "have-nots," this approach argues that, in the twenty-first century, multiple career paths need to be open to students. A one-size-fits-all curriculum is not only wrong for the job market of the twenty-first century but also may increase the dropout rate and drive students away from successful educational opportunities and job employability.

At the same time, "multiple paths" also need to mean the same thing in different locales. Children of the middle and upper classes are not often introduced to career paths in the vocational and service sectors, for example, or encouraged to attend a community college. If by "multiple paths" all that occurs is that children in low-income neighborhoods have a few additional opportunities that are regularly afforded to all children in upper-income families, then very little will change. One of the challenges for the poor is that they frequently are not able to see the sorts of career opportunities that exist. The potential exists that greater curricular offerings can broaden horizons and, in doing so, educational and economic opportunity.

A European Alternative to "College for All"

The United States has had a long history of the twin ideas of American exceptionalism and individual ability. Indeed, since the founding of the country, a discourse has developed around the idea that America is unique and that an individual can do whatever he or she desires if the government does not intrude. Such an assumption, in part, has led to the idea that everyone should have the same opportunity for college. Furthermore, if individuals have the same opportunity, they "will be all they can be," to paraphrase a popular jingle. One alternative, however, is how education and opportunity have been conceived in Germany and other European countries.

Comparative data with OECD countries highlight how America's current educational structure is neither exceptional nor geared for individual opportunity. Youth unemployment is higher, and the number of youth in stable employment five years after leaving education is lower than in other advanced industrialized economies (Hoffman 2011, 3). One assumption that European countries and the United States share is that youth with low skills and low educational levels are at risk. As outlined earlier, the countries diverge with regard to America's position vis-à-vis educational opportunity and Europe's specific policies aimed at vocational training for youth. Such training links education to labor market needs and includes workplace learning. Students in high schools in Germany go outside the school to be trained for specific skills in the workplace that will enable them to assume a career.

The integration of work and learning is something that has been critiqued quite severely in the United States, in large part because of a history of discrimination against particular groups of individuals—racial and ethnic minorities, in particular. A great deal of research has pointed out how individuals in the early twentieth century were trained for the workforce in a manner that suggested the purpose of education was to make individuals submissive workers (Bowles and Gintis 1976). Such a critique suggested that the schooling that America provided ran counter to the ethos of individualism. The same line of research continued through the 1980s, where the important work by Jeannie Oakes (1987) on tracking highlighted how ability grouping largely failed, and those who were tracked were the same sort of individuals who were tracked at the start of the century—students of color.

European countries also have been concerned with tracking. It is worth quoting Nancy Hoffman (2011) at length here:

> Concern about the potentially pernicious effects of early tracking continues to preoccupy the OECD countries. They keep data and are sensitive to the relationship between parental education and income and schools results. ... Tracking takes two forms in the OECD countries: in Austria, Germany, Switzerland, and the Netherlands students choose or are placed into a vocational or academic pathway between the ages of 10 and 12. The Nordic countries and Australia have comprehensive schools through the end of lower secondary school, with everyone following the same curriculum. Then at age 15 students and their families have a choice of a university or vocational pathway. (18)

Although European countries attempt to avoid the sorts of tracking that concern those in the United States, the outcomes remain relatively the same. Three differences, however, exist between the United States and a country such as Switzerland or Germany. First, those who are tracked find jobs and careers, rather than dropping out or being unemployed, as is frequently the case in the United States in the twenty-first century. Second, wages for the working class tend to be higher in European countries than in the United States; one of America's problems is the huge discrepancy in wages and income. Third, the apprentice-ships and traineeships offered in Europe are more advanced than what was once defined as vocational education. In Europe, high-tech, cutting-edge training tends to be part of the vocational framework rather than part of tertiary education.

Here's how the German apprenticeship model works. Students are apprentices at an employer four days a week; they are in school only one day a week. As in the United States, this form of training is free, and the training lasts about three years. The employer pays minimum wage for the students, and they provide on-the-job training. But they also have a say in what the curricula and training should be. When the training is over, the student and the employer can continue the job, but neither the student nor employer is stuck with the other. The engagement between school and businesses is quite firm and set in a way that is rare in the United States. As one observer of the training that Germany provides has commented, "On-the-job training is likely the biggest lever America can pull to close the skills gap. Sadly, only a handful of American companies operate anything resembling an apprenticeship program" (University Ventures 2013, 2).

In a school-to-work system, employers play a significant role in what students learn and how they are trained. They also may pay for part of the training or apprenticeship. Such a relationship has frequently been resisted in the United States, in part because of a fear that a corporate agenda would train "workers" in a manner that would make them compliant. Although one may agree with such sentiments, a sustained and systemic relationship with school systems and employers is largely absent in the United States. The result is that America's college graduates leave school without being prepared for a particular career. Two-thirds of all Germans, however, have an occupational qualification by the time they are twenty (Hoffman 2011, 100).

My purpose here is neither to give an extended exegesis on German education nor to suggest that such a model is perfect. In Europe, for example, there tends to be an overreliance on a single indicator, such as performance on a standardized test. However, as Norton Grubb (2008) and others have noted (Grubb and Lazerson 2012), viable alternatives exist to the increasingly common assumption that all one hundred ninth graders should be prepared and go to college, and if they do not, either something is wrong with the system or something is wrong with them. As Ben Levin and Lauren Segedin (2011) have noted, "Studying what other systems do is a worthwhile activity not because it gives us answers, but because it gives us questions and ideas. … It tells us that there are other ways to get to a goal and broadens our thinking about what these might be" (7). Hence, a variety of possibilities might exist that actually better serve the populace and the individual than the assumption that everyone should go to college.

The reasons for dropping out of high school tend to be similar across countries and schools—academic ability, boredom, a lack of relevant curricula, and personal problems, to name a few—but the solutions to resolving these problems differ. Countries other than the United States have a viable alternative to mainstream education geared toward college preparation. Linkages to the labor market and a career get set early in a child's schooling in Europe, whereas career-based discussions, in the United States, largely take place in postsecondary education.

Conclusion

This is a text without a conclusion, or, at least, I am unconvinced of the appropriate solution, much less what the appropriate policies might be to advance a solution that pertains centrally to our theme of rethinking education and poverty. The United States is on the horns of a dilemma. Unquestionably, the country needs to make dramatic strides in improving access to higher education. More students need to be college ready, and more students need to graduate from two-and four-year institutions. But roughly 40% of the population does not need to attend higher education. This population's attendance will neither raise overall wages nor employment, and the citizenry cannot afford the revenue necessary for everyone to participate in higher education. Additionally, a college preparation curriculum is likely to increase dropout rates in high school.

However, the history of in e quality that has existed in the United States is likely to ensure certain outcomes. The poor, students of color, and other historically marginalized populations would likely be overrepresented in the non-college-going populations. The pervasive strength of those among the entitled classes will surely strengthen social capital for their children (Bourdieu 1986), whereas college-going networks will not be so strong in low-income neighborhoods.

A country that prides itself on the idea of educational opportunity needs to come to grips not simply with schooling, but with wealth inequality. In a fair society where people are paid similar wages, attending college would not be nearly as critical as it is today. College-educated workers earn almost twice as much an hour as their high school–educated counter parts (Tierney and Hentschke 2011). Education has long been seen as a route out of poverty and into the middle class. But it seems clear that education also should prepare people for a wide array of careers and citizenship. There has recently been a great deal of discussion about measuring academic readiness for college (Maruyama 2012; Porter and Polikoff 2012). To be sure, what one needs to succeed in college must be investigated and refined. But perhaps an additional priority ought to be a fulsome discussion about what the opportunities should be when students graduate from high school and how these opportunities might be more closely targeted to particular careers and employment. Such a discussion also needs to be linked to a larger conversation in the country about wealth disparities and how to reduce income in equality.

Acknowledgments

The author wishes to thank Shaun Harper, Adrianna Kezar, James Minor, and Laura Perna for helpful comments on an earlier draft of this chapter.

References

Amelga, Makeda. 2012. *College and Career Readiness: A Quick Stats Fact Sheet*. Washington, DC: National High School Center at the American Institutes for Research. http://www.businessweek.com/articles/2012-04-09/why-college-isnt-for-everyone.

Ansalone, George. 2001. "Schooling, Tracking, and Inequality." *Journal of Children and Poverty* 7 (1): 33–49.

Archbald, Doug, and Elizabeth Farley-Ripple. 2012. "Predictors of Placement in Lower Level versus Higher Level High School Mathematics." *High School Journal* 96 (1): 33–51.

Bailey, Thomas, Dong Wook Jeong, and Sung-Woo Cho. 2009. *Referral, Enrollment, and Completion in Developmental Education Sequences in Community Colleges* (CCRC Working Paper No. 15). New York: Teachers College, Columbia University.

Balfanz, Robert, and Vaughan Byrnes. 2012. *The Importance of Being in School: A Report on Absenteeism in the Nation's Public Schools*. Baltimore: Johns Hopkins University Center for Social Organization of Schools.

Berliner, David C. 2006. "Our Impoverished View of Educational Reform." *Teachers College Record* 108 (6): 949–95.

Betts, Julian R., Andrew C. Zau, and Karen Volz Bachofer. 2013. *College Readiness as a Graduation Requirement: An Assessment of San Diego's Challenges*. San Francisco: Public Policy Institute of California. http://www.ppic.org/main/publication.asp?i=1049.

Bishop, John H., and Ferran Mane. 2004. *Raising Academic Standards and Vocational Concentrators: Are they Better Off or Worse Off?* (CAHRS Working Paper No. 04-12). Ithaca, NY: Cornell University, School of Industrial and Labor Relations, Center for Advanced Human Resource Studies. http://digitalcommons.ilr.cornell.edu/cahrswp/16/.

Bourdieu, Pierre. 1986. "The Forms of Capital." In *Handbook of Theory and Research for the Sociology of Education*, edited by J. G. Richardson. 241–58. New York: Greenwood Press.

Bowles, Samuel, and Herbert Gintis. 1976. *Schooling in Capitalist America: Educational Reform and the Contradictions of Economic Life*. New York: Basic Books.

Cardoza, Kavitha. 2012. "Graduation Rates Increase around the Globe as U.S. Plateaus." *American University Radio*. February 21. http://wamu.org/news/morning_edition/12/02/21/graduation_rates_increase_around_the_globe_as_us_plateaus.

Carnevale, Anthony P., Stephen J. Rose, and Ban Cheah. 2013. *The College Payoff: Education, Occupations, Lifetime Earnings*. Washington, DC: Georgetown University Center on Education and the Workforce.

Carnevale, Anthony P., Nicole Smith, and Jeff Strohl. 2010. *Help Wanted: Projections of Jobs and Education Requirements through 2018.* Washington, DC: Center for Education and the Workforce, Georgetown University. http://cew.georgetown.edu/jobs2018/.

Dewey, John. 1916. *Democracy and Education: An Introduction to the Philosophy of Education.* New York: Macmillan.

Douglass, John Aubrey. 2011. "Revisionist Reflections on California's Master Plan at 50." *California Journal of Politics and Policy* 3 (1): 1–36.

Gardner, Howard. 1993. *Multiple Intelligences: New Horizons in Theory and Practice.* New York: Basic Books.

Geiser, Saul, and Richard C. Atkinson. 2013. "Beyond the Master Plan: The Case for Restructuring Baccalaureate Education in California." *California Journal of Politics and Policy* 4 (1): 67–123.

Grubb, W. Norton. 2008. "Challenging the Deep Structure of High School: Weak and Strong Versions of Multiple Pathways." In *Beyond Tracking: Multiple Pathways to College, Career, and Civic Participation*, edited by Jeannie Oakes and Marisa Saunders, 197–212. Cambridge, MA: Harvard Education Press.

Grubb, W. Norton, and Marvin Lazerson. 2012. "The Education Gospel and Vocationalism in U.S. Higher Education: Triumphs, Tribulations, and Cautions for Other Countries." In *Work and Education in America*, edited by Antje Barabasch and Felix Rauner, 101–21. New York: Springer.

Harris, Angel L. 2011. *Kids Don't Want to Fail: Oppositional Culture and the Black-White Achievement Gap.* Cambridge, MA: Harvard University Press.

Haskins, Ron, and Cecilia Elena Rouse. 2013. *Time for Change: A New Federal Strategy to Prepare Disadvantaged Students for College.* Prince ton, NJ: Princeton University-Brookings Institute. http://www.brookings.edu/research/papers/2013/05/07-disadvantaged-students-college-readiness-haskins.

Heckman, James J., Jora Stixrud, and Sergio Urzua. 2006. "The Effects of Cognitive and Noncognitive Abilities on Labor Market Outcomes and Social Behavior." *Journal of Labor Economics* 24 (3): 411–82.

Hoffman, Nancy. 2011. *Schooling in the Workplace.* Cambridge, MA: Harvard Education Press.

Johnson, Hans, and Ria Sengupta. 2009. *Closing the Gap: Meeting California's Need for College Graduates.* San Francisco: Public Policy Institute of California. http://www.ppic.org/main/publication.asp?i=835.

Levin, Ben, and Lauren Segedin. 2011. *International Approaches to Secondary Education.* Toronto, Canada: Higher Education Quality Council of Ontario.

Lewin, Tamar. 2010. "Once a Leader, U.S. Lags in College Degrees." *New York Times.* July 23. http://www.nytimes.com/2010/07/23/education/23college.html.

Lin, Barbara. 2006. *Access to A–G Curriculum at San Jose Unified School District. Center for Latino Policy Research Brief* 2 (1): 1–2. http://escholarship.org/uc/item/92k987pp. Lucas, Samuel R. 1999. *Tracking Inequality: Stratification and Mobility in American High Schools.* New York: Teachers College Press.

Lumina Foundation. 2013. *A Stronger Nation through Higher Education.* http://www.luminafoundation.org/stronger_nation/.

Maruyama, Geoffrey. 2012. "Assessing College Readiness: Should we be Satisfied with ACT or other Threshold Scores?" *Educational Researcher* 41 (7): 252–61.

National Center for Public Policy and Higher Education. 2010. *Beyond the Rhetoric: Improving College Readiness through Coherent State Policy*. http://www.highereducation.org/reports/college_readiness/CollegeReadiness.pdf.

Oakes, Jeannie. 1985. *Keeping Track: How Schools Structure Inequality*. New Haven, CT: Yale University Press.

—. 1987. "Tracking in Secondary Schools: A Contextual Perspective." *Educational Psychologist* 22 (2): 129–53.

Ogbu, John U., ed. 2008. *Minority Status, Oppositional Culture, and Schooling*. New York: Routledge.

Owen, Stephanie, and Isabel V. Sawhill. 2013. *Should Everyone Go to College?* Washington, DC: Brookings Institute.

Porter, Andrew C., and Morgan S. Polikoff. 2012. "Measuring Academic Readiness for College." *Educational Policy* 26 (3): 394–417.

Roderick, Melissa, Jenny Nagaoka, and Vanessa Coca. 2009. "College Readiness for All: The Challenge for Urban High Schools." *Future of Children* 19 (1): 185–210.

Rosenbaum, James E., Jennifer L. Stephan, and Janet E. Rosenbaum. 2010. "Beyond One-Size-Fits-All College Dreams: Alternative Pathways to Desirable Careers." *American Educator* 34 (3): 2–13.

Rumberger, Russell W. 2011. *Dropping Out: Why Students Drop Out of High School and What Can Be Done about It*. Cambridge, MA: Harvard University Press.

Samuelson, Robert J. 2012. "It's Time to Drop the College-for-All Crusade." *Washington Post*. May 27. http://articles.washingtonpost.com/2012-05-27/opinions/35456501_1_college-students-josipa-roksa-private-colleges-and-universities.

Sanoff, Alvin P. 2006. "A Perception Gap Over Students' Preparation." *Chronicle of Higher Education*. March 10. http://chronicle.com/article/A-Perception-Gap-Over/31426.

Symonds, William C., Robert B. Schwartz, and Ronald Ferguson. 2011. *Pathways to Prosperity: Meeting the Challenge of Preparing Young Americans for the 21st Century*. Cambridge, MA: Harvard University Graduate School of Education. http://dash.harvard.edu/bitstream/handle/1/4740480/Pathways_to_Prosperity_Feb2011-1.pdf?sequence=1.

Taylor, Paul, Rich Morin, Rakesh Kochlar, Kim Parker, D'Vera Cohn, Mark Lopez, Richard Fry, Wendy Wang, Gabriel Velasco, Daniel Dockterman, Rebecca Hinze-Pifer, and Soledad Espinosa. 2010. *How the Great Recession Has Changed Life in America*. Washington, DC: Pew Research Center.

Tierney, William G., and Guilbert C. Hentschke. 2007. *New Players, Different Game: Understanding the Rise of For-Profit Colleges and Universities*. Baltimore: Johns Hopkins University Press.

—. 2011. *Making It Happen: Increasing College Access and Attainment in California Higher Education*. La Jolla, CA: National University System Institute for Policy Research.

University of California. 2007. *Major Features of the California Master Plan for Higher Education*. Oakland, CA: Author. http://www.ucop.edu/acadinit/mastplan/mpsummary.htm.

University Ventures. 2013. "The Skills Gap and the Spit-Take." *UV Letters* 3 (21). http://universityventuresfund.com/publications.php?title=the-skills-gap-and-the-spit-take.

U.S. Department of Education. 2012. *Fall Enrollment Survey*. Washington, DC: National Center for Education Statistics, Integrated Postsecondary Education Data System. http://nces.ed.gov/programs/projections/projections2021/tables/table_20.asp.

Vedder, Richard. 2012. "Why College Isn't for Everyone." *Bloomberg Businessweek*. April 9. http://www.
businessweek.com/articles/2012-04-09/why-college-isnt-for-everyone.

Vedder, Richard, Christopher Denhart, and Jonathan Robe. 2013. *Why Are Recent College Graduates Underemployed? University Enrollments and Labor-Market Realities*. Washington, DC: Center for College Affordability and Productivity. http://centerforcollegeaffordability.org/uploads/Underemployed%20Report%202.pdf.

White House. (n.d.). "Higher Education." http://www.whitehouse.gov/issues/education/higher-education.

Educating Homeless and Highly Mobile Students

Implications of Research on Risk and Resilience

BY ANN S. MASTEN, ARIA E. FIAT, MADELYN H. LABELLA,
AND RYAN A. STRACK

S chools in many districts across the United States have seen a dramatic increase in the numbers of students experiencing homelessness over the past 3 decades. Rates of homelessness among families with children and youth increased sharply in the 1980s and 1990s and then surged again with the onset of the Great Recession during the first decade of the 21st century. The federal response to the crisis of homelessness in children included enactment of the McKinney-Vento Homeless Assistance Act (reauthorized under the No Child Left Behind Act; see Samuels, Shinn, & Buckner, 2010, for this history). McKinney-Vento legislation, intended to address the educational challenges of homeless students, guaranteed homeless students the right to enroll in school immediately; to attend their school of origin if that is preferred and feasible; to receive transportation for school and educational services comparable to other students; and to not be stigmatized or segregated on the basis of their homeless status. The law established funding and procedures for the appointment of a local homeless education liaison for every public school district, as well as a state coordinator. The law also mandated that the numbers of children and youth enrolled in school would be collected by state and local agencies and compiled by the National Center for Homeless Education, which operates the U.S. Department of Education's (ED's) technical assistance and information center for its Education of Homeless Children and Youth Program.

Schools around the country, particularly in urban districts, continue to face many challenges in meeting the needs of students who experience homelessness. In 2010–2011, over 1 million students were identified as homeless under the ED criteria, a 13% increase over the previous year, and in 2012–2013, that number reached 1,240,925 (National Center for Homeless Education, 2014). ED defines homeless individuals as those "who lack a fixed, regular, and adequate nighttime residence," including children and youth living in shelters, motels, or vehicles or at campgrounds; on the street; or in abandoned buildings or other inadequate situations or who are doubled up because of loss of housing, economic hardship, or similar reasons; as well as those awaiting foster placement (see U.S. Code, Title 42, Chapter 119, Subchapter I, § 11302). The ED definition is similar to, but broader than, the definition used by Housing and Urban Development (HUD); unlike HUD, ED includes individuals who are doubled up.

The educational success of homeless children has been a central focus of the first author's research program for more than 20 years in collaboration with regional school districts and shelter providers (Masten et al., 2014). In this commentary, we provide an overview of this research on educational risks and resilience of homeless and highly mobile (HHM) students in the context of additional research on school adjustment in homeless children. In the first section we describe the high cumulative risk faced by homeless children and the persistent achievement disparities our research has revealed. In the second section we highlight findings on the promotive and protective factors associated with school readiness and success in school. In the final section we discuss the translational applications of our findings, with a particular focus on implications for school psychology practice and policy, as well as directions for future research.

High on a Continuum of Risk

Early research on children experiencing homelessness focused on the high prevalence of health, educational, and behavioral problems seen in this population (Masten, 1992; Rafferty & Shinn, 1991). Children who were homeless (with or without their families) shared many of the risk factors often observed in circumstances of extreme poverty, along with the additional challenges of residential instability, including school mobility. Associated risks included sociodemographic risk factors (e.g., single-parent households, low maternal education, unemployed parents) and adverse life experiences (e.g., child maltreatment, domestic violence, divorce, loss or separation from parents, incarcerated parent, foster care).

Early studies compared risk levels of children living with families in shelters with those of children from a similar socioeconomic background who were not currently homeless. Results showed considerable overlap in adversities but suggested that homeless families had experienced more cumulative risk, particularly in relation to recent stressful life events and financial problems. In our first study of families residing in an emergency shelter, we conducted a survey of parents and their 8- to 17-year-old children (Masten, Miliotis, Graham-Bermann, Ramirez, & Neemann, 1993). We compared data from questionnaires completed by 93 parents and 159 children in the shelter with data from 53 families with 62 children from a very low-income housed comparison group recruited to match the sheltered sample on sociodemographic background. The two groups differed significantly on family income, with homeless families reporting significantly lower incomes than their housed counterparts. An interesting finding was that 10% of the housed sample reported they had previously been homeless, suggesting these two samples likely shared risk for homelessness. Rates of lifetime adverse experiences looked very similar between the two groups, with the exception that the homeless sample of children had changed schools significantly more often. In contrast, large differences were found in the number of recent (past 12 months) stressful life events reported by parents and adolescents in the homeless sample compared with the housed sample, underscoring the surge in adverse life events associated with homelessness. Children in the homeless sample reported having fewer friends and spending less time with friends, and they also were more likely to expect they would live in a shelter as adults. Both samples, homeless and housed, had elevated scores on a measure of externalizing problems. In the combined samples, high cumulative chronic risk exposure, recent life events, and parent distress predicted more internalizing and externalizing problems. Housing status did not have unique effects once these other risk factors were accounted for, suggesting that homelessness functioned as a marker of high cumulative risk.

The pattern of results from this study suggested an underlying continuum of risk, with children staying in shelters at greater risk than their housed low-income peers. Subsequent data and reviews have continued to support that conclusion (Bassuk, Richard, & Tsertsvadze, 2015; Brumley, Fantuzzo, Perlman, & Zager, 2015; Samuels et al., 2010).

Educational Risk

From the beginning, evidence on risks associated with homelessness in children raised concerns about education. Early evidence indicated that in addition to many risk factors for academic and behavioral problems shared by other impoverished children, homeless students had additional challenges related to repeated school changes, frequent absences, and other barriers to school access (Masten, 1992; McChesney, 1993; Molnar, 1988; Rafferty & Rollins, 1989). Children experiencing homelessness often had high rates of grade retention and school mobility and lower than average grades or test scores. For example, in our first study (Masten et al., 1993), we found that 38% of homeless children aged 8 to 17 years had repeated a grade, and they changed schools more frequently than currently housed low-income peers in the comparison group. Another of our early studies, which focused on achievement in homeless African American children (who represented the majority of children staying in shelters in the region), found that 80% of the children aged 6 to 11 years scored in the bottom quartile on a standardized test (Masten et al., 1997). In addition, scores based on the individual testing in this study were strongly related to school records of achievement and classroom teacher ratings of behavior.

Findings From Administrative Data on Achievement Disparities

The services mandated by the McKinney-Vento Homeless Assistance Act led to substantial improvements in access to education for children experiencing homelessness (Miller, 2011). The requirements for reporting on the numbers of homeless children attending school also resulted in important new opportunities for analysis of administrative data.

The Minneapolis Public Schools (MPS) were among the many districts that responded to McKinney-Vento requirements by appointing a homeless liaison, establishing a reliable system for identifying HHM students, and boosting services for HHM students. As part of its routine responsibilities, the MPS Research, Evaluation, and Assessment Department (REA) also administered standardized testing in reading and mathematics. To track educational progress of individuals and the school population as a whole, REA adopted tests designed for growth analyses to document year-to-year growth. By the 2003–2004 school year, all testing and tracking procedures were in place to accumulate reliable data year over year.

A collaborative team, including REA leadership and statisticians and the HHM liaison, as well as faculty and graduate students from the University of Minnesota, began to analyze these data in de-identified form to understand the big picture of risk and resilience and to inform practices and policies designed to meet the needs of HHM students. The findings not only showed striking risk gradients but also highlighted the variability in and resilience among children who were identified as HHM under federal guidelines.

Our first set of analyses of administrative data drew on testing results across three school years (2003–2004 to 2005–2006). It was fortuitous that the district switched from testing each spring (2004, 2005) to fall testing (2005), which made it possible to examine the infamous effect of summer vacation on learning. Alexander, Entwisle, and Olson (2001) previously found that the summer effect was more pronounced for low–socioeconomic status (SES) children, and we expected to see similar patterns in the administrative data. For this study, four cohorts of students were studied separately based on their grade at Time 1; scores were available for students beginning in second, third, fourth, and fifth grade over the three time points (Obradović et al., 2009). On the basis of administrative data on HHM status and National School Lunch Program (NSLP) eligibility each year, three mutually exclusive groups were formed to study cumulative risk: HHM (all children who were identified at any time in the study window under McKinney-Vento guidelines); low income (eligible for reduced-price or free meals but not identified as HHM at any time during the study window); and advantaged or low risk (never identified by the district as HHM or receiving NSLP benefits; i.e., all other students).

As reported by Obradović et al. (2009), we used linear mixed models to study intraindividual growth in achievement over time with these data. School records also provided important data on common covariates of achievement such as gender, attendance, special education placement, English language learner (ELL) status, and racial or ethnic identity, which allowed us to account for and study their role. Overall, these covariates showed expected links to achievement (e.g., better attendance was associated with better achievement). Even with these covariates controlled, findings indicated substantial achievement gaps between advantaged and disadvantaged students, as well as a significant gap between the low-income and HHM groups, consistent with the expected continuum of risk. These differences were evident both in reading and in mathematics beginning in second grade, and the gaps did not close, instead sometimes widening over time. A classic summer effect was observed for all students, with a larger summer effect for low-SES students (including the HHM group). Consistent with study hypotheses, low-SES students showed almost no gains during the summer and often showed declines.

In our next analysis of achievement growth across different levels of risk, we were able to analyze data spanning five testing periods (fall 2005 to fall 2009), using all the test data available for students in third through eighth grades, when the same tests were administered in this district (Cutuli et al., 2013). We again used growth modeling to study intraindividual learning, but this time, we used an accelerated longitudinal design to combine all of the data into growth curves spanning third to eighth grades in reading and mathematics. We also divided the NSLP-eligible students into two groups, reflecting those who qualified for free lunch at any point during the study window and those who qualified for reduced-price meals but not free lunch. Thus, for this project, we compared four groups, again expecting a continuum of risk.

Results of the Cutuli et al. (2013) analyses showed dramatic achievement disparities. The results for mathematics are displayed in Figure 15.1. Beginning in third grade, the HHM group showed significantly lower achievement on average than all other groups, with achievement gaps persisting or widening over time. Scores were consistent with the hypothesized continuum of risk: The free-lunch group had lower achievement than the group receiving reduced-price lunch, which in turn scored lower than the general group. There was a notable difference between the two groups eligible for different levels of NSLP benefits. The group qualifying for reduced-price lunch (eligibility based on family income from 130% to 185% of the federal poverty line) but not free lunch (<130% of the poverty line) tracked the national norm reference point on this test quite closely. In contrast, the free-lunch group had much lower scores and, similar to the HHM group, showed a growing achievement gap in math among the later grades.

Another notable finding from this analysis was the sheer number of students identified as HHM over the 6-year window for the administrative data used to designate group status. Close to 14% of the students in this study fell into the HHM group based on cumulative data. Moreover, risk associated with HHM status was chronic and persistent. Children in the HHM group, regardless of when the identification occurred, showed significantly lower achievement in math and reading beginning in the first year of testing in third grade and persisting in ensuing years.

We also found evidence of acute risk, suggesting academic problems may increase around the time of homeless episodes. Students generally achieved at lower levels in years immediately after identification as HHM compared with their achievement at other times. In addition, the growth rate for mathematics, but not for reading, slowed for individual children in the year after identification as HHM. Although both mathematics and reading were affected by chronic risks associated with HHM status, mathematics appeared to be particularly sensitive to the acute disruptions to learning that may accompany residential instability and stresses of homelessness.

Similar to findings from the previous study, achievement differences associated with risk level were marked and significant when gender, ELL status, special education, and ethnicity

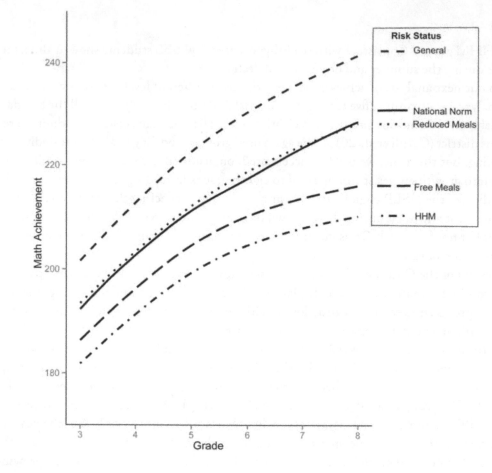

FIGURE 15.1   **Achievement trajectories based on growth analyses**

Note. Achievement trajectories are shown for mathematics scores on a standardized test for 26,474 students, with pooling of data from five consecutive assessments (fall 2005 to 2009). The average observed scores for the four groups, as well as the national average score, are shown. HHM = homeless and highly mobile. Reprinted with permission from Wiley-Blackwell from *Child Development* by Cutuli et al. (2013). Copyright 2012 by Cutuli et al. and Society for Research in Child Development.

were controlled (Cutuli et al., 2013). The homeless group had lower attendance overall than all other groups.

Recent research drawing on administrative data from another urban school district confirms the value of administrative data for studying educational risk. Brumley et al. (2015) used an integrated data system to analyze the risks for educational problems in a large cohort of first-grade children. Results corroborated earlier evidence of higher levels of specific risks and cumulative risk exposure in the group that had experienced homelessness (defined conservatively by a history of staying in a shelter) compared with housed low-income peers. Homelessness was associated with numerous well-established risk factors for child development, including birth problems, low maternal education, a teenage mother, maltreatment, and history of lead exposure. Once all of the risks investigated in this study were considered, homelessness showed a unique association with social engagement problems

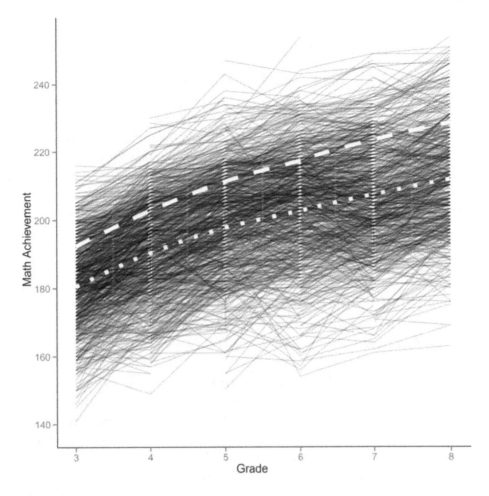

FIGURE 15.2   **Variability among homeless students for mathematics achievement**

Note. Individual achievement trajectories of homeless and highly mobile students are depicted by black lines. The dashed white line represents the mean national achievement level, and the dotted white line is 1 *SD* below the national normative mean. Reprinted with permission from Wiley-Blackwell from *Child Development* by Cutuli et al. (2013). Copyright 2012 by Cutuli et al. and Society for Research in Child Development.

at school, but not reading or academic engagement problems. For the latter two outcomes, higher cumulative risk in the homeless subsample accounted for their educational risk.

Findings From Administrative Data on Resilience

In addition to illustrating academic risks, our research documented substantial evidence of resilience. We observed marked variability within the HHM groups in the Obradović et al. (2009) study, with many children showing good achievement over time. Approximately 60% of the HHM students had scores within a standard deviation or better on the achievement test trajectories, and 20% scored above the national average. The control variables showed some relation to the achievement of HHM students but did not account for the variability.

We also observed striking differences in achievement within the HHM group in the Cutuli et al. (2013) study, as shown in Figure 15.2. Close to half of the students in this large group of HHM students (45%) scored in the average range or better in mathematics and reading over time, even though the overall average was low for the HHM students as a whole. This finding again invited the questions, What makes a difference? How do we account for this variability? The control variables, common covariates of achievement, explained some risk-group differences, but most of the variance was left unexplained. These questions led us to consider additional administrative data that gradually became available, such as earlier achievement, but also studies with direct assessment of potential protective factors that schools do not typically assess. These ongoing questions inspired a search for protective factors, both with district-level data and through direct assessment of families staying in emergency shelters.

Resilience in HHM Students: Searching for Malleable Protective Factors

It was clear in our earliest studies of children in HHM situations that some children were manifesting academic resilience—that is, doing well in the school context despite their experiences of adversity and disadvantage. The correlates of better achievement and school adjustment often reflected typical promotive and protective factors observed in the broader literature on resilience (Masten, 2014; Masten et al., 2014). These factors included attributes of the child (e.g., good cognitive skills) and attributes of the family (e.g., close parent–child relationships or parent involvement in education; Masten et al., 1997; Miliotis, Sesma, & Masten, 1999).

In the course of our large studies of administrative data, we tested the role of early reading skills as a predictor and moderator of risk (Herbers et al., 2012). Scores on reading tests in first grade predicted third-grade reading and mathematics scores, as well as the rate of learning over time (third to eighth grade) in both areas of academic achievement. The significance of reading was even greater for the highest risk students (the free-lunch and HHM groups described earlier), with reading showing a significant moderating effect on the predictive significance of risk group. The interaction effects suggest that early reading skills may be a protective factor for later learning among the most disadvantaged students, as well as a harbinger of future achievement.

Beginning in 2006, we initiated a series of studies focused on direct assessments of children and parents in shelters that were focused on identifying malleable promotive or protective factors for school success. Parenting and children's executive function (EF; described in detail later) held particular interest for us because of their salience in the developmental literature on resilience among disadvantaged children.

We have used multiple methods to assess parenting quality, including the Five Minute Speech Sample (e.g., Narayan, Herbers, Plowman, Gewirtz, & Masten, 2012) and direct observations of parent–child dyads in structured sessions that are later coded using standardized coding systems (e.g., Herbers, Cutuli, Supkoff, Narayan, & Masten, 2014). We have used multiple strategies for coding parenting skills and the quality of parent–child interaction, ranging from microsocial coding using State Space Grid techniques (e.g., Herbers et al., 2014) to more global coding with validated rating scales, including the Family Interaction Task codes originally developed by Forgatch and DeGarmo (1999). Results of our recent studies of parenting quality suggest that effective parenting is related to better EF skills in children (Herbers et al., 2014) and moderates the risk of academic problems in young HHM students (Herbers et al., 2011). Our results are consistent with the hypothesis that one way effective parenting "goes to school" is mediated by the EF skills of their children. Similarly, another research group recently found that inhibitory control skills mediated effects of risk on achievement problems in highly mobile preschool-aged children (Schmitt, Finders, & McClelland, 2015).

Executive functions refer to the neurocognitive processes involved in goal-directed, voluntary control of attention; working memory; and self-control of emotions and behavior that develop rapidly in preschoolers and continue to develop into early adulthood (Zelazo & Carlson, 2012). EF development is influenced by brain maturation and socialization, and these skills can be disrupted or damaged by adverse experiences that result in high levels of biological stress (Blair & Raver, 2012; Hackman, Gallop, Evans, & Farah, 2015). Teachers value EF because children's self-control is fundamental for learning in a classroom context, and numerous studies have shown the importance of these skills for school readiness and success (Blair & Raver, 2015). Our work was among the earliest to document the significance of directly assessed EF skills for school success in HHM children (Masten et al., 2012; Obradović, 2010). We were keenly interested in EF skills as a resilience factor because there was considerable evidence that these skills were malleable, in both preschool children and older students (Diamond & Lee, 2011; Raver et al., 2011; Riggs, Jahromi, Razza, Dillworth-Bart, & Mueller, 2006; Zelazo & Carlson, 2012).

We have investigated multiple components of EF since 2006 using a variety of measures administered to children while they were staying in emergency shelters. We have tested a variety of EF tasks and adapted some of the most promising tasks for greater suitability in testing EF skills in diverse young children. Results have corroborated the validity of these skills as correlates and predictors of school success, including academic achievement, social competence with peers, relationships with teachers, and classroom conduct (Herbers et al., 2014; Lafavor, 2012; Masten et al., 2012; Obradović, 2010). EF skills are distinct from, although closely related to, general cognitive abilities (as measured by IQ tests) and show unique predictive significance for homeless children's school success with measures of intellectual functioning controlled (Masten et al., 2012).

In a recent study, still under way, we evaluated the potential of innovative EF measures, particularly computerized assessments of EF skills, for screening school readiness in preschoolers (Wenzel et al., 2013). In collaboration with the early childhood screening team in the MPS, we recruited families participating in the district's regular prekindergarten screening for an optional child EF assessment, completed at the same time as the screening itself. Over 90% of families participating in the regular screening consented to participate in our study, producing a sample of 3-to 5-year-old children. Concurrent validity was excellent, with an EF composite score correlating highly ($r = 0.76$ for 471 English-speaking children) with scores on the Minneapolis Preschool Screening Instrument–Revised (MPS, 2007), a measure of cognitive school readiness used by multiple districts in this metropolitan area. We are now observing our participants administratively to track how they do in school based on grades, district standardized testing, and state benchmark tests, as well as attendance and other indicators of positive school engagement. Early data are very promising that EF tests will have value added for preschool screening.

In our most recent work, we also have begun to study the role of biological processes in risk and resilience of HHM students (Masten et al., 2014). Specifically, we are investigating how EF skills are related to measureable biological markers of stress, such as salivary cortisol levels, gene expression in saliva, and hair cortisol levels. Early results indicated that salivary cortisol levels were related to EF performance during in-shelter testing sessions (Cutuli, 2011). Further research is under way to investigate how positive and negative life experiences affect the activity of stress-relevant genes, as well as the accumulation of the stress hormone cortisol in hair. The goal of extending our measures to a biological level is to better understand the processes underlying risk and resilience related to stress, parenting, and EF.

Moving Toward Intervention: Improving EF Skills to Promote School Readiness

Evidence from our research implicated EF skills as having potential influence on school success in HHM students, a promising finding that was corroborated by the work of other investigators (e.g., Schmitt et al., 2015). As a result, we began developing and testing interventions to promote resilience by building EF skills during the preschool years, taking advantage of the natural window of opportunity when EF skills develop rapidly and brain plasticity is high (Zelazo & Carlson, 2012). Targeting foundational skills in homeless preschoolers has the potential to promote school readiness and initiate a positive cascade of academic competence, mitigating achievement gaps in the long term (Heckman, 2006; Masten, 2011). Previous research had shown the benefits of targeted EF interventions, including individual training programs (Espinet, Anderson, & Zelazo, 2012; Rueda, Rothbart, McCandliss, Saccomanno, & Posner, 2005) and adapted classroom curricula (Diamond, Barnett, Thomas, & Munro, 2007; Raver et al., 2011; Riggs et al., 2006). However, there were no existing programs known to be effective for HHM children at very high risk of academic difficulties. We endeavored to fill this gap by developing a brief but intensive EF intervention suitable for use with highly mobile families.

In 2010, with support from a local funder and in collaboration with community partners, we developed and piloted a 3-week program designed to boost EF skills in homeless children attending the shelter preschool just before entering kindergarten (Casey et al., 2014). Encouraged by the success of this pilot, we developed a multicomponent EF intervention designed for use with HHM families, with curricular components appropriate for any preschool classroom. Because reflection and cognitive reprocessing play a central role in EF skills (Espinet, Anderson, & Zelazo, 2012), our theory of change focused on boosting the amount and quality of reflection training and practice the child received at the individual, family, and classroom levels. Our 3-week-long intervention included teacher training in a flexible classroom curriculum of EF-focused activities; parent psychoeducation about children's developing self-regulatory abilities; and one-on-one scaffolded training, intended for children who lack the individual EF skills to benefit meaningfully from group interventions (Casey et al., 2014; Masten et al., 2014). Early results have been promising, with teachers and parents enthusiastic about the materials and activities, as well as measurable changes observed in child performance and behavior. However, further enhancements, iterative improvements, and rigorous testing of the intervention still lie ahead.

Implications for School Psychology Practice, Training, Research, and Policy

Our research is consistent with a larger body of evidence documenting marked risk and resilience with respect to educational success in HHM preschoolers and older students. In conclusion, we highlight implications of the evidence for school psychology practice, training, research, and policy.

Implications for Practice: Assessment and Placement

The variability in school readiness and achievement among HHM-identified students underscores the importance of outreach to ensure that these students participate in routine assessments, prekindergarten screening, and other opportunities for early identification of learning problems and needs. All too often, we have encountered children staying in shelters who fell through the cracks of screening, referral, and learning enrichment or special education programs that might have boosted their school readiness and success. Instead, these children often fall far behind their peers before they connect with appropriate supports and services. Mobility itself is a critical barrier to adequate screening and follow-through. Given the high return on investment during early childhood, it is particularly important to screen children in shelters for school readiness, with proactive identification of any special education needs.

Mobility also creates issues in placement of HHM students, sometimes leading to high concentrations of HHM students in schools and classrooms with high turnover rates. This is a structural problem that perpetuates a suboptimal learning environment in these classrooms, both for HHM students and for other students. Fantuzzo, LeBoeuf, & Rouse (2014) have shown that a high concentration of HHM students in a school is associated with lower reading achievement and attendance rates for children at that school. The high cumulative risk observed for many HHM students also poses challenges for teachers faced with many children struggling to overcome the effects of stress and other serious barriers to learning.

Implications for Practice: The Value of Data

Some of the most compelling evidence on the risks and resilience of HHM children in recent years has resulted from analyses of high-quality administrative or integrated data, often provided by research, evaluation, and testing departments in school districts. For example, the findings from our growth analyses of longitudinal administrative data on achievement in the MPS have been widely cited and also presented to local, state, national, and international policy audiences. Results of Cutuli et al. (2013) have been presented to the local school board, as well as the Minnesota legislature, and were cited in a recent report of the U.S. Government Accountability Office (2014) entitled *Education of Homeless Students: Improved Program Oversight Needed*. Our analyses were possible because of the quality of data available in the MPS and the collaboration of district and university colleagues working together. Such data are compelling to policymakers who can make more resources available to school systems and shelter providers. Data also can inform districts about progress in meeting the needs of HHM students, ranging from transportation to summer school programs, and provide evidence on the success of district efforts to address achievement disparities.

Implications for Training and Professional Development

Homelessness among students is disturbingly common in many districts and classrooms, and therefore, it is vitally important that school personnel have adequate training on the issues and rights of HHM students, as well as the significance of school personnel's role in promoting resilience among these students. In many ways, the teachers, school psychologists, and other personnel encountered by HHM students and their parents represent the best opportunities for these highly disadvantaged families to connect with the educational resources and protective influences crucial to the success of these children. Although professional development needs to be tailored to the specific roles of the various staff, all school personnel need to understand the threatening situations often faced by these children, as well as their federally mandated rights and their potential for success. Avoiding stigma is paramount, so professional development should emphasize that many children who experience homelessness succeed, particularly in a context of well-timed and targeted protections.

Implications for Early Childhood Education

Findings indicating that the achievement gaps for HHM students emerge early and persist also underscore the importance of early and stable preschool programming for children already exposed to homelessness or at very high risk of homelessness. Multiple investigators have called for early interventions for children at risk because of homelessness (e.g., Brumley et al., 2015; Masten et al., 2014). Access to high-quality programs may be particularly important for these children given the evidence that quality matters for early childhood interventions for high-risk children (Heckman, 2006; Reynolds, Temple, White, Ou, & Robertson, 2011). Early childhood programs that emphasize EF skill development may promote long-term learning by building self-regulatory skills necessary for school success (Diamond et al., 2007; Raver et al., 2011).

Implications for Future Research

Since the 1980s, research has advanced on the academic risk and resilience of HHM children, yet much remains to be done (Cutuli & Herbers, 2014; Masten et al., 2014; Miller, 2011). Further research is needed to differentiate the effects of residential mobility, school mobility, and high cumulative risk (Miller, 2011; Schmitt et al., 2015). In addition, there is much more research focused on the educational risks associated with homelessness than there is on the educational successes of HHM students and the processes that may facilitate their resilience. Understanding the processes that promote success are important for supporting resilience in these and other high-risk children (Cutuli & Herbers, 2014; Masten, 2014).

The field needs innovative and tailored interventions but also research on how well they work. To date, relatively little research exists on the effectiveness of any interventions designed to promote school success or learning in HHM students (Casey et al., 2014). Given the prominence of homelessness as an indicator of academic risk and the striking achievement gaps revealed in recent studies for many HHM students, evidence-based interventions are crucial for addressing the needs of many individual children experiencing homelessness and for addressing the intransigent achievement gaps observed in many school districts. Research on predictors of resilience among HHM students, although limited, suggests several promising directions for intervention development and targeting. These include access to summer programs, computer training, and high-quality early childhood programs for children and youth experiencing homelessness, as well as interventions to support effective parenting and children's EF skills (Buckner, Mezzacappa, & Beardslee, 2003, 2009; Casey et al., 2014; Cutuli & Herbers, 2014; Herbers et al., 2011, 2014).

Implications for Policy

The evidence on risks and protective factors suggests multiple strategies for school programming to promote academic success in HHM students. First, it is important for schools to accurately identify HHM students. This can be done in part through partnerships with local housing agencies and emergency shelters; however, these methods may not identify children who are in inadequate living situations (e.g., living in cars or at campsites) or doubled up with other families. Research suggests that parents and youth may be reluctant to disclose their HHM status because of concerns about privacy and stigma (Ausikaitis et al., 2014; Comey, Litschwartz, & Pettit, 2012). Community outreach during school enrollment may help to educate families about the school's nonjudgmental response to homelessness and resources to provide services. In addition, staff should be trained to consider potential signs of homelessness (e.g., hunger, absenteeism).

Next, schools must ensure that children identified as meeting ED criteria for homelessness receive the services to which they are entitled. This is the specific charge of the homeless education liaison, who serves as an important connection for homeless students and families. The homeless education liaison can provide support and guidance about services and academic enrichment programs available to homeless children, as well as immediate school placement if these children are coming to a new community. To avoid disruption in schooling, it is imperative that schools provide all of the needed evaluations and referrals as quickly as feasible.

Given the stability of low achievement trajectories among HHM students who have fallen behind, these students may require intensive academic support and summer programming to have a chance to catch up. Programs to encourage attendance also are important given the frequency of absenteeism observed among many (although not all) homeless students. Any disciplinary actions that remove children from school also would likely exacerbate this problem, and it is important to consider the possibility of homelessness when children are frequently tardy or absent (Ausikaitis et al., 2014; Comey et al., 2012). Homeless children also may need access to school supplies and digital tools for school, including computers, as well as quiet places to do homework. Families may need guidance about how to access such resources.

The Importance of School Psychologists

School psychologists have a special role to play in facilitating school success among HHM students because of school psychologists' multifaceted roles in assessing the needs of students and promoting students' success, both individually and at the level of ecological systems in the school context (Burns, 2013). It is important for school psychologists to understand the characteristics and implications of homelessness and mobility in order to establish appropriate interventions and accommodations for students experiencing homelessness. It is essential for schools to accurately identify and document the status of HHM students so that federally mandated rights are met and services provided (e.g., free meals, transportation). Connecting with the homeless education liaison will be important to ensure that these mandated services are provided. In addition, some (although not all) HHM students may have vulnerabilities related to high cumulative risk that need to be considered to best serve these students. For example, homeless children exposed to domestic or community violence may benefit from individual or group counseling for students exposed to such violence. School psychologists can help HHM students secure access to social skills training and mental health services as needed (Moore, 2013; Tobin & Murphy, 2013).

School psychologists can also help establish academic stability in the midst of residential mobility, educating HHM families about their children's right to stay at their school of origin if that is desired and feasible. When school changes do occur, school psychologists can work to preserve educational continuity, ensuring that a new school acquires school records and reviews previous academic interventions to support learning. School psychologists also can facilitate academic planning for HHM students during the school year, helping to coordinate support across teachers and service providers.

School psychologists also have an important role to play in assessment, both at the individual level and at the school level. Testing procedures need to accommodate the situation of homeless students who may miss testing dates. Outreach may be important to ensure that HHM children are included in screening and other testing sessions that may open opportunities for enrichment and special educational programming. It is also important to consider the appropriateness of measures used for evaluation, as well as the timing of evaluation. Very few measures have been well validated for use with extremely impoverished children who also may be under considerable stress from co-occurring traumatic events that precipitate a homeless episode. School psychologists play a vital role in selecting suitable measures and interpreting results, being mindful of the shortcomings in validity of many tests for HHM students.

Last but certainly not least, school psychologists can play a facilitating role in educating parents and supporting the school engagement of families dealing with homelessness. HHM parents may not be aware of the potential detriments of school mobility or the rights mandated by HHM status for their children, including transportation to their children's school of origin. Parents in this situation may need extra support to feel welcomed and empowered as partners in their children's education.

Conclusion

Over the past 3 decades, we have made great strides in understanding the needs and strengths of homeless students. Although far from done, this work has practical implications for identifying and supporting academic success among these students. School personnel in general and school psychologists in particular have central roles to play in promoting resilience in children challenged by homelessness and all of its attendant risks to educational success.

References

Alexander, K. L., Entwisle, D. R., & Olson, L. S. (2001). Schools, achievement, and inequality: A seasonal perspective. *Educational Evaluation and Policy Analysis, 23,* 171–191. doi:10.3102/01623737023002171

Ausikaitis, A. E., Wynne, M. E., Persaud, S., Pitt., R., Hosek, A., Reker, K., ... Flores, S. (2014). Staying in school: The efficacy of McKinney-Vento Act for homeless youth. *Youth & Society.* Advance online publication. doi:10.1177/0044118X14564138

Bassuk, E. L., Richard, M. K., & Tsertsvadze, A. (2015). The prevalence of mental illness in homeless children: A systematic review and meta-analysis. *Journal of the American Academy of Child and Adolescent Psychiatry, 54,* 86(2), 86–96. doi:10.1016/j.jaac.2014.11.008

Blair, C., & Raver, C. C. (2012). Child development in the context of adversity: Experiential canalization of brain and behavior. *American Psychologist, 67*, 309–318. doi:10.1037/a0027493

Blair, C., & Raver, C. C. (2015). School readiness and self-regulation: A developmental psychobiological approach. *Annual Review of Psychology, 66*, 711–731. doi:10.1146/annurev-psych-010814-015221

Brumley, B., Fantuzzo, J., Perlman, S., & Zager, M. L. (2015). The unique relations between early homelessness and educational well-being: An empirical test of the continuum of risk hypothesis. *Children and Youth Services Review, 48*, 31–37. doi:10.1016/j. childyouth.2014.11.012

Buckner, J. C., Mezzacappa, E., & Beardslee, W. R. (2003). Characteristics of resilient youths living in poverty: The role of self-regulatory processes. *Development and Psychopathology, 15*, 139–162. doi: 10.1017.S0954579403000087

Buckner, J. C., Mezzacappa, E., & Beardslee, W. R. (2009). Self-regulation and its relations to adaptive functioning in low-income youths. *American Journal of Orthopsychiatry, 79*, 19–30. doi:10.1037/ a0014796

Burns, M. K. (2013). Contextualizing school psychology practice: Introducing featured research commentaries. *School Psychology Review, 42*, 334–342.

Casey, E. C., Finsaas, M., Carlson, S. M., Zelazo, P. D., Murphy, B., Durkin, F., … Masten, A. S. (2014). Promoting resilience through executive function training for homeless and highly mobile preschoolers. In S. Prince-Embury & D. H. Saklofske (Eds.), *Resilience interventions for youth in diverse populations* (pp. 133–158). New York, NY: Springer.

Comey, J., Litschwartz, L., & Pettit, K. L. S. (2012). Housing and schools: Working together to reduce the negative effects of student mobility (Urban Institute Brief 26). Washington, DC: Urban Institute.

Cutuli, J. J. (2011). *Context, cortisol, and executive functions among children experiencing homelessness* (PhD dissertation). University of Minnesota, Minneapolis, MN.

Cutuli, J. J., Desjardins, C. D., Herbers, J. E., Long, J. D., Heistad, D., Chan, C.-K., … Masten, A. S. (2013). Academic achievement trajectories of homeless and highly mobile students: Resilience in the context of chronic and acute risk. *Child Development, 84*, 841–857. doi:10.1111/cdev.12013

Cutuli, J. J., & Herbers, J. E. (2014). Promoting resilience for children who experience family homelessness: Opportunities to encourage developmental competence. *Cityscape, 16*, 113–139.

Diamond, A., Barnett, W. S., Thomas, J., & Munro, S. (2007). Preschool program improves cognitive control. *Science, 318*, 1387–1388. doi:10.1126/ science.1151148

Diamond, A., & Lee, K. (2011). Interventions shown to aid executive function development in children 4 to 12 years old. *Science, 333*, 959–964. doi:10.1126/science.1204529

Espinet, S. D., Anderson, J. E., & Zelazo, P. D. (2012). N2 amplitude as a neural marker of executive function in young children: An ERP study of children who switch versus perseverate on the dimensional change card sort. *Developmental Cognitive Neuroscience, 2*, S49–S58. doi:10.1016/j.dcn.2011.12.002

Fantuzzo, J. W., LeBoeuf, W. A., & Rouse, H. L. (2014). An investigation of the relations between school concentrations of student risk factors and student educational well-being. *Educational Researcher, 43*, 25–36. doi:10.3102/0013189X13512673

Forgatch, M. S., & DeGarmo, D. S. (1999). Parenting through change: An effective prevention program for single mothers. *Journal of Consulting and Clinical Psychology, 67*, 711–724. doi:10.1037/0022-006X. 67.5.711

Hackman, D. A., Gallop, R., Evans, G. W., & Farah, M. J. (2015). Socioeconomic status and executive function: Developmental trajectories and mediation. *Developmental Science*. doi:10.1111/desc.12246

Heckman, J. J. (2006). Skill formation and the economics of investing in disadvantaged children. *Science, 312*, 1900–1902. doi:10.1126/science.1128898

Herbers, J. E., Cutuli, J. J., Lafavor, T. L., Vrieze, D., Leibel, C., Obradović, J., & Masten, A. S. (2011). Direct and indirect effects of parenting on the academic functioning of young homeless children. *Early Education & Development, 22*, 77–104. doi:10.1080/10409280903507261

Herbers, J. E., Cutuli, J. J., Supkoff, L. M., Heistad, D., Chan, C.-K., Hinz, E., & Masten, A. S. (2012). Early reading skills and academic achievement trajectories of students facing poverty, homelessness, and high residential mobility. *Educational Researcher, 41*, 366–374. doi:10.3102/0013189X12445320

Herbers, J. E., Cutuli, J. J., Supkoff, L. M., Narayan, A. J., & Masten, A. S. (2014). Parenting and co-regulation: Adaptive systems for competence in children experiencing homelessness. *American Journal of Orthopsychiatry, 84*, 420–430. doi:10.1037/h0099843

Lafavor, T. L. (2012). *The impact of executive function and emotional control and understanding on the behavioral functioning and academic achievement of children living in emergency homeless shelters* (PhD dissertation). University of Minnesota, Minneapolis, MN.

Masten, A. S. (1992). Homeless children in the United States: Mark of nation at risk. *Current Directions in Psychological Science, 1*, 41–44. doi:10.1111/1467-8721.ep11509730

Masten, A. S. (2011). Resilience in children threatened by extreme adversity: Frameworks for research, practice, and translational synergy. *Development and Psychopathology, 23*, 141–154. doi:10.1017/S0954579411000198

Masten, A. S. (2014). *Ordinary magic: Resilience in development.* New York, NY: Guilford Press.

Masten, A. S., Cutuli, J. J., Herbers, J. E., Hinz, E., Obradović, J., & Wenzel, A. J. (2014). Academic risk and resilience in the context of homelessness. *Child Development Perspectives, 8*, 201–206. doi:10.1111/cdep.12088

Masten, A. S., Herbers, J. E., Desjardins, C. D., Cutuli, J. J., McCormick, C. M., Sapienza, J. K., … Zelazo, P. D. (2012). Executive function skills and school success in young children experiencing homelessness. *Educational Researcher, 41*, 375–384. doi:10.3102/0013189X12459883

Masten, A. S., Miliotis, D., Graham-Bermann, S., Ramirez, M., & Neemann, J. (1993). Children in homeless families: Risks to mental health and development. *Journal of Consulting and Clinical Psychology, 61*, 335–343. doi:10.1037/0022-006X.61.2.335

Masten, A. S., Sesma, A., Si-Asar, R., Lawrence, C., Miliotis, D., & Dionne, J. A. (1997). Educational risks for children experiencing homelessness. *Journal of School Psychology, 35*, 27–46. doi:10.1016/S0022-4405(96)00032–5

McChesney, K. Y. (1993). Homeless families since 1980, Implications for education. *Education and Urban Society, 25*, 361–380.

McKinney-Vento Homeless Assistance Act of 1987, Pub. L. No. 100-77, 101 Stat. 482, 42 U.S.C. § 11301 *et seq.* (1987).

Miliotis, D., Sesma, A., & Masten, A. S. (1999). Parenting as a protective process for school success in children from homeless families. *Early Education and Development, 10*, 111–133. doi:10.1207/s15566935eed1002 2

Miller, P. M. (2011). A critical analysis of the research on student homelessness. *Review of Educational Research, 81*, 308–337. doi:10.3102/0034654311415120

Minneapolis Public Schools. (2007). *Technical manual for the Minneapolis Preschool Screening Instrument–Revised*. Minneapolis, MN: Author.

Molnar, J. (1988). *Home is where the heart is: The crisis of homeless children and families in New York City*. New York, NY: Edna McConnell Clark Foundation.

Moore, J. (2013). Resilience and at-risk children and youth. *National Center for Homeless Education*.

Narayan, A. J., Herbers, J. E., Plowman, E. J., Gewirtz, A. H., & Masten, A. S. (2012). Expressed emotion in homeless families: A methodological study of the five-minute speech sample. *Journal of Family Psychology, 26*, 648–653. doi:10.1037/a0028968

National Center for Homeless Education. (2014). *Education for Homeless Children and Youth (EHCY) Federal Program Profile*. Greensboro, NC: Author.

Obradović, J. (2010). Effortful control and adaptive functioning of homeless children: Variable-focused and person-focused analyses. *Journal of Applied Developmental Psychology, 31*, 109–117. doi:10.1016/j.appdev.2009.09.004

Obradović, J., Long, J. D., Cutuli, J. J., Chan, C.-K., Hinz, E., Heistad, D., & Masten, A. S. (2009). Academic achievement of homeless and highly mobile children in an urban school district: Longitudinal evidence of risk, growth, and resilience. *Development and Psychopathology, 21*, 493–518. doi:10.1017/S0954579409000273

Rafferty, Y., & Rollins, N. (1989). *Learning in Limbo: The Educational Deprivation of Homeless Children*. New York, NY: Advocates for Children.

Rafferty, Y., & Shinn, M. (1991). The impact of homelessness on children. *American Psychologist, 46*, 1170–1179. doi:10.1037/0003-066X.46.11.1170

Raver, C. C., Jones, S. M., Li-Grining, C., Zhai, F., Bub, K., & Pressler, E. (2011). CSRP's impact on low-income preschoolers' preacademic skills: Self-regulation as a mediating mechanism. *Child Development, 82*, 362–378. doi:10.1111/j.1467-8624.2010.01561.x

Reynolds, A. J., Temple, J. A., White, B. A., Ou, S.-R., & Robertson, D. L. (2011). Age 26 cost–benefit analysis of the child–parent center early education program. *Child Development, 82*, 379–404. doi:10.1111/j.1467-8624.2010.01563.x

Riggs, N. R., Jahromi, L. B., Razza, R. P., Dillworth-Bart, J. E., & Mueller, U. (2006). Executive function and the promotion of social–emotional competence. *Journal of Applied Developmental Psychology, 27*, 300–309. doi: 10.1016/j.appdev.2006.04.002

Rueda, M. R., Rothbart, M. K., McCandliss, B. D., Saccomanno, L., & Posner, M. I. (2005). Training, maturation, and genetic influences on the development of executive attention. *Proceedings of the National Academy of Sciences of the United States of America, 102*, 14931–14936. doi:10.1073pnas.0506897102

Samuels, J., Shinn, M., & Buckner, J. C. (2010). *Homeless children: Update on research, policy, programs, and opportunities*. Washington, DC: Office of the Assistant Secretary for Planning and Evaluation, U.S. Department of Health and Human Services.

Schmitt, S. A., Finders, J. K., & McClelland, M. M. (2015). Residential mobility, inhibitory control, and academic achievement in preschool. *Early Education and Development, 26*, 189–208. doi:10.1080/10409289.2015.975033

Tobin, K., & Murphy, J. (2013). Addressing the challenges of child and family homelessness. *Journal of Applied Research on Children: Informing Policy for Children at Risk, 4*(1), 1–29. doi:10.1542/peds.2011-2663

U.S. Government Accountability Office. (2014). *Education of homeless students: Improved program oversight needed* (GAO-14-465). Washington DC: Author.

Wenzel, A. J., Berghuis, K. J., Hillyer, C., Seiwert, M. J., Anderson, J. E., Zelazo, P. D., … Masten, A. S. (2013, March). *Validity of executive function assessment for early childhood screening in an urban school district.* Poster presentation at the Society for Research in Child Development Biennial Meeting, Seattle, WA.

Zelazo, P. D., & Carlson, S. M. (2012). Hot and cool executive function in childhood and adolescence: Development and plasticity. *Child Development Perspectives, 6*, 354–360. doi:10.1111/j.1750-8606.2012.00246.x

Family Resources as Protective Factors for Low-Income Youth Exposed to Community Violence

BY CECILY R. HARDAWAY, EMMA STERRETT-HONG,
CYNTHIA A. LARKBY, AND MARIE D. CORNELIUS

Introduction

Community violence is a source of trauma and chronic stress for adolescents growing up in neighborhoods where crime and violence are prevalent (Jain and Cohen 2013). Defined as "deliberate acts intended to cause physical harm against a person or persons in the community" (Cooley-Quille et al. 1995, p. 1364), community violence can involve fights, stabbings, and shootings. Adolescence is a particularly important developmental stage to study the effects of community violence. Adolescents are experiencing greater levels of autonomy and independence from the nuclear family (Steinberg 2008; Whitmire 2000), while at the same time are being exposed to more community influences, potentially including community violence. Consistent with this idea, studies have linked older youth age with higher levels of exposure to community violence (Martin et al. 2013; Stein et al. 2003).

Relative to both children and adults, adolescents face an elevated risk of becoming victims of and witnesses to many forms of community violence. A report from the National Center for Juvenile Justice showed that, from 1994 to 2010, adolescents ages 12–17 were more than twice as likely as adults to be victims of simple assault and other types of serious violent crimes (Sickmund and Puzzanchera 2014). In 2013, homicide was the third leading cause of death for youth in this same age group (Centers for Disease Control and Prevention, National Center for Injury Prevention and Control 2015). Moreover, according to the National Survey of Children's Exposure to Violence, roughly 42 % of youth ages 14–17 have witnessed an assault in their community, 10% have witnessed a shooting, and 1 % have witnessed a murder during the past year (Finkelhor et al. 2009). African American youth are especially susceptible to exposure to community violence. African American youth witness more violence than other youth and are more likely to be victims of assault and serious crime compared to other youth (Crouch et al. 2000; Gaylord-Harden et al. 2011; Sickmund and Puzzanchera 2014; Wilson et al. 2012).

Exposure to community violence during adolescence is a risk factor for internalizing (e.g., anxiety and depression) and externalizing problems (e.g., aggression and delinquency)— both of which pose serious risks for compromised functioning in adulthood (Brook et al. 2013; Mason et al. 2010; Yaroslavsky et al. 2013). Although studies have consistently linked exposure to community violence to negative outcomes for adolescents, much still needs to be learned about factors that protect youth exposed to community violence (Jain and Cohen 2013). The current study aims to address these gaps in the literature. Specifically, we examined whether kinship support and parental involvement help buffer low-income youth from emotional and behavior problems associated with exposure to community violence. During adolescence, as in earlier developmental stages, youth continue to be significantly influenced by parenting behaviors, but relationships with other adults may become more meaningful and impactful as the social networks of youth expand during adolescence (Kahn and Antonucci 1980). We hypothesized that kinship support and parental involvement would attenuate longitudinal associations between adolescents' exposure to community violence and internalizing and externalizing behaviors during adolescence. Our investigation of family-level protective factors is shaped by work indicating that families play a key role in building youth's capacity to appraise and cope with stressors in adaptive ways (Foster and Brooks-Gunn 2009; Kliewer et al. 1994).

Although exposure to community violence is a risk factor for internalizing and externalizing problems, not all youth exposed to community violence experience problems as a result. Studies showing an association between exposure to violence and psychological and behavioral problems typically find only small to medium effect sizes (Fowler et al. 2009; Wilson and Rosenthal 2003). Individual differences in outcomes associated with exposure to community violence may be explained by variation in protective factors or individual, family, and community resources that youth possess or have at their disposal (SmithBattle 2009). As such, identifying protective factors that foster continued adaptation or recovery after exposure to community violence remains an important area for research (Margolin 2005).

This study is undergirded by the concept of resilience defined as "relative resistance to environmental risk experiences, or the overcoming of stress or adversity" (Rutter 2006, p. 2). Resilience is not a static trait or individual characteristic that can be measured directly, however it is evinced when individuals experience relatively better outcomes than other individuals exposed to similar levels of adversity (Rutter 2012). Individual, family, and community protective factors can help promote resilience by mitigating the effects of risks (Rutter 2012). The broader literature on resilience as well as the literature on community violence point to the potential of family support to act as a buffer against negative outcomes associated with exposure to community violence (Luthar and Zelazo 2003).

Interaction models are used to test whether hypothesized protective factors moderate the effects of risks (Masten 2001). The present study draws on resilience research to better understand the nature of interactions between exposure to violence and hypothesized protective factors. We are particularly interested in what Luther and colleagues term *protective-stabilizing* patterns of interaction in which a risk factor is less strongly related to symptoms when a protective factor is present (Luthar et al. 2000). That is, a buffering effect is shown such that symptoms that would be expected to result from exposure to a particular risk are diminished or stabilized by a protective factor. This study examines the protective effects of kinship support and parental involvement on youth internalizing and externalizing problems, in order to help understand conditions under which exposure to community violence is less strongly associated with youth behavior problems and to better inform interventions for youth exposed to community violence.

Kinship Support

Kinship support refers to the provision of emotional, social, and financial assistance by extended family members, such as grandparents, aunts, and uncles, to children and parents. This support often occurs in the context of extended family relationships characterized by physical proximity and interdependence (e.g., Lamborn and Nguyen 2004; Pallock and Lamborn 2006). Kinship support is associated with a variety of youth outcomes, including lower levels of emotional and behavioral problems (Johnson et al. 2011; Taylor 2010). Theorists have described how the activation of extended kinship care support often occurs in circumstances in which families face stressors, such as poverty, discrimination, and crime, providing a compensatory or protective function (Garcia Coll et al. 1996; Masten and Coatsworth 1998). Historically, African American values related to the importance of interpersonal relationships and broad definitions of family (Johnson and Staples 2005; Sudarkasa 1997) have supported a broad inclusion of relatives and fictive kin in the activities of nuclear families (e.g., Jones and Lindahl 2011). Thus, extended family members are intimately involved in the child-rearing and household activities in many African American families (Boyd-Franklin 1989; Franklin 1997). Kinship support is linked to better anger management in African American youth growing up in high risk neighborhoods (Stevenson 1997). In addition, kinship support has been found to lessen the association between negative contextual influences, including financial stress and maladaptive parenting practices, and youth internalizing and externalizing difficulties (Taylor 2010; Taylor et al. 2014).

Kinship support has shown protective effects in the context of other environmental stressors; however, a paucity of studies have examined the role of kinship support—particularly support from extended family members—in the context of community violence. One cross-sectional investigation found that kinship support moderated the relation between exposure to community violence and complex post-traumatic stress disorder among African American children, such that the association between exposure to community violence and complex post-traumatic stress disorder was weaker when children had higher levels of kinship support (Jones 2007). However, studies have yet to address similar research questions with longitudinal data on adolescents and in relation to other socioemotional adjustment outcomes beyond complex post-traumatic stress disorder.

Although little attention has been paid to kinship support as a moderator of the influence of community violence on youth externalizing and internalizing difficulties, support for possible protective effects can be drawn from empirical investigations of mechanisms of the influence of community violence on youth. In terms of externalizing problems, community violence has been found to increase the likelihood of youth behavior problems due to increased exposure to negative role models, negative peers, and increased accessibility of illegal activity (Fowler et al. 2009). Since kinship support is a vehicle for providing positive role models and extra monitoring (Pallock and Lamborn 2006; Taylor et al. 1993), it may reduce interaction with negative role models and peers as well as opportunities to engage in illegal activity, and, thus, act as a protective factor against developing externalizing problems. The picture with regard to internalizing symptoms is more complicated. It has been postulated that community violence increases physiological reactivity, fears, and self-blame, as well as interferes with affect regulation, which can lead to anxiety and depression (Cooley-Quille et al. 2001; Fowler et al. 2009). Whether kinship support has the potential to impact physiological reactivity, fears, self-blame, and affect regulation, and thus can act as a buffer against the development of internalizing problems, has been under-studied.

Parental Involvement

Parental involvement encompasses behaviors and practices that foster positive parent-adolescent relationships and provide emotional and instrumental support. Involved parents are adept at communicating, expressing affection, and spending time with their children (Collins et al. 2000). Studies have shown that important dimensions of parental involvement have salutary effects on adolescent socioemotional adjustment. For example, positive parent–child relationships are related to socioemotional adjustment indirectly through adolescents' self-esteem (Barber et al. 2003) and ability to self-regulate (Brody et al. 2002). Further, family routines, parental monitoring, and parental supportiveness promote positive socioemotional functioning (Hair et al. 2008). Adolescents who feel supported by their parents may appraise threats as less dangerous and cope with stress in more adaptive ways than peers who lack this positive family resource (Aceves and Cookston 2007; Kliewer et al. 1994).

Although some evidence suggests that parental involvement is an especially important source of protection for youth living in dangerous neighborhoods with concentrated poverty (Dearing 2004; Loukas and Prelow 2004), only a small number of studies have specifically investigated whether parental involvement acts as a buffer in the context of exposure to community violence. The few studies in this area have focused on a limited set of outcomes and have yielded mixed results. Brookmeyer et al. (2005) found that parental support moderated the relationship between witnessing violence and violence perpetration, such that the relationship between witnessing violence and violence perpetration was not significant for boys with average or high levels of parental support but was significant for boys with low levels of parental support. Other studies have found direct effects of parental involvement on adolescent outcomes but have not found evidence that parental involvement has a protective effect. For example, Pearce et al. (2003) found that parental involvement was not protective against externalizing problems when adolescents were exposed to high levels of violence. Similarly, McMahon et al. (2013) found that parental support did not moderate the association between violent victimization and symptoms of anxiety and depression. Variability in the operationalization of exposure to community violence (i.e., witnessing and victimization assessed separately or combined) as well as differences in the focal outcomes examined in each study may account for disparate findings. It is possible that, in the context of youth exposure to community violence, parental involvement may be protective against some types of maladjustment and not others. Given the paucity of research on parental involvement as a moderator of exposure to violence and the narrow focus of existing studies, more investigations that include multidimensional conceptualizations of parental involvement that capture both emotional and instrumental support provided by parents are needed.

Environmental stress theory (McKelvey et al. 2015; Wandersman and Nation 1998) postulates that community violence may lead to increased emotional and behavioral difficulties by making youth feel insecure about themselves and the world around them and by causing impairment in their relationships, including the ability of their parents to adequately monitor their behaviors and attend to their emotional needs. To the extent that parental involvement helps youth develop emotional security and also takes the form of parental monitoring and emotional support, it may help buffer youth exposed to community violence from increases in both externalizing and internalizing difficulties.

The Current Study

The primary goal of this study was to identify moderators of the association between exposure to community violence and socioemotional adjustment, using a sample predominately comprised of low-income African American youth born to women who were once adolescent mothers. The hypothesized moderators examined were kinship support and parental involvement. These moderators were selected because they represent family factors that research suggests may be protective in the context of community violence and because each of these moderators are potentially modifiable through intervention. Kinship support and parental involvement were hypothesized to act as *protective-stabilizing* moderators. It was expected that kinship support and parental involvement would be associated with positive outcomes for youth and that adolescents exposed to violence in the context of high levels of parental involvement would show fewer internalizing and externalizing problems than their peers with low levels of parental involvement. It is also predicted that relationship between exposure to community violence and externalizing problems would be weaker for youth with high levels of kinship support. Due to the limited empirical work conducted specifically on kinship support as a moderator, our examination of whether kinship support would moderate the association between community violence and internalizing problems is considered exploratory.

The current study makes several important contributions to the literature on community violence and adolescents' socioemotional adjustment as measured by internalizing and externalizing behaviors. We focus on family-level moderators of the impact of community violence that have received limited attention in the literature. Our study uses a multidimensional measure of parental involvement as a way of extending previous studies that have almost exclusively focused on singular dimensions of parental involvement. Another contribution is our focus on kinship support—a culturally-relevant variable that may be a particularly important resource for African American adolescents who face some of the highest levels of exposure to community violence (Crouch et al. 2000; Voisin 2007). Most studies that examine family-level support focus on the immediate family and have not adequately addressed important resources provided by extended family members. Our use of a longitudinal design and inclusion of controls for prior behavior also represent important contributions given that most previous studies have been cross-sectional.

Methods

Sample and Participant Selection

Data for this study are drawn from the Teen Mother Study, which is part of the Maternal Health Practices and Child Development project, a consortium of studies on the long-term effects of prenatal substance use. This study was a naturalistic examination of substance use during pregnancy among teenagers and the effects of substance exposure on offspring outcomes. Pregnant adolescents were recruited from the Magee-Womens Hospital prenatal clinic in Pittsburgh, Pennsylvania from 1990 to 1994. There was no oversampling of substance use; all pregnant adolescents who attended the prenatal clinic were eligible for the study. Participants were seen during a prenatal visit in the first half of pregnancy and at delivery with their newborn infants. The initial participation rate was 99 %. There were 413 live born singletons at the delivery phase. Follow-up visits were conducted with mothers and their children in our laboratory when offspring were ages 6 (1995–2000), 10 (2000–2005), and 14 and 16 (2005–2011). The Institutional Review Boards of the Magee-Womens Hospital and the University of Pittsburgh approved each phase of this study. More detailed information on study protocol and sample descriptives can be found in other publications (Cornelius et al. 2002; Cornelius et al. 2012).

Mothers and children were interviewed by trained interviewers and completed self-report measures in office. At each assessment, the teenage mothers reported on their sociodemographic information, psychological symptoms, parenting, and home environment. At the age 14- and 16-year assessments, the children reported their own behavior.

The present study focuses on the offspring at the 14- and 16-year follow-up phases. Sample sizes at 14 and 16 years were 318 and 334, representing retention rates of 77 and 81 % of the total number at birth, respectively. The final sample for the current study is comprised of 312 adolescents. Of the 312 adolescents, 71 % were African American and 29 % were White.

The majority of their mothers were unmarried (72 %). Ninety-one percent of mothers had completed at least 12 years of school and mean monthly household income was $2257 (*SD* = $1709) at age 14. The sample included 156 girls and 156 boys. Mean adolescent age was 14.49 years (*SD* = 0.59: range = 13.85–16.28) and 16.49 years (*SD* = 0.58: range = 15.93–19.53) at the 14- and 16-year follow-up phases, respectively. Families who were included in the sample for the present study did not significantly differ from those who were not included with respect to annual household income, primary caregiver education level, maternal age, child gender, and employment status at the birth assessment. Youth included in the analytic sample were more likely to be born to unmarried mothers than youth not included in the analytic sample χ^2 (1, N = 413) = 5.87, p < .05 and African Americans were more likely to be included in the analytic sample than Whites χ^2 (1, N = 413) = 6.59, p < .05.

Measures

The independent variable (exposure to community violence) and moderating variables (kinship support and parental involvement) were assessed at age 14. Dependent variables (internalizing and externalizing problems) were assessed at age 16. Covariates from age 10 were also included. Descriptive statistics and bivariate correlations between study variables are shown in Table 16.1.

Exposure to Community Violence

At age 14, adolescents completed a modified version of the Screen for Adolescent Violence Exposure (SAVE), a self-report scale that assesses lifetime exposure to community violence (Hastings and Kelley 1997). A sample of 1200 inner-city adolescents was used to develop the SAVE empirically; excellent reliability (alpha coefficients ranged from .65 to .95) and validity were demonstrated (Hastings and Kelley 1997). A subset of 14 items focusing on victimization by violence (e.g., "had shots fired at me" and "someone has pulled a knife on me") and witnessing violence (e.g., "seen someone get shot" and "have seen someone get killed") comprised the exposure to violence measure. Adolescents indicated on a 2-point scale (0 = *no*, 1 = *yes*) whether they had been exposed to each form of violence. Responses were summed to form the total score (α = .72).

Kinship Support

The Kinship Support Scale (Taylor et al. 1993) measures social support provided by adult relatives to adolescents and their families. The 13-item scale taps three areas of support, including socialization and entertainment, advice and counseling, and problem solving. A sample item is, "When we have to make important family decisions, we ask our relatives for advice," with responses ranging from 4 (*strongly agree*) to 1 (*strongly disagree*; α = .89). The measure has demonstrated good internal reliability in previous studies with similar samples (Kenny et al. 2003; Taylor et al. 1993).

TABLE 16.1 Intercorrelations between study variables

Study variable	Mean	SD	1	2	3	4	5	6	7	8	9	10	11
1. Male	–	–	–										
2. White	–	–	-.06	–									
3. Maternal education	12.60	1.31	.07	-.00	–								
4. Child physical abuse	6.15	2.39	.05	-.10	.07	–							
5. Internalizing problems (10)	5.82	5.20	-.06	.10	-.03	.05	–						
6. Externalizing problems (10)	9.83	7.90	.18**	-.04	-.11	.10	.53**	–					
7. Community violence	2.19	1.99	.09	-.24**	-.05	.29**	-.01	.11	–				
8. Kinship support	41.21	6.69	.05	-.17**	-.02	-.26**	-.04	.01	-.08	–			
9. Parental involvement	29.47	4.53	.05	-.08	.02	-.17**	-.08	-.05	.05	.30**	–		
10. Internalizing problems (16)	8.22	7.14	-.17**	.02	-.01	.15*	.19**	.03	.15*	-.20**	-.23**	–	
11. Externalizing problems (16)	11.47	8.18	-.03	-.07	-.01	.16*	.12*	.17**	.22**	-.13*	-.19**	.56**	–

Numbers in parentheses represent the age at which the variable was assessed

* $p<.05$; ** $p<.01$

Parental Involvement

Parental involvement was assessed using the acceptance/ involvement subscale of the Parenting Style Index (Stein-berg et al. 1992; Steinberg et al. 1991). Adolescents completed this subscale at age 14. This subscale presents adolescents with a series of 9 statements that focus on the extent to which they perceive their parents as "loving, responsive, and involved" (e.g., "I can count on my parent(s) to help me out, if I have some kind of a problem") (Steinberg et al. 1992, p. 1270). Responses are indicated on a 4-point scale, ranging from 1 (*strongly agree*) to 4 (*strongly disagree*; $\alpha = .76$).

Internalizing Problems

The Youth Self-Report and Profile (YSR; Achenbach and Rescorla 2001) was used to assess internalizing problems. At age 16, adolescents responded to a series of statements on a 3-point response scale (0 = *not true*, 1 = *somewhat or sometimes true*, 2 = *very true or often true*), indicating how well each statement described their behavior. The internalizing problems scale is comprised of the anxious/depressed symptoms (e.g., "I feel worthless or inferior"), withdrawn/depressed symptoms (e.g., "There is very little that I enjoy"), and somatic complaints (e.g., "I feel dizzy or lightheaded") subscales (31 items; $\alpha = .88$).

Externalizing Problems

Externalizing problems were assessed at age 16 with the YSR (Achenbach and Rescorla 2001). Adolescents completed the externalizing scale of the YSR, which is comprised of the aggressive behavior (e.g., "I am mean to others") and delinquent behavior subscales (e.g., "I break rules at home, school, or elsewhere"). The sum of the 32 items was used as the score for this variable ($\alpha = .89$).

Covariates

Mothers completed the internalizing problems (32 items; $\alpha = .86$) and externalizing problems (33 items; $\alpha = .91$) scales of the Child Behavior Checklist at age 10, (CBCL; Achenbach 1991). These scales parallel the internalizing and externalizing problem scales measured by the YSR. However, the YSR externalizing problems scale contains additional items focusing on alcohol and tobacco use and breaking rules that are not included in the CBCL. Four other covariates, race (0 = African American, 1 = White), maternal education at age 10 (number of years), child sex (0 = female, 1 = male) and history of physical abuse, were also included in this study. Adolescents' history of physical abuse (5 items; $\alpha = .75$) was assessed at age 14 with the Childhood Trauma Questionnaire (Bernstein and Fink 1998).

Data Analysis

Path analysis in Mplus version 6.11 was used to test the hypothesized models (Muthén and Muthén 1998–2007). Mplus handles missing data using full information maximum likelihood estimation (FIML), which yields parameter estimates that tend to be less biased than those generated by ad hoc missing data techniques (e.g., listwise deletion; Schafer and

Graham 2002). Unlike imputation methods for handling missing data, which assign values for each missing data point, FIML uses an iterative procedure to generate the parameters of the population most likely to have produced the available sample data.

Two models were tested for each hypothesized moderator—one model that did not include an interaction term (main effects model) and a second model that did (interaction effects model). All models included both internalizing and externalizing problems simultaneously as outcomes. Interactions were tested and probed in the manner recommended by Aiken and colleagues (Aiken and West 1991; Cohen et al. 2003). Continuous predictor variables included in models were converted to z-scores, and interaction terms were the product of two z scores. For significant interaction terms, simple slopes were calculated and plotted for high (1 SD above the mean) and low (1 SD below the mean) levels of the moderator variable. All models were evaluated based on the size and significance of the coefficients as well as model fit. Acceptable model fit was indicated by nonsignificant Chi square values, RMSEA values of <.06, CFI and TLI values of ≥.95, and SRMR values of equal to or <.08 (Schreiber 2008).

Results

Frequencies of Lifetime Violence Exposure

Table 16.2 presents the prevalence of different types of exposure to community violence. Almost 80 % of youth experienced one or more types of community violence. Seeing someone get beaten up (72 %), seeing someone get badly hurt (44.4 %), seeing someone pull a gun on someone else (22.7 %), having to run for cover when people started shooting (21.9 %), and seeing someone pull a knife on someone else (18.3 %) were most frequently reported.

TABLE 16.2 Frequencies of lifetime violence exposure at age 14

Item	%
Seen someone get beaten up	72.0
Seen someone get badly hurt	44.4
Seen someone pull a gun on someone else	22.7
Had to run for cover when people started shooting	21.9
Seen someone pull knife on someone else	18.3
Seen someone get shot	10.0
Have been badly hurt by someone else	9.0
Seen someone get attacked with a knife	9.0
Seen someone get killed	3.9
Someone pulled a gun on me	2.9

Had shots fired at me	2.6
Someone pulled a knife on me	1.3
Have been attacked with a knife	1.0
Been shot	.3

Internalizing Problems

Main Effects

Exposure to community violence was related to more internalizing problems in the model for kinship support ($B = .88, p < .05$) and parental involvement ($B = 1.09, p < .01$). Higher levels of kinship support and parental involvement were related to fewer internalizing problems ($B = -1.13, p < .05$; $B = -1.47, p < .01$, respectively).

Two-Way Interactions

As previously described, two-way interaction terms were created to determine whether the potential moderators modified relations between exposure to community violence and internalizing and externalizing behaviors. Contrary to our hypotheses, neither of the interaction terms significantly predicted internalizing problems (see Tables 16.3, 16.4).

Externalizing Problems

Main Effects

Exposure to community violence was related to more externalizing problems in the model for kinship support ($B = 1.34, p < .01$) and parental involvement ($B = 1.53, p < .01$). Higher levels of parental involvement were related to fewer externalizing problems ($B = -1.47$, $p < .01$), but kinship support was not ($B = -.88, p > .05$).

Two-Way Interactions

Kinship support moderated the relation between exposure to community violence and externalizing problems, ($B = -1.19, p < .01$; see Table 16.3). The relation between exposure to violence and externalizing problems was significant at low but not high levels of kinship support, indicating that kinship support acted as a *protective-stabilizing* moderator. The simple slope of the relation between violence exposure and externalizing problems for youth 1 SD below the mean of kinship support was 2.56, $t(312) = 3.99, p < .01$, and the simple slope for youth 1 SD above the mean of kinship support was .19, $t(312) = .31, p > .05$ (Fig. 16.1).

Parental involvement also moderated the association between exposure to community violence and externalizing problems, $B = -1.04, p < .05$. The simple slope for youth 1 SD below the mean of parental involvement was 2.59, $t(312) = 3.97, p < .01$ and the simple slope for youth 1 SD above the mean of parental involvement was .51, $t(312) = .79, p > .05$ (Fig. 16.2). As was the case with kinship support, the relation between exposure to

TABLE 16.3 Structural equation models examining main and interactive effects of kinship support

	Main effects model				Interactive effects model			
	Internalizing		Externalizing		Internalizing		Externalizing	
	B (S.E.)	β	B (S.E.)	β	B (S.E.)	β	B (S.E.)	β
Predictor variables								
Male	-2.41 (.79)	-.17**	-1.21 (.92)	-.07	-2.34 (.79)	-.17**	-1.05 (.91)	-.06
White	.06 (.92)	.00	-.78 (1.07)	-.04	.08 (.92)	.01	-.71 (1.05)	-.04
Maternal education	.02 (.40)	.00	.11 (.47)	.01	.02 (.40)	.00	.10 (.47)	.01
Child physical abuse	.49 (.44)	.07	.51 (.51)	.06	.36 (.45)	.05	.18 (.52)	.02
Internalizing problems (10)	1.09 (.35)	.15**	—	—	1.11 (.35)	.16**	—	—
Externalizing problems (10)	—	—	1.46 (.42)	.18**	—	—	1.55 (.42)	.19**
Community violence	.88 (.42)	.12*	1.34 (.49)	.16**	.90 (.42)	.13*	1.38 (.48)	.17**
Kinship support	-1.13 (.44)	-.16*	-.88 (.51)	-.11	-.97 (.46)	-.14*	-.46 (.52)	-.06
Violence × kinship support	—	—	—	—	-.45 (.36)	-.08	-1.19 (.41)	-.18**

Fit indices	χ^2	df	RMSEA	CFI	TLI	SRMR
Model summary						
Main effects model	9.19	7	.03	.99	.96	.02
Interactive effects model	.91	5	.00	1.00	1.10	.01

Predictors in the main effects model accounted for 11 and 10 % of the variance in internalizing and externalizing problems, respectively.

Predictors in the interactive effects model accounted for 12 and 12 % of the variance in internalizing and externalizing problems, respectively

* $p<.05$; ** $p<.01$

TABLE 16..4 Structural equation models examining main and interactive effects of parental involvement

| | Main effects model | | | | Interactive effects model | | | |
| | Internalizing | | Externalizing | | Internalizing | | Externalizing | |
Predictor variables	B (S.E.)	b	B (S.E.)	b	B (S.E.)	b	B (S.E.)	b
Male	-2.37 (.78)	-.17**	-1.11 (.91)	-.07	-2.30 (.78)	-.16**	-1.02 (.90)	-.06
White	.38 (.89)	.02	-.58 (1.03)	-.03	.37 (.89)	.02	-.58 (1.02)	-.03
Maternal education	.09 (.39)	.01	.17 (.46)	.02	.08 (.39)	.01	.16 (.46)	.02
Child physical abuse	.43 (.43)	.06	.40 (.50)	.05	.30 (.44)	.04	.17 (.51)	.02
Internalizing problems (10)	1.02 (.35)	.14**	—	—	1.06 (.35)	.15**	—	—
Externalizing problems (10)	—	—	1.38 (.42)	.17**	—	—	1.48 (.42)	.18**
Community violence	1.09 (.41)	.15**	1.53 (.48)	.19**	1.11 (.41)	.16**	1.55 (.48)	.19**
Parental support	-1.47 (.40)	-.21**	-1.47 (.46)	-.18**	-1.43 (.40)	-.20**	-1.41 (.46)	-.17**
Violence × kinship support	—	—	—	—	-.60 (.38)	-.09	-1.04 (.44)	-.13**

Fit indices	χ^2	df	RMSEA	CFI	TLI	SRMR
Model summary						
Main effects model	6.81	7	.00	1.00	1.00	.02
Interactive effects model	1.07	5	.00	1.00	1.09	.01

Predictors in the main effects model accounted for 13 and 12 % of the variance in internalizing and externalizing problems, respectively.

Predictors in the interactive effects model accounted for 14 and 13 % of the variance in internalizing and externalizing problems, respectively

* $p<.05$; ** $p<.01$

community violence and externalizing problems was significant at low but not high levels of parental involvement. Thus, parental involvement appears to be operating as a *protective-stabilizing* moderator.

Discussion

Neighborhoods as contexts for development play a powerful role in shaping young people's experiences during childhood and adolescence (Garcia Coll et al. 1996; Leventhal and Brooks-Gunn 2000). Studies with increasingly sophisticated designs are highlighting neighborhood disadvantage, in particular, as a highly salient risk factor for child mental health and behavior problems (Goodnight et al. 2011; Leventhal and Brooks-Gunn 2011). Residence in high-poverty neighborhoods often goes hand-in-hand with chronic exposure to risks factors (e.g., crime and violence) that threaten positive development and limit access to resources that foster positive development (e.g., institutional resources, recreational facilities, and quality schools; Guerra and Williams 2006).

This study focuses on community violence as a risk factor for mental health and behavior problems in low-income youth. We use longitudinal data to examine kinship support and parental involvement as moderators of the association exposure to violence and adolescent socioemotional adjustment (i.e., internalizing and externalizing problems). Consistent with our hypotheses, we found that exposure to community violence was related to internalizing and externalizing problems. Moreover, high levels of kinship support and parental involvement weakened the association between exposure to community violence and externalizing problems. However, contrary to our prediction, none of the moderators

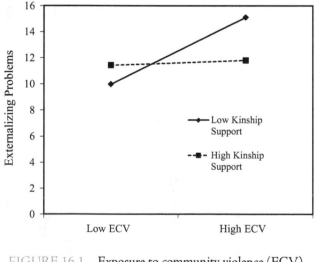

FIGURE 16.1   Exposure to community violence (ECV)
9 kinship support predicting externalizing problems

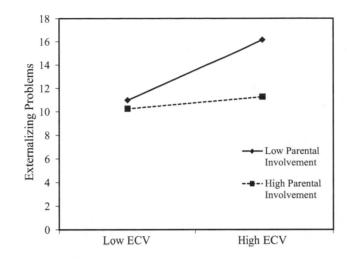

FIGURE 16.2 Exposure to community violence (ECV)
9 parental involvement predicting externalizing problems

examined showed significant interactions with exposure to community violence predicting internalizing problems.

Our results are congruous with prior literature showing relationships between exposure to community violence and internalizing and externalizing behaviors (Fowler et al. 2009). Community violence can lead to internalizing problems, such as anxiety and depression, by causing adolescents to believe the world is unsafe and unpredictable, exposing them to a chronic sense of loss due to death or maiming of community members, and increasing their overall stress (Cooley-Quille et al. 2001; LeDoux 1993). Pathways through which community violence may heighten the risk for externalizing problems include exposure to negative role-models, aggressive thoughts and response styles, and desensitization to violence (Mrug et al. 2008; Ng-Mak et al. 2002; Robinson et al. 2011). In line with other studies, both kinship support and parental involvement attenuated the positive association between exposure to community violence and externalizing problems (Proctor 2006). Kinship support and parental involvement may weaken this association by helping to provide models for appropriate behavior. Involved parents and extended family members may also provide additional monitoring and supervision of youth which could decrease their exposure to negative role models or decrease their opportunities for engaging in delinquent behavior. Another potential explanation is that parents and extended family members may provide outlets for youth to verbally express their feelings about community violence instead of reacting with physical aggression.

Consistent with previous studies that have examined links between exposure to community violence and both internalizing and externalizing problems (Hardaway et al. 2012; Li et al. 2007), we did not find moderating effects for internalizing problems. Further research is required to determine whether these findings reflect a larger pattern.

Internalizing problems typically are less apparent than externalizing problems. Studies have shown that, when multiple informants rate children's internalizing and externalizing problems, informants' ratings of externalizing problems tend to agree more than informants' ratings of internalizing problems, suggesting that informants are better able to detect and agree on problem behaviors that are more observable (De Los Reyes and Kazdin 2005). As such, parents are less likely to notice and try to intervene when internalizing behaviors are present. Research also suggests that parents are not always aware of their children's exposure to community violence (Ceballo et al. 2001). As a result, relationships that are generally warm and caring may not be enough to overcome internalizing problems that stem from exposure to community violence. Research also suggests that exposure to community violence affects the way adolescents appraise threats and that threat appraisal is related to internalizing but not externalizing problems. Combined, these threads of research indicate that adolescents exposed to violence may benefit from interventions focused on changing cognitive processes (i.e., threat appraisals) related to violence exposure, direct communication with parents about these experiences, and in some cases professional psychological help.

Our failure to find moderating effects of internalizing problems may also be due to the way internalizing problems were measured. In the current study, symptoms of anxiety and depression where combined in one internalizing problems scale. Some work suggests that exposure to community violence may affect depression and anxiety differently. One study showed that the relation between exposure to community violence and depression was curvilinear, whereas the relation between exposure to community violence and anxiety was linear (Gaylord-Harden et al. 2011). Combining symptoms of depression and anxiety may have obscured interactive effects that operate differently in their prediction of symptoms of depression versus anxiety. Future studies should examine protective factors for symptoms of depression and anxiety separately.

Limitations and Strengths

The results of the current study should be interpreted in light of some limitations. One limitation involves the measurement of exposure to community violence. The measure used in the current study does not assess the location in which youth were exposed to violence. Some work suggests that violence exposure is differentially related to socioemotional adjustment outcomes depending on the location in which it occurs (Mrug and Windle 2010). Also, our measure of exposure to violence assessed lifetime exposure, thus we were unable to pinpoint the timeframe in which violence exposure occurred. There is some evidence that suggests that more recent violence exposure may be more strongly related to symptoms (Brandt et al. 2005). Another limitation is that this study relied on adolescent self-report measures for the focal constructs, thus some of the observed relationships could be artifacts of shared method variance. Our results are, however, in line with those reported in multiple informant studies. In addition, our sample was comprised of youth born to adolescent mothers, which may in some ways limit generalizability. Studies suggest the offspring of teenage mothers have outcomes similar to other children born to mothers who delayed child bearing but have similar socioeconomic backgrounds (SmithBattle 2009). Therefore, our findings are likely generalizable to other low-income adolescents.

Despite these limitations, this study has several strengths. We focused on family-level moderators that to this point have received little attention in the research literature. Another strength of this study is its longitudinal design. To date, most studies that have examined moderators of exposure to community violence have been cross sectional. By using longitudinal data, we were able to control for possible preexisting differences in socioemotional adjustment. Moreover, we controlled for exposure to child physical abuse, increasing confidence that the significant findings are due to exposure to community violence and not other forms of violence.

Future Directions and Implications

One key area for future research is identifying factors that protect youth against internalizing problems. This study and others have found fewer if any protective factors that reduce the risk of internalizing problems associated with exposure to community violence (Hardaway et al. 2012; Li et al. 2007). The results from this study suggest that greater attention should be paid to culturally-relevant protective factors that may be important in helping adolescents cope with violence exposure. This is particularly important given that racial and ethnic minority youth are disproportionately exposed to community violence (Crouch et al. 2000; Voisin 2007). The current study and other recent work suggests that extended family support and adherence to cultural values such as *familismo* (for Latino youth) are coping resources that may be particularly important for minority youth (Kennedy and Ceballo 2013). Importantly, although it did not buffer youth from the impact of community violence on internalizing symptoms, parental involvement exhibited a direct association with lower levels of internalizing symptoms. Thus, developers of interventions may want to include a focus on increasing parental involvement when addressing depression and anxiety among youth in high-violence neighborhoods. In addition to examining family-level protective factors, more work needs to focus on modifiable, extra-familial protective factors that can reduce the consequences of community violence on internalizing symptoms. Recent studies have identified participation in extracurricular activities and neighborhood collective efficacy as moderators of exposure to community violence (Francois et al. 2012; Hardaway et al. 2012; Jain et al. 2012). After protective factors are identified, it will also be important for future studies to contribute to understanding processes that underlie protection or exactly how certain protective factors reduce risk.

In contrast to the results for internalizing problems, both parental involvement and kinship support acted as protective factors against the development of externalizing problems. Practitioners should stress to parents living in violent communities the importance of maintaining close relationships with their teens by modeling ways to effectively manage anger and interpersonal altercations, monitoring their teen's whereabouts, and serving as consistent, stable sources of emotional support. Parents should also be advised that continued contact with kin—the larger network of family relationships—can provide their adolescent offspring with additional resources for support, monitoring and modeling behaviors. In addition, extended family members can be informed of their potential to positively influence youth living in dangerous communities. Practitioners and interventions should encourage parents and extended family members to collaborate in creating a network of adult support to youth to provide supervision, positive role-modeling, and opportunities for youth to discuss ways to express anger and handle interpersonal difficulties in a healthy, productive manner.

Conclusion

The developmental stage of adolescence brings newfound autonomy, increased mobility, and expanded social networks. Unfortunately, these new forms of independence likely contribute to the increase in risk for exposure to community violence that also occurs during adolescence. National statistics indicate that adolescents are victimized by violence more frequently than any other age group and that witnessing serious acts of violence is prevalent among youth. Exposure to community violence is associated with a host of socioemotional adjustment problems, including internalizing and externalizing problems. This study examined whether kinship support and parental involvement moderate the association of exposure to community violence to adolescent internalizing and externalizing problems. The findings from this study suggest that support from both parents and extended family may help mitigate some of the negative effects of exposure to community violence. Specifically, this study found that both kinship support and parental involvement moderated the association between exposure to community violence and externalizing problems—although neither moderated the effect of community violence on internalizing problems. These findings highlight the important role that family relationships may play in mitigating some of the negative consequences of community violence for adolescents through high levels of parental involvement and support from extended family.

Acknowledgments

This study was supported by grants from the National Institutes of Health (NIDA: DA09275, NIAAA: AA022473, AA007453, PI: M. Cornelius; NIDA: DA019482, PI: C. Larkby).

Authors' Contributions

CH conceived of the study, designed the study, performed the statistical analysis, and drafted the manuscript. ES provided input on the study design and helped draft the manuscript. CL and MC assisted in drafting and editing the manuscript.

Conflict of interest

The authors report no conflicts of interest.

References

Aceves, M. J., & Cookston, J. T. (2007). Violent victimization, aggression, and parent-adolescent relations: Quality parenting as a buffer for violently victimized youth. *Journal of Youth and Adolescence, 36*(5), 635–647.

Achenbach, T. M. (1991). *Integrative guide for the 1991 CBCL/4–18, YSR, and TRF profiles*. Burlington, VT: University of Vermont, Department of Psychiatry.

Achenbach, T. M., & Rescorla, L. A. (2001). *Manual for the aseba school-age forms & profiles*. Burlington, VT: University of Vermont, Research Center for Children, Youth, & Families.

Aiken, L. S., & West, S. G. (1991). *Multiple regression: Testing and interpreting interactions*. Newbury Park, CA: Sage.

Barber, C. N., Hall, J., & Armistead, L. (2003). Parent-adolescent relationship and adolescent psychological functioning among African-American female adolescents: Self-esteem as a mediator. *Journal of Child and Family Studies, 12*(3), 361–374.

Bernstein, D. P., & Fink, L. (1998). *Childhood trauma questionnaire: A retrospective self-report manual*. San Antonio, TX: The Psychological Corporation.

Boyd-Franklin, N. (1989). *Black families in therapy: A multisystems approach*. New York, NY: Guilford Press.

Brandt, R., Ward, C. L., Dawes, A., & Flisher, A. J. (2005). Epidemiologial measurement of children's and adolescents' exposure to community violence: Working with the current state of the science. *Clinical Child and Family Psychology Review, 8*(4), 327–342.

Brody, G. H., McBride Murry, V., Kim, S., & Brown, A. C. (2002). Longitudinal pathways to competence and psychological adjustment among African American children living in rural single-parent households. *Child Development, 73*(5), 1505–1516.

Brook, J. S., Lee, J. Y., Finch, S. J., Brown, E. N., & Brook, D. W. (2013). Long-term consequences of membership in trajectory groups of delinquent behavior in an urban sample: Violence, drug use, interpersonal, and neighborhood attributes. *Aggressive Behavior, 39*(6), 440–452.

Brookmeyer, K. A., Henrich, C. C., & Schwab-Stone, M. (2005). Adolescents who witness community violence: Can parent support and prosocial cognitions protect them from committing violence? *Child Development, 76*(4), 917–929.

Ceballo, R., Dahl, T. A., Aretakis, M. T., & Ramirez, C. (2001). Inner-city children's exposure to community violence: How much do parents know? *Journal of Marriage and Family, 63*(4), 927–940.

Centers for Disease Control and Prevention, National Center for Injury Prevention and Control. Web-based Injury Statistics Query and Reporting System (WISQARS) [Online]. (2005). [cited June 2015]. www.cdc.gov/injury/wisqars.

Cohen, J., Cohen, P., West, S. G., & Aiken, L. S. (2003). *Applied multiple regression/correlation analysis for the behavioral sciences* (3rd ed.). Mahwah, NJ: Erlbaum.

Collins, W. A., Maccoby, E. E., Steinberg, L., Hetherington, E. M., & Bornstein, M. H. (2000). Contemporary research on parenting: The case for nature and nurture. *American Psychologist, 55*(2), 218–232.

Cooley-Quille, M., Boyd, R. C., Frantz, E., & Walsh, J. (2001). Emotional and behavioral impact of exposure to community violence in inner-city adolescents. *Journal of Clinical Child Psychology, 30,* 199–206.

Cooley-Quille, M. R., Turner, S. M., & Beidel, D. C. (1995). Emotional impact of children's exposure to community violence: A preliminary study. *Journal of the American Academy of Child and Adolescent Psychiatry, 34*(10), 1362–1368.

Cornelius, M., Goldschmidt, L., Day, N., & Larkby, C. (2002). Alcohol, tobacco, and marijuana use among pregnant teenagers: Six-year follow-up of effects on offspring growth. *Neurotoxicology and Teratology, 24,* 703–710.

Cornelius, M., Goldschmidt, L., De Genna, N., & Larkby, C. (2012). Effects of prenatal cigarette smoke exposure on behavior dysregulation among 14-year-old offspring of teenage mothers. *Maternal Child Health Journal, 16,* 694–705.

Crouch, J. L., Hanson, R. F., Saunders, B. E., Kilpatrick, D. G., & Resnick, H. S. (2000). Income, race/ethnicity, and exposure to violence in youth: Results from the national survey of adolescents. *Journal of Community Psychology, 28*(6), 625–641.

De Los Reyes, A., & Kazdin, A. E. (2005). Informant discrepancies in the assessment of childhood psychopathology: A critical review, theoretical framework, and recommendations for further study. *Psychological Bulletin, 131,* 483–509.

Dearing, E. (2004). The developmental implications of restrictive and supportive parenting across neighborhoods and ethnicities: Exceptions are the rule. *Journal of Applied Developmental Psychology, 25*(5), 555–575.

Finkelhor, D., Turner, H., Ormond, R., & Hamby, S. (2009). Violence, abuse, and crime, exposure in a national sample of children and youth. *Pediatrics, 124,* 1411–1423.

Foster, H., & Brooks-Gunn, J. (2009). Toward a stress process model of children's exposure to physical family and community violence. *Clinical Child and Family Psychological Review, 12,* 71–94.

Fowler, P. J., Tompsett, C. J., Braciszewski, J. M., Jacques-Tiura, A. J., & Baltes, B. B. (2009). Community violence: A meta-analysis on the effect of exposure and mental health outcomes of children and adolescents. *Development and Psychopathology, 21*(1), 227–259.

Francois, S., Overstreet, S., & Cunningham, M. (2012). Where we live: The unexpected influence of urban neighborhoods on the academic performance of African American adolescents. *Youth & Society, 44*(2), 307–328.

Franklin, J. H. (1997). African American families: A historical note. In H. P. McAdoo (Ed.), *Black families* (3rd ed., pp. 5–8). Thousand Oaks, CA: Sage.

Garcia Coll, C., Crnic, K., Lamberty, G., Wasik, B. H., Jenkins, R., Garcia, H. V., & McAdoo, H. P. (1996). An integrative model for the study of developmental competencies in minority children. *Child Development, 67,* 1891–1914.

Gaylord-Harden, N. K., Cunningham, J. A., & Zelencik, B. (2011). Effects of exposure to community violence on internalizing symptoms: Does desensitization to violence occur in African American youth? *Journal of Abnormal Child Psychology, 39,* 711–719.

Goodnight, J. A., Lahey, B. B., Van Hulle, C. A., Rodgers, J. L., Rathouz, P. J., Waldman, I. D., & D'Onofrio, B. M. (2011). A quasi-experimental analysis of the influence of neighborhood disadvantage on child and adolescent conduct problems. *Journal of Abnormal Psychology, 121*(1), 95–108.

Guerra, N. G., & Williams, K. R. (2006). Ethnicity, youth violence, and the ecology of development. In N. G. Guerra & E. P. Smith (Eds.), *Preventing youth violence in a multicultural society* (pp. 17–45). Washington, DC: American Psychological Association.

Hair, E. C., Moore, K. A., Garrett, S. B., Ling, T., & Cleveland, K. (2008). The continued importance of quality parent-adolescent relationships during late adolescence. *Journal of Research on Adolescence, 18*(1), 187–200.

Hardaway, C. R., McLoyd, V. C., & Wood, D. (2012). Exposure to violence and socioemotional adjustment in low-income youth: An examination of protective factors. *American Journal of Community Psychology, 49*(1–2), 112–126.

Hastings, T. L., & Kelley, M. L. (1997). Development and validation of the screen for adolescent violence exposure (SAVE). *Journal of Abnormal Child Psychology, 25*(6), 511–520.

Jain, S., Buka, S. L., Subramanian, S. V., & Molnar, B. E. (2012). Protective factors for youth exposed to violence: Role of developmental assets in building emotional resilience. *Youth Violence and Juvenile Justice, 10,* 107–129.

Jain, S., & Cohen, A. K. (2013). Fostering resilience among urban youth exposed to violence: A promising area for interdisciplinary research and practice. *Health Education & Behavior, 40,* 651–662.

Johnson, J. E., Esposito-Smythers, C., Miranda, R., Rizzo, C. J., Justus, A. N., & Clum, G. (2011). Gender, social support, and depression in criminal justice-involved adolescents. *International Journal of Offender Therapy and Comparative Criminology, 55*(7), 1096–1109.

Johnson, L. B., & Staples, R. (2005). *Black families at the crossroads: Challenges and prospects.* San Francisco, CA: Jossey-Bass.

Jones, J. M. (2007). Exposure to chronic community violence: Resilience in African American children. *Journal of Black Psychology, 33*(2), 125–149.

Jones, D. J., & Lindahl, K. M. (2011). Coparenting in extended kinship systems: African American, Hispanic, Asian heritage, and Native American families. In K. M. Lindahl & J. P. McHale (Eds.), *Coparenting: A conceptual and clinical examination of family systems* (pp. 61–79). Washington, DC: American Psychological Association.

Kahn, R. L., & Antonucci, T. C. (1980). Convoys over the life course: Attachment, roles and social support. In P. Baltes & O. Brim (Eds.), *Life span development and behavior* (Vol. 3, pp. 253–286). San Diego, CA: Academic Press.

Kennedy, T. M., & Ceballo, R. (2013). Latino adolescents' community violence exposure: After-school activities and familismo as risk and protective factors. *Social Development, 22*, 663–682.

Kenny, M. E., Blustein, D. L., Chaves, A., Grossman, J. M., & Gallagher, L. A. (2003). The role of perceived barriers and relational support in the educational and vocational lives of urban high school students. *Journal of Counseling Psychology, 50*(2), 142–155.

Kliewer, W., Sandler, I., & Wolchik, S. (1994). Family socialization of threat appraisal and coping: Coaching, modeling, and family context. In F. Nestmann & K. Hurrelmann (Eds.), *Social networks and social support in childhood and adolescence* (pp. 271–291). Berlin, Germany: Walter De Gruyter.

Lamborn, S. D., & Nguyen, D.-G. T. (2004). African American adolescents' perceptions of family interactions: Kinship support, parent-child relationships, and teen adjustment. *Journal of Youth and Adolescence, 33*(6), 547–558.

LeDoux, J. E. (1993). Emotional networks in the brain. In M. Lewis & J. M. Haviland (Eds.), *Handbook of emotions* (pp. 109–118). New York: Guilford Press.

Leventhal, T., & Brooks-Gunn, J. (2000). The neighborhoods they live in: The effects of neighborhood residence on child and adolescent outcomes. *Psychological Bulletin, 126*(2), 309–337.

Leventhal, T., & Brooks-Gunn, J. (2011). Changes in neighborhood poverty from 1990 to 2000 and youth's problem behaviors. *Developmental Psychology, 47*(6), 1680–1698.

Li, S. T., Nussbaum, K. M., & Richards, M. H. (2007). Risk and protective factors for urban African American youth. *American Journal of Community Psychology, 39*(1), 21–35.

Loukas, A., & Prelow, H. M. (2004). Externalizing and internalizing problems in low-income latino early adolescents: Risk, resource, and protective factors. *Journal of Early Adolescence, 24*(3), 250–273.

Luthar, S. S., Cicchetti, D., & Becker, B. (2000). The construct of resilience: A critical evaluation and guidelines for future work. *Child Development, 71*(3), 543–562.

Luthar, S. S., & Zelazo, L. B. (2003). Research on resilience: An integrative review. In S. Luthar (Ed.), *Resilience and vulnerability: Adaptation in the context of childhood adversities* (pp. 510–549). New York: Cambridge University Press.

Margolin, G. (2005). Children's exposure to violence: Exploring developmental pathways to diverse outcomes. *Journal of Interpersonal Violence, 20*(1), 72–81.

Martin, L., Revington, N., & Seedat, S. (2013). The 39-item Child Exposure to Community Violence (CECV) scale: Exploratory factor analysis and relationship to PTSD symptomatology in trauma-exposed children and adolescents. *Internatioal Journal of Behavioral Medicine, 20*, 599–608.

Mason, W. A., Hitch, J. E., Kosterman, R., McCarty, C. A., Herrenkohl, T. I., & David Hawkins, J. (2010). Growth in adolescent delinquency and alcohol use in relation to young adult crime, alcohol use disorders, and risky sex: A comparison of youth from low-versus middle-income backgrounds. *Journal of Child Psychology and Psychiatry, 51*(12), 1377–1385.

Masten, A. S. (2001). Ordinary magic: Resilience processes in development. *American Psychologist, 56*, 227–238.

Masten, A. S., & Coatsworth, J. D. (1998). The development of competence in favorable and unfavorable environments: Lessons from research on successful children. *American Psychologist, 53*(2), 205–220.

McKelvey, L. M., Conners-Burrow, N. A., Mesman, G. R., Pemberton, J. R., & Casey, P. H. (2015). Promoting adolescent behavioral adjustment in violent neighborhoods: Supportive families can make a difference. *Journal of Clinical Child & Adolescent Psychology, 44*, 157–168.

McMahon, S. D., Coker, C., & Parnes, A. L. (2013). Environmental stressors, social support, and internalizing symptoms among African American youth. *Journal of Community Psychology, 41*(5), 615–630.

Mrug, S., Loosier, P. S., & Windle, M. (2008). Violence exposure across multiple contexts: Individual and joint effects on adjustment. *American Journal of Orthopsychiatry, 78*(1), 70–84.

Mrug, S., & Windle, M. (2010). Prospective effects of violence exposure across multiple contexts on early adolescents internalizing and externalizing problems. *Journal of Child Psychology and Psychiatry, 51*(8), 953–961.

Muthén, L.K., & Muthén, B.O. (1998–2007). *Mplus user's guide*. Los Angeles: Muthén & Muthén.

Ng-Mak, D. S., Salzinger, S., Feldman, R., & Stueve, A. (2002). Normalization of violence among inner-city youth: A formulation for research. *American Journal of Orthopsychiatry, 72*(1), 92–101.

Pallock, L. L., & Lamborn, S. D. (2006). Beyond parenting practices: Extended kinship support and the academic adjustment of African-American and European-American teens. *Journal of Adolescence, 29*, 813–828.

Pearce, M. J., Jones, S. M., Schwab-Stone, M. E., & Ruchkin, V. (2003). The protective effects of religiousness and parent involvement on the development of conduct problems among youth exposed to violence. *Child Development, 74*(6), 1682–1696.

Proctor, L. J. (2006). Children growing up in a violent community: The role of the family. *Aggression and Violent Behavior, 11*(6), 558–576.

Robinson, W. L., Paxton, K. C., & Jonen, L. P. (2011). Pathways to aggression and violence among African American adolescent males: The influence of normative beliefs, neighborhood, and depressive symptomatology. *Journal of Prevention and Intervention in Community Psychology, 39*(2), 132–148.

Rutter, M. (2006). Implications of resilience concepts for scientific understanding. *Annals of the New York Academy of Sciences, 1094*(1), 1–12.

Rutter, M. (2012). Resilience as a dynamic concept. *Development and Psychopathology, 24*(2), 335–344.

Schafer, J. L., & Graham, J. W. (2002). Missing data: Our view of the state of the art. *Psychological Methods, 7*(2), 147–177.

Schreiber, J. B. (2008). Core reporting practices in structural equation modeling. *Research in Social & Administrative Pharmacy, 4*, 83–97.

Sickmund, M., & Puzzanchera, C. (Eds.). (2014). *Juvenile offenders and victims: 2014 National report*. Pittsburgh, PA: National Center for Juvenile Justice.

SmithBattle, L. (2009). Reframing the risks and losses of teen mothering. *MCN: The American Journal of Maternal/Child Nursing, 34*(2), 122–128.

Stein, B. D., Jaycox, L. H., Kataoka, S., Rhodes, H. J., & Vestal, K. D. (2003). Prevalence of child and adolescent exposure to community violence. *Clinical Child and Family Psychology Review, 6*, 247–264.

Steinberg, L. (2008). A social neuroscience perspective on adolescent risk-taking. *Developmental Review, 28*, 78–106.

Steinberg, L., Lamborn, S. D., Dornbusch, S. M., & Darling, N. (1992). Impact of parenting practices on adolescent achievement: Authoritative parenting, school involvement, and encouragement to succeed. *Child Development, 63*(5), 1266–1281.

Steinberg, L., Mounts, N. S., Lamborn, S. D., & Dornbusch, S. M. (1991). Authoritative parenting and adolescent adjustment across varied ecological niches. *Journal of Research on Adolescence, 1*(1), 19–36.

Stevenson, H. C, Jr. (1997). "Missed, dissed, and pissed": Making meaning of neighborhood risk, fear and anger management in urban black youth. *Cultural Diversity and Mental Health, 3*(1), 37–52.

Sudarkasa, N. (1997). African American families and family values. In H. P. McAdoo (Ed.), *Black families* (3rd ed., pp. 9–40). Thousand Oaks, CA: Sage.

Taylor, R. D. (2010). Risk and resilience in low-income African American families: Moderating effects of kinship social support. *Cultural Diversity and Ethnic Minority Psychology, 16*(3), 344–351.

Taylor, R. D., Budescu, M., Gebre, A., & Hodzic, I. (2014). Family financial pressure and maternal and adolescent socioemotional adjustment: Moderating effects of kin social support in low income African American families. *Journal of Child and Family Studies, 23*(2), 242–254.

Taylor, R. D., Casten, R., & Flickinger, S. M. (1993). Influence of kinship social support on the parenting experiences and psychosocial adjustment of African-American adolescents. *Developmental Psychology, 29*(2), 382–388.

Voisin, D. R. (2007). The effects of family and community violence exposure among youth: Recommendations for practice and policy. *Journal of Social Work Education, 43*(1), 51–66.

Wandersman, A., & Nation, M. (1998). Urban communities and mental health: Psychological contribution to understanding toxicity, resilience, and interventions. *American Psychologist, 53*, 647–656.

Whitmire, K. A. (2000). Adolescence as a developmental phase: A tutorial. *Topics in Language Disorders, 20*, 1–14.

Wilson, W. C., & Rosenthal, B. S. (2003). The relationship between exposure to community violence and psychological distress among adolescents: A meta-analysis. *Violence and Victims, 18*(3), 335–352.

Wilson, H. W., Woods, B. A., Emerson, E., & Donenberg, G. R. (2012). Patterns of violence exposure and sexual risk in low-income, urban African American girls. *Psychology of Violence, 2*, 194–207.

Yaroslavsky, I., Pettit, J. W., Lewinsohn, P. M., Seeley, J. R., & Roberts, R. E. (2013). Heterogeneous trajectories of depressive symptoms: Adolescent predictors and adult outcomes. *Journal of Affective Disorders, 148*, 391–399.